DATA STRUCTURES OUTSIDE IN
With Java™

Sesh Venugopal

Rutgers University

PEARSON

Prentice
Hall

Upper Saddle River, New Jersey 07458

Library of Congress Cataloging-in-Publication Data

Venugopal, Sesh.
  Data Structures Outside In with Java / Sesh Venugopal.
    p. cm.
  ISBN 0-13-198619-8
  1. Data structures (Computer science) 2. Java (Computer program language)
I. Title.
  QA76.9.D35V46 2006
  005.13'3–dc22

                                                    2006031108

Vice President and Editorial Director, ECS: *Marcia J. Horton*
Executive Editor: *Tracy Dunkelberger*
Associate Editor: *Carole Snyder*
Editorial Assistant: *Christianna Lee*
Executive Managing Editor: *Vince O'Brien*
Managing Editor: *Camille Trentacoste*
Production Editor: *John Shannon*
Director of Creative Services: *Paul Belfanti*
Creative Director: *Juan Lopez*
Cover Design Director: *Jayne Conte*
Cover Designer: *Bruce Kenselaar*
Managing Editor, AV Management and Production: *Patricia Burns*
Art Editor: *Gregory Dulles*
Director, Image Resource Center: *Melinda Reo*
Manager, Rights and Permissions: *Zina Arabia*
Manager, Visual Research: *Beth Brenzel*
Manager, Cover Visual Research and Permissions: *Karen Sanatar*
Manufacturing Manager, ESM: *Alexis Heydt-Long*
Manufacturing Buyer: *Lisa McDowell*
Executive Marketing Manager: *Robin O'Brien*
Marketing Assistant: *Mack Patterson*

© 2007 Pearson Education, Inc.
Pearson Prentice Hall
Pearson Education, Inc.
Upper Saddle River, NJ 07458

Printed in the United States of America

10 9 8 7 6 5 4 3 2 1

ISBN: 0-13-198619-8

Pearson Education Ltd., *London*
Pearson Education Australia Pty. Ltd., *Sydney*
Pearson Education Singapore, Pte. Ltd.
Pearson Education North Asia Ltd., *Hong Kong*
Pearson Education Canada, Inc., *Toronto*
Pearson Educación de Mexico, S.A. de C.V.
Pearson Education—Japan, *Tokyo*
Pearson Education Malaysia, Pte. Ltd.
Pearson Education, Inc., *Upper Saddle River, New Jersey*

To my mother and father

Preface

There are two broad approaches to studying data structures.

One is the "inside-out" approach in which the implementation of the data structure, i.e., *how* it is built, is learned either before or in conjunction with its application to problem solving. In other words, start from the nucleus of the data structure and build outward to its use in a problem.

The inside-out approach, however, is discordant with the manner in which software is built in practice out of libraries of objects that are known only through their application programming interfaces (**API**s). Here, the "outside-in" approach becomes the norm: a component or object is first—and often only—seen via its interface, which characterizes its behavior and therefore its suitability for a given application. That is, *what* a component does precedes how it is built.

Outside-in: From price-tagged interface to implementation

In this book, we are interested in the interface as well as the implementation of data structures. We follow the outside-in approach to presenting them because it will enable students to easily apply in practical software development what they learn in class. Our approach is outlined in the following sequence of steps.

1. **Introduce a data structure by narrating its properties and use in applications.**

   This step familiarizes the student with the characteristic behavior of the data structure, setting the stage for the encapsulation of data and operations into a Java class.

2. **Formalize the characteristic properties of a data structure by presenting the public interface of a Java class that implements the data structure.**

   This step defines the set of operations that may be applied on the data structure, formulated from the discussion in Step 1. With the interface, there also comes a "price tag"—the running times of the interface operations.

   The price tag is an important consideration in the selection of data structures for an application. It may be argued that the price tag determination may only be made after the data structure is implemented. While this is true, the outside-in approach that is used to build software in practice typically separates the group of people who work with the outside from the group of people who build the inside. The outside group must rely on all, and only, that information that comes with the interface. Having a price tag with the interface is critical for the outside group to evaluate and choose the best objects possible for the application at hand.

   To be consistent with this approach, we have attached the price tag to the interface, but made a working compromise: in the interface, specify the minimal requirements of the implementation so that the running times of the operations stay within the price tag.

   We admit that this blurs the separation between interface and implementation, while recognizing that part of the issue is also that the same person—the student—is working with both the outside and the inside, albeit at different times. The best way for the student to approach the interface-implementation separation is to first imagine that he or she is a client of the data structure, with full cognizance of the interface and the price tag, and then imagine being the implementor of the data structure, who has been told what limitations (price tag) to work with to build the structure.

3. **Further illustrate the use of a data structure by writing Java applications using its class interface presented in Step 2.**

   This step gives the student a clear practical understanding of how to build an application in Java using a data structure whose public interface is known, but whose internal implementation is hidden.

   Steps 2 and 3 strongly emphasize the interface of a data structure. By repeatedly building applications using only the public interface of data structures, the student gets a practical feel for software development using components whose internal implementation details need not (and indeed, may not) be available.

4. **Design and implement the data structure, i.e., develop the code for the Java class whose interface was presented in Step 2, analyze the running times of its operations, and verify them against the price tag.**

   This step emphasizes code reuse in one of two forms: (a) *composition:* using previous data structures as component (Java) objects in building, or composing, a new data structure, or (b) *inheritance:* building a new data structure by inheriting from a previously built data structure (Java class).

   While we are following an outside-in approach, this "in" part does not degenerate into using classes from the Java collections framework. Instead, it is on an equal footing with the "outside" part, with a detailed understanding of the implementation so that the student learns all aspects of building data structures, including evaluating the tradeoffs involved in choosing among a set of candidate implementations.

Apart from providing a consistent pedagogical form, these steps help students to understand and apply the important object-oriented design principles of encapsulation, separation of interface from implementation, and code reuse.

Prerequisites in Java

This book assumes a CS1-level background in Java 1.5, with the following specific coverage: program structure, data types, control structures for decision and repetition, including the if, if-else, for, while, and repeat statements, and arrays. It also assumes that the student is familiar with the widely used String class.

Chapter 1 is a Java primer on object-oriented programming that starts by assuming this CS1-level background, and introduces objects and classes, inheritance, the Object class, exceptions, core input and output features, class packaging, and access control. In the context of input/output, the java.util.StringTokenizer and the java.util.Scanner (new to Java 1.5) classes are described, with a discussion of their typical usage.

The primer also introduces specifically design-oriented features, including polymorphism, abstract classes, and interfaces.

The last section discusses the new Java 1.5 generics, an indispensable tool for building usable and robust data structures. This discussion also details the design and use of the `java.util.ArrayList` class, which is a very useful component in implementing container structures, or collections.

Paths through the book

An essential course focusing on the basic data structures and sorting algorithms, preceded by reviewing/learning the required Java tools and techniques in two weeks, could cover Chapters 1–10, skipping Section 10.7 (AVL Tree), and Chapters 12–13, skipping Sections 13.3 (Heapsort) and 13.4 (Radix sort).

A course that could conduct the Java due diligence in lab instead of lecture could add Heap from Chapter 11, and Heapsort and Radix sort from Sections 13.3 and 13.4 respectively.

Advanced material could be incorporated by covering AVL trees from Section 10.7, and Chapters 14 and 15 on graphs. In case of time limitation, Chapter 14 would suffice to familiarize students with graph algorithms, while leaving out the implementation details of Chapter 15.

A two-course sequence could cover the entire book, including much of the Java background material in Chapter 1. The first course could cover Chapters 1 through 9, up to and including Binary Tree/General Tree, and the second could cover the rest of the chapters, starting with Binary Search Tree/AVL Tree of Chapter 10.

Pedagogical structures.

- Every chapter, except the preliminary Chapters 1 and 2, begins with a list of **Learning Objectives.** This gives a precise overview of the learning material in the chapter.
- Key points in every chapter are presented in the following format:
  These key points are also itemized in the end-of-chapter summary.
- Public interfaces of Java classes for data structures are presented as figures in the following format:

Class classname

Constructors

Signature and description of each public constructor

Methods

Running time (price tag), signature, and description of each public method

- Every complete Java class implementation is presented in the following style:

    Class File number   *Class File Name*

    Class outline, with some constructors/methods possibly filled in

- Throughout the book, we use algorithms written in pseudo-code, providing language-independent descriptions of processes. These algorithms appear with a header of the form:

Algorithm name_of_algorithm

The notations used in the pseudo-code are self-explanatory.
- Every chapter except Chapter 2 concludes with a listing of **Summary** points. These include the key points in the chapter, as well as other important points to remember, including specific Java issues.
- Every chapter except Chapter 2 tests the student's understanding of the material in the form of exercises and programming problems:

    - **Exercises**, which are, for the most part, conceptual language-independent material, especially focusing on work-through reviews, abstract design issues, and time-space analysis.
    - **Programming Problems**, which focus on building Java classes, especially focusing on design/implementation alternatives and code reuse.

Acknowledgments

I would like to thank the Data Structures teams in the Computer Science department at Rutgers University with whom I have taught this course for over more than a decade, and who have provided direct as well as indirect input that has helped shape this book. Special thanks to current and former faculty members Diane Souvaine, Ken Kaplan, Miles Murdocca, and Don Smith for discussing and reviewing the content.

Many thanks to my friends and former graduate student colleagues Nathalie Japkowicz, George Katsaros, and Dan Arena for carefully reviewing the initial C++ draft, Gabriela Hristescu for providing help with typesetting aspects, and Sri Divakaran for reviewing parts of the Java manuscript. Several students in my data structures class of Fall 1997 read the first complete draft of this book and gave valuable feedback. Thanks to them all, especially Alex Chang, for being such a tremendously loyal fan of the book. Thanks also to the students in Fall 2002 and Spring 2003 who pointed out various errors and other shortcomings in an earlier version that was customized for Rutgers.

Thanks are also due to the Data Structures faculty at Middlesex County College, and my former colleagues when I was working at Lucent Technologies with whom I discussed the material in this book at some point or the other. Special thanks to Tom Walsh at Lucent for cheering me on.

Thanks to all the reviewers who helped make this a better book: Barbara Goldner at North Seattle Community College, Mark Llewellyn at University of Central Florida, Chris Dovolis at University of Minnesota, Iyad A. Ajwa at Ashland University, Minseok Kwon at Rochester Institute of Technology, George Rouskas at North Carolina State

University, Roxanne Canosa at Rochester Institute of Technology, Mary Horstman at Western Illinois University, Ray Whitney at University of Maryland, University College, and Robert P. Burton at Brigham Young University.

The editorial team at Prentice Hall have supported me in all aspects of this project. Thanks to my editor Tracy Dunkelberger for believing that this book project would be a worthwhile enterprise, for her cheery confidence that kept me on an even keel, and for making this book real. Thanks to Christianna Lee and Carole Snyder for guiding me through the review process, and for responding to all my questions with patience and grace.

John Shannon, Irwin Zucker, Camille Trentacoste and the production staff at Laserwords helped correct the numerous typographical and grammatical errors that had crept into the book, and formatted the pages to make sure they were presentable. Due to their diligence and expertise, you, dear reader, are spared my inadvertent mistakes or plain ignorance in these areas. For this, my sincere appreciation and thanks to all of them.

I am deeply grateful to the members of my family and that of my wife's for their advice and encouragement, and for being there to pep me up when things didn't seem to be going too well at times. I would specially like to thank my parents, my mother-in-law, and my wife's grandparents for their constant support. Above all, thanks to my father, C.N. Venugopal, and to my wife's grandfather, Dr. Hayrettin Tanacan, for their special participation. Although both of them are far removed from computers in general, and Data Structures in particular, they took the pains to go through my book to try and understand exactly what it was that I was trying to write that was taking so long!

Thanks to my wife, Zehra Tulin, for her help in many ways during the writing of this book, and more importantly, for her love and support at all times. And an extra big hug to my son Amar whose unfailing pride in his dad spurs me on.

Finally, thanks to all the students who took my classes in various subjects at Rutgers University and Middlesex County College over the years. They have been instrumental in my growth as an educator, and I hope this book can serve as a token of my gratitude to each and every one of them.

In closing, I would be very happy to hear from you about this book—what you liked, what you did not care for, and the errors you found, if any. You can reach me by email at *sesh_venugopal@rutgers.edu*. Your feedback will help me serve you better.

Sesh Venugopal

Piscataway, New Jersey
November, 2006

List of Class Files

Contents

C H A P T E R   1

Object-Oriented Programming in Java

This chapter describes the key features and mechanisms that comprise object-oriented programming in Java, specifically tailored for use in the rest of this book.

The discussion starts with the basics of objects and classes, including encapsulation, class construction and the members of a class, invocation of methods and method overloading, and references to objects. It then moves on to inheritance and the implementation of the is-A design idea, the reuse of code, method overriding, and the Object class.

Using exceptions as a mechanism to handle errors is an important part of Java programming and is explored in detail next. This is followed by a discussion of the most commonly used Java features for input and output.

The maintainability of Java programs is improved by dividing it into packages of related classes, and by specifying appropriate access levels for classes and its members. Two sections are devoted to the understanding of how to make Java applications maintainable.

The next four sections are on polymorphism, abstract classes, and interfaces, which comprise the core of good design practice in building Java applications.

The section following this discusses generics, a major new feature introduced in Java 1.5. Generics are of great importance in building usable and robust data structures.

1.1   OBJECTS AND ENCAPSULATION

Java is an object-oriented language. This means that the components that make up a Java application are considered to be objects that interact with each other, much as in the real world. This object-oriented approach allows us to write Java programs that can model a range of problems, from the simplest to the most sophisticated, with a natural conversion of a problem into a Java-based design.

1.1.1   Objects

Consider modeling a television set so that it can be simulated on a computer for testing its parts. A Java program written for this simulation would model the TV as an object.

A TV is activated when it is powered on. From this moment on, at every point of time until its power is switched off, the TV can be manipulated by changing its volume, the channel it is tuned to, its brightness and contrast, and so on. When it is powered off, the TV is still there, and it may even retain its latest settings for the next time it is switched on.

Programs may also model nonphysical objects. Say you write software for a graphical drawing package. This package would have to internally keep track of all the figures the user draws on the drawing pad, so it knows when, where, and how to display the figures on the pad. When the user quits a drawing session, the package must save all the figures the user has drawn so far so that the drawing can be re-created the next time the user starts up the program and recalls the saved drawing.

One of the most basic drawing elements is a rectangle. A drawing may have many rectangles—the drawing package will create a `Rectangle` object to model each of them. Each rectangle will have an (x, y) location on the plane (referring to, say, the top-left corner of the rectangle), and will have a width, w, and a height, h.

1.1.2   Lifetime, State, and Messages

In a Java program, the simulation of a TV set starts with the creation of a TV object. This TV object will exist as long as the simulation runs; i.e., the *lifetime* of a TV object is equal to the duration of the simulation.

During its lifetime, the *state* of the TV may be changed by sending it *messages* to switch channels, change volume, and so on. The ways in which we can change its state are defined beforehand by the object and are not changeable during its lifetime. Also, the TV is unable to change its own state unless induced by a message sent by an external source. When a message is sent to the TV, it *knows* what to do, i.e., exactly *how* to respond to the message.

The state of a TV object in a Java program comprises a set of attributes, each of which is a variable with a certain value. The values of all the attributes together determine a current state—if any of these values is changed, the state is changed. The behavior of a TV object comprises of a set of operations, each of which may be triggered by a message.

An operation may change the state of the TV (e.g., change volume) or simply access some attribute of the current state (e.g., recall channel). The variables of the TV object are its data, and the operations are its functions. The data and functions are therefore *encapsulated,* or enclosed, within a single entity that is the TV object. In Java, the data are called *fields,* and the operations, *methods.* Thus, a Java object encapsulates fields and methods, which constitute the object's *members.*

Analogously, a `Rectangle` object comprises the fields for its x and y coordinates, and its width and height values, w and h, and methods that allow the manipulation of the `Rectangle`, such as drawing the rectangle on the display, moving it, resizing it, and so forth.

1.1.3 Clients of an Object

In object-oriented programming parlance, the sender of messages to an object is usually referred to as the *client* of that object. An object may have several clients that send messages to it at different points in the lifetime of the object. Note that the client of an object is itself another piece of program code, not a human. This is why it is better to use the term "client" rather than "user."

1.1.4 Separation of Interface from Implementation

What an object is capable of doing is its behavior, which is available to its clients via its methods, or *interface.* (Some data members may also belong to the interface, but such members do not participate in the state of the object. See Section 1.2.5.) Exactly *how* this behavior is implemented by the object is not known to its clients; that is completely up to the object. Thus the interface of an object is clearly separated from its implementation.

This separation is a cornerstone of object-oriented programming, and is of tremendous advantage to clients. They can "write to" an interface with the guarantee that even if the object changes the way it implements the interface, the clients of the object do not have to write their code because the *interface itself is not changed.*

1.2 CLASSES

A *class* serves as a blueprint from which any number of objects may be created. When we say "Honda Civic," we refer to a class of *cars.* The particular Honda Civic in your garage is an object of this class. That is, each object is an *instance* of its class.

We will use two examples, a TV class and a `Rectangle` class, to explain the various aspects of classes.

```
public class TV {
  // static fields
  public static final int MAX_VOLUME = 10;
  public static final int DEFAULT_CHANNEL = 2;
  public static final int DEFAULT_VOLUME = 4;

  // instance (state) fields
  int channel, volume;

  // constructor with parameters
```

```java
  public TV(int channel, int volume) {
    this.channel = channel;
    this.volume = Math.min(volume, MAX_VOLUME);
  }

  // no-arg constructor
  public TV() {
    this(DEFAULT_CHANNEL, DEFAULT_VOLUME);
  }

  // state-update method
  public void switchChannel(int newChannel) {
    channel = newChannel;
  }

  // state-update method
  public void changeVolume(int newVolume) {
    volume = Math.min(newVolume, MAX_VOLUME);
  }

  // state-access method
  public int recallChannel() {
    return channel;
  }
}


public class Rectangle {
  // static fields
  public static final int DEFAULT_WIDTH = 5;
  public static final int DEFAULT_HEIGHT = 5;

  // instance (state) fields
  private int x, y, w, h;

  // constructor specifying all field values
  public Rectangle(int x, int y, int w, int h) {
    this.x = x; this.y = y; this.w = w; this.y = y;
  }

  // constructor specifying only x and y
  public Rectangle(int x, int y) {
    this(x, y, DEFAULT_WIDTH, DEFAULT_HEIGHT);
  }

  public void moveTo(int x, int y) { // state update
    this.x = x; this.y = y;
  }

  public void resize(int w, int h) { // state update
    this.w = w; this.h = h;
  }

  public int getX() { // state access
    return x;
  }
```

```
public int getY() { // state access
  return y;
}

public int getWidth() { // state access
  return w;
}

public int getHeight() { // state access
  return h;
}

public String toString() { // string representation
  return x + "," + y + "," + w + "," + h;
}
}
```

1.2.1 State and Behavior

A class encapsulates state and behavior for its objects.

The state of any object of class TV is defined by its fields `channel` and `volume`. A TV object's behavior is defined by the three methods `switchChannel`, `changeVolume`, and `recallChannel`. Of these, `switchChannel` and `changeVolume` change the state of the TV, but `recallChannel` simply accesses the state.

Note that the field `MAX_VOLUME`, which is defined to be `static`, is not considered a part of the state. The reason for this is explained in Section 1.2.5.

In the class `Rectangle`, fields x, y, w, and h define the state of any `Rectangle` object. The behavior of such an object is defined by the methods `moveTo`, `resize`, `getX`, `getY`, `getWidth`, and `getHeight`.

The method `toString` does not participate in defining the behavior of a `Rectangle` object; rather, it returns a `String` representation of the object. This method is special in a sense that is described in Section 1.4.

The class, field, and method declarations in the classes TV and `Rectangle` use the keywords `public`, `private`, `static` and `final`. We discuss the `static` and final keywords in Section 1.2.5, and the `public` and `private` keywords in Section 1.8.

1.2.2 Method Overloading

The *signature* of a method is its name, and the number, sequence, and types of its parameters. The return type is *not* part of the signature.

For instance, all these following methods have the same signature:

```
int stuff(int x, int y) { ... }
float stuff(int x, int y) { ... }
int stuff(int y, int x) { ... }
```

That is, for the compiler, these three methods are the same.

In a class, no two methods can have the same signature—if they do, the compiler treats this an ambiguity and does not compile the class.

Now suppose we wanted to add an operation or feature to the Rectangle class that would tell whether a point was contained in it. We could add the following method to the Rectangle class to implement this operation:

```
public boolean contains(int px, int py) {
   return px >= x && px <= x+w && py >=y && py <= y+h;
}
```

The idea of containment can be extended to check whether a rectangle contains another inside it. That is, we can make this operation work for rectangles just as we did for points:

```
public boolean contains(Rectangle other) {
   return other.x >= x && other.y >= y &&
          (other.w + other.x - x) <= w &&
          (other.h + other.y - y) <= h;
}
```

Now, class Rectangle consists of two methods named contains. However, the signatures of these methods are different because they have different types of arguments. The contains method is said to be *overloaded*.

A method in a class is said to be overloaded if there is at least one other method in the class that has the same name but a different signature.

1.2.3   Object Creation, Constructors, Garbage Collection

A new TV object may be created as follows:

```
TV myTV = new TV();
```

The left-hand side of the statement declares myTV to be a *reference* of *type* TV. The right-hand side, which is the keyword new followed by a call to the TV class's no-arg constructor, creates a TV object. Assigning the right-hand side to the left means that the reference myTV now refers to an actual TV object.

All objects must be created with new. Without this, but only the declaration, there is no real object. For instance,

```
TV aTV;
```

simply establishes that the name aTV will refer to a TV object; but at this point aTV does not refer to anything.

New object creation actually occurs in two phases. Creating a new TV object with new TV() should be read as new TV + TV(). That is:

1. The new TV part (without the parentheses after TV) creates a new TV object by allocating memory space for it, and initializes all its fields to their default values, depending on type. So, for instance, an int field is initialized to zero, and a String field is initialized to null.

2. The TV() part then calls the no-arg constructor on this new TV object to (re)initialize its state as required.

A constructor is like a method in that it may accept parameters, but it is not really a method. Two syntactic differences distinguish it from a method:

- It has the same name as its class.
- It has no return value.

Importantly, a constructor is only called once for an object, when the object is created with new.

No-arg constructor.   A constructor that takes no parameters, or arguments, is called a *no-arg* constructor. A class may have at most one no-arg constructor. The TV class has a no-arg constructor, which was used to initialize a new TV object earlier.

The Rectangle class does not have a no-arg constructor. So we cannot create a Rectangle object like this:

```
Rectangle rect = new Rectangle(); // error, no no-arg constructor
```

Parametered constructors.   The no-arg constructor of the TV class initializes a new TV object with the channel set to 2 and the volume set to 4, by default. If TV objects need to be created with other initial values for channel or volume, the *parametered* constructor may be used instead:

```
TV aTV = new TV(4,5);
```

As for a Rectangle object, it may be created by specifying its location as well as its width and height, or just its location, in which case default values are supplied for the width and the height. Each of these options may be exercised by calling either parametered constructor of the Rectangle class.

Constructor code reuse.   The no-arg constructor of the TV class, when invoked on a new TV object, initializes its channel field to DEFAULT_CHANNEL (2) and volume field to DEFAULT_VOLUME (4), but it does so in an (apparently) strange way:

```
public TV() {
  this(DEFAULT_CHANNEL, DEFAULT_VOLUME);
}
```

The this statement calls the parametered constructor of the TV class, which, in turn, initializes the channel and volume fields to the specified argument values.

The no-arg constructor could have been equivalently written as:

```
public TV() {
  channel = DEFAULT_CHANNEL;
  volume = DEFAULT_VOLUME;
}
```

However using this(...) is better because it reuses the code of the parametered constructor.

As in the TV class, the two-arg constructor in the Rectangle class calls the four-arg constructor in turn, sending it the x and y values it got, and the default values for w and h.

Explicit reference to current object.   There is another use of the keyword this, as shown in the code for the parametered constructor of the TV class:

```
public TV(int channel, int volume) {
  this.channel = channel;
  this.volume = Math.min(volume, MAX_VOLUME);
}
```

The keyword this is a reference to the object on which the constructor is invoked. That is, this.channel and this.volume refer to the fields channel and volume of the object on which the constructor has been called.

The keyword this may be used in any method or constructor of a class. In the above constructor, using the keyword this is essential, since otherwise the parameters channel and volume would be indistinguishable from the fields of the same names. Writing channel or volume in the constructor would always refer to the parameters, which would *hide* the class fields of the same name.

Compiler-supplied default constructor.   What if a class does not define a constructor? Then the compiler *implicitly* supplies a *default* constructor, which is a no-arg construction with an empty body, i.e., one that does nothing. By implicit, we mean that the compiler carries out the action without programmer intervention.

For instance, suppose we design a class LazyTV, which is identical to TV, except that it does not have any constructors. Then the Java compiler would implicitly supply a default constructor which is effectively the following:

```
public LazyTV() { }    // does nothing
```

If the default constructor does nothing, how would a new TV object be initialized? Recall that writing new LazyTV() results in a two-phase process. In the first phase, the new LazyTV part (without the parentheses after LazyTV) creates a new LazyTV object by allocating space for it, and initializing the fields in the object to default initial values based on their types. In this case, both channel and volume are initialized to 0. Subsequently, in the second phase, the default constructor is called, which does nothing.

Even when we create an object in class TV, which does define constructors (i.e., there will not be a default constructor supplied by the compiler):

```
TV someTV = new TV(5, 7);
```

the fields channel and volume of object someTV are first each default-initialized to 0, and subsequently changed (reinitialized) to 5 and 7 by the parametered constructor that is called.

Garbage collection.   The memory space occupied by an object is reclaimed by the *garbage collector* when the object is no longer in use. Consider the following pair of statements:

```
Rectangle rect = new Rectangle(10,10);
rect = new Rectangle(5,5);
```

The second statement assigns a new `Rectangle` object to the reference `rect`. At this point, the first `Rectangle` object `(10,10)` has no variable referring to it. Thus, it is not accessible any more, and is considered to be no longer in use.

When an object is no longer in use, it technically ceases to exist. It is up to the garbage collector to (a) identify that an object is not in use, and (b) determine, subsequent to this identification, the best time to reclaim the space used by this object. The garbage collector is always silently running in the background, intruding every now and then (without programs noticing this intrusion) to carry out its task.

Thus, memory allocated when a new object is created is automatically garbage collected when it is no longer in use. This language-design strategy does away with potential memory problems that are the bane of programming languages like C and C++. Two frequent memory-related problems in these languages are (a) the programmer "forgets" to free up space that was allocated earlier but is no longer required (wasteful) and (b) the programmer tries to use memory that was freed up earlier, without realizing that it no longer belongs to the program (dangerous).

1.2.4   Method Invocation

An object may be sent a message by invoking one of its methods:

```
myTV.changeVolume(4); // send a changeVolume message
rect.moveTo(7,8);     // send a moveTo message
```

The myTV and `rect` objects respond to these messages by executing their respective methods, which, in each of these cases, results in a change in the object's state.

In the following, the overloaded `contains` method of the `Rectangle` is invoked through object `rect`:

```
rect.contains(4,5); // contains a point?
rect.contains(new Rectangle(2,3)); // contains a rectangle?
```

1.2.5   Static Fields and Methods

Static fields.   Every TV object has its own instance, or copy, of the fields `channel` and `volume`. Consider the following statements:

```
TV tv1 = new TV(4,6);
TV tv2 = new TV(4,6);
tv1.switchChannel(5);
System.out.println(tv1.recallChannel()); // 5
System.out.println(tv2.recallChannel()); // 4
```

Switching the channel on `tv1` does not affect the channel setting on `tv2` because their respective channel fields are separate and different.

Occasionally, several objects of a class may share a common resource. This resource is a property of the class as a whole, *not copied* in every object of the class. Such a classwide resource is declared using the *modifier* `static`.

The TV class defines a `static` field, `MAX_VOLUME`, which is used to set a limit on the value of the `volume` field, both in the parametered constructor and in the `changeVolume` method.

All TV objects will be able to share the MAX_VOLUME resource. Since it is a property of the class, not of any specific object, it may be accessed by using the *class name* instead of an object name:

```
System.out.println("Max volume is " + TV.MAX_VOLUME)
```

Since all objects have access to a static field, it can also be accessed via an object, as in:

```
System.out.println("Max volume is " + myTV.MAX_VOLUME)
```

Access via the class name is recommended because it is then obvious that the field is static, and also underscores the meaning of a field being static.

Constants.   The keyword final is another modifier used for the field MAX_VOLUME of class TV. It indicates that once a value is assigned to this field, it may not subsequently change, i.e., the field serves as a *constant*. In general, there is no obligation that a static field also be final.

Static methods.   Another use of the static modifier is to define *utility methods*. A utility method is one that applies to the class rather than any particular object of that class. Therefore, a utility method is invoked through the name of the class that contains it, and not through an object.

For example, the String class in Java defines the utility method valueOf:

```
public static String valueOf(boolean b)
```

This method accepts a boolean value b, and returns the string "true" or "false" depending on whether b is true or false. It may be invoked as follows:

```
boolean b = true;
String.valueOf(b);
```

The String class defines several other overloaded valueOf methods that return appropriate string representations of other primitive data types as well as objects.

An extreme example of the use of utility methods is the class Math in the java.lang package. *All* the methods in this class are static, and so are its fields. The Math class serves as a repository of some standard mathematical functions. For instance, here is how we can find the square root of a number by invoking the static method sqrt:

```
double x = Math.sqrt(3.9);
```

In the TV class, we used the static method min of the Math class:

```
public TV(int channel, int volume) {
  this.channel = channel;
  this.volume = Math.min(volume, MAX_VOLUME);
}
```

A static method *may not* refer to a nonstatic field in the class.

Controlling number of instances using static method.   One special use of `static` methods is to control the number of instances of a class that may be created in an application. Suppose we define a class called `DrawingManager` that keeps track of all figures (rectangles, points, etc.) in a drawing application, and does various other managerial activities. We only need one `DrawingManager` object in the application. How do we enforce this constraint? (Sure, the application can be responsible enough to only create one instance, but mistakes happen, and a program must protect itself against errors to the extent possible.)

The first thing to do in the `DrawingManager` class is to not have any constructors. Otherwise, there is nothing to prevent the application from issuing two or more calls to new. Note that not writing any constructor at all does not help, because we know that the compiler will then write in a default constructor. So we write a constructor, but we turn it off using the `private` modifier:

```
private DrawingManager() { }
```

The `private` keyword is discussed in Section 1.8. Here it means that if you write this:

```
DrawingManager dm = new DrawingManager();
```

the compiler will call an error because the constructor is not visible outside the class. However, it may be used within the class, as seen in the following discussion.

The second thing to do (after making sure not to define a constructor) is to define a method that can deal out the one instance of `DrawingManager` when needed. In other words, whenever the application needs the `DrawingManager` instance, it will call this method.

```
public static DrawingManager getInstance() { ... }
```

This method must be `static` because it cannot be called on a `DrawingManager` object. In fact, the very first time this method is called, a new (and only) `DrawingManager` object will be created and returned. Subsequently, the same `DrawingManager` object will always be returned on every call. Let's fill in the method body to do this:

```
public static DrawingManager getInstance() {
  if (instance == null) {
     instance = new DrawingManager();
  }
  return instance;
}
```

The third thing to do is to define the `instance` field, again as a `static` variable because it is effectively the property of the class.

```
private static DrawingManager instance = null;
```

This field is explicitly initialized to null, just to be safe, although when the application starts running, all static fields of a class are initialized to their default values based on type. This is analogous to how all the fields of an object are default-initialized when it is created.

Also, this field is marked `private` so that it will not be accidentally accessed directly when it is null. (The `private` keyword is discussed in more detail in Section 1.8.) All accesses are thus forced to be made through the `getInstance` method, which correctly handles the `null` case.

Putting it all together, here is an outline of the `DrawingManager` class:

```
public class DrawingManager {
  ...
  private static DrawingManager instance = null;

  private DrawingManager() { }
  ...
  public static DrawingManager getInstance() {
    if (instance == null) {
        instance = new DrawingManager();
    }
    return instance;
  }
}
```

Special static method main.   In a Java *application* (as opposed to an applet), the `main` method is declared to be `static`:

```
public static void main(String args[])
```

1.2.6   Object References

When an object is created using the new construct, it is assigned space in memory. An object's name, such as the name myTV or `rect` we used earlier, is a reference to this space in memory.

The following pair of statements:

```
TV first = new TV(7, 3);
TV second = new TV(7, 3);
```

creates two physically distinct TV objects, each initialized to channel 7, volume 3. On the other hand, the following pair of statements:

```
TV first = new TV(7, 3);
TV second = first;
```

creates only one TV object (in the first statement) that is referenced, or referred to, by two names.

By the same token, consider what happens when a method that takes some object as parameter is called. For instance, take the method `contains` of the `Rectangle` class that accepts another `Rectangle` object as parameter. Here is a call to this method:

```
Rectangle rect1 = new Rectangle(3,4);
Rectangle rect2 = new Rectangle(4,5);
boolean b = rect1.contains(rect2);
```

The method `contains` that accepts a `Rectangle` object as parameter names its parameter, `rect`. When this method is called above, and `rect2` is passed as the matching argument to this parameter, when the method executes, its `rect` refers to the *same* object as `rect2`, *not a different copy* of it.

Occasionally, one might want to *clone* an object. Cloning an object means making another physically distinct object that is identical to the first, down to its current state. This topic is examined in more detail in Section 1.4.3.

1.3   INHERITANCE

A color TV is a special type of TV. A car is a special type of vehicle. Being *special* is relative to something that is nonspecial; the special entity has a little extra something relative to the nonspecial entity. *Modeling this notion of specialization in a way that leads to reuse of code is the basis of inheritance in object-oriented programming.*

1.3.1   Superclass and Subclass

Suppose class B is a specialization of class A. This means that the fields and methods of a class A are *inherited* (and therefore reused) by class B. In Java, the inheriting class (B) is called the *subclass,* and the class from which it inherits (A) is called its *superclass.* A superclass-subclass relationship is graphically expressed with an arrow from the subclass to the superclass.

A   (superclass)

B   (subclass)

Inheritance, in general, implements an important design situation: several classes share common data and behavior, but each provides its own special data and behavior that make it different from the other classes.

For instance, cars and motorcycles are both motorized vehicles. They are both capable of moving, they both have engines, and they both run by burning fuel. But a car is different from a motorcycle in that it has four wheels instead of two, is covered instead of open, and has a steering wheel instead of a steering bar.

We could model this system using three classes: superclass `MotorVehicle` captures the commonality of features and behavior between its subclasses `Car` and `Motorcycle`, while the latter implement their respective specializations.

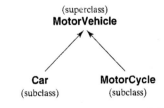

(superclass)
MotorVehicle

Car
(subclass)

MotorCycle
(subclass)

The code in `MotorVehicle` is reused by each of `Car` and `Motorcycle`. This design is schematically expressed in a *class inheritance hierarchy* (often simply referred to as a class hierarchy)

Inheritance requires an *is-A* relationship between the class that inherits and the class that is inherited from. Every `Car` *is A* `MotorVehicle`, but the converse is not true.

Let us take an example to illustrate the different aspects of inheritance in detail. Suppose we were to define a specialization of the TV class called `StereoTV`; i.e., `StereoTV` is a subclass of TV. In Java, the keyword extends is used in the class definition of StereoTV to indicate that it is a subclass of TV, shown below:

```java
public class StereoTV extends TV {
  // special fields
  int balance;
  int leftVolume;
  int rightVolume;
  public static final int MAX_BALANCE = 10;
  public static final int MIN_BALANCE = -10;

  // constructor with parameters
  public StereoTV(int channel, int volume, int balance) {
    super(channel, volume);    // invoke superclass constructor
    checkSetBalance(balance);
    setLeftRight();
  }

  // no-arg constructor
  public StereoTV() {
    this(2, 4, 0);
  }

  // special methods
  public int getBalance() {
    return balance;
  }

  public void setBalance(int balance) {
    setCheckBalance(balance);
    setLeftRight();
  }

  // overrides changeVolume of superclass TV
  public void changeVolume(int newVolume) {
    super.changeVolume(newVolume);
    setLeftRight();
  }

  // helper method
  void checkSetBalance(int balance) {
    if (balance < 0) {
        this.balance = Math.max(balance, MIN_BALANCE);
    } else {
        this.balance = Math.min(balance, MAX_BALANCE);
    }
  }

  // helper method
  void setLeftRight() {
    float fraction = Math.abs(balance)*1.0 / MAX_BALANCE;
    if (balance < 0) {
        leftVolume = this.volume;
        rightVolume = (1 - fraction)*leftVolume;
        rightVolume = leftVolume - rightVolume;
    } else {
        rightVolume = this.volume;
```

```
        leftVolume = (1 - fraction)*rightVolume;
        leftVolume = rightVolume - leftVolume;
    }
  }
}
```

StereoTV is a specialization of TV in that it provides an additional feature called balance that may be used to bias the volume toward one audio channel (not to be confused with the TV channel) or the other, defined by the fields leftVolume and rightVolume.

A neutral balance has a value of 0—the volume is equal on the left and right audio channels. A negative (positive) balance indicates that the bias is toward the left (right) audio channel; the volume on the other audio channel is proportionally reduced. The maximum balance on either the negative or the positive side cannot exceed an absolute value of 10, defined by the fields MAX_BALANCE and MIN_BALANCE.

Consider a balance of −5, and a volume set to 5. Then the bias toward the left is 50% (*balance/maximum* = 5/10 = 0.5), i.e., the volume on the right is reduced by $5 * 0.5 = 2$ (integer truncation), which gives a final right channel volume of $5 - 2 = 3$. The left channel volume is 5.

There are two methods in StereoTV, namely checkSetBalance and setLeftRight, that serve as helpers to the other methods of the class, and are not accessible for direct use by a client because they are not declared public. (The accessibility of fields, methods, and classes is discussed in detail in Section 1.8.)

We will explain the construction of StereoTV, as well the different aspects of inheritance, in the following discussion.

1.3.2 Inherited and Specialized Fields

When a class B is subclassed from A, it inherits all the *inheritable* fields of A. For now, let us assume that all fields of a class are inheritable. (In Section 1.8, we will see exactly how a field qualifies as inheritable.) This means that B can treat the inherited fields of A *as its own*. In other words, it is as if B wrote the inherited code for itself.

Class StereoTV inherits the fields MAX_VOLUME, channel and volume from class TV. In addition, it introduces the following five fields: balance, leftVolume, rightVolume, MAX_BALANCE, and MIN_BALANCE. Of these, the last two are not *instance* variables, but

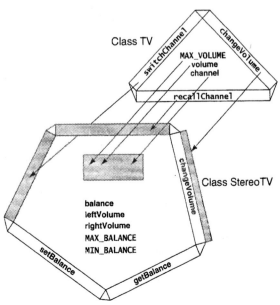

classwide (static) constants (final). These five additional fields are responsible for making StereoTV special with respect to TV; thus we sometimes refer to them as special fields.

1.3.3 Constructors

A superclass constructor is not inherited by its subclass.

There is a common pattern to the code of the constructors and other methods of StereoTV: first handle the part inherited from the superclass, if applicable, and then handle the specialization part.

Constructor with parameters.   Here is the constructor that accepts three arguments:

```
public StereoTV(int channel, int volume, int balance) {
  super(channel, volume);
  checkSetBalance(balance);
  setLeftRight();
}
```

First handle the part inherited from the superclass. In this case, first initialize the part inherited from the superclass—and what better way to do this than to invoke the superclass constructor?

```
super(channel, volume);
```

The keyword super followed by an argument list invokes the superclass, or TV, constructor, which initializes the volume and channel fields, as seen earlier.

Then handle the specialization part. In this case, initialize the balance, leftVolume, and rightVolume fields. This is done by calling on the helper methods checkSetBalance and setLeftRight, respectively.

The method checkSetBalance ensures that the specified balance is within bounds. If an out-of-bound balance is specified, it is replaced by the appropriate bounding balance value and then assigned to balance.

Method setLeftRight initializes the leftVolume and rightVolume fields based on the bias specified by balance—the details were explained earlier.

No-arg constructor.   As in the class TV, the no-arg constructor simply invokes the other constructor:

```
this(2, 4, 0);
```

with initialization values of 2 and 4 respectively for channel and volume, and 0 for balance.

1.3.4 Object Creation

A StereoTV object may be created as follows:

```
StereoTV stv = new StereoTV(4, 5, 0);
```

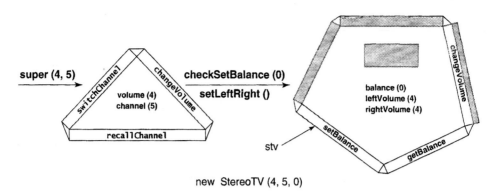

super (4, 5)

checkSetBalance (0)

setLeftRight ()

volume (4)
channel (5)

recallChannel

balance (0)
leftVolume (4)
rightVolume (4)

stv

new StereoTV (4, 5, 0)

The preceding figure shows the superclass and subclass parts of this object being initialized.

Of course, we may alternatively create a StereoTV object using the no-arg constructor:

```
StereoTV nextStv = new StereoTV();
```

1.3.5   Inherited and Specialized Methods

As with the fields of a class, the inheritable methods of a class A are inherited by its subclass B. Again, let us for the moment assume that all the methods of a class are inheritable, pending a detailed discussion of inheritability in Section 1.8. Thus, the methods switchChannel, changeVolume, and recallChannel of class TV are all inherited, and the code for each reused, by StereoTV.

StereoTV itself introduces three additional methods: getBalance, setBalance, and changeVolume.[1] The first two methods go hand-in-hand with the balance field in providing the StereoTV's specialization.

But the case of changeVolume is puzzling: if it is inherited from TV, what is the purpose of redoing it, and how can one prevent it from conflicting with the inherited changeVolume? These questions are answered in Section 1.3.6.

Now let us see how getBalance and setBalance are implemented.

First handle the inherited part. This does not apply, since these methods are specifically meant to handle only the specialization part.

Then handle the specialization part. Thus, getBalance simply returns the current state (value) of the balance field, while setBalance repeats the code used by the constructor to initialize balance, as well as leftVolume and rightVolume:

```
public void setBalance(int balance) {
  checkSetBalance(balance);
  setLeftRight();
}
```

---

1. The methods checkSetBalance and setLeftRight are not relevant because they are simply helpers and do not provide new functionality to clients.

1.3.6   Method Overriding

When the *same functionality* is provided by the superclass and its subclass, but the underlying *implementations are different,* the subclass *overrides* the implementation of the superclass. Both TV and StereoTV provide a functionality or capability called changeVolume, but StereoTV implements it differently from TV because it has to handle the leftVolume and rightVolume fields in addition to the inherited volume field.

The clients are not aware of exactly how these implementations differ; all they see is that the method changeVolume of StereoTV *has the same signature* as its counterpart in TV. Thus, in syntactic terms, a method in a subclass overrides another in a superclass if the methods have the same signature.

Here again is the StereoTV version of changeVolume:

```
public void changeVolume(int newVolume) {
  super.changeVolume(newVolume);
  setLeftRight();
}
```

First handle the inherited part. What better way to do this than to invoke the superclass version of changeVolume:

```
super.changeVolume(newVolume);
```

The keyword super is used to invoke a superclass method. This delegates taking care of the volume field to the superclass.

Then handle the specialization part. In this case, the leftVolume and rightVolume fields are updated by a call to the helper method setLeftRight.

In sum, from the point of view of inheritance, there are three kinds of methods a subclass may implement:

- A method special to the subclass, i.e., that provides new functionality not available in the superclass. Such a method typically does not reuse any code from the superclass and only has to deal with the specialization part.
- A method inherited from the superclass. In this case, all the code from the superclass implementation is reused, and there is no specialization part.
- A method that overrides an inherited method. Here, typically the overriding method reuses some code from the superclass, and implements some of its own specialization.

1.4   THE Object CLASS

When a class A is defined that does not explicitly extend another class, it is implicitly assumed to extend a class called Object, which is in the package java.lang. (Packages are discussed in detail in Section 1.7.) Then, any class that extends A also extends Object, by transitivity. Thus, *every* class in Java ultimately extends the Object class.

For example, the classes TV and Rectangle are direct descendants of the Object class, and StereoTV is a second-level descendant. Since Object is at the root of the Java class hierarchy, it is the superclass of all classes. Therefore, an Object type reference may refer to an object of any class:

```
Object tv = new TV(7, 3);
Object str = "A string object";
```

There are two sets of methods in Object, general utility methods, and methods that support *threads*. The discussion of threads is beyond the scope of this book. Some of the more frequently used utility methods are briefly described below. Each of these methods is inherited by all classes; a class may wish to (and most likely would want to) override one or more of these methods to provide its own specific implementation.

1.4.1   The equals Method

Following is the declaration of the equals method:

```
public boolean equals(Object obj)
```

This method compares the object on which it is invoked with the object referred to by the specified obj argument. It returns true if these objects have *equal value,* and false otherwise.

The default implementation of this method in Object assumes that an object is only *equal to itself.* The following example, based on the Rectangle class of Section 1.2, shows that the equals method is equivalent to the == operator.

```
Rectangle rect1 = new Rectangle(1,2,3,4);
Rectangle rect2 = new Rectangle(1,2,3,4);
Rectangle rect3 = rect1;

if (rect1 != rect2)) {    // this is true
    System.out.println("rect1 and rect2 refer to different objects");
}

if (!rect1.equals(rect2)) {    // this is true
    System.out.println("rect1 is not equal to rect2");
}

if (rect1 == rect3) {    // this is true
    System.out.println("rect1 and rect3 refer to the same object");
}

if (rect1.equals(rect3)) {    // this is true
    System.out.println("rect1 is equal to rect3");
}
```

It is clear the default implementation of equals in the Object class checks whether two objects are *physically the same*. Thus, rect1 is not equal to rect2 even though they have the same values for all the fields—they are different objects, created by separate invocations of new. However, rect1 is equal to rect3—they both refer to the same physical object.

In the geometric sense, we want two rectangles to be equal to each other if their widths and heights are equal. In the example above, we want rect1 to be equal to rect2. To implement this notion of equality, we would have to write an equals method in the Rectangle class that would override the equals method inherited from the Object class:

```
public class Rectangle {
   ...
   public boolean equals(Object obj) {
      if (obj != null && obj instanceof Rectangle) {
         Rectangle other = (Rectangle)obj;
         return this.w == other.w && this.h == other.h;
      }
      return false;
   }
}
```

Get to know this method well because it is idiomatic in its construction. Every time we write a method that overrides the equals method of the Object class, we will use this pattern:

- The if condition is exactly as above, with the name of the class for which this method is implemented being substituted for Rectangle.
- In the body, the parameter reference is explicitly cast to the type of the object on which this method is invoked.
- The body evaluates to true or false based on the specific requirement of the class.
- The last statement (outside the if) returns false.

Let us analyze the if condition check in more detail. First of all, we need to return false if the parameter is a null reference; i.e., the object on which this method is invoked (referred to by this) is not equal to a null object.

We also need to return false if the parameter refers to an object that is not an instanceof type Rectangle. In Section 1.9.4 you will learn that X is an instanceof Y if X refers to an object that is of type Y or any subclass of Y. Thus, in our method, if the parameter does not refer to a Rectangle (or a subclass of Rectangle) object, we cannot go on with the equality check because we depend on w and h being defined as fields of the parameter object.

If the conditions in the check are met, the body is assured that the parameter object is indeed a non-null Rectangle (or subclass of Rectangle) object, and as a result, the width and height of this can be respectively compared with the width and height of the parameter. However, before accessing the w and h fields of the object referred to by obj, the latter must be explicitly cast (another example of casting down the hierarchy) to type Rectangle. The reason for this is explained in Section 1.9.3.

1.4.2   The toString Method

This method writes out a string representation of an object's value:

```
public String toString() { ... }
```

This is extremely useful as a debugging tool, as well as a tool to print the value of an object to an output stream. Typically, a class would override the Object class implementation of this method, as we did in the Rectangle class:

```
public class Rectangle {
   ...
   public String toString() {
     return x + "," + y + "," + w + "," + h;
   }
}
```

Thus:

```
Rectangle rect = new Rectangle(3,4,5,6);
System.out.println(rect);    // prints 3,4,5,6
```

We could have written:

```
System.out.println(rect.toString());
```

but the explicit toString() call in this situation is redundant. The reason is that whenever a variable is sent as an argument to the System.out.println() or System.out.print() method, it is automatically converted to a string. If the variable is an object reference, this conversion is done by automatically calling the toString method on the referred object. If this object's class forgot to define a toString method, the inherited toString from the Object class is used, which returns a useless string representation.

1.4.3   The clone Method

At the end of Section 1.2, we remarked that cloning an object means making a physical copy with the same state as the source object. The default way to clone an object is to use the clone method of the Object class:

```
protected Object clone()
throws CloneNotSupportedException { ... }
```

But simply invoking this inherited method in some class is not going to do it. Suppose we want to make a clone of a TV object, c. If we do the following:

```
TV myTV = new TV();   TV newTV = myTV.clone();
```

then based on the definition of the TV class we have seen earlier, the clone method will "throw an exception" called CloneNotSupportedException. Exceptions, including the throws clause in the header of a method as shown above, are discussed in detail in Section 1.5.

In order to *enable* cloning of its objects, a class *must* declare itself to implement an interface called Cloneable, defined in java.lang. (Interfaces are discussed in Section 1.12.) Thus:

```
public class TV implements Cloneable {
    ...
}
```

TV objects may then be cloned as follows:

```
TV myTV = new TV(4, 5);
TV newTV = myTV.clone();      // channel=4, volume=5
if (newTV != myTV) {      // true since not same object
    newTV.switchChannel(7);      // channel=7, volume=5
}
```

The statement:

```
TV newTV = myTV.clone();
```

creates another object, which is a physical copy of the object referred to by myTV. After this statement, newTV and myTV refer to two different objects that happen to have the same state, i.e., the clone starts out with the same field values as the object from which it was cloned. Subsequent to this, any changes made to the clone, newTV, has no effect on the object from which it was cloned; they lead separate lives.

It is worthwhile to summarize how clonability was implemented in this example:

- Any class that permits its objects to be cloned must implement the interface java.lang.Cloneable. This interface has no methods.
- The implementation of clone in Object assigns the instance fields of the cloned object to the corresponding instance fields of the clone. In our example, these are the fields channel and volume. This makes the clone start out with the same state as the object from which it was cloned.
- The Object.clone method creates an object of the same type as the one being cloned. In our example, this means that the cloned object is guaranteed to be of type TV, and *not* Object, even though it is Object that really does the cloning.

1.5   EXCEPTIONS

Say we write the following program to find the factorial for an integer greater than zero:

```
01 public class Factorial {
02     public static void main(String[] args) {
03         int n = Integer.parseInt(args[0]);
04         int fact = 1;
05         while (n > 1) {
```

```
06        fact = fact * n;
07        n--;
08      }
09      System.out.println(n + "! = " + fact);
10    }
11 }
```

Then we compile and run this program:

```
> javac Factorial.java
> java Factorial 10
10! = 3628800
```

Here is another run:

```
> java Factorial 1o
Exception in thread "main" java.lang.NumberFormatException:
                            For input string: "1o"
        at java.lang.NumberFormatException.forInputString(
                            NumberFormatException.java:48)
        at java.lang.Integer.parseInt(Integer.java:456)
        at java.lang.Integer.parseInt(Integer.java:497)
        at Factorial.main(Factorial.java:3)
```

(The first two lines of the output have been wrapped over to the next line to fit the format of this page.)

We mistyped the number 10 as "1o", with the letter o instead of the digit 0. The program crashes with an error message from the *virtual machine*. The program failed because an *exception* was *thrown* at some point in the execution. The error message details both the sequence of actions from the time the program started executing to the time the exception was thrown, and the exception itself. We will get to the details of what an exception is, and the mechanism used to throw exceptions, but first let us start by understanding exactly what sequence of incidents culminated in this error.

1.5.1 Interpreting an Exception Message

The first line of the error message corresponds to the latest incident.

If we want to follow the sequence of actions from the time the program started executing, which was the earliest incident in this story, we would have to start reading the error message starting with the last line:

```
at Factorial.main(Factorial.java:3)
```

The sequence that led to the final error started in the main method of class Factorial, on line 3. Line 3 of the Factorial class calls the method parseInt of the `Integer` class with the argument `args[0]`, which is the first argument to the program, "1o" in the example.

On to the second line of the error message, which describes the next incident:

at java.lang.Integer.parseInt(Integer.java:497)

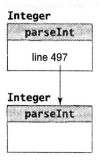

At this time, program execution is in the `parseInt` method of `java.lang.Integer`, on line 497. Since this is a Java API class, we are not familiar with the code in it, but we can infer that this is where the program attempted to interpret the letter "o" in our mistyped "1o" as a digit.

Going up one more line in the error message to the next incident, we see the following:

at java.lang.Integer.parseInt(Integer.java:456)

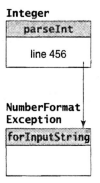

Again, since we do not know the code for `java.lang.Integer`, we cannot say much except to broadly infer that some action is being taken here to handle the problem of not being able to interpret "o" as a digit.

Further up the error message chain, we are at this line:

at java.lang.NumberFormatException.forInputString(
                    NumberFormatException.java:48)

Execution has now proceeded to the forInputString method of the java.lang.Number
FormatException class, on line 48. This is where we have a first look at the exception
itself.

This java.lang.NumberFormatException is a class that encapsulates an exception
object that represents a specific kind of error: that an attempt was made to interpret
a string as a number (integer) but the interpretation failed because the string was not
formatted correctly as a number.

Finally, an additional error line is printed:

```
Exception in thread "main" java.lang.NumberFormatException:
                        For input string: "1o"
```

and the program stops running.

It so happens that this exception sequence is actually printed by the virtual machine,
or VM (launched by the java command), that is running our program, and not by the
program itself.

The entire chain of events, starting from the VM executing the program all the way
to the NumberFormatException, and the reverse flow of control, in which an exception
makes its way all the way back to the VM, is shown in the following figure.

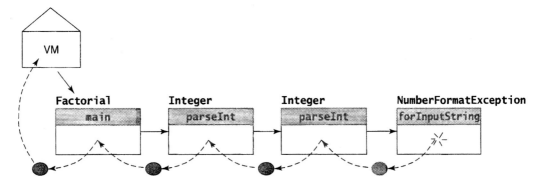

In fact, we can condense the chain of incidents to just two lines and know exactly
what happened:

```
Exception in thread "main" java.lang.NumberFormatException:
                        For input string: "1o"
...
        at Factorial.main(Factorial.java:3)
```

That is, line 3 of our code started the process that ended in an error, which resulted
in the java.lang.NumberFormatException exception being thrown, for string "1o". We
know this was the argument to the program, passed on to Integer.parseInt on line 3
of our code.

Identifying and reporting errors is a major component of any program, and Java's
support for the programmer toward this is the concept of exceptions and the rules
governing how to use them. It is important to understand why exceptions are better than
other, homegrown ways of handling errors.

1.5.2   Homegrown Error Handling

The following example takes two strings as arguments for the first and last names of a person, and prints them out as lastname, firstname.

```
01 public class Names {
02    public static void main(String[] args) {
03       String fname = args[0];
04       String lname = args[1];
05       System.out.println(lname + ", " + fname);
06    }
07 }
```

Let as compile and run this program:

```
> javac Names.java
> java Names Michael Jordan
Jordan, Michael
```

What does the program expect from its arguments? First of all, there must be two arguments—running it with fewer than two arguments would not make sense, and would be considered an error. Also, the first argument is expected to be a first name, and the second a last name, but there is no way to check this in a program because names are proper nouns.

Next, each of the arguments must have at least one character—an empty name has no meaning, and would be considered an error. So you can run the program like this, with quotes around the arguments:

```
> java Names "Michael" "Jordan"
Jordan, Michael
```

and it would be just the same as before, but if you run the program like this:

```
> java Names "" "Jordan"
Jordan,
```

it prints the last name followed by a comma, and then nothing because the first name is of length zero. This is an error, and should be reported, instead of printing a strange-looking incomplete output.

How to make our program catch and report these two errors? Here's one way:

```
01 public class Names {
02    public static void main(String[] args) {
03       if (args.length != 2) {
04          System.err.println("expected usage: java Names " +
05                             "<firstname> <lastname>");
06          System.exit(1);
07       }
08
09       String fname = args[0];
10       if (fname.length() == 0) {
11          System.err.println("error: firstname is length zero");
12          System.exit(1);
13       }
```

```
14
15      String lname = args[1];
16      if (lname.length() == 0) {
17          System.err.println("error: lastname is length zero");
18          System.exit(1);
19      }
20
21      System.out.println(lname + ", " + fname);
22  }
23 }
```

The approach here is to detect the error as soon as it could have happened, print an error message to the error stream System.err (discussed in Section 1.6), and exit the program right there, with a System.exit(1). By convention, a nonzero argument to System.exit indicates an error.

This is a "torpedo" approach to error handling where any error will bring the program crashing down right away without any hesitation. But many times we want a more nuanced approach, where the error is identified and reported, at which point a calculated decision can be made whether to continue the program or halt it.

Let's revisit the factorial program and write it a little differently by creating a separate method to compute the factorial, and calling this method from the main method:

```
01 public class Factorial {
02    public static void main(String[] args) {
03       int n = Integer.parseInt(args[0]);
04       System.out.println(n + "! = " + fact(n));
05    }
06
07    private static int fact(int n) {
08       int fact = 1;
09       while (n > 1) {
10          fact = fact * n;
11          n--;
12       }
13       return fact;
14    }
15 }
```

As before, if we run this program with an argument that cannot be interpreted as a number, the program will crash due to the java.lang.NumberFormatException. But try this:

```
> javac Factorial.java
> java Factorial -5
-5! = 1
```

This is not correct. The argument, -5, passes the number format check because it is a legal integer, but the factorial of -5 is not defined, and the attempt to compute it should have been reported as an error. One way you might think of reporting the error is by having the fact method return 0 in case of an error, instead of simply terminating the program.

Then, when program control returns from fact, have the caller check the return value and report an error if it is 0 as shown in the following code.

```
01 public class Factorial {
02   public static void main(String[] args) {
03     int n = Integer.parseInt(args[0]);
04     int f = fact(n);
05     while (f == 0) {
06       System.out.println("error: factorial only works with " +
07                           "positive integers, your input was " + n);
08       System.out.print("\tPlease enter a positive integer => ");
09       n = readInput();
10       f = fact(n);
11     }
12     System.out.println(n + "! = " + f);
13   }
14
15   private static int fact(int n) {
16     if (n < 1) {
17       return 0;
18     }
19     int fact = 1;
20     while (n > 1) {
21       fact = fact * n;
22       n--;
23     }
24     return fact;
25   }
26
27   private static int readInput() { ... }
28 }
```

The burden of taking action on an error is moved from the callee to the caller, and this is usually advantageous because the caller has more contextual information, and therefore is able to handle problems more judiciously. In the preceding code, the caller is the main method. The writer of this method knows that the input is coming from a user, not from another part of the program, to which this error should propagate. So the writer uses this contextual information to prompt the user for a correct input instead of terminating the program.

Now let's add another requirement to the program. Since factorials can get very large, beyond a point they cannot be represented in an integer variable. Note that the answer 16! is smaller than for 15 and is thus incorrect. Then 17! is reported as a negative number, again incorrect. These point to the inability of an integer variable to hold 16! and 17! (and larger).

```
> java Factorial 14
14! = 1278945280
> java Factorial 15
15! = 2004310016
> java Factorial 16
16! = 2004189184
> java Factorial 17
17! = -288522240
```

Thus we should limit our program to only accept integer arguments between 1 and
15. We can add another condition inside the `fact` method:

```
01 public class Factorial {
02   public static void main(String[] args) {
03     int n = Integer.parseInt(args[0]);
04     int f = fact(n);
05     while (f == 0 || f == -1) {
06       if (f == 0) {
07         System.out.println("error: factorial only works with " +
08                             "positive integers, your input was " + n);
09         System.out.print("\tPlease enter a positive integer => ");
10       } else { // f == -1
11         System.out.println("error: factorial only works with " +
12                             "integers from 1 to 15, your input was " + n);
13         System.out.print("\tPlease enter an integer between 1 and 15 => ");
14       }
15       n = readInput();
16       f = fact(n);
17     }
18     System.out.println(n + "! = " + f);
19   }
20
21   private static int fact(int n) {
22     if (n < 1) {
23       return 0;
24     }
25     if (n > 15) {
26       return -1;
27
28     }
29     int fact = 1;
30     while (n > 1) {
31       fact = fact * n;
32       n--;
33     }
34     return fact;
35   }
36
37   private static int readInput() { ... }
38 }
```

What `fact` is doing is *coding* error messages and passing them back, and the caller is then
deciphering the code and handling them as needed. This approach works because `fact`
returns a result, but what if a method does not return a result?

Consider writing a program that prints a pattern like this:

```
*
* *
* * *
* * * *
```

The input to this program is the number of lines to be printed, and the input has to be an integer greater than zero. We also want the input to be at most 20. Here is the program:

```
01 public class Pattern {
02    public static void main(String[] args) {
03       int n = Integer.parseInt(args[0]);
04       print(n);
05    }
06
07    private static void print(int n) {
08       if (n < 1) {
09          // don't know how to tell caller there's an error
10          return;
11       }
12       if (n > 20) {
13          // don't know how to tell caller there's an error
14          return;
15       }
16       for (int line=1; line <= n; line++) {
17          for (int star=1; star <= line; star++) {
18             System.out.print("* ");
19          }
20          System.out.println();
21       }
22    }
23 }
```

We have a problem here: print cannot tell the caller that there is an error when the parameter n is outside the required limits. We could force the print method to return an int just so that we can return an error code, but this would blatantly violate the design of the program, forcing methods to do things they should not be doing. The more liberties we take like this, the more difficult it gets to ensure that the program will work correctly when more and more features are added. There is another, more important reason for not returning an error code, which has to do with how software is built.

A software application is developed by many people working in groups. The group, say, that works on developing useful code libraries or structures is different from the group that uses these libraries in another part of the application. In the case of the factorial application, imagine that there is an application that performs various mathematical computations, factorial being only one of them. There is one group in charge of writing up a library of mathematical functions, including fact, that will be used in the application, and a different group that will use these functions to, say, plot them on a graphing window.

How fast and how well the application can be built depends on how independently these different groups can work, building their respective parts (subsystems) of the application in parallel. In order to do this, they will need to understand how different subsystems interact with each other. This means that the inputs and outputs of the subsystems, in other words their interfaces, must be clearly defined. And part of the clarity of definition is *separating normal flow in and out of methods from error-based or exceptional flows.*

In particular, having a method's return value mean either a correct result or an error code is dangerous because it confuses the issue and weakens the link between the method and its caller. And, of course, in the case of methods that do not return a value, the approach to force error coding would be more convoluted, and therefore more error-prone.

Java's mechanism of using exceptions is a uniform, well-engineered process that separates normal execution from error situations. An exception is an *object,* and at the point where an error is detected, an exception object must be created and *thrown,* which launches a separate control flow in the program that is orchestrated by the virtual machine. We call this the exceptional control flow, or just exceptional flow.

1.5.3 Throwing an Exception

Here is the Names program reworked to throw exceptions.

```
01 public class Names {
02   public static void main(String[] args) {
03     if (args.length != 2) {
04       throw new IllegalArgumentException("usage: java Names " +
05                                    "<firstname> <lastname>");
06     }
07
08     String fname = args[0];
09     if (fname.length() == 0) {
10       throw new IllegalArgumentException("firstname is " +
11                                    "length zero");
12     }
13
14     String lname = args[1];
15     if (lname.length() == 0) {
16       throw new IllegalArgumentException("lastname is "+
17                                    "length zero");
18     }
19
20     System.out.println(lname + ", " + fname);
21   }
22 }
```

As soon as an error is detected, an exception is thrown. Before you throw an exception, you need to choose an appropriate exception object. There are many exception classes available in the Java API, tailormade for various types of error conditions. Most exceptions in general-purpose applications can be encapsulated by using one of the Java API exceptions.

In the names example, the error is that the arguments to the program are incorrect. This is a very common type of error in many programs, and the java.lang.Illegal-ArgumentException is a perfect fit for this kind of error. After you pick an appropriate exception class, you need to create a new object of that class. There are usually two constructors for any exception: a no-arg constructor, and another constructor that accepts a single argument called *detailed message*. The second constructor is preferred when you want to give more information about the error than what is suggested by the name of the exception. In our code above, all three exceptions are `IllegalArgumentException` objects, but each carries a different detailed message.

After the exception object is created, you need to `throw` it. The moment the exception is thrown, the method from where it is thrown is *exited*, as if you had *returned* from the method right there. No other statements in the method are executed, and control goes back to the caller. However, this is a different, exceptional control path, which is handled differently by the virtual machine. Let's see how this works in the names example. Below is the sample code and an illustration:

```
> javac Names.java
> java Names Madonna " "
Exception in thread "main" java.lang.IllegalArgumentException:
                          lastname is length zero
        at Names.main(Names.java:16)
```

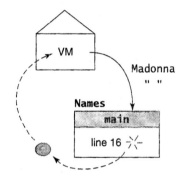

This looks much like our very first look at exceptions, where we tracked the `NumberFormatException`. In this execution of the Names program, the `main` method throws an `IllegalArgumentException` at line 16 because the last name length is zero. Since the `main` method has no caller, the exception is taken over by the virtual machine, which prints out the first line of the error message. Since it " " also knows the entire control sequence of any Java program it runs, it prints the second line which tells where the exception originated. Finally, the virtual machine stops the program.

Now let's rework the `Factorial` program using exceptions and removing all error handling code from the `main` method:

```
01 public class Factorial {
02    public static void main(String[] args) {
03       int n = Integer.parseInt(args[0]);
04       int f = fact(n);
05       System.out.println(n + "! = " + f);
06    }
07
08    private static int fact(int n) {
09       if (n < 1) {
10          throw new IllegalArgumentException(n + " < " + 1);
11       }
12       if (n > 15) {
13          throw new IllegalArgumentException(n + " > " + 15);
14       }
15       int fact = 1;
```

```
16     while (n > 1) {
17         fact = fact * n;
18         n--;
19     }
20     return fact;
21   }
22 }
```

Let us compile and run this program with -15 as argument:

```
> javac Factorial.java
> java Factorial -15
Exception in thread "main" java.lang.IllegalArgumentException: -15 < 1
        at Factorial.fact(Factorial.java:10)
        at Factorial.main(Factorial.java:4)
```

When the exception is thrown, the control flow is no longer normal. The exceptional flow does not go to the statement in the `main` method immediately after the call to `fact`, which is the `System.out.println` statement. Instead, it passes *through* the `main` method, and then on to the virtual machine, which writes out the error message, along with the sequence of method calls in reverse order, starting with the method that threw the exception.

Now let's take a different approach, and have the `main` method *intercept* any exception that is thrown by `fact`.

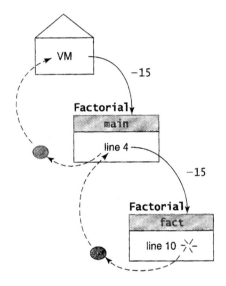

1.5.4 Catching an Exception

```
01 public class Factorial {
02   public static void main(String[] args) {
03     int n = Integer.parseInt(args[0]);
04     int f=0;
05     try {
06         f = fact(n);
07     } catch (IllegalArgumentException e) {
08         throw new IllegalArgumentException(n + "<1 or >15");
09     }
10     System.out.println(n + "! = " + f);
11   }
12
13   private static int fact(int n) {
```

```
14      if (n < 1) {
15          throw new IllegalArgumentException(n + " < 1");
16      }
17      if (n > 15) {
18          throw new IllegalArgumentException(n + " > 15");
19      }
20      int fact = 1;
21      while (n > 1) {
22          fact = fact * n;
23          n--;
24      }
25      return fact;
26   }
27 }
```

An exception that is thrown by a method can be caught by the caller of the method. To do this, the caller has to enclose the method call in a so-called try block, following which is a catch block, as in lines 05-09 above.

Imagine that the Factorial program is executed again, with an argument of -15. The main method is called, which first parses the argument into the integer n. Then it executes the call to fact, which is inside the try block. We know that an exception is going to be thrown by fact. The exception comes back to the main method, but will only *stop* there *if the exception is caught*. How is this determined?

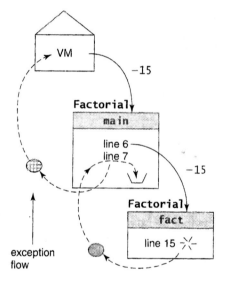

Think of it as the call returning from fact (in an exceptional flow of control), then looking to see if there is a catch block at the end of the try with the *same exception type as the exception that was thrown*. If so, the statements within the catch block are executed. If not, the exception is not caught, and it propagates up to the previous method in the call sequence.

The catch block looks just like a method, with a single argument that is an exception object, and a body within braces. In our example, the exception object is of type IllegalArgumentException, which matches the type of the thrown exception. The exception object is given the local name e for possible use inside the catch block. The body of this block is executed, which throws a new exception object, again of type IllegalArgumentException, but with a consolidated message that gives both ends of the acceptable range of inputs—in the figure the two exception objects are different. That is, while fact treats each end of the range as a separate case, the caller tries to prevent errors in future runs by laying out the error in more detail.

Since an exception is thrown, no subsequent statements in the main method are executed, and the method is exited. The virtual machine then takes over the exception, prints an error message, and stops the program. Here is the result of running Factorial again, with -15 as the argument:

```
> java Factorial -15
Exception in thread "main" java.lang.IllegalArgumentException:
                                    -15<1 or >15
        at Factorial.main(Factorial.java:7)
```

If, on the other hand, we run Factorial with the argument 5, no exception is thrown by fact, the catch block is never entered, and control will jump over the catch block to line 10, where the value of 5! is printed.

Note that the variable f is declared before the try block, instead of:

```
try {
    int f = fact(n);
} catch (IllegalArgumentException e) {
    throw new IllegalArgumentException(n + "<1 or >15");
}
System.out.println(n + "! = " + f);
```

This would result in a compilation error, because f would not be visible in the print statement, which is outside the try block.

The program design we adopted above simply had the main method provide an additional layer of exception, so if an exception was thrown by fact, the program would eventually terminate. We could have designed the program differently. Instead of having the catch block throw a new exception, we could have dealt with the original exception by prompting the user for a legal input, as we did earlier. In which case, the try-catch combination might look like this:

```
02 public static void main(String[] args) {
03    int n = Integer.parseInt(args[0]);
04    int f=0;
05    boolean done=false;
06    while (!done) {
07       try {
08          f = fact(n);
09          done = true;
10       } catch (IllegalArgumentException e) {
11          System.out.println(e.getMessage());
12          System.out.print("\tPlease enter an integer between 1 and 15 => ");
13          n = readInput();
14       }
15    }
16    System.out.println(n + "! = " + f);
17 }
```

The entire try-catch combination is now inside a while loop that will spin until a correct input is entered and its factorial computed. The new design is best explained by means of a sample run:

```
> java Factorial -15
-15 < 1
Please enter an integer between 1 and 15 => 22
22 > 15
Please enter an integer between 1 and 15 => 10
10! = 3628800
```

Since the argument to the program is -15, the call to fact on line 8 results in an exception. When the exceptional flow of control comes to main, it jumps directly into the catch block, skipping over line 9. In the catch block, line 11 prints the detailed message (-15 < 1) carried by the exception. This is done by calling the method getMessage on the exception object.

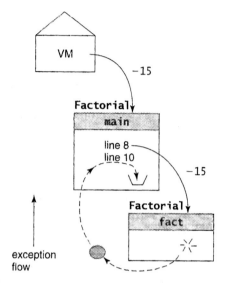

Next, line 12 is executed, which prompts the user for a correct input, an integer between 1 and 15. The user enters 22 to this prompt, which is returned by a call to readInput on line 13. This terminates the execution of the catch block. Since done was not reset to true, control goes back into the body of the while loop.

Control flows exactly the same way again, with the only difference being the detailed message (22 > 15). This time, on being prompted for an integer between 1 and 15, the user does enter a legitimate input, 10, and once again, control goes back into the while loop. Now the call to fact returns in a normal flow, with the value of 10! stored in f. Then the statement on line 9 is executed, which sets done to true. The catch block is not entered at all, the while loop is exited, the print statement on line 16 is executed, and the program terminates normally.

The try block in this example shows that it can contain several statements, only some of which may throw exceptions. What if there is a block of statements in which there are two statements that throw different types of exceptions?

We can modify the previous example so that the main method also catches the NumberFormatException. We will change the design of the program a bit so that it does not accept any arguments. Instead it asks for input from the user. This makes for a better program than having the user start by sending an argument to the program, and if that is incorrect, switching to giving an input to a program prompt.

```
02 public static void main(String[] args) {
03    if (args.length > 0) {
04       System.err.println("usage: java Factorial");
05       System.err.println("ignoring arguments");
06    }
```

```
07    int n=0;
08    int f=0;
09    boolean done=false;
10    while (!done) {
11        try {
12            System.out.print("\tPlease enter an integer between 1 and 15 => ");
13            n = readInput();
14            f = fact(n);
15            done = true;
16        } catch (NumberFormatException e) {
17            System.out.println("Input is not an integer");
18        } catch (IllegalArgumentException e) {
19            System.out.println(e.getMessage());
20        }
21    }
22    System.out.println(n + "! = " + f);
23 }
```

Assume that the readInput method throws a NumberFormatException if a non-integer string is input. There are now two catch blocks after the try block, one to intercept the NumberFormatException that may be thrown on a call to readInput on line 13, and the other to intercept the IllegalArgumentException that may be thrown on a call to fact on line 14.

Here is the sequence of actions that will take place if you run the program as follows:

```
> java Factorial
        Please enter an integer between 1 and 15 => lo
Input is not an integer
        Please enter an integer between 1 and 15 => 10
10! = 3628800
```

On being prompted to enter an integer between 1 and 15, the user types "lo" by mistake, with the letter "o". This input is read by readInput, which tries to parse the string and throws a NumberFormatException. The exception control comes back to main and jumps to the end of the try block, that is, to line 16.

At this point, it looks at the exception parameter type NumberFormatException in the catch block on line 16, finds a match with it, and executes the body, which prints the message

```
Input is not an integer
```

The reason for this catch block is to print a better message than the one carried as a detailed message by the NumberFormatException, which reads:

```
For input string: "lo"
```

After the body of the first catch block has been executed, *control skips over the next* catch *block, i.e., it does not enter this block* (which catches the IllegalArgumentException). Since done has not been set to true, the while loop is re-entered.

The user is again prompted for an integer, types 10, the factorial is computed and returned on line 14, the boolean done is set to true on line 15, and the end of the try block is reached without any exceptions being thrown by any of the called methods. Control skips over the catch blocks, and the factorial of 10 is printed.

In summary, say there are several catch blocks after a try block. When an exception generated by one of the statements in the try block is intercepted, control jumps to the end of the try block, and the exception parameter type of every catch block is checked in sequence. For the first exception type that matches the intercepted exception type, the corresponding catch block is executed, and control skips over all subsequent catch blocks.

If there are several catch blocks after a try block, it does not matter in what order they are coded *so long as no two of the exception types are in the same path in the exception class hierarchy.* Specifically, they don't have to match the order of the statements in the try block that give rise to the corresponding exception types. When the type of the intercept exception is compared against the catch exception types, at most one of the catch types will match.

However, in the example we just discussed, say we flipped the order of the catch blocks so that the IllegalArgumentException comes first:

```
11    try {
12       System.out.print("\tPlease enter an integer between 1 and 15 => ");
13       n = readInput();
14       f = fact(n);
15       done = true;
16    } catch (IllegalArgumentException e) {
17       System.out.println(e.getMessage());
18    } catch (NumberFormatException e) {
19       System.out.println("Input is not an integer");
20    }
21 }
```

Let's compile this new program:

```
> javac Factorial.java
Factorial.java:18: exception java.lang.NumberFormatException has already
          been caught
          } catch (NumberFormatException e) {
          ^
1 error
```

This message makes sense when you find out that NumberFormatException is *a subclass of* IllegalFormatException. It will be matched against the first catch block, and will never get to the second. This means that if there are two catch blocks with exception types E1 and E2, and E1 is a subclass of E2, then the E1 catch block must *precede* the E2 catch block.

Sometimes it is helpful to have a catch-all block that can handle several kinds of intercepted exceptions at once, in the same manner. The next section shows how.

1.5.5   Exception Class

All exceptions are subclasses of the java.lang.Exception class. There is a hierarchy of classes above Exception as well.

The Exception class defines two basic constructors, a no-arg constructor and a constructor with a single String argument that can carry detailed messages. All subclasses of Exception also define these two constructors. There are two other constructors whose usage is more specialized, but we will not include them in this discussion.

We have seen that NumberFormatException is a subclass of IllegalArgumentException, but the latter is a subclass of Exception. Say we wanted to change the implementation of the main method of the Factorial example so that we have a single catch block that handles all input errors. Then we could have that catch block use the type Exception for its parameter instead of a specific subtype:

```
    ...
11 try {
12     System.out.print("\tPlease enter an integer between 1 and 15 => ");
13     n = readInput();
14     f = fact(n);
15     done = true;
16 } catch (Exception e) {
17     System.out.println("Input is not an integer between 1 and 15");
18 }
    ...
```

Let's run this new program with the same inputs as the earlier run:

```
> java Factorial
        Please enter an integer between 1 and 15 => 1o
Input is not an integer between 1 and 15
        Please enter an integer between 1 and 15 => 10
10! = 3628800
```

Since NumberFormatException and IllegalArgumentException are subclasses of Exception, they both match the Exception type in the catch block.

This catch-all block is convenient because the action required from the user is the same in both exception cases, which is that the user enter an integer between 1 and 15. But the error message that is printed is not very clear in the case when the user types a "1o". The message does not say the string is malformed, and a user who mistyped "10" as "1o" might well look at the message and not realize that the input string has an "o" character instead of the digit "0".

It would be better to extend the catch block by printing the detailed message of the intercepted exception:

```
    ...
16 } catch (Exception e) {
17     System.err.println(e.getMessage());
18     System.out.println("Input is not an integer between 1 and 15");
19 }
    ...
```

In addition to the String getMessage() method, the Exception (and its subclasses) defines another useful method called void printStackTrace(). This is the method used by the virtual machine to print the entire sequence of method calls up to the point where the exception was thrown.

The following is a stack trace we saw in the very first example of this section:

```
> java Factorial lo
Exception in thread "main" java.lang.NumberFormatException:
                                    For input string: "lo"
      at java.lang.NumberFormatException.forInputString(
                                 NumberFormatException.java:48)
      at java.lang.Integer.parseInt(Integer.java:456)
      at java.lang.Integer.parseInt(Integer.java:497)
      at Factorial.main(Factorial.java:3)
```

IllegalArgumentException is a subclass of Exception, but it is not an immediate subclass. Instead, it is an immediate subclass of RuntimeException, which is in turn a subclass of Exception. (Just as a reminder, all of these are in the java.lang package.) There are other exception classes that are in a hierarchy that descends directly from Exception, and thereby hangs a tale. We will explore this story in the context of our discussion of input and output, which follows. There, you will also see how to write your own exception class.

1.6   INPUT AND OUTPUT

Inputs to a program and outputs from it can be done either via the terminal or through files. The Java API has a wide variety of input-output (IO) classes for many different requirements. In particular, we will see how the java.util.Scanner class introduced in Java 1.5 can do much of the basic and most frequently needed IO functions.

1.6.1   Terminal-Driven IO

The simplest output method is to print something to the terminal:

Code	Output

`System.out.println("First line");`
`System.out.println("Second line");`
`System.out.print("Word1;");`
`System.out.print("Word2\n");`
`System.out.println("The end");`
	First line
	Second line
	Word1;Word2
	The end

java.lang.System is a special class that contains a (static) field called out. This field is of type java.io.PrintStream, and is called the *standard output stream*, connected to the terminal by default. There is also a *standard error stream*, defined by a static field called err, that is also connected by default to the terminal. This stream is used to print error messages.

The PrintStream class defines methods print, which prints the given string argument, and println, which prints the given string argument followed by a newline character. The `print` variant can be made to look like `println` by simply appending a newline character, '\n', to the end of the string argument.

The simplest input method is to enter data via the terminal. The `System.in` field is the `standard` input stream, connected to the terminal by default. But an input stream in Java can contain either text data or binary data. In order to read text, we need to put an interpreter around `System.in` that can parse the input as text. There is an ideal class for this, `java.util.Scanner`, that has a number of methods to read different types of data. Here is an example with various data items typed to the terminal, and read in using the Scanner class:

Code	Terminal

```
Scanner sc = new Scanner(System.in);        string
String str = sc.next();                                echo:string
System.out.println("\techo:" + str);        25
int i = sc.nextInt();                                  echo:25
System.out.println("\techo:" + i);          32.6
float f = sc.nextFloat();                              echo:32.6
System.out.println("\techo:" + f);          the end
str = sc.next();                                       echo:the
System.out.println("\techo:" + str);
```

There are several things to note in this code segment.

First, there is both input and output being done at the terminal—the output lines echo the input, for confirmation.

Second, the `Scanner` methods `next()`, `nextInt()`, and `nextFloat()` respectively read a string, an integer, and a floating-point number from input. There are various other methods in the `Scanner` class, including some that read other types of data such as `double`.

Third, when you run this program, you will see nothing until you type the first line, "string". You see nothing because the program waits on input when it executes the `sc.next()` statement. After you type the line and hit enter, it reads the input as a string. That is, hitting enter gets the program out of waiting, it reads in the entire line. The statement immediately after it then echoes the string that was read. This process is repeated for the next three reads—the program waits, you type the input and hit enter, the program reads the line, and it echoes what it read.

Fourth, the last echo only prints "the" but the input line was "the end". The reason is that the `next()` method extracts the next *token* from the input. A token is a sequence of non-white-space characters. White spaces include blank space, tab, and newline characters. When the string "the end" is accepted by the program, the `next()` method only extracts the first token, "the", and this is echoed. If you wanted to print the token "end" also, you would have to write another `sc.next()` statement. Then, since there is an unextracted token, "end" in the program, this additional call to `next()` would extract that token *without having to wait for new input*.

Note that when you enter a line of input, that line is a string of characters by default. Therefore, if the first line of input to the preceding example was 25 instead of `string`, the program would read 25 as a string of characters. On the other hand, if the second line of input was string, then you would get the following exception:

```
> java IO
25
        echo:25
string
Exception in thread "main" java.util.InputMismatchException
        at java.util.Scanner.throwFor(Scanner.java:819)
        at java.util.Scanner.next(Scanner.java:1431)
        at java.util.Scanner.nextInt(Scanner.java:2040)
        at java.util.Scanner.nextInt(Scanner.java:2000)
        at IO.main(IO.java:7)
```

This InputMismatchException is thrown because the sc.nextInt() method cannot interpret string as an integer.

Having the user run the program and just see a blank screen is not a good idea because there is no way for the user to know that the program is waiting for an input, let alone to know what kind of input. A program that asks for input from the terminal should prompt the user for the input:

Code	Terminal

```
Scanner sc = new Scanner(System.in);
System.out.print(
        "Enter a string => ");
System.out.println("\techo:" +
                sc.next());
System.out.print(
        "Enter an integer => ");
System.out.println("\techo:" +
                sc.nextInt());
System.out.print(
        "Enter a real number => ");
System.out.println("\techo:" +
                sc.nextFloat());
```

```
Enter a string => string
        echo:string
Enter an integer => 25
        echo:25
Enter a real number => 32.6
        echo:32.6
```

Using print instead of println in the prompts makes for a better user interface.

The user can interact with a program via the terminal (standard input and output) for small amounts of data. When the volume of IO data becomes large, or when a program needs to be run on many different inputs, it is easier to put the data in files for the program to read from or write into.

1.6.2   File-Based IO

Reading from a file.   Reading from a file can be very easily accomplished by setting up a Scanner to get input from that file instead of from System.in. Say we want to write a program that would read a large set of floating-point numbers (such as exam scores of students) from a file called "scores" and compute the average of these scores. Here is a program to do just that:

```
01 import java.util.*;
02 import java.io.*;
03
04 public class IO {
05    public static void main(String[] args) {
06       Scanner sc = new Scanner(new File("scores"));
07       float sum = 0;
08       int n=0;
09       while (sc.hasNextFloat()) {
10          sum += sc.nextFloat();
11          n++;
12       }
13       System.out.println("avg = " + sum/n);
14    }
15 }
```

To begin with, there are two things to note in this program. On line 6, where the Scanner is set up, the parameter is a File object. This File object is itself constructed by pointing it to the disk file "scores". The File class is in the package java.io. The second thing is that on line 9 the condition of the while loop calls the Scanner method hasNextFloat(), which returns true if there are any more real numbers to be read. There are similar methods to check for the existence of more data of other types.

In the input file, the numbers can be in any sequence, not necessarily one per line. Also, if there is more than one number on a line, there can be any number of spaces between them. Thus the following variations of the input file will give the same result:

```
2.5                    .    2.5      .    2.5 6.8 5.7 10.2 19
6.8    5.7  10.2       .    6.8      .
19                     .    5.7      .
                       .    10.2     .
                       .    19       .
```

The nextFloat method starts from wherever it left off in the previous call and looks for a non-whitespace character, skipping over all whitespace characters in between. Remember that whitespace characters are spaces, new lines, and tabs. Then, when it sees the first non-whitespace character, it starts accumulating a sequence of non-whitespaces into a token, breaking off when it encounters a whitespace character. The token accumulated is then interpreted or parsed as a floating-point number.

Let's compile the IO program:

```
> javac IO.java
IO.java:6: unreported exception java.io.FileNotFoundException;
          must be caught or declared to be thrown
Scanner sc = new Scanner(new File(''scores''));
                  ^
1 error
```

The error has to do with the creation of a File object in line 6—what if the file is not on disk? When we learned about exceptions in Section 1.5, we never once came across a compiler error of this kind. Every situation we looked at entailed an exception being thrown when a program is running. In a similar vein, we would expect that when the IO program runs, a `FileNotFoundException` is thrown if the file "scores" is not found. However, here the compiler is getting involved, and this program does not compile because, as the error message spells out, this exception must be *caught or declared to be thrown*. The reason for this new development, which is a essentially a stricter check in the use of exceptions, is that `FileNotFoundException` is what is called a *checked* exception.

Checked and unchecked exceptions.   If you look again at the exception class hierarchy, you will see that `FileNotFoundException` is a subclass of `java.io.IOException`, which in turn is a subclass of `Exception`. Contrast this with, say, `IllegalArgumentException`, which is a subclass of `RuntimeException`. All subclasses, immediate or otherwise, of `RuntimeException` are called *unchecked* exceptions, while all other exceptions are called *checked* exceptions. See Figure 1.1.

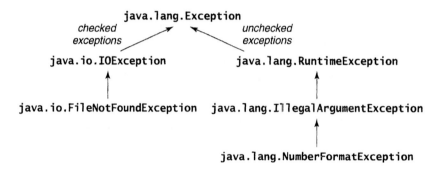

FIGURE 1.1: Checked and Unchecked Exceptions. Unchecked exceptions are descendants of `RuntimeException`.

As this makes clear, `FileNotFoundException` (and `IOException`) are checked exceptions. The rule when using checked exceptions is that if a method M gets a checked exception back from a call to another method, then M must either catch this checked exception or throw it. Throwing the exception, in this context, means simply passing it along, and is achieved by adding a new `throws` clause to the method header. See Figure 1.2.

Here is what we would do to the `main` method header in our example, to throw, or pass along, the `FileNotFoundException`:

```
public static void main(String[] args)
throws FileNotFoundException {
    ...
}
```

As always, the decision of whether to catch an exception or pass it along depends on whether or not the method in question can do anything useful after catching the exception.

Although an unchecked `RuntimeException` can be thrown by a method without a corresponding `throws` declaration in its header, it is often the practice to include unchecked exceptions in a throw clause. The reason is that a client that calls this method can then know of all the exceptions that may be thrown, and prepare to catch or pass them

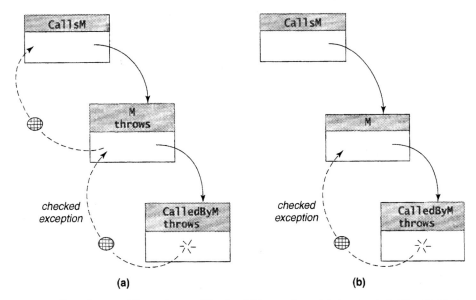

FIGURE 1.2: Catching or Throwing a Checked Exception. (a) Method CalledByM throws a checked exception and has a throws clause in its header. Method M does the same. (b) Method CalledByM throws a checked exception and has a throws clause in its header. Method M catches the exception thrown by CalledByM and does not throw any exceptions, so it does not have a throws clause in its declaration.

along as appropriate. If the client does not know of an exception that may be thrown by a method, then it has no way of recovering from the exception.

Writing to a file. Writing text to a file is done by setting up a File object as we did for reading, and then creating a java.io.PrintWriter object with this File as the target. Here is a program that reads a set of names from a file in which each name is stored as a first name and last name pair, and writes the names to another file, in last name–comma–first name format.

```
01 import java.util.*;
02 import java.io.*;
03
04 public class NamesFilter {
05    public static void main(String[] args)
06    throws FileNotFoundException {
07       Scanner sc = new Scanner(new File(args[0]));
08       PrintWriter pw = new PrintWriter(new File(args[1]));
09       while (sc.hasNext()) {
10          String fname = sc.next();
11          String lname = sc.next();
12          pw.println(lname + "," + fname);
13       }
14       pw.close();
15    }
16 }
```

Line 8 sets up a `PrintWriter`, which defines `print` and `println` methods (among others) that can then be used to write output. As seen in line 14, *it is important to close* the `PrintWriter` object when all output has been written, otherwise some of the written output may not appear in the target file.

1.6.3 String Tokenizing

Say we want to write a program that would reverse the process of the `NamesFilter` program, that is, read from a file that contains names in last name–comma–first name format, and write out a file that has the names in first name–last name format. Here is our first attempt at this:

```
01 import java.util.*;
02 import java.io.*;
03
04 public class NamesFilterRev {
05    public static void main(String[] args)
06    throws FileNotFoundException {
07       Scanner sc = new Scanner(new File(args[0]));
08       PrintWriter pw = new PrintWriter(new File(args[1]));
09       while (sc.hasNext()) {
10          String lname = sc.next();
11          String fname = sc.next();
12          pw.println(fname + " " + lname);
13       }
14       pw.close();
15    }
16 }
```

When you run this program, you will see that the `next` call on line 11 throws an exception *when there are an odd number of lines in the input file.*

What happens is that every call to `next` will read the *entire last name–comma–first name* string because there is no whitespace between the names, only a comma character. Recall from Section 1.6.1 that `nextInt` extracts tokens, and a token is a sequence of non-whitespace characters. Here is what the output file would look like for the sample input file:

Input file	Output file
Federer,Roger	Agassi,Andre Federer,Roger
Agassi,Andre	Becker,Boris Sampras,Pete
Sampras,Pete	
Becker,Boris	

This is what happens. In the first iteration through the `while` loop, the `next()` on line 10 reads `Federer,Roger` as a single token and assigns it to `lname`. Then the `next()` on line 11 reads `Agassi,Andre` as the next token and assigns it to `fname`. Then, on line 12, the string `Agassi,Andre  Federer,Roger` is printed out. The same process is repeated in the second iteration of the `while` loop for the third and fourth lines. The program does not crash, but the output is obviously wrong.

On the other hand, if there was only one line in the input file, then the next()
on line 10 would read that whole line as a single token, leaving no more tokens for
the next() on line 11, resulting in an exception being thrown. The workaround is
to use ',' as a *delimiter* character, so that a token is a sequence of non-whitespace
and non-comma characters. This can be done by setting the delimiter of the Scanner
appropriately with its useDelimiter method, but instead we will use another class called
java.util.StringTokenizer because this was the way to go before the Scanner class
was introduced, and it is useful to learn how StringTokenizer works.

Here is our reworked program:

```
01 import java.util.*;
02 import java.io.*;
03
04 public class NamesFilterRev {
05   public static void main(String[] args)
06   throws FileNotFoundException {
07     Scanner sc = new Scanner(new File(args[0]));
08     PrintWriter pw = new PrintWriter(new File(args[1]));
09     while (sc.hasNext()) {
10       String name = sc.next();
11       StringTokenizer st = new StringTokenizer(name,",");
12       String lname = st.nextToken();
13       String fname = st.nextToken();
14       pw.println(fname + " " + lname);
15     }
16     pw.close();
17   }
18 }
```

The while loop reads one line at a time—the line is read in the call to next() on line
10. This line is the entire last name–comma–first name string. After the name is read,
a new StringTokenizer object is created with this name as the target, and with the ','
character as the token delimiter, as coded on line 11. The method nextToken() called
on a StringTokenizer object returns the next token that is extracted, interpreted as a
string. Since ',' is the delimiter, the first token is the last name, and the second token is
the first name.

When a delimiter is explicitly specified to the StringTokenizer, the whitespace
characters (blank space, newline, tab) are no longer treated as delimiters. If you needed
to tokenize a string based only on whitespace delimiters, you would set up the tokenizer
without explicitly specifying delimiters:

```
StringTokenizer st = new StringTokenizer(str);
```

The StringTokenizer can be used to tokenize a string with more than one possible
delimiter. So, for instance, suppose that in NamesFilter we had written out the names in
the form last name–comma–space–first name. Then, in NamesFilterRev, we would set
up the StringTokenizer on line 11 as follows:

```
11          StringTokenizer st = new StringTokenizer(name,", ");
```

The second argument is a delimiter string that consists of all possible delimiters, so a token is a sequence of characters, none of which is a delimiter specified in the delimiter string.

With the java.lang.System, java.util.Scanner, java.util.StringTokenizer, java.io.File, and java.ioPrintWriter classes, we can do most of the regular kinds of IO. The java.io package has many other classes that are useful in special situations, including classes that can read and write binary data.

1.6.4   Writing an Exception Class

Now that we have seen both checked and unchecked exceptions, we are ready to write our own, or *user-defined*, exception classes.

There are numerous exception classes defined in the Java API for different kinds of errors. Still, you may have need for an exception that can describe a very specific kind of error condition in your application for which none of the exceptions in the Java API is just the right fit. You can then define your own exception class. Here are two examples:

```
public class MyCheckedException          public class MyUncheckedException
    extends Exception {                       extends RuntimeException {

    public MyCheckedException() {            public MyUncheckedException() {
        super();                                 super();
    }                                        }

    public MyCheckedException(               public MyUncheckedException(
            String message) {                        String message) {
        super(message);                          super(message);
    }                                        }
}                                        }
```

As you can see, all you need to do is simply extend either Exception or RuntimeException depending on whether you want a checked exception or an unchecked one. Then define the two basic constructors, a no-arg constructor that calls the superclass no-arg constructor, and a constructor that accepts a detailed message string as argument and calls the corresponding superclass constructor. We remarked in Section 1.5.5 that the Exception class has two other constructors whose usage is more specialized. If need be, we can also have our exception class define constructors analogous to these specialized constructors.

1.7   CLASS PACKAGES

A typical software application will have a large number of classes, and managing them can be cumbersome and prone to errors. However, large applications naturally consist of subsystems that perform different functions. The classes in the application can be grouped according to the subsystem to which they belong, structuring the code in a way that makes for easier management. Such grouping can be done in Java using *packages*.

1.7.1   Java Packages

Java comes with a class library—the Java Application Programming Interface, or API—that itself is a large collection of many hundreds of classes. These classes are categorized into many packages. The core classes in the API, including the String class, are in the java.lang package. Classes that support input and output are in the java.io package, including the File class and the IO exception classes that we saw in Section 1.6. The java.util package is a menagerie of classes that are useful in many general applications. This package includes the Scanner class we saw in Section 1.6, and a class called ArrayList that we will see in Section 1.13. These two classes are frequently used in this book. The following figure illustrates this package structure.

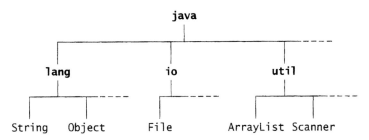

One of the things you want to get used to when dealing with packages is to refer to classes by their *fully qualified* names. A fully qualified name is the name of the class prefixed with the package to which it belongs. For example, java.lang.String is the fully qualified name of the String class, and java.util.Scanner is the fully qualified name of the Scanner class.

How does this packaging process affect how you write programs in Java? The first thing to know is that whenever you write a Java class, it is automatically placed in a special anonymous, catch-all package, unless you take explicit action to place it in a named package of your choosing. However, you cannot place your Java class in any of the Java API packages. If you write, say, five classes, they will all be placed by default in the no-name package, so they will end up belonging to the same package.

Now let us see how to use a class from one of the Java API packages in a class that you want to build. Say you write a class called MyClass that compares two strings sent as arguments to it and writes them out in alphabetical order. In order to do this, you use the String class that is in the java.lang package. Here is the code:

```
public class MyClass {
  public static void main(java.lang.String[] args) {
    javaz.lang.String str1 = args[0];
    java.lang.String str2 = args[1];
    if (str1.compareTo(str2) < 0) {
      System.out.println(str1 + "," + str2);
    } else {
      System.out.println(str2 + "," + str1);
    }
  }
}
```

We have used the fully qualified name, java.lang.String, wherever we refer to the String class. But the line

```
public static void main(java.lang.String[] args) {
```

looks strange because we are used to seeing String[] args, not java.lang.String[] args. What we can infer from this is that we do not have to use the fully qualified name of the String class. The reason is that java.lang is a special package. It is used so often in programs that classes belonging to it do not need to be fully qualified when they are used.

If, in this same program, you wanted to use the java.util.ArrayList class, then you would have to fully qualify it. Now say you needed to refer to the ArrayList in 10 different places in your program. Then you would need to write java.util.ArrayList 10 times. This gets tedious, but Java has a nice workaround. In the very first line of your class file, you write an *import* statement:

```
import java.util.ArrayList;

public class MyClass { ... }
```

Then, wherever you want to refer to java.util.ArrayList, you just write ArrayList without the qualifying package name prefix.

Let's take this a step further. Suppose you wanted to use five different classes from java.util in your program. You can use the workaround to type five lines of import at the top of your class file. This too begins to get tedious, and yet again, there is another workaround. You change the import statement to this:

```
import java.util.*;

public class MyClass { ... }
```

Using the '*' is called wildcarding because it can match anything that is a fit. At every place where you write ArrayList, the compiler checks against the import, sees the java.util.*, knows to then check whether ArrayList is in the package java.util, and finds a match. That is, the '*' matches ArrayList.

Many classes typically use several classes from the java.io package and from the java.util package. A class such as this would then do the following at the top of its Java source file:

```
import java.util.*;
import java.io.*;
...
```

1.7.2 Organizing Packages

So far we have seen how to use classes from the Java API packages. We will now turn to categorizing the classes we write for an application into our own named packages. First of all, the names we choose for our packages must not conflict with the names of the java packages. For instance, we cannot name a package java.io. Package names do not need a '.' in them. Java packages are named with a java. prefix, because the '.' actually has a specific function here that will become clear after we have seen a little more of how to name packages.

Suppose you are building a game program, and you have classified the program into subsystems including actors, scenarios, and weapons. Then you implement all aspects of the game that have to do with the actors in classes that are in a package called actors, implement all scenarios classes in a scenarios package, and all weapons classes in a weapons package. You need to tell the compiler what class goes into what package, and the way you do it is with a *package* statement at the top of the file, even before the import statement, if any.

For instance, say there is a class called LightSaber in the weapons package. Here is how you would make this known to the compiler:

```
package weapons;

// import statements if any
...

public class LightSaber { ... }
```

You would need to write a package statement just like this one on the very first line of each Java source file that implements a weapons package class, as also for the classes in the other packages.

There is another setup that the compiler requires for it to recognize packages correctly, and that has to do with how the Java source files are organized in the filesystem on disk. Say your application is under a root directory or folder called game. Under the game folder, you need to create a folder for each package with the same name as the package. So you will have one folder called weapons, another called scenarios, and a third called actors. Once these folders are created, you need to put all the Java source files for classes in the weapons package under the weapons folder, and similarly organize the Java source files for other classes under their respective package folders. This structure is shown in the figure below:

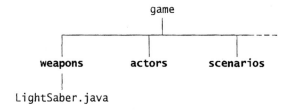

When you compile a class that belongs to a package by running javac from the command line, you have to make sure that you are positioned in the right folder. In the game example, in order to compile LightSaber, you will need to be in the game folder (*not* in the weapons folder), and run javac like this:

```
game> javac weapons/LightSaber.java
```

Assuming no compilation errors, this will result in the creation of a class file, LightSaber.class, in the weapons folder. The fully qualified name of the LightSaber class is now weapons.LightSaber.

Classes within the same package can refer to each other without using fully qualified names, just like referring to java.lang classes. Say LightSaber refers to another class, Sword, from the same weapons package. See the figure below:

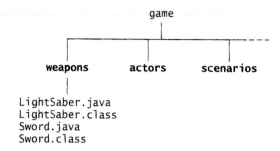

Then you can just do this in LightSaber:

```
package weapons;

public class LightSaber {
  Sword sword;
  ...
}
```

That is, a reference to Sword is not fully qualified, and neither is there an import statement such as import weapons.Sword or import weapons.*. LightSaber belongs to the weapons package, so when it is compiled, any non-fully-qualified name is automatically looked up in weapons for a match. Since classes in the same package will typically tend to refer to each other quite often, this is a special provision in Java to alleviate the developer's tedium.

When an application gets large, you may need to organize your subsystems into smaller subsystems. You can do this to any number of hierarchical levels, and the package organization can then mirror the system hierarchy. For instance, say you wanted to further subdivide the actors subsystem into sub-subsystems jedi, clones, and so on. Then, each jedi sub-subsystem class can be placed in a jedi package, each clones class in a clones package, and so on.

Since jedi and clones are already under actors, the package name for any class in these packages will have two levels of nesting. For instance, say you write a MaceWindu class in jedi. Then you will have to write a package statement in the class like this:

```
package actors.jedi;

// import statements if any
...

public class MaceWindu { ... }
```

This Java source file will be placed in a folder called jedi that you will need to create under the actors folder.

In order to compile the MaceWindu class, you will *still* be in the game folder, from where you will issue the following command:

```
game> javac actors/jedi/MaceWindu.java
```

This will create a MaceWindu.class file under the jedi folder. The fully qualified name of this class is actors.jedi.MaceWindu.

You may want to make the top-level of the game application itself a part of the package hierarchy, analogous to how the Java API has java itself as the first part of the package hierarchy, shown in the figure below:

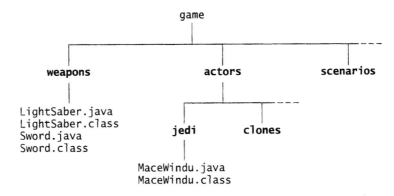

In this case, you would prefix all package names with game: LightSaber would have a package statement that reads package game.weapons, and MaceWindu would have a package statement that reads package game.actors.jedi. Finally, when compiling any of the classes in the game application, you would need to be in the folder, say myapps, that contains the game folder:

```
myapps> javac game/weapons/LightSaber.java
myapps> javac game/actors/jedi/MaceWindu.java
```

Say a class called game.scenarios.Endor needs to access some classes in game.actors.jedi and some classes in game.weapons. In order to do this, the Endor class would need either to (a) use the fully qualified names of the required classes wherever they are referred to, or (b) add one import statement with the fully qualified name of each required class (so references to these classes in the rest of the program need not use fully qualified names), or (c) add one import statement with a wildcard for each of the packages (and again, refer to them elsewhere without having to use fully qualified names). The last alternative is the most convenient:

```
package game.scenarios;

import game.weapons.*;
import game.actors.jedi.*;

public class Endor {
```

```
LightSaber ls = new LightSaber();
MaceWindu mw = new MaceWindu();
  ...
}
```

Note that even though Endor and the classes to which it refers are under game at the top level, the referred classes must still be fully qualified (either in the import or directly at the place of reference) by prefixing the game. part. See the figure below:

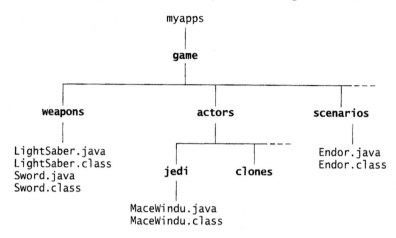

1.7.3   Name Conflict Resolution

Since all class names must be fully qualified when used, you may have two classes with the same name as long as their fully qualified names are different. Suppose in each of the game packages, you want to write a class that displays an image or set of images to the screen. You can have a Display class in each of the packages, without conflict, since with fully qualified names, they will be different from each other: game.weapons.Display, game.actors.jedi.Display, and game.scenarios.Display.

Even when all fully qualified names are distinct, confusion may arise if there is a conflict between two classes with the same name because of how they are imported and how they are referred to. Consider a situation in which you are writing a data structures collection of classes, in a package called structures. In this collection, you have written a class called Stack, so its fully qualified name is structures.Stack. Then you write another class called WebHistory that uses a Stack object to maintain history of visited web pages. It also uses the java.util.Scanner object. Here is what you do:

```
package structures;

import java.util.*;

public class WebHistory {
  ...
  Stack stk = new Stack();
  Scanner sc = new Scanner(System.in);
  ...
}
```

Since Stack is in the same package, structures, as WebHistory, you don't specifically import it, and neither do you use its fully qualified name.

Now it turns out that there is also a Stack class in the java.util package . When you compile the WebHistory class, and the line Stack stk = new Stack() is reached, the compiler will first look under package structures (because it is the package to which the class being compiled belongs) to see if there is a Stack class. If there is one, that is the class which will be used.

When the line Scanner sc = new Scanner(System.in) is reached, the compiler will first look in structures to possibly find a matching class called Scanner. It won't, and will move on to look in java.lang. There is no Scanner class in java.lang either, so finally the compiler will look in java.util because the import statement in the WebHistory source file says to look there. Here it does find a Scanner class, which is the one that will be used.

What if you had really wanted to use the java.util.Stack class instead of structures.Stack in WebHistory? In this case, writing the program as above won't work. Instead, you will have to fully qualify the name Stack wherever it is referred to:

```
package structures;

import java.util.*;

public class WebHistory {
    ...
    java.util.Stack stk = new java.util.Stack();
    Scanner sc = new Scanner(System.in);
    ...
}
```

As a matter of policy, it is wise to use the fully qualified name of a class wherever it is referenced, *if there is a class with the same name* in the *namespace* of the application. The namespace of the application is the collection of all the classes in all packages that are visible to the compiler.

In Section 1.8, we will look at the restrictions that can be placed on accessing classes from other packages, in order to enable better management of code.

1.8   ACCESS CONTROL

The local variables of a method (including its parameters) are *visible* only in the body of that method. What is the visibility of a class? Of a field of a class? Of a method of a class?

Every field and method of a class, as well as its constructors, may be declared with one of the following *access control modifiers*: public, private, or protected. These respectively define *public, private,* and *protected* levels of accessibility. If no access control modifier is specified, a *package* level of accessibility is assumed.

1.8.1   Private Access

This is the most restricted level of accessibility. A field or method declared private is only accessible in the class itself.

1.8.2 Package Access

A field or method (or class) for which no access control modifier is specified is accessible, as well as inheritable, by any class in its package. No class outside the package may access or inherit it.

Recall that if a class is not declared to belong to a specific package (i.e., there is no package statement), it is placed in an anonymous catchall package shared by all other classes for which a package name is not specified.

In Section 1.3, we assumed that all the fields of TV were inheritable by StereoTV, even though they were not declared public. This assumption would be valid if TV and StereoTV belonged to the same package.

There are two ways we can make these classes belong to the same package. One is to not name any package for either and let them fall into the catchall package. The other is to code a package name, say television, for each class:

```
package television;                    package television;
public class TV { ... }                public class StereoTV extends TV { ... }
```

Actually, there is yet another means by which we could make the fields of TV inheritable to StereoTV.

1.8.3 Protected Access

A protected field or method (or class) is inherited by subclasses and is also accessible to classes within the same package. We may think of this as

```
protected = package classes + nonpackage subclasses
```

So protected provides more access than *package* but less than public.

If we didn't want TV and StereoTV to be in the same package, we could make the fields of TV inheritable by StereoTV (in general, by any subclass of TV) by making them protected:

```
public class TV {
  protected int channel;
  protected int volume;
  ...
}
```

1.8.4 Public Access

A public field or a method is accessible *anywhere the class is accessible*. Also, it is inheritable by subclasses.

This is the most liberal level of accessibility. All the *methods* of class TV and class StereoTV are declared public, and, since the respective classes themselves are declared public, these methods are accessible anywhere.

Except for the static fields, none of the *fields* of TV or StereoTV are declared public. In fact, since they have no access control modifiers, they are accessible only within the same package.

1.8.5 An Example

Let us look at an example to see exactly how access control works. In the figure that follows classes A, B, and C are defined in the same package, abcpackage.

```
package abcpackage;          package abcpackage;          package abcpackage;

class B {                    public class A {             class C extends B {

    int bpack;                   private int apriv;            public void m() {

    public void m() {            protected int aprot;              A a = new A();

        A a = new A();           public int apubl;                 a.apriv = 10;

        a.aprot = 10;            int apack;                        a.apack = 15;

    }                            . . .                             B b = new B();

}                            }                                     bpack = 5;

                                                               }

                                                           }
```

OK, public · OK, same package · OK, public · NOT OK, private · OK, same package · OK, same package · OK, same package

Three other classes, D, E, and F, are defined in a different package, defpackage.

Class D extends A. It inherits apubl and aprot, but not apriv or apack. So apack cannot be accessed in D, as shown in the following figure:

```
package defpackage;          package defpackage;          package defpackage;

public class D               public class E {             public class F
    extends A {                  B b;                          extends A {
                                                                     
    int dpack;                   public void m() {             public void m() {

    public void m() {                aprot = 5;                    A a = new A();

        aprot = 5;               }                                 a.aprot = 5;

        apack = 10;          }                                     a.apack;

    }                                                          }

}                                                          }
```

D: OK, inherited from A · NOT OK, not inherited from A
E: NOT OK, not visible · NOT OK, not accessible
F: NOT OK, not accessible via a

B is not visible to class E because B is package-private, and E is in a different package than B. The variable aprot is defined as protected in A, and is not visible to E because E is neither in the same package as A nor a subclass of A.

The errors in class F are interesting. Class F is in a different package than A, so the field apack is not inherited. However, field aprot *is* inherited. This is exactly like what we see in class D. However, in class F, the references to aprot and apack are via the object a, in which the rules of accessibility defined above do not apply. Only the public members of a class can be accessed via its instances.

1.9 POLYMORPHISM

We will now recap our earlier discussion in Section 1.2.6 on references and the objects they refer to. When we say that a reference ref is of type ClassA, we mean that ref is *declared* as follows:

```
ClassA ref;
```

This declaration type of a reference is also known its *compile* time type, or *static* type.

When we say that an object is of type ClassA, we mean that it was created as follows:

```
new ClassA();
```

(We assume a no-arg constructor for ClassA here, but any constructor would do.)

To make the reference, ref, of type ClassA refer to an object of type ClassA, we can bring the above statements together as follows:

```
ClassA ref = new ClassA();
```

Here, ref is now said to have a *run time* type, or *dynamic* type, of ClassA. Recall a couple of earlier examples of declaration and object creation:

```
StereoTV stv = new StereoTV(4, 5, 0);
```

and

```
TV myTV = new TV(4, 5);
```

In each of these, the static type of the reference is the same as its dynamic type.

1.9.1 Polymorphic Reference

Now suppose class ClassC subclasses ClassB, which in turn subclasses ClassA, and we set up references r1, r2, and r3 as follows:

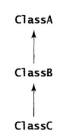

ClassA

ClassB

ClassC

```
ClassA r1 = new ClassA();
ClassB r2 = new ClassB();
ClassC r3 = new ClassC();
```

Now consider the following statements:

```
ClassA ref;   // ref declared of type ClassA
ref = r1;     // ref refers to a ClassA object
ref = r2;     // ref refers to a ClassB object
ref = r3;     // ref refers to a ClassC object
```

Reference ref takes on a different "form" in each statement. In the second statement it behaves like a ClassA object, in the third like a ClassB object, and in the fourth like a ClassC object. In other words, ref demonstrates *polymorphic* behavior.

Polymorphic literally means "many forms." Polymorphism in the context of object-oriented programming means that we can use a reference of a superclass type to refer to an object of that type, as well as any subclass type, any number of levels down the class inheritance hierarchy. In other words, the static type of a reference can be the same as its dynamic type or a superclass (not necessarily immediate) of its dynamic type.

In the example given above, ClassA is the root of the hierarchy, ClassB is an immediate subclass, and ClassC is a subclass two levels down.

Recall that inheritance captures an *is-A* relationship between subclass and superclass. In the example, every ClassB objects *is-A* ClassA object. Therefore, a reference of type ClassA should also be able to refer to a ClassB object. (Think of the example of Car subclassing MotorVehicle. You can *refer* to a car as a motor vehicle, but not the other way around.) Similarly, every ClassC object is-A ClassA object; thus, a reference of type ClassA should also be able to refer to a ClassC object.

How can we use polymorphism to advantage? Suppose we have the following set of statements in our program:

```
...
TV tv = null;
if (<condition>) {
    tv = stv;      // reference to a StereoTV object
} else {
    tv = myTV;     // reference to a TV object
}
...
tv.changeVolume(7);
```

In the last statement, method changeVolume is invoked via the reference tv. We have no way of knowing until runtime whether the method will be invoked on a StereoTV object or to a TV object, since tv could refer to either depending on how the condition check turns out. But we are guaranteed that changeVolume will be invoked on the appropriate object at runtime, depending on what tv refers to. This is polymorphic behavior on the part of tv.

If polymorphism were not supported, we would have to define two types of references—TV and StereoTV—and write code that would be longer and harder to maintain.

The support the language provides in order to make this kind of referencing legal is described below.

1.9.2   Casting up the Class Hierarchy

When we write:

```
ref = r2;
```

we are assigning a reference of type ClassB to a reference of type ClassA. The types on the two sides of the assignment are different, but Java allows us the freedom to do this because the reference on the left is of a type that is a superclass of the reference on the right. Java performs an *implicit* cast of r2 to the type of ref. That is, the following

```
ref = (ClassA)r2;
```

is done implicitly—the compiler does it without programmer intervention. This is called *casting up* the class (inheritance) hierarchy, since the cast is toward the root.

An implicit cast up the class hierarchy is also done in the case of:

```
ref = r3;    // implicit cast two levels up
```

with the cast traveling two levels up the hierarchy.

This implicit "upward" cast is the *language support for polymorphism.*

1.9.3   Casting Down the Class Hierarchy

Consider the following:

```
...
TV tv = null;
if (<condition>) {
    tv = stv;    // reference to a StereoTV object
} else {
    tv = myTV;   // reference to a TV object
}
...
tv.setBalance(7);
```

The last statement

```
tv.setBalance(7);
```

would be incorrect if tv *were to refer to* a TV *object,* since TV does not define a setBalance method. But the statement would be correct if tv were indeed to refer to a StereoTV object. However, the compiler is conservative about this, and flags the statement as an error, period. This is justifiable, because here tv is *not* used in a polymorphic sense. Although one can use a superclass reference to refer to a subclass object, one cannot use it to invoke a method that is special only to the subclass. Once "specialty" sets in, polymorphism is no longer active.

If we know *for sure* that tv indeed refers to a StereoTV object, there is a workaround. We may invoke the setBalance method by *forcing* a cast *down* the class hierarchy:

```
TV tv = stv;
((StereoTV)tv).setBalance(2);    // cast down
```

Casting down the hierarchy has to be done when we need to force nonpolymorphic behavior on a reference. One has to be careful in doing this, because if the reference we are casting actually refers to the superclass type object, and not to an object of the subclass type to which it is being cast, the program will blow up at runtime. This would happen, for example, if we had done the following in the original example to "fool" the compiler:

```
...
TV tv = null;
if (<condition>) {
    tv = stv;    // reference to a StereoTV object
} else {
    tv = myTV;   // reference to a TV object
}
...
((StereoTV)tv).setBalance(7);  // fooled the compiler
```

If tv does refer to a TV object, the invocation of setBalance will be rejected at runtime. But there is another, safer workaround, described in the following.

1.9.4   The instanceof Operator

Java provides the instanceof operator to determine the relationship between a reference and the type of object to which it refers at runtime. In general,

```
X instanceof Y
```

is true if X refers to an object whose type is either Y or a subclass (any number of levels down the class hierarchy) of Y.

Recall the hierarchy of classes ClassA, ClassB, and ClassC introduced in Section 1.9.1. After the following statements:

```
ClassA ref;
ref = r1;    // behaves as a ClassA object
```

the statement

```
ref instanceof ClassA
```

is true. After the following:

```
ref = r2;    // behaves as a ClassB object
```

both of the statements given below are true:

```
ref instanceof ClassB
ref instanceof ClassA
```

Finally, after the following:

```
ref = r3;    // behaves as ClassC object
```

the statements:

```
ref instanceof ClassC
ref instanceof ClassB
ref instanceof ClassA
```

are all true.

To wrap up, let's revisit the example of Section 1.9.3, in which we forced a downward cast on the reference tv, but were liable to get "caught" at runtime if the reference turned out to refer to a TV object. We can prevent this potential runtime error by using the instanceof operator to check whether the object to which tv refers is indeed an *instance of* StereoTV before casting it:

```
...
TV tv = null;
if (<condition>) {
   tv = stv;     // reference to a StereoTV object
} else {
   tv = myTV;    // reference to a TV object
}
...
if (tv instanceof StereoTV) {
   ((StereoTV)tv).setBalance(7);  // avoid run time error
}
```

1.10   ABSTRACT CLASSES

Suppose we were building a graphical geometry application in which we wanted to implement objects for a variety of geometric shapes, such as line segments, rectangles, circles, and so on. For every such object, we want to be able to *draw* it, *scale* it by a specified factor, *translate* it by a specified amount, and *rotate* it by a specified angle. All geometric objects share these four common operations, but exactly *how* each operation is implemented differs from shape to shape.

We could build a class hierarchy in which Shape is the superclass, with LineSegment, Rectangle, and Circle as its subclasses. We can write code like this:

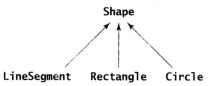

```
Shape s1 = new LineSegment();
s1.draw(...);     // line segment draws itself
Shape s2 = new Circle();
s2.draw(...);     // circle draws itself
...
// s1 has undergone changes, can't tell at compile time what actual
// shape s1 now refers to
s1.scale(...);    // but we can scale it all the same
```

Knowing that s1 (and s2) always refer to Shape objects, it is safe to invoke any of the operations defined for Shape, and to rely on the fact that the actual object will take care of drawing itself appropriately. This is another instance of polymorphism, and results in simple and elegant code.

1.10.1   Abstract Class Shape

Now we come to the crux of the matter. The class Shape itself is not *real*—it does not make sense to create a Shape object, as for example:

```
Shape s = new Shape();    // can't do this
```

That is, Shape is an *abstract* class. It declares certain operations that *must* be supported by any subclass of Shape, but itself *does not implement* any of them because it doesn't know how to.

1.10.2 Abstract Class Properties

```
public abstract class Shape {
  protected String color;
  public Shape() {
    color = "black";
  }
  public void
    setColor(String color) {
      this.color = color;
  }
  public String
    getColor() {
      return color;
  }
  public abstract
    void draw();
  public abstract
    void move(int toX, int toY);
  public abstract
    void rotate(int degrees);
  public abstract
    void scale(float factor);
}


public class Rectangle
       extends Shape {
  ... // fields
  public Rectangle() {
    super();
    ...
  }
  public void
    draw() {...}
  public void
    move(int toX, int toY) {...}
  public void
    rotate(int degrees) {...}
  public void
    scale(float factor) {...}
}
```

We note several properties of abstract classes.

- A class declared with modifier abstract is an abstract class—it is not possible to create objects of this class.
  Shape is an abstract class, and thus we cannot create Shape objects.

- If a class not declared abstract has an abstract method, it would result in a compile-time error.

- An abstract class may define fields that can be inherited by its subclasses.
  The field color in the abstract Shape class is an example.

- An abstract class may define one or more constructors. Since clients may not create abstract class objects, the constructor(s) is for the use of subclasses—the constructor(s) may perform initialization for the part inherited by subclasses.
  In our example, Shape defines a no-arg constructor that initializes the color to a default black value.

- An abstract class may define non-abstract methods. The methods setColor and getColor in the Shape class are examples.
  In fact, all methods of an abstract class may be nonabstract, in which case only the class declaration with the abstract modifier identifies it as such.

- Each subclass of an abstract class may override one or more of the abstract methods inherited by it, with implementations that effectively make those method nonabstract.
  In our class hierarchy, every subclass of Shape would implement the methods draw, translate, rotate, and scale, as, for example, the Rectangle class, which can be designed as a subclass of Shape. The example shown is only a skeleton.

- A subclass of an abstract class need not override all the inherited abstract method with implementations. If the subclass does not provide an implementation for at least one inherited abstract method, it remains an abstract class.

The java.util.Dictionary class is an abstract class subclassed by the nonabstract java.util.Hashtable class, a useful structure for efficient storage and retrieval of data.

1.11   A GAME PARK EXAMPLE

We have studied polymorphism and abstract classes in the preceding sections. Let us strengthen our understanding by using these concepts in an example, that of building a slice of a game park application. The main component of this application that is of relevance to us here is how to model the relationship between the current set of animals in the game park: lions, tigers, horses, donkeys, and zebras. We would like to group these animals based on a natural classification, as in the following figure:

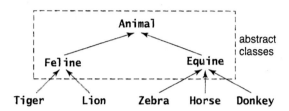

When the application is running, we want to be able to populate it with instances of different animals. Tigers and lions are felines, and share common properties, which can be abstracted into a Feline class. However, no actual Feline object is ever created in the application because this class only represents an idea, that of being a feline. Similarly, Equine abstracts and stores common properties of all equines. Finally, at the top of the hierarchy is the class Animal, which abstracts and stores the common properties of all animals, including felines and equines.

Here is sample code for some of these classes, with the method definitions establishing commonalities and differences between them:

```java
public abstract class Animal {
  public void run() {
    System.out.println("run");
  }
}
```

```java
public abstract class Feline {
  public void roar() {
    System.out.println("roar!");
  }
}
public class Tiger
      extends Feline {
  public void roar() {
    System.out.print("Tiger: ");
    super.roar();
  }

  public void run() {
    System.out.print("Tiger: ");
    super.run();
  }
}
```

```java
public abstract class Equine {
  public void trot() {
    System.out.println("trot");
  }
}
public class Zebra
      extends Equine {
  public void trot() {
    System.out.print("Zebra: ");
    super.trot();
  }

  public void run() {
    System.out.print("Zebra: ");
    super.run();
  }
}
```

The property of running is common to all animals, and so a run method is defined in the top-level Animal class. Felines roar but equines do not, and equines trot but felines do not, so there is a branching in the properties, with the class Feline defining a roar method, and the class Equine defining a trot method. Both these classes inherit the run method from Animal, of course.

The Tiger class is not abstract, and redefines the inherited roar and run methods to first print itself out, and then call the superclass definitions of these methods respectively. If roar were called on a Tiger object, we would see Tiger roar! in the output. Similarly, Zebra redefines the trot and run methods to identify itself first, and then call the respective superclass definitions.

Let's put together a small application to show how we can refer to each animal at different levels of specificity: either as the most general level of animal, or the intermediate level of feline or equine, or the most specific level of tiger, zebra, and so on. We will accomplish this concisely using polymorphism. Here is the program in its entirety, following which we will look at each method in more detail.

```java
public class GamePark {

    static Animal[] animals = new Animal[5];

    public static void main(String[] args) {
        populateAnimals();
        makeAnimalsRun();
        System.out.println();
        makeEquinesTrot();
    }

    static void populateAnimals() {
        animals[0] = new Tiger();
        animals[1] = new Lion();
        animals[2] = new Zebra();
        animals[3] = new Horse();
        animals[4] = new Donkey();
    }

    static void makeAnimalsRun() {
        for (int i=0; i < 5; i++) {
            animals[i].run();
        }
    }

    static void makeEquinesTrot() {
        Equine[] equines = new Equine[3];
        equines[0] = (Equine)animals[2];
        equines[1] = (Equine)animals[3];
        equines[2] = (Equine)animals[4];
        for (int i=0; i < 2; i++) {
            equines[i].trot();
        }
    }
}
```

Compile and execute this program:

```
> javac GamePark.java
> java GamePark
Tiger: run
Lion: run
Zebra: run
Horse: run
Donkey: run

Zebra: trot
Horse: trot
Donkey: trot
```

The main method does three things: populate animals, make all of them run, and make all the equines trot. Each of these activities is performed by a different method, and each method tells us something specific about polymorphism.

Consider the populateAnimals method. The array animals is declared to hold Animal entries. That is, the static or compile time type of each animals[i] reference is Animal. But the dynamic of runtime type of each is different, as can be seen in the figure alongside. This is the "ground floor" of polymorphism, enabled by our class design hierarchy with Animal at the top.

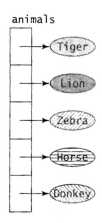

The method makeAnimalsRun reaps the benefit of the seed sown by the populateAnimals method. It uses *dynamic binding* to *bind* the call to method run to the dynamic type of reference animals[i], and not the static type. Thus, when run is called on animals[0], the method executed is that of the class Tiger, which is exactly what is needed. Contrast this 100% polymorphic code with a totally nonpolymorphic version:

100% polymorphic	**Totally nonpolymorphic**
``static void makeAnimalsRun() {
for (int i=0; i < 5; i++) {
animals[i].run();
}
}```	```static void makeAnimalsRun2() {
((Tiger)animals[0]).run();
((Lion)animals[1]).run();
((Zebra)animals[2]).run();
((Horse)animals[3]).run();
((Donkey)animals[4]).run();
}```

In the nonpolymorphic version, each animals[i] is first cast into a static type that matches its dynamic type, and then the run method is invoked. This code would work, but it is unnecessarily complex, and does not use the power of polymorphism with dynamic binding. Moreover, this code does not scale well—what if there were 100 animals, and you needed to make them all run? Writing 100 lines of code, one per animal, would be terribly tedious and error-prone.

Last look at the method `makeEquinesTrot`, which shows again how to use polymorphism effectively in conjunction with dynamic binding. The lesson here is that since we are only looking at equines, we need to have the static type set to `Equine`, not `Animal` because the `trot` method is not defined on `Animal`. In sum, the static type must be set to the highest possible level in the hierarchy, one that has the subhierarchy of interest under it.

1.12   INTERFACES

In Section 1.1.4 we discussed the importance of separating the interface of a class from its implementation. While the `public` methods (and fields) of a class constitute an *implicit* public interface, Java provides a construct called `interface` that may be used to define an *explicit* interface.

1.12.1   The Java `interface` Construct

An `interface` is like an abstract class in which none of the methods are implemented and there are no instance variables. That is, if there are any fields at all, they must be `static`.

Let's take the example we did in Section 1.10, that of `Rectangle` extending the abstract class `Shape`, and rework it using interfaces. We define an interface called `ShapeInterface` as follows:

```
public interface ShapeInterface {
  void draw();
  void move(int toX, int toY);
  void rotate(int degrees);
  void scale(float factor);
}
```

Note the following features of an interface definition:

- In the declaration, the keyword `class` is replaced by the keyword `interface`.
- All the methods are implicitly `public` and `abstract` simply by virtue of being a part of the interface. One may explicitly add the keywords `public` and `abstract` to every method, but this is *not recommended.*
- Fields, if any, are implicitly `public`, `static`, and `final`. More descriptively, if there are any fields at all in an interface, they may only be publicly available classwide constants.

1.12.2   Implementing an Interface

A class may conform to an interface by specifying that it `implements` that interface. This means that the class implements *all* the methods prescribed by the interface, but is not restricted to only these methods—it may also implement other methods not specified by the interface.

Now let us redo the `Rectangle` class from Section 1.10 by having it implement `ShapeInterface` instead of extending the abstract class `Shape`.

```java
public class Rectangle implements ShapeInterface {
  protected String color;
  ...    // other fields
  public Rectangle() {
    color = "black";
    ...
  }
  public void setColor(String color) {
    this.color = color;
  }
  public String getColor() {
    return color;
  }
  public void draw() { ... }
  public void move(int toX, int toY) { ... }
  public void rotate(int degrees) { ... }
  public void scale(float factor) { ... }
}
```

Apart from implementing all the methods prescribed by `ShapeInterface`, class `Rectangle` implements additional methods `setColor`, and `getColor`. In contrast, when `Rectangle` was built by extending abstract class `Shape`, it inherited the code for these methods from the latter.

A noteworthy observation is that *any class that extends* `Rectangle` *will implicitly implement* `ShapeInterface`: all the interface methods, being `public`, are inherited by any subclass of `Rectangle`.

1.12.3 Interface as a Type

An interface defines a type just as a class does. So, for instance, one may declare a reference of type `ShapeInterface`:

```java
ShapeInterface c = new Rectangle();
```

This is similar to the situation where a reference of static type A may refer to any object of type A or any subclass of A. The analogy is that any reference of interface type X may refer to any object of type Y, provided that Y implements X.

1.12.4 The Need for Interfaces

Consider the following set of classes that may form part of a (highly simplistic and incomplete) graphic windowing system.

There are two classes, Terminal and Frame, that model different types of virtual windows, and a class called Manager that is in charge of managing these windows.

Let us start with a Terminal class that serves as a command-line interface to the operating system. It has width and height attributes. It provides, among other capabilities, methods that read from and write to the screen. Most relevant to us is the fact that it provides *methods to open, close, and destroy it.*

Next, class Frame implements a work area with a menu bar, typically found in applications such as word processors and drawing packages. As in Terminal, Frame also *provides methods to open, close, and destroy it.*

Finally, we have a Manager class that manages graphic objects, and among them, specifically those that may be *opened, closed, and destroyed.*

```
public class Terminal {
  int width, height;
  ...
  public String readLine() {...}
  public void
    writeLine(String line) {...}
  ...
  // what we are really looking at
  public void open() {...}
  public void close() {...}
  public void destroy() {...}
}

public class Frame {
  int width, height;
  MenuBar menubar;
  ...
  public void saveFile();
  public void openFile();
  ...
  // what we are really looking at
  public void open() {...}
  public void close() {...}
  public void destroy() {...}
  ...
}

public class Manager {
  ...
  public void manage(
    (any object that may
     be opened, closed or
     destroyed) {...}
  ...
}
```

Here is the problem: exactly what *type* of object do we specify as the argument to the manage method of the Manager class? This type of object must not only match Terminal and Frame, but also instances of any other class that implements open, close, and destroy methods.

A manageable interface. It is clear that we need to define a new type that prescribes these methods. In other words, we need an interface such as the Manageable interface below:

```
public interface Manageable() {
  void open();
  void close();
  void destroy();
}
```

Now we can fill in the argument type in the manage method of class Manager:

```
public void manage(Manageable obj) { ... }
```

Thus, manage will deal with any object that implements the Manageable interface, including Terminal and Frame, both of which are slightly modified:

```
public class Terminal implements Manageable { ... }
public class Frame implements Manageable { ... }
```

This example illustrates but one instance of a generic situation where building an interface is necessary. Suppose classes A and B (not necessarily related) implement a common set of functions which is of interest to a third class, C. C performs certain tasks on any classes (and only those classes) that implement this set of functions. *Then the common set of functions is abstracted out into an interface, say* I. A *and* B *both implement* I, *while* C *performs certain tasks on any class that implements* I.

In our example, A is class Terminal, B is Frame, C is Manager, manage is the method that implements "certain tasks," and I is Manageable.

A class may implement more than one interface. Suppose the Rectangle class implements the interface ShapeInterface as well as the GraphicInterface interface. Then it would be defined as:

```
public class Rectangle implements ShapeInterface, GraphicInterface
```

1.12.5 Extending Interfaces

Like classes, interfaces may be extended. In the following example, RDevice is an interface that specifies a computer device that can read magnetic or optical media such as a hard drive or a CD. RWDevice is an interface that specifies a computer device that can not only read but also write to an optical or magnetic medium. Since a read-write device is a read device and then some, the specification of RWDevice extends that of RDevice.

As an example, see that a DVDPlayer will implement RDevice, and a DVDBurner, which extends DVDPlayer, will implement RWDevice.

```
public interface RDevice {
  void read(...);
  ...
}

public interface RWDevice
extends RDevice {
  void write(...);
  ...
}
```

```
public class DVDPlayer implements RDevice {
  public void read(...) { ... }
}

public class DVDBurner extends DVDPlayer
implements RWDevice {
  public void write(...) {
    ...
  }
}
```

1.13 GENERICS

Many applications need to store collections of objects. A drawing application will need to store all its rectangles, circles, points, and so on, i.e, all Shape objects (recall our discussion of the Shape class in Section 1.10). An application that manages appointments will need to store Appointment objects, where each Appointment object would include the data, time, location, and description of an appointment. It would be useful for such applications to have a readily available collection class that they can use to store and manipulate the objects under consideration. Such manipulation would include adding to the collection, removing from the collection, searching in the collection, and similar functions.

Now suppose you are building a collection class such that it can be used by many different applications. It would be impractical to build one collection class for Shape objects, another for Appointment objects, and so on. Moreover, you could not possibly know beforehand what types of objects would need to be stored by the large number of applications that may potentially use your class. You need to take a different approach to building your collection class: it has to be *generic* enough to hold any type of object, the type being decided at the time the collection is actually used by an application.

One way to genericize your class would be to use the catchall Object class to stand for the objects held, because you know that any type of object–including Shape and Appointment—is ultimately an Object type.

Suppose you name your class MyCollection. Further, suppose you define methods add and remove that can be used by an application to respectively add objects to and remove objects from the collection.

```
public class MyCollection {
    ...
    public void
        add(Object o) {...}
    public Object
        remove() {...}
}
```

Every reference in your class to any object in its collection would use the Object type; i.e., it converts the particular type of object to Object. On the other hand, when an object is retrieved from the collection, the application can convert it back to the particular type.

```
public class ShapeApp {
    ...
    MyCollection myc =
        new MyCollection();
    myc.add(new Rectangle(3,4));
    ...
    Rectangle rect =
        (Rectangle)myc.remove();
    ...
}
```

Note that the former conversion is a class cast going up the class hierarchy (as we saw in Section 1.9.2), while the latter is a class cast going down the hierarchy (as we saw in Section 1.9.3).

However, there is a problem. There is no way for the collection to tell whether all the objects in the collection are alike, because the genericization process has reduced all of them to mere Objects. So an application could quite easily mix Apple objects with Orange objects within a single collection without knowing that it did so (by accident) and then get into trouble when it retrieves them from the collection and tries to compare apples with oranges. This Objectification strategy is not reliable enough. What to do?

Java has a solution. You define your class to accept objects of some generic type, say T. You need not call this generic type T—it is simply a placeholder, or tag. By convention, T is used, and it stands for "template." (Alternatively, a type template is denoted as E instead of T.)

```
public class MyCollection<T> {
    ...
}

public class TVApp {
    MyCollection<TV> myc =
        new MyCollection<TV>();
    myc.add(new TV(3,4));
    myc.add(new TV(4,5));
    ...
    TV myTv = myc.remove();
    ...
```

A generic class is said to be a template that can be concretized to contain objects of any particular type when the generic class itself is instantiated.

To continue our understanding of generics, we now turn to a very useful collection class defined in the Java libraries.

1.13.1 Using `java.util.ArrayList` for Collections

The `ArrayList` is a generic array that can resize itself automatically on demand. Consider the following usage of the `ArrayList` class:

```
ArrayList<String> al = new ArrayList<String>(5);
for (int i=0; i < 5; i++) {
   al.add(new String(i));
}
// automatic resizing when one more item is added
al.add(new String(5));
```

In the first line, `al` is declared to be of type `ArrayList<String>`. The `<String>` part concretizes the generic `ArrayList` with type `String`, which is a commitment to only have `String` items in the array list.

The right-hand side of the first line sets up an instance of a `String`-specific array list with an initial *capacity* of 5. The capacity of an array list at any time is the number of array locations for which memory space has been set aside.

In the `for` loop, `String` objects are added to this array list. Every time the `add` method is called, the given object is appended to the end of the list, and the *size* of the array list is increased by one. As long as the size is less than the capacity, the memory space available is unchanged.

When an attempt is make to add the sixth object, after exiting the `for` loop, the array list sees that it is full to capacity. In order to make room for the new object, it resizes itself. The Java API specification for the `ArrayList` class does not say exactly how much additional space is allocated. For the purpose of illustration, let us assume the capacity is doubled. In our example, the following actions are carried out:

- A new array of capacity 10 (double the previous capacity of 5) is allocated.
- All items from the old array are copied to the new.
- The new item to be added is appended to this new array.
- The internal reference to the collection is switched from the old array to the new array—the old array is ready to be garbage collected.

This process will be repeated if the array list is full to capacity (all 10 locations are filled), and a new item is asked to be added. Then the actions listed above are carried out, starting with the allocation of a new array of size 20.

The `ArrayList` class has numerous methods to add and remove items, as well as methods to get the current size (i.e., the actual number of items in the array), get an item at a given index (this is a constant time operation because the basis is an array), replace an item at a given index with a new item, and so on. There is also another useful no-arg constructor that sets up an `ArrayList` with a default initial capacity.

1.13.2   The `java.util.ArrayList` Public Interface

The class header of the `java.util.ArrayList` and the declarations of its public members give us a good idea of how to genericize a class.

The first step is to define the class to accept a type parameter:

```
public class ArrayList<E> ...
```

The type parameter is given a name (here the name is E), which can then be referred to everywhere in the class where the type needs to be genericized. As we saw earlier, this generic name is completely up to the class implementer, although it is typically either E or T.

Next up are the constructors. A constructor is defined as always, as, for example:

```
public ArrayList() ...
```

Note than when we create a new `ArrayList` object, we say:

```
ArrayList<String> al = new ArrayList<String>() ...
```

On the right-hand side, the object type is first set to `ArrayList<String>`, and then *its* no-arg constructor is called. (Recall from Section 1.2.3 that object creation is a two-phase process.) In other words, the object is created with the specific type concretization to `String`, and the constructor is defined in this type context, so it does not need a type qualifier.

Methods in the `ArrayList` class refer to the generic type parameter in their header, if needed. So, for instance, the method add is defined to accept an object of the parameter type E:

```
public boolean add(E o) ...
```

Note that this parameter E refers to the *same* E that was declared in the class header. Which means that if a client concretizes the `ArrayList` class to type `String`, then the add method would accept a `String` object.

As another example, consider the method remove:

```
public E remove(int index) ...
```

This method returns an object of generic type E, again the same E that was specified in the class header. If E is concretized to `String`, then this method should be read as

```
public String remove(int index) ...
```

The `ArrayList` class highlights some of the aspects of genericizing the public interface of a class. Let's take this to the next step by studying how to implement a generic class of our own that maintains an array of objects in sorted order. In the process, we will also learn about generic interfaces and how to implement them.

1.13.3 Implementing a Generic Class

Say we want to implement an array that stores its contents in sorted order. We would like to make this class generic, so that any client-specified type of objects can be stored, so long as they are sortable. Here is a first sketch of our class, SortedArray, which will use the ArrayList to store its contents.

```
public class SortedArray<T> {
   private ArrayList<T> items;

   public SortedArray() { ... }
   public SortedArray(int cap) { ... }
   public int indexOf(T item) { ... }
   public T get(int i) { ... }
   public int size() { ... }
   public boolean remove(T item) { ... }
   public void add(T item) { ... }
}
```

All references to T in the SortedArray class are to the one and the same T defined in the class header. The name T used to genericize SortedArray is in turn used to concretize the ArrayList component:

```
private ArrayList<T> items;
```

Suppose a client of SortedArray concretizes the generic type T to Integer:

```
SortedArray<Integer> myArray = new SortedArray<Integer>(10);
```

Then this concrete Integer type "matches" the template type T in the SortedArray class header, and, consequently, everywhere else in the class. In particular, it matches the T in:

```
private ArrayList<T> items;
```

which results in items being concretized to ArrayList<Integer>.

We can implement the constructors and all the methods except add by simply passing the buck to the corresponding constructors and methods of the ArrayList class.

Continuing the concretization of T to Integer, each of the constructors sets up items to be a new ArrayList<Integer> object.

The indexOf method accepts an Integer as parameter and checks this against the Integer-ized items. The get method returns the (Integer) item at position i of the array, and the size method returns the number of entries in the array.

```
public class SortedArray<T> {
   private ArrayList<T> items;

   public SortedArray() {
      items = new ArrayList<T>();
   }

   public SortedArray(int cap) {
      items = new ArrayList<T>(cap);
   }

   public int indexOf(T item) {
      return items.indexOf(item);
   }

   public T get(int i) {
      return items.get(i);
   }

   public int size() {
      return items.size();
   }
```

The remove method accepts an Integer as parameter and removes it (if it
exists) from items. This leaves the add
method.

```
public boolean remove(T item) {
    return items.remove(item);
}

public void add(T item) {...}
}
```

When a new item is added, it must be inserted in the correct sorted position. This gives rise to certain wrinkles in both the code and the genericization process.

1.13.4 Implementing a Generic Interface

In this example, when 7 is to be added
to the sorted array, it is compared
against array items, starting with the
first. But each comparison needs to
tell whether 7 is greater than an array
item or not. At the first item encountered for which 7 is not greater than
the item (8, in the example), the scan stops, and 7 is inserted just before the item. This maintains the sorted order of the array.

The new requirement now is the comparison for *greater than*. How can it actually be coded into the add method? Consider this:

```
public void add(T item) {
    int i=0;
    while (i < items.size()) {
        if (item._____(items.get(i))) {
            break;
        }
        i++;
    }
    // item must be inserted at i
    items.add(i,item);
}
```

The last line calls a variation of the add method in ArrayList that is documented as follows in the Java API specification:

> public void add(int index, E element)
>
> Inserts the specified element at the specified position in this list. Shifts the element currently at that position (if any) and any subsequent elements to the right (adds one to their indices).

How to fill in the blank so that we can check whether item is less than the i-th entry in items? What method can we call on T-type objects (the generic type parameter) that will do this check? All we know is that any type would subclass Object, so the only comparison method we can legitimately use is the equals method.

The answer is to define T to be not just any type, but a type that provides a method to perform the less-than comparison we need. This is an ideal place to use an interface that prescribes a less-than comparison method, and to stipulate in our class definition that T must be a type that implements this interface.

Let us develop such an interface, called `MyComparable`, shown below:

```
public interface MyComparable<T> {
  boolean lessThan(T other);
  boolean greaterThan(T other);
}
```

Note that this is a generic interface which can be applied to any type of object.

Example: Making integers conform to `MyComparable<T>`.   Consider building a class that encapsulates an integer value and implements the `MyComparable` interface for comparisons between integers. Following is an example of such a class.

```
public class IntItem implements MyComparable<IntItem> {

  public final int value;

  public IntItem(int value) {
    this.value = value;
  }

  public boolean lessThan(IntItem other) {
    return this.value < other.value;
  }

  public boolean greaterThan(IntItem other) {
    return this.value > other.value;
  }
}
```

The `IntItem` class instantiates the generic type `T` of the interface `MyComparable` with the concrete type `IntItem`, which is the class type itself. Consequently, the methods `lessThan` and `greaterThan` also concretize this generic type `T` of their respective parameters with the type `IntItem`.

Interface `java.lang.Comparable`.   While the example given above illustrated the use and implementation of an interface to solve the comparing-for-less-than (and greater-than) problem, we do not really need to define our own `MyComparable`-like interface. Since searching a sorted list and sorting an unsorted list are frequent operations in computing, the Java language defines a generic interface called `Comparable<T>` for this purpose.

This interface prescribes a single method with one of three possible return values: zero (equal objects), positive integer ("this" object greater than parameter), or negative integer ("this" object less than parameter).

Several of the Java language classes implement this interface, including `String` and `Integer`—String implements `Comparable<String>`, and `Integer` implements `Comparable<Integer>`.

```
Integer two = new Integer(2);
Integer three = new Integer(3);
int c = two.compareTo(three);
if (c == 0) {
    System.out.println("two is equal to three");
} else if (c < 0) {
    System.out.println("two is less than three");
} else { // c > 0
    System.out.println("two is greater than three");
}
c = "two".compareTo("three"); // used with Strings
System.out.println("result = " + c); // > 0
```

The IntItem class we defined earlier is no longer needed—we can use the Integer class, instead.

Now reconsider our SortedArray class, and the method add at which we were stuck. Making the class generic by using a type parameter T is not sufficient—we cannot tell if there is a less-than method in the class type that will concretize T when SortedArray is used. But we now know that we need to stipulate that T be a type that implements the Comparable interface. To do this, Java defines the following syntax:

```
public class SortedArray<T extends Comparable<T>> ...
```

Note that the keyword extends is used, and *not* the keyword implements.

Then, in the add method, we can fill in the blank like this:

```
if (item.compareTo(items.get(i)) <= 0) {
```

Every concrete instance of T will implement the compareTo method, which will return a value less than (or equal to) zero if the target item (item) is less than (or equal to) the parameter item (items.get(i)).

Since the String and Integer classes (among others) in the java.lang package implement the Comparable<T> interface, we can use the SortedArray class with either, as shown below:

```
public class MyApplication {
  public static void main(String[] args) {
    SortedArray<String> sas = new SortedArray<String>();
    sas.add("Jack");
    sas.add("Jill");
    sas.add("Hill");
    System.out.println(sas.indexOf("Hill"));  // 0
    sas.remove("Hill");
    System.out.println(sas.indexOf("Jack"));  // 0
  }
}
```

1.13.5   Static Template Methods

Suppose we build an application class called `Sorter` that accepts either a sequence of integers or a sequence of strings, in any order, and prints them out in sorted order. Let's put this application together piece by piece, starting with the `main` method that asks whether the user wants to input integers or strings.

Depending on whether the user wants to sort integers or strings, the method `sortIntegers` or `sortStrings` is called:

```
import java.util.*;
public class Sorter {
  public static void main(
                     String[] args) {
    Scanner sc =
           new Scanner(System.in);
    System.out.print("Integers (i) " +
             "or Strings (s) ? => ");
    char c = sc.next().charAt(0);
    if (c == 'i') {
      sortIntegers(sc);
    } else {
      sortStrings(sc);
    }
  }
  ...
}
```

```
static
void sortIntegers(Scanner sc) {
  sortedArray<Integer> sa =
    new SortedArray<Integer>();
  System.out.print(
    "Enter integer, or " +
    "'q' if done => ");
  while (sc.hasNextInt()) {
    sa.add(sc.nextInt());
    System.out.print(
       "Enter integer, or " +
       "'q' if done => ");
  }
  print(sa);
}
```

```
static
void sortStrings(Scanner sc) {
  SortedArray<String> sa =
    new SortedArray<String>();
  System.out.print(
    "Enter string, or " +
    "'-1' if done => ");
  String str = sc.next();
  while (!str.equals("-1")) {
    sa.add(str);
    System.out.print(
       "Enter string, or " +
       "'-1' if done => ");
    str = sc.next();
  }
  print(sa);
}
```

Both of these methods end up calling `print` at the end, to print the sorted array. How to implement `print`? Since it may be called with either `SortedArray<String>` or `SortedArray<Integer>`, it must be genericized. Here is our first attempt at implementing `print`:

```
static void print(SortedArray<T> sa) {
  for (int i=0; i < sa.size(); i++) {
    System.out.println(sa.get(i));
  }
}
}
```

However, when `Sorter.java` is compiled with the above, the following error message is printed:

```
> javac Sorter.java
Sorter.java:37: cannot find symbol
symbol  : class T
```

```
location: class Sorter
    static void print(SortedArray<T> sa) {
                                ^
1 error
```

The issue here is that a type name, T, is used without having been defined. When we defined the SortedArray class, we defined the type name T in the class header. As a result, every (nonstatic) method in the class could use the name T to refer to this same type. Now, Sorter itself is not genericized as a whole, but we need to genericize the single static method print. In order to do this, we need to add a type definition to the header of the method before the return type specification:

```
static <T> void print(SortedArray<T> sa) {
```

When we compile, we can see that we are on the right track, but we are stopped short by the following error:

```
> javac Sorter.java
Sorter.java:37: type parameter T is not within its bound
    static <T> void print(SortedArray<T> sa) {
                    ^
1 error
```

Since we had defined the type parameter to SortedArray as T extends Comparable<T>, we need to be consistent in the print method. But we don't place the bound on T where it is used:

```
static <T> void print(SortedArray<T extends Comparable<T>> sa) {
```

Rather, we place the bound on T where it is defined:

```
static <T extends Comparable<T>> void print(SortedArray<T> sa) {
```

Here is the correct print method in its entirety:

```
static <T extends Comparable<T>> void print(SortedArray<T> sa) {
  for (int i=0; i < sa.size(); i++) {
    System.out.println(sa.get(i));
  }
}
```

Static template method in generic class.   In the previous discussion, we saw how to define a generic static method in a class that was not genericized, by defining a template type in the context of the method itself, i.e. in the method header. What if we want to define a generic static method in a class that is already generic?

As an example, suppose we want to define a static method in the generic SortedArray<T> class that would take an unsorted array, and return a sorted version of this array in an SortedArray<T> object. Here's a first attempt at defining such a method:

```
public class SortedArray<T extends Comparable<T>> {
  ...
  public static SortedArray<T> sort(T[] arr) {
```

```
    SortedArray<T> sarr = new SortedArray<T>(arr.length);
    for (int i=0; i < arr.length; i++) {
        sarr.add(arr[i]);
    }
    return sarr;
}
```

Since we have already defined T in the class header, can we not refer to that same T in the method, just as we did in the definition of the nonstatic methods?

It turns out that we cannot reuse the class definition of T. When we compile the attempt shown above, we get the following errors:

```
> javac SortedArray.java

SortedArray.java:42: non-static class T cannot be referenced from a static
    context public static SortedArray<T> sort(T[] arr) {
                                 ^
SortedArray.java:42: non-static class T cannot be referenced from a static
    context public static SortedArray<T> sort(T[] arr) {
                                                    ^
SortedArray.java:43: non-static class T cannot be referenced from a static
        context SortedArray<T> sarr = new SortedArray<T>(arr.length);
                            ^
SortedArray.java:43: non-static class T cannot be referenced from a static
        context SortedArray<T> sarr = new SortedArray<T>(arr.length);
                                                   ^
4 errors
```

The message is pretty clear: the T defined in the class header *only applies to instance objects*. This means that static methods are not included in the scope of the class-level generic type parameter.

So we need to use the same approach as in the Sorter class print method, which is to define a method-specific type parameter:

```
public static <T extends Comparable<T>> SortedArray<T> sort(T[] arr) {
    SortedArray<T> sarr = new SortedArray<T>(arr.length);
    for (int i=0; i < arr.length; i++) {
        sarr.add(arr[i]);
    }
    return sarr;
}
```

The T defined here *will not conflict* with the T defined in the header—they are separate, independent T's.

In closing, generic classes are an important addition to Java, and are very useful in building many of the data structures we will study in this book.

1.14 SUMMARY

- The two defining characteristics of object-oriented programming are encapsulation, in which data and methods are packaged within a class, and inheritance, in which a (sub)class that specializes another (super)class inherits the latter's data and methods.
- Encapsulation separates interface from implementation, making for code that is robust and easy to maintain.

- Reusing an encapsulation means using an object time and again as a component in other objects: this is reuse by composition.
- A class is a blueprint for the creation of objects, and prescribes the state attributes and behavior of its instances or objects.
- An object once created is alive so long as there is at least one reference to it. When there are no longer any references to an object, it is automatically reclaimed by the garbage collector, which can then recycle the space used by this object.
- A message to an object leads to the invocation of a method in that object.
- Two methods in a class with the same name but different signatures are said to be overloaded.
- Overloaded methods provide similar functionality in slightly different contexts. The similarity in function is indicated by the common method name, while the difference in context is indicated by the difference in either types or numbers of parameters.
- If a class does not implement any constructor, then the compiler introduces a default constructor, which is a constructor that does not take any arguments and has an empty body.
- Static fields and methods are properties of the class, and not specific to any object—they can be used directly via the class name, without going through an object.
- Inheritance implements the is-A design idea, and makes it possible to build class hierarchies that accurately model application systems.
- When a subclass inherits the data and methods (both are program code) from its superclass, it is said to reuse the inherited code.
- A method in a subclass that has the same signature as a method inherited from its superclass is said to override the inherited method. An overriding method specializes the functionality of the overridden method.
- All classes in Java implicitly extend a root class called `Object`.
- The `Object` class provides several methods that have default implementations, including the methods `equals`, `toString`, and `clone`. All classes inherit these methods, but most would want to override them in order to provide their own specific implementations.
- Java programs use exceptions to signal errors.
- Exceptions are of two kinds: unchecked or runtime exceptions, and checked or compile-time exceptions.
- A method that throws a checked exception must declare a throws clause in its header for this exception. This requirement does not apply to unchecked exceptions.
- Input and output connected to the terminal can be done via the `System.in`, `System.out`, and `System.err` streams.
- The `java.util.Scanner` and `java.util.StringTokenizer` classes are adequate for most kinds of input processing.
- Large Java applications are typically organized into packages of classes.
- The package hierarchy in a Java application has a one-to-one correspondence with the organization of the constituent classes on the filesystem.

- Access to any member of a class—its fields and methods—can be at four different levels from most restricted to least restricted: private, package, protected, and public.
- Polymorphism means that a superclass reference can refer to an object of any of its subclasses along an inheritance hierarchy. This means that a superclass reference can behave like an object of any of its subclasses, thus the term polymorphism, or "many forms."
- The type used to declare a reference is its static, or compile-time, type, while the type of the object it points to is its dynamic, or runtime, type.
- The importance of polymorphism is that a message sent via a superclass reference can invoke the corresponding method in any of its subclasses; exactly which subclass's method is invoked depends on the subclass object to which the reference refers.
- An abstract class cannot be instantiated—it serves only as a repository in which to gather the fields and methods common to all its superclasses.
- Classes not related by inheritance often need to be brought under the common umbrella of an interface by a third class so that the latter may apply one or more common operations to objects of these classes.
- An interface may extend another interface, just as a class may extend another class.
- A generic class is one that allows a choice of client-defined types to concretize it.
- A generic class defines a parameter type in its header.
- The parameter type defined in a generic class header applies only to instance members; static methods, if generic, need to define a separate local type parameter in the method header.
- An interface can be made generic, just like a class.

1.15 EXERCISES

E1.1. For each of the following objects, think of at least two fields that may hold its state, and at least two operations that may determine its behavior. At least one of these operations must be a state access operation, and at least one must be a state update operation.
  (a) Radio
  (b) Word
  (c) Circle
  (d) RoadIntersection
  (e) Car
  (f) Modem

E1.2. Briefly describe all the uses of static fields.

E1.3. Briefly describe the ways in which static methods may be used.

E1.4. Can a static method reference a nonstatic field in its class? Explain. Can a nonstatic method reference a static field? Explain.

E1.5. When defining a class, it is always safe to define one particular kind of field as public. Identify this kind of field and say why it is safe.

E1.6. If one were to order the access control levels from least restrictive to most restrictive, what would the order be?

E1.7. A field x in a public class A is declared protected.

  (a) Can code in another class in the same package access x? What if the class is in another package?

  (b) Would a class B that extends A inherit this field if B is in the same package as A? In a different package?

  Would either of your answers change if A were not declared public?

E1.8. Given the following declarations:

```
public class A { ... }
public class B extends A { ... }
public class C extends A { ... }
A a; B b; C c;
```

which of the following statements would compile without errors?

  - b = new B();
  - a = new B();
  - a = new C();
  - b = new A();
  - b = new C();

For those statements that would not compile, how would you fix the error while preserving the sense of the statement?

E1.9. How would a compiler know whether two methods in a class were overloaded? Whether a method in a subclass overrides a method in a superclass?

E1.10. Explain how an exception generated as a result of a call from within a try block navigates a sequence of catch blocks at the end of the try.

E1.11. Suppose there are two classes A and B, and B extends A. There is a field public int x defined in A, inherited by B. Given the following:

```
A a = new A();
B b = new B();
a.x = 5;
System.out.println(b.x);
```

What would be printed? What can you say, in general, about inherited fields based on the above: how are they "shared" between subclass and superclass?

E1.12. With exactly the same situation as in Exercise E1.11 above, *except* that x is declared public static, what would be printed by the same set of statements as in that exercise? What can you say, in general, about static inherited fields based on the above: how are they "shared" between subclass and superclass?

E1.13. You are given the following Java files:

```
package drawingpad;             package drawingpad;
public class Palette {          public abstract class Shape {
  ...                             ...
}                               }

package drawingpad.util;
public class StorageManager {
  ...
}
```

Show how these source files are organized in the filesystem. Then show how you would compile each of these classes.

E1.14. How is an interface different from an abstract class? Can all interfaces be replaced by abstract classes, so that no program would ever need to use interfaces?

E1.15. Design an example scenario, with as few classes as possible, where an interface is effectively used, and describe this interface.

E1.16. When and why would you make a class generic?

E1.17. Why does a static method of a generic class need a separate template type declaration in its header?

1.16   PROGRAMMING PROBLEMS

P1.1. For each of the objects listed in Exercise E1.1, define a class with your answers to the questions asking for at least two fields and two operations. You don't have to write code for the methods: simply give the declarations and put in a line or two of comments describing what they do.

P1.2. Write a program that would read a spreadsheet of student exam scores from a file and print each student's total score on all exams. Your program should also print the average score of all students for each exam. The file is organized as follows: There is one student record per line. Each student record has multiple columns: the first column is in the format <last name, first name>, and each subsequent column is an exam score. There is a ':' between every two columns. You may assume that each score is a real number between 0 and 100. Your program should accept two arguments: the name of the input file, and the name of the file to which the score report is to be written. Throw exceptions as necessary.

P1.3. Implement a class called Word that contains a single field: a String in which to store the word. A Word may only consist of alphabetic characters. Your class must support the following operations (when we say "this word," we are referring to the object on which the operation is invoked):

- Tell whether this word is a proper noun. A proper noun begins with a capital letter; no other letters are capitalized. (Ignore the fact that words that begin a sentence start with a capital letter but are not necessarily proper nouns.)
- Tell whether this word is an acronym—all letters are capitalized.
- Tell whether another word is the same as this word, ignoring case.
- Tell whether another word is the same as this word, taking case into account.
- Return the length of this word.
- Clone this word.

Define a constructor that would accept a String as an argument. It must throw an IllegalArgumentException if the supplied String is not a word.

P1.4. In Problem P1.3 we defined a proper noun and an acronym. These are both special types of words, and may therefore be defined as classes that extend Word: ProperNoun extends Word, and Acronym extends Word. Reimplement Word by getting rid of the operations that can tell whether a word is a proper noun or an acronym. Then implement ProperNoun and Acronym. All three classes must now provide the last three operations listed in Problem P1.3. Make sure to reuse as much code as possible.

P1.5. Most board games have pieces that move across the board with certain set rules about how far and in which direction they may move. In the following set of problems, you will set up the infrastructure for a board game. Start by defining an *abstract* class called Piece with the following fields that describe the piece:

- Its name.

- Its color. A piece may be black, white, red, blue, or green.
- Its position. Assume that the games for which a piece may be used are played on 8 × 8 grid boards—the position is a coordinate *(i,j)* on such a board, with each coordinate taking on a value between 0 and 7. (The top-left corner of the board is taken to be the origin, (0,0).)

All pieces can make a move to the left or a move to the right. However, how far they go either left or right in one move is not known. Implement:

- A public method in `Piece` to move the piece left or right by one space. This method should accept a direction parameter. If a move is requested that would take the piece off the edge of the board, simply return without doing anything.
- Protected methods in `Piece` to move the piece left or right by as many spaces as needed. Both of these methods will accept number of spaces as parameter. As before, if a move is requested that would take the piece off the edge of the board, simply return without doing anything.

Also define operations to retrieve values of the various attributes, as well as the `toString` method to print a string representation. Define a constructor that accepts name, color, and location of the piece. Finally, ensure that all parameters to methods are legal values. (Would you find it useful to define constants for left and right directions, as well as for all valid colors?)

P1.6. A **slow** piece is a piece that moves left or right *exactly one step* in every move. Define a class called `SlowPiece` that extends `Piece`, implementing a constructor and redefining the inherited `toString` method.

P1.7. A **fast** piece is a piece that can move left or right *as many steps as specified*. Define a class called `FastPiece` that extends `Piece`, implementing a constructor and redefining the inherited `toString` method. In addition, define a public move method that accepts a direction and a number of spaces to move. (Why did we not have to define a move method in `SlowPiece`?)

P1.8. A **flexible** piece is one that can move right or left as well as up or down—this leads to **slow flexible** and **fast flexible** pieces. Extend the class hierarchy developed so far in Problems P1.5 through P1.7 to include these two new kind of pieces. First, define an interface called `Flexible` that prescribes up and down directions as constants. Then define class `SlowFlexible` that implements `Flexible` and extends `SlowPiece`, and class `FastFlexible` that implements `Flexible` and extends `FastPiece`. Define methods in these classes as needed.

P1.9. Define a class called `Board` that would hold an image of the 8 × 8 game board. Each position of the board either contains a piece or is empty. Since the pieces move around on the board, any location may contain any type of piece at any given time. The board should be able to accept messages to do the following:

- Add a new piece to the board only if none exists at the new piece's intended location.
- Move a piece at a given location in a given direction by a given number of spaces.
- Print itself out, showing the color and type of each piece on the board at its current location.

Remember that only flexible pieces will accept a move-up or move-down message, and only a fast piece will be able to move more than one space at a time. (Hint: you may have to use the `instanceof` operator to enforce correct typing when a move is called for.)

P1.10. Write an application called `PracticeMoves` that would accept commands from input to create pieces and move them on an 8 × 8 game board, and print the board. You may use the following command syntax, with each command appearing on a new line. A nonemphasized word implies that it appears verbatim in the command; an emphasized word stands for several possibilities that are explained. A word in square brackets implies it is optional.

- create *location* [fast] [flexible]

  Create a piece and place it in a given initial *location* of the form *x y*. By default a piece is slow and nonflexible.

- move *location direction* [*spaces*]

  Move a piece, where *direction* is one of "left," "right," "up," or "down," of which the last two only apply to flexible pieces. The optional *spaces,* which is only applicable to fast pieces, specifies how many places to move the piece.

- print

  Print the board.

- help

  List all the commands that can be issued.

Identify all the places in your code where polymorphism is used.

P1.11. The class hierarchy built in Problems P1.5 through P1.8 may not result in the most amount of code reuse possible for the given system. Suppose we tried an alternative design in which class `Piece` is *not* abstract, and includes an additional field called *speed* which is either fast or slow. It implements the move-left and move-right operations; depending on whether *speed* is fast or slow, the number of steps may or may not be specified. A constructor expects the client to specify whether the piece is slow or fast.

Next, instead of an interface `Flexible`, a class `FlexiblePiece` that extends `Piece` is built, which provides the move-up and move-down operations. Implement this hierarchy.

P1.12. Rewrite the `Board` and `PracticeMoves` classes for the new class design of Problem P1.11.

(a) Does the design of Problem P1.11 reuse more code than than that of Problems P1.5 through P1.8?

(b) Does the new design introduce design loopholes that could be misused by a client?

(c) Does the new design make either the code within the classes `Piece` and `FlexiblePiece` or the code within the classes `Board` or `PracticeMoves` more cumbersome?

(d) Is introducing an additional *speed* field in the new *Piece* class and making it nonabstract a liability rather than an asset? In other words, is it more trouble than it is worth?

P1.13. Suppose you want to design and implement a class that may be used by any application that deals with objects that have color. One application may be a graphics application that enables users to draw colored shapes. Another may be an application that models a store in which all products have colors. Whatever the application may be, your class—say we call it `ColorOrganizer`—is capable of grouping all its objects by color. That is, all red objects will be together, all blue objects will be together, and so on.

Here are the following guidelines for you to build `ColorOrganizer`:

- Define an interface that will prescribe a method that will define equality between two colors.
- Genericize the `ColorOrganizer` class by defining a type parameter that is bounded by this interface.
- Define instance methods in `ColorOrganizer` to do the following as *efficiently* as you can make them:
  - Add a colored object to this `ColorOrganizer` instance.
  - Remove an object from this `ColorOrganizer` instance and return it.
  - Tell how many objects in this `ColorOrganizer` instance have the same color as a given object.
  - Tell how many different colors of objects there are in this `ColorOrganizer` instance.
  - Tell how many objects there are of a given color in this `ColorOrganizer` instance.
  - List the number of objects of each color that are in this `ColorOrganizer` instance.
- Define a static method in `ColorOrganizer` that will take an array of colored objects and return a `ColorOrganizer` version comprising the colored objects grouped according to color.

CHAPTER 2

The Big Picture

2.1   WHAT ARE DATA STRUCTURES?
2.2   WHAT DATA STRUCTURES DO WE STUDY?
2.3   WHAT ARE ABSTRACT DATA TYPES?
2.4   WHY OOP AND JAVA FOR DATA STRUCTURES?
2.5   HOW DO I CHOOSE THE RIGHT DATA STRUCTURES?

The big picture comprises answers to several questions that capture the essence of data structures, and their place in programming.

We start with the critical first question: *What are data structures?* Once we know what data structures are, our obvious next question is: *What data structures do we study?* The answer to this question enumerates a collection of the so-called "classic" data structures in computer science that have found common appeal and wide usage.

The next pair of questions ask about the *perspective* from which we view and build data structures. The first of these, *What are abstract data types?*, seeks to understand how data structures may be perceived by a program as *abstract data types*, or *ADTs*, and why this is a useful perspective. The second question, *Why OOP and Java for data structures?*, seeks to understand why data structures need to be studied in the context of OOP or *object-oriented programming*, and why we favor Java as the medium in which to implement the object-oriented programming paradigm.

The last question is concerned with evaluating the merit of a data structure. *How do I choose the right data structures* for my program? The answer to this question helps select data structures based on their *appropriateness* and *efficiency* for the application at hand. The answer also helps us to build new data structures, since designing and implementing a data structure is a special case of designing and implementing an application program.

This book also covers some essential sorting algorithms. While the algorithms do not introduce any new data structures not already covered in the rest of the book, they emphasize the importance of the role some of the data structures play in their efficient implementation.

2.1   WHAT ARE DATA STRUCTURES?

A **newspaper** is an aggregation, or collection, of **pages.**
    Each **page** has a collection of **headings.**
        Under each **heading** is a set of **columns.**
            Each **column** consists of numerous **paragraphs.**
                Each **paragraph** consists of several **sentences.**
                    Each **sentence** consists of a set of **words** and **punctuation.**
                    Each **word** is a set of characters.
                    Each **punctuation** is a character.
                    Each **character** is ?

A data structure is an aggregation of data components that together constitute a meaningful whole.

The components themselves may be data structures. If the newspaper is a data structure, then so are each of its pages, and so are each of its headings, and so on. One can peel a data structure like an onion, exposing lower-level data structures, until one comes to a stop at some "atomic" unit.

The determination of what constitutes an atomic unit depends on the observer. As a reader of the newspaper, I am content to stop at the characters that make up a word—the character is the atomic unit. But as one who prints the paper, I need to know what goes into making that character appear on the page in ink—for me, the lithographic components that go into printing characters are the atomic units.

2.2   WHAT DATA STRUCTURES DO WE STUDY?

We are most likely to have already encountered the *array* data structure. An array is an aggregation of entries arranged in contiguous fashion with the provision of a single-step random access to any entry. We do not think of the array as a formal data structure because it is built into most programming languages.

While the array is a powerful data structure, and fits into almost all programming situations, there are numerous other situations where more sophisticated data structures are required. Over the years, several *classic* data structures have been recognized for their importance in serving the needs of programmers. A more or less standard subset of these classic data structures is covered in this book.

The data structures covered in this book may be broadly classified as either *linear* or *nonlinear* data structures, based on how the data is conceptually organized or aggregated. But data organization is not the only means of classifying data structures. One may classify data structures according to the physical or abstract systems they model. For instance, trees model hierarchies and graphs model symmetric or asymmetric relationships. This is a more informative and useful way of defining graphs and trees than simply labeling them both as nonlinear data structures.

In this book, we are primarily interested in striking a balance between bringing out the commonalities among data structures and showcasing their individualism. With this in mind, we study the following data structures.

Linear structures.   The *list, queue,* and *stack* are referred to as *linear collections*. Each of them is a repository that stores its entries in a linear sequence, and in which entries may be added or removed at will. They differ in the restrictions they place on how these entries may be added, removed, or accessed.

List

A *list* is a linear collection of entries in which entries may be added, removed, and searched for without restriction. There are two kinds of lists: *ordered list,* in which the entries are maintained in sorted order, and *unordered list,* in which the entries are not arranged in any particular order.

Queue

A *queue* is a linear collection in which entries may only be removed in the order in which they are added. More specifically, if entry x is added before entry y, then y may not be removed before x. The *queue* is commonly referred to as a first-in, first-out (*FIFO*) data structure. There is typically no provision to search for an entry in the *queue*.

Stack

A *stack* is different from a *Queue* in the fundamental respect that entries may be only be are removed in the reverse order in which they are added, i.e., the last entry added is the first one to be removed. The *stack* is commonly referred to as a last-in, first-out (*LIFO*) data structure. As in the *queue*, there is typically no provision to search for an entry in the *stack*.

Trees.   The data structures in the *trees* category share a common nonlinear *arrangement* that is conceptually modeled after the trees we see around us in nature. But this model is useful to a limited extent: the various tree structures covered here vary widely in the physical and abstract systems they model.

Binary Tree

As a data structure that models a physical or abstract system, a *binary tree* consists of entries each of which contributes to the tree as a whole based on its *position* in the tree. Moving an entry from one position to another changes the meaning of the *binary tree*.

General Tree

A *general tree* models a hierarchy such as the organizational structure of a company, or a family tree. As a nonlinear arrangement of entries, it is a generalization of the binary tree structure, hence the name.

Binary Search Tree

The *binary search tree* has the same structural form as the *binary tree,* but each entry in the *binary search tree* is self-contained: it does not contribute differently if its position in the tree is changed, nor does the tree as a whole carry a meaning that is tied to the relative arrangement of the entries.

The *binary search tree* is a repository of entries, arranged (effectively) in sorted order: it is a tree analogue of the *ordered list.* Entries may be added, removed, and searched for at will.

AVL Tree

The *AVL tree* is a special, *height-balanced,* binary search tree. An ordinary binary search tree provides a mechanism to search for entries in it; the *AVL tree* derives its importance from the fact that it speeds up this search process to a remarkable degree.

Heap as a Priority Queue

A priority queue is a specialization of the FIFO *queue* in that its entries are assigned priorities. Of all the entries in a priority queue, the entry with the highest priority is the one to leave first. If we were to group data structures according to their role or behavior, the priority queue structure would be placed in the same category as the FIFO *queue.* Here we have chosen to classify it based on its conceptual structure: it is implemented as a *heap,* which is a special kind of binary tree structure.

Updatable Heap

Once an entry is added to a simple priority queue, i.e., a *heap,* its priority may not change. Often, one wants to be able to change the priority of an entry when it is in the priority queue: this calls for an *updatable heap,* i.e., a heap with updatable priorities. The implementation of an *updatable heap* raises several issues of safety and efficiency that require a more sophisticated solution than the regular *heap.*

Hash table.   The *hash table* stores entries with the sole aim of enabling efficient search. However, unlike the *binary search tree,* the *hash table* does not arrange its entries in effective sorted order and does not have a tree structure. The implementation of an efficient hash table requires a sound knowledge of certain mathematical properties of numbers and of so-called *hash functions* that manipulate numbers.

Graphs.   Graphs model relationships. A general tree is a special kind of graph, since a hierarchy is a special system of relationships among entities. Graphs may be used to model systems of physical connections, such as the World Wide Web (web pages and the links between them), computer networks, and airline routes, as well as abstract relationships, such as course-pre-requisite structures.

Once we are able to appropriately model a system as a graph, we may use one or more standard graph algorithms to answer certain questions we may ask of the system. For instance, after modeling a complete airline routing system, we may ask: What is the fastest way to get from point A to point B? The *shortest-paths* algorithm can answer our question.

2.3   WHAT ARE ABSTRACT DATA TYPES?

Software developers have long struggled with the issue of writing code that is robust, easy to maintain, and reusable. Out of this effort to write better code arose a new metaphor for using and building data structures: *a data structure is an abstract data type.* There was no new development in the data structures themselves; what changed, with significant impact on code development, was the way they were packaged.

An abstract data type, or ADT, highlights the notion of *abstractness.* When we say "data type," we generally refer to the primitive data types built into a language, the most common ones being integer, real, character, and boolean. Now consider an integer in a programming language such as Java. An integer, we know, is most likely implemented, or represented, in four bytes in the computer. However, when we use integers, *we do not worry at all about its internal representation.* What we do know, and care about, is that we can perform certain operations on integers that are guaranteed to work the way they are intended to. Again, exactly *how these operations are implemented by the compiler in machine code is of no concern.* Last, we know that even if we run our program on a different machine, the *behavior of an integer does not change, even though its internal representation may change.*

What the software community observed is that programmers use primitive data types purely via their operational *interface*—say, '+', '-', '*', '/' for integers—while language designers and compiler writers were responsible for *designing* the interface for these data types, as well as for *implementing* them. As far as the programmers were concerned, the implementation of the data types was hidden from view, and abstracted out into the interface—that is all they saw. For them, the primitive data types were *abstract* entries, although for the language designer or compiler writer, they are not. Thus abstraction is relative to the point of view.

The viewer sees the TV in terms of its volume, contrast, brightness, and other controls. This is the operational interface of the TV, depicted by the outermost circle. Going one level lower, the TV itself is built out of various components. One of these may be a programmable chip. The TV manufacturer buys this chip off-the-shelf and connects it to the other components. In order to do this correctly, the manufacturer has to know the operational interface of

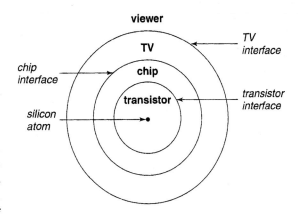

the chip, which is available as a specification manual. This is depicted by the circle that divides the TV from the chip.

Peeling off one more layer, we see that the chip consists of transistors, among other things. Again, the chip manufacturer may want to treat the transistor as an abstract entity, dealing with it based on its operational specification alone. The transistor itself is made of silicon, whose constituent atoms are the bottom line in this system of abstractions. In sum, "abstraction" is a relative term, depending on where the interface line is drawn.

A primitive data type is abstract on one side of a interface line, which is the line between the high-level language program and the compiler. This insight led to the obvious (in hindsight) generalization: if one could move the dividing line a little further toward the program, and away from the compiler, one could get higher and higher levels of abstraction. But since the dividing line is really intruding into the programmer's domain, these higher-level abstractions began to be referred to as *user-defined types*.

Data structures may be built as user-defined abstract data types. A data structure is a package, possibly consisting of several layers of abstraction, since it may in turn be built out of other data structures.

Let us take a *stack* of integers as an example. In the preceding section, we learned that a stack is a linear structure in which entries are taken out (*popped*) in the reverse order in which they are added (*pushed*). That is, if 10, 20 and 30 are pushed onto a stack in this sequence, successive pops will retrieve these entries in the order 30, 20, and 10. A *stack* (of integers) may be built using a *list* (of integers), which in turn may be built using an array (of integers).

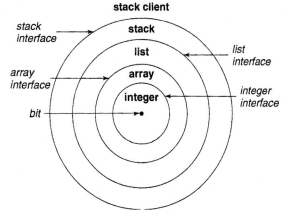

In this example, the integer and array are language-defined types, while the *stack* and *list* are user-defined types.

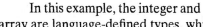

At the beginning of this section we said that the idea of abstract data typing arose out of a need to develop code that was robust, easy to maintain, and reusable. Since an ADT makes a clean separation between interface and implementation, the user only sees the interface and therefore does not need tamper with the implementation. On the other hand, if the implementation of an ADT changes, the code that uses the ADT does not break, since the interface remains the same. Thus, the "wall of abstraction" makes the code more robust: both the user and the builder of the ADT see an unchanging interface.

The responsibility of maintaining the implementation is separated from the responsibility of maintaining the code that uses an ADT. This makes the code easier to maintain. Moreover, once an ADT is built, it may be used multiple times in various contexts. For example, the *list* ADT may be used directly in application code, or may be used to build another ADT, such as a *stack*.

Abstract data typing is an effective approach to code development, but how does one ensure that developers actually use this approach? What would really help is the means to automatically check whether code violates the separation between interface and implementation, and also, a set of tools that makes it easy for the programmer to reuse code. Object-oriented programming is a paradigm that addresses exactly these issues, among several others.

2.4   WHY OOP AND JAVA FOR DATA STRUCTURES?

First, what does object-oriented programming (OOP) have to do with data structures? We have already come part of the way toward an answer to this question by answering a related question: what does abstract data typing have to do with data structures? We now need to answer the connecting question: how does OOP *implement* abstract data typing?

The OOP paradigm views the program as a system of interacting objects. Objects in a program may model physical objects such as cars and networks, or abstract entities such as words and game strategies. An object is said to *encapsulate* state and behavior. The state of an object is its current "situation"; its behavior is defined by a set of operations that may be used to change or access its state. For instance, the state of an integer, treated as an object, is its current value, and its behavior is the set of arithmetic operations that may be applied to integers.

An object's behavior is its interface to the user—the user may manipulate the object via this interface. Exactly how this behavior is implemented (and how the state is stored) is not visible to the user. In object-oriented programming, a *class* is the template out of which several objects may be created. The class is analogous to the ADT, and an object is analogous to a variable of an ADT.

In the OOP world, the user of an object is called its *client*. Objects interact by sending messages to each other. So, for instance, object A may be a client of object B, and may prod B to do something by sending a message to it. This results in some operation in B's interface being performed, which may either send back to the client, A, information about B's current state, or may result in updating B's state.

As an example, consider the *stack* ADT from Section 2.3. We observed that a *stack* may be built using a *list* ADT. The following figure shows how a *stack* object interacts with its clients, and in turn, how it behaves as a client of its component *list* object.

As can be seen, the *Stack* interface defines four operations: *push, pop, getSize,* and *isEmpty.* These operations constitute the behavior of the *stack* object. The state of the *stack* object is determined by the current number and positions of its constituent entries. The *stack* object, in turn, contains a *list* object, which implements its state, and the behavior of the *stack* object is implemented in terms of the *list* object's behavior. Arrows indicate messages from client to object.

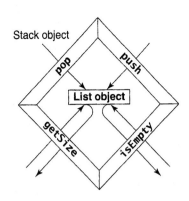

A client of a *stack* object may send it *push* and *pop* messages, which result in its state being updated. On the other hand, *getSize* and *isEmpty* messages simply query the state of the *stack* without updating it.

Now let us look at the implementation of the *stack* object. It uses a *list* object to implement its state, i.e., the entries of the *stack* are actually stored in this *list* object. The *list* object acts like a proxy for the *stack.* Accordingly, the *stack* interface operations are implemented in terms of a corresponding set of *list* interface operations. In effect, the *stack* is a client of the *list* object it contains. If the client of the *stack* sends it a *getSize* message, the *stack* in turns sends a similar message to the *list* object. The answer sent back by the *list* object is then transmitted back to the *stack*'s client.

We can draw a picture for a *list* object that contains an array object, analogous to the figure above. The *stack* object is now the client of the *list* object, which, in turn, is the client of the constituent array object. The array object serves as a proxy for the *list* object.

Objects once built may be reused several times, in just the way ADTs are intended to be reused. In this type of reuse, an object is built by using another, internal object to implement its state—this is called *reuse by composition.* The term "composition" is used because one object is *composed of* (contains) one or more other objects that are being reused. In OOP terminology, we say that the containing object *has-A* contained object. This is the case, for instance, when we build a *stack* object by reusing a *list* object as a component: the *stack has-A list.*

The other kind of reuse afforded by OOP, quite different from composition, is called *reuse by inheritance.* Data structures may be built by *inheriting* from other data structures; typically, if data structure A inherits from data structure B, then every A object is *is-A* B object, but the reverse is not true. For example, one may build an AVL tree by inheriting from a *binary search tree,* since every AVL tree is *is-A* special, height-balanced, binary search tree. However, every binary search tree is not an AVL tree.

Reuse by inheritance breaks the "wall of abstraction" between objects. Inheriting means sharing the implementation code: the *AVL tree* reuses the code in the *binary search tree* implementation. Clearly, the inheriting entity sees *behind* the inherited entity's interface, i.e., breaks the wall.

Our approach in the study of data structures strives to consistently bring out the separation between interface and implementation, between the client's view of an object and its internal implementation details. When we introduce a data structure, we first get familiar with its behavior, *what* it is intended to, by using it in applications that act as its clients. Then we cross the abstraction wall and go over to the other side, where we study *how* to implement it.

In implementing a data structure, we choose between reuse by composition and reuse by inheritance, depending on the situation. We also study the implementations of several related data structures together, since related data structures very often reuse the same component structures.

A language that implements the OOP paradigm ensures automatically that a program written in that language strictly follows the OOP tenets of (a) separation of interface from implementation by encapsulation, and (b) code reuse through inheritance when (and only when) permitted. In other words, the designer of a data structure can indicate, in an OOP language, exactly how its interface is separated from its implementation, and can rest assured that any violation of this design will be automatically caught by the compiler. Also, the designer can indicate exactly how the code that implements a data structure can be reused by other structures by inheritance, and can depend on the language to enforce this reuse policy.

There are currently two popular languages that implement the OOP paradigm: C++ and Java. We have chosen Java to implement all the data structures in this book, as well as the associated application programs that use these data structures.

Java is a safe implementation of the object-oriented programming paradigm. Object-oriented programming is a natural medium in which data structures can be built; Java carries us further by enabling us to write our data structures *cleanly* and *quickly,* with a minimum of fuss. A discussion of the merits and drawbacks of Java is beyond the scope of this book; however, there is no lack of publicly available material that do this well.

The *class* construct is the bedrock of Java programs. A Java program is a collection of classes, and all objects are instances of classes. In other words, a class serves as a blueprint for the creation of objects, just as a Ford Explorer design specification would serve as a blueprint for the manufacture of Ford Explorers. An ADT is implemented as a class in Java.

We eschew the traditional term *abstract data type* in favor of the more modern *class,* because *class* has a much broader practical appeal. It can serve both as an ADT and also as its implementation, depending on whether we view, from the outside, the public interface presented by a class, or, from the inside, its implementation details.

2.5 HOW DO I CHOOSE THE RIGHT DATA STRUCTURES?

When writing a program, one of the first steps is determining or choosing the data structures. What are the "right" data structures for the program? The *interface* of operations supported by a data structure is one factor to consider when choosing between several available data structures. But that's not all. Another, extremely important factor is the *efficiency* of the data structure: how much *space* does the data structure occupy, and what are the *running times* of the operations in its interface?

Interface. If our program is going to implement a printer queue, then we need the *queue* data structure. But what if we need to maintain a collection of entries in no particular order, as, for instance, a list of friends to invite to a party? A *stack* or *queue* would work, provided we simply add names as they come and print them all out at the end. But if we wanted to look up certain names to see if they were in the list, then we couldn't use the *stack* or *queue,* because they do not support search operations. An *unordered list* would be the appropriate data structure in this case. In sum, we choose the structure whose interface fits most closely with the requirements of the application.

As is evident from the preceding discussion, it is not too difficult to fit the requirements of the application to the operations supported by a data structure. It is more of a challenge to choose from a set of candidate data structures that all meet the operational requirements.

A data structure may provide a *minimal* set of operations that characterize its behavior, with the advantage of being *easily understood*. The fewer the operations that constitute the interface, the easier it is to learn how to use the data structure. For instance, the *stack* data structure may provide, at the bare minimum, three operations: push, pop, and isEmpty.

In contrast to the minimal interface approach, a data structure may provide a set of additional operations that are not absolutely essential, but make it more *flexible* or easy to use. For example, the client of a *stack* may frequently want to know how many entries are in it. This can be determined by using another *stack* and popping all the entries from the first into the second while keeping a running count. Then one has to repeat this process to restore the contents of the second stack back to the first. Clearly, if the *stack* were to come with an additional operation, say *getSize,* that returned the number of entries in it, the client would be spared a lot of grief.

It is tempting to go overboard and equip an object with a large number of operations, with the intention of helping its clients. This may, in fact, create just the opposite effect: the client may be overwhelmed, and have a hard time trying to separate the wheat from the chaff, in selecting those operations that are most useful while discarding those that are simply add-ons. Therefore, when we build increasingly complex programs, we have to pay a great deal of attention to choosing between minimal structures and flexible ones, while trying to find a happy medium.

The lessons we learn about selecting the "right" data structures to *use* in an application program apply equally well to *building* data structures. After all, implementing a data structure also requires us to think about what other data structures we could use as the constituent components.

Whenever we study a data structure in this book, we start by understanding its characteristic behavior, i.e., *what it is meant for,* in the context of some situations or applications for which it provides an ideal fit. Then we specify the list of operations in a typical implementation of this data structure, with a discussion of what these operations do, and why it makes sense to include them in the interface. In Java terms, we describe the *public methods of the class* that implements that data structure.

Running time.   What we have seen is how to fit the interface to the requirement. But there is another, equally important, and sometimes contradictory factor to consider: the running time of each operation in the interface. A data structure with the best interface fit may not be the best overall fit if the running times of its operations are not up to the mark.

In general, when we have more than one data structure implementation whose interfaces satisfy our requirements, we may have to select one based on comparing the running times of the interface operations, as well as the space consumed by the data structure. Often, time is traded off for space—i.e., more space is consumed to increase speed, or a reduction in speed is traded for a reduction in the space consumption.

For each data structure we study, we present the running time of each operation in its interface. This is the *price tag* of the implementation, and is a quantitative measure of a more general *efficiency* cost. This, in turn, begs the question: how do we measure efficiency? That is the subject of the next chapter.

CHAPTER 3

Efficiency of Algorithms

Efficiency is a measure of speed and space consumption. In this chapter, we will focus on measuring the speed of a program, also called it's running time or execution time, and describe a general quantitative standard for it. This standard is the *order* of complexity and is denoted by the letter O, read as *big oh*.

The space consumption, or requirement, may be also represented using *big O*, and is always *less than or equal to* to the time requirement. Therefore, we do not explicitly discuss the space requirement in this chapter.

Learning Objectives

- Identify the basic operations in an algorithm.
- Determine the running time of an algorithm by counting its basic operations.
- Express the running time of an algorithm as a function of the input size.
- Understand the asymptotic growth of functions.
- Derive the *big O* order of the running time.
- Study some typical running time orders that arise in computing.
- Explore multivariable order, relative order, and arithmetic with orders.
- Describe worst-case and average running times.

3.1 POLYNOMIAL ARITHMETIC: A RUNNING EXAMPLE

In this section, we introduce basic polynomial arithmetic, used as a running example throughout the chapter to illustrate the various aspects of determining running time.

Tuple representation. A polynomial may be represented as an *ordered tuple* of coefficients whose length is equal to the degree of the polynomial plus one. For example, the polynomial:

$$4x^5 - 2x^3 + 2x + 3$$

may be written as the following ordered tuple:

$$(4, 0, -2, 0, 2, 3)$$

Addition/subtraction. To add two polynomials on paper, we would line them up one below the other in such a manner that the coefficients of the same degree term appear along the same column:

$$
\begin{array}{lllllllllll}
P_1 & = & + & 4x^5 & & & - & 2x^3 & + & 2x & + & 3 \\
P_2 & = & & & + & 8x^4 & + & 4x^3 & - & 3x & + & 9 \\
\hline
P_1 + P_2 & = & + & 4x^5 & + & 8x^4 & + & 2x^3 & - & x & + & 12
\end{array}
$$

Using the ordered tuple notation, we simply add up the entries according to position:

$$
\begin{aligned}
P_1 + P_2 & = (4, 0, -2, 0, 2, 3) + (0, 8, 4, 0, -3, 9) \\
& = (4, 8, 2, 0, -1, 12)
\end{aligned}
$$

Note that P_2 needs to have a zero in the leftmost position, since the degree of P_1 is one more than that of P_2. Also, both P_1 and P_2 have a zero for the second-degree term.

Subtracting one polynomial from another is done similarly.

Multiplication. Multiplication is performed much like the multiplication of two decimal numbers. For example:

$$
\begin{aligned}
P_1 & = 3x^2 + x + 2 \\
P_2 & = x^3 - 3 \\
P_1 * P_2 & = (3, 1, 2) * (1, 0, 0, -3)
\end{aligned}
$$

may be worked out as follows, with every coefficient of the first polynomial multiplied by every coefficient of the second:

$$
\begin{array}{rrrrrr}
 & & 3 & 1 & 2 & \\
 & 1 & 0 & 0 & -3 & \\
\hline
 & & -9 & -3 & -6 \\
 & 0 & 0 & 0 \\
 0 & 0 & 0 \\
3 & 1 & 2 \\
\hline
3 & 1 & 2 & -9 & -3 & -6
\end{array}
$$

The resulting polynomial is thus:

$$3x^5 + x^4 + 2x^3 - 9x^2 - 3x - 6$$

Evaluation and Horner's rule.   Suppose we wanted to evaluate the polynomial

$$p = 4x^4 - 2x^3 + 5x^2 + 10x - 15$$

at $x = 2$. If we simply plug in the value of x in every term, we end up separately computing x^5, x^4, x^3, and x^2. Overall these will add up to $4 + 3 + 2 + 1 = 10$ multiplications.

A better way to do this is to use *Horner's rule*, which avoids such repeated multiplications by noting that if, for instance, x^4 has been computed, then x^5 may be obtained with just one additional multiplication: $x * x^4$. This is applied recursively across the polynomial to reduce the overall number of multiplications. Here is how the polynomial is evaluated, with the parentheses determining the order of evaluation of subexpressions:

$$((((4)x - 2)x + 5)x + 10)x - 15$$

Now there are only four multiplications.

3.2   BASIC OPERATIONS

As an end-user of a program, when we speak of its running time, we usually refer to the wall-clock time, as in "The spell-checker took 10 minutes to check my document." While the wall-clock time is what the lay person relies on to measure program speed, it is not necessarily a reliable means of knowing whether a program is fast or slow, since several other factors may cloud the issue.

For instance, suppose you wanted to compare the speed of your spell-checker with that of your friend's. He says, "Mine ran in under five minutes," but you are not about to admit defeat that easily. So you ask him certain questions. "What is the speed of your CPU?" "Did you have any other programs running at the same time?" "How long is your document?" And so on. What you are trying to do is to level the playing field by ensuring that your respective spell-checkers ran under the *same environment*, so that you can make a fair comparison.

What we need is to be able to measure the running time independent of such peripheral issues as the machine on which the measurement is being made (*CPU speed*) and the operating system environment in which the program is running (*system load*). Measuring the running time with a stop-watch or by plugging in calls to the system clock within the program brings these issues into play, and is not generally reliable. Instead, what we need to measure are the basic operations.

MEASURING RUNNING TIME

The most reliable way to measure the running time is to count the number of times the basic operations that contribute to the running time are executed. The running time is proportional to this count.

What are these basic operations? They depend on what the program does. Table 3.1 lists some programs and the corresponding basic operations they perform that contribute to the running time.

TABLE 3.1: Basic operations performed by some sample programs.

Program	Basic Operation
Sorting a set of integers	Comparing two integers
Copying a file into another	Copying a byte
Adding two polynomials	Adding two coefficients

The running time in the first program is proportional to the number of pair-wise comparisons, in the second to the number of bytes in the input file, and in the third to the number of coefficient additions. From now on, instead of constantly saying "running time is proportional to," we will simply say "running time is."

In Table 3.1 we refer to the running times of *programs*. In truth however, we are not concerned with the programming language in which a program is written so much as the algorithm it implements. In other words, it is more important to be able to think of the program as an algorithm or sequence of steps that is *independent of any programming language*. This would enable us to exclude from our count irrelevant operations that do not involve basic operations, such as loop index increments and loop termination conditions.

ALGORITHM IMPLEMENTED BY A PROGRAM IS IMPORTANT

In analyzing the running time of a program, it is important to think of it as an algorithm, i.e., a sequence of steps independent of the programming language in which it may be implemented.

Table 3.1 listed one basic operation in each row. In general, algorithms consist of more than one basic operation. Sometimes we count all of them, other times a single *dominant* one.

Example: Polynomial evaluation.   We saw in Section 3.1 how to evaluate a polynomial at a given x value. In the naive evaluation scheme, where we simply plugged in the value of x in every term and computed the powers separately, we end up performing the following numbers of operations:

- ten multiplications for evaluating the powers of x
- four multiplications with coefficients for the first four terms
- four additions across the evaluated terms

In all, we perform 14 multiplications and 4 additions. It is obvious that we will be performing many more multiplications than additions. Moreover, multiplication is typically faster than addition. Thus, multiplications are the dominant basic operations.

Example: Weighted average.   Imagine that you are browsing the web, and you have a "hot" list of several favorite sites you visit often. You are interested in determining the average response time over a day's session in which you visit each site on your hot list several times.

The response time on visiting a site may be different at different times of the day. However, it is likely that some sites get hit much more often than other sites, so we will focus on the differences between response times of different sites rather than different response times for the same site. In keeping with this, let us assume that the response time for site i is fixed at t_i, with the sites being numbered 1, 2, ..., n.

If the number of times you visited site i is f_i, the total response time for this site is $f_i * t_i$. The total response times over all sites is:

$$f_1 * t_1 + f_2 * t_2 + \cdots + f_n * t_n$$

For the average response time over all sites, we divide the above quantity by the number of sites, n.

For $n = 50$, this computation would take 50 multiplications, 49 additions, and one division. It is clear that the number of multiplications would be exactly one more than the number of additions, no matter how many sites there are. And there is always exactly one division. In this case, we can choose both additions and multiplications as the dominant basic operations.

Next, we need to relate the running time of an algorithm to the size of the input(s) on which it operates.

3.3   INPUT SIZE

Suppose we measure the running times of two sorting algorithms, A and B, by counting the respective number of comparisons. We run these algorithms on the *same input,* and come up with the following: A makes 35 comparisons, and B makes 40. Can we say that A is faster then B, on any common input?

It is not clear that we can say this—what if the input size were to change? Would A still be faster than B? It is clear that a single raw number of comparisons such as the above is not going to tell us much—we need to observe what happens when A and B are run on inputs of various sizes. Specifically, what we need is the number of comparisons as a *function of the input size.*

BASIC OPERATIONS AND INPUT SIZE

In analyzing the running time of an algorithm, it is important to relate the number of basic operations to the size of the input, i.e., the number of basic operations must be expressed as a function of the input size.

Table 3.2 lists the input sizes of the sorting, file copying, and matrix-vector multiplication algorithms discussed above.

The input size is not restricted to a single variable. In the case of polynomial addition, there are two inputs: the ordered tuple for the first polynomial, of size $n + 1$ (degree plus one), and the ordered tuple of the second polynomial, of size $m + 1$. For the sake of

TABLE 3.2: Input sizes for various algorithms.

Algorithm	Input Size
Sorting	n: the number of integers to be sorted
File Copying	n: the number of bytes in the input file
Polynomial Addition	n: degree of first polynomial
	m: degree of second polynomial

simplicity, we ignore the constant 1 (which is, in general, insignificant compared to n and m) and treat the sizes as n and m, respectively.

3.4 ASYMPTOTIC GROWTH OF FUNCTIONS

Back to the sorting algorithms A and B introduced at the beginning of Section 3.3. Let n be the size of the input common to both algorithms. Now suppose A performs

$$3n - 10$$

comparisons, and B performs

$$2n + 10$$

comparisons on this input.[1] Then, if $n = 15$, A makes 35 comparisons, and B makes 40. However, if $n = 20$, they both make the same number of comparisons, 50. If n is increased beyond this, say to 25, then A makes 65 comparisons, while B makes only 60. In fact, for all $n > 20$, B makes fewer comparisons than A, i.e., B is faster than A.

Clearly, what mattered was the constant that multiplied n in the number of comparisons, not the constant that was added or subtracted. Hence, when we measure the running time as a function of n, *we can ignore the additive constants*. But that is only half the story.

Consider two algorithms P and Q that perform the same task, but P performs

$$f_p = 4n + 20$$

basic operations, and Q,

$$f_q = 2n^2 - 10$$

basic operations, defined for all $n > 2$. Figure 3.1 illustrates the growth of these functions against n.

For $n = 3$ and $n = 4$, Q performs fewer operations than P, therefore Q is faster. But for $n = 5$, they both perform the same number of operations. For *any* $n > 5$, P performs fewer operations than Q, i.e., P is faster.

This leads to an important general concept, called *asymptotic growth* of functions.

The term *asymptotic* has to do with the idea of *a large enough N:* there is no limit on how large N can be, as long as *beyond* that N, one function is always greater than the other. In the preceding example, we say that P is asymptotically faster than Q.

---

1. These comparisons are only defined for $n > 3$.

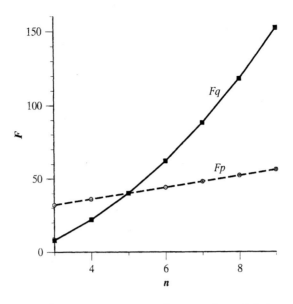

FIGURE 3.1: Growth of Functions. For $3 \leq n < 5$, the curve for f_q is below that of f_p. At $n = 5$, they intersect. Thereafter, for all $n > 5$, the curve for f_q is always above that for f_p.

ASYMPTOTIC GROWTH OF FUNCTIONS

Given two functions $f(n)$ and $g(n)$, if there is an integer N such that for all $n > N, f(n)$ is always greater than $g(n)$, then $f(n)$ is said to grow asymptotically faster than $g(n)$.

Furthermore, it is important to determine the *rate at which a functions grows faster than another.* The following table illustrates how f_q outstrips f_p as n increases.

n	f_p	f_q
5	40	40
10	60	190
20	100	790
50	220	4990

Clearly, f_q grows by leaps and bounds compared to f_p. This is because the dominant term in f_q is *quadratic* (degree 2), while that in f_p is only *linear* (degree 1), even though the multiplicative constant in the former is less than that in the latter. In this case, the *constants that multiply the dominant terms do not matter.*

P's linear running time is in a different class, or *order of complexity,* than Q's quadratic running time. We say that Q's running time is *of the order n^2,* while P's is *of the order n.*

This idea of the order is important, since a difference in order is immediately apparent in a difference in wall-clock time, for any nontrivial input size. In fact, for larger and larger input sizes, the difference in order becomes increasingly significant, which leads us to the notion of big oh, or big O.

3.5   ORDER AND BIG OH

In comparing the running times of algorithms, it is important to determine the order of running time, shorn of multiplicative and additive constants. Algorithms with the same running time order are considered to be in the same speed league. The notation O, called *big oh* or *big O*, is a concise notation for the order. So we write $O(n)$ to mean "of the order n," and $O(n^2)$ to mean "of the order n^2."

A formal definition of big O follows from the definition of the asymptotic growth of functions in the preceding section.

BIG O

Given two functions $f(n)$ and $g(n)$, $f(n) = O(g(n))$ if and only if there exists a constant c such that $c * g(n)$ grows asymptotically faster than $f(n)$.

For instance, suppose $f(n) = 4n + 20$ and $g(n) = n$. Then, for $c = 5$, $c * g(n)$ grows asymptotically faster than $f(n)$. Hence, $4n + 20 = O(n)$. In other words, $4n + 20$ is of the order of n.

While one can always work at determining an N for asymptoticity as described in the preceding section, and a c as shown above, there is a sequence of steps one can follow to directly determine the big O order of a given function without having to explicitly determine N and c. Suppose we have computed the running time for an algorithm (basic operations) as a function of n, the input size. The following describes how to derive the *big O* order.

DERIVING THE BIG O ORDER

1. Replace all additive constants in the running time with the constant 1.
2. Retain only the highest-order term in this modified running time.
3. If the highest-order term is not 1, remove the constant (if any) that multiplies this term.

You are left with the *big O* order.

What do we mean by the *highest-order term?* Usually, we are faced with power terms such as n, n^2, or $n^{1.5}$; in these cases, the term with the highest power is the highest-order term. Occasionally, we may run into somewhat more complex terms, such as $n * \log(n)$, and it may be difficult to determine whether this term is, say, of a higher order than $n^{1.5}$. For quick reference in such situations, in Section 3.5.3 we establish a relative ordering among commonly encountered terms.

Let us now work out some examples of determining the *big O* running time order.

Example: Polynomial evaluation.   In Section 3.1 we saw that a simple way to evaluate a polynomial such as the following:

$$P = 4x^4 - 2x^3 + 5x^2 + 10x - 15$$

at a given value of x is to compute each power of x separately, then multiply these powers with the respective coefficients and add these together.

Let us generalize this to a polynomial of degree n. Assume that none of the coefficients is zero, so we have to evaluate the powers

$$x^n, x^{n-1}, x^{n-2}, \ldots, x^3, x^2$$

The first one would take $n - 1$ multiplications, the second $n - 2$ multiplications, the third $n - 3$ multiplications, and so on. In all, the number of multiplications performed would be:

$$(n - 1) + (n - 2) + (n - 3) + \cdots + 2 + 1 = n(n - 1)/2 = n^2/2 - n/2$$

Further, each term except the constant needs one coefficient multiplication, for a total of n multiplications. Thus, the grand total number of multiplications is:

$$\frac{n^2}{2} - \frac{n}{2} + n$$

Choosing multiplications as the dominant basic operations, the above is also the running time.

Now, let us apply the rules to derive the big O order.

1. *Replace all additive constants in the running time with the constant 1.*

   There are no additive constants in the running time, so nothing is done in this step.

2. *Retain only the highest-order term in this modified running time.*

   The highest-order term is $n^2/2$, which we retain. This is the new running time at this point.

3. *If the highest-order term is not 1, remove the constant (if any) that multiplies this term.*

   The constant in question is $1/2$; when we remove it, we are left with n^2.

Thus, the big O running time order is $O(n^2)$. Note that the input size is n, the degree of the polynomial[1]. $O(n^2)$ therefore means that the running time is quadratic in the size of the input.

Example: Polynomial evaluation using Horner's rule.   We noted that the simple evaluation scheme is very inefficient relative to the Horner's rule for evaluation—the latter performs far fewer multiplications.

To reiterate Horner's rule, the above polynomial is evaluated using the following parenthesization scheme:

$$((((4)x - 2)x + 5)x + 10)x - 15$$

---

1. The input is the tuple representation, which is actually of size $n + 1$, but we ignore the 1 relative to n.

Now there are only four multiplications, and still only four additions.

The key observation here is that, the number of multiplications is equal to the degree of the polynomial. Thus, if the degree of the polynomial is n, the number of multiplications is n, for a big O running time order of $O(n)$, which is linear in the size of the input. This is far superior to the previous quadratic running time; recall the difference illustrated by f_p and f_q in Section 3.4.

Next, we explore some typical running time orders encountered in computing and understand how they relate to each other.

3.5.1   Typical Running Time Orders

In Table 3.3, there are several running times listed in the first column. The corresponding entries in the second column are their respective *big O* orders, obtained by applying the three rules we saw earlier in this section. The last column lists the informal terms used to refer to these orders, as, for instance, "running time is linear in the input size," or "running time is quadratic in the input size." Let us go over each of these orders in order to get a better understanding.

Constant.   The constant order, $O(1)$, means that the running time is independent of the input size. In other words, the running time remains the same, however much the input size is increased or decreased. A good example of an $O(1)$ running time is the operation of accessing the i-th element in an array. No matter how many entries the array contains (input size), this operation always takes one step. This, of course, is the single biggest advantage of using an array.

Linear.   We will encounter the linear order, $O(n)$, quite frequently in the following chapters. One of the simplest linear algorithms is the one used to find the maximum (or minimum) of n values in an array.

The classic algorithm to find the maximum of a list of values starts by setting the maximum to the first value. Then it compares the second value against the maximum and updates the maximum if the second value happens to be larger. And so on, until each value is compared against whatever happens to be the maximum at that time, and the maximum is updated if needed. Thus, $n - 1$ comparisons are made in all, for an order of $O(n)$.

TABLE 3.3: Typical running time orders.

Running Time	Order	Informal Term
10	$O(1)$	Constant
$3n + 25$	$O(n)$	Linear
$1.5n^2 + 25n - 55$	$O(n^2)$	Quadratic
$250n + 10n \log n + 25$	$O(n \log n)$	*en log en*
$3 \log n + 30$	$O(\log n)$	Logarithmic
$10n^3 + 2n$	$O(n^3)$	Cubic
$12 * 2^n$	$O(k^n)$	Exponential

Quadratic.   We have so far seen a simple-minded polynomial evaluation scheme as an example of a quadratic, or $O(n^2)$, algorithm. Let us take one more example.

Sorting algorithms provide fertile ground for the quadratic order. A host of sorting algorithms are described in Chapter 13, but let us take a simple sorting algorithm called **selection sort** to illustrate our point.

Here is selection sort on an array of length 6. The algorithm makes five passes over the array, working on increasingly smaller sub-arrays of sizes 6, 5, 4, 3, and 2 respectively.

3	9	2	5	8	7

Pass 1

3	7	2	5	8	9

Pass 2

3	7	2	5	8	9

Pass 3

3	5	2	7	8	9

Pass 4

3	2	5	7	8	9

Pass 5

2	3	5	7	8	9

In the first pass, it finds the maximum of all values, 9, and swaps this with the last value, 7. Thus 9 has now gone to its correct position in the sorted array. This last position is ignored for the rest of the algorithm.

In the second pass, the value 8 happens to be both the maximum and the last, so it is exchanged with itself. And so on, until the algorithm terminates when there is exactly one value, 2, remaining to be sorted.

We can formalize the selection sort algorithm as follows.

algorithm selectionSort(A, n)

input: array A, of length n

for (p from 1 to n-1) do
    $max \leftarrow$ maximum of $A[0]$ through $A[n - p]$
    $maxpos \leftarrow$ position of max
    $A[maxpos] \leftarrow A[n - p]$
    $A[n - p] \leftarrow max$
endfor

Observe that when p is 1, the elements examined are $A[0]$ through $A[n - 1]$; when p is $n - 1$, the elements examined are $A[0]$ through $A[1]$.

The process of finding the maximum is the usual sequential scanning algorithm, and is not elaborated here.

To analyze the running time of selection sort, we take a pair-wise comparison between array entries as the basic operation. In the first pass, $n - 1$ comparisons are made to find the maximum of n entries. In the second pass, $n - 2$ comparisons are made to find the maximum of $n - 1$ entries, and so on. The total number of comparisons made over all the passes of the algorithm is given by:

$$(n - 1) + (n - 2) + (n - 3) + \cdots + 2 + 1 = n(n - 1)/2$$

We saw an identical result earlier in the polynomial evaluation example, and we know that the above is $O(n^2)$. To summarize, the size of the input is n, and the running time of selection sort is quadratic in the size of the input.

Example: Apparently quadratic, actually linear.   The fact that the order must be related to the input size cannot be overemphasized. Following is an example of a very simple algorithm that looks as if it is quadratic but is actually linear.

Consider a 2-D array of size $n \times n$. Applications that deal with 2-D arrays usually initialize all the array entries at some point. Let us consider an algorithm that does this. It goes over all n^2 entries of the array, and assigns some value to each. Taking assignments as our basic operations, we have a total of n^2 assignments for a running time of $O(n^2)$.

This seems like a quadratic order, but *look at the size of the input*. It is n^2, the size of the 2-D array. If the size of the array is doubled, the number of assignments made will be doubled too, not quadrupled. The mathematical way to reconcile this is to replace the size of the input with another variable, say m. That is, let $m = n^2$. Then the running time is $O(m)$, *linear in the input size*.

Logarithmic, $n \log n$, cubic.   We will defer the explanation of the logarithmic order, $O(\log n)$, to the discussion of the binary search algorithm in Section 5.2.

The *en log n* order, $O(n \log n)$, is encountered in this book in the discussion of some of the sorting algorithms covered in Chapter 13.

Any algorithm that takes $O(n^3)$ time soon becomes impractical for large n. We do not encounter the cubic order $O(n^3)$ in this book.

Exponential.   The exponential is of the form $O(k^n)$, where k is some constant independent of the input size n. This order is most often encountered in algorithms that explore "all possible options" (applying *brute force*) in solving a particular problem.

The exponential order is an indication of the *severe* impracticality of an algorithm, save for very small values of n. For example, an exponential algorithm with a running time of 2^n will consume over a million units of time for an input size even as small as 20 ($2^{20} = 1024 \times 1024 > 1,000,000$). One can clearly see that the running time will be a nightmarish number when n is, say, of hundreds order.

Example: Subset sum.   Given n integers $I_1, I_2, \ldots, I_n$, we would like to know if there is a subset of these integers that sums up to another given integer K.

The problem may be solved by a "try all possibilities" approach. Each possibility is a combination of some subset of integers expressed as a binary n-tuple, as, for instance, $(1, 1, 0, 0, \ldots, 0, 1)$. This n-tuple represents a combination that includes I_1 and I_2 (a 1 in the first and second positions of the tuple), does not include I_3 and I_4 (0 in the third and fourth positions), and so on. The sum of the included integers can then be compared against K.

The solution thus boils down to generating all possible such tuples. Since there are n positions in a tuple, and each position can have a 0 or 1 value, the number of possible tuples is 2^n, which is exponential in the size of the input, n.

3.5.2 Multi-Variable Order

In all the examples of algorithms we have seen so far, we could express the size of the input to each algorithm in terms of a single variable, say n. On occasion, we may devise an algorithm for some problem whose input size is expressed in two or more, mutually independent variables.

Note that in Table 3.2, the last row indicates that polynomial addition is one such example, where there are two polynomials that are input, one of degree n and the other of degree m. These two polynomials are independent of each other, which means n and m are also mutually independent.

Let us analyze the running time of polynomial addition and obtain a big O order.

Example: Polynomial addition.   As we saw earlier in Section 3.1, adding two polynomials using the tuple representation involves "lining" them up by matching the coefficients of same-degree terms, and then adding these coefficients pair-wise.

Call the polynomials P and Q. Let the degree of P be n, and that of Q be m. When we align the coefficients of P and Q, there would be some coefficients of either P or Q that "stick out" if the degrees of P and Q are not the same. So, for example, if the degree of P is less than the degree of Q, then there will be $n + 1$ pair-wise coefficient additions (including the constant term), and the remaining coefficients of Q that "stick out" are copied directly into the result.

In this case we need to consider both additions and copying (assignment) as basic operations since the two polynomials may not be of the same degree, and there will always be some copying to be done. Let us count the additions and copying separately and then add them up.

Observe that the number of additions will be equal to the *minimum* of the degrees P and Q plus 1, i.e., $\min(m, n) + 1$.

The number of direct copies made of coefficients will be equal to the difference between the maximum degree and the minimum degree. For example, if the degree of P is 3, and that of Q is 5, then the number of direct copies made $= 5 - 3$ for the two coefficients of Q that "stick out." More formally, the number of direct copies made is $\max(m, n) - \min(m, n)$

Adding the above additions and copies we get:

$$\min(m, n) + 1 + \max(m, n) - \min(m, n) = \max(m, n) + 1$$

for an order $O(\max(m, n))$. This is a strange-looking creature which we have not encountered before but we can make one simple observation here that will put us on more familiar ground: this order is *linear in the size of the input*. The size of the input is $n + m$, and the order is linearly proportional to this size.

3.5.3   Relative Order

We can establish a relative ordering among the running-time orders listed in Table 3.3. We have also included the terms $\sqrt{n}$ and $n\sqrt{n}$. In this ordering, x precedes y if x grows slower than y. We use the symbol $<$ to indicate this, with the understanding that it is not meant to be a simple arithmetic comparison.

$$1 < \log n < \sqrt{n} < n < n \log n < n\sqrt{n} < n^2 < n^3 < k^n$$

To put it another way, if algorithm X has a running time of $O(\log n)$, and algorithm Y has a running time of $O(n)$, then the running time of Y grows faster than the running time of X, i.e., X is faster than Y.

Remember that these are big O, asymptotic orders, so any pair of relationships above will hold for particular large values of n at which point one function will cross "under" the other and stay that away forever. For instance, $\log n$ is a lower-complexity *order* than n. If there is an algorithm whose running time is, say, $1000 \log n$, and another whose running time is $2n$, then until n gets to be somewhere in the 5000 range, the first algorithm will run slower than the second, although its big O order is less than that of the second.

And the moral of the story—we see that big O orders are exactly that: *orders*. They are not exact numbers, and they are only applicable if the asymptoticity, or growth, of n (of whatever the input size parameters are) is kept in mind. Exercises E3.5 and E3.6 reinforce this discussion.

3.5.4 Order Arithmetic

Often, we may want to add the running times of different algorithm components, each of which has been independently analyzed. For example, an algorithm may have two components, the first with a running time of $O(n)$, and the second with a running time of $O(n \log n)$. Then we may add them together to obtain $O(n + n \log n)$. But since the term $n \log n$ dominates, we reduce this to $O(n \log n)$.

By the same token, it is imprecise to write $O(n + n^2)$; instead we write $O(n^2)$, since n^2 is a higher order than n. In general, we observe the following rule:

VARIABLES IN THE ORDER FUNCTION

For each variable that appears in the input size of an algorithm, there must be at most one term in that variable in the order function for the running time of that algorithm.

Notice we say "at most one", not "exactly one"; if an input size variable does not appear in the order function, it means that the corresponding time (or space) requirement does not depend on that variable.

3.6 WORST-CASE AND AVERAGE

Often, there is a progression of running times from *the best-case running time* to the *average running time,* and on to the *worst-case* running time. Consider searching for a "target" element in an array (of size n) by comparing the target with the first entry, then the second, and so on. In the best case, a match is found after only one comparison: $O(1)$. In the worst case, a match is found only after comparing every entry in the array: $O(n)$. On the average, a match will be found after approximately $n/2$ comparisons, which is again $O(n)$.

Of these, the worst-case running time offers a *guarantee* that the running time will never be worse than it. In practice, this is an important requirement, and more often than not, running times are worst-case running times unless otherwise specified.

The best-case running time is of little practical significance, in that it neither offers a bulwark against "pathological inputs" that the worst-case running time does, nor does it offer a sense of what may be usually expected, as the average running time does.

The average running time, however, is the most significant of all, because it is the *expected* running time. In other words, if we were to run a program, we would *expect* to see its average running time, and we would *at worst* see the worst-case running time. The problem with the average running time is that it is often hard to determine *analytically*; more often than not, the average running time is empirically approximated by running a number of carefully constructed experiments.

And finally, a note on vocabulary.

COMPLEXITY AND WORST-CASE

Often, computer scientists say "time complexity" to mean running time, and "space complexity" to mean space requirement. And when they just say "complexity" without qualifying it, they usually mean time complexity. Further, if they do not specify average or worst-case, they mean worst-case.

Let us strengthen our understanding of the worst-case running time by studying one more example.

Example: Bubble sort.   Here is another sorting algorithm that may serve as an alternative to the selection sort algorithm presented in Section 3.5.1.

As with selection sort, the bubble sort algorithm makes several passes over the list of values to be sorted, but there are major differences in exactly how it works out each pass, and also exactly how many passes it makes.

Let us start by looking at how bubble sort executes a single pass.

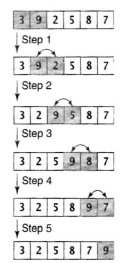

In the first pass on this example array, the algorithm executes five steps. (1) The first value, 3 is compared against the second value 9. Since the first is not greater than the second, nothing more is done. (2) The second value, 9 is compared against the third value, 2. Now, since the second is greater than the third, the values are exchanged. (3) Values 9 and 5 are exchanged. (4) Values 9 and 8 are exchanged. (5) Values 9 and 7 are exchanged.

The value 9, which is the maximum of all values, eventually makes its way, or *bubbles* through, to the last position of the array. Subsequently, as in selection sort, this position is ignored.

Note that five comparisons and four data exchanges are made in the first pass.

In the second pass, four pair-wise comparisons are made $(1 - 2, 2 - 3, 3 - 4, 4 - 5)$, with two data exchanges (3 with 2, and 8 with 7), so that 8 bubbles through to its rightful position at location 5 of the array.

Starting the third pass, the entries of the array are:

2, 3, 5, 7, 8, 9

but effectively, only the first four entries are considered. In this pass, three pair-wise comparisons are made, without any data being exchanged at all. *Since there are no data exchanges, it must be that the array is sorted.* Thus, the algorithm terminates at this point, without making any more unnecessary passes through the array.

The total number of comparisons made is $5 + 4 + 3 = 12$, while the total number of data exchanges is $4 + 2 = 6$.

The bubble sort algorithm offers a spectrum of running times, *depending on the arrangement of data in the input array.* Clearly, for this example, bubble sort performs fewer operations than the worst possible, since it stopped after the third pass.

Following is the bubble sort algorithm.

algorithm bubbleSort(A, n)

input: array A, of length n

$done \leftarrow$ false, $p \leftarrow 1$
while (not *done* and $p \leq n$) do
    $done \leftarrow$ true
    for (i from 0 to $n - p - 1$)
        if $(A[i] > A[i + 1])$ then
            exchange $A[i]$ with $A[i + 1]$
            $done \leftarrow$ false
        endif
    endfor
    $p \leftarrow p + 1$
endwhile

Observe the following:

- The **while** loop terminates on one of two conditions: either there has been no exchange of entries in some pass, indicated by a true value for *done,* or all $N - 1$ passes have been made over the array.

- The inner **for** loop performs one pass over the array. The usage of the pass variable p is similar to that of variable p used in the selection sort algorithm shown in Section 3.5.1.

The key observation here is that before a pass is initiated, *done* is set to true by default (just outside the **for** loop). Then, if an exchange is made in the pass, *done* is immediately set to false, implying that one more pass will have to be made (assuming, of course, that there is more than one entry left to be examined). If no exchange of entries takes place, *done* remains true, thereby forcing the enclosing **while** loop to terminate before it iterates for the next pass.

Let us now do a general worst-case analysis of bubble sort. We observe that the number of comparisons is always fixed for a given number of entries: if there are n entries, $n - 1$ comparisons are made. The number of data exchanges is variable, and can never be more than the number of comparisons. Therefore, we choose comparisons, the dominant operations, as the basic operations.

In the worst case, the algorithm will be forced to go through all the passes. As in selection sort, when the effective array size is 1, the algorithm will terminate, so there are

$n - 1$ passes in all. Just as in selection sort, there will be $n - 1$ comparisons in the first pass, $n - 2$ in the second, and so on, for a total of:

$$(n - 1) + (n - 2) + (n - 3) + \cdots + 2 + 1 = n(n - 1)/2$$

Yet again, we have a $O(n^2)$ algorithm, but only for the *worst-case*.

Just for curiosity's sake, what is the best-case number of comparisons? The best case will occur when the input array is already sorted; the algorithm will make one pass, with $n - 1$ comparisons and no data exchanges, and terminate. Thus the best-case big O order is $O(n)$, linear in the input size.

3.7 SUMMARY

- The most reliable way to measure the running time of an algorithm is to count the number of basic operations it performs. The running time is proportional to this count.
- In order to analyze the running time of a program, it is important to think of it as an algorithm independent of the programming language in which it is implemented. This algorithm is then analyzed.
- It is important to express the count of the basic operations of an algorithm as a function of the input size variables.
- Given two functions $f(n)$ and $g(n)$, if there is an integer N such that for all $n > N$, $f(n)$ is always greater than $g(n)$, then $f(n)$ is said to grow asymptotically faster than $g(n)$.
- Given the running time of an algorithm, its big O order may be derived by the following steps:

  1. Replace all additive constants in the running time with the constant 1.
  2. Retain only the highest-order term in this modified running time.
  3. If the highest-order term is not 1, remove the constant (if any) that multiplies this term.

- Some typical running time orders are: $O(1)$ (constant), $O(n)$ (linear), $O(n^2)$ (quadratic), $O(n^3)$ (cubic), $O(n \log n)$ (*en log en*), $O(\log n)$ (logarithmic), $O(k^n)$ (exponential).
- These typical orders may be arranged in order of relative asymptotic growth from slowest to fastest as follows:

$$1 < \log n < n < n \log n < n^2 < n^3 < k^n$$

- The running times of different components of an algorithm analyzed independently may be added together to obtain the running time of the algorithm itself.
- For each variable that appears in the input size of an algorithm, there must be at most one term in that variable in the order function for the running time.
- The worst-case running time of an algorithm offers a guarantee that the running time will never be worse than itself.

- The average running time of an algorithm is its expected running time, on average. It is usually hard to analytically determine the average running time of an algorithm.
- Time complexity means the same as running time, and space complexity means the same as space requirement.
- The term complexity used without any qualifier means time complexity.
- If there is no reference to worst-case or average complexity order, it usually means worst-case.
- The space requirement of an algorithm is always less than or equal to the time requirement.

3.8   EXERCISES

E3.1. An algorithm searches a database for a person's name, in order to retrieve the associated phone number. What are the basic operations performed by this algorithm?

E3.2. Given the functions $f_a = 10n^2 + n - 10$, and $f_b = n^3$:
   (a) What is the lowest positive integer value of n beyond which one function is always greater than the other?
   (b) In relative terms, which function grows asymptotically slower?

E3.3. Referring to the polynomial multiplication scheme described in Section 3.1:
   (a) What are the basic operations?
   (b) Is there a dominant basic operation?
   (c) How many basic operations are performed in multiplying $3x^2 + x + 2$ with $x^3 - 3$?
   (d) In general, if one polynomial is of degree p, and the other, of degree q, how many basic operations would be performed by the multiplication scheme?
   (e) Write your answer to the above as a big O order.

E3.4. Write each of the following running times as a big O order.
   (a) $13n^2 - 2n + 56$
   (b) $2.5 \log n + 2$
   (c) $n * (12 + \log n)$
   (d) $1 + 2 + 3 + \cdots + n$
   (e) $\log n^2 + 10$
   (f) $\log n^2 + n \log n$

E3.5. We saw the following relative arrangement of big O complexities from fastest to slowest:

$$1 < \log n < n < n \log n < n^2 < n^3 < k^n$$

Assuming a multiplicative constant of 5 for every one of these, draw a table with these as columns. In the first row, for each column, fill in the value of the corresponding complexity function for $n = 2^3 = 8$. Then fill subsequent rows similarly using $n = 2^k$, $k = 7, 9, 10, 20, 30$. See the relative difference in growth rates as n grows very large.

E3.6. Repeat Exercise E3.5, this time with different constants for the different functions (columns). That is, assume the following "real" functions corresponding to the sequence of big O orders:

$$1000000, 100000 \log n, 10000n, 1000n \log n, 100n^2, 10n^3, 2^n$$

When you fill in the rows, mark the transition points when a later column function value gets to be greater than earlier column value. Write up your conclusion about how to use the big O's in this particular context.

E3.7. An algorithm prints the following pattern:

```
*
*   *
*   *   *
*   *   *   *
*   *   *   *   *
```

(a) What are the basic operations performed by the algorithm that you would count toward its running time?

(b) Count the number of these basic operations.

(c) The number of lines printed in the preceding pattern is five. Assume that the algorithm can extend this pattern for any number of lines (line number i has i stars). If the number of lines, n, is an input to the algorithm, how many basic operations are performed as a function of n?

(d) Write your answer to the above question as a big O order.

E3.8. Given an array consisting of integers in the following order:

```
19, 2, 7, 10, 9, 5, 15
```

Imagine this array is sorted using selection sort as described in Section 3.5.1 and the **selectionSort** algorithm. Answer the following questions.

(a) How many pair-wise value comparisons are made?

(b) How many data exchanges are made?

(c) Could you have arrived at the number of comparisons by simply plugging in the appropriate value for n in $n(n - 1)/2$?

(d) Would the number of comparisons change if the array was instead ordered in reverse?

E3.9. Consider that the array in Exercise 3.8 is now sorted using bubble sort as described in Section 3.6 and the **bubbleSort** algorithm. Answer the following questions.

(a) How many pair-wise value comparisons are made?

(b) How many data exchanges are made?

(c) Is the number of comparisons made the best (least) possible? If not, what is the best (least) possible number of comparisons the algorithm could make, assuming the array entries were arranged accordingly in the input?

(d) Is the number of comparisons made the worst possible? If not, what is the worst possible number of comparisons the algorithm could make, assuming the array entries were arranged accordingly in the input?

(e) Could you obtain the worst-case value of the above question by just plugging in the appropriate value for n in $n(n - 1)/2$?

(f) Would the number of best and worst comparisons change if the array was ordered in reverse?

E3.10. A spreadsheet keeps track of student scores on all the exams in a course. Each row of the spreadsheet corresponds to one student, and each column in a row corresponds to his/her score on one of the exams. There are r students and c exams, so the spreadsheet has r rows and c columns.

Consider an algorithm that computes the total score on all exams for each student, and the average class score on each exam. You need to analyze the running time of this algorithm.

(a) What are the basic operations you would count toward the running time?

(b) What is the worst-case running time as a total count (not big O) of these basic operations?

      (c) What is the big O running time?

      (d) Is your algorithm linear, quadratic, or some other order?

E3.11. Two people compare their favorite playlists for matching songs. The first playlist has n songs, and the second has m. Each is stored in an array, in no particular order. Describe an algorithm to find the common songs in these lists (intersection).

      (a) What is the worst-case big O running time of your algorithm? Make sure to state the basic operations used in your analysis of running time.

      (b) What is the best-case big O running time of your algorithm? Explain clearly, including all book-keeping needed to achieve this best case.

E3.12. Repeat Exercise 3.11 to find common songs in two playlists, but this time assume that each list is sorted in alphabetical order of songs. Can you devise a faster algorithm than the one in Exercise 3.11 to take advantage of the alphabetical ordering? What is the worst-case big O running time of your algorithm? Is the average big O running time the same as the worst case or different? Explain.

E3.13. The Fibonacci series of numbers is a favorite of mathematicians, and goes as follows:

      0, 1, 1, 2, 3, 5, 8, 13, 21, ...

The first two numbers are 0 and 1, and every subsequent number is the sum of the previous two. Devise an algorithm that would print all the numbers in the Fibonacci series up to some given limit n. That is, the greatest Fibonacci number printed would be less than or equal to n. What is the worst-case big O running time of your algorithm? Is the average big O running time the same as the worst case or different? Explain.

E3.14. A card-game program keeps a deck of cards in an array. Give an algorithm to "unshuffle" the deck so that all the cards of a suit are grouped together, and within each suit, the cards are in ascending order of rank—consider the ace as the lowest-ranked card. Since there are only 52 cards, space is not an issue, so you can use extra space if needed. The only constraint is that your algorithm be as fast as possible.

      What is the worst-case big O running time of your algorithm? What are the basic operations you used in your analysis? Is the average big O running time different from the worst case?

E3.15. There is a highway with n exits numbered 0 to $n - 1$. You are given a list of the distances between them. For instance:

Exits:	0	1	2	3	4	5
Distances:	5	3	4	2	8	6

The distance from the start of the highway to exit 0 is 5, from exit 0 to 1 is 3, and so on.

      You have to devise an algorithm that would calculate the distance between any two exits. Imagine that this distance function is called millions of times by applications that need this information, so you need to make your algorithm as fast as possible.

      Describe your algorithm. What is the worst-case big O running time? Make sure to state all the parameters you use in the analysis and relate them to the algorithm.

CHAPTER 4

Unordered List

The unordered list is a simple linear collection of items. It can be used as a basic tool in a variety of applications that do not require that items be stored in any particular relative order.

Learning Objectives

- Describe the properties of an unordered list.
- Study sequential search and analyze its worst-case and average running times.
- Discover how the entries in a list may be dynamically rearranged to achieve better search times.
- Understand the public interface of an unordered list class in Java and the running times of its methods.
- Develop a set of classes for an expense-processing application based on an unordered list.
- Understand how object-oriented programming can be used to write a single piece of code in Java that can perform equality checking based on different criteria for different input objects.
- Learn what linked lists are, why they are useful, and how to build and manipulate them.
- Implement a linked list class in Java and analyze the running times of its methods.
- Implement an unordered list class in Java using a linked list component.

4.1 UNORDERED LIST PROPERTIES

A simple yet useful application of a list is in keeping track of daily expenses. When we spend money on something we consider important enough to be tracked, we write it down in an expense list. It would be useful to write a program that maintains an expense list like the one shown below of all recorded expenses, that can be used to find quick answers to simple budgeting questions.

Expense List

Date	Amount	Item
2005/01/03	50.00	Shoes
2005/01/03	78.95	Clothes
2005/01/03	50.00	Shoes
2005/02/03	19.55	Food
2005/05/03	34.00	Entertainment
	. . .	
2005/06/20	78.00	Clothes
2005/06/15	255.00	Jewelry
2005/06/19	64.00	Sports
	. . .	

For each expense, we store the date of the expense, the amount of the expense, and the item for which the expense was incurred.

There is no particular order in which items are listed. Most of them are naturally arranged according to date. However, sometimes, an expense may be added to the list that is dated earlier than some existing entries (as, for instance, the entries for Jewelry and Sports).

Also, there may be duplicate entries—the same date and price for the same item (as for Shoes).

UNORDERED LIST

An unordered list is a linear collection of entries whose relative positions with respect to one another is irrelevant.

A note of clarification is needed here. Technically, any list is ordered in the sense that every entry has a predecessor and a successor; i.e., the order is dictated by the physical arrangement of the entries. However, our sense of "order" here is related to the relative arrangement of entries based on their *values*. So when we say that a list is unordered, we mean that the physical arrangement has no relationship to any meaning, or value, associated with the data. Thus, one could think of an unordered list as an "unsorted" list.

When we maintain an expense list, we would like to answer the following kinds of questions:

- What is the maximum (or minimum) expense, and on what item?
- What is the average expense?
- What is the total amount spent on a given item?
- What is the itemwise breakup of expenditures?
- What is the total amount spent in a given time period?

All these questions may be answered by scanning such a list from the beginning and terminating when our question is answered. For instance, to answer the question "What was the total amount spent on clothes?", we step through the items in the list from beginning to end. Each time we see "clothes" in the Item column, we add the associated amount in the Amount column to an accumulating sum.

Operations. While there are several operations that one would like to perform on an unordered list, it is useful to first define the fundamental operations a list *must* support.
Table 4.1 summarizes these operations.

TABLE 4.1: Fundamental list operations.

Operation	Description
Append	Add an entry at the end of the list
Enumerate	Step through all the list entries
Remove	Delete a specific entry from the list
Contains	Search the list to determine whether it contains a specific entry

A primary fundamental operation is adding an entry to the list. Since the entries in the list are in no particular order, we usually add at the end, i.e., *append*. Another fundamental list operation is the ability to *enumerate* the list, i.e., step through all the entries from beginning to end. Yet another fundamental operation is to *remove* an entry from the list. Finally, an important operation is to search the list to see if it *contains* a specific entry.

Apart from the operations listed in Table 4.1, other, nonfundamental operations, such as determining the number of entries and checking whether a list is empty, may be also supported to facilitate ease-of-use, instead of having the application implement them by using the fundamental operations.

There are several important issues involved in searching a list with the *contains* operation. The mechanism adopted is called *sequential search*. We will explore sequential search in detail in the following section.

4.2   SEQUENTIAL SEARCH

The operation *contains* searches for a specified item (called the *target*) in the list. Since the list is unordered, the only way to conduct the search is to look at every element in *sequence,* i.e., one after another, and *compare* it against the target. If a match is found, the operation returns *true,* otherwise it returns *false.* The former result is a *successful search,* and the latter, an *unsuccessful search* or *failed search.*

SEQUENTIAL SEARCH

A target is compared against every entry in the list in sequence, one after the other. If the target matches an entry, the search is successful. If no match is found, the search is unsuccessful.

Now that we have the basic idea down, let us play with some numbers. Let us first of all assume that we are conducting a search in a list that contains *n* elements.

What is the *best*-case number of comparisons for a successful search? If you said one, you would be right on—if the very first element compared against the target is a match, then we have succeeded with only a single comparison.

What is the *worst*-case number of comparisons for a successful search? If you said *n*, you answer would be right on the money again—in the worst case, we would have to compare *every* element against the target, and we would not succeed until the last, or *n*-th, comparison.

What is the number of comparisons for an unsuccessful search? Again, it is *n*; we know that the search is a failure only (and immediately) after we have compared every element against the target. In fact, the last comparison decides whether we are in a worst-case successful situation or a failure situation. Since there is only one way to fail, there is no difference between best-case and worst-case failures.

What is the *average* number of comparisons for a successful search? One intuitive guess would be $n/2$, for number of items divided by 2. Another guess would be $(n + 1)/2$, for the average of the best and worst cases.

Which, if either, of these guesses is correct? Can we substantiate the correct answer with a formal mathematical derivation?

4.2.1 Average Case Analysis

Let us start by clearly defining the problem in the context of searching for an entry in a data structure:

AVERAGE NUMBER OF COMPARISONS FOR SEARCH

The number of comparisons required, on average, to search for any element in the structure.

This definition is not restricted to sequential search, nor is it restricted to an unordered list. It is applicable to any kind of search in any kind of structure in which a target is compared against the elements in the structure.

In order to apply this definition to compute the average number of comparisons, we need to convert it to a mathematical form. The mathematical definition follows an age-old idea: if we had to find the average of *n* numbers, we would add up the numbers and divide by *n*. Consequently, if the elements are numbered 1 through *n*, and it takes C_i comparisons to find success at the *i*-th element, then the average number of comparisons is simply:

$$\frac{C_1 + C_2 + \cdots + C_n}{n}$$

Let us apply this to sequential search. In a sequential search of a list, it takes one comparison to succeed at the first element, two comparisons to succeed at the second element, and so on, as shown in Figure 4.1.

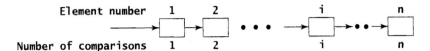

FIGURE 4.1: Sequential Search. Elements are compared against the target in sequence starting with first element. The i-th element would be matched against the target in the i-th comparison. Success at the i-th element would thus result after i comparisons.

In general, it takes i comparisons to succeed at the i-th element, i.e., $C_i = i$. Plugging these values into the above formula, we get, for the average number of comparisons:

$$\frac{1 + 2 + \cdots + n}{n} = \frac{n(n + 1)}{2} \times \frac{1}{n} = \frac{n + 1}{2}$$

There is, however, an implicit assumption in this:

We are assuming that any element is searched for with the same likelihood as any other. In other words, if there are n elements, we are assuming that any one element has a 1/n chance, or probability, of being searched.

Let us take an example for which we do not make this assumption. Suppose we maintain a list of seven elements with an uneven distribution of probabilities of search per element, as shown below.

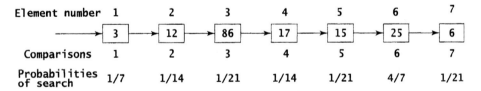

Verify that the search probabilities add up to 1. Note that 3 is twice as likely to be searched as 17, and 25 is four times as likely.

The average number of comparisons cannot be computed as before by adding all the comparisons and dividing by 7; we need to take the search probabilities into account. For each element, we take the product of the number of comparisons for that element with the probability of searching for it, and then add all these products. This works out to:

$$1 \times \frac{1}{7} + 2 \times \frac{1}{14} + 3 \times \frac{1}{21} + 4 \times \frac{1}{14} + 5 \times \frac{1}{21} + 6 \times \frac{4}{7} + 7 \times \frac{1}{21} = \frac{99}{21} = 4.7$$

In fact, this is a fundamental formula that works for *any* search algorithm on *any* data structure. The P_i's are either given or assumed, and are independent of the data structure and the search algorithm. In other words, the distribution of searches over the various elements is determined by the users of the data structure, and not by what specific

---

AVERAGE NUMBER OF COMPARISONS FOR SEARCH WITH PROBABILITIES

Let the data structure contain n elements, and let the probability of searching for element i be P_i. Suppose that a given search algorithm requires C_i comparisons to successfully search for element i. Then the average number of comparisons required for successful search of any element is:

$$P_1 * C_1 + P_2 * C_2 + \cdots + P_n * C_n$$

---

data structure is used or how the searches are performed. For a given data structure (e.g., an unordered list) and a given search algorithm (e.g., a sequential search), we would have to compute the C_i's (as we did earlier).

If we assume equal search probabilities, P_i would be $1/n$. For sequential search on an unordered list, we would then arrive at $(n + 1)/2$ for the average number of comparisons, which tallies with one of the intuitive guesses.

What is the importance of this average-case analysis?

4.2.2   Rearranging Data Based on Search Patterns

Look again at the preceding example, and see how the entries are positioned in the list. If 25 is four times as likely to be searched as 3, shouldn't 25 be all the way up front so that we incur fewer comparisons when we search for it? In fact, we would pay the lowest cost for the average number of comparisons if we were to *arrange the elements from first position to last position based on the decreasing search probabilities.*

REARRANGING DATA

The lowest number of average comparisons for search in a list is obtained if the entries of the list are arranged in decreasing order of search probabilities from beginning to end.

This rearrangement of data has nothing to do with the attributes of the entries. Put differently, the list is still unordered with respect to the values of these attributes. So, for instance, an expense list may be rearranged as above, but it would still be unordered with respect to dates, expense amounts, or expense items.

The foregoing discussion assumes that the search probabilities are all known beforehand. It may be possible to arrive at a distribution of probabilities in an installation where the pattern of searches has stabilized over time. However, in new situations where the search is being applied, or in situations where there is no stability in the pattern of searches, there is a simple technique that can be applied dynamically during a search.

If a search is made for element x of the list, then after this element is found, it is simply *moved to the front of the list.* Thus, the more often an entry is searched for, the more toward the front of the list it will be. In turn, this means that the most frequent searches will use up the least number of comparisons. This *move-to-front* scheme works well in practice and is easy to implement. We will return to it in the exercises at the end of the chapter.

We have explored searching in a list in great detail because it is the most important operation a list could support, and also the richest in the options it provides for implementation. The other operations, including the fundamental ones listed in Table 4.1 are simpler. Our next task is to implement a list in Java.

4.3 A List CLASS

Figure 4.2 shows the public interface of an unordered list class named List.

As an example, we can construct and populate a list of String items as follows:

```
List<String> shoppingList = new List<String>();
shoppingList.add("Carrots");
shoppingList.add("Bread");
shoppingList.add("Milk");
shoppingList.add("Honey");
```

We remove "Bread" as follows:

```
shoppingList.remove("Bread");
```

On the other hand, if we were to do following:

```
shoppingList.remove("Missing");
```

we would get a NoSuchElementException thrown back.

The methods contains, remove, and removeAll all involve search, and are self-explanatory.

Enumeration.   The items of a List object may be enumerated with a simple device called a **cursor,** which steps through the list one item at a time. To start the enumeration, a call is made to the first method. This sets the cursor at the first item of the list, and returns that item. Every subsequent call to the next method moves the cursor to the next item, and returns that item. When the cursor is at the end of the list, any subsequent call to next will return null.

Here is an example that enumerates the shopping list:

```
String item = shoppingList.first();
while (item != null) {
  System.out.println(item);
  item = shoppingList.next();
}
```

Running times.   Any application that needs to store an unordered collection of any type of object can use the List class designed above without knowing how the List is implemented. The running times listed in Figure 4.2 do, however, constrain the implementation in the following ways.

Class structures.linear.List<T>

Constructors

List( )
Creates an empty unordered list.

Methods

$O(1)$ **void add(T item)**
Adds specified item to the end of this list.

$O(1)$ **int size( )**
Returns the number of elements in this list.

$O(1)$ **boolean isEmpty( )**
Returns true if this list is empty, false otherwise.

$O(n)$ **boolean contains(T item)**
Returns true if item is in this list, false otherwise.

$O(1)$ **void clear( )**
Removes all the elements in this list, i.e. empties this list.

$O(n)$ **void remove(T item)**
Removes first occurrence of specified item from this list.
Throws **NoSuchElementException** if item is not in this list.

$O(n)$ **void removeAll(T item)**
Removes all occurrences of specified item from this list.
Throws **NoSuchElementException** if item is not in this list.

$O(1)$ **T first( )**
Returns the first element in this list, null if list is empty.

$O(1)$ **T next( )**
Returns the next element in this list, relative to a previous call
to **first** or **next.** Returns null if there no more elements.

FIGURE 4.2: A Generic Unordered List Class. Only the public interface is shown. Duplicate items are permitted. Running times assume an implementation that keeps direct references to the first and last items, a count of number of items, and a cursor that can enumerate items sequentially; n is the number of items in the list.

The first constraint is that an implementation should be able to access the last item in the list in $O(1)$ time, so that the add method can be implemented in $O(1)$ time.

The second constraint is that an implementation should maintain a count of the number of items in the list. The size method can then simply return this count, for an $O(1)$ running time. Also, the isEmpty method can be implemented in $O(1)$ time.

The third constraint is that an implementation should be able to empty the list in $O(1)$ time, and thus the clear method should run in $O(1)$ time.

The fourth constraint is that an implementation has to use a cursor to enumerate a list, so that each of the enumeration methods first and next can be implemented in $O(1)$ time.

The methods contains, remove, and removeAll all involve conducting a sequential search on the list, thereby requiring $O(n)$ time in the worst case. This set of running times is not a constraint on the implementation; rather, it is an algorithmic limitation that cannot be violated by any implementation.

In summary, the running times that go with a class interface are as much a part of the specification as the method signatures. In other words, every interface comes with a price tag, and this price tag places some constraints on the implementation.

4.4 AN ExpenseList CLASS USING List

Let us exercise the List class by designing and implementing an expense list program based on the discussion in Section 4.1.

Our primary focus will be on building an ExpenseList class that will support operations for maintaining expenses. We will use the generic List class as a component, implementing all the ExpenseList class methods by reusing code from one or more of the appropriate List class methods.

Class apps.linear.Expense

Fields

> **Calendar date**
>> Stores the expense date.
>
> **float amount**
>> Stores the expense amount.
>
> **String item**
>> Stores the expense item.
>
> *SimpleDateFormat sdf*
>> Static field that formats the expense date to "yyyy/mm/dd".

Constructors

> **Expense(Calendar expDate, float expAmount, String item)**
>> Creates an expense instance with given date, amount, and item.

Methods

$O(n)$	**boolean equals(Object exp)**
	Overrides the Object class' equals method. Returns true if this expense is equal to the argument expense, i.e. if the respective dates, amounts, and items are the same.
$O(n)$	**String toString( )**
	Overrides the Object class' toString method. Returns a string representation of this expense.
$O(1)$	**String getDate( )**
	Returns a string representation of this expense's date, as "yyyy/mm/dd".
$O(1)$	*Calendar getCalendar(int year, int month, int date)*
	Utility (static) method that constructs a Calendar instance out of year, month, and date. Months are numbered starting with 0 for Jan.
$O(1)$	*Calendar getCalendar(String date)*
	Utility (static) method that constructs a Calendar instance out of a string of the form "yyyy/mm/dd".
$O(1)$	*String getDate(Calendar date)*
	Utility (static) method that returns a string representation of a Calendar date.

FIGURE 4.3: An Expense Class. Only the public interface is shown. The parameter n in the running times is the length of an Expense instance, varying according to the lengths of the item and amount fields. The length of date is fixed, the same for any expense.

In order to build the ExpenseList class, we first need to define the type of expense entry that is to be stored in the expense list. Every expense entry will consist of the amount of the expense, the date of the expense, and the item for which the expense was incurred. We can wrap all this information in a class called Expense, and have ExpenseList instances consist of several Expense instances.

4.4.1 Expense Class Interface

Figure 4.3 shows the public interface of an Expense class.

Since the Expense class is essentially a glue that holds together the components of any expense, and these components will be accessed quite often, the fields are declared public so that they can be directly accessed by clients without having to go through accessor (getter) methods. As we will see shortly, there are no private members at all in this class.

The java.util.Calendar class is ideal for storing dates. In general, a date could include time as well, in hours, minutes, and seconds. However, for this application we will restrict a date to year, month, and day of month.

The java.util.SimpleDateFormat class is used to format Calendar dates into readable strings. There are a variety of formats that can be specified via SimpleDateFormat. In this application, we will use the format "yyyy/mm/dd" to represent dates.

Let us see how these classes are used in the implementation of the Expense class.

4.4.2 Expense Class

Class File 4.1. *Expense.java*

```
01 package apps.linear;
02
03 import java.text.SimpleDateFormat;
04 import java.util.Calendar;
05 import java.util.Scanner;
06
07 public class Expense {
08
09   public Calendar date;
10   public float amount;
11   public String item;
12   public static final SimpleDateFormat sdf = new SimpleDateFormat("yyyy/MM/dd");
13
14   public Expense(Calendar expDate, float expAmount, String expItem) {
15     date = expDate;
16     amount = expAmount;
17     item = expItem;
18   }
19
20   public boolean equals(Object other) {
21     if ((other != null) && (other instanceof Expense)) {
22       Expense another = (Expense)other;
23       return (item.equals(another.item) &&
24               date.equals(another.date) &&
25               amount == another.amount);
26     }
```

```
27       return false;
28     }
29
30     public String toString() {
31       return String.format("%s\t%.2f\t%s",
32                   sdf.format(date.getTime()), amount, item);
33     }
34
35     public String getDate() {
36       return sdf.format(date.getTime());
37     }
38
39     public static Calendar getCalendar(int year, int month, int date) {
40       Calendar cal = Calendar.getInstance();
41       cal.set(year, month, date, 0, 0, 0);
42       return cal;
43     }
44
45     public static Calendar getCalendar(String date) {
46       Scanner sc = new Scanner(date).useDelimiter("/");
47       return getCalendar(sc.nextInt(), sc.nextInt()-1, sc.nextInt());
48     }
49
50     public static String getDate(Calendar date) {
51       return sdf.format(date.getTime());
52     }
53 }
```

Method getDate on lines 35–37 shows how to format a Calendar date using the SimpleDateFormat class: (a) set up an instance of SimpleDateFormat with the required format (the static instance sdf in our implementation, with the format "yyyy/MM/dd"), (b) use the Calendar class's getTime method to get the equivalent Date instance, and (c) call the format method on the SimpleDateFormat instance with the Date instance as argument.

The method getDate on lines 50–52 does the same thing on the argument date. In other words, this getDate is a *utility method* housed in the Expense class, and it is a static method because it does not apply to any specific instance of Expense.

The utility method getCalendar on lines 39–43 shows how to create a Calendar instance from year, month, and day in two steps. First, get a default Calendar instance from the static getInstance method of the Calendar class—note that this is different from the usual creation of a new instance using a constructor. Once the default instance is obtained, call its set method to set its year, month, and day fields with the first three arguments, and its hours, minutes, and seconds with the next three arguments—zeros here, since we are using dates without time.

The other utility getCalendar method, on lines 45–48, performs the same function as the previous one, except that it takes a date string of the form "yyyy/mm/dd" as its argument. This method parses the date string into its year, month, and day components, and calls the first getCalendar variant. Note that months are numbered 0 through 11.

With the Expense and List classes at hand, we can now build an ExpenseList class. First, let us look at the public interface of this class, following which we discuss its implementation.

4.4.3 ExpenseList Class Interface

Figure 4.4 shows the public interface of an ExpenseList class.

Observe that the core List methods all reappear in the ExpenseList class: add, size, isEmpty, contains, clear, remove, first, and next. The rest are specialized methods that provide capabilities required of the ExpenseList class that are above and beyond the core operations provided by the List class.

Class apps.linear.ExpenseList

Constructors

ExpenseList( )
Creates an empty expense list.

Methods

$O(1)$ **void add(Expense exp)**
Adds specified expense to the end of this list.

$O(1)$ **int size( )**
Returns the number of expenses in this list.

$O(1)$ **boolean isEmpty( )**
Returns true if this list is empty, false otherwise.

$O(n)$ **boolean contains(Expense exp)**
Returns true if specified expense is in this list, false otherwise.

$O(n)$ **Expense get(Expense exp)**
Returns the entry that matches specified expense; null if no match.

$O(1)$ **void clear( )**
Removes all the expenses in this list (i.e., empties the list).

$O(n)$ **void remove(Expense exp)**
Removes specified expense from this list.
Throws **NoSuchElementException** if exp is not in list.

$O(n)$ **float avgExpense( )**
Returns the average of all expense amounts in this list.

$O(n)$ **float maxExpense( )**
Returns the maximum of all expense amounts in this list.

$O(n)$ **float minExpense( )**
Returns the minimum of all expense amounts in this list.

$O(n)$ **float amtSpentOn(String item)**
Returns the total amount spent on specified item.

$O(n)$ **float amtSpentDuring(Date from, Date to)**
Returns the amount spent during the specified time period.

$O(1)$ **Expense first( )**
Returns the first expense element in this list.

$O(1)$ **Expense next( )**
Returns the next expense element in this list, relative to a previous call
to **first** or **next**. Returns null if there no more elements.

FIGURE 4.4: **An ExpenseList Class.** Only the public interface is shown. All running times are directly related to those of the List class; n is the number of items in the list.

Let us see now see how the ExpenseList class is implemented.

4.4.4 ExpenseList Class Implementation

As we said earlier, the ExpenseList class uses the List class as a component by calling methods in the List class's public interface. Note that the generic List class is instantiated with the Expense type because the list will hold Expense objects.

Class File 4.2. *ExpenseList.java*

```
package apps.linear;

import java.util.NoSuchElementException;
import java.util.Calendar;
import structures.linear.List;

public class ExpenseList {
  List<Expense> expenses;

  public ExpenseList() { expenses = new List<Expense>(); }
  public void add(Expense exp) { expenses.add(exp); }
  public int size() { return expenses.size(); }
  public boolean isEmpty() { return expenses.isEmpty(); }
  public boolean contains(Expense exp) { return expenses.contains(exp); }
  public void clear() { expenses.clear(); }
  public void remove(Expense exp) { expenses.remove(exp); }
  public Expense first() { return expenses.first(); }
  public Expense next() { return expenses.next(); }
  public float maxExpense() { ... }
  public float minExpense() { ... }
  public float avgExpense() { ... }
  public float amountSpentOn(String expItem) { ... }
  public float amountSpentDuring(Calendar from, Calendar to) { ... }
  public Expense get(Expense getExp) { ... }
}
```

Methods that wrap List counterparts.   We observed in Section 4.4.3 that a subset of the methods of ExpenseList correspond one-to-one with their List counterparts. These are the sequence of methods from add to next.

Each of these methods is a single line of implementation that invokes the List counterpart method on the expenses object. The running time of each of these methods is thus the same as the running time of the invoked List counterpart, and may be read off Figure 4.2.

Methods that are special to ExpenseList.   The rest of the methods in ExpenseList are special in that they have no counterpart in the List class.

Of these, the methods maxExpense, minExpense, and avgExpense share a common feature: they all need to scan every expense entry in the list and process the amount part of the entry. They differ in minor respects in the way they process the expenses. Here are minExpense (maxExpense is analogous) and avgExpense:

```
public float minExpense() {
  float min=Float.MAX_VALUE;
  Expense exp = expenses.first();
  while (exp != null) {
    float amt = exp.amount;
    if (amt < min) {
      min = amt;
    }
    exp = expenses.next();
  }
  return min;
}
```

```
public float avgExpense() {
  float sum=0;
  Expense exp = expenses.first();
  while (exp != null) {
    sum += nextExpense.amount;
    exp = expenses.next();
  }
  return sum/expenses.size();
}
```

The time requirement of each of these methods is $O(n)$ if there are n expense entries in the list. Every invocation of first or next method of the List class takes $O(1)$ time, as listed in Figure 4.2. Since there are $n + 1$ such calls (one call to first, $n - 1$ calls to next, and an additional call to next that will return null) the total running time is $O(n)$.

The methods amountSpentOn and amountSpentDuring involve sequential search: amountSpentOn matches the item component of every expense against the item in hand (target item), whereas amountSpentDuring compares the date component of every item against the date in hand.

```
public float
amountSpentOn(String expItem) {
  float sum=0;
  Expense exp =
    expenses.first();
  while (exp != null) {
    if (expItem.equals
          (exp.item)) {
      sum += exp.amount;
    }
    exp = expenses.next();
  }
  return sum;
}
```

```
public float
amountSpentDuring(Calendar from,
                  Calendar to) {
  float sum=0;
  Expense exp = expenses.first();
  while (exp != null) {
    if (!(exp.date.before(from) ||
         exp.date.after(to))) {
      sum += exp.amount;
    }
    exp = expenses.next();
  }
  return sum;
}
```

The running time of both methods is is $O(n)$ for a list of n expenses. Observe that in the method amountSpentDuring, the Calendar class methods before and after are used to select only those expenses whose dates are neither before nor after the range of dates sent as arguments to the method.

There is one aspect of the ExpenseList class implementation that needs to be examined in greater detail. In the contains method, the call to the List class's contains method searches the list for an expense that matches the given expense. How does the contains method of the List class know when two Expense instances are equal? Moreover, can the rules be changed according to need, so that, say, at certain times expenses can be made equal if their items match, but at other times they can be made equal if their dates match?

The get method also checks whether two Expense objects are equal:

```
public Expense get(Expense getExp) {
  Expense exp = expenses.first();
  while (exp != null) {
    if (exp.equals(getExp)) {
        return exp;
    }
    exp = expenses.next();
  }
  return null;
}
```

In fact, this method itself is rather peculiar. It accepts an Expense object as argument, and returns a matching Expense object from the expense list. Are these two Expense objects different? If not, why bother with this method? If they are different, how come they match? The idea here is again connected to a deeper notion of equality. Time to explore.

4.4.5 Equality of Objects and Searching

Here is method contains once again:

```
public boolean contains(Expense exp) {
  return expenses.contains(exp);
}
```

To understand it better, let us rewrite the method by implementing a search in the method itself instead of calling on the analogous List method:

```
public boolean contains(Expense exp) {
  Expense nextExpense = expenses.first();
  while (nextExpense != null) {
    if (exp.equals(nextExpense)) return true;
    nextExpense = expenses.next();
  }
  return false;
}
```

Look at the statement that calls the equals method:

```
if (exp.equals(nextExpense)) return true;
```

The notion of equality here is defined by the equals method of the exp object or the Expense class. The Expense class, as listed in Section 4.4.2, defines two expenses to be equal if they have the same item, amount, and date. This is a catchall definition that serves as a reasonable default.

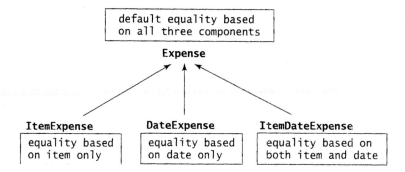

FIGURE 4.5: **Specific Equality by Extension.** The classes `ItemExpense`, `DateExpense`, and `ItemDateExpense` each extend (i.e., are subclasses of) `Expense` with the sole purpose of defining specialized equality checks.

But what if we wanted to know whether we had incurred any expense on a particular day, say 2005/2/15 (i.e., as explained earlier, February 15, 2005)? To do this, we would need to redefine the equality of expenses in terms of date only, *so that we can search by date.* On the other hand, if we wanted to know whether we had incurred any expense on a certain item, say "Shoes," we would need to redefine equality in terms of item, *so that we can search by item.* Or we may want to search by both date and item, as in the expense on "Shoes" on 2005/2/15.

How can an application manage such multiple definitions of equality?

Class specialization for special equality. The solution is to define special classes that extend the `Expense` class, with the sole aim of implementing special, and different, kinds of equality of expenses. Figure 4.5 illustrates this design.

The definitions for these subclasses follow a common pattern, as seen in the definition of `ItemExpense`.

Class File 4.3. *ItemExpense.java*

```
package apps.linear;

import java.util.Calendar;

public class ItemExpense extends Expense {
  public
  ItemExpense(Calendar expDate, float expAmount, String expItem) {
    super(expDate, expAmount, expItem);
  }

  public boolean equals(Object other) {
    if ((other != null) && (other instanceof Expense)) {
        Expense another = (Expense)other;
        return (item.equals(another.item));
    }
    return false;
  }
}
```

The subclasses DateExpense and ItemDateExpense are defined in an analogous manner, differing in their definitions of the equals method.

Searching in ExpenseList. Imagine that we have created an ExpenseList instance called budget and populated it with a number of Expense objects, with expenses like those listed in the example of Section 4.1.

Now suppose we want to determine whether budget contains any purchase of shoes. In order to do this, we define a target object of type ItemExpense and send it as the parameter to the contains method of ExpenseList:

```
ItemExpense itemExp = new ItemExpense(null, 0, "Shoes");
if (budget.contains(itemExp))
    ...
```

In the diagram shown below, we can follow the bouncing ball in the sequence of actions triggered by the call to contains:

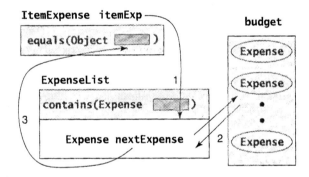

(1) An ItemExpense object, itemExp, is sent as actual argument to method contains in ExpenseList. Note that the parameter exp of contains will match any actual argument that is either an Expense object or an object of a subclass of Expense, such as ItemExpense.

(2) An Expense object, nextExpense, is picked up from budget.

(3) This nextExpense object is shipped as the actual argument to the equals method of itemExp, which compares the item component of itemExp against the item component of nextExpense for equality.

Note the line in the itemExp method that reads:

```
if ((other != null) && (other instanceof Expense))
```

It is crucial to ask for an instance of Expense, and *not* of ItemExpense. The latter check would fail, because the budget list is populated with Expense objects, not ItemExpense objects. While it is true that every ItemExpense object is an instance of Expense, the converse is not true.

Since we know that only the item components will be compared, we can safely send in our itemExp object with a null value for date and zero for amount.

About keys. Let us revisit the get method. An Expense object is sent in as argument, and a matching Expense object is returned. Is the matching object the same as the object sent in? What is a *match,* anyway? To understand this method, let us first define the *key* part of an object.

KEY PART OF AN OBJECT

The key part of an object is the part used as the basis of comparing against another object for equality.

For example, the key part of an ItemExpense object is its item field.

The get method is useful for extracting an *entire* object from the list by matching its key part with a specified key. In other words, the argument sent to get would only have the key part filled in, and the return value would be an object whose key part matched the specified key.

To illustrate, consider Figure 4.5 once again. In a DateExpense object of the three fields date, amount, and item, only the date field would participate in equality checking, i.e., date is the key. On the other hand, in an ItemDateExpense object, the key would comprise two fields: item and date.

Now let us assume that we have built an ExpenseList called budget in which each entry is a DateExpense object. At some point we would like to know how much we spent on a given item, say Shoes on a particular day, say 2005/9/15. We can get an answer to this question as follows:

```
Calendar dt = Expense.getCalendar("2005/9/15");
Expense qExp = new ItemDateExpense(dt, null, "Shoes");
Expense aExp = budget.get(qExp);
if (aExp != null) {     // there was a match
    System.out.println("Amount spent = " + aExp.amount);
}
```

We only send in the key part, which is the date and the item, and get returns the entire matching entry (including amount), if any.

We have seen how to implement an ExpenseList class using the List class interface. Our next task is to figure out how to implement the List class. First we must decide what data structure to use to store the items in a list.

An obvious solution is to use an array, but removing items from anywhere in the list would leave holes in the array. If the holes are left as is, then we will end up using more space than necessary. Also, search times would be greater than $O(n)$, since the search would have to step through (and over) all the holes. On the other hand, if the holes are patched up by compacting the array, we would be doing a lot of data movement within the array. All in all, the array is not a good solution. Neither is the ArrayList class in the java.util package, since it is built on an array.

What we need is a data structure that allows random insertion and deletion of items anywhere in the structure without suffering the penalty of either wasted space or data moves. The *linked list* is just this kind of structure, and we will study it next and then use it to implement the List class. In later chapters, we will see how the linked list can also be used to implement several other data structures.

4.5 LINKED LIST

An array stores a collection of data in a contiguous memory area. This is what makes accessing an array entry at a given index an $O(1)$ operation: knowing the memory address of the first entry of the array, the address for an entry at any index can be computed by simply adding an offset that is the product of the index and the size of each entry.

Allocating space for an array is a one-shot deal, because space once allocated can neither be grown nor shrunk. In order to not run out of space, or waste too much space, an application would need to know how many data entries need to be stored before allocating array space for storage. This is often not possible, and so more space than needed would typically have to be allocated, just to be safe.

The linked list is a fundamental data structure in computing that overcomes this problem by allocating units of space on demand, and hooking up these units via a homegrown mechanism known as linking. The units of space are called *nodes,* and each node, when allocated, can come from anywhere in memory, unrelated to any previously allocated node.

Here is the conventional schematic representation of a linked list consisting of four nodes.

A null link is drawn as a backslash character.

L is an access pointer that refers (points) to the beginning of the list.

Each node has a data part, and a link (pointer) that hooks this node to the next node in the linked list.

LINKED LIST

A linked list is a linear structure consisting of nodes. Each node has a data part that holds the client-supplied information, and a link that refers to the next node in the linked list.

The links bind together the nodes, which are disparate memory areas, to provide *apparent contiguity.*

To access the entries of the linked list, a reference to its first entry is all we need. Given this reference, we can access any entry by simply following the chain of links. When an entry is removed from a linked list, all that needs to be done is to have its predecessor's link refer to its successor—this effectively delinks or cuts out the to-be-removed entry

TABLE 4.2: Array vs linked list. A comparison of the capabilities and limitations of the array and linked list structures.

Operation	Array	Linked List
Access	Random, single step	No random access, need to always start at the beginning and skip over intervening entries
Insertion/ Deletion	Need to move entries over	No perturbation of entries
Storage	Allocated in one shot, thus drawback of underestimating/overestimating space requirement	Allocated only when needed, but links consume additional space

from the list. Similarly, an entry may be inserted anywhere in the list without having to move other entries to create space. We will study these operations in detail soon.

Before we go further, let us compare the array and linked list structures on the basis of their capabilities and limitations, summarized in Table 4.2.

For the requirements of insertion, deletion, and storage space, the linked list offers definite advantages compared to an array. However, the biggest drawback of the linked list is its inability to perform random access for any entry in a single step. Thus, the linked list is an extremely useful structure *provided that direct access to entries is not a key requirement.*

Let us take a closer look at how some of the linked list operations may be implemented. The first thing to do is to define a class for the nodes of the linked list.

4.5.1 Node

Here is a definition of a generic node that holds an object of some generic type T. Each node holds an object of some generic type T. Observe that a node is defined in terms of itself: the next field of the node class is a reference to another Node<T> object, just like itself. This is a so-called *self-referential* structure.

When several nodes are strung together, they will all have data of the same type. It is possible to mix and match data types in the nodes of a linked list by changing the Node definition to contain catchall Object instances.

```
class Node<T> {
  T data;
  Node<T> next;
  Node(T data, Node<T> next) {
    this.data = data;
    this.next = next;
  }
}
```

```
class Node {
  public Object data;
  public Node next;
  public Node (Object dat) {
    data = dat;
    next = null;
  }
}
```

4.5.2 Insertion

There are basically three cases to cover, with small differences in implementation: adding to the beginning of the list, adding to the end of the list, and adding in between two nodes of the list. It's all a question of hooking up the links correctly and ensuring that the insertion works *independent of how many entries are already in the list, including an empty list.*

Adding a new node as the first node of the list is the simplest. The following figure illustrates the sequence of steps in the insertion.

This shows an insertion at the front of a linked list.

(1) Create a new node.
(2) Make the new node's next link refer to the first entry of the list.
(3) Make the reference to the first node of the list now refer to the new node.

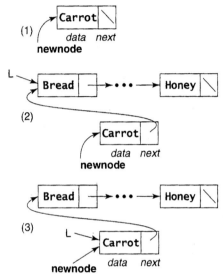

The code for this insertion is as follows, assuming that L refers to the first node of the list:

```
Node<String> newnode =
    new Node<String>("Carrot",null);
newnode.next = L;
L = newnode;
```

Note that this works even if L is null to begin with—the next link of the new node is correctly assigned null (which it already is after construction), and L is now the first and only node in the linked list.

There is an even more compact way in which to write this:

```
L = new Node<String>("Carrot", L);
```

Trace this code by hand, and verify that it is equivalent to the original version. What if we wanted to insert a new node immediately *after* a specified node, say P, in the list?

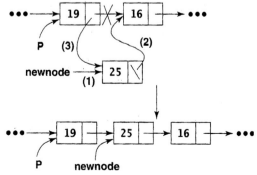

(1) Create a new node.
(2) Make the new node's next link refer to the node following *P.*
(3) Update the next link of the node to which *P* refers to now refer to the new node.

Again, these steps may be translated into the following code:

```
Node<Integer> newnode = new Node<Integer>(25,null);
newnode.next = P.next;
P.next = newnode;
```

Finally, adding a new node as the last entry of a linked list is just a special case of the above, with P as the last entry of the original list.

In all the cases of insertion detailed above, care should be taken to follow the sequence of steps as is. Switching the sequence of steps is an invitation to disaster. For instance, in the insertion of 25, if we switched steps (2) and (3) and wrote the following code,

```
Node<Integer> newnode = new Node<Integer>(25,null);
P.next = newnode;
newnode.next = P.next;
```

the second step would break the link to the node that has 16 a little too early. Then, in the third step, the next field of newnode would end up pointing to newnode itself, since P.next, on the right-hand side, is pointing to newnode by now.

SEQUENCE OF STEPS IN LINKED LIST INSERTIONS AND DELETIONS

Inserting a node into or deleting a node from a linked list follows a strict sequence of steps. Changing the order of the steps in the sequence would lead to incorrect results.

4.5.3   Deletion

Once again, we can identify three basic deletion situations: deleting the first node, deleting the last node and deleting some in-between node. Let us go over the third case for illustration, assuming that P refers to the node *preceding* the node to be deleted. The sequence of steps here is exactly the reverse of that followed in the insertion of a node after a specified node:

```
Node<String> oldnode = P.next;
P.next = oldnode.next;
```

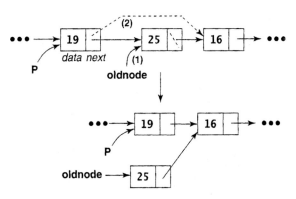

The first step gets a reference to the node to be deleted, oldnode, via the reference, P, to the previous node. The second step delinks this node from the linked list.

Note that oldnode.next still points to the same node in the linked list it was pointing to earlier, but this is irrelevant. Say the method that contains this code defines oldnode locally. Then, when the method terminates, this temporary reference is discarded, and the virtual machine will thereafter garbage collect the old linked list node that was delinked.

Deleting the first node is a special case where the list reference, L, would simply be made to point to L.next:

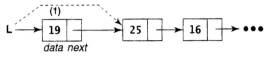

```
L = L.next;
```

Deleting the last node looks like a special case, but the code we wrote for the "general" case would still work, since oldnode.next would just be null, and the next field of P would be (correctly) assigned to this null pointer.

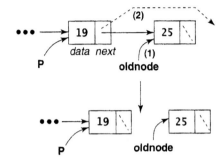

A final special case is that of deleting a node that happens to be the only node in a linked list, i.e., it is both the first node and the last node. In this case, there would be no previous node, and the deletion would simply have to set the list reference, L, to null.

After L is reset, the deleted node would have no reference to it from the program and would be garbage collected.

Deleting a linked list node is a consequence of deleting a data entry that happens to be at that node. This in turn requires that we first traverse the list and locate this entry, and thus the node that contains it.

4.5.4 Access

Stepping through, or *traversing,* all the entries of a linked list from beginning to end following the chain of references is a useful operation in practice. Moreover, this process may be enhanced to search for and locate specific nodes. The list traversal code below prints the contents of each node, assuming that L refers to the first node.

```
Node<String> nextNode = L;}
while (nextNode != null) {
   System.out.println(
            nextNode.data);
   nextNode = nextNode.next;
}
```

Now assume that we want to delete, in a linked list of strings, the first occurrence of the string "Carrot". Our first task is to locate the node that contains this string:

```
Node<String> nextNode = L;
while (nextNode != null) {
   if ("Carrot".equals(
            nextNode.data)) {
      break;
   } else {
      nextNode = nextNode.next;
   }
}
if (nextNode != null) {
   // value found
   // but we needed to stop at the node prior to this!!
```

We can't delete nextNode unless we have a reference to the node prior to it, and in the code above we managed to overshoot this previous node. One way to correct this is to use two variables to traverse the list, the second lagging the first by one node:

```
Node<String> nextNode = L;
Node<String> P = null;
while (nextNode != null) {
   if ("Carrot".equals(
            nextNode.data)) {
      break;
   else {
      P = nextNode;
      nextNode = nextNode.next;
   }
}
if (nextNode != null) { // value found
   // now we have P referring to the predecessor of nextNode
   . . .    // delete nextNode
```

after one iteration

4.5.5 Circular Linked List

It is often useful to have instant access to both the first *and* last entries of a linked list. This can be achieved by maintaining two access variables. But there is another way, and that is to have a single reference to the last entry, and *have the last entry refer back to the first.* In other words, we maintain a **circular linked list,** or CLL, for short.

CIRCULAR LINKED LIST

A circular linked list is a linked list in which the last node refers back to the first.

(a) A single variable provides direct access to the last entry, and access to the first entry in one additional step. (b) A single-entry list has the next part of the entry referring to itself.

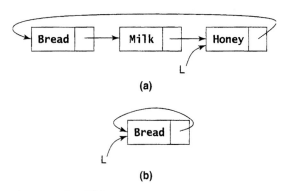

(a)

(b)

Given that L refers to the last entry, the first entry is simply L.next. And if L == L.next, that means there is exactly one entry in the CLL.

Let's try to code a couple of operations on the CLL.

Insertion.   How about inserting a new node as the *first* entry?

```
Node<String> newnode =
    new Node<String>("Carrot", null);
// link from newnode to first node
newnode.next = L.next;
// link from last node to new node
L.next = newnode;
```

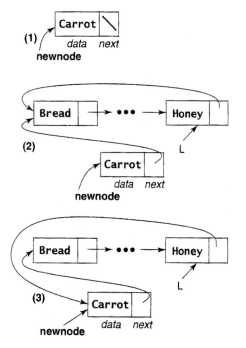

Once L.next is understood to be the first node, this code is identical to the insertion of a node at the beginning of a noncircular linked list. The only problem is, this code will *not work if the list is empty,* i.e., L is null to begin with.

The line

```
newnode.next = L.next
```

will raise a java.lang.NullPointerException on L.

That is, there is an attempt to access an object via a null pointer.

To avoid this problem, we need to make a special check for L, something we did not have to do with the noncircular list. Here's the corrected code:

```
Node<String> newnode = new Node<String>("Carrot", null);
if (L == null) {
    newnode.next = newnode;    // refers to itself
    L = newnode;
} else {
    newnode.next = L.next;
    L.next = newnode;
}
```

Deletion.   Now let's try deleting the last node. In the noncircular linked list, we discovered that in order to delete a node we need to have access to the node preceding it. A circular linked list is no different in this respect. We have to find the predecessor to the last node, L, by traversing the list from the beginning. Let's assume that P is this predecessor node, and that it has already been located.

Then, the code to delete the last node is:

```
Node<String> oldnode = L;
// delink last node from list
P.next = oldnode.next;
// set L to the predecessor,
// the new last node
L = P;
```

This code assumes that there are at least two nodes in the list. If the list has only one node, L will simply be set to null.

Finally, let us write the code for traversing the entire list. In the case of a noncircular list, the stopping condition was simple—the scan terminates when the scanning reference or pointer becomes null. In the circular linked list, however, the termination condition is that the scanning pointer returns to the starting position.

This is a first attempt at writing the traversal code with the new termination condition, with the variable L referencing the last node (assuming that the list is not empty, i.e., L is not null).

```
Node<String> nextNode = L;
System.out.println(nextNode.data);
while (nextNode.next != L) {
    nextNode = nextNode.next;
    System.out.println(nextNode.data);
}
```

This works, but here is another way, using a do loop instead of a while loop, which is often useful when dealing with circular linked lists. Again, this assumes that the list is not empty.

```
Node<String> nextNode = L;
do {
    System.out.println(nextNode.data);
    nextNode = nextNode.next;
}
while (nextNode != L);
```

Let's use what we have learned to design and implement a LinkedList class.

4.6   A LinkedList CLASS

This class is designed with the aim of providing clients with a flexible tool that can be used to perform a variety of tasks. The List class is only one of many classes that may be built using the LinkedList. Thus, the operations supported by LinkedList are numerous,

Class structures.linear.LinkedList<T>

Constructors

LinkedList( )
Creates an empty linked list.

Methods

$O(1)$ **void add(T item)**
Adds specified item to the end of this linked list.

$O(n)$ **void insertAt(T item, int index)**
Adds specified item to this linked list at specified index. Index must refer to an existing position in the list; the existing entry will be moved over.
Throws **IndexOutOfBoundsException** if the index is < 0 or ≥ number of entries.

$O(n)$ **void remove(T item)**
Deletes first occurrence of specified item from this linked list.
Throws **NoSuchElementException** if the item is not in this linked list.

$O(n)$ **T removeAt(int index)**
Deletes from this linked list the entry at the specified index, and returns the deleted entry.
Throws **IndexOutOfBoundsException** if the index is < 0 or ≥ number of entries.

$O(n)$ **void removeAll(T item)**
Deletes all occurrences of specified item from this linked list.
Throws **NoSuchElementException** if the item is not in this linked list.

$O(n)$ **void clear( )**
Deletes all entries from this linked list.

$O(n)$ **void setAt(T item, int index)**
Sets the entry at the specified index to the specified item.
Throws **IndexOutOfBoundsException** if the index is < 0 or ≥ number of entries.

$O(n)$ **T getAt(int index)**
Returns the entry at the specified index of this linked list.
Throws **IndexOutOfBoundsException** if the index is < 0 or ≥ number of entries.

$O(n)$ **int indexOf(T item)**
Returns the index in this linked list of the specified item, –1 if not found.

$O(1)$ **int size()**
Returns the number of entries in this linked list.

$O(1)$ **boolean isEmpty()**
Returns true if this linked list is empty, false otherwise.

FIGURE 4.6: A Generic Linked List Class Public Interface. Running times assume one-step access to both ends of the linked list; n is the number of entries in the list.

TABLE 4.3: Classification of LinkedList methods according to functionality.

Functionality	Method(s)
Insertion	add, insertAt
Deletion	remove, removeAt, removeAll, clear
Update	setAt
Access	getAt, indexOf, size, isEmpty

and at a lower level of abstraction, including ones that offer position-based access to the linked list elements.

The public interface of a generic LinkedList class is shown in Figure 4.6.

The LinkedList class methods may be classified according to functionality as summarized in Table 4.3.

Running times.   The basic unit time operations that count toward the running time are the following:

- Retrieving a reference, as in Node x = p.next
- Updating a reference, as in p.next = x
- Retrieving or updating the size (number of items) of the linked list.
- Comparison between a pair of data items stored in the linked list.

The methods add, size, and isEmpty have a worst-case running time of $O(1)$. All the other methods have a worst-case running time of $O(n)$ for a list of n elements. The running times will become evident when we see the implementation that follows.

Here is an implementation of the LinkedList class, based on a circular linked list.

Class File 4.4. *LinkedList.java*

```
package structures.linear;

import java.util.NoSuchElementException;

class Node<T> {
  T data; Node<T> next;
  Node (T dat) {
      data = dat; next = null;
  }
}

public class LinkedList<T> {

  Node<T> tail; int count;

  public LinkedList() { tail = null; count = 0; }
  public boolean contains(T item) { return indexOf(item) >= 0; }
  public int size() { return count; }
  public boolean isEmpty() { return count == 0; }
  public void add(T item) { ... }
  public void insertAt(T item, int index) { ... }
```

```
    public void remove(T item) { ... }
    public T removeAt(int index) { ... }
    public void removeAll(T item) { ... }
    public void clear() { tail = null; count = 0; }
    public void setAt(T item, int index) { ... }
    public T getAt(int index) { ... }
    public T get(T item) { ... }
    public int indexOf(T item) { ... }
}
```

The file LinkedList.java contains one public class, LinkedList. It also has a nonpublic helper Node class, with which we are already familiar. A source file can have at most one public class, but any number of nonpublic classes. In this case, since Node<T> has no modifier, it is a package-private class, visible to all classes in the same package, structures.linear.

In the LinkedList class, the field tail makes it clear that this class is implemented as a circular linked list, since there is no field that points to the front of the linked list. The count field keeps track of the number of entries in the linked list at any time.

Let us go over some of the methods according to the categories listed in Table 4.3, namely *insertion, deletion, update,* and *access.*

Insertion methods.   The add method is used to add an entry to the end of the list, and has a straightforward implementation:

```
public void add(T item) {
    Node<T> itemnode = new Node<T>(item);
    if (count == 0) { // empty list
        itemnode.next = itemnode;
    } else {
        itemnode.next = tail.next;
        tail.next = itemnode;
    }
    tail = itemnode;
    count++;
}
```

An empty list at the time of add is a special case and is handled appropriately.

The insertAt method has a broader application, and may be called whenever an entry is to be *inserted* in the strict sense. If the index supplied is *i*, then there must be an existing entry at position *i* ($0 < = i < n$, where *n* is the number of entries in the list).

```
public void insertAt(T item, int index) {
    if (index < 0 || index > count) {
        throw new
            IndexOutOfBoundsException(index + " < 0 or > " + count);
    }
    // find predecessor
    Node<T> pred = tail;
    for (int i=0; i < index; i++) {
        pred = pred.next;
    }
```

```
// insert after pred
Node<T> itemnode = new Node<T>(item);
itemnode.next = pred.next;
pred.next = itemnode;
count++;
}
```

The new entry is inserted to take the place of the existing (old) entry at index *i;* after the insertion, the old entry is at position *i* + 1, and the entries following it will all have their positions increased by one. Note, in particular, that insertion cannot be done on an empty list, nor can it be used to add an entry to the end of the list. For the latter, the add method must be used.

In order to insert an item at a particular place, we need to have a reference to the entry that immediately precedes it, i.e., its predecessor. In this case, it happens to be the entry at position index-1, referred to as pred, which is accessed by traversing the list in the for loop. As a special case, if the insertion is done at index 0, the predecessor is taken to be the last entry of the linked list. In this case, the initial setting of pred to tail will also be the eventual setting—the for loop will terminate without any iteration.

Deletion methods.   The most interesting of the deletion methods is removeAll, which deletes all the occurrences of a given item.

```
public void removeAll(T item) {
    if (count == 0) {
        throw new
            NoSuchElementException();
    }
    // step through all entries
    Node<T> prev=tail;
    Node<T> curr=tail.next;
    int oldcount = count;
    for (int i=0; i < oldcount; i++) {
        // delete matching item
        if (item.equals(curr.data)) {
            prev.next = curr.next;
            curr.data = null;
            curr.next = null;
            count--;
        } else {
            prev = curr;
        }
        curr = prev.next;
    }
    if (count == oldcount) {
        // no match
        throw new
            NoSuchElementException();
    }
    if (count == 0) { tail = null; }
    else { tail = prev; }
}
```

As we discovered earlier, when we first learned how to delete a node from a linked list, it is helpful to track through the list using two references. In the removeAll method, the reference prev is one step behind curr. The initial value of curr is last.next, the first entry in the list. Since this is a circularly linked list, the initial value of prev is not null, but tail instead.

The for loop steps curr (and therefore prev) through each entry in the list, matching the data in curr with the specified item. If a match is found, the curr node is deleted, and the count of entries decremented by one—note that prev should not be advanced in this case. If a match is not found, prev is advanced. In either case, curr is advanced by setting it to prev.next (*not* curr = curr.next, why?), and the scan continues.

While most of the work is done in the for loop, we need to be sure that the tail variable has a legal value before the method terminates. Of special concern is the situation where all entries in the list are deleted, in which tail needs to be set to null—this is done in the last if. If the list is not empty at the end of the for loop, curr and prev will end up referring to the first and last nodes in the list respectively (which may not be the same as the first and last nodes of the original list), and tail is thus set to prev in the last else.

Of the other two deletion methods, remove calls removeAt, after getting the index of the item using the method indexOf:

```java
public void remove(T item) {
   int i = indexOf(item);
   if (i == -1) {
      throw new NoSuchElementException();
   }
   removeAt(i); // reuse
}
```

The method removeAt does all the heavy lifting:

```java
public T removeAt(int index) {
   if (index < 0 || index >= count) {
      throw new
         IndexOutOfBoundsException(index + " < 0 or >= " + count);
   }
   T ret = null;    // for return
   if (index == 0) {
      ret = tail.next.data;    // save for return
      if (count == 1) { // single element, special case
         tail = null;
      } else { // at least two entries
         tail.next = tail.next.next;
      }
      count--;
   } else { // at least two entries, and index > 0
      // find the entry just prior to index
      Node<T> prev=tail.next;
      for (int i=0; i < index-1; i++) {
         prev = prev.next;
      }
      // remove after prev
      Node<T> curr = prev.next;
      ret = curr.data;    // save for return
      prev.next = curr.next;
      curr.next = null;
      count--;
      if (curr == tail) {
         tail = prev;
      }
   }
   return ret;
}
```

Update method. There is only one update method, setAt, which is fairly straight-forward:

```
public void setAt(T item, int index) {
  if (index < 0 || index >= count) {
     throw new
        IndexOutOfBoundsException(index + " < 0 or >= " + count);
  }
  Node<T> curr=tail.next;
  for (int i=0; i < index; i++) {
     curr = curr.next;
  }
  curr.data = item;  // update
}
```

The main work of this method is to traverse the list to get to the required node, after which it is a simple matter to set the data at that node to the specified item.

Access methods. Of the access methods listed in Table 4.3, the method getAt is a traversal of the list, while the method indexOf is an implementation of sequential search.

```
public T getAt(int index) {
  if (index < 0 || index >= count) {
     throw new
        IndexOutOfBoundsException(
        index + " < 0 or >= " + count);
  }
  // skip over preceding nodes
  Node<T> curr=tail.next;
  for (int i=0; i < index; i++) {
     curr = curr.next;
  }
  return curr.data;
}
```

```
public int indexOf(T item) {
  if (count == 0) {
     return -1;
  }
  // step through list nodes
  Node<T> curr=tail.next;
  for (int i=0; i < count; i++) {
     if (item.equals(curr.data)) {
        return i;
     }
     curr = curr.next;
  }
  return -1;
}
```

The third access method, get is identical in logic to the indexOf method except that it returns the matching item if found. So the method body for get is the same as the code for indexOf, except that return -1 becomes return null, and return i becomes return curr.data.

With such a flexible tool as the LinkedList class, it is a simple matter to (finally) implement the List class, with a significant amount of code reuse.

4.7 List CLASS IMPLEMENTATION

Let us do a quick review of what we have done so far. We started with the List interface and used it to build an ExpenseList class, which populated a list with Expense objects. Thinking of how to implement the List class, we saw that using an array or the java.util.ArrayList class would not be a good choice. The LinkedList class, on the other hand, would be an ideal fit.

Just as we implemented the ExpenseList class using the List class as a component, so we can build the List class using the LinkedList class as a component. That is, every List instance will contain an instance of the LinkedList class. Then, each method of the List class (except for first and next) implements its functionality by simply invoking, on this LinkedList instance, the analogous method of the LinkedList class. This is clear in the implementation that follows.

Class File 4.5. *List.java*

```
package structures.linear;

import java.util.NoSuchElementException;

public class List<T> {
  LinkedList<T> elements;
  int cursor;

  public List() { elements = new LinkedList(); cursor = -1; }
  public void add(T item) { elements.add(item); }
  public int size() { return elements.size(); }
  public boolean isEmpty() { return elements.isEmpty(); }
  public boolean contains(T item) { return elements.indexOf(item) != -1;}
  public void remove(T item) { elements.remove(item); }
  public void removeAll(T item) { elements.removeAll(item); }
  public void clear() { elements.clear(); }
  public T first() {
    if (elements.size() == 0) { return null; }
    cursor = 0;
    return elements.getAt(cursor);
  }
  public T next() {
    if (cursor < 0 || cursor == (elements.size()-1)) {
        return null;
    }
    cursor++;
    return elements.getAt(cursor);
  }
}
```

To implement enumeration via the first and next methods, the List defines a cursor field, which is initialized to -1 in the constructor.

Whenever the first method is called, a check is made to see if there are any items at all in the list, by calling the LinkedList method size on the component linked list elements. If the list is empty, the method returns null. Otherwise, the cursor is reset to 0, thereby referring to the first element in the list. The getAt method of the LinkedList class is then called to access this first element.

Whenever the next method is called, the cursor is first checked to see if it is not -1 and that it is not already at the last element. If the cursor is at -1, it would mean that first was never called. If the cursor is already at the last element, any call to next cannot proceed any further. The method returns null in both these cases.

As an exercise, verify the running times of the List methods listed in Figure 4.2.

4.8   SUMMARY

- An unordered list is a linear collection of entries whose relative positions with respect to each other is irrelevant.
- An unordered list is characterized by four main operations: appending an entry to the list, removing an entry from the list, enumerating the entries in the list, and searching for an entry in the list.
- An entry is searched for in an unordered list using sequential search.
- In sequential search, a target is compared against every entry in the list in sequence, one after the other. If the target matches an entry, the search is successful. If no match is found, the search is unsuccessful.
- The average number of comparisons for successful search in a data structure is the number of comparisons required, on average, to search for any element in the structure.
- The average number of comparisons for successful search in a data structure is given by the formula:

$$P_1 * C_1 + P_2 * C_2 + \cdots + P_n * C_n$$

  where P_i is the probability of searching for the i-th element, C_i is the number of comparisons required to find that element, and n is the number of elements.
- In the absence of specific information about probabilities, each element is assumed to be searched with the same probability as any other element, which implies that $P_i = 1/n$ in the above formula, for all i.
- The lowest number of comparisons on average for successful search in a list is obtained if the entries of the list are arranged in decreasing order of search probabilities from beginning to end.
- The notion of the equality of objects is specific to a client, and is implemented in a client class by overriding the default implementation.
- The key part of an object is the part used as the basis of comparing against another object for equality.
- A linked list is a linear structure consisting of nodes. Each node has a data part that holds the client-supplied information, and a link that refers to the next node in the linked list.
- The linked list's main advantage over an array is that space for nodes is allocated only when needed, thereby avoiding over/underestimating the space required. Its main disadvantage is that a direct one-step access to a specified position of the list is no longer possible.
- Inserting a node into or deleting a node from a linked list follows a strict sequence, and violating this sequence leads to disastrous results.
- A circular linked list is one in which the last node refers back to the first.
- An unordered list class may be implemented using a linked list object as a component. Then the methods of the list class can, in turn, invoke the appropriate methods of the linked list class to get their work done, thereby reusing a significant amount

of code. Since this reuse is achieved by using a *component* (linked list) object, it is code reuse by composition.

- Code reuse by composition is also demonstrated in the implementation of the ExpenseList class, which uses an unordered list component.

4.9 EXERCISES

E4.1. Given the following list of integers:

    3, 9, 2, 15, -5, 18, 7, 5, 8

answer the following questions pertaining to sequential search on this list.
(a) What is the number of comparisons made for an unsuccessful search?
(b) What is the average number of comparisons for a successful search, assuming that all entries are searched with equal probability?

E4.2. For the same list of integers as in Exercise 4.1 above, suppose that the search probabilities are respectively the following:

    0.1, 0.3, 0.05, 0.2, 0.05, 0.1, 0.05, 0.1, 0.05

The first probability corresponds to searching for 3, the second to 9, and so on.
(a) What is the average number of comparisons for successful search?
(b) Give *one* rearrangement of the list entries that would result in the lowest number of comparisons on average for successful search? What is this number?

E4.3. With reference to the "move-to-front" method of rearranging the entries of a list described in Section 4.2.2, answer the following questions:
(a) Beginning with the list of Exercise 4.1, show the state of the list after all of the following searches have been made: 12, 18, 15, 18, −5, 9, 19, 8.
(b) What is the total number of comparisons made in the above searches?
(c) If the list were *not* rearranged after every search, what would be the total number of comparisons made for the same sequence of searches as in the first question?

E4.4. You are given an unordered list of six elements with the following probabilities of searching for the elements in positions 1 through 6: 0.1, 0.1, 0.15, 0.15, 0.25, 0.25. If a sequential search were to scan for the target *backwards* through the list, what would be the average number of comparisons for successful search?

E4.5. In Section 4.2.1 we computed the average number of comparisons for *successful* sequential search on a list of length n to be $(n + 1)/2$. What is the average number of comparisons for an unsuccessful search?

E4.6. Suppose you are given a list that supports only the operations *append, remove,* and *enumerate,* as described in the first three rows of Table 4.1. Give an algorithm describing how you would perform each of the following operations *in terms of the given operations.*
(a) Empty a list (i.e., remove all the entries)
(b) Remove all occurrences of a given item from a list
(c) Obtain the size (i.e., the number of entries) of a list
(d) Search for a given item in the list, returning true or false depending on whether the item is found or not

E4.7. For each of the required operations in Exercise 4.6 above, obtain the running time in big O. Choose comparison of entries and copying entries as the basic operations.

E4.8. A **set** consists of entries that are in no particular order, *without any duplicates*. It supports (apart from others) three fundamental operations:

- *Union* with another set: the set on which this operation is invoked is modified to contain the members that are either in itself or in the given set.
- *Intersection* with another set: the set on which this operation is invoked is modified to contain the members that are common to itself and the given set.
- *Difference* with another set: the set on which this operation is invoked is modified to contain only entries that are not also members of the given set.

(a) Can a set be implemented using an unordered list?

(b) If so, describe how each of the above set operations can be implemented in terms of the unordered list operations *append, remove, enumerate,* and *contains*.

E4.9. Suppose you are given a linked list with four nodes, and a new node to be inserted *after* the node containing c.

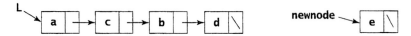

(a) Illustrate the steps you would take to perform this insertion by drawing them clearly on the figure. You *may not* assume that you have a ready-made reference to any node except the first prior to insertion.

(b) Treating reference updates, as in

```
L.next = newnode
```

and reference accesses, as in

```
Node<String> x = L.next
```

as basic operations, count the number of basic operations made in the above insertion.

E4.10. In the list of Exercise E4.9, suppose the node containing b is to be deleted.

(a) Illustrate the steps you would take to perform this deletion, drawing them clearly in the figure. You *may not* assume that you have a ready-made reference to any node except the first prior to deletion.

(b) Again, treating reference updates as well as a reference accesses as basic operations, count the number of basic operations made in the above deletion.

E4.11. You are given the following circular linked list, and a new node to be inserted *after* the node containing d.

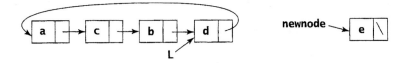

Answer the same questions as in Exercise E4.9.

E4.12. With the same circular linked list as in Exercise E4.11, the node d has to be deleted. Answer the same questions as in Exercise E4.10.

E4.13. Verify that the running times of the LinkedList class methods are as presented in Section 4.6, with the basic operations specified there.

E4.14. Using the known running times of the LinkedList class methods, verify that the running times of the List class methods are as presented with its interface in Figure 4.2.

4.10   PROGRAMMING PROBLEMS

P4.1. Given a noncircular linked list with a reference L to its first node, tell in *one short sentence* what the following method returns:

```
<T> Node<T> mystery(Node<T> L) {
  Node<T> p = L;
  Node<T> q = L;
  while (q.next != null) {
    q = q.next;
    if (q.next != null) {
        q = q.next;
        p = p.next;
    }
  }
  return p;
}
```

(Hint: trace the code for one-node and two-node lists, then for three-node and four-node lists, and see if a pattern emerges.)

P4.2. This problem mirrors Exercise E4.6. For each of the questions in that exercise, implement a client method (i.e., a method that is outside the List<T> class) with the following specifications:

(a) <T> void empty(List<T> L)

(b) <T> void removeAll(List<T> L, T item)

(c) <T> int size(List<T> L)

(d) <T> boolean contains(List<T> L, T item)

P4.3. Suppose that some clients of the ExpenseList class find its interface too cumbersome, with too many methods. One solution is to combine the methods avgExpense, maxExpense, and minExpense, int one method:

```
float[] avgminmaxExpense()
```

that returns an array of length 3, containing the average, maximum, and minimum expenses respectively. Your method should make *exactly one scan* of the expense list.

P4.4. This problem pertains to the method contains of the ExpenseList class. Write code fragments for each of the following, using method contains, and the Expense, ItemExpense, DateExpense, and ItemDateExpense classes.

(a) Determine whether there is any expense on the item "Shoes".

(b) Determine whether there is any expense for the date 2005/5/3/.

(c) Determine whether there is any expense for "Shoes" on 2005/5/3.

P4.5. Implement a method:

```
float totalExpense(ExpenseList L, String item)
```

that would return the total expense in list L, for the given item. For instance, if item were "Shoes", this method would add up all the expenses for shoes found in the list, and return the total. (Hint: use the method get of the ExpenseList class with an appropriate ItemExpense object.)

P4.6. Given a noncircular linked list with a reference L to its first node, write a method:

```
<T> Node<T> reverse(Node<T> L)
```

that would return a new list (reference to the first node) that contains the entries of the given list L in reverse order. The given list must not be changed. See the following figure.

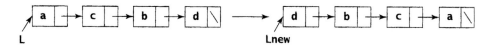

P4.7. Given a noncircular linked list, convert it to a CLL and return a pointer to the last node:

```
<T> Node<T> convert2CLL(Node<T> L)
```

P4.8. You are given a noncircular linked list consisting of characters, with a reference L to its first node. Write a method:

```
<T> boolean isPalindrome(Node<T> L)
```

that would tell whether the entries spell the same forwards and backwards (i.e., the entries form a palindrome). For instance, the entries were 'a', 'b', 'b', and 'a' form a palindrome. (Hint: you may call the reverse method of Problem 4.6.)

P4.9. Given two CLLs, Node L1 and Node L2 (i.e., L1 and L2 refer to the *last* nodes of the respective CLLs), write a method:

```
<T> Node<T> append(Node<T> L1, Node<T> L2)
```

that would append the second list to the end of the first. The method must return a reference to the last node of the enhanced list. It *may not* use any extra space, either for nodes or for the entries in the nodes.

P4.10. Given a CLL, Node<T> L (i.e., L refers to the *last* node of the CLL), write a method:

```
<T> Node<T> evenList(Node<T> L)
```

that would return a reference to the last node of a linked list obtained by extracting the even-positioned nodes of L—the first node is assumed to in position 1. When the method s is done, L would still refer to the first node, but the rest of this list would consist of the odd-positioned nodes of the original list. The following figure may help you understand the problem better.

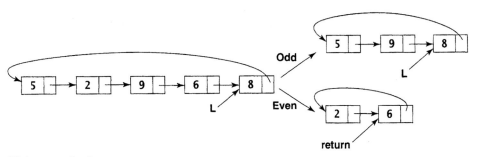

P4.11. Write a method:

```
<T> Node<T> joinLists(Node<T> Odds, Node<T> Evens)
```

that would *merge* two CLLs Odds and Evens (i.e., Odds and Evens refer to the last nodes of the respective linked lists) into a single list. In the result list, the nodes of the Odds list must be in the odd-numbered positions (1, 3, 5, etc.), and those of the Evens list must be in the even-numbered positions. You should not use any extra space for nodes or data entries in the nodes.

P4.12. Suppose the LinkedList class did not define a count field. Reimplement the following methods:

(a) `int size()`

(b) `boolean isEmpty()`

P4.13. Write an application class called WordCount that would print the number of occurrences of each word (ignoring case) in an input text file. Use a list to store (word,count) pairs. (Note that if a word is immediately followed by punctuation without any spacing, you should strip the punctuation before using the word.)

P4.14. Reimplement all the methods of the LinkedList class using a noncircular linked list. Compute and tabulate the running times of the constructor and all the methods of this new class.

P4.15. A *doubly linked list* (DLL) is a linked list in which each node has a *previous* link, in addition to the next link, that points to the previous node in the linked list. The previous link of the first node is null.

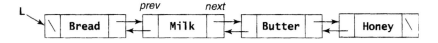

(a) Write a DLLNode<T> class.

(b) Implement a method addFront that adds a new item to the front of a doubly linked list, and returns the new front node reference.

```
<T> DLLNode<T> addFront(DLLNode<T> front, T item)
```

(c) Implement a method deleteFront that deletes the first item from a doubly linked list, and returns the new front node reference. Your method should throw a NoSuchElementException if the list is empty.

```
<T> DLLNode<T> deleteFront(DLLNode<T> front)
```

(d) Implement a method delete that deletes the first occurrence of a given item from a doubly linked list, and returns the new front node reference. Your method should throw a NoSuchElementException if the list does not contain this item.

`<T> DLLNode<T> delete(DLLNode<T> front, T item)`

(e) Implement a method deleteAll that deletes all occurrences of a given item from a doubly linked list, and returns the new front node reference. Your method should throw a NoSuchElementException if the list does not contain this item.

`<T> DLLNode<T> deleteAll(DLLNode<T> front, T item)`

P4.16. A *circular doubly linked list* (CDLL) is a doubly linked list in which the previous link of the first node points to the last, and the next link of the last node points to the first. If there is only one node, both links of this node point to itself.

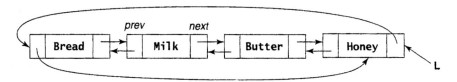

Reimplement of all the methods listed in Problem P4.15 using a CDLL.

CHAPTER 5

Ordered List

The ordered list is a linear collection of entries, with the additional property that all the entries are arranged in ascending or descending order of keys. This ordering speeds up the process of searching for an entry in the list, a feature that is the cornerstone of the ordered list.

Learning Objectives

- Describe the properties of an ordered list, and compare them with those of an unordered list.
- Study binary search and analyze its worst-case running time.
- Understand how a Java interface can be designed to ensure that an ordered list consists only of objects that may be sorted.
- Design the public interface of an ordered list class in Java, and determine the running times of its methods.
- Learn how to merge two ordered lists in an efficient manner.
- Develop a list consolidation application based on merging, using the ordered list class.
- Implement an ordered list class in Java using an array list component.

5.1 INTRODUCTION

Suppose you plan to throw a big graduation party. You start preparing for the party and draw up an initial list of invitees. Since you foresee a lot of activity with this list in terms of people being added or deleted or some information being changed, you would rather have a program maintain the list for you on your computer.

If you don't care about the order in which the names are listed, your program can build an unordered list, with new names added to the end of the list.

On the other hand, if you were to maintain the names of your invitees in alphabetical order, your program would use an ordered list. Any new name inserted into the list would be inserted in its *correct place* in the list.

ORDERED LIST

An ordered list is a linear collection of entries in which the entries are arranged in either ascending order or descending order of keys.

The *key* part of an entry object that serves as the basis of the ordering may vary depending on what kind of entries are stored in the ordered list. For instance, if you store the names and phone numbers of the invitees, the name is the key because the invitees are listed in alphabetical order of names.

There are several advantages to maintaining the names in alphabetical order. First, if you were to simply check the names against the ones you have in mind, it would be much easier to do so if the list were alphabetized by name. Second, as we will soon see, merging two lists of names is much easier if they are both in alphabetical order.

The third advantage is a more general one, applicable to any sorted list: a faster search for any particular key. In this example of a list of names, we can search for any particular name much faster than if the names were maintained in an arbitrary order.

In an unordered list, we use sequential search to look for a key (target). In the worst case, we may end up comparing the key of every entry in the list against the target key, leading to a running time of $O(n)$ for a list containing n entries.

Searching for a key in an ordered list can be done significantly faster. Think of how we search for a name in a phone book. We don't search linearly; instead, we "jump" over pages, narrowing down our search very quickly. In particular, we don't look at every entry in the phone book.

Searching in an ordered list is similar, and follows a process called *binary search*. Binary search in a list of n entries takes only $O(\log n)$ time in the worst case.

There is an enormous difference between $O(n)$ and $O(\log n)$, the difference becoming increasingly significant with bigger and bigger n. Consider a typical phone book that has at least a million entries. Here is a quick back-of-the-envelope calculation: if it takes one second to compare two names, sequential search could take up to a million seconds, or 11 days! Binary search, on the other hand, would take up to $\log 1000000$ seconds, or only about 20 seconds.

Exactly how does binary search work, and why does it take only $O(\log n)$ time?

5.2   BINARY SEARCH

One bright day your colleague, Binary Tom, sets up a challenge. "Think of a number between 1 and 63," he says. You think of 55. Upon which BT declares, "I bet I can guess your number within 11 tries." This is how the exchange goes ...

```
BT: ''Is it equal to 32?''   You: ''No.''
BT: ''Is it less than 32?''  You: ''No.''
BT: ''Is it equal to 48?''   You: ''No.''
BT: ''Is it less than 48?''  You: ''No.''
BT: ''Is it equal to 56?''   You: ''No.''
BT: ''Is it less than 56?''  You: ''Yes.''
BT: ''Is it equal to 52?''   You: ''No.''
BT: ''Is it less than 52?''  You: ''No.''
BT: ''Is it equal to 54?''   You: ''No.''
BT: ''Is it less than 54?''  You: ''No.''
```

The next guess is going to be BT's last chance.

```
BT: ''Is it equal to 55?''
```

Yes! What was Binary Tom's strategy, and how did he know beforehand that he would be able to guess your number within exactly 11 tries?

5.2.1   Divide in Half

Going over Tom's sequence of questions in detail, you gradually discover his strategy. With every pair of questions, he *cut down the possible range of numbers by half*. In his mind's eye he was seeing the range dwindling like this, all the way down to 55:

$1\text{--}63 \rightarrow 33\text{--}63 \rightarrow 48\text{--}63 \rightarrow 48\text{--}56 \rightarrow 49\text{--}56 \rightarrow 53\text{--}56 \rightarrow 54\text{--}56 \rightarrow 55$

But how did Tom know that he would only need up to 11 questions? Analyzing carefully, you take out paper and pencil and start drawing up the following table with two columns. On the left, you write the step number, and on the right, you write the range in that step. The 11 questions came from using two questions for all but the last step, in which only one question was used: $2 \times 6 - 1$ questions in all.

Progress

Step	Range
1	63
2	31
3	15
4	7
5	3
6	1

You begin to see a pattern in the numbers in the right-hand column: the numbers go as powers of 2 minus 1, ending with $2^1 - 1 = 1$. You list out the table again to capture this pattern, reversing it so the right-hand column begins with 1 in the first row, and attempting to generalize it.

Finally, you arrive at the answer. Given a maximum bound N that can be expressed as $N = 2^k - 1$, any number between 1 and N can be guessed in $2k - 1$ guesses. All you need to do is to obtain k:

$$k = \log_2 (N + 1)$$

Pattern

Step	Range	Range Related to Step No.
1	1	$2^1 - 1$
2	3	$2^2 - 1$
3	7	$2^3 - 1$
4	15	$2^4 - 1$
...	...	...
k	–	$2^k - 1$

Now you can play the same game as Tom. "Think of a number between 1 and 1,048,575." You know that 1,048,575 is $2^{20} - 1$, so you need at most 39 guesses. "I bet I can guess your number within 39 tries."

5.2.2 Algorithm

This guessing strategy can be translated into the binary search algorithm applied on an array in which the entries are arranged in ascending order of keys.

Here is a binary search for the key 19 in the array. The search key is known as the *target*, which is first compared against the middle entry of the array. The middle position is computed as $(0 + 9)/2 = 9/2 = 4$, using integer division. Since the entry at this position, 26, is greater than the target, *the target cannot be in the right half of the array.* Therefore, in the next step, the effective subarray under consideration is the one between the positions 0 (left end) and 3 (right end).

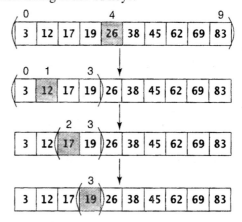

This process continues, with the next midpoint being 1, computed as $(0 + 3)/2$. Now the middle entry, 12, is less than the target, 19. So the target cannot be in the left half of the subarray. The right half of the subarray is delimited by position 2 (left end) and 3 (right end).

In Step 3, the midpoint is 2, computed as $(2 + 3)/2$. Since the entry at this position, 17, is less than the target, 19, we once again go to the right half, which is bounded by the positions 3 and 3 (i.e., a subarray with only one entry).

In the last step, this middle entry 19 is found to be equal to the target, and the search terminates successfully.

The general binary search algorithm follows.

Algorithm binarySearch(A, n, t)

input: array A of length n, target t

$left \leftarrow 0$
$right \leftarrow n - 1$
while ($left \le right$) do
    $mid \leftarrow (left + right) / 2$
    if ($t == A[mid]$) then
        break out of while loop
    else
        if ($t < A[mid]$) then
            $right \leftarrow mid - 1$
        else
            $left \leftarrow mid + 1$
        endif
    endif
endwhile

if ($left \le right$) then
    display "found at position", mid
else
    display "not found"
endif

The subarray under consideration at any step is bounded by the positions *left* and *right*. The midpoint is computed as $mid = (low + high)/2$, and the result is truncated down to an integer.

If the middle element is equal to the target, the search terminates successfully. Otherwise, since the array is ordered, one more comparison is made to determine whether to proceed with the search in the left half or right half of the array (i.e., half the array is taken out of future consideration).

This process is repeated until a match occurs (success) or there are no more entries in the array left to compare against the target (failure). There are no more entries to examine when the *left* and *right* indices cross over—see the *while* loop check.

Trace the algorithm on the preceding array with 20 as target, instead of 19. See how the *left* and *right* indices cross over at the end, resulting in failure to find the target.

Running-time analysis.   In every step, the algorithm first makes one comparison to determine whether the target is equal to the middle entry. If not, one more comparison is made to go left or right. Thus, two comparisons are made to go from a subarray to the next half subarray.

When a search terminates successfully, as in the example, only one comparison (equality) is made in the last step. Thus, $2 \times 3 = 6$ comparisons are made in the first three steps, followed by one comparison in the last step, for a total of seven comparisons in all. This example, in fact, illustrates the worst-case number of comparisons for success.

On the other hand, if the search fails to find the target, two comparisons are made in the last step, in an attempt to go left or right. Then, *before beginning the next step*, it is discovered that the delimiters have crossed over, and no next step is taken. In the example, if the target were 20 instead, the search would terminate *after one more comparison*—the search needs to proceed in a subarray to the right of 19, but there is no such subarray. This is a failed search, after eight comparisons. *The number of comparisons for a worst-case failed search is always one more than the number of comparisons for a worst-case successful search.*

Let us formalize all this. Let there be n entries in the array, and to begin with, let us assume that $n = 2^k - 1$. Arguing along the same lines as in the guessing game of the preceding section, we find that it takes $2k - 1$ comparisons for worst-case success, and $2k$ for worst-case failure. Since $k = \log(n + 1)$,[1] we have $2\log(n + 1) - 1$ comparisons for worst-case success, and $2\log(n + 1)$ comparisons for worst-case failure.

What if n is not of the form $2^k - 1$? It turns out that we can represent the number of comparisons in general as $2\lceil\log(n + 1)\rceil - 1$ for worst-case success, and consequently as $2\lceil\log(n + 1)\rceil$ for worst-case failure, where, $y = \lceil x \rceil$ means that y is the *smallest integer greater than or equal to* x. For instance, $\lceil 2.3 \rceil = 3$.

BINARY SEARCH, WORST-CASE COMPARISONS

The worst-case number of comparisons for binary search of an array with n entries is $2\lceil\log(n + 1)\rceil - 1$ for success, and $2\lceil\log(n + 1)\rceil$ for failure.

In summary, the number of comparisons made by binary search for both successful and unsuccessful search is $O(\log n)$ in the worst case. Just as with sequential search, we can also compute the average number of comparisons for successful and failed searches. This computation for some specific arrays is explored in the exercises. The *general* average case analysis is presented in Section 10.8.

It is important to note that this fast binary search, of the order $O(\log n)$, is possible on an array, but not on a linked list. Every step of binary search accesses the middle entry of the list. In an array this is a direct access that takes $O(1)$ time. However, in a linked list of length n, accessing the middle entry would take $O(n)$ time, since it would have to start at the beginning of the list and run its way down all the entries that precede the middle one. This access time would play a dominant role in the running time of the entire algorithm, which would end up being greater than $O(\log n)$.

Let us now turn our attention to designing an OrderedList class that will support binary search. Different OrderedList instances may store different *types* of elements; for example, a program may maintain an ordered list of people's names (strings) in alphabetical order, or, say, an ordered list of student records keyed on student ID. In order for binary search to work correctly, independent of the type of entries stored in the ordered list, we need to build some scaffolding, as will be explained in the next section.

5.3   ORDERING: INTERFACE java.lang.Comparable

In Section 4.4.5, we had to solve the problem of how to make a class that used a generic equals method work with objects of any type. We learned how to construct a hierarchy

---

1. We omit the base 2 for convenience, since most logarithms in computing are to the base 2

of classes in order to implement a specific client-defined kind of equality that would solve our problem in an elegant manner.

We are now faced with a similar but somewhat more challenging problem. Unlike an unordered list, an ordered list method that either searches for or inserts an entry would not only need to tell whether two entries are *equal,* but also whether one entry is *less than* or *greater than* another, as illustrated by the binary search process. In order to make our OrderedList admit only items that can be compared for ordering, it can implement the Comparable<T> interface, as we did for the SortedArray class in Section 1.13.3.

Example: Making expenses conform to Comparable.   Recall the classes Expense, ItemExpense, DateExpense, and ItemDateExpense from Section 4.4.5 and Figure 4.5. There we only had to be concerned with appropriately redefining the equals method. How would we modify these classes, and the class hierarchy, to enable us to store their instances in the OrderedList class?

The place to start is the root of the class hierarchy, Expense. We would have to first have this class implement the interface Comparable<Expense>, and therefore define the method compareTo, which would compare two Expense objects based on date, item name, and amount. Here is an outline of the modified Expense class:

```
public class Expense implements Comparable<Expense> {
   ...
   public int compareTo(Expense other) {
      if (this.date.before(other.date)) return -1;
      if (this.date.after(other.date)) return 1;
      int c = this.item.compareTo(other.item);
      if (c != 0) return c;
      if (this.amount == other.amount) return 0;
      if (this.amount > other.amount) return 1;
      return -1;
   }
   ...
}
```

As you can see from the code, we must decide what it means for one Expense object to be less than or greater than another because three fields are involved in the comparison. Specifically, the fields need to be given a relative-precedence order in the comparison process. Here we have elected to give date the highest precedence, followed by item, and finally amount.

Thus, when two Expense instances are compared, their respective dates are compared first. If the dates are not equal, then the invoking (this) instance is declared to be less than or greater than the other according to whether the former chronologically precedes or follows the latter, and this terminates the Expense comparison. Only if the dates are not equal does the Expenses comparison proceed with the comparison of the respective items, possibly working its way through to comparing the respective amounts as well, if needed.

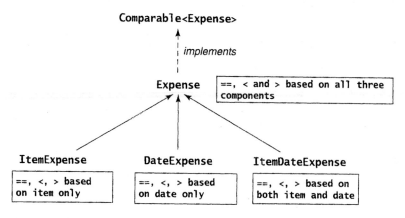

FIGURE 5.1: Specific Equality, Less than, and Greater than. Expense implements interface Comparable<Expense>, and therefore defines method compareTo, which compares all three components of two Expense objects. The classes ItemExpense, DateExpense, and ItemDateExpense each extend (i.e., are subclasses of) Expense, and redefine the inherited compareTo method appropriately.

Having modified the Expense class, the classes DateExpense, ItemExpense, and ItemDateExpense would each extend Expense, as before. Since Expense already implements Comparable<Expense>, these classes would also *implicitly* implement Comparable<Expense> (i.e., they *do not* explicitly state that they implement Comparable<Expense>).

Each of the classes DateExpense, ItemExpense, and ItemDateExpense would therefore inherit the compareTo method from Expense, but would override it to base the comparison on *date* only, *item* only, and *date* as well as *item*, respectively. See Figure 5.1.

5.4   AN OrderedList CLASS

Figure 5.2 shows the public interface of the class.

Note the class header:

```
OrderedList<T extends Comparable<T>>
```

This is analogous to the SortedArray class header we saw in Section 1.13.3. The OrderedList class must only admit instances of classes T that implement the Comparable<T> interface.

We have defined this class with the constraint that there are *no duplicate entries*—two entries are duplicates of each other if their respective *keys* are equal. Observe that several operations that were defined on the unordered list (Figure 4.2) are also defined on the ordered list, including add and remove. The new OrderViolationException is discussed shortly.

Method binarySearch. The binarySearch method is the cornerstone of this class. It conducts a binary search of the ordered list for a given key and returns a position.

Class
structures.linear.OrderedList<T extends <Comparable<T>>

Constructors

OrderedList(int capacity)
Creates an empty ordered list with specified initial capacity.
OrderedList( )
Creates an empty ordered list with default initial capacity.

Methods

$O(1)$ **void add(T item) throws OrderViolationException**
Adds new item to the end of this list.
$O(n)$ **void add(int pos, T item) throws OrderViolationException,**
       IndexOutOfBoundsException
Adds new item to this list at the specified position.
$O(n)$ **void insert(T item) throws OrderViolationException**
Inserts specified item at appropriate position in this list.
$O(1)$ **int size( )**
Returns the number of items in this list.
$O(1)$ **boolean isEmpty( )**
Returns true if this list is empty, false otherwise.
$O(\log n)$ **int binarySearch(T item)**
Conducts a binary search for specified item in this list. Returns pos.
If item is found, pos is the location of the item in this list. If item is
not found, pos < 0, and **abs**(pos) is one more than its would-be location.
$O(1)$ **T get(int pos) throws IndexOutOfBoundsException**
Returns the item at the specified position of this list.
$O(n)$ **void remove(T item) throws NoSuchElementException**
Removes the specified element from this list.
$O(n)$ **void remove(int pos) throws IndexOutOfBoundsException**
Removes from this list the item at the specified position.
$O(1)$ **void clear( )**
Removes all the entries from this list (i.e., empties it out).
$O(1)$ **T first( )**
Returns the first element of this list, null if list is empty.
$O(1)$ **T next( )**
Returns the next element in this list, relative to a previous call to **first** or **next**.
Returns null if there no more elements.

FIGURE 5.2: A Generic Ordered List Class. Only the public interface is shown. Duplicate keys are not permitted. Sorted array storage is required; n is the number of entries in the list.

If the key is indeed in the list, the method returns the position at which the key is found. If the key does not exist in the list, the function returns a negative position whose absolute value is *one more than* the position at which the key would appear *were it to be stored in the list*.

Consider, for example, the following ordered list of integers:

2, 5, 8, 19, 25, 36, 55

A call to binarySearch for key 19 would return 3, the position at which 19 is found. On the other hand, a call to BinarySearch for key 30 would return -6, meaning that (a) 30 is not in the list, and (b) if it were to be added to the list, it would fall into position $6 - 1 = 5$.

The reason for the loaded return value for failure is that often we want to know if a key exists in the list, and if not, insert an entry with that key. If the search were to just return, say, -1 to indicate failure, then a subsequent insertion would redo the search process in order to find where the entry needs to be inserted. To avoid this redundant work, the search method returns a "would-be" position, which can then be directly used to insert an entry, using the insert method.

Exceptions. We are familiar with the exceptions NoSuchElementException and IndexOutBoundsException from Section 4.6—both of these are runtime exceptions, the former defined in the java.util package, and the latter in the java.lang package. The exception OrderViolationException is a new exception that is not in the Java language libraries. We define it here for the following reason.

Suppose the key 6 is to be inserted at position 2 in the following list, using the add(int, T) method:

2, 5, ⎡8⎤, 19, 25, 36, 55

The key 8 is currently at position 2. On inserting the key 6, the list is updated as follows:

2, 5, ⎡6⎤, 8, 19, 25, 36, 55

But what if one attempts to insert the key 7 at position 2 in the new list? This should be detected as an attempt to violate the order of the list (since 7 is not less than 6, the key currently at position 2), and an exception should be thrown. Since there is no exception that fits this requirement in the Java packages, we define a tailor-made exception called OrderViolationException, in the package structures.linear.

While the preceding example describes the need for the OrderViolationException using the insert method as an example, a violation of order may also occur when the add(T) or insert(T) method is invoked.

Method add(T) requires that the key of the item to be added (to the end of the list) be larger than any existing key in the list (i.e., the new key is larger than that of the current last item of the list).

Method insert(T) requires that the key of the item to be added not match with the key of an existing item (i.e., the new key should not be a duplicate of an existing key). In fact the add methods will also detect an attempt to add a duplicate key, and throw an instance of the OrderViolationException.

The OrderViolationException here to detect duplicates should really have been named, say, DuplicateOccurrenceException. However, we opted to not define an additional exception, electing to have the OrderViolationException do double duty, and documenting the usage clearly in the interface.

The implementation of OrderViolationException appears in Section 5.7.

Running times.   Since binary search can only be performed on an array in $O(\log n)$ time, any implementation of the OrderedList class must store its entries in an array-based structure.

Of the methods for adding to the list and removing from the list, only the add(T) method is $O(1)$ time, since in an array it would simply assign the new item to the position one beyond the current last item, without disturbing the array in any other way. The other methods would, in general, need array items to be moved around to either accommodate the new item in the case of adding, or to close the hole in the case of removing. In the worst case, this could result in all n array items being moved, for a time of $O(n)$.

So how does an ordered list stack up against an unordered list?

PRIMARY ADVANTAGE OF ORDERED LIST

The primary advantage of an ordered list implemented using an array-based structure is that searching for an entry in an ordered list using binary search is significantly faster than searching for an entry in an unordered list using sequential search.

But there is no free lunch. The penalty for the fast search is paid in adding and deleting entries, as we have just seen.

PRIMARY DISADVANTAGE OF ORDERED LIST

The primary disadvantage of an ordered list implemented using an array-based structure is that inserting or deleting an entry takes upto $O(n)$ time, compared to only $O(1)$ time in an unordered list.

Table 5.1 compares the running times of the basic operations in an unordered list and ordered list, and pinpoints the tradeoffs.

TABLE 5.1: **Running Times of Basic Operations: Unordered List vs Ordered List.** The ordered list is assumed to be implemented using an array. The ordered list gains in search time, but loses in time for adding an entry.

Operation	Unordered List	Ordered List
Insert	$O(1)$	$O(n)$
Remove	$O(n)$	$O(n)$
Search	$O(n)$	$O(\log n)$

Addressing the tradeoff seen Table 5.1, when do we choose to maintain an ordered list? If we never store more than a handful of entries (say, less than 50), we may want to go with the unordered list to avoid the overhead of data movement while not losing much by way of increased search time. On the other hand, if we have a large number of entries (in the hundreds or more), and do many more searches than insertions (searches in phone books and through directory assistance are much more frequent than new names being added), then the ordered list is a clear winner.

Let us now turn to a very interesting application of ordered lists, that of *merging* two ordered lists.

5.5   MERGING ORDERED LISTS

Suppose you get your roommate to co-host your graduation party. You decide to maintain two separate lists of friends who are invited. An invitee may call either of you to confirm. You may therefore find that some invitees' names appear in both lists.

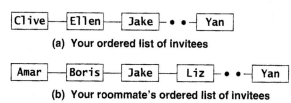

(a) Your ordered list of invitees

(b) Your roommate's ordered list of invitees

If an invitee calls to cancel, you cannot simply delete that invitee from your list. For one thing, there is no guarantee that the invitee's name is on your list—it may on your roommate's list instead. This is the case with Liz. For another, the invitee's name may appear in both lists, in which case deleting the name from your list *alone* will not suffice. This is the case with Jake—you and your roommate *both* would have to delete Jake's name from your respective lists. How to handle this in a convenient manner?

You put your heads together and come up with the following scheme. Instead of immediately trying to delete an invitee's name from a list, you will postpone the deletion to a later point, when each of you has had a chance to examine the other's list. In the meanwhile, you will keep a record of all the deletions that will eventually have to be made.

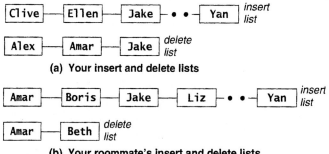

(a) Your insert and delete lists

(b) Your roommate's insert and delete lists

In sum, you and your roommate will *each keep two lists:* one list (the *insert* list) in which all insertions are made as before, and another list (the *delete* list) to record all deletes. A confirming invitee's name gets added to the insert list, and a canceling invitee's name gets added to the delete list.

Finally, on the morning of the party (at which time you "freeze" your lists), you and your roommate get together to arrive at the final list of invitees. You carry out the following sequence of actions:

- **Merge** your separate insert lists into a single ordered insert list, without duplicates.

- **Merge** your separate delete lists into a single ordered delete list, without duplicates.

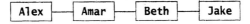

- **Delete,** from the merged insert list, all the names that appear in the merged delete list. More accurately, do a *difference* of the merged insert list with the merged delete list, keeping only those names in the merged insert list that do not appear in the merged delete list. This latter definition is more accurate because there may be names in the merged delete list (e.g., Alex and Beth) that do not appear in the merged insert list—this could happen if Alex called and said he would not be able to attend the party, not knowing that his name was not on the invitee list to begin with. The resulting insert list is the final list of invitees.

All that remains to be done is to figure out how to *merge* two ordered lists into a single ordered list, fast.

5.5.1 Two-Finger Merge Algorithm

The following figure shows how an ordered list is merged into another.

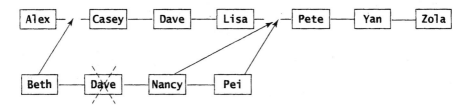

As we saw earlier in this section, if an ordered list is implemented as an array to facilitate fast binary search, inserting into an ordered list can be expensive because it typically involves moving all the entries over to create a spot for the new entry. Consequently, while *in concept* we follow the insertion approach of the above figure, *in practice* we will build a separate third list to hold the merged entries, as can be seen below.

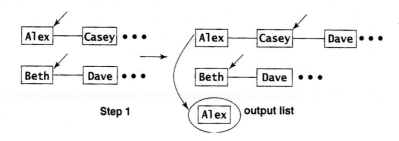

Step 1

output list

The merging algorithm maintains two "fingers" that start by pointing at the first entry of either list. These two entries are compared. In our example, Alex is compared with Beth. The smaller keyed entry is appended to the result list, and the finger that pointed to this entry is moved over one step along that list. In our example, Alex is placed in the result list and the finger moves up to point to Casey.

In the second step, Beth is appended to the output list, and in the third step, Casey is moved to the output list.

At the beginning of Step 4, the finger on the first list points to Dave, and the finger on the second list points to Dave. Since these entries are identical, only one copy of Dave is appended to the output list; *both* fingers are then moved over to the next entry in their respective lists.

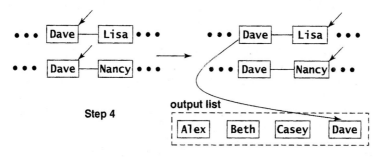

Step 4

output list

In Step 5, Lisa is compared with Nancy, and Lisa is added to the output list. In Step 6, Pete is compared with Nancy, and Nancy is added to the output list. Then Pete is compared with Pei, and Pei is added to the output list.

All the entries of the second list have now been transferred to the output list, shown in the figure below, leaving the rest of the entries in the first list, namely Pete, Yan, and Zola. These leftover entries are then simply appended to the output without having to make any more comparisons. This is the *cleanup* phase of the merge process.

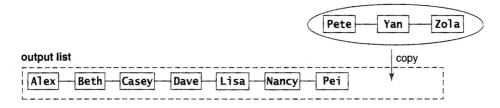

output list

Algorithm merge($L1$, $L2$, $L3$)

Input: ordered lists $L1$, $L2$
Output: merged ordered list $L3$

$L3 \leftarrow$ empty
$f1 \leftarrow$ finger at first entry of $L1$
$f2 \leftarrow$ finger at first entry of $L2$

while (neither $f1$ nor $f2$ is
        beyond the end of its list) do
  if $f1$'s entry $<$ $f2$'s entry then
    append $f1$'s entry to $L3$
    move $f1$ to next entry in $L1$
  else if $f2$'s entry $<$ $f1$'s entry
    append $f2$'s entry to $L3$
    move $f2$ to next entry in $L2$
  else
    append $f1$'s entry to $L3$
    move $f1$ to next entry in $L1$
    move $f2$ to next entry in $L2$
  endif
endwhile

if $f1$ is beyond end of $L1$ then
  append remaining $L2$ to $L3$
endif

if $f2$ is beyond end of $L2$ then
  append remaining $L1$ to $L3$
endif

Each iteration of the *while* loop results in one entry being added to the output list. Note that in the loop, the block of statements after the second *else* are executed if the entries being compared are identical—in this case, only one copy is appended to the output list, $L3$, but both fingers are moved up. This ensures that the output list does not carry duplicates. The two *if* statements after the *while* loop clean up the leftover entries.

Running-time analysis. What are the basic operations? Certainly, every comparison adds to the running time. But what about the cleanup, the copying of all remaining entries of an input list to the output list, when the other input list has been fully processed? This could be a significant contribution to the running time, *depending on how the ordered list is implemented.* For now, we will only count comparisons as the basic operations.

Let the first list contain m entries and the second list contain n entries. We will start by examining the best case—namely, the case in which the least number of comparisons is made. Clearly, the more entries we append to the output in the cleanup phase (in which no comparisons are needed), the fewer comparisons we need to make. This would happen if all the entries of one list were less than all the entries of the other list.

In the next figure, the double-headed arrows show the comparisons made. Every entry in the "lesser" list is compared with the first entry of the "greater" list, found to be smaller in key, and therefore appended to the output list. In the cleanup, all the entries of the greater list are appended to the output without further comparisons.

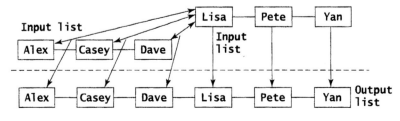

Let us assume that the *m*-list entries are all less than the *n*-list entries. Then every entry of the *m*-list will be compared with the first entry of the *n*-list and appended to the output. When the *m*-list is exhausted, the *n* list is simply appended to the output in the cleanup phase. In all, *m* comparisons are made. It helps even more if $m < n$, for the best possible of best cases. Thus, the best-case number of comparisons is $min(m, n)$.

MERGING ORDERED LISTS, BEST-CASE NUMBER OF COMPARISONS

Given two ordered lists of lengths *m* and *n* respectively, the best-case number of comparisons is $min(m, n)$, when all the entries of the shorter list are smaller than all the entries of the other list.

Naturally, the worst-case scenario would occur when no entry from either list gets a free ride into the output list—in other words, *every entry undergoes a comparison before it can be appended to the output list*. Of course, the last entry to go into the output list will not be compared, because there is nothing to compare it against, so it is the only entry that gets a free ride. Since there are $m + n$ entries in the output list, the worst-case number of comparisons is $m + n - 1$.

It is instructive to characterize the relative ordering of keys in the two lists that would result in the worst-case number of comparisons. One immediate situation that comes to mind is when the keys of the two lists are ordered in "zig-zag," or alternating, fashion, as in the following figure.

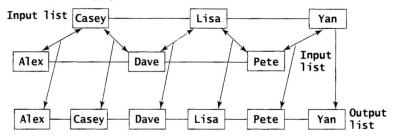

It would be nice if this were the only type of situation that results in the worst-case number of comparisons, since it is not very likely that the lists to be merged have the highly specific property of having alternating keys.

Unfortunately, there is a more general (less constrained) worst-case situation: *the last output entry is from one list and the second-to-last output entry is from the other, with no constraints in the relative interlist ordering of the other entries*. (Can you reason why this situation would still result in $m + n - 1$ comparisons?)

5.6 LIST CONSOLIDATION USING OrderedList

Our goal is to implement the list consolidation process described in the example of party lists just before Section 5.5.1 using the OrderedList class.

There are two merge operations in this algorithm. These merge operations are applied on lists that may contain common keys. The algorithm for merging listed in

> # MERGING ORDERED LISTS, WORST-CASE NUMBER OF COMPARISONS
>
> Given two ordered lists of lengths m and n respectively, the worst-case number of comparisons is $m + n - 1$, guaranteed to occur if the last two entries of the output list are respectively the last entries of the input lists.

algorithm **merge** of Section 5.5.1 preserves only one copy of a pair of common keys in the resulting list—that is, this merge algorithm is computing the *union* of two ordered lists.

By analogy, in the example of the party lists deleting the entries of the merged delete list from the merged insert list is the same as computing the *difference* of the first list and the second (i.e., the result is the list of all entries that are in the first list *but not* in the second). This can be implemented by making small modifications to the **merge** merge (union) algorithm. Specifically, two modifications need to be made if we want to compute $L_1 - L_2$.

- In the *while* loop, if a pair of entries are equal (the last *else* in the *if*), *neither* is appended to the output.
- In the cleanup following the *while* loop, *only* L_1 is appended to the output.

Often, we want to compute the *intersection* of two ordered lists. This is in the same league as union and difference, and can also be implemented by modifying the union algorithm.

5.6.1 Merger: A Utility Class

What we have covered is a *family* of merge algorithms. It therefore makes design sense to put these together under one roof. An appealing solution is to define a class called Merger that would provide three methods: union, difference, and intersection. This class simply provides a set of utility methods for OrderedList objects. We will call such a class a *utility* class.

An important feature of a utility class is that it does not allow for the creation of objects because there is no notion of state for the class—creation of objects is prevented by defining a *private* no-arg constructor. The java.lang.Math class is an appropriate analogy—it provides a set of methods, all static, that are used to manipulate numbers. The Math class cannot be used to create Math objects because there is no notion of a mathematical object with state.

> # UTILITY CLASS
>
> A utility class serves as a repository of static utility methods for objects of a certain kind, in which object creation is disallowed by defining a single, private no-arg constructor.

An outline of such a Merger class is shown in Figure 5.3.

```
package structures.linear;

public class Merger {

  // an inaccessible no-arg constructor
  private Merger( ) { }

  // Appends to the end of LOut, the entries of LIn starting at pos.
  private static <T extends Comparable<T>>
    void append(OrderedList LOut, OrderedList LIn, int pos) {
    while (pos < LIn.size()) {
        LOut.add(LIn.get(pos++));
    }
  }

  public static <T extends Comparable<T>>
    OrderedList<T> union(OrderedList<T> first,
            OrderedList<T> second) { ⋯ }
  public static <T extends Comparable<T>>
    OrderedList<T> difference(OrderedList<T> first,
            OrderedList<T> second) { ⋯ }
  public static <T extends Comparable<T>>
    OrderedList<T> intersection(OrderedList<T> first,
            OrderedList<T> second) { ⋯ }
}
```

FIGURE 5.3: Outline of Merger Class. A private no-arg constructor is defined to prevent creation of objects. All methods are defined static.

All methods of the Merger class are static and may be invoked via the class name. Observe how they are declared, with a T extends Comparable<T> after the static modifier, but before the return type, OrderedList<T>. Recall our discussion of static template methods in Section 1.13.5.

The **merge** algorithm is implemented in the method union:

```
01 public static <T extends Comparable<T>>
02 OrderedList<T> union(OrderedList<T> first, OrderedList<T> second) {
03
04   if (first.isEmpty()) {
05       OrderedList<T> result = new OrderedList<T>(second.size());
06       append(result, second, 0);
07       return result;
08   }
09
10   if (second.isEmpty()) {
11       OrderedList<T> result = new OrderedList<T>(first.size());
12       append(result, first, 0);
13       return result;
14   }
15
```

```
16    // neither is empty, get those fingers moving
17    int size1 = first.size();
18    int size2 = second.size();
19    OrderedList<T> result = new OrderedList<T>();
20    int firstFinger = 0, secondFinger = 0;
21    while (firstFinger < size1 && secondFinger < size2) {
22        // get the entries pointed to by the fingers
23        T firstItem = first.get(firstFinger);
24        T secondItem = second.get(secondFinger);
25        int c = firstItem.compareTo(secondItem);
26        if (c == 0) {
27            result.add(firstItem);
28            firstFinger++; secondFinger++;
29        } else if (c < 0) {
30            result.add(firstItem);
31            firstFinger++;
32        } else {
33            result.add(secondItem);
34            secondFinger++;
35        }
36    }
37
38    // tie up loose ends
39    if (firstFinger < size1) {
40        append(result, first, firstFinger);
41    }
42    if (secondFinger < size2) {
43        append(result, second, secondFinger);
44    }
45    return result;
46 }
```

The lists *L1* and *L2* of the algorithm are the parameters first and second, respectively. The list *L3* of the algorithm is the new OrderedList<T> instance returned by the method.

The first two if statements, on lines 4–8 and 10–14 respectively, check for the easy processing conditions where one of the lists is empty. In either case, the nonempty list is simply appended to the output list, and the method terminates after returning this output list. If neither list is empty, the *while* loop of the algorithm is implemented on lines 21–36.

The union method can serve as a reference for implementing the difference and intersection methods. This is followed up in the programming problems at the end of the chapter.

5.6.2 A Consolidation Class

With the Merge class at our disposal, we move forward towards our goal of implementing the list consolidation process. The lists we want to work with contain the names of people that we would store as String objects, so we will instantiate the generic OrderedList<T> class with String for T.

```
01 public class Consolidate {
02
03    static <T extends Comparable<T>> void printList(OrderedList<T> ol) {
04        T item = ol.first();
05        if (item == null) return;
06        System.out.print(item);
07        while ((item = ol.next()) != null) {
08            System.out.print(" - " + item);
09        }
10        System.out.println();
11    }
12
13    public static void main(String[] args)
14    throws java.io.IOException {
15
16        java.util.Scanner sc = new java.util.Scanner(new File(args[0]));
17        OrderedList<String> YInsList = new OrderedList<String>();
18        while (sc.hasNext()) {
19            YInsList.add(sc.next());
20        }
21        sc = new Scanner(new File(args[1]));
22        OrderedList<String> RmInsList = new OrderedList<String>();
23        while (sc.hasNext()) {
24            RmInsList.add(sc.next());
25        }
26        sc = new Scanner(new File(args[2]));
27        OrderedList<String> YDelList = new OrderedList<String>();
28        while (sc.hasNext()) {
29            YDelList.add(sc.next());
30        }
31        sc = new Scanner(new File(args[3]));
32        OrderedList<String> RmDelList = new OrderedList<String>();
33        while (sc.hasNext()) {
34            RmDelList.add(sc.next());
35        }
36
37        OrderedList<String> MergedInsList =
38                    Merger.union(YInsList, RmInsList);
39        OrderedList<String> MergedDelList =
40                    Merger.union(YDelList, RmDelList);
41        OrderedList<String> FinalList =
42                    Merger.difference(MergedInsList, MergedDelList);
43        printList(FinalList);
44    }
45 }
```

The main method reads names from input using instances of Scanner, and builds an ordered list of StringItem objects out of these names. The four lists—*YInsList* (your insert list), *YDelList* (your delete list) *RmInsList* (your roommate's insert list), *RmDelList* (your roommate's delete list)—are available in different input files, whose names are sent as arguments to the program.

5.7 OrderedList CLASS IMPLEMENTATION

Our expectation all along has been that the ordered list is implemented using an array-based structure, so that binary search on the list can be performed in $O(\log n)$ time. It is useful to have an array that can grow automatically to accommodate new entries—the java.util.ArrayList class meets this requirement. We will use an ArrayList<T> instance as a component in the OrderedList class.

Class File 5.1. *OrderedList.java*

```java
package structures.linear;

import java.util.ArrayList;
import java.util.NoSuchElementException;

public class OrderedList<T extends Comparable<T>> {

  ArrayList<T> elements;
  int cursor;

  public OrderedList(int cap) {
    elements = new ArrayList<T>(cap);
    cursor = -1;
  }
  public OrderedList() {
    elements = new ArrayList<T>();
    cursor = -1;
  }
  public int size() { return elements.size(); }
  public boolean isEmpty() { return elements.isEmpty(); }
  public void clear() { elements.clear(); }
  public T get(int pos) {
    if (pos < 0 || pos >= elements.size()) {
        throw new IndexOutOfBoundsException(
                    "pos < 0 or >= " + elements.size());
    }
    return elements.get(pos);
  }
  public T first() {
    if (elements.size() == 0) {
        return null;
    }
    cursor = 0;
    return elements.get(cursor);
  }
  public T next() {
    if (cursor < 0 || cursor == (elements.size()-1)) {
        return null;
    }
    cursor++;
    return elements.get(cursor);
  }
}
```

```
public int binarySearch(T item) { ... }
public void add(T item) { ... }
public void add(int pos, T item) { ... }
public void insert(T item) { ... }
public void remove(T item) { ... }
public void remove(int pos) { ... }
}
```

Fields and Constructors. The OrderedList class field, elements, is the component ArrayList (generic) instance that stores the list entries in order. The other field, cursor, is used to implement enumeration. The pair of constructors correspond to the underlying ArrayList constructors.

Method binarySearch. In essence, this is an implementation of the **binarySearch** algorithm of Section 5.2.2, with some smarts thrown in.

```
01 public int binarySearch(T item) {
02    if (elements.size() == 0) { // not found
03        return -1;
04    }
05    int lo=0, hi=elements.size()-1;
06    int mid=0;
07
08    while (lo <= hi) {
09        mid = (lo+hi)/2;
10        int c = item.compareTo(elements.get(mid));
11        if (c == 0) { return mid; }
12        if (c < 0) { hi = mid - 1; }
13        else { lo = mid + 1; }
14        }
15    }
16
17    if (item.compareTo(elements.get(mid)) < 0) {
18        return(-(mid+1));
19    } else {
20        return(-(mid+2));
21    }
22 }
```

The first smart move is to exit early if the list itself is empty (lines 2–4). The return value is -1 because $abs(-1) - 1 = 0$ is the position at which the target would find itself if it were added to the list.

The second smart move is the handling of the generalized failure situation, on lines 17–21, following the termination of the while loop. One of the values $-(mid + 1)$ or $-(mid + 2)$ is returned according to whether the target item is less than the mid entry or not. You may verify that these return values work correctly.

Let us now take one representative insertion method, add(int,T), and one representative deletion method, remove, to complete our discussion of the OrderedList class.

Methods to insert item.   There are two methods, add(T) and insert(T), which respectively append an item to the list, and insert it at the correct position in the list.

```java
public void add(T item) {
   int pos = elements.size();
   if (pos > 0) {
      T pred = elements.get(pos-1);
      if (item.compareTo(pred) <= 0)
      {
         throw new
         OrderViolationException();
      }
   }
   elements.add(item);
}
```

```java
public void insert(T item) {
   if (elements.size() == 0) {
      elements.add(item);
      return;
   }
   int pos = binarySearch(item);
   if (pos >= 0) {
      throw new
      OrderViolationException();
   } else {
      elements.add(-pos-1, item);
   }
}
```

The add method checks to make sure that the current item, which is the would-be predecessor of the new item, is strictly less than the latter. Otherwise, either there is an attempt to insert a duplicate (if they are equal), or there is an out-of-order situation, and an OrderViolationException is raised.

The insert method first checks for the easy case of an empty list, in which case the new item is simply added to the end. Otherwise, the correct position for the new item is found with a call to binarySearch. Remember that if binarySearch returns a positive value, it means that the target exists in the list. In insert this would mean an attempt to insert a duplicate entry, and an OrderViolationException is raised. Otherwise, if binarySearch returns a negative value, that value is used (after changing sign and subtracting 1) as the correct index of the new item, and is added with a call to the method add(int, T). The latter method is discussed below.

The method add(int, T) is different from the above insertion methods in that an index for insertion is given as an argument.

```java
public void add(int pos, T item) {
   if (pos < 0 || pos >= elements.size()) {
      throw new IndexOutOfBoundsException(
                "pos < 0 or >= " + elements.size()+1);
   }
   if (pos > 0) { // there is a predecessor
      if (item.compareTo(elements.get(pos-1)) <= 0) {
         throw new OrderViolationException();
      }
   }
   if (pos < (elements.size()-1)) { // there is a successor
      if (item.compareTo(elements.get(pos-1)) >= 0) {
         throw new OrderViolationException();
      }
   }
   elements.add(pos, item);
}
```

The first task is to ensure that the given index position is legal. Following this, a more important condition needs to be satisfied before the insertion can be accomplished: the item to be inserted must be strictly greater than its predecessor (if any), and strictly less than its successor (if any). If either of these *ordering* conditions is violated, an `Order-VioulationException` is raised.

Following is the definition of the `OrderViolationException` class.

Class File 5.2. *OrderViolationException.java*

```
01 package structures.linear;
02
03 public class OrderViolationException extends RuntimeException {
04    public OrderViolationException() {
05       super();
06    }
07
08    public OrderViolationException(String s) {
09       super(s);
10    }
11 }
```

Methods to delete item.   The two delete methods are `remove(T)` and `remove(int)`.

```
public void remove(T item) {              public void remove(int pos) {
   if (elements.size() == 0) {               if (pos < 0 ||
      throw new                                  pos >= elements.size()) {
      NoSuchElementException();                 throw new
   }                                            IndexOutOfBoundsException(
   int pos = binarySearch(item);                "pos < 0 or >= " +
   if (pos < 0) {                                elements.size());
      throw new                              }
      NoSuchElementException();             elements.remove(pos);
   }                                      }
   elements.remove(pos);
}
```

The first method uses `binarySearch` to locate the specified item. After the item is located, the `ArrayList` method `remove(int)` is invoked on `elements` to delete the item.

The second method ensures that the index is legal, following which it too invokes the `ArrayList` method `remove(int)`.

5.8   SUMMARY

- An ordered list is a linear collection of entries arranged in sorted order of keys.
- The primary advantage of an ordered list, assuming it is implemented as an array, is that searching for an entry in an ordered list using binary search is significantly faster than searching for an entry in an unordered list using sequential search.

- The primary disadvantage of an ordered list, assuming it is implemented as an array, is that adding an entry takes up to $O(n)$ time, compared to only $O(1)$ time to add an entry to an unordered list.

- The worst-case number of comparisons for binary search of an array with n entries is $2\lceil \log(n + 1)\rceil - 1$ for success, and $2\lceil \log(n + 1)\rceil$ for failure, which is $O(\log n)$ for both.

- Given two ordered lists of lengths m and n respectively, the best-case number of comparisons to merge these lists is $min(m, n)$, when all the entries of the shorter list are smaller than all the entries of the other list.

- Given two ordered lists of lengths m and n respectively, the worst-case number of comparisons to merge these lists is $m + n - 1$. This is guaranteed to occur when the last two entries of the output list are delete respectively the last entries of the input lists.

- All objects admitted to an ordered list are required to implement methods that compare pairs of objects for equality, less than, and greater than. In order to comply with this requirement, a Java interface is designed that prescribes these methods, and all ordered list objects are required to implement this interface.

- A utility class is one that serves as a repository of `static` utility methods that operate on objects of a certain type, and in which object creation is disallowed by defining a single, `private` no-arg constructor.

- The ordered list is implemented using a vector to ensure fast, $O(\log n)$, binary search.

5.9   EXERCISES

E5.1. Consider binary search on the ordered array used as an example in Section 5.2.2.
  (a) List the values according to the number of comparisons it would take to find them. In other words, list all values that can be found with one comparison, all values that can be found with three comparisons, and so on.
  (b) What is the average number of comparisons required to find any of the values in the array, assuming they are all searched with equal probabilities. (Hint: Use the answer to the first part, and the formula given in Section 4.2.1.)
  (c) What would be the average number of comparisons if you were to use *sequential search*, instead?

E5.2. The worst-case number of comparisons for binary search of an array with n entries is $2\lceil \log(n + 1)\rceil - 1$ for success.
  (a) What is the worst-case number of comparisons for success for $n = 16$? Let this value be k.
  (b) What is the *smallest value* of n for which the worst-case number of comparisons for success is $k + 2$?

E5.3. Suppose we have an ordered list of n entries, and we search for a target t in it, using the following *modified sequential search* algorithm:

```
set current to first entry
while (current is within list) do
  if (t == current entry) break    { success }
  else if (t < current entry) break   { failure }
  else set current to next entry
  endif
endwhile
```

(a) What is the worst-case number of comparisons for a *successful* search?

(b) What is the average number of comparisons for an *unsuccessful* search? Assume that all failure possibilities are equally likely. Clearly show your derivation. (Hint: determine all the possible "positions" at which failure can occur, and the number of comparisons for each position. Then apply the formula for average comparisons given in Section 4.2.1, using equal probabilities.)

E5.4. The **binarySearch** algorithm of Section 5.2.2 first checks whether the target is equal to the current middle entry, before proceeding to the left or right halves if required. There is another variant of binary search which postpones the equality check until the very end. This version is presented below—we call it **lazy binary search:**

Algorithm lazyBinarySearch(A, n, t)

$$left \leftarrow 0$$
$$right \leftarrow n - 1$$
while ($left < right$) do
    $mid \leftarrow (left + right)/2$
    if ($t > A[mid]$) then
        $left \leftarrow mid + 1$
    else
        $right \leftarrow mid$
    endif
endwhile

if ($t == A[left]$) then
    display "found at position", *left*
else
    display "not found"
endif

(a) Trace this algorithm on the example array of Section 5.2.2 with 19 as the target. How many comparisons does it make?

(b) Trace the algorithm on this array with 26 as the target. What is the number of comparisons made?

(c) How many comparisons does this algorithm makes in general for an array of size *n*? Give an exact figure, not big *O*.

(d) Under what conditions is it preferable to use this version instead of the original binary search version?

E5.5. Given an ordered list, A, of size *n*, and an unordered list, B, of size *m*, you are required to find their intersection (i.e., the set of elements common to both A and B). Assume that neither A nor B has duplicate entries.

Give the running time, in big O, for each of the following ways of computing the intersection, assuming that the ordered list is implemented using an array.

(a) For every element in A, find a match in B.

(b) For every element in B, find a match in A. Under what conditions is the first method more efficient than the second?

E5.6. Suppose you are given two ordered lists of integers:

$$2, 6, 7, 9, 25, 32$$

and

$$-5, 6, 10, 12, 17, 25, 35, 45, 55, 63$$

How many comparisons (exact, not big O) would it take to obtain the following, using the two-finger **merge** algorithm of Section 5.5.1, or a minor variation of it?

(a) A merged ordered list that contains no duplicates (i.e. *union*).

(b) A "merged" ordered list that contains only those integers in the first list that are not in the second list (i.e. *difference*).

(c) A "merged" ordered list that contains only those integers that are common to both lists (i.e. *intersection*).

E5.7. In the running-time analysis of the **merge** algorithm in Section 5.5.1, we said that whether or not to count the direct copies of entries to the output list depended on how the ordered list was implemented. Considering that the ordered list is implemented using an array, how many entries would be directly copied to the output in each of the cases of *union, difference,* and *intersection* in Exercise E5.6 above?

E5.8. Suppose we now make the following assumptions: (a) the ordered list is implemented using a *linked list;* (b) two ordered lists are merged in such a way that the nodes of the input lists are physically moved (not copied) to the merged list in the appropriate order. The (leftover) input lists are no longer needed after the merge is done.

Then, considering comparisons as well as access or update of node references as basic operations, how many basic operations would it take to do each of the *union, difference,* and *intersection* operations of Exercise E5.6? (Hint: appending a linked list to another does not require stepping through all the nodes.)

E5.9. If the ordered list were to be implemented as a linked list, what would be the running times of the operations *add, remove,* and *contains*. Note that *add* must add a new entry to the appropriate position in the list.

E5.10. Assume that the ExpenseList class of Section 4.4, which was an unordered list, is maintained as an *ordered list* instead, using the date field of every Expense entry as the ordering criterion. In other words, ExpenseList is arranged in chronological order of expenses. Instead of using a List as a component, the ExpenseList class now uses an OrderedList.

(a) Describe clearly (in English or pseudo-code) how you would reimplement the method amtSpentDuring.

(b) For a list of n entries, what would be the running time of your implementation if there are d expense entries in the list for the given time period?

E5.11. Now assume that ExpenseList is maintained in alphabetical order of items, and thus, instead of using a List component, the ExpenseList class uses an OrderedList component.

(a) Describe clearly (in English or pseudo-code) how you would reimplement the method amtSpentOn.

(b) What would be the running time (in big O) of your implementation, for a list of n expense entries and k distinct items?

E5.12. An alternative algorithm for searching on an ordered array of size N works as follows: It divides the array into M contiguous blocks each of size B. For simplicity you may assume that B divides N without remainder. Here is the algorithm to search for a key k:

> Compare k with the entries B, $2B$, $3B$, and so on. In other words, compare k with the last entry in each block. If k is equal to the entry $i * B$ for some $i \leq M$, then stop with success. Otherwise, if $k > M * B$, stop with failure.
>
> If neither of the above conditions is true, then it must be that $k < i * B$ for some $i \leq M$. Perform a sequential search on the block of entries from $(i - 1) * B + 1$ to $i * B - 1$. Stop with success if k is equal to some entry in this block, otherwise stop with failure.

(a) What is the worst-case number of searches for success?

(b) What is the *average* number of comparisons for a successful search on an array of size N? Assume that all the entries in the array are searched with equal probability.

E5.13. At the end of Section 5.5.1 we stated that the worst-case number of comparisons, $m + n - 1$, for merging two ordered lists of length m and n, would occur if the last output entry is from one list, and the second-to-last output entry is from the other. Argue that this statement is true.

E5.14. Integers in computers are represented in a fixed extent of memory. The typical width of an `int` is 4 bytes. This obviously limits the numerical value of an integer one can store and manipulate in a computer—the typical value works out to about 12 decimal places. One way to get around this limitation is to represent an integer as a sequence of digits, very similar to the polynomial representation of Section 3.1. Then one can use integers of as many digits as one wishes.

If you were to build a class called `BigInt` to implement an unlimited-width integer, what operations would your class support? List the name of each operation, along with a brief description of its function.

E5.15. A polynomial may be represented as an ordered list as follows: for every term in the polynomial, there is one entry in the ordered list, consisting of the term's coefficient *and* degree. The entries are ordered according to descending values of degree; zero-coefficient terms are not stored.

(a) Show, by drawing a figure, how the polynomial

$$4x^5 - 2x^3 + 2x + 3$$

may be represented as an ordered list.

(b) Give *efficient* algorithms for the following based on this ordered-list representation of a polynomial.

  (i) Evaluating a polynomial at a given x value.

  (ii) Adding two polynomials to give a third: $r = p + q$.

  (iii) Multiplying two polynomials to give a third: $r = p * q$.

(c) Compute the running times (big O) of the above algorithms.

5.10 PROGRAMMING PROBLEMS

P5.1. Suppose you were to write an application that dealt with 2D geometry. One of the components of your application is a `Point` class of which there will be many instances that you would like to store in an `OrderedList`. Implement this `Point` class, defining fields and methods as appropriate. Two points are equal if they have the same x and y coordinates. A point is less than another point if its distance from the origin is less than that of the other.

P5.2. You can implement an "inverse" phone book by storing phone numbers, and associated names, in an `OrderedList`. That is, the phone number is the key by which the phone book is ordered. Implement a `Phone` class that has a phone number and an associated name (owner of the number) so that its instances can be stored in an `OrderedList`. Pay particular attention to how you will implement the `compareTo` method.

P5.3. Having implemented the `Phone` class in Problem P5.2, define a class called `PhoneBook` that uses an `OrderedList` instance to store `Phone` instances. Flesh out the class as follows:

  (a) Implement a no-arg constructor that sets the `OrderedList` component to empty.

  (b) Implement a method that adds a `Phone` instance to the phone book.

  (c) Implement a method that removes a `Phone` instance from the phone book.

  (d) Implement a method that searches for a `Phone` instance in the phone book and returns the associated name. This is the "inverse" look-up.

Each of these methods should run as fast as you can make it.

P5.4. Suppose you had to implement both a regular phone book (ordered by name associated with phone number) and an inverse phone book with the same set of phone number–name combinations. The `Phone` class you implemented in Problem P5.2 is used for the inverse phone book. How will you design a class that can be used for the regular phone book? The two classes are required to share as much code as possible either by inheritance or by some other means. Design such a pair of classes—you may keep the `Phone` class as is, or you can change it if you want to meet the new requirement.

P5.5. Write an additional `OrderedList` class method:

```
int lazyBinarySearch(T item)
```

that would implement the `lazyBinarySearch` algorithm of Exercise E5.4.

P5.6. Write a method:

```
boolean blockSearch(T item)
```

that would implement the search technique of Exercise E5.12.

P5.7. Complete the `Merger` class of Figure 5.3 by implementing the `intersection` and `difference` methods. Use the implementation of the `union` method as a reference.

P5.8. Suppose we had two linked lists, `Node<T extends Comparable<T>> L1` and `Node<T extends Comparable<T>> L2`, where `L1` is a reference to the first node of one linked list, and `L2`, a reference to the first node of the other. Use the following definition of a linked list node:

```
public class Node<T extends Comparable<T>> {
  public T data;
  public Node<T> next;
  public Node(T data, Node<T> next) {
    this.data = data;
    this.next = next;
  }
}
```

The entries in these linked lists are in sorted (ascending) order. Write a method merge:

```
<T extends Comparable<T>> Node<T> merge(Node<T> L1, Node<T> L2)
```

that would merge these linked lists by simply moving the nodes of L1 and L2 into the merged list, without using extra space for nodes or entries in the nodes. At the end of the method, L1 and L2 are no longer relevant, and the returned entity is a reference to the first node of the merged list.

P5.9. The following problems mirror Exercise E5.10 and Exercise E5.11. Assume that the expenses field of the ExpenseList class is now an OrderedList object.

(a) Implement your design for the method amtSpentDuring of Exercise E5.10, assuming that expenses are ordered chronologically.

(b) Implement your design for the method amtSpentOn of Exercise E5.11, assuming that expenses are stored in alphabetical order of items.

P5.10. Which of the methods of the OrderedList class would change if the entries of the list were to be maintained in *descending* order of values? Reimplement these methods, and analyze their running times in big O.

P5.11. Reimplement the OrderedList class using a LinkedList instead of an ArrayList as the component that maintains the entries. Analyze the running times of the methods in big O.

P5.12. In Problem P4.13, you implemented WordCount using an unordered list. Reimplement that program using an OrderedList instance to store words and their associated counts. Which implementation would be faster? Explain, clearly describing every parameter that affects the running time in either implementation.

CHAPTER 6

Queue

The queue data structure uses an underlying linear storage organization, while presenting an abstraction that models real-life queues. A classic application is the print queue in a computing environment, which we will study at length in this chapter.

Learning Objectives

- Describe the behavior of a queue.
- Enumerate the primary operations supported by a queue.
- Learn about the UNIX print queue, the main commands that can be issued to it, and how these commands may be mapped to the operations of the queue data structure.
- Understand the public interface of a queue class in Java and the running times of its methods.
- Implement a print queue class in Java using the queue class.
- Study the implementation of the queue class, and the tradeoffs involved in choosing between candidate storage components.

6.1 QUEUE PROPERTIES

The name of this data structure says it all. Its behavior mimics that of our everyday queues—lines in which people "queue up" to be served, in a *first-come, first-served* manner.

People join a queue at its end, or *rear,* and leave the queue after reaching the *front* and being served. On the other hand, people do change their minds after being in the queue for a while, and leave abruptly without reaching the front and being served. This is quite reasonable, and it *does not violate* the first-come, first-served policy because the person who leaves the queue before reaching the front does not get served.

As another example, consider the typical computing environment in which queues are used to process requests for service on shared resources. One such shared resource is a printer, to which users submit print jobs that are serviced using a first-come, first-served policy. The computer system enforces this policy by maintaining a print queue.

The print queue is actually maintained by a program called a *print spooler*. The spooler is in charge of adding any newly arrived print job to the queue at the rear (*enqueueing*), and taking a print job off the front of the queue (*dequeueing*) and sending it to the printer when the printer becomes free.

A job that is in the queue may be dequeued before it reaches the front. This could happen if a user gets impatient. A user, for instance, may decide to dequeue the job and either resubmit it later or submit it to a different printer.

The first-come, first-served policy is also known as *first-in, first-out*, or FIFO for short.

QUEUE

A queue is a linear collection of entries in which, for every pair of entries x and y, if x leaves from the front of the queue before y, then x must have entered the queue before y.

Note that the FIFO policy is applicable only for entries that are served; that is, they reach the front of the queue and are then removed. Entries may leave the queue without reaching the front; in this case, the FIFO rule does not apply. In other words, x may enter the queue before y, and yet y may leave the queue before x, provided y is not served.

Operations. Table 6.1 lists a set of operations a queue is expected to support.

TABLE 6.1: Queue operations.

Operation	Description
Enqueue	Add an entry to the rear of the queue
Dequeue	Remove the entry at the front of the queue
Enumerate	List all the entries in the queue
IsEmpty	Tell if the queue is empty
Size	Tell how many entries are in the queue

The operations *enqueue* and *dequeue* define the queue. While one could design a queue class with just these defining operations plus a bare minimum that includes enumeration, empty check, and size, other operations may be needed in order to effectively serve a wide range of applications that use a queue. One such application is the print queue in a UNIX environment.

6.2   UNIX PRINT QUEUE

In a UNIX operating system environment, a user who wants to submit a print job types the `lpr` command, at which time the job gets queued up at the printer.[1] Following is the simplest form of the `lpr` command:

`lpr` *filename*

Usually, before issuing the `lpr` command, a user will check the status of the printer queue using the `lpq` command:[2]

`lpq`

The output of this command looks something like the following:

	Owner	**Job**	**File**
active:	swilliams	309	wimbledon
	ronaldinho	300	wcsoccer
	marionjones	312	fleetfoot
	swilliams	267	usopen

All the current entries in the queue are listed: the very first entry is currently being printed (*active*), and the entries following it will be printed in the order shown.[3] Each job is given a unique integer id (second column); apart from this, a job has an associated owner name, and the name of the file to be printed in that job. Note that the same user may have more than one job waiting in the queue.

Occasionally, the printer will run into trouble and will sit there without printing anything until somebody notices the problem and fixes the printer. During this time, the print queue begins to grow, and users may want to pull their print requests out. To delete their print requests, they would have to issue the `lprm` command.[4] Here is the first version,

`lprm`

which deletes the job that is currently active (being printed), provided it belongs to the person who issued the `lprm` command. For example, given the status of the printer queue shown above, only swilliams can issue the `lprm` command and succeed in removing the active job. A variation of the `lprm` command is the following:

`lprm` *jobid*

This removes the job whose id is *jobid,* again provided that it belongs to the user who issued the `lprm` command. Last, the variant:

`lprm --`

removes *all* the jobs owned by the user who issued this command.

---

1. Some UNIX versions use the `lp` command.
2. Some UNIX versions use the `lpstat` command.
3. Different UNIXes may have somewhat different styles of print queue display.
4. Some UNIX versions use the `cancel` command.

Clearly, while the *lpr* and *lpq* commands can be directly supported by the *enqueue* and *enumeration* operations of the queue data structure, only the simplest version of *lprm* (remove active job) can be supported by *dequeue*.

The other operations can, in principle, be implemented in terms of the *dequeue* and *enqueue* operations. However, this is an unnecessary burden on the clients of the queue, and may result in making their implementation inefficient. The more advisable course of action would be to have the queue support selective removal of entries from anywhere in the queue, as well as other operations that may be useful in other applications.

Let us turn our attention to the public interface of a queue class that attempts to achieve this compromise.

6.3   A QUEUE CLASS

Figure 6.1 shows the public interface of a generic queue class.

Class structures.linear.Queue

Constructors

  Queue( )
    Creates an empty queue.

Methods

$O(1)$	**void enqueue(T item)**	
	Adds specified item at the rear of this queue.	
$O(1)$	**T dequeue( )**	
	Removes and returns the item at the front of this queue.	
	Throws **NoSuchElementException** if queue is empty.	
$O(1)$	**int size( )**	
	Returns the number of items in this queue.	
$O(1)$	**boolean isEmpty( )**	
	Returns true if this queue is empty, false otherwise.	
$O(n)$	**int positionOf(T item)**	
	Returns the position of the specified item in this queue, if found, and -1 if not found. Position 0 is the front of the queue.	
$O(1)$	**void clear( )**	
	Removes all the elements in this queue (i.e., empties this queue).	
$O(n)$	**void remove(T item)**	
	Removes first occurrence (from front) of specified item from this queue. Throws **NoSuchElementException** if item is not in the queue.	
$O(n)$	**void removeAll(T item)**	
	Removes all occurrences of specified item from this queue. Throws **NoSuchElementException** if item is not in the queue.	
$O(1)$	**T first( )**	
	Returns the first item in the queue (front), null if the queue is empty.	
$O(1)$	**T next( )**	
	Returns the next item in the queue relative to a previous call to **first** or **next.** Returns null if the end of the queue is reached.	

FIGURE 6.1: A Generic Queue Class. Only the public interface is shown. Running times assume an implementation that maintains direct references to the front and rear, and a running count of number of items, *n*, in queue.

The methods enqueue, dequeue, first, next, isEmpty, and size implement the basic operations listed in Table 6.1. Method positionOf is useful to examine the progress of a specific entry through the queue.

One may think of a queue as a specialized (restricted) unordered list in that the entries are not ordered with respect to any of their attributes. Except for the methods dequeue and positionOf, all the other methods supported by this Queue class have their functional counterparts in the List class of Section 4.3. Method enqueue is identical in functionality to the List class method add, and the other methods are identically named in both Queue and List.

Running times of methods.   The fundamental operations on a queue are performed at its rear (enqueue) or front (dequeue). An efficient implementation would maintain a *direct reference* to the rear, and another to the front, making these positions accessible in one step—that is, in $O(1)$ time. Therefore, the methods enqueue and dequeue can be implemented in $O(1)$ time.

Moreover, an implementation can maintain a running count of the number of entries in the queue, incrementing it by one when an item is enqueued, and decrementing by one when an item is dequeued. Thus, the methods size and isEmpty can also be implemented in $O(1)$ time.

Apart from the running times of the methods already discussed above, those of the other methods follow from the running times of the same-named unordered list methods listed in Figure 4.2. Note that method positionOf implements a sequential search on the queue.

6.4 A `PrintQueue` CLASS USING QUEUE

We described the operations of a UNIX print queue in Section 6.2. The time has come to concretize that discussion by building a working print queue class. Figure 6.2 shows the public interface of this class, called PrintQueue. This class is in a package we develop called apps.linear.unixPrinter, which contains other support classes to be discussed shortly.

Every entry in the print queue will encapsulate three attributes of a print job: its job id, the owner of the job, and the name of the file that needs to be printed. The methods of the PrintQueue class will be implemented by calling appropriate Queue class methods to reuse as much code as possible.

In designing this class we encounter the same issue as for the ExpenseList class in Section 4.4: we would want to search for entries in the queue based on different search criteria at different times. For instance, the second version of lrpm listed in Figure 6.2 searches the queue entries matching both owner name and job id, while the third version, lprmAll, searches only on the owner name.

We know what the print queue has to do to deal with this issue: follow the strategy outlined in Section 4.4.5, specifically that in Figure 4.5, where we had a basic Expense class from which we subclassed three other classes.

Job class hierarchy.   Here we will define a basic Job class that will stand for the type of all objects in the queue. In other words, whenever a new job is submitted to the queue, it will be enqueued as a Job object.

Class apps.linear.unixPrinter.PrintQueue

Constructors

PrintQueue( )
>Creates an empty print queue.

Methods

void lpr(String owner, int jobId, String file)
>Enqueues a job with the specified owner name, job id, and file name.

void lpq(PrintWriter pw)
>Prints all the entries in this queue.

void lprm(String owner)
>Removes the active job at the front of this queue if its owner name
>matches the specified owner name; throws **NoSuchElementException** otherwise.

void lprm(String owner, int jobId)
>Removes the job with the specified jobId from this queue if its owner
>name matches the specified owner name; throws **NoSuchElementException** otherwise.

void lprmAll(String owner)
>Removes all jobs in this queue that have been submitted by specified owner;
>throws **NoSuchElementException** if there is no matching job.

FIGURE 6.2: **PrintQueue: A UNIX Print Queue Class.** The public interface is shown.

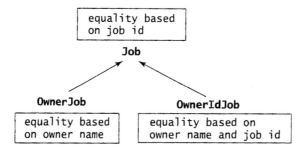

FIGURE 6.3: **Job Class Hierarchy.** The Job class overrides the equals method of its superclass, Object. The classes OwnerJob and OwnerIdJob are subclasses of Job that override the equals method inherited from Job.

From this Job class we will subclass two other classes, OwnerJob and OwnerIdJob. The equals method of the OwnerJob class will compare owner names, while that of the OwnerIdJob class will compare owner names as well as job ids. Since the job id is the only unique identifier for every job, the Job class's equals method will compare job ids only. This class hierarchy is illustrated in Figure 6.3.

These classes are helpers of the PrintQueue class and are not visible to the clients of PrintQueue. Consequently, they are not implemented as public classes. The complete definitions of the Job, OwnerJob, and OwnerIdJob appear below, in the file *Job.java*.

Class File 6.1. *Job.java*

```java
package apps.linear.unixPrinter;

class Job {
  String owner;
  int id;
  String file;

  Job(String ownerName, int jobId, String fileName) {
    owner = ownerName;
    id = jobId;
    file = fileName;
  }
  public String toString() {
    return new String(owner + " " + id + " " + file);
  }
  public boolean equals(Object other) {
    if ((other != null) && (other instanceof Job)) {
        //equality based on job id only
        Job another = (Job)other;
        return (id == another.id);
    }
    return false;
  }
}

class OwnerJob extends Job {
  OwnerJob(String owner, int jobId, String fileName) {
    super(owner, jobId, fileName);
  }
  public boolean equals(Object other) {
    if ((other != null) && (other instanceof Job)) {
        //equality based on job owner only
        Job another = (Job)other;
        return (owner.equals(another.owner));
    }
    return false;
  }
}

class IdOwnerJob extends Job {
  IdOwnerJob(String owner, int jobId, String fileName) {
    super(owner, jobId, fileName);
  }
  public boolean equals(Object other) {
    if ((other != null) && (other instanceof Job)) {
        //equality based on both owner and id
        Job another = (Job)other;
        return (owner.equals(another.owner) &&
                id == another.id);
    }
    return false;
  }
}
```

Note that `toString` and `equals` are both declared `public`, even though the classes themselves are not public. The reason is that these methods override their `Object` class counterparts; an overriding method cannot provide less accessibility than the overridden method, and both `toString` and `equals` are declared `public` in the `Object` class.

ACCESSIBILITY OF AN OVERRIDING METHOD IN JAVA

Suppose class B extends class A. Then any method in B that overrides an inherited method from A cannot be less accessible than the inherited method.

Armed with all the proper tools, we are now ready to implement the `PrintQueue` class. The complete class code follows.

Class File 6.2. *PrintQueue.java*

```java
package apps.linear.unixPrinter;

import java.util.NoSuchElementException;
import java.io.PrintWriter;
import structures.linear.Queue;

public class PrintQueue {
  Queue<Job> printQ;

  public PrintQueue() {
    printQ = new Queue<Job>();
  }
  public void lpr(String owner, int jobId, String file) {
    printQ.enqueue(new Job(owner,jobId,file));
  }
  public void lpq(PrintWriter pw) {
    Job job = printQ.first();
    while (job != null) {
        pw.println(job);
        job = printQ.next();
    }
  }
  public void lprm(String owner, int jobId) {
    if (printQ.isEmpty()) {
        throw new NoSuchElementException();
    }
    // remove entry that matches owner and id
    printQ.remove(new IdOwnerJob(owner, jobId, null));
  }
  public void lprm(String owner) {
    if (printQ.isEmpty()) {
        throw new NoSuchElementException();
    }
    Job front = printQ.first();
    if (owner.equals(front.owner)) {
        printQ.dequeue();
```

```
    } else {
        throw new NoSuchElementException();
    }
  }
  public void lprmAll(String owner) {
    if (printQ.isEmpty()) {
        throw new NoSuchElementException();
    }
    // remove all entries with matching owner
    printQ.removeAll(new OwnerJob(owner, 0, null));
  }
}
```

Fields and constructors.   The only field is a Queue<Job> object, printQ, that holds the entries in the print queue. The constructor, therefore, simply creates an empty printQ.

Method lpr   The method lpr accepts all the required information needed to add a new job to the print queue, constructs a Job object out of this information, and passes it on to printQ.enqueue.

Method lpq   Method lpq is a simple output function that involves enumerating and printing all the entries of printQ. Since each entry is a Job object, printing it out will automatically lead the compiler to invoke the Job class method toString that lists the owner, id, and file.

Versions of lprm   The different versions of lprm primarily illustrate the context-dependent implementation of the generic equality that we have repeatedly come across.
    The version of lprm that dequeues an active job based on the owner's name:

```
public void lprm(String owner)
```

is actually the odd version out.
    The other two have much more in common in the way they implement equality: they both need to create a new object of a specific type (OwnerJob or OwnerIdJob), depending on whether only the owner names are to be compared for equality, or both owner name and job id are to be used in the comparison.

Running times of methods.   The following table summarizes the running times of the PrintQueue methods.

PrintQueue Method	Queue Method Invoked	Running Time
lpr	enqueue	$O(1)$
lpq	first, next	$O(n)$
lprm(owner)	first, dequeue	$O(1)$
lprm(owner,jobid)	remove	$O(n)$
lprmAll(owner)	removeAll	$O(n)$

The running times of the `PrintQueue` methods depend on the running times of the `Queue` methods that are invoked. Figure 6.1 listed the running times of the `Queue` methods. So, for instance, `lpr` simply invokes `enqueue`, and since the running time of `enqueue` is $O(1)$, that of `lpr` is also $O(1)$. On the other hand, `lpq` invokes `first`, and then repeatedly invokes `next`, for a total time of $O(n)$.

Let us go on to an implementation of the `Queue` class, once again discovering how code reuse by composition makes for an easy implementation.

6.5   QUEUE CLASS IMPLEMENTATION

There are two main choices of tools available with which we can build the `Queue` class. One choice is to use an array-based contiguous storage scheme that lets us perform direct access of any position in $O(1)$ time. The other choice is to use a linked list. Let us examine both choices.

6.5.1   Design 1: Using Array-Based Storage

Array list.   Since a queue can grow dynamically, we can use `ArrayList` to accommodate growth on demand. Assume that we fix the lower end of an array list (the 0-th position) as the front of the queue, and the higher end as the rear. Two indices, *front* and *rear,* are maintained to point to the respective ends of the queue.

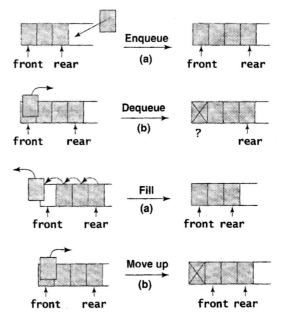

When an item is enqueued, the rear index is advanced by one, and the item is filled in at the new position. But when we dequeue an entry, the 0-th position becomes empty.

How do we handle this empty spot?

One solution is to fill up the "hole" created by the dequeued entry by moving all the entries over by one position toward the beginning of the array list, as illustrated by (a). This would be a very expensive proposition if the queue had a large number of entries. Each dequeue operation would take $O(n)$ time—a very inefficient implementation.

On the other hand, instead of filling up the hole, we could simply move the front index up by one every time an entry is dequeued, as illustrated by (b).

This maintains an $O(1)$ time to dequeue, but leads to another problem, namely, a significant wastage of space. Every time an entry is dequeued, the space it occupied is essentially given up for lost—that space is never used again.

Here is a special case in which two entries are enqueued, following which there is a sequence of one enqueue and one dequeue, repeated several times.

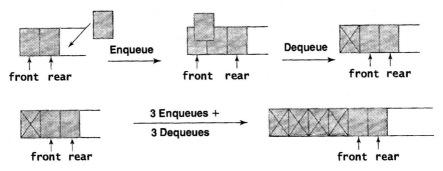

Every enqueue and dequeue pair results in yet another array location being wasted. The more inserts and deletes there are, the more locations will be wasted. The solution to the problem is to use the second approach (moving the front index up) on a fixed-length array, and *recycle* space. This is called the *circular array* approach.

Circular array. The top half shows how, when the end of the array is hit, the subsequent enqueues wrap back to the beginning of the array to reclaim lost space.

The bottom half shows a conceptual view of the circular array, with the indexes of the array positions labeled in the inner circle. There are two unused positions, 1 and 2.

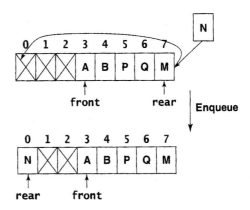

While wrapping back is a reasonable option, there are several issues that need to be examined. First, in the noncircular case we could tell exactly how many entries there were in the queue by simply looking at the difference between the front and rear indexes (plus one), since the rear index was always greater than the front. In the case of the circular array, this is no longer true—when

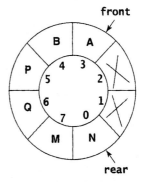

the queue wraps back, the rear index becomes *less than* the front index!

Now how can we tell how many entries there are in the queue? If the rear index is less than the front index, then the gap between the rear and front is the *unused space*. Since we can find the amount of this unused space by subtracting the rear index from the front index (minus one), we can compute the used space by subtracting this unused space from the length of the array. In the example, *before enqueueing,* the unused space is $(front - rear) - 1 = (3 - 1) - 1 = 1$, and the used space is therefore $8 - 1 = 7$.

But that's not all. When we start out with an empty queue, what do we set the front and rear indexes to be? It may be easier to decide this if we assume that one entry has been enqueued. Then we know that the front and rear indexes must both be 0, the first position of the array, since the front and rear are the same for a single-entry queue. Now what happens if this entry is dequeued? The front index is advanced by one—it becomes 1. The rear index remains at 0—it is an empty queue. Therefore, *in an empty queue,* the rear index is one less than the front index. In fact, we can choose front and rear to be *any* pair of positions such that the rear is one position less than the front when we start out with an empty queue.

Suppose we start with an empty queue and keep enqueueing items until there is no more space. Then the queue is full, and the rear index keeps advancing until it ends up coming to one position behind the front index, *just as in the case of the empty queue.*

An empty queue looks the same as a full queue when you inspect the rear and front indices.

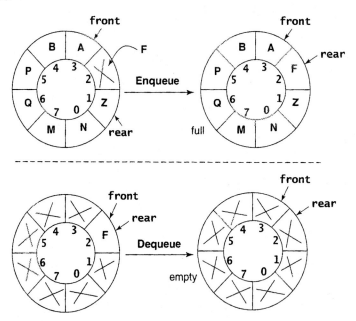

When the rear index is two positions behind the front, there is one unused space. When an entry is enqueued, the rear advances to one position behind front, and the queue is full.

When the rear and front indexes are at the same position, the queue has one entry. When this entry is dequeued, the front advances, so that once again rear is one position behind front, but this time the queue is empty.

In other words, if you take a snapshot of the queue indexes at some point in time, you will not be able to tell an empty queue from a full queue. There is a simple solution to this problem: keep a count of the number of entries in the queue, starting with 0 when the queue is created. Then, every time an item is enqueued or dequeued, increase or decrease the count by one, respectively.

All the issues we have discussed until now require careful bookkeeping to get things straight. A more serious issue with using an array is the inherent space underestimation or overestimation problem. Since the array is to be allocated a priori, we run into the problem of wasting space because we have allocated too much of it, or of running out of space too soon.

In sum, using array-based storage, whether an array list or a circular array, comes with drawbacks that may be unacceptable. A more attractive solution is to use a linked list instead.

6.5.2   Design 2: Using `LinkedList`

If we use a linked list, we have the `LinkedList` class ready at hand. To implement the Queue class, we can draw on our experience of building the `List` class in Section 4.7 using a `LinkedList` object.

Class File 6.3. *Queue.java*

```
package structures.linear;

import java.util.NoSuchElementException;

public class Queue<T> {

  LinkedList<T> list;
  int cursor;

  public Queue() { list = new LinkedList<T>(); cursor = -1; }
  public void enqueue(T item) { list.add(item); }
  public T dequeue() {
    if (list.isEmpty()) {
        throw new NoSuchElementException();
    }
    return list.removeAt(0);
  }
  public int size() { return list.size(); }
  public boolean isEmpty() { return list.isEmpty(); }
  public int positionOf(T item) { return list.indexOf(item); }
  public void clear) { list.clear(); }
  public void remove(T item) { list.remove(item); }
  public void removeAll(T item) { list.removeAll(item); }
  public T first() {
    if (list.size() == 0) { return null; }
    cursor = 0;
    return list.getAt(cursor);
  }
  public T next() {
    if (cursor < 0 || cursor == (list.size()-1)) { return null; }
    cursor++;
    return list.getAt(cursor);
  }
}
```

All the hard work we did to build the LinkedList class is really paying off. What could be easier than this implementation? Recall that the LinkedList class used a circular linked list for its implementation, and the add method added a new item to the end of the linked list. So the queue is a linked list with its front at the first node, and its rear at the last node.

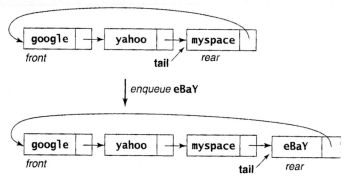

There are a couple of implementation details regarding exceptions that need to be highlighted.

Exception filtering.   The body of the dequeue method could have been alternatively implemented as follows:

```
return list.removeAt(0);
```

In other words, without the if statement. However, in this version, if the linked list were empty, this line of code would get an IndexOutOfBoundsException thrown, as documented in the LinkedList interface of Figure 4.6. This exception would then be passed along to the client that called the dequeue method, resulting in confusion—the client does not supply an index argument to the dequeue method, so what is the meaning of the IndexOutOfBoundsException?

This confusion can be cleared up by supplying a more meaningful exception to the client. The dequeue method first checks whether the list is empty, and if so, it throws the NoSuchElementException, which whether tells the client that there is no element to be dequeued. Only if the list is not empty is the subsequent code executed, which at this point is guaranteed not to throw the IndexOutOfBoundsException exception. What we have done here is to filter the IndexOutOfBoundsException.

FILTERING EXCEPTIONS

When class *A* reuses an instance of class *B* as a component, exceptions thrown by methods of *B* may have to be caught by *A* in order to reinterpret them for clients of *A*. We call this *filtering* an exception. The reason for filtering is that to the clients of *A*, the fact that *A* contains *B* may be hidden, and an exception thrown by *B* that makes its way to the client of *A* without being filtered may not impart appropriate meaning to the client.

6.6   SUMMARY

- The queue data structure implements the first-in, first-out (FIFO) abstraction.
- A queue is a linear collection of entries in which, for every pair of entries x and y, if x leaves from the front of the queue before y, then x must have entered the queue before y.
- An entry may leave a queue before reaching the front. In that case, the entry is not served.
- There are two fundamental operations supported by a queue: enqueue and dequeue.
- A queue class may provide more than just the fundamental enqueue and dequeue operations to facilitate ease of use.
- A queue may be viewed as a specialized or restricted unordered list. Several unordered list operations are also applicable to the queue.
- A print queue in UNIX can be implemented using the queue data structure.
- Implementing a UNIX print queue using the Queue class requires the Queue clients to build a class hierarchy that will enable the matching of a queue entry against a specific item based on either job id, job owner, or both.
- If class B extends class A, then any method in B that overrides an inherited method from A cannot be less accessible than the inherited method.
- An array list may be used to implement the queue, but this would result in an implementation that is either inefficient in time (every dequeue takes $O(n)$ time) or wasteful of space usage.
- A circular array may be used to implement a queue, with the attendant problem of overestimating or underestimating the space requirement associated with the static allocation of an array.
- A linked list is better than either an array list or a circular array to implement a queue. The Queue<T> class can then use a LinkedList<T> object as its storage component.
- When class A reuses an instance of class B as a component, exceptions thrown by methods of B may have to be caught by A in order to reinterpret them for clients of A. We call this *filtering* an exception. The reason for filtering is that to the clients of A, the fact that A contains B may be hidden, and an exception thrown by B that makes its way to the client of A without being filtered may not impart appropriate meaning to the client.

6.7   EXERCISES

E6.1. Write an algorithm that would read a sequence of characters from the input, terminated by a newline character, and enqueue them in a queue.

E6.2. Suppose a queue is maintained as a circular array, as described in Section 6.5.1. Assuming the array is of length 7, show the contents of the array, as well as the positions of the indexes *rear* and *front,* at the end of each of the following steps:

    (a) Start with an empty queue, setting the front index to 0, and the rear index to an appropriate value.

    (b) Enqueue the characters A, C, D, F.

    (c) Dequeue three characters.

    (d) Enqueue the characters W, P, Q, R, X, J.

    (e) Dequeue four characters.

    (f) Dequeue the rest of the characters in the queue.

E6.3. Repeat Exercise E6.2 assuming that the queue is maintained as an array list. How many array list positions are left unused at the end of the operations?

E6.4. Repeat Exercise E6.2 assuming that the queue is maintained as a circular linked list. What will be the equivalent of the front and rear indexes in the linked list? Show the linked list at the end of each step.

E6.5. Suppose the queue data structure is implemented using a circular array. What would be the running times (big O) of each of the queue operations listed in the public interface of the Queue class in Figure 6.1? Assume that the queue maintains a running count of the number of entries in the queue at any time.

E6.6. A *double-ended queue* is a special type of queue in which adds and deletes are supported at both ends, meaning that *enqueue* and *dequeue* can be done at the front as well as the rear. Thus, it supports four fundamental operations: *enqueueFront*, *enqueueRear*, *dequeueFront*, and *dequeueRear*.

Discuss the suitability of each of the following storage implementations for a double-ended queue, arguing as we did in Section 6.5.

    (a) Array list

    (b) Array

    (c) Linked List

    (d) Doubly Linked List

E6.7. Suppose you were given a queue that *did not* include operations for enumeration, and you wanted to define an operation called *peek* that would return the entry at the front of the queue without removing it. Write an algorithm for *peek* in terms of the operations *enqueue, dequeue*, and *isEmpty*. You may use other, temporary queues, if necessary. What is the running time of your algorithm in big O?

E6.8. Suppose we consider implementing an ordered list using a queue. What would be some major drawbacks of this approach?

E6.9. Suppose there is a long line of people at a check-out counter in a store. Suddenly, another one opens up, and to ensure fairness, every alternate person is directed to the new counter. In other words, people in the first, third, fifth, etc., positions are moved to the new counter in the same relative order. Assuming that the lines are represented by two queues, write an algorithm that would "split" the original queue as described above, and send the alternate entries to the new, initially empty queue.

E6.10. A queue that models a line of people waiting at a check-out counter in a store may be considered as an ordered list, sorted according to arrival times—the person who arrives earliest ("smallest" arrival time) is at the front. This problem addresses the opposite of the preceding one. Suppose there are lines (queues) at two check-out counters. One of them suddenly closes, and the people in that line need to be merged with the other line. In order to ensure fairness, the new queue must be arranged in order of arrival times. Assuming that there is a record of the arrival times of every person in both lines, write an algorithm that would perform this merge.

E6.11. A *priority queue* is a queue in which every entry has an associated priority, so that on a dequeue, the entry with the highest priority is removed. What data structure would you use to store the priority queue entries, and how would you design the enqueue and dequeue operations?

6.8   PROGRAMMING PROBLEMS

P6.1. Implement a client method (*not* in the Queue<T> class):

```
<T> void readAndEnqList(Scanner sc, Queue<T> q)
```

that would read a list of names, one per line, from an input stream using the scanner sc, and enqueue them in the queue q. The class Queue<T> is the one listed in Figure 6.1.

P6.2. Implement a method:

```
void removeLast(Queue<String> q, String str)
```

that would remove *only the last* occurrence of the specified string, str, from the queue q of strings. The last occurrence is defined as the one farthest from the front of the queue. (Hint: you may need to use another, temporary queue.)

P6.3. Implement the algorithm for *peek* that you designed in Exercise E6.7, using a Queue<T> class that does not support enumeration.

```
<T> T peek(Queue<T> q)
```

P6.4. Suppose the Queue<T> class did not support the removeAll method. Implement the following method that would remove all occurrences of the specified item from the specified queue:

```
void removeAllOccurrencesOf(Queue<T> q, T item)
```

(Hint: you may need to use another, temporary queue)

P6.5. We would like to add the following method to the PrintQueue class listed in Figure 6.2:

```
void lprmId(int jobId)
```

This method would remove a job from the print queue with the specified job id. If there is no such job, it would return silently.
    Implement this method.

P6.6. Write a method:

```
Queue<T> splitQueue(Queue<T> q)
```

to implement your algorithm of Exercise E6.9. The original queue is the parameter, q, and the new queue is the returned object.

P6.7. Write a class called Deq<T> that implements a double-ended queue as described in Exercise E6.6. Your class should support the following methods: enqueueFront, enqueueRear, dequeueFront, dequeueRear, isEmpty, and size. Use a circular linked list from scratch (do *not* use the LinkedList class) to implement the queue storage.

P6.8. Write a class called CircularQueue<T> that implements a queue using a circular array. You need only implement the methods enqueue, dequeue, size, isEmpty, isFull, first, and next. Devise exceptions called QueueFullException and

QueueEmptyException to throw when enqueue is called on a full queue and dequeue is called on an empty queue, respectively.

P6.9. Implement a `PriorityQueue<T extends Comparable<T>>` class, using the `Queue<T>` class to store all entries. Your class should define dequeue, enqueue, isEmpty, size, and peek methods, and have each of these call on appropriate Queue methods to get its work done.

CHAPTER 7

Stack

The stack data structure uses an underlying linear storage organization, while presenting a very simple yet powerful abstraction to its clients. As we will see in this chapter and some of the subsequent ones, the stack is one of the most ubiquitous data structures in computing.

Learning Objectives

- Describe the behavior of a stack.
- Enumerate the primary operations supported by a stack.
- Examine several applications of the stack, including parentheses matching, evaluating postfix expressions, and the conversion of an infix expression to postfix form.
- Understand the public interface of a stack class in Java and the running times of its methods.
- Develop a postfix package in Java to implement postfix expression evaluation.
- Study the implementation of a stack class in Java, and the tradeoffs involved in choosing between candidate reusable components.

7.1 STACK PROPERTIES

Consider surfing the Web on a browser, where a sequence of *back* clicks loads the browser with Web pages in reverse order of visit. That is, the *last* visited page is the *first* loaded when going back. Another example is that of the *undo* operation in a text editor—a chain of *undo*s erases actions in the sequence latest to earliest.

A *stack* is a collection of entries that demonstrates exactly this **last-in, first-out** behavior, called LIFO for short.

STACK

A stack is a linear collection of entries in which, for every entry y that enters the stack after another entry x, y leaves the stack before x.

The difference between the FIFO behavior of a queue and the LIFO behavior of a stack is a reflection of the contrasting nature of the applications that use them. A queue models a real-life queue, and all reasonable real-life queue behavior traits are captured in the queue's operations. A stack, on the other hand, *memorizes* things and recalls them in reverse order, serving an entirely different class of applications that model such behavior.

Operations. A stack can be imagined as an upright box; the top is open and the bottom is closed. An entry is always added, or *pushed*, onto the top of stack. An entry is always removed, or *popped*, also from the top of stack.

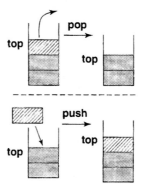

Thus the stack supports two fundamental operations: *push* and *pop*. These are the defining, or characteristic, operations. Enumeration, empty check, and size are usually added as basic operations because they are very frequently needed in applications.

Table 7.1 summarizes these operations.

TABLE 7.1: Stack operations.

Operation	Description
Push	Add an entry to the top of stack
Pop	Delete the entry at the top of stack
Enumerate	List all the entries in the stack
IsEmpty	Tell if the stack is empty
Size	Tell how many entries are in the stack

Compare this with the queue operations listed in Table 6.1. Now let us see how a stack can be used by studying some classic applications.

7.2 STACK APPLICATIONS

In this section, we discuss three applications that use a stack.

7.2.1 Parentheses Matching

A compiler checks expressions in a program to ensure that all parentheses are matched. This is a static situation—the entire expression is available at the time of parentheses checking.

On the other hand, good text editors match parentheses on the fly. On typing a closing parenthesis, the user is shown the companion opening parenthesis, if there is one that matches the closing parenthesis. If there is no matching opening parenthesis, the user is alerted to this fact immediately.

A closing parenthesis matches the latest opening parenthesis. In implementing the matching, opening parentheses need to be stored when encountered, and recalled in reverse order whenever closing parentheses are encountered. This is a clear invitation to use a stack.

What to store in a stack. It seems a little redundant to explicitly store opening parentheses in a stack that can only contain opening parentheses.

In the example of a text editor that matches parentheses, what the editor wants to do is to show the user *which* opening parenthesis was matched by a closing parenthesis. The location of every opening parenthesis in the text is what needs to be stored, not the parenthesis itself.

When the user types an opening parenthesis, the text editor could push its location onto the stack. When a closing parenthesis is typed, the location at the top of the stack is popped and used to address the matching opening parenthesis in the text.

In evaluating an expression, if the compiler were to make an initial scan over it to simply match parentheses without regard to operands and operators, it would not even need to use a stack to store opening parentheses. Instead, it could simply keep a running count of opening parentheses, adding one when a new opening parenthesis is encountered, and subtracting one when a closing parenthesis is encountered. If the count becomes negative at any point, the expression (at that point) contains an unmatched closing parenthesis. On the other hand, if at the end of scanning the expression the count is not zero, it is evident that the expression contains unmatched opening parentheses.

7.2.2 Postfix Expression Evaluation

We write arithmetic expressions in Java like so:

```
-a / (b + c) * d - e
```

This is an *infix* expression, in which every binary operator appears *between* the values (operands) on which it operates, and every unary operator appears *immediately before* the operand on which it operates. The operands are either variables or constants specified in the expression or the results obtained by evaluating subexpressions. The multiplication and division operators are given higher precedence than the addition and subtraction operators in evaluation.

Consider the expression:

```
2 - 3 + 5 * 2 * 3 + 4
```

When scanning the expression, evaluation has to be done based on precedence of operators, equivalent to placing parentheses as follows:

```
(((2 - 3) + ((5 * 2) * 3)) + 4)
```

Clearly, evaluation cannot be done on the fly with a simple left-to-right scan; some back-and-forth movement is needed to enforce this precedence. If we insist that evaluation proceed strictly left-to-right, we need to parenthesize the expression appropriately:

```
(2 - 3 + 5) * 2 * 3 + 4
```

A different form of expression, called *postfix,* does away with the need for parentheses. In a postfix expression, as shown below, an operator always follows the operands or subexpressions on which it operates. It may be evaluated by scanning once from left to right. The order of operands in a postfix expression is the same as in the equivalent infix expression.

Infix	**Postfix**
a + b * c - d	a b c * + d -
(a + b) * c - d	a b + c * d -
a + b * c - f / d	a b c * + f d / -
a + b * (c - f) / d	a b c f - * d / +
2 - 3 + 5 * 2 * 3 + 4	2 3 - 5 2 * 4 * + 4 +

A general postfix expression is best defined by describing how it is evaluated *using a stack,* as illustrated in Figure 7.1.

This evaluation procedure may be used to detect illegal postfix expressions. There are two conditions that must be met for the evaluation process to terminate successfully:

- When an operator is encountered, there must exist a most recent pair of operands or temporary results on the stack for application.
- When the scanning of the expression is complete, there must be exactly one value on the stack.

If either condition is violated, the input expression is not a legal postfix expression.

For instance, when the expression "b c + d * -" is evaluated, the stack would contain the single value $(b + c) * d$ after scanning the * and applying it to the top two entries. The next operator, '-', would see only one entry on the stack. The expression is therefore not in postfix form.

The expression "b c + d * e" is not a legal postfix expression either, because the stack would have two entries when the scanning is complete: the bottom entry would be the value $(b + c) * d$, and the top entry would be e.

Armed with the knowledge gained so far, we can write an algorithm (shown below) to evaluate a given postfix expression. For the sake of simplicity, we restrict ourselves to expressions in which every operand is an integer and every operator is one of '+', '-', '*', or '/', as, for instance, "23 12 + 2 * 150 3 / - 8 /", which evaluates to 2.5.

FIGURE 7.1: Stack-Based Evaluation of Postfix Expression. The expression is scanned left to right. When an operand is encountered, it is pushed on the stack. When an operator is encountered, the top two entries on the stack are popped, the operation is performed, and the result of the operation is pushed back on the stack. The evaluation terminates when the expression has been completely scanned, at which point the lone entry on the stack is the result.

algorithm postfixEvaluation

expr ← input postfix expression string
tok ← first token of *expr*
while (*tok* is not empty) do
    if (*tok* is an operator) then
        topval ← pop stack
        nextval ← pop stack
        result ← apply *tok* on
            topval and *nextval*
        push *result* on stack
    else
        value ← *tok* string converted to
            integer
        push *value* on stack
    endif
    tok ← next token of *expr*
endwhile

result ← pop stack

Every iteration of the while loop processes one token of the input expression. Once a token is obtained, it is checked to see whether it is an operator or an operand.

If the token is an operator, the top two values on the stack are popped, the appropriate operation performed, and the resulting value pushed back on stack. On the other hand, if the token is an operand, it must be first converted to the corresponding numeric value. For instance, the token "1234" is just a string of digit characters, and must be converted to its numeric integral value.

When all the tokens are parsed (i.e., the expression has been completely scanned), the algorithm terminates by displaying the single entry on the stack, which is the result of the evaluation.

Since division is one of the permitted operators, we need a stack that can store real numbers. The entire expression is first read in as a string. To process the expression, we need to be able to differentiate between operands and operators. We assume that there is some mechanism to *parse* the expression string and return the next *token* (operand or operator) when we need it. Since the operands are integers, a token is either a sequence of digits or one of the four legal operators. The parsing mechanism will treat any character other than these (such as blank spaces) as token *separators* that can be ignored.

There are two possible errors that may be encountered by the algorithm. One is that of insufficient operands, and the other is that of too many operands. Both of these are a result of the expression being illegal.

The insufficient-operands case is detected when the token is an operator but the stack has fewer than the two operands on which the operator must be applied. This would happen, for instance, on an illegal expression such as a +. The too-many operands case is detected after the while loop when the stack has more than one entry in it. This would happen, for instance, on an illegal expression such as a b.

7.2.3   Infix to Postfix Conversion

In the preceding section we described the evaluation of postfix expressions. However, programs typically only recognize expressions that are in infix form. Thus there is an intermediate step in which a compiler converts an infix form to its postfix equivalent before evaluating it. Here is an algorithm that can be used to convert an infix expression to postfix form.

algorithm infixToPostfix

expr ← input infix expression string
tok ← first token of *expr*
while (*tok* is not empty) do
    if (*tok* is...) then output *tok*
    if (*tok* is...) then push *tok* on stack
    else if (*tok* is an operator) then
        if (top of stack is '(') or stack is empty) then
            push *tok* on stack
        else if (*tok* has higher priority than stack top) then
            push *tok* on stack
        else
            pop stack and write popped value to output
            push *tok* on stack
        endif
    else if (*tok* is a closing parenthesis) then
        pop operators and write to output
            until a '(' is encountered
        pop '(' but don't write it to output
    endif
    tok ← next token of *expr*
endwhile
pop all operators and write to output

Note that multiplication and division have higher priority than addition or subtraction—we will restrict our expression to these four operators. A stack is used to store opening parentheses as well as operators.

This algorithm assumes that all the parentheses in the expression are matched, and that the operands and operators form a legal infix expression.

The algorithm does one simple scan of the input. If the length of the input is n, this algorithm takes $O(n)$ time. In other words, it is a linear time algorithm.

7.3   A Stack CLASS

Figure 7.2 lists the public interface of a generic stack class.

Class structures.linear.Stack<T>

Constructors

> **Stack( )**
>> Creates an empty stack.

Methods

$O(1)$ **void push(T item)**
> Adds new item to the top of this stack.

$O(1)$ **T pop( )**
> Removes and returns the item at the top of this stack.
> Throws **NoSuchElementException** if the stack is empty.

$O(1)$ **int size( )**
> Returns the number of elements in this stack.

$O(1)$ **boolean isEmpty( )**
> Returns true if this stack is empty, false otherwise.

$O(1)$ **void clear( )**
> Removes all the elements in this stack, i.e. empties it out.

$O(1)$ **T first( )**
> Returns the top entry of the stack; null if stack is empty.

$O(1)$ **T next( )**
> Returns the next entry of the stack going from top to bottom;
> null if bottom of stack has been reached.

FIGURE 7.2: A Generic Stack Class. Only the public interface is shown. Running times assume an implementation that keeps a reference to the top of stack, as well as a running count of number of items, n, in the stack.

Note that the only entry that can be removed is the one at the top of the stack; entries "under" the top cannot be removed.

7.4   A POSTFIX EXPRESSION EVALUATION PACKAGE

We want to build a PostfixEvaluator class that will evaluate a postfix expression as described in Section 7.2.2. We will build the class in a such way that an application can see the evaluation in slow motion (i.e., step by step) if desired. Figure 7.3 is a sample run of an application built around the postfix evaluator.

Every step of the evaluation processes one token of the expression. In Figure 7.3, when the evaluator has run for three steps, the tokens processed so far and the contents of the stack are both displayed. After one more step—that is, after detecting the token '+', the top two operands on the stack are added and their result is pushed back on the stack.

Then the evaluator is run to completion, and the final result displayed. The evaluator can be restarted with a new expression if desired, or the application can be terminated at any point.

```
Enter the postfix expression below
   ==> 12.5 15.6 10.8 + -

Choose a command:    runall     runsome     restart     quit
   Enter command => runsome
Evaluate how many steps? => 3

      Processed : 12.5 15.6 10.8


              ------------>
   Stack : | 12.50 | 15.60 | 10.80
              ------------>


Choose a command:    runall     runsome     restart     quit
   Enter command => runsome
Evaluate how many steps? => 1

      Processed : 12.5 15.6 10.8 +


              ------------>
   Stack : | 12.50 | 26.40
              ------------>


Choose a command:    runall     runsome     restart     quit
   Enter command => runall
      Result => -13.90

Choose a command:    runall     runsome     restart     quit
   Enter command => quit
```

FIGURE 7.3: Postfix Evaluation: The evaluator can be run either to completion or in stop-and-go fashion.

7.4.1 Class PostfixEvaluator

The class PostfixEvaluator and all its support classes are packaged in apps.linear. postfix. PostfixEvaluator is the only class that reveals a public interface to be used by clients—all other classes in the package are satellites of this class, and do not declare any methods as public.

Figure 7.4 is an outline of the PostfixEvaluator class.

This class responds to different events or messages. A message sent to a PostEvaluator object results in some actions being performed depending on the type of message sent. These message types and the resultant actions are summarized in Table 7.2.

Each message type corresponds to one method in the class. A design of this kind relies on keeping the classes simple and having them rely on one another to get a task done by apportioning pieces of it. There are four support classes: java.util.StringTokenizer, which parses the postfix expression into tokens and deals them out one at a time;

```
package apps.linear.postfix;
import java.util.StringTokenizer;
import java.util.NoSuchElementException;
import java.io.PrintWriter;

public class PostfixEvaluator {
  StringTokenizer exprTok;
  StatusKeeper exprStatus;
  StackKeeper postStack;

  public PostfixEvaluator() {
    postStack = new StackKeeper();
    exprStatus = new StatusKeeper();
  }
  public void printStatus(PrintWriter pw) {
    pw.println();
    exprStatus.printStatus(pw);
    pw.println();
    postStack.printStack(pw);
    pw.println();
  }
  public void init(String expr) { ··· }
  public float runAll(PrintWriter pw)
    throws IllegalExpressionException { ··· }
  public void runSome(int howManySteps, PrintWriter pw)
    throws IllegalExpressionException { ··· }
}
```

FIGURE 7.4: **Outline of PostfixEvaluator class.** exprTok, exprStatus, and postStack are objects that support the evaluator. The methods runAll and runSome each throw an IllegalExpressionException if the expression is not in postfix form.

TABLE 7.2: PostfixEvaluator messages and actions.

Message	Action
init	Initialize all objects to evaluate a specified postfix expression
runAll	Run the evaluator to completion and return the result
runSome	Run the evaluator only for a specified number of steps
printStatus	Print the current status of the evaluation process

StatusKeeper, which keeps track of the portion of the expression that has been processed so far; StackKeeper, which maintains the evaluation stack; and IllegalExpressionException, which defines a specialized *checked* exception for this application. The last three classes are in the apps.linear.postfix package.

An application that needs to evaluate a postfix expression starts off by creating and initializing a PostfixEvaluator object.

Then it can send a runAll message to this object to evaluate and produce the result in one shot. Or it can send several runSome messages to perform partial evaluations, interspersing these messages with printStatus messages to watch the action. In any case, one message to runA11 is always required in order to terminate the evaluation and obtain the result. The application can restart the evaluator on an expression (or a new expression) by sending it an init message.

The action in the evaluator revolves around the runSome method. The example that follows shows how this method cycles through one step of the evaluation process by sending messages to the supporting objects. The postfix expression that is being evaluated is "25 12 + 13 -".

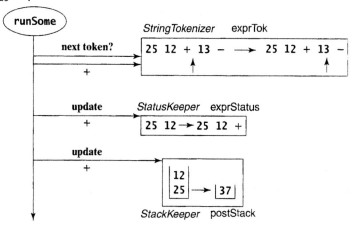

The subexpression "25 12" has already been processed just before runSome performs the step that is illustrated—processing the next token, +.

On receiving a nextToken message from runSome, exprTok returns the token + and updates itself. Method runSome then sends an update message to exprStatus along with the token +. Finally, runSome sends an update message to postStack, which performs an evaluation and updates the stack.

Next, let us take a closer look first at the support classes, and then at the Postfix-Evaluator class, in the postfix package.

7.4.2 Class StatusKeeper

Class File 7.1. *StatusKeeper.java*

```
package apps.linear.postfix;

import java.io.PrintWriter;

class StatusKeeper {
  StringBuffer status;

  StatusKeeper() { status = new StringBuffer; }
  void init() { status.setLength(0); }
  void update(String token) { status.append(token + " "); }
  String getStatus() { return status.toString(); }
  void printStatus(PrintWriter pw) { pw.println("   Processed : " + status);
  }
}
```

The status of the evaluator is the expression processed so far. This starts out being nothing, so the length of the buffer is set to zero in the `init` method.

Every time a token is processed and `update` is invoked, the status is appended by appending this token (along with a blank space) to the status buffer. At the end of processing, therefore, the status buffer will contain the complete input expression.

7.4.3 Class StackKeeper

Here is the complete StackKeeper class.

Class File 7.2. *StackKeeper.java*

```
package apps.linear.postfix;

import java.util.NoSuchElementException;
import java.io.PrintWriter;
import structures.linear.Stack;

class StackKeeper {
   static final char[] operators = {'+', '-', '*', '/'};
   Stack<Float> evalStack;

   StackKeeper() { evalStack = new Stack<Float>(); }
   void init() { evalStack.clear(); }
   int size() {
       return evalStack.size();
   }
   void update(String token) {
       if (isOperator(token)) {
           evaluate(token.charAt(0));
       } else {
           evalStack.push(Float.valueOf(token));
       }
   }
   float getTop() {
       Float top = evalStack.first();
       if (top == null) {
           throw new NoSuchElementException();
       }
       return top;
   }
   boolean isOperator(String instr) { ... }
   void evaluate(char op) { ... }
   void printStack(PrintWriter pw) { ... }
}
```

Fields. The field `operators` lists all possible operators that may be used in an expression. This field is a class variable shared by all StackKeeper instances and is therefore declared as `static`.

The field `evalStack` is the stack used to evaluate the expression. It will store operands and the result of evaluating subexpressions. Since these are floating-point numbers in general, we need to instantiate the generic Stack class with the Float type before use.

Initialization.   Recall from Table 7.2 that method init is called before an expression is evaluated. It clears evalStack of all its entries (i.e., empties it out).

Method isOperator.

```
boolean isOperator(String instr) {
   if (instr.length() > 1) {
      return false;
   }
   char c = instr.charAt(0);
   for (int i=0;
        i < operators.length;
        i++) {
      if (c == operators[i]) {
         return true;
      }
   }
   return false;
}
```

This method determines if the specified token is one of the four listed operators.

Since the operators, according to field operators, are all single-character strings, if the specified argument has a length greater than 1, it is not an operator.

If it is indeed an operator, it is first converted to a char, and then compared with each of the characters listed in operators for a match, in the for loop.

Method evaluate.   This method applies an operator to the top two elements on the stack. It must ensure that the top-of-stack element is the *second* operand, and that the one below it is the *first*.

```
void evaluate(char op) {
   Float topval = evalStack.pop();
   Float nextval = evalStack.pop();
   float tempval=0;
   switch (op) {
      case '+': tempval = nextval + topval; break;
      case '-': tempval = nextval - topval; break;
      case '*': tempval = nextval * topval; break;
      case '/': tempval = nextval / topval; break;
   }
   evalStack.push(tempval);
}
```

Note that auto unboxing is applied on each of the evaluation statements in the switch block, where the Float variables nextval and topval are unboxed to the float type in order to apply an arithmetic operation. Then, in the last statement, auto boxing is applied to tempval to convert it to Float for pushing on the stack.

Method update.   Depending on whether the token to be processed is an operator or not, either the evaluate method is invoked, or the token is pushed on evalStack.

Method `printStack`

This method prints an image of the stack.

```
void printStack(PrintWriter pw) {
  pw.println("              ----------->");
  pw.print("   Stack :");

  Stack<Float> tempStack = new Stack<Float>();
  Float obj = evalStack.first();
  while (obj != null) {
    tempStack.push(enum.nextElement());
    obj = evalStack.next();
  }

  obj = tempStack.first();
  while (obj != null) {
    pw.print(String.format(" | %.2f", obj));
    obj = tempStack.next();
  }
  pw.println();
  pw.println("                ----------->");
}
```

A temporary stack, `tempStack`, is set up in which all the evaluation stack items are transferred, so that their order in `tempStack` is reversed with respect to the order in `evalStack`. Then, by going through `tempStack` from top to bottom (which is how the enumeration methods `first` and `next` traverse a stack), the items are printed as they would appear from *bottom* to *top* in `evalStack`.

7.4.4   Class `PostfixEvaluator` Implementation

We will now flesh out the outline in Figure 7.4 to pull together all the classes we have discussed so far.

Method `init` sends an `init` message to each of `postStack` and `exprStatus`, which end up initializing themselves; that is to say, `postStack` empties its stack, and `exprStatus` empties its buffer.

```
public void init(String expr) {
  postStack.init();
  exprStatus.init();
  exprTok = new StringTokenizer(expr);
}
```

Method `runAll` simply passes the buck to `runSome` by calling on it to process *all the tokens* of the expression in one shot.

```
public float runAll(PrintWriter pw)
throws IllegalExpressionException {
  // process all remaining tokens of expression
  runSome(exprTok.countTokens(), pw);

  // stack must have one entry, the result, at the end
  if (postStack.size() > 1) {
    throw new
      IllegalExpressionException("insufficient operators");
  }

  return postStack.getTop(); // result
}
```

Note that in the first statement, the StringTokenizer method countTokens returns the number of tokens that *remain to be enumerated*. In other words, the value returned by countTokens is the number of times the method nextToken will return a token before returning null. This is useful because runAll may be called after several calls to runSome, in which case the evaluation has to complete from where it left off, not start from scratch.

At the end of the run, the stack must contain exactly one element, which is the result of the evaluation. If it contains more than one element, this means that the number of operators was insufficient—recall our discussion of error conditions at the end of Section 7.2.2—and an exception called IllegalExpressionException (defined in the apps.linear.postfix package) is thrown. This potential error condition is checked in the if statement. Here is the class file for this exception:

Class File 7.3. *IllegalExpressionException.java*

```
package apps.linear.postfix;

public class IllegalExpressionException extends Exception {

  public IllegalExpressionException() {
    super();
  }

  public IllegalExpressionException(String s) {
    super(s);
  }
}
```

This is a checked exception because it extends the Exception class, and not the RuntimeException class. Since it is checked, a method that throws a new instance of this exception must declare that it throws the exception, as seen in the headers for the methods runAll and runSome.

Method runSome is the core part of the evaluator.

```
public void runSome(int howManySteps, PrintWriter pw)
throws IllegalExpressionException {
  int step=0;
  while (exprTok.hasMoreTokens()) {
    if (step == howManySteps) {
        return;
    }

    String nextTok = exprTok.nextToken();
    exprStatus.update(nextTok);
    try {
        postStack.update(nextTok);
    }
    catch (NoSuchElementException f) {
        // not enough entries on stack for evaluation
        printStatus(pw);
        throw new
            IllegalExpressionException("insufficient operands");
    }

    step++;
  }
}
```

The while loop performs the actions depicted in the example of Section 7.4.1.

The exception handling in the catch block is particularly noteworthy. The post-Stack.update method, called in the try block, would throw a NumberFormatException if an operand is not a legal floating-point number, and a NoSuchElementException if it tries to evaluate but does not find sufficient elements on the stack. From the point of view of runSome, the NumberFormatException cannot be handled, so it just passes this on to its (runSome's) caller. Since this is a runtime exception, it is not declared as thrown by runSome in its header. On the other hand, the NoSuchElementException is caught by runSome in order to do two things:

- Print the current evaluation status so that the calling application gets as much information as possible about the source of the exception.
- Throw an IllegalExpressionException, in order to deliver the most precise and complete information about the cause of the exception. This is much better than just passing through the NoSuchElementException, which, in this context, is not informative enough. Note that we used the same line of reasoning of exception filtering as discussed in Section 6.5.

One final comment. If an application runs through the entire expression by only calling runSome one or more times, it would still need to call runAll in the end in order to get the result off the stack.

7.5   Stack CLASS IMPLEMENTATION

We evaluate two alternatives for storing the stack entries: an array list and a linked list.

7.5.1   Design 1: Array List for Storage

An instance of the ArrayList class is used as a component in the Stack class, with the last entry of the array list as the top of the stack, as shown below.

Consider the correspondence between the core Stack methods and ArrayList methods. The Stack enumeration methods first and next can be implemented by running an index backward through the ArrayList component, because the first entry in the enumeration is the top of stack as defined by the Stack interface of Figure 7.2.

Stack	Array List
push	add
pop	remove(n-1)
isEmpty	isEmpty
size	size
clear	clear

You can verify that the running times of the Stack methods using this design alternative would match the expected running times listed in Figure 7.2.

7.5.2   Design 2: Linked List for Storage

We will use the LinkedList class of Section 4.6 to store the stack entries. The only question here is: Which end of the list should be used for the pushes and pops? We want to do both these operations in $O(1)$ time.

LinkedList implements a circular linked list in which an addition could be done at either end in $O(1)$ time. However, while deletion from the front can be done in $O(1)$ time, deletion from the rear can only be done in $O(n)$ time. Thus, we would need to use the front of the list as the top of stack.

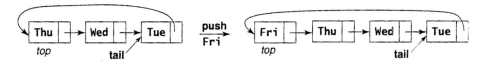

Class File 7.4. *Stack.java*

```
package structures.linear;

import java.util.NoSuchElementException;

public class Stack<T> {
  LinkedList<T> list;
  int cursor;

  public Stack() { list = new LinkedList<T>(); cursor = -1; }
  public void push(T item) {
```

```
   if (list.size() == 0) {
       list.add(item);
   } else {
       list.insertAt(item, 0); // add to front
   }
}
public T pop() {
   if (list.isEmpty()) {
       throw new NoSuchElementException();
   }
   return list.removeAt(0); // first entry
}

public int size() { return list.size(); }
public boolean isEmpty() { return list.isEmpty(); }
public void clear() { list.clear(); }
public T first() {
   if (list.size() == 0) {
       return null;
   }
   cursor = 0;
   return list.getAt(cursor);
}
public T next() {
   if (cursor < 0 || cursor == (list.size()-1)) {
       return null;
   }
   cursor++;
   return list.getAt(cursor);
}
}
```

Observe that in the method push we cannot use the insertAt method of the LinkedList class if the list is empty. As specified in the LinkedList interface listed in Figure 4.6, using the insertAt method requires insertion in the strict sense—the insertion effectively takes the position of an existing entry. So when the list is empty, we use the add method instead.

Knowing the running times of the LinkedList methods (Figure 4.6), we can verify that the running times of the Stack methods are as listed in Figure 7.2. Let us do this for the push and pop methods—the rest are left as an exercise.

Let us first recall the worst-case running times of the LinkedList methods. The add, size, and isEmpty methods take $O(1)$ time, while the other methods all take $O(n)$ time.

The Stack push method calls the LinkedList method add or insertAt(item,0). The add method takes $O(1)$ time. The insertAt(item, index) method takes $O(n)$ time in the worst case, but insertAt(item,0) only takes $O(1)$ time because it needs to add a new item at the front of the linked list, which is accessible in $O(1)$ time.

The Stack pop method calls the LinkedList method removeAt(0). The removeAt (index) method takes $O(n)$ time in the worst case, but removeAt(0) only takes $O(1)$ time because it removes the *first* entry, which only takes $O(1)$ time, as stated at the beginning of this section.

7.6   SUMMARY

- The stack data structure implements the last-in, first-out (LIFO) abstraction.
- A stack is a linear collection of entries in which, for every entry y that enters the stack after another entry x, y leaves the stack before x.
- A stack memorizes things and recalls them in reverse order.
- There are two fundamental operations supported by a stack: push and pop.
- Every infix expression can be written unambiguously in postfix form without parentheses.
- A postfix expression can be evaluated by using a stack with a single left-to-right scan of the expression.
- A stack class in Java may define more than just the fundamental push and pop methods in its interface in order to provide better efficiency and ease of use.
- A stack is a powerful tool for parentheses matching or, in general, for matching entities that must occur in opening and closing pairs.
- An infix expression may be converted in $O(n)$ (linear) time into the equivalent infix form, using a stack.
- A stack class may be implemented using an array list or a linked list as component, with careful attention being paid to the "end" at which push and pop are performed, in order to maintain $O(1)$ time for these operations.

7.7   EXERCISES

E7.1. Convert the following infix expressions to postfix:
  (a) a + (b * c) / (d + f)
  (b) (((2 + 3) * 5) - 15)
  (c) a + (3 - p * r) / q - x
E7.2. Convert the following postfix expressions to infix:
  (a) a b c + * d -
  (b) a b c + / e *
  (c) a d - e f * + a f + /
E7.3. Trace the postfix evaluation algorithm **postfixEvaluation** of Section 7.2.2 on the following postfix expressions:
  (a) 10 3 4 - 5 * /
  (b) 3 15 5 4 2 * - + +
  Answer in the style of Figure 7.1 by showing, at every step, the postfix expression parsed so far, and the contents of the stack.
E7.4. Trace the infix-to-postfix conversion algorithm **infixToPostfix** of Section 7.2.3 on the following infix expressions:
  (a) a + b + c - d
  (b) (((2 + 3) * 5) - 15)
  (c) 3 * ((5 + 4) * 2) - 15 / 3
  Answer by showing, at every step, the infix expression parsed so far, and the contents of the stack.
E7.5. Verify that the infix-to-postfix conversion algorithm **infixToPostfix** takes $O(n)$ time. Explain your line of reasoning.

E7.6. Add error checking to the infix-to-postfix conversion algorithm **infixToPostfix** to detect mismatch of parentheses. Your improved algorithm should display an appropriate error message and immediately terminate if it detects a mismatch of parentheses.

E7.7. In the infix-to-postfix conversion algorithm **infixToPostfix** what is the associativity of operators that have the same precedence? For instance, would the expression

    a + b - c

be evaluated in a left-to-right manner

    ((a + b) - c)

or in a right-to-left manner?

    (a + (b - c))

E7.8. Referring to Exercise E7.7, if operators other than +, -, *, and / were involved, and each operator came with an additional specification of whether it associated left to right or right to left, how would you change the **infixToPostfix** algorithm to account for this?

E7.9. Suppose we run a parentheses matcher that scans some text and simply tells whether the parentheses are matched: *yes* if they are matched, and *no* if they are not. Show what such a matcher would store on the stack by illustrating the scanning process on the following:
(a) (a + (b * c) + d)
(b) ((a + b * (c + d))
(c) a - (b * (c + d) - (e / f))

E7.10. Another form of an expression that does away with parentheses is the *prefix* form. In this form, an operator precedes its operands, or the subexpressions on which it operates. The following table shows the prefix equivalents of some infix expressions.

Infix	Prefix
a + b * c - d	- + a * b c d
(a + b) * c - d	- * + a b c d
a + b * c - f / d	- + a * b c / f d
a + b * (c - f) / d	+ a / * b - c f d
2 - 3 + 5 * 2 * 3 + 4	+ + - 2 3 * * 5 2 3 4

(a) Convert the infix expressions of Exercise 7.1 to prefix form.
(b) Convert the following prefix expressions to infix form:
   i. * + a b c
   ii. - / a + b c d
   iii. * / - + a b c d e

E7.11. Can you write an algorithm to evaluate a prefix expression using a *single* stack?

   • What are the potential implementation complications that may arise in your scheme, compared to the postfix evaluation algorithm **postfixEvaluation?**

- Would these problems be overcome if you were to use an additional stack for the evaluation? Explain.

E7.12. You are given a stack S that contains a number of items (it could even be empty). Describe how you would use an auxiliary stack T to count the number of items in $S;$ at the end of your algorithm, S must be unchanged. You may only use the *push, pop,* and *isEmpty* operations on either stack.

E7.13. With the same conditions as in Exercise E7.12—stack S and auxiliary stack T, and the *push, pop, isEmpty* operations—describe how you would delete, from S, every occurrence of a given item, leaving the order of the remaining items in S unchanged.

E7.14. How would you build a queue using one or more stacks? Specifically, using one or more stacks, write algorithms for the queue operations *enqueue* and *dequeue* in terms of the stack operations *push, pop,* and *isEmpty*.

E7.15. A *double-ended queue* is a special type of queue in which adds and deletes are supported at both ends (i.e., *enqueue* and *dequeue* may be done at the front as well as the rear). Thus, it supports four fundamental operations: *enqueueFront, enqueueRear, dequeueFront,* and *dequeueRear*.

Give algorithms to implement these operations by using two stacks and their *push, pop,* and *isEmpty* operations.

E7.16. A palindrome is a string that reads the same both backwards and forwards. Give an algorithm using a stack and a queue to detect whether a given string is a palindrome.

E7.17. Describe how you could use one array to store two independent stacks. If the size of the array is n, the two stacks together can hold up to n entries. A client should be able to push an entry on either stack so long as at least one location in the array is free.

7.8 PROGRAMMING PROBLEMS

P7.1. Implement the parentheses-matching algorithm described in Section 7.2.1 by writing a method:

```
boolean parenMatch(String s)
```

that will accept a string containing several opening and closing parentheses, and will return `true` if the parentheses match, and `false` otherwise. You may assume that a parenthesis is a separate token.

P7.2. Consider a more general "bracket"-matching program that detects matching pairs of '(' and ')', '[' and ']', and '{' and '}'. Let us call this program *matcher*. The matcher scans text that contains the above tokens, and determines whether they are matched up. Implement a method:

```
boolean match(String s)
```

that will accept a string containing several of the above to-be-matched tokens, and will return `false` if there is a mismatch, and `true` otherwise.

If there are several possible implementations, describe each of them, explain which is most efficient in time, and implement it.

P7.3. Suppose that the Stack class interface of Figure 7.2 consisted only of the three methods push, pop, and isEmpty. Implement the following client method (*not* in the Stack class):

```
<T> int size(Stack<T> S)
```

to return the number of items in a given stack S. Use your answer to Exercise 7.12.

P7.4. In the light of Problem P7.3, argue in favor of introducing the size method in the Stack class, as we have done in Figure 7.2. Is your argument based on (a) efficiency, (b) ease of use, or (c) both? Explain.

P7.5. The design of the package postfix could be modified by introducing a class called Operator and reimplementing the class StackKeeper to account for the new design. In this problem, you will design the Operator class, and in the next you will reimplement the StackKeeper class.

Design the Operator class as follows:

(a) Encapsulate the set of permitted operators. Should this be instance data or class data?

(b) Encapsulate the actual operator, which would be one of the operators in the permitted set.

(c) Implement a constructor:

```
Operator(String s)
```

that will accept a string and create an operator out of it. Your constructor should throw an exception if the string supplied is not a permitted operator. Would you throw a runtime exception or a checked exception? Design your own exception class if you need to.

(d) Implement a method:

```
isOperator(String s)
```

that will tell whether a given string is a permitted operator or not. Should this method be a class method or an instance method?

(e) Implement a method:

```
float evaluate(float p, float q)
```

that will apply *this* operator (i.e., the actual operator encapsulated) to the given float operands, and return the resulting float value. Note that the order of parameters must be maintained in the application of the operator (i.e., p is the *first* operand, and q is the *second*).

P7.6. Now reimplement the StackKeeper class to use the Operator class defined in Problem 7.5 above. Do away with methods that are no longer required, and reimplement those that need to be changed. Do you have to add any new methods?

P7.7. Compare the new postfix package as detailed above in Problems P7.5 and P7.6 with the old postfix package as described in the text. Do you think the new package is better designed? How would you compare the respective efficiencies in space and time of the old and new packages?

P7.8. Write a class called InfixToPostfix to convert an infix expression to an equivalent postfix expression using the **infixToPostfix** algorithm of Section 7.2.3. Follow the style of the PostfixEvaluator class, with init, runAll, runSome, and printStatus methods. In each step of the conversion, one input token should be processed. The method runAll should return the output expression as a String.

   The InfixToPostfix class needs two helper classes analogous to the StatusKeeper and StackKeeper classes used by PostfixEvaluator. Can any of these classes be reused directly? If not, define new classes, reusing as much code as possible.

P7.9. Implement a class ArrayStack using the class java.util.ArrayList (instead of a linked list) as the component that stores the entries, following the design ideas discussed in Section 7.5.1. Implement a default constructor, and the same methods as in the Stack class.

P7.10. Implement a stack class with the same public interface as in Figure 7.2, using a linked list built *from scratch* (i.e., not reusing the LinkedList class). What are the pros and cons of this implementation, as compared to reusing the LinkedList class?

CHAPTER 8

Recursion

Recursion is a problem-solving paradigm that may be applied to several of the data structures and algorithms we study in this text. In this chapter, we will study recursion from the ground up, learn how to define data structures and algorithms recursively, and work through the implementation of recursion in Java programs.

Learning Objectives

- Describe the components of a recursive definition.
- Learn how to construct recursive definitions.
- Learn how to implement recursive definitions as Java methods.
- Study the forward and backing-out phases of the execution of a recursive method.
- Explore the application of recursion to solving linked list problems.
- Understand how recursion works on problems in which data is stored in an array.
- Review all the aspects of a recursive solution by applying recursion to solve the towers of Hanoi puzzle.
- Learn how recursion is implemented using a stack.
- Enumerate the drawbacks of recursion.
- Get to know tail recursion, and see how tail recursive methods can be transformed by replacing recursion with iteration.

8.1   RECURSIVE DEFINITIONS

An onion is a sphere that has an outer layer, inside which is a smaller onion.

In other words, an onion is made up of smaller and smaller onions, revealed by peeling it layer by layer until there is nothing left.

RECURSIVE DEFINITION

A recursive definition of an entity defines the entity in terms of itself.

Recursive definitions are also called *self-referential* definitions, since the definition of an entity makes a reference to itself in the definition.

Let us now look at the recursive definitions of some data structures and mathematical functions to get a better grasp of this fundamental idea.

8.1.1   List

Here is the recursive definition of a list:

RECURSIVE DEFINITION OF LIST

A list is either empty or consists of a first entry followed by a list.

Observe that each level of recursion has its own "first" entry. If we apply the general recursive-list definition to the outermost level of the list, it would *specifically* read:

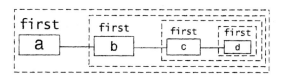

The list consists of a first entry, 'a', followed by a list.

We can apply the definition to any level of recursion. For example, if we apply it to the innermost level, it would specifically read:

The list consists of a first entry, 'd', followed by a list.

What happens if we then take the leftover list, call it *leftover* from the preceding definition, and apply the general recursive definition to *it*? Well, as can be seen in the same figure, there is nothing following 'd', *so it must be that the definition of leftover collapses into the part that says*:

A list is either empty, ...

In other words, *leftover* is an empty list.

This first part of the general recursive definition is called the *base condition,* meaning the condition at which the definition *does not recurse* any more. When the list is empty, there is nothing more to recurse on.

We can define the base condition, alternatively referred to as base *case,* as follows:

BASE CONDITION (CASE) OF A RECURSIVE DEFINITION

Every recursive definition must have at least one condition, called its base condition or base case, at which the definition does not recurse (i.e., does not refer to itself).

If there were no base case, the recursive definition would spin endlessly in an *infinite recursion.* In the case of the list, it would mean that the definition could be applied to the list over and over again without ever hitting the base condition, which would only be possible if the list were infinitely long.

For every *finite* list, however, there must be a terminating condition—namely, the base condition. In this regard, you may notice that in the general recursive definition of the list, there is no reference to the *size* of the list. If we assume that the list is finite, it follows that the size of the *contained* (or leftover) list is smaller than the size of the *containing* list. Specifically, the contained list contains one less entry than the containing list.

Breaking and making a list.   A recursive definition of a data structure such as a list can be used to break it down, item by item, by decomposing, or "eating away," a list, first entry by first entry, all the way down until there is nothing left (i.e., the leftover list is empty).

On the other hand, as shown in the next figure, we can work this process backwards. Starting with an empty list, we can build up bigger and bigger lists by using the recursive definition to add one entry at a time to the *front* of the growing list.

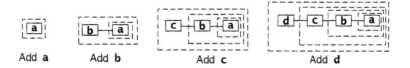

Add **a**   Add **b**   Add **c**   Add **d**

Given a sequence of entries to be entered into a list, the recursive definition places them in reverse order. In other words, the first entry to be added turns out to be the last entry in the "final" list.

RECURSIVELY BUILDING A DATA STRUCTURE

The recursive definition of a data structure may be used to build it from scratch.

Let us try to work out another recursive definition, say for an ordered list.

8.1.2   Ordered List

We can start with the known, that is, the definition of a list, and simply substitute *ordered list* for list:

> *An ordered list is either empty or consists of a first entry followed by an ordered list.*

We see immediately that this does not carry the most crucial information: the relative ordering of entries. How can we work this into our first-cut definition?

To do this, we need to take the *smallest possible step* to get from "here" to "there." Focus on the first entry that has been peeled out. How does the value of the first entry relate to the rest of the list? It is less than or equal to the values of all the remaining entries in the list. Here is our new, improved (correct) definition:

RECURSIVE DEFINITION OF ORDERED LIST

An ordered list is either empty or consists of a first entry followed by an ordered list, and the value of the first entry is less than or equal to the values of all the entries in the following ordered list.

At this point, it is useful to visualize a metaphor that binds the peeled-out portion of the recursion with the rest of the recursion. We will use the informal idea of a **glue** that binds these two parts. In the case of a list, the glue is the *link* between the first entry and the remaining list. In the case of the ordered list, it is not only the link between the first entry and the rest of the list, but also the *condition* that the value of the first entry be less than or equal to the values of the remaining entries. So the glue does not necessarily have to be a physical link—it can be a mathematical construct.

A precise definition of this glue is essential to building recursive programs, say for building a list recursively, since it is crucial to know exactly how to implement the binding of the list constructed up to a certain point, with a new entry.

Recursive definitions do not have to be restricted to data structures. In fact, recursive definitions have their basis in mathematics, where they are called **inductive** definitions. A great many mathematical functions can be defined recursively. Let us take a couple of classic instances to further illustrate recursive definitions.

8.1.3   Factorial Function

We know that the factorial of N is $1 \times 2 \times 3 \times \ldots \times N - 1 \times N$. A factorial function, *fact,* can be recursively defined as follows:

$$
\begin{aligned}
fact(n) &= 1, \text{if } n = 1 \\
&= n \times fact(n - 1), \text{if } n > 1
\end{aligned}
$$

Here, the first line:

$$fact(n) = 1, \text{if } n = 1$$

is the base case, and thus the definition of factorial at $n = 1$ is not recursive.

If $n > 1$, however, $fact(n - 1)$ is the recursive part, which is the factorial of a smaller instance, namely $n - 1$.

Here is a recursive definition of $fact(4)$. In the case of the list, the "glue" that bound together the first entry of the list and the rest of the

list was a physical link. In the case of the factorial, a multiplication ties together the "first entry" (at whatever level of recursion is being considered) with the rest of the factorial.

Another way to read the definition is that if $fact(n - 1)$ *were known*, then $fact(n)$ could be computed by multiplying the former by n. Thus, if $fact(n)$ is the whole onion, then n is the outer layer that is peeled out, leaving $fact(n) - 1$ inside. In reverse, if $fact(n - 1)$ were available, then $fact(n)$ could be obtained by gluing the n on top of it, by multiplication.

We raised a subtle but very crucial point when we said "if $fact(n - 1)$ *were known*." The words "were known" assume the existence of $fact(n - 1)$ at face value. We will see that for a long-term grasp of recursive definitions, this face-value assumption is critical—it is the "blind faith" factor.

8.1.4 Fibonacci Sequence

Another well-known mathematical function has to do with the so-called **Fibonacci** sequence of numbers:

$$0, 1, 1, 2, 3, 5, 8, 13, 21, 34, \ldots$$

in which the first two numbers are defined to be 0 and 1, and every subsequent number is the sum of the previous two numbers in the sequence. Thus, the sequence in general can be expressed as the values of the Fibonacci function, F:

$$F_0, F_1, F_2, F_3, \ldots$$

where F is defined as follows:

$$F(n) = 0, \text{if } n = 0$$
$$= 1, \text{if } n = 1$$
$$= F(n - 1) + F(n - 2), \text{if } n > 1$$

There are two base cases: the right-hand sides of the first and second lines. Recall our earlier definition of base case: every recursive definition has *at least* one base case, meaning *one or more* base cases.

This is also our first exposure to a recursive definition that consists of *two* recursive subexpressions. Specifically, $F(n)$, the containing entity, is recursively defined in terms of two subexpressions, $F(n - 1)$ and $F(n - 2)$.

Finally, let us phrase the definition in terms of our blind-faith factor. If $F(n - 1)$ and $F(n - 2)$ *were available,* then $F(n)$ could be obtained by gluing them together by addition.

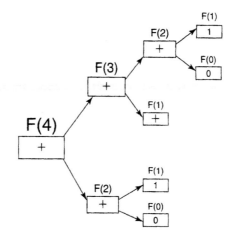

As can be seen in the figure that follows, the definition of $F(4)$ spins off two chains of recursion, one on $F(3)$ and another on $F(2)$, each of which in turn spins off two chains, and so on. Every chain ends in either $F(0)$ or $F(1)$, which are the base cases.

Blind faith is well and good, but the computer is an unforgiving creature. The best way to develop blind faith is through experience, by seeing several instances where it works. This brings us to recursive programs.

8.2   RECURSIVE PROGRAMS AND BACKING OUT

In this section we will write several recursive programs, some of which will implement the recursive definitions we have seen earlier, and others that will offer new insights into recursion. Overall, these programs will help us to learn the nitty-gritty of implementing recursion.

8.2.1   Computing the Factorial

A recursive program implements a recursive definition. In Java, a recursive program is always implemented as a recursive method.

Returning to our simple factorial function example of Section 8.1.3, a recursive method that implements it would look like the following, assuming N > 0:

```
int fact(int N) {
    if (N == 1) {
        return 1;
    } else {
        return N*fact(N-1);    // recursive call
    }
}
```

The wonderful thing about the implementation is that it so faithfully mimics the recursive factorial definition. This is true of most recursive programs: the implementation is easy once the definition is correctly in place.

WRITING A RECURSIVE METHOD

The main work in writing a recursive method to solve a problem is to come up with a clear and correct recursive definition for the solution.

We know that a recursive definition is one that defines something in terms of itself. Obviously, then, a recursive method is one that solves a problem by *applying itself recursively* to solve smaller and smaller instances of the problem until it "eats away" the entire input. We say that a recursive method *calls itself*—note how this is apparent in the method shown above, where the construct

```
fact(N-1)
```

is placed inside the method `fact`. Stated more clearly, there is a place in the method where the method calls itself with an argument, $N - 1$, that is one less than the parameter value, N, of the containing method.

A RECURSIVE METHOD CALLS ITSELF

A recursive method contains one or more lines where the method is called with the same number and type of arguments as the parameters in the method.

This figure shows how the factorial recursion code given above results in the `fact` function calling itself repeatedly for an initial argument of $N = 4$. In the forward phase of the recursion, a call to `fact` is made with $N = 4$. Then `fact` spins off copies of itself to compute the factorial of increasingly smaller values of N, until $N = 1$ is reached.

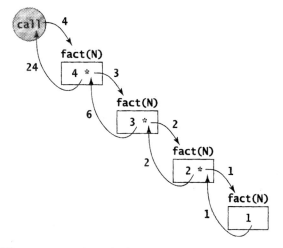

Meanwhile each of the previously spun-off copies is waiting for its immediate successors to return with its answer. As soon as it gets an answer from its successor, it multiplies the answer by the N value it is holding on to, and sends the new answer to its waiting predecessor. This is the backing-out phase.

The forward and backing-out phases can be likened to the following. Suppose there are four friends, Samir, Jane, Hiromi, and Andrey, whom you call on to find the answer to *fact*(4). You pass your request to Samir. On getting the number 4, Samir decides to play it smart. Instead of computing the whole thing himself, he holds on to the number 4 and *asks Jane* to compute *fact*(3).

Samir now waits for Jane to give him the answer. Jane plays a similar game: she holds on to 3, and asks Hiromi to compute and return to her the answer for *fact*(2). Hiromi, in turn, holds on to 2, and asks Andrey to compute and return to her the answer to *fact*(1).

The buck stops at Andrey—the forward phase is done, because Andrey realizes that he doesn't have to call on anyone: the answer to *fact*(1) is 1, the base case, and he is about to return the answer to Andrey.

FORWARD PHASE

Every recursion has a forward phase in which a call at every level except the last spins off a call to the next level and waits for the latter call to return control to it.

A snapshot at this point would show Samir, Jane, and Hiromi frozen in their places, waiting for an answer to come back. This is the end of the forward phase.

In the backing-out phase, Andrey sends 1 to Hiromi. Andrey's work is done. Hiromi unfreezes, multiplies this with the 2 that she is holding on to, and sends the result, 2, to Jane. At this point, Hiromi's work is done. Jane multiplies this with her 3, and sends a 6 back to Samir, and her work is done. Samir multiplies this with his 4 to obtain 24, passes it on to you, and is done.

BACKING OUT PHASE

Every recursion has a backing-out phase in which a call at every level except the first passes control back to the previous level, at which point the call waiting at the previous level wakes up and resumes its work.

A last comment before we go on: we can write the `fact` method more compactly, without the `else` part, as follows:

```
int fact(int N) {
    if (N == 1) return 1;
    return N*fact(N-1);    // recursive call
}
```

Note that if the condition `N == 1` is true, the method exits with a return value of 1 and the second line is never reached. On the other hand, if this condition is false, control simply "falls through" to the second line, as required.

We will now review our understanding of the forward and backing-out phases of recursion by examining a recursive method for the Fibonacci function.

8.2.2 Computing the Fibonacci Sequence

Again, the method mimics the definition in Section 8.1.4 line for line:

```
int Fibo(int N) {
    if (N == 0) return 0;
    if (N == 1) return 1;
    return Fibo(N-1) + Fibo(N-2) ;      // two recursive calls
}
```

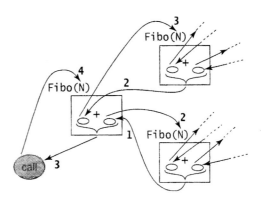

The figure shows the forward and backing-out phases of the recursion for the first two levels. A call to F(N) is made with $N = 4$. This call in turn makes a call to $F(3)$. It then waits until the $F(3)$ call returns, following which it makes a call to $F(2)$.

While every call waits on two subsequent calls, these waits are not simultaneous. For example, $F(4)$ *first* waits on $F(3)$. When $F(3)$ returns, $F(4)$ grabs the value returned by $F(3)$ and holds on to it. *Next*, it spins off a call to $F(2)$, and then waits again. Then, when $F(2)$ returns, it grabs the value returned by $F(2)$, and adds it to the value from $F(3)$ that it had been holding on to earlier, following which it returns this value to the caller, and its work is done.

In general, every call except the $F(0)$ and $F(1)$ calls exhibits a *wait-wakeup-wait-wakeup* cycle of behavior. Which means that for every call there are two forward phases and two backing-out phases.

Having strengthened our understanding of implementing recursion on some mathematical functions, let us return to recursion on data structures, starting with recursion on linked lists. At the design level, this is really about recursion with higher-level lists, which we discussed in Section 8.1.1. However, since a linked list is used to implement a list, our recursive programs will deal with linked lists. What this essentially means is that we will have to concentrate more on the nitty-gritty of the "physical" links (glue) that tie the entries together.

8.2.3 Recursion with Linked Lists

Several linked list operations may be implemented using recursion. Let us assume that we have a noncircular linked list. As defined in Section 4.5, assume that the linked list consists of Node<T> objects, where the Node<T> class contains two components, data and next. Further, assume that we have a reference, called first, to the first node of this linked list. Since the list is noncircular, the next component of the last node in the list is null.

Counting number of nodes.   How can we implement a recursive method that would count the number of nodes in the linked list, given a reference to its first node? The first step is to come up with a recursive definition.

First, let us quickly go over the definition of a linked list:

RECURSIVE DEFINITION OF LINKED LIST

A linked list is either empty or consists of a first node whose next field references the rest of the linked list.

Note how many implementation (nitty-gritty) details appear in this definition, in contrast to the "clean" definition of a list presented in Section 8.1.1.

Now let us try a recursive definition of the number of nodes in a linked list:

RECURSIVE DEFINITION OF NUMBER OF NODES IN LINKED LIST

The number of nodes in an empty linked list is zero; otherwise, it is one (for the first node) plus the number of nodes in the rest of the linked list.

Here is the code, in a method called countNodes:

```
<T> int countNodes(Node<T> first) {
    if (first == null) return 0;
    return 1 + countNodes(first.next);
}
```

You may want to verify that this method works correctly by building a picture of its forward and backing-out phases.

Printing entries backwards.   Another interesting piece of code is one that would print the entries of a linked list backwards. The key is the fact that in recursion each level waits until the next level returns. So, if the linked list is traversed front to back recursively, but the entry at any level is printed *after* the call to the subsequent level returns, the entire linked list would be printed backwards. In short, printing is done during the backing-out phase, not the forward phase.

```
<T> void printBackwards(Node<T> first) {
    if (first != null) {
        printBackwards(first.next);    // forward phase
        System.out.println(first.data);    // backing out phase
    }
}
```

Splitting a linked list in two. Finally, a relatively harder example to drive the point home. Here we will use recursion to split a linked list into odd nodes and even nodes without using any extra space. Essentially, this involves modifying the references that link the nodes together, as shown in this figure.

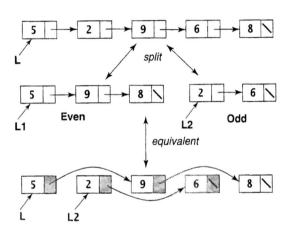

Looking at the bottom-most linked list in the figure, it is clear that the reference to the original list is also the reference to the even list. By a deft sequence of changes to all next components except for the last node, the list is split in two, with a new reference to the first node of the odd list.

How can we express the split process recursively? How about:

> *The linked list consists of the first node, the second node, and the rest of the linked list. Recursively split the rest of the list into rest-even and rest-odd linked lists. Then hook up the next field of the first node to the rest-even linked list, and the next field of the second node to the rest-odd linked list.*

Unlike the usual recursive definition of a list or linked list, where only the first entry or node is peeled, here we have been forced to peel both the first and second nodes to accurately express the recursion.

Now let us take a shot at the code for the split, writing a method that would accept a reference to the original list, and return a reference to the odd list after splitting.

```
<T> Node<T> split(Node<T> L) {
    first = L;
    second = L.next;
    restEven = second.next;
    restOdd = split(restEven);
    first.next = restEven;
    second.next = restOdd;
}
```

The only problem is that this won't always work. In referring to L.next, we are assuming that L is not null (i.e., the list has at least one node), and in referring to second.next, we are assuming that second is not null (i.e., the list has at least two nodes). This little program will crash if the list is empty or has only one node.

But this can easily be fixed by putting in the appropriate checks to detect these conditions. If the list is empty or has only one node, a null value should be returned because there is no question of an odd list. Here is the modified code:

```
<T> Node<T> split(Node<T> L) {
    if (L == null || L.next == null) return null;
    ...
    // the rest exactly as before
    ...
}
```

8.3 RECURSION ON AN ARRAY: BINARY SEARCH

In Section 5.2 we studied binary search, in which a sorted array of entries is repeatedly divided in half, until either the target is found and the search terminates with success, or there is no more room for halving the array, and the search terminates with failure. We came up with an iterative algorithm for binary search, presented in Section 5.2.2.

Our objective in this section is to reformulate binary search on an array of size n as a recursive process. The first question is: what is the smallest step we can take to peel the process? It is the comparison of the middle entry with the target. Depending on how this comparison turns out, we are either done, or we go to the left half of the array, or we go to the right half of the array.

But what happens when we go to the left or right half? We *repeat the binary search process on a smaller array,* exactly the condition that suggests that we have a recursive situation.

The next question is: how do we define this smaller array? It is not as clean as a linked list, where there is a first entry, and the rest of the list is simply referenced by the next field of the first entry. In binary search, we have a nonlinear situation, and the only way to define a subarray is to define its *bounds*.

We have seen how the bounds are set and how they change in the course of binary search, in the iterative binarySearch algorithm of Section 5.2.2.

Algorithm recBinarySearch(A, t, left, right)

input: array *A*, target *t*,
       subarray limits *left*, *right*

if (*left* > *right*) then
    display "not found"
else
    mid ← (*left* + *right*) / 2
    if (*t* == A[*mid*]) then
        display "found"
    else if (*t* < A[*mid*]) then
        recBinarySearch(*A*, *t*, *left*, *mid-1*)
    else
        recBinarySearch(*A*, *t*, *mid+1*, *right*)
    endif
endif

As in the iterative version, *left* and *right* respectively denote the left and right ends of the array. Also, the bounds change after one comparison in exactly the same manner as in the iterative version.

All that is left to be accounted for is the base case. In other words, when does the recursion terminate? We know that binary search terminates on success or failure; each of these cases must also terminate the recursion. Therefore, there are two base cases for the recursion: (a) when the target matches a "middle" entry at some level of recursion, or (b) when the *left* and *right* delimiters cross over each other.

8.4   TOWERS OF HANOI: AN APPLICATION

Let us apply all that we have learned so far to solving a classic problem— the game called the *Towers of Hanoi*.

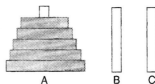

A   B   C

The setup is shown in the figure that follows: there are three towers or pegs, *A*, *B*, and *C*, and a pile of disks of various sizes. To begin with, all the disks are on peg *A*.

The object of the game is to move all the disks from peg *A* to *C*, using *B* as an intermediate, or "scratch," peg, while obeying two rules: (a) only one disk can be moved at a time, and (b) a larger disk can never go on top of a smaller one.

Legend has it that this game was played as a religious rite with three diamond needles and 64 golden disks, and the end of the game was supposed to mark the end of the world.

Our aim is to write a recursive program that will print each move made in transferring a stack of *n* pegs from *A* to *C*.

8.4.1   A Recursive Definition

The first, and most critical, step toward our recursive program is to develop a clear *recursive definition* of the solution. Let us build up some confidence by trying our hand with the simplest cases and see how we do.

The smallest instance of the problem is when there is only one disk in the stack (i.e., *n* = 1). The solution is trivial: simply move the disk from peg *A* to *C*, and we are done. What if there are two disks (i.e., *n* = 2)? Again, the solution is not hard: get the top disk out of the way by moving it to *B*, move the bottom disk to *C*, and reclaim the top disk by moving it from *B* to *C*.

Clearly, the case of $n = 1$ is a base case, and we can write it out as follows:

BASE CASE OF TOWERS OF HANOI

When $n = 1$, move a disk from *A* to *C*.

We need to be able to express the solution for $n = 2$ in a recursive manner. In order to do that, we need to build a pattern—let us try $n = 3$.

With three disks, we extend the idea we adopted for $n = 2$. Now, instead of moving one disk out of the way, we **move** *two* disks out of the way, from *A* to *B*. Then, as in the two-disk case, we move the bottom disk from *A* to *C*. Finally we **move** the two disks from *B* to *C*.

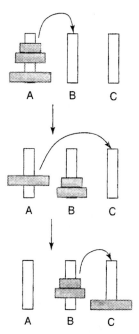

There is a subtlety here which you may have caught: the first and last **move**s in the above solution (highlighted in bold face) are not simple moves, since we are not allowed to move two disks at a time. They are subproblems, to be solved in their own right. But each of these subproblems needs us to move *two* disks from one peg to another, *which we already know how to do*. Thus we have the makings of a recursive process here, but we need to iron out one additional detail.

Note that the two-disk problem, as described earlier, moved two disks from *A* to *C*. But in the three disk problem, the first two-disk subproblem moves disks from *A* to *B*, and the second two-disk subproblem moves disks from *B* to *C*. There is really no inconsistency here, provided we *parametrize* the source, destination, and intermediate pegs.

In other words, it does not really matter what the *specific* source, destination, and intermediate pegs are. The *pattern* for moving two disks from *A* to *C*, using *B* as the intermediate, is the same as moving two disks from *A* to *B* using *C* as the intermediate.

Now we are in a position to summarize our solution for $n = 3$:

- **move** two disks from *A* to *B*, using *C* as the intermediate peg
- move a disk from *A* to *C*
- **move** two disks from *B* to *C*, using *A* as the intermediate peg

By treating steps 1 and 3 as two-disk subproblems and clearly rephrasing them in terms of the solution to $n = 2$, we arrive at a recursive definition:

RECURSIVE DEFINITION OF TOWERS OF HANOI SOLUTION
FOR $n = 3$

- Solve the Towers of Hanoi problem for $n = 2$, with source peg A, destination peg B, intermediate peg C
- move a disk from A to C
- Solve the Towers of Hanoi problem for $n = 2$, with source peg B, destination peg C, intermediate peg A

The above is a *specific* recursive definition that works for $n = 3$. To take it to the limit, let us "unravel" the recursive solutions for $n = 2$ above and get the moves printed step by step:

- move a disk from A to C
- move a disk from A to B
- move a disk from C to B
- move a disk from A to C
- move a disk from B to A
- move a disk from B to C
- move a disk from A to C

Let us do one last specific case, $n = 4$, but this time we can jump directly to the recursive solution:

RECURSIVE DEFINITION OF TOWERS OF HANOI SOLUTION
FOR $n = 4$

- Solve the Towers of Hanoi problem for $n = 3$, with source peg A, destination peg B, intermediate peg C
- move a disk from A to C
- Solve the Towers of Hanoi problem for $n = 3$, with source peg B, destination peg C, intermediate peg A

All we did was recurse on $n = 3$ subproblems instead of $n = 2$. We see a pattern for solving the *general* Towers of Hanoi problem (i.e., for n disks): we need to solve two $n - 1$ subproblems, between which is sandwiched the base case of $n = 1$. So, finally, here is our general recursive solution:

RECURSIVE DEFINITION OF TOWERS OF HANOI SOLUTION FOR ANY *n*

- Solve the Towers of Hanoi problem for $n - 1$, with source peg *A*, destination peg *B*, intermediate peg *C*
- move a disk from *A* to *C*
- Solve the Towers of Hanoi problem for $n - 1$, with source peg *B*, destination peg *C*, intermediate peg *A*

That's it. We can move on to the recursive program that implements this definition.

8.4.2   A Recursive Program

To complete our discussion, let us write a method called hanoi to solve our problem. As we have seen time and again, once we have a precise recursive definition, the recursive program simply falls into place. From the definition, it is evident that our method must accept the following parameters: the size of the stack of disks, *n;* the source peg; the destination peg; and the intermediate peg.

Here is the code for this method:

```
void hanoi(int n, char src, char dest, char interm) {
    // swap destination and intermediate pegs
    hanoi(n-1, src, interm, dest);
    // base case
    System.out.println("move a disk from " + src + " to " + dest);
    // swap source and intermediate pegs
    hanoi(n-1, interm, dest, src);
}
```

Note that this method is even more general than our recursive definition of the solution: the source, intermediate, and destination pegs could be anything, not only *A, B,* and *C.*

Finally, this method could easily be embedded within a simple application class whose main method would accept a value for *n,* and the names of the three pegs, and invoke the hanoi method to print the moves of the solution.

8.5   RECURSION AND STACKS

Let us now take a close look at the *mechanism* by which a recursive program is actually implemented by the compiler. In Section 8.2 we saw how a recursion executes its forward and backing-out phases. The order in which the recursive process backs out is the reverse of the order in which it goes forward. During the backing-out process, some action may be performed that involves recalling something that has been stored in the forward process.

This requirement of storing something and recalling for later use in reverse order of storage is ideally supported by a stack. Little surprise, then, that the compiler *uses a stack to implement recursion.*

The following figure shows how the factorial recursion of Section 8.2.1 is implemented using a stack.

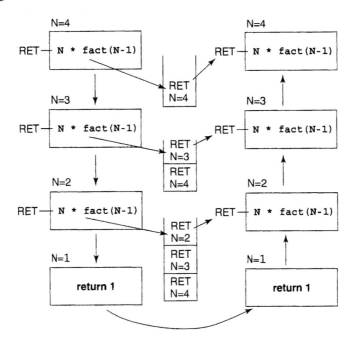

In the code for the fact method, the line return N*fact(N-1) is where a recursive call is made. This is also the line where the call must return so that the multiplication can be performed. The location of this line of code, indicated by RET, needs to be stored on the stack.

In the forward phase, prior to transferring control to a called method, the return address, RET, and the value of parameter *N* are pushed on the stack. In the backing-out phase, when a call finishes executing, the return address at the top of the stack is popped, so that control can be returned to this address, and the value of *N* is popped so that the appropriate state of the caller can be restored.

Note that the return address, RET, or location is the same for any level of recursion because the method executed is the same at any level; however, the values of the local variables and parameters, characterizing the *state* of the method, change in each call.

To summarize:

- In the forward phase, the values of local variables and parameters, and the return address are pushed on the stack for every level of the recursion
- In the backing-out phase, the stacked address is popped and used to return to executing the rest of the code in the calling level, and the stacked local variables and parameters are popped and used to restore the state of that call

8.6   DRAWBACKS OF RECURSION

The main drawback of recursion is the amount of stack space that is used to implement it. Another, less frequently occurring drawback is that certain computations may be performed redundantly. We examine both these drawbacks in the light of the applications we have studied so far.

Recursion consumes stack space.   Every recursive method call produces a new instance of the method, one with a *new set of local variables* (including parameters). Before this new instance starts executing, local information (variables and parameters) pertaining to the calling instance is stored on the stack, to be picked up on return.

The total stack space used depends upon the level of nesting of the recursion process, and the number of local variables and parameters. As we observed in Section 8.5, the number of local variables and parameters does not change from one level of recursion to another, since the same code is being executed at every level, although with a different state or set of values of these variables and parameters.

Let us return to our very first example of recursion, that of computing the factorial of a number. While this is a classic example because of its simplicity, it is also the last thing one would want to write as a recursive program in practice. A recursive version would suffer an enormous overhead: the recursion terminates only when $N = 1$, and in the meanwhile, local information pertaining to each of the calls to fact(N), fact(N-1), and so on, all the way down to fact(2) is stored on the stack. In sum, fact(N) would consume $O(N)$ worth of stack space.

Recursion may perform redundant computations.   Consider again the recursive computation of the Fibonacci sequence as illustrated in Section 8.1.4. Note that in computing $F(4)$, $F(2)$ is computed *twice,* a clear case of redundant computation. The instance of $F(4)$ only reveals the tip of the iceberg.

What if we wanted to compute $F(5)$? If you draw the recursive levels of computation for this in a manner similar to that for $F(4)$, you will observe that $F(3)$ is computed twice, each of which involves a computation of $F(2)$, and there is another computation of $F(2)$ by itself. Things thus get worse as we recursively compute the Fibonacci sequence for bigger and bigger numbers. Not to mention the stack space that is being used up by the recursive implementation.

In sum, one has to weigh the simplicity of the code delivered by recursion against its drawbacks as described above. When a relatively simple iterative solution is possible, it is definitely a better alternative. In the next section, we see how one specific recursive code pattern tells us that an iterative solution exists.

8.7   TAIL RECURSION

Say a method makes a recursive call. If, upon return from the recursive call, it does nothing but return the result of the call (or just returns if the method has no return value), the method is said to be *tail recursive.* Here are two methods, one of which is tail recursive, and the other is not.

Tail Recursive	**Not Tail Recursive**

```
<T> void traverse(
        Node<T> first) {
    if (first == null) {
        return;
    }
    System.out.println(first.data);
    traverse(first.next);
}
```

```
<T> void printBackwards(
        Node<T> first) {
    if (first == null) {
        return;
    }
    printBackwards(first.next);
    System.out.println(first.data);
}
```

A tail recursive method can *always* be rewritten without using recursion, and instead using iteration. This saves stack space, and results in better efficiency. Some compilers will automatically transform a tail recursive method into an iterative version.

The binary search algorithm of Section 8.3 (and its implementation) is tail recursive. The factorial method fact of Section 8.2.1 and the Fibonacci method Fibo of Section 8.2.2 are both non–tail recursive methods, but they can be both be transformed into tail recursive variants. The key is to use one or more *accumulators* as parameters to the method.

As written in Section 8.2.1, method fact is not tail recursive because upon return from the recursive call, there is a multiplication with the local N before returning from the method. We will use an accumulator called result as a parameter, and rewrite the method. This method will be *driven* by another method—this latter driver is the method called from elsewhere in the program.

Tail Recursion	**Driver**

```
int tailRecFact(int N, int result) {
    if (N == 1) {
        return result;
    }
    return tailRecFact(N-1, N*result);
}
```

```
int fact(int N) {
    return tailRecFact(N, 1);
}
```

Similarly, Fibo can be transformed into a tail recursive method, this time using two accumulators:

Tail Recursion	**Driver**

```
int tailRecFibo(int N, int next,
            int result) {
    if (N == 0) {
        return result;
    }
    return tailRecFibo(N-1,
                next + result,
                next);
}
```

```
int Fibo(int N) {
    return tailRecFibo(N, 1, 0);
}
```

The following table lists the values of the parameters in successive calls to `tail-RecFibo`, to help us visualize the progression for N = 5:

N	next	result
5	1	0
4	1	1
3	2	1
2	3	2
1	5	3
0	8	5

So `Fibo(5, 1, 0)` will return a result of 5.

When we see a tail recursive method, we are assured that there is an iterative alternative, so we may as well work out and write the iterative version.

The iterative version for factorial is very simple, and uses three variables worth of space for `result`, `i`, and N. Thus it consumes only $O(1)$ space.

```
int fact(int N) {
    int result = 1;
    for (int i=2; i <= N; i++) {
        result *= i;
    }
    return result;
}
```

Let us write an iterative solution to compute the Fibonacci number for N. What we need is to start at the base case(s), as we did with the factorial computation, and work our way up. At every point we need to remember the previous two numbers so that we can add them up.

As can be seen, the key is in observing that the previous two numbers form a window that moves up by one step in every iteration.

The window starts with the base case numbers 0 and 1, and in the first iteration the next number, 1 is computed. In the second iteration, the window moves up by one step to cover the second number of the preceding iteration, namely 1, and the new number computed, namely 1. And so on. Once this becomes clear, the iterative code is simple.

The iterative version, illustrated to the right, uses space worth five variables, again $O(1)$. There are no redundant computations: every intermediate Fibonacci number is computed exactly once.

```
int Fibo(int N) {
    int a = 0; int b = 1;
    for (int i=2; i <= N; i++) {
        fib = a + b; a = b; b = fib;
    }
    return fib;
}
```

The problem of printing backwards and the towers of Hanoi problem have solutions that are not transformable to tail recursive versions. There is no iterative solution to these problems, and recursion is the only recourse. In the following chapters we will see several more instances of recursion in action, many of them genuinely recursive in that they do not have iterative solutions. It will become increasingly clear that recursion is not an afterthought, but a way of thinking about problems from the get-go.

8.8 SUMMARY

- A recursive definition of an entity defines the entity in terms of itself.
- Every recursive definition must have at least one condition, called its base condition or base case, at which a definition does not recurse (i.e., does not refer to itself).
- A recursive definition that does not encounter a base case, or has no base case, would spin endlessly—this is called an infinite recursion.
- A data structure may be built from scratch by using its recursive definition.
- A recursive definition of a problem involves a so-called blind-faith factor that presupposes that a smaller instance of the problem can be solved by applying the same recursive definition to it.
- The main work in writing a recursive method to solve a problem is to work out a clear and correct recursive definition for the solution.
- A recursive method contains one or more calls to itself.
- The execution of every recursive method consists of forward and backing-out phases.
- A recursion that involves an array needs to carry the limits of the subarray for each level of the recursive process.
- A recursive definition or implementation consists of one "small step" which is then glued with the result of one or more recursive calls.
- The mechanism of recursion is implemented by means of a stack, in which, at every recursive call, the caller stores the values of its local variables and parameters, as well as an address to which the "called" must return upon its completion.
- The main drawback of recursion is that it consumes stack space.
- Another drawback of recursion is that it may perform redundant computations.
- A method is tail recursive if, upon returning from the recursive call, it does nothing else but return.
- Every tail recursive method can be transformed into one that does not use recursion but is iterative.
- An iterative solution is much more efficient than a recursive solution for a problem because it does not need to use any stack space at all.

8.9 EXERCISES

E8.1. Trace the recursive computation of the Fibonacci function $F(5)$ by drawing a figure similar to the one for $F(4)$ in Section 8.1.4. Count the number of additions performed overall. Compare this with the number of additions performed by the iterative version of Section 8.7.

E8.2. Consider the trace of the fact recursion implementation using a stack illustrated in Section 8.5. Counting the storage of a return address and a parameter as one unit of space each, what is the maximum units of space at any point in the stack? What would be your answer for the computation of fact(6) instead of fact(4)?

E8.3. Trace the recursive computation of the method Fibo of Section 8.2.2 called with $N = 4$ using a stack. Again, counting the storage of a return address and a parameter as each one unit of space, what is the maximum units of space at any point in the stack?

E8.4. Trace the countNodes method of Section 8.2.3 in a manner analogous to the trace of the fact method illustrated in Section 8.2.1. Assume that the linked list has four entries (it doesn't matter what these entries are). Show the actual sublist under consideration at every level of the recursion.

E8.5. Trace the printBackwards method of Section 8.2.3 in a manner analogous to the trace of the fact method illustrated in Section 8.2.1. Assume that the linked list has four entries, "May," "August," "January," and "December," in that order. Show the actual sublist under consideration at every level of the recursion, and the output at the end of each step of the backing-out phase.

E8.6. Trace the split method of Section 8.2.3 in a manner analogous to the trace of the fact method illustrated in Section 8.2.1. Clearly show the states of the lists first and second at every level of the recursion, both in the forward phase and in the backing-out phase.

E8.7. In a manner analogous to the trace of the fact method illustrated in Section 8.2.1, trace the recBinarySearch algorithm of Section 8.3 on the binary search example of Section 5.2.2, searching for target 19 in the given array. Show the actual subarray being considered at every level of the recursion. How many comparisons are made in all? How does this compare with the number of comparisons in the iterative version?

E8.8. Repeat Exercise E8.7, but this time with a stack, showing the contents of the stack as it grows in the forward phase of the recursion. (Hint: the array name, the bounds of the subarray, the local variable *mid*, the target *t*, and the return address are stacked for every recursive call. Observe that there are two possible return addresses.)

Counting the storage of a return address, a local variable, and a parameter as each one unit of space, what is the maximum units of space at any point in the stack?

E8.9. Work out by hand the moves made in solving the towers of Hanoi puzzle for $n = 4$. How many moves were made?

E8.10. Write a recursive definition for an ordered list in which the entries are arranged in *descending* order of values.

E8.11. Write a recursive definition for a function $S(N)$ that is the sum of all integers from 1 to N. What prevents your definition from being an infinite recursion?

E8.12. Write a recursive definition for the power function N^I, where N and I are integers, and $I \geq 0$.

E8.13. The greatest common divisor (GCD) of two integers m and n, $m \geq n$, is defined as follows: If n is 0, then the GCD is m. Otherwise, the GCD is the GCD of n and the remainder of m divided by n. For instance, the GCD of 5 and 3 is 1, obtained as follows: GCD(5,3) is in turn GCD(3,2), which is in turn GCD(2,1), which is in turn GCD(1,1), which is in turn GCD(1,0), which is 1.

Write a mathematical recursive definition of the GCD function.

E8.14. You are given a list of integers. Write a recursive definition of the maximum-valued entry in the list.

E8.15. A string of characters is defined as a palindrome if it reads the same both forwards and backwards. For example, the string "abba" and "madam" are palindromes. Write a recursive definition of a palindrome. (The empty string and a single-character strings are considered to be palindromes.)

8.10   PROGRAMMING PROBLEMS

P8.1. Implement a Java application class called Towers consisting of a main method and the hanoi method of Section 8.4.2. Your application must accept a value for *n*, the number of disks, and print out the moves required to solve the puzzle for *n* disks. It should also print the *number* of moves made.

Run your program on different values of *n*, starting with 2 and incrementing by 1 every time. What is the lowest value of *n* at which it makes more than 1,000 moves? Do you see a pattern that relates the number of moves to the value of *n*? What kind of running-time order does this indicate?

P8.2. You are given the following listMystery method:

```
<T> int listMystery(Node<T> L) {
    if (L == null) return 0;
    if (L.data > 0) {
        return 1 + listMystery(L.next)
    } else {
        return listMystery(L.next)
    }
}
```

Describe in one sentence what this method does when called with a reference to the first node of a linked list of integers?

Write a recursive definition for the function implemented by this method.

P8.3. You are given the following listMystery2 method:

```
<T> void listMystery2(Node<T> prev, Node<T> L) {
    if (L == null) return;
    listMystery2(L, L.next);
    L.next = prev;
}
```

Suppose you are given a linked list whose first node is referenced by LL. Describe in one sentence what the above method would do if called as follows:

```
listMystery2(null, LL)
```

P8.4. Write a recursive method:

```
<T> Node<T> merge(Node<T> L1, Node<T> L2)
```

that would merge two *sorted* linked lists L1 and L2 of integers. Your method should return a reference to the first node in the merged list, and should *not use any additional space for nodes*. In other words, your merged list must consist of only those nodes that were in L1 or L2.

P8.5. Write a recursive method:

```
<T> void insert(Node<T> L, Node<T> newNode)
```

that would insert a new node at the *end* of a linked list whose first node is refer-enced by L.

P8.6. Write a recursive sequential search method:

```
<T> boolean
contains(Node<T> L, T item)
```

that would search for item item in the linked list referenced by L, and return true or false, respectively, depending on whether the item is found or not.

P8.7. Write a recursive method to reverse the entries in a queue. For instance, if the queue had entries A, B, C, the method would transform the queue into C, B, A.

```
<T> void reverse(Queue<T> queue)
```

P8.8. Write a recursive method to print the following X pattern:

```
X       X
  X   X
    X
  X   X
X       X
```

The parameter to the method is the height of the X. The height of the sample X above is 5.

P8.9. Given a string of characters stored in an array, write a boolean recursive method, isPalindrome, that would determine whether the string is a palindrome or not. You may assume that all the locations of the array are filled. A zero-length string (empty string) is considered to be a palindrome.

P8.10. The *Ackermann* function takes two integer arguments m and n, and is defined as follows for *initial m* and *n* both greater than 0:

- if $m = 0$ then *Ackermann* equals $n + 1$
- if $n = 0$ then *Ackermann* equals *Ackermann*$(m - 1, 1)$
- if neither m nor n is 0, then *Ackermann* equals *Ackermann* $(m - 1, Ackermann(m, n - 1))$

The *Ackermann* function grows amazingly fast, and takes a very large number of calls to be evaluated. For instance, evaluation of *Ackermann*$(3, 4)$ requires over $10,000$ calls.

Implement this function and test it out for values of m and n. At what values of m and n does it take more than a million calls to evaluate this function?

P8.11. The function $C(n, k)$ gives the number of ways in which we can select (choose) k objects out of n. For instance, if there are three candies in lemon, cherry, and apple flavors, we can choose two of these three in three ways: (1) lemon and cherry, (2) lemon and apple, or (3) apple and cherry. Choosing two of three is represented by $C(3, 2)$.

We can determine $C(n,k)$ for any n and k using the following definition:

$$C(n,k) = \begin{cases} 1 & \text{if } k = 0 \\ 1 & \text{if } k = n \\ 0 & \text{if } k > n \\ C(n-1,k-1) + C(n-1,k) & \text{if } 0 < k < n \end{cases}$$

(a) Trace the computation of $C(5,3)$ in a manner similar to that of the trace of the $F(4)$ in Section 8.1.4. Are any redundant computations performed?

(b) Implement the function $C(n,k)$ as a Java method.

P8.12. Here's a recursive method to count the number of nodes in a linked list:

```
<T> int countNodes(Node<T> first) {
    if (first == null) {
        return 0;
    }
    return 1 + countNodes(first.next);
}
```

Transform this method into a tail recursive version.

P8.13. Write a tail recursive method to remove all occurrences of an item from a linked list:

```
<T> Node<T> removeAll(Node<T> first, T item) {
```

The method should return a reference to the first node of the resulting list.

CHAPTER 9

Binary Tree and General Tree

Two-way decision-making is one of the fundamental concepts in computing, and a host of mechanisms and structures have been devised to implement this concept in programming. One such key data structure is the binary tree.

While a binary tree models two-way decisions or choices, a general tree models hierarchies such as family trees, employee hierarchies in organizations, and file system hierarchies in operating systems. A hierarchy represents multi-way choices, and in this sense, the general tree is an extension of the binary tree.

Learning Objectives

- Describe a binary tree in terms of its structure and components, and learn recursive definitions of the binary tree and its properties.
- Study standard tree traversals in depth.
- Develop a binary tree class interface based on its recursive definition.
- Learn about the signature of a binary tree and understand how to build a binary tree given its signature.
- Understand Huffman coding, a binary tree–based text-compression application, and use the binary tree class to implement Huffman coding.
- Implement the binary tree class.
- Study how tree traversals may be implemented nonrecursively using a stack.
- Describe the properties of a general tree.
- Learn the natural correspondence of a general tree with an equivalent binary tree, and the signature of a general tree.

9.1 BINARY TREE PROPERTIES

Most of the concepts and terminology we use in *computer* binary trees are derived from *natural* trees, as you can observe in Figure 9.1.

9.1.1 Components

Let us now go over the binary tree example in Figure 9.1(b) and see how different components of this tree are named. To start with, a binary tree consists of **nodes** and **branches.** A node is a place in the tree where data is stored. In the example, A through F are the labels for the nodes of the binary tree.

There is one special node called **root.** The root is the "starting point" of the tree. In Figure 9.1, node A is the root.

The nodes are connected to each other by links or branches. But there is a precise way in which these branches are laid out. First of all, a branch is either a *left* branch or a *right* branch, as is illustrated in Figure 9.1(b).

Here is where the concept of *binary*ness comes in. A branch signifies a decision path—a choice that connects one node to another. Consider node B in Figure 9.1(b). There are two choices at B, expressed as left-branch B--C and right-branch B--D. Thus binary means that there are *at most two choices.*

Accordingly, a node is said to have at most two **children.** Thus, node B has children C and D. In turn, B is the parent of C as well as D. C is the **left child** of B, and D is its **right child.**

A node that does not have any children is called a **leaf;** leaves are the "end nodes" of a binary tree. Thus, C, H, I, and G are leaf nodes in the binary tree of Figure 9.1(b). Nonleaf nodes are called **internal nodes.**

We said that a node may have *at most two children.* The leaves have no children. In the binary tree of Figure 9.1(b), nodes F and A have one child each; all other nonleaf nodes have two children.

There is a single **path** from any node to any other node in the tree. If we were to trace the path from root A to node E in Figure 9.1(b), it would consist of the following series of branches:

```
A--B, B--D, D--E
```

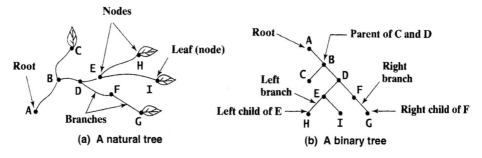

FIGURE 9.1: (a) A natural tree, and (b) its computer counterpart, a binary tree.

Convince yourself that there is no other way to reach E from A. How about the path from node H to node F? It involves going "up" the tree, first to parent E, then to E's parent, D, and then going "down" to D's child, F, resulting in the following series of branches:

```
H--E, E--D, D--F
```

In a binary tree data structure, *data items stored at the nodes of the tree are identified by the relative positions of the nodes.* For instance, leaf I in the tree of Figure 9.1(b) is in a fixed position relative to the other nodes in the tree, and specifically, relative to the root. The tree as a whole carries a meaning that would change if the relative positions of the data in the tree were to change.

RELATIVE POSITIONS OF NODES

A binary tree is defined by the relative positions of the data in its nodes, and the tree as a whole carries a meaning that would change if the relative positions of the data in the tree were to change.

These ideas are described in the next section with examples.

9.1.2 Position as Meaning

If-then-else tree. As can be seen in the figure, the if-then-else tree is a binary tree that represents an if-then-else construct in a program. Every node in this tree is a conditional expression that evaluates to *yes* or *no*. If it evaluates to yes, the left branch (if any) is taken, and if it evaluates to no, the right branch (if any) is taken. Note that every single path in this tree represents one execution path that can be traced by the program.

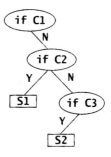

As with the leaves of Figure 9.1, in the if-then-else tree the statement S1 can be distinguished from S2 by simply describing the sequence of conditions in the path from the root to either statement. In other words S1 is executed if C1 is false, and C2 is true. Interchanging the positions of S1 and S2 would change the meaning of the entire program that the tree represents.

20-questions tree. As the next figure illustrates, the 20-questions tree is a depiction of the game of "20 questions."[1] In this game, one person thinks of an entity (animal or person, inanimate object, etc.), and others try to guess what the entity is by asking a series of up to 20 questions. The person who thought of the entity may only answer these questions with a *yes* or *no*.

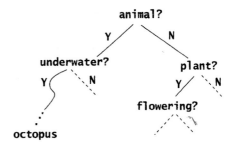

Based on the reply to each question, the group can narrow down the possibilities. The final answer depends on the sequence of answers given to the questions. As with the if-then-else tree, a leaf node is an entity that can be distinguished from any other leaf-level entity by describing the path from the root to that leaf. So an octopus is an *animal* that lives *underwater*. Once the sequences of questions are laid out in the tree, the node that contains *octopus* had better not switch its position with the one that contains *flowering plant*.

Expression tree. The expression tree, shown in the next figure, is a binary tree that represents the evaluation of the arithmetic expression (f + ((a * b) - c)). The relative positions of the nodes in the tree determine the value of an expression. In this sense, the whole is more than

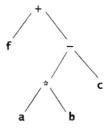

the sum of the parts. If the * were interchanged with the +, we would get an entirely different value, (f * ((a + b) - c)), and a different expression tree.

The expression tree is different from the if-then-else and 20-questions trees in that the root does not act as a "source" from which all things flow. To write the expression represented by such a tree, we start at a leaf node and work our way through the tree in a particular sequence. Later, we will return to this sequence and study it in more detail.

A few other interesting properties of binary trees (and some more terminology) up next.

9.1.3 Structure

We need to build some terminology and tools that will help us codify the structure of a binary tree. An obvious first measure is a count of the number of nodes in the tree. However, two trees with the same number of nodes may not have the same structure. The

---

1. This was inspired by an example in *Data Structures and Other Objects*, by Savitch and Main.

following figure shows all the different binary tree structures that can be built out of two and three nodes, respectively. There are two different tree structures that can be built out of two nodes, and five different structures out of three nodes.

(a)   (b)   (c)   (d)   (e)   (f)   (g)

Another useful attribute of a node is its distance from the root, called its **depth.** Distance is counted in number of branches from the root. So the depth of the root itself is zero.[1] Nodes at the same depth are said to be at the same **level,** with the root being at level zero. The **height** of a tree is the maximum level (or depth) at which there is a node. Alternatively, the height of a tree is the distance of the farthest leaf from the root.

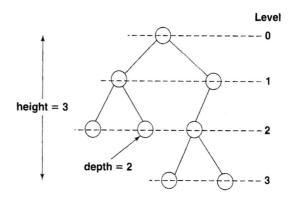

There are two special types of binary trees, **strictly binary** and **complete,** that merit consideration.

STRICTLY BINARY TREE

A strictly binary tree is one in which every node has either no child or two children (i.e., no node can have only one child).

The expression tree is a strictly binary tree, because every internal node is a *binary* operator and must therefore have two children.

COMPLETE BINARY TREE

In a complete binary tree, every level but the last must have the maximum number of nodes possible at that level. The last level may have fewer than the maximum possible, but they should be arranged from left to right without any empty spots.

The following figure shows some examples and counter-examples of strictly binary and complete binary trees.

---

1. Numbering may also be done starting with level 1 at the root, instead of 0.

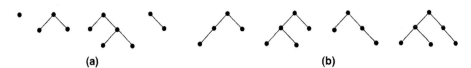

(a)   (b)

Of the four trees shown in (a), the first three are strictly binary, but the fourth is not. Of the four trees in (b), the first two are complete and the last two are not. Which trees in (a) and (b) are both complete and strictly binary? Which trees are neither?

This brings us to another interesting aspect of binary trees: the maximum number of nodes per level, and therefore, the maximum number of nodes in the tree. At level i, there can be at most 2^i nodes. Let the height of a binary tree be h. Then the maximum number of nodes that can be accommodated at the last level of this tree is 2^h. The capacity of this tree, N_{max} (i.e., the maximum number of nodes it can contain), is the following, obtained by adding the maximum number of nodes over all the levels:

$$N_{max} = 2^0 + 2^1 + 2^2 + \cdots + 2^{h-1} + 2^h = 2^{h+1} - 1$$

This result leads to the following important corollary, one we will use on numerous occasions:

MAXIMUM NUMBER OF NODES IN A BINARY TREE

Let a binary tree contain N_{max} nodes, the maximum number of nodes possible for its height, say h. Then, $h = \log(N_{max} + 1) - 1$.

9.1.4 Recursive Definitions

We can recognize a binary tree if we see one, but how can we program a computer to recognize one? It turns out that the binary tree lends itself very well to a recursive definition.

RECURSIVE DEFINITION OF BINARY TREE

A binary tree is either empty or consists of a special node called root that has a left subtree and a right subtree that are mutually disjoint binary trees.

We can use this recursive definition to build a binary tree from scratch. Or, going the other way, given a binary tree, we can trace its construction by applying the recursive definition to break it up into smaller and smaller subtrees until we hit bottom (i.e., the empty tree). This is depicted in Figure 9.2.

Tree T can be decomposed into its "atomic" units (i.e., empty trees) by repeatedly applying the recursive definition to it, its component subtrees, its subtrees' subtrees, and

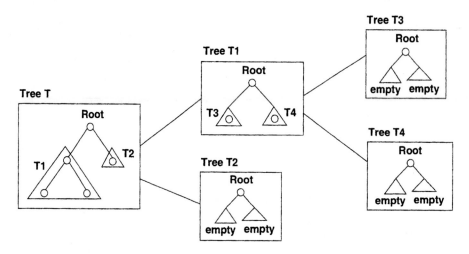

FIGURE 9.2: **Recursive Tree Construction and Decomposition.** Going left to right, we apply the recursive definition to break down T to empty trees. Going right to left, we construct T by applying the recursive definition.

so on, until empty subtrees are reached. The empty tree is the base case of the recursive definition.

We can build the binary tree T using the following sequence of steps:

- Starting with an empty tree, T2, make a root node for it.
- Starting with an empty tree, T3, make a root for it.
- Starting with an empty tree, T4, make a root for it.
- Starting with an empty tree, T1, make a root for it. Make T2 the left subtree of this root. Make T3 the right subtree of this root.
- Starting with an empty tree, T, make a root for it, Make T1 the left subtree of this root. Make T2 the right subtree of this root.

We can write a program that could build such a binary tree in incremental steps and ensure that the tree it builds is in fact a binary tree.

Several attributes that characterize a binary tree can also be defined recursively—for instance, the number of nodes and the height.

RECURSIVE DEFINITION OF NUMBER OF NODES

The number of nodes in an empty binary tree is zero. Otherwise, the number of nodes is one plus the number of nodes in the left and right subtrees of the root.

Note how closely this definition follows the recursive definition of the binary tree itself, as does the following definition of tree height.

RECURSIVE DEFINITION OF HEIGHT

The height of an empty binary tree is −1. Otherwise, the height is one plus the maximum of the heights of the left and right subtrees of the root.

The height of an empty tree is defined to be −1, and thus the height of a single-node tree is (correctly) computed to be 0.

9.2 BINARY TREE TRAVERSALS

Traversing or stepping through the entries of a linear structure was easy because there was one obvious way to go: start from the beginning and go to the end, in sequence. The binary tree, on the other hand, has no obvious traversal sequence. The starting point is obviously the root, but then what? Which way to turn first, left or right? And which way to turn after that? And so on.

Moreover, at every turn you take, you have to come back and take the *other* turn to finish up. The deeper you go in the tree following a particular path, the more unexplored directions you need to put on the back-burner to be followed when the path is retraced. Trouble is, how to remember what directions were not taken, and therefore need to be returned to?

To restore a semblance of order to this situation of seemingly endless possibilities, four standard traversals are defined on a binary tree. These are the **preorder, inorder, postorder,** and **level-order** traversals. All but the last are recursively defined; in this sense, level-order traversal is the odd one out.

A good example to illustrate these traversals is the expression tree of Section 9.1.2. At that time we wrote down, in infix form, the expression represented by the tree, and remarked that there is a particular sequence in which the tree nodes are traversed to produce this form. It turns out that this sequence is the inorder traversal. Let us begin with the inorder traversal and understand exactly how it works.

The key first step is to view the tree as a recursive structure, shown here for an expression tree. Once this is recognized, we traverse in the required order. Another important visual idea is to imagine empty subtrees to the left and right of leaf nodes f, a, b, and c to complete the recursive definition—as we know, these empty subtrees terminate the recursion.

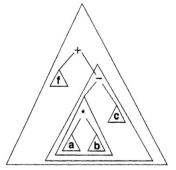

The traversals employ an action called *visit* that does something at a node. Visiting a node could be a simple action, such as printing the contents of the node, or something more complex or application-specific.

Following is a recursive definition of inorder traversal.

INORDER TRAVERSAL OF TREE T

First recursively traverse the *L*eft subtree of T, then *V*isit the root of T, then recursively traverse the *R*ight subtree of T.

Needless to say, there is nothing to be done when the tree is empty. The abbreviations *V, L,* and *R* for visit, left traverse, and right traverse, respectively, can very concisely describe the traversal: inorder traversal is **LVR.**

The figure shows how the flow of program control goes through every node, and is a nonrecursive view of inorder traversal in which the traversal starts and ends at the root, encountering every node three

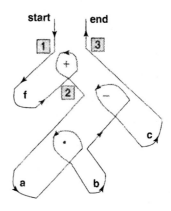

times during the traversal process. After the last encounter, the node is left behind forever, and the thread of control returns to its parent.

NONRECURSIVE VIEW OF TRAVERSALS

A traversal encounters each node in the tree three times: when entering the node from its parent, when returning from traversing its left subtree, and when returning from traversing its right subtree. Depending on whether a node is visited in the first, second, or third encounter, we have a preorder, inorder, or postorder traversal, respectively.

We will return to this idea in Section 8.5 when we see how a recursive traversal may be implemented nonrecursively using a stack.

Following are the recursive definitions of preorder and postorder traversals.

PREORDER TRAVERSAL OF TREE T

First *V*isit the root of T, then recursively traverse the *L*eft subtree of T, then recursively traverse the *R*ight subtree of T.

POSTORDER TRAVERSAL OF TREE T

First recursively traverse the *Left* subtree of T, then recursively traverse the *Right* subtree of T, then *V*isit the root of T.

The inorder traversal of an expression tree produces the infix form of the expression. One can thus deduce that a preorder traversal will produce the prefix form, and the postorder traversal, the postfix form—see the following table.

Traversal	Expression	Form
Preorder	+ f - * a b c	Prefix
Inorder	f + a * b - c	Infix
Postorder	f a b * c - +	Postfix

Finally, we must not forget level-order traversal. Here is the definition:

LEVEL-ORDER TRAVERSAL OF TREE T

Starting at the root level, go level by level in T, *v*isiting the nodes at any level in left-to-right order.

The following figure shows all four traversals on a couple of trees.

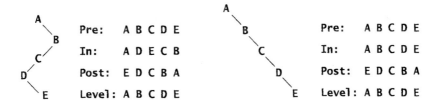

As we mentioned earlier, the traversals (particularly the recursive ones) provide the basis for designing algorithms to extract different types of information about a binary tree by simply tailoring the definition of *visit* according to need. Here are a couple of instances:

- The *number of nodes* can be computed by using a postorder traversal to implement the recursive definition outlined earlier. The count (at the root) cannot be computed until the count of the left subtree (traverse left) and the count of the right subtree (traverse right) are computed first. Thus, *visiting* a node in this case can be implemented as summing the counts of the number of nodes in the left and right subtrees and adding one for the node being visited.

- The *height* can be computed analogously.

TAILORING THE DEFINITION OF VISIT

The standard traversals can be used to process information in a tree by appropriately defining what actions are performed when a node is visited.

Next, we explore a `BinaryTree` class.

9.3   A `BinaryTree` CLASS

Figure 9.3 shows the public interface of a generic binary tree class.

Class structures.tree.BinaryTree<T>

Fields

> **BinaryTree<T> left, right, parent**

Constructors

> **BinaryTree( )**
> Creates an empty binary tree.

Methods

$O(1)$ **void makeRoot(T data)**
     Creates a root node for this tree with the specified data.
     Throws **TreeViolationException** if this tree is not empty.
$O(1)$ **void setData(T data)**
     Sets the data at this tree node to the specified data.
$O(1)$ **T getData( )**
     Retrieves the data stored at this tree node.
$O(n)$ **BinaryTree<T> root( )**
     Returns the root of the tree in which this tree is a subtree.
$O(1)$ **void attachLeft(BinaryTree<T> tree)**
     Attaches the specified tree as the left subtree of this tree node.
     Throws **TreeViolationException** if this tree node already has a left subtree.
$O(1)$ **void attachRight(BinaryTree<T> tree)**
     Attaches the specified tree as the right subtree of this tree node.
     Throws **TreeViolationException** if this tree node already has a right subtree.
$O(1)$ **BinaryTree<T> detachLeft( )**
     Detaches the left subtree from this tree node and returns the detached tree.
     Returns null if this node does not have a left subtree.
$O(1)$ **BinaryTree<T> detachRight( )**
     Detaches the right subtree from this tree node and returns the detached tree.
     Returns null if this node does not have a right subtree.
$O(1)$ **boolean isEmpty( )**
     Returns true if this tree is empty, otherwise returns false.
$O(1)$ **void clear( )**
     Empties out this binary tree, and detaches it from its parent node.

FIGURE 9.3: A Generic Binary Tree Class. Only the public interface is shown; n is the number of nodes in the tree.

The most noteworthy design feature of this class is that it is based on the recursive tree definition. To understand the implications of this design decision, consider the following example.

First, create the trees P and Q:

```
BinaryTree<String> P =
       new BinaryTree<String>();
BinaryTree<String> Q =
       new BinaryTree<String>();
```

Next, convert the empty trees to single-node trees:

```
P.makeRoot("root");
Q.makeRoot("leftOfP");
```

Then attach Q as the left subtree of P:

```
P.attachLeft(Q);
```

This line of code speaks to the recursive definition of the tree, consistent with the way we recursively built binary trees in Section 9.1.4.

Next, we create a single-node tree, R, and attach it as the right subtree of Q:

```
BinaryTree<String> R =
       new BinaryTree<String>();
R.makeRoot("rightOfQ");
Q.attachRight(R);
```

When we say that P is a binary tree, we are actually referring to the root of the tree. Clearly, once we have a reference to the root, we have access to all the nodes under it (i.e., the entire tree). This is analogous to the linked list, where a reference to the first node also (transitively) referred to the entire list.

We can access all the nodes of the tree P as follows:

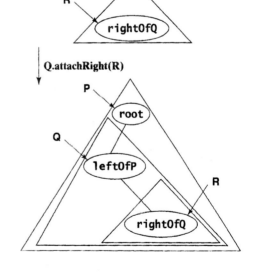

```
BinaryTree<String> Pleft = P.left;     // same as Q
BinaryTree<String> Qright = P.left.right;    // same as R
BinaryTree<String> Rroot = R.root();    // same as P
```

Note that root() takes one all the way up following the chain of parents. Rroot could also be obtained as:

```
Rroot = R.parent.parent;
```

The structure of the tree can be easily navigated because the children and parent links of a node are publicly accessible.

It is interesting to see how to delete a single node from a tree. For instance, if we want to delete node Q from the final tree of the preceding figure, we have to delink Q from its parent and its child, and attach Q's child to Q's parent:

```
BinaryTree<String> Qparent = Q.parent;
Q = Qparent.detachLeft();
BinaryTree<String> Qright = Q.detachRight();
Qparent.attachLeft(Qright);
```

At this point, Q is an independent, single-node tree. The code given above is equivalent to the following one-liner:

```
Q.parent.attachLeft(Q.parent.detachLeft().detachRight());
```

A little hard to understand, as one liners go, so let us try to take it one step at a time. Q.parent.detachLeft() detaches Q from P and returns Q, on which detachRight is invoked. The latter detaches R from Q and returns R, which serves as an argument to Q.parent.attachLeft() to complete the connection of R to P.

Finally, with this BinaryTree class, writing the recursive traversal procedures is a breeze. Here is inorder traversal, implemented as a method that takes a binary tree as parameter and simply prints the data at a node when it visits that node.

```
<T> void inorder(BinaryTree<T> tree) {
    if (tree != null) {
        inorder(tree.left);
        System.out.println(tree.getData());
        inorder(tree.right);
    }
}
```

Running times of methods.   Methods makeRoot, setData, and getData all involve reading or writing data once into a node. This read or write can be counted as a unit time operation, and as a result the running times of each of these methods is $O(1)$.

Assuming that any implementation of the BinaryTree class keeps a pointer to the root node, checking for whether the tree is empty is equivalent to checking whether this pointer is null. This is a unit time operation and isEmpty; therefore is an $O(1)$ time method.

Also, method `clear` would simply have to set the root pointer to null, effectively breaking the one and only access point to the rest of the tree—all the tree nodes will be subsequently garbage collected. Thus the `clear` method can be implemented in $O(1)$ time.

The `attachLeft` and `attachRight` methods simply link the parent pointer of the parameter tree node to the receiving tree node, and the children pointers of the receiving tree node to the parameter tree node. Setting up these links is a total of three pointer settings—a constant number of pointer settings, each of which takes unit time, for a running time of $O(1)$. The running times of `detachLeft` and `detachRight` can be analogously shown to be $O(1)$.

The `root` method can, in the worst case, be called on a leaf node that is at the greatest possible depth in the tree. In this case, the `root` method implementation would have to go all the way up the tree, taking $O(h)$ time, where h is the height of the tree. Furthermore, for a tree containing n nodes, the height could be as much as $n - 1$ in the case where the tree is entirely lopsided. In other words, if every node (except the root) is the left (resp. right) child of its parent, then we have a tree that is lopsided to the left (resp. right). Thus, the worst case time for the `root` operation is $O(n)$.

9.4   STORING AND RECREATING A BINARY TREE

Imagine a computer helpline that uses a *preconstructed* binary tree to ask a sequence of questions, and navigate down the tree based on the caller's response:

```
Helper: ''Does the power light come on?''
Caller: ''Yes.''
Helper: ''When you boot up, do you hear clicking and
        whirring sounds?''
Caller: ''No.''
...
```

Each node in such a tree is a question from the helper. The helper asks questions stored in the tree by starting with the question at the root node (the power light question, in this example), and depending on a yes/no answer to this question, either takes the left branch or the right. The process continues until a leaf node is hit—each leaf node is a diagnosis.

If the diagnosis is incorrect, it may be that an insufficient number of questions have been asked. The caller may help by suggesting an additional question or two that will disambiguate the diagnosis and solve the problem. These questions may be added to the tree at the appropriate places in the hierarchy, and subsequently used to help diagnose similar problems. In this sense, the tree *learns* along the way.

A binary tree like the one in a computer helpline can be used as a database. It is loaded from a file into memory when a dialogue session is to be conducted—in other words, a caller gets online and starts up a dialogue. When the caller disconnects, the tree is stored back (possibly updated) into this file at the end of the session.

Since the tree needs to stored at the end of a session, and loaded back at the beginning of the next session, the tree is *persistent* between sessions (i.e., its state is stored away to be retrieved later). There has to be some way of specifying or encoding the structure of a binary tree in plain-text (nongraphical) format. This is applicable to any persistent data structure.

9.4.1 Signature of a Binary Tree

SIGNATURE OF A DATA STRUCTURE

The signature of a data structure is an encoding of the structure and its contents in plain-text format that can be stored off-line (on disk) and used to recreate the data structure in memory when needed.

The signature of a linear structure is trivial: one simply stores (and subsequently loads) the entries in sequence. The signatures of nonlinear structures in general, and of binary trees in particular, are not this obvious.

Consider a tree with three nodes, A, B, and C, where A is the root, B is its left child, and C is its right child. We could store this tree as the sequence A followed by B, followed by C, with the understanding that the first entry is the root, the second is the left child of the root, and the third is its right child.

What if our tree grew bigger by adding on D and E as the left and right children, respectively, of C? If we stored them in the sequence A, B, C, D, E, we wouldn't be able to tell later whether D and E were the children of C or B. Both possibilities would be covered by the stored sequence.

What we have described above is a storage scheme corresponding to the level-order traversal. Unfortunately, a level-order sequence does not *uniquely* identify a binary tree. In other words, given a level-order sequence, one can, in general, construct more than one binary tree out of it.

Since we are considering tree traversals as potential candidates for uniquely specifying a tree, how about looking at the inorder, preorder, and postorder traversals? It doesn't take us too long to discover that any of these traversals by itself is not a unique specification. For each, we can construct more than one tree with the same traversal sequence, as in the following examples:

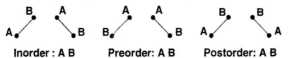

Inorder : A B   Preorder: A B   Postorder: A B

If one traversal sequence alone does not do it, what if we were take a *pair* of traversals as a unique tree specification? Consider the preorder and inorder traversals, for instance. The preorder traversal is **V L R,** while the inorder is **L V R.** We observe that the *root* of the tree is the first node to be visited in preorder—this is the **V.** But by looking at the rest of the preorder traversal, we can't tell which nodes appear in the left subtree of **V,** and which appear in the right subtree.

However, we have the inorder traversal to help us out. We observe that the *same* **V** appears in the inorder traversal, and because the inorder traverses the left subtree first, then the **L** in the inorder traversal comprises all the nodes in the left subtree of **V,** and the **R** comprises all the nodes in the right subtree.

Thus the the preorder and inorder traversals together determine a unique binary tree. So do the postorder and inorder traversals. The only difference in the latter is that the **V** in postorder, which is the root of the binary tree, appears at the end. So the postorder traversal is read backward if we are mapping to a tree starting at its root. Also, going backward, the right subtree appears before the left subtree.

The postorder and preorder traversals *do not* determine a unique binary tree. It is easy to demonstrate this with an example. Consider, for instance, the second pair of trees in the set of examples above. For *either* tree in this pair, the preorder sequence is A B, and the postorder sequence is B A.

SIGNATURE OF A BINARY TREE

The signature of a binary tree can be either of the following pairs of traversals: (a) preorder and inorder, or (b) postorder and inorder.

For the following discussion, we will choose the preorder and inorder traversal pair as the *signature* of a binary tree, and learn how to devise an algorithm to build a tree from its signature.

9.4.2 Building a Binary Tree from its Signature

The algorithm for building a binary tree from its signature follows from the preceding discussion. See the following example.

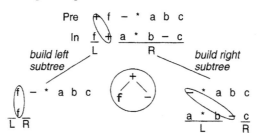

The preorder traversal for the current subtree is scanned left to right. The symbol (e.g., +) at the current position in the scan is the root of the current subtree. This symbol is matched against the inorder traversal of the subtree. The symbols (e.g., f) to the left of the matched symbol in the inorder traversal form the left subtree of the matched symbol, and those to the right (e.g., a * b - c) form the right subtree. This process is repeated recursively.

Next, we will implement this algorithm in a Java program. To keep things simple, we assume that the tree we are about to build stores Strings. The input file contains the inorder and preorder traversal sequences of a tree, and each item in a sequence is a String. The expression tree of Section 9.1.2 is used as an example to illustrate the tree-building process.

We will write two methods that can be embedded in any application class with appropriate modifiers: one to read in the traversal sequences from the input file into two arrays, and another to build the tree from these arrays.

Method buildFromSignature. Our first method, buildFromSignature, asks for the input file name and then proceeds to read it. The first line of the file is assumed to contain the number of nodes in the tree. For our example tree, this would be 7. Following this is the preorder sequence, one entry per line, which is

```
+ f - * a b c
```

for the expression tree, followed by the inorder sequence, which is

```
f + a * b - c
```

for the expression tree. After reading the input, this method calls the recursive tree-building method called buildTree, and returns the tree it constructs.

```
BinaryTree<String> buildFromSignature()
throws IOException {
  // reader for standard input
  BufferedReader stdinbr = new BufferedReader(
           new InputStreamReader(System.in));

  System.out.print("File name? => ");
  System.out.flush();
  String file = stdinbr.readLine();
  // scanner for file specified by user
  Scanner sc = new Scanner(new File(file));
  int numNodes = sc.nextInt();
  String[] preorder = new String[numNodes];
  String[] inorder = new String[numNodes];

  for (int i=0; i < numNodes; i++) {
      preorder[i] = sc.next();
  }
  for (int i=0; i < numNodes; i++) {
      inorder[i] = sc.next();
  }
  //call recursive buildTree method
  return buildTree(preorder, 0, inorder, 0, numNodes-1);
}
```

Method buildTree. The following code for the buildTree method completes the program.

```
BinaryTree<String> buildTree(String[] pre, int i,
           String[] in, int lo, int hi) {

  if (i >= pre.length || lo > hi) {
      return null;    // down to an empty subtree
  }

  //root is first in preorder
  BinaryTree<String> myTree = new BinaryTree<String>();
  myTree.makeRoot(pre[i]);
```

```
// search for pre[i] in in[lo..hi]
int j;
for (j=lo; j <= hi; j++) {
    if (pre[i].equals(in[j])) {
        break;
    }
}

// build left and right subtrees recursively
BinaryTree<String> leftSub = buildTree(pre, i+1, in, lo, j-1);
BinaryTree<String> rightSub = buildTree(pre, i+j-lo+1, in, j+1,hi);

// attach them to the root and return
myTree.attachLeft(leftSub);
myTree.attachRight(rightSub);
return myTree;
}
```

Figure 9.4 illustrates the entire process on the expression tree.

We now turn to a classic application of binary trees: text compression using a scheme called Huffman coding.

9.5   HUFFMAN CODING

Text compression is of enormous importance in practice. One of the earliest and most well known instances of text compression is in the construction of the Morse code for sending information by telegraph. In recent times, file compression has become ubiquitous—almost everyone is familiar with compressing and decompressing files.

Apart from reducing file space on disk to as much as one third the original, current text-compression techniques make it practical to transmit large volumes of data in compressed form across networks.

Numerous techniques are used for text (and nontext) compression. In general these techniques may be broken up into two categories: *statistical coding* techniques and *dictionary coding* techniques.

9.5.1   Statistical and Dictionary Coding

Statistical coding techniques rely on compressing text by coding the component symbols based on the frequency of their occurrence. Thus, the more often a symbol occurs, the smaller is its code. The Morse code is an example of this. A scheme called arithmetic coding holds much promise today.

The dictionary coding approach, on the other hand, assigns codes to certain contiguous strings of characters. The codes, and the corresponding strings, are stored in a dictionary used by the decoder. Currently, the Ziv-Lempel coding schemes enjoy wide popularity.

Huffman coding is a statistical coding method that was invented by D. A. Huffman of M.I.T. in 1952. While current techniques may be superior to Huffman coding in practice, the significance of Huffman coding is that it sparked further research into devising

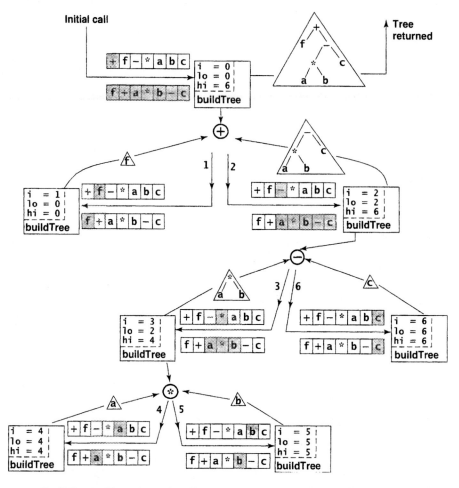

FIGURE 9.4: **Building a Tree from its Signature.** Each box is one copy of the `buildTree` method. The subtree to be built by a recursive call has, as its root, the entry at index `i` of the preorder array. All the entries in this subtree are enclosed between indexes `lo` and `hi` of the inorder array. The arrays are shaded according to the values of `i`, `lo`, and `hi`. Numbers along the arrows that trace the process indicate the sequence in which the recursion proceeds.

approaches that evolved into the current techniques. The Huffman coding technique assigns codes to symbols by building a binary tree from which the codes can be read off.

9.5.2 Algorithm

The Huffman coding algorithm builds a binary tree called the Huffman tree. Each symbol comes with a probability that indicates the likelihood of the symbol's occurring in any single character position of the text. One important assumption we will make here is that the probabilities are input to the Huffman coding algorithm in *sorted ascending order*. This assumption will be used to select the appropriate data structures in the construction of the binary tree.

Following is the algorithm to construct the Huffman tree, illustrated with an example in which the input symbols and probabilities are: a(0.1), w(0.1), u(0.1), e(0.2), t(0.2), and $(0.3).

Algorithm huffmanCoding

1. Construct a single-node binary tree for each of the symbols. Place these binary trees in a queue S, in increasing order of probability.

2. Pick the two smallest-weight trees, say A and B, from S and T, as follows:

   (a) If T is empty, A and B are respectively the front and next-to-front entries of S. Dequeue them from S.

   (b) If T is not empty,

      i. A is the smaller-weight tree of the trees at the front of S and the front of T. Dequeue A.

      ii. B is the smaller-weight tree of the trees at the front of S and the front of T. Dequeue B.

3. Construct a new tree, P, by creating a root and attaching A and B as the subtrees of this root. The weight of P is the combined weights of A and B.

4. Add P to the queue T.

5. Repeat steps 2 through 4 until S is empty.

In the algorithm, we use the term *weight* of a binary tree to mean the sum of the probabilities of the symbols contained in the tree.

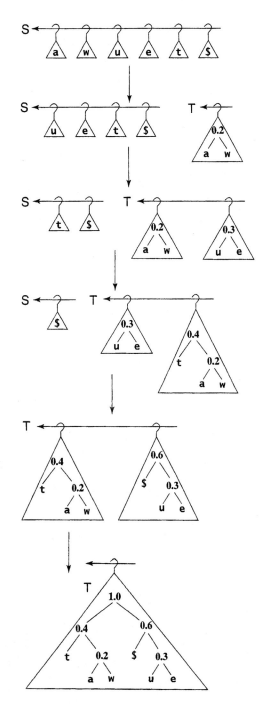

It will become apparent, too, that all the symbols are at the leaves of the trees. The algorithm maintains two queues that we will refer to as S and T respectively. Both start out being empty initially.

When the algorithm stops, T will contain a single tree, say H. The leaves of H will contain the input symbols. To read off the code for any symbol, trace the path from the root to the leaf, recording a 0 for a left branch and a 1 for a right branch in the path. The bit string so constructed is the code for that symbol.

The tree in (b) is equivalent to the tree in (a), constructed out of the same input set of symbols and probabilities, with a different shape but the same average code length of 2.5 per symbol.

The codes for the symbols of tree (a) are:

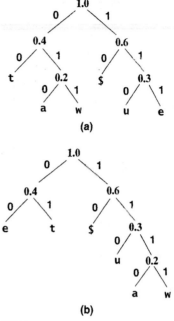

```
a:010, w:011, u:110, e:111, t:00, $:10
```

9.5.3 Average Code Length and Prefix Property

The *average code length* is the sum of the products of the code lengths and the corresponding probabilities of occurrence:

$$(3 \times 0.1) + (3 \times 0.1) + (3 \times 0.1) + (3 \times 0.2) + (2 \times 0.2) + (2 \times 0.3) = 2.5$$

The tree in (b) above may be an alternative result of the construction algorithm. Which one of (a) or (b) is constructed depends on how ties are broken when picking the minimum-weight tree from S and T. You may verify that the tree in (b) has the same average code length as the one in (a).

Finally, an important property of Huffman codes is that no code is a prefix of another, which follows from the fact that all the symbols are at the leaves of the Huffman tree. For, if a symbol were at an internal node, then that symbol's code would be a prefix to the codes of all the symbols in its subtree.

This *prefix property* is essential to decode a message. Here is an example:

```
0100011110011111001011000111
```

This message is decoded by reading it one bit at a time and tracing a path down the Huffman tree. The direction of the next branch to be taken at any node in the tree is determined by the next bit of the message. When a leaf node is reached, the symbol stored at that leaf is output to the decoded text, and a new path is started from the root of the tree.

The sample message breaks down as follows, where each group of bits is a path from the root to a leaf:

```
010 00 111 10 011 111 00 10 110 00 111
```

and is therefore decoded into:

```
ate$wet$ute
```

If, instead of being assigned a variable-length code, each character was assigned a 3-bit code (since there are six characters, a 3-bit code is the least length required to encode them all), the length of the encoding for the string `ate$wet$ute` would be $3 \times 11 = 33$, instead of 28 as above.

Next, we will use the `BinaryTree` class to implement Huffman coding.

9.5.4 A Huffman Class Using `BinaryTree`

We will now develop a class called `Huffman` to implement Huffman encoding and decoding on a set of symbols with given probabilities of occurrence. There are two distinct stages to using the `Huffman` class: building the tree (encoding), followed by repeated decoding of encoded strings.

The class provides three public methods: a constructor that will build the tree,

```
public Huffman(char[] symbols, float[] probs)
```

a method that will return the code for a specified symbol,

```
public String getCode(char symbol)
```

and a method that will decode a given Huffman-coded binary string,

```
public String decode(String code)
```

Supporting this public interface is a host of nonpublic methods, whose functions will become clear when we go over the code for the public methods.

There is one implementation detail in particular that needs to be described up front. Although all the nodes in a `Huffman` tree store data of type `float`, the data in the leaves is interpreted differently from that in the internal nodes. The data in a leaf node is actually an integer value, which is an index into a pair of parallel arrays, one of which holds the symbols, and the other, the probabilities of the symbols. The data in an internal node is the sum of the probabilities associated with its children.

Here is an outline of the `Huffman` class file. A detailed explanation follows, along with the complete code.

Class File 9.1. *Huffman.java*

```
package apps.tree;

import structures.tree.BinaryTree;
import structures.linear.Queue;
import java.util.NoSuchElementException;
```

```
import java.util.ArrayList;

public class Huffman {

    char[] symbols;      //all input symbols
    float[] probs;       //all input probabilities
    ArrayList<BinaryTree<Float>> locations;    //all leaf node locations
    String[] codes;    //codes for all symbols

    Queue<BinaryTree<Float>> leaves;
    Queue<BinaryTree<Float>> trees;
    BinaryTree<Float> huffman;

    public Huffman(char[] symbols, float[] probs) { ... }
    public String decode(String code) { ... }
    public String getCode(char symbol) { ... }
    void buildLeaves() { ... }
    BinaryTree<Float> selectMin() { ... }
    float getProb(BinaryTree<Float> tree) { ... }
    void buildTree(BinaryTree<Float> first, BinaryTree<Float> second) { ... }
    void buildAll() { ... }
    int treeHeight(BinaryTree<Float> tree) { ... }
    void processCodes() { ... }
}
```

Fields.   The instance variables of the Huffman class may be divided into three groups: input variables, output variables, and process variables. The input variables are symbols and probs for the input symbols and their respective probabilities of occurrence. The output variables are codes and huffman, with the obvious uses. The array list locations keeps pointers to the respective leaf nodes for the symbols—this is particularly useful when encoding the symbols. The queues leaves and trees are used to construct and process the Huffman tree. In fact, leaves is analogous to the queue S of the algorithm **huffmanCoding,** and trees is analogous to the queue T.

Tree construction.   The tree construction departs a little from the picture shown in the figure accompanying the **huffmanCoding** algorithm in that the leaves of the Huffman tree store integer *index* values and not the symbols. That is, the symbol that corresponds to a leaf node is located in the symbols array at the index stored in this node. The following figure shows all the data structures of class Huffman as they would appear when construction of the Huffman tree is completed for the example shown with algorithm **huffmanCoding.**

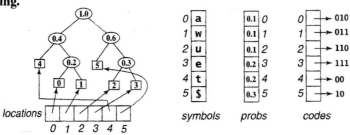

Note that the arrays symbols, probs, codes and the array list locations are all parallel, in that the same index in all the arrays gives information about one and the same symbol.

Constructor and support methods.   The following constructor builds the Huffman tree.

```
public Huffman(char[] symbols, float[] probs) {
  this.symbols = symbols;
  this.probs = probs;
  locations = new ArrayList<BinaryTree<Float>>(symbols.length);

  if (symbols.length == 0) {
    huffman = null;
    return;
  }

  // if there is only one symbol, create a tree with root
  // and left child, and return
  if (symbols.length == 1) {
    BinaryTree<Float> leaf = new BinaryTree<Float>();
    leaf.makeRoot(0f);
    locations.add(leaf);
    huffman = new BinaryTree<Float>();
    huffman.makeRoot(probs[0]);
    huffman.attachLeft(leaf);
    return;
  }

  leaves = new Queue<BinaryTree<Float>>();
  trees = new Queue<BinaryTree<Float>>();

  // build the queue of leaf nodes
  buildLeaves();

  // extract first two leaf nodes
  BinaryTree<Float> first = leaves.dequeue();
  BinaryTree<Float> second = leaves.dequeue();

  // build new tree and add to queue trees
  buildTree(first, second);

  // now the rest of the huffman tree construction
  buildAll();

  // and now for the final tree
  huffman = trees.dequeue();

  // finally, read off and store the codes
  processCodes();
}
```

The case of an empty input—symbols.length == 0—is handled in the first if statement, and the case of a single symbol in the input—symbols.length == 1—is handled in the second if statement. Both these cases are treated separately from the rest in order to avoid needlessly building the queues leaves and trees. Moving on to the general case of more than one symbol in the input, the leaves queue is created, and then is built by a call to the helper method buildLeaves.

As shown, the implementation of this method does the following: it creates a single-node tree for each of the symbols in the for loop; it creates a new leaf node and sets the data of this node to the index for the corresponding symbol; it adds a reference to this node at the same index in the locations array list; and it adds this single-node tree to the leaves queue.

```
void buildLeaves() {
    for (int i=0; i < symbols.length;
        i++) {
        BinaryTree<Float> leaf =
            new BinaryTree<Float>();
        leaf.makeRoot((float)i);
        locations.add(leaf);
        leaves.enqueue(leaf);
    }
}
```

Following the call to buildLeaves, the constructor calls the method buildTree to prime the trees queue, sending this method the first two leaf-node trees.

The method buildTree, shown here, is responsible for putting together a new tree given a left subtree and a right subtree. It uses the method getProb to extract the weights of the specified subtrees, and sets the weight of the new tree to the sum of these weights. Once the tree is built, it is enqueued in the trees queue. Note that the call to the method makeRoot of the BinaryTree<Float> class uses auto boxing to send in a float argument to match the declared Float parameter of makeRoot.

```
void buildTree(
    BinaryTree<Float> first,
    BinaryTree<Float> second) {
    float prob1 = getProb(first);
    float prob2 = getProb(second);
    BinaryTree$<$Float$>$ both =
        new BinaryTree<Float>();
    both.makeRoot(prob1 + prob2);
    both.attachLeft(first);
    both.attachRight(second);
    trees.enqueue(both);
}
```

As you can see, method getProb checks whether the parameter tree is a leaf. Recall that for a leaf node, the data is an index into the parallel arrays, including probs. Also note that auto unboxing is used to assign the returned Float from method getData to the float variable index, as well as in the last line, to return data from an internal node.

```
float getProb(
    BinaryTree<Float> tree) {
    if (tree.left == null &&
        tree.right == null) {
        float index = tree.getData();
        return probs[(int)index];
    }
    return tree.getData();
}
```

After the first nonleaf subtree is built, the `Huffman` class constructor calls method `buildAll` to build the rest of the tree. This method calls the `selectMin` method, which is implemented as follows:

```
BinaryTree<Float> selectMin() {
  BinaryTree<Float> first = leaves.first();
  BinaryTree<Float> second = trees.first();

  float prob1 = getProb(first);
  float prob2 = getProb(second);
  if (prob1 < prob2) {
    leaves.dequeue();
    return first;
  } else {
    trees.dequeue();
    return second;
  }
}
```

This method looks at the first entry in each of the `leaves` and `trees` queues, and returns the one that has the smaller probability.

In the `buildAll` method, which is implemented here, the first `while` loop is used as long as there is at least one entry in the `leaves` queue. However, there may an be iteration of this loop that starts when there is exactly one entry in the `leaves` queue, and that is the first to be picked as having the minimum probability when compared with the probability associated with the first entry in the `trees` queue. In this case, the `else` part of the `if` statement in this loop will kick in, since `selectMin` needs both its parameters to be nonempty.

When all the leaves are done being picked, the second `while` loop iterates over the `trees` queue, picking the first two entries, and building subtrees, until there is exactly one entry left, which is the final Huffman tree.

```
void buildAll() {
  while (!leaves.isEmpty()) {
    BinaryTree<Float> first =
      selectMin();
    BinaryTree<Float> second =
      null;
    if (!leaves.isEmpty()) {
      second = selectMin();
    } else {
      second = trees.dequeue();
    }
    buildTree(first, second);
  }

  while (trees.size() > 1) {
    BinaryTree<Float> first =
      trees.dequeue();
    BinaryTree<Float> second =
      trees.dequeue();
    buildTree(first, second);
  }
}
```

This final tree is retrieved by the `Huffman` class on returning from the call to `buildAll`. Following this, method `processCodes` is called to read off the codes for the symbols from the tree and store them in the array codes. While this step is not strictly required, it makes the task of subsequently obtaining the code for a symbol much more efficient—the tree does not have to be traversed every time the code for a symbol is requested.

Reading off the codes. Here is the implementation of method processCodes.

```
void processCodes() {
  int height = treeHeight(huffman);
  char[] codeString = new char[height];

  codes = new String[symbols.length];

  // use locations[] to access a leaf and go towards the root
  // filling in the code backwards in codeString
  for (int i=0; i < locations.size(); i++) {
      int index = height;
      BinaryTree<Float> node = locations.get(i);
      BinaryTree<Float> parent = node.parent;
      while (parent != null) {
          index--;
          if (node == parent.left) {
              codeString[index] = '0';
          } else {
              codeString[index] = '1';
          }
          node = parent;
          parent = node.parent;
      }
      // create a String from codeString and fill in codes
      codes[i] = new String(codeString, index, height-index);
  }
}
```

Since the array list locations provides direct access to the leaf nodes, we can read the code for any symbol by starting at the leaf node for that symbol and following the parent links all the way up to the root, implemented in the for loop.

This would, of course, mean that we are reading the code for the symbol backwards, but that is easily corrected by filling in the code in an array character by character, going back to front in the array. We will use a scratch space character array called codeString for this purpose. In order to allocate space for codeString, we need to know the maximum code length of any symbol, which in turn is the height of the Huffman tree. The height can be computed recursively, implemented in the method treeHeight as follows:

```
int treeHeight(BinaryTree<Float> tree) {
    if (tree == null) { return -1; }
    // recursive height computation
    return Math.max(treeHeight(tree.left), treeHeight(tree.right)) + 1;
}
```

In method processCodes, once the root is reached, the portion of codeString that has been filled up is converted into a String—the last statement in the for loop. This is the Huffman code for the symbol under consideration. The String constructor used here is defined as follows in the java.lang.String class:

```
public String(char value[], int offset, int count)
```

This constructs a new String whose value is the subarray of characters in value[] beginning at the index offset, and of length count.

Encoding and decoding messages.   Once the Huffman tree is constructed, a coding program can use it to encode (compress) a text file thus: for every symbol that needs to be encoded, the getCode method is invoked to obtain its code (bit string), which is then written to the output. At the decoding end, the entire encoded message is passed in to the method decode, which spits out the original message.

Method getCode starts out by obtaining, for the given symbol, its index position in the codes array. This is done with a sequential search of the symbols array. But why go backward?

Recall our discussion in Section 4.2.1 of the average-case analysis of sequential search and the rearranging of data based on search patterns. We discovered then that we obtain the optimal average-case search cost if we perform sequential search on an array whose entries are arranged in *decreasing* order of search frequencies.

```
public String getCode(
                char symbol) {
    int i;
    // backward sequential search
    for (i=symbols.length-1; i >= 0;
          i--) {
        if (symbol == symbols[i]) {
            break;
        }
    }
    if (i < 0) {
        throw new
            NoSuchElementException();
    }
    return codes[i];
}
```

The symbols array is analogous, except that its entries are arranged in *increasing* order of search frequency. When decoding the message, the symbol that will be encountered most frequently, and therefore will make the greatest number of calls to getCode, is the one stored in the last entry of symbols. So we search backwards in symbols, thereby ensuring that the average search time over all searches is optimal.

Finally, method decode uses the prefix property of the Huffman code to implement the decoding process.

```
public String decode(String code) {
    StringBuffer decoded = new StringBuffer();
    int i=0;
    while (i < code.length()) {
        BinaryTree<Float> node = huffman;
        // down to leaf
        while (node.left != null || node.right != null) {
```

```
    if (code.charAt(i++) == '0') {
        node = node.left;
    } else {
        node = node.right;
    }
}
// reached a leaf node
float index = node.getData();
decoded.append(symbols[(int)index]);
}
return decoded.toString();
}
```

Starting with the complete coded string, code, it goes down the tree from the root, making a left turn if the next character in the code is 0, or a right turn if it is 1. When it reaches a leaf node, it has decoded a part of the code string into the text symbol corresponding to the leaf node. This text symbol is appended to an accumulator, decoded, which is a StringBuffer instance.

The process starts up again to decode the next symbol, now starting at the code string at the index beyond the part that has been used up so far, and continues until the entire code string has been used up—this is the iteration of the outer while loop.

After the entire code string has been decoded, the decoded buffer is converted into a String and returned.

9.6   BinaryTree CLASS IMPLEMENTATION

Clients of the binary tree get to go anywhere in the tree, and attach or detach other trees to any node. The implementation must be tailored to provide this kind of freedom by more or less laying open the entire tree structure for the clients to work with. In particular, *the recursive nature of the binary tree must be fully visible to clients.* Consequently, the binary tree has four fields, namely data, left, right, and parent. The first stores the data and is the only nonpublic field. The rest are links that set up the recursion, since each of them is a reference to a binary tree.

The example given here helps us to recall the recursiveness of the binary tree structure. A binary tree consists of four fields: data, left, right, and parent. (a) In an empty binary tree, all four fields are null. (b) In a nonempty binary tree, at least the data field is not null. This is the root. (c) One or more of the other fields could also be nonnull, linked to other binary trees. A binary tree is *always* the root of some subtree, and can also be the subtree of another binary tree.

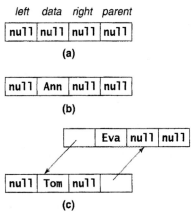

So here is the recursive BinaryTree implementation.

Class File 9.2. *BinaryTree.java*

```java
package structures.tree;

public class BinaryTree<T> {

  protected T data;
  public BinaryTree<T> left;
  public BinaryTree<T> right;
  public BinaryTree<T> parent;

  public BinaryTree() {
    data = null;
    left = null;
    right = null;
    parent = null;
  }

  public void makeRoot(<T> data) {
    if (this.data != null) {
        throw new TreeViolationException();
    }
    this.data = data;
  }

  public void setData(<T> data) {
    this.data = data;
  }

  public <T> getData() {
    return data;
  }

  public void attachLeft(BinaryTree<T> tree) {
    if (left != null) {    // left subtree already exists
        throw new TreeViolationException();
    }
    if (tree != null) {
        tree.parent = this;
        left = tree;
    }
  }

  public void attachRight(BinaryTree<T> tree) {
    if (right != null) {    // right subtree already exists
        throw new TreeViolationException();
    }
    if (tree != null) {
        tree.parent = this;
        right = tree;
    }
  }
```

```
public BinaryTree<T> detachLeft() {
  BinaryTree<T> retleft = left;
  left = null;
  return retleft;
}

public BinaryTree<T> detachRight() {
  BinaryTree<T> retright = right;
  right = null;
  return retright;
}

public boolean isEmpty() {
  return data == null;
}

public void clear() {
  left = null; right = null; data = null; parent = null;
}

public BinaryTree<T> root() {
  if (parent == null) {     // this itself is the root
      return this;
  }
  BinaryTree<T> nextParent = parent;
  //follow parent links to go to root
  while (nextParent.parent != null) {
      nextParent = nextParent.parent;
  }
  return nextParent;
}
}
```

Constructor, single-node tree, exception.   The constructor creates an empty binary tree that can be converted to a single-node tree by setting up the root in method make-Root. In makeRoot, the exception TreeViolationException (in the structures.tree package) is thrown if there is already a data-filled root node. Specifically, the root of a tree can be set up only if the tree is empty (i.e., data is null).

Here is the implementation of the TreeViolationException class:

Class File 9.3. *TreeViolationException.java*

```
package structures.tree;

public class TreeViolationException extends RuntimeException {
  public TreeViolationException() {
    super();
  }

  public TreeViolationException(String s) {
    super(s);
  }
}
```

Building up and breaking down.   Whether we are putting together trees to build bigger ones, or breaking them down into their components, we need the "core four" methods, which comprise two complementary pairs: `attachLeft` and `attachRight`, `detachLeft` and `detachRight`.

The specified binary tree is attached as the right subtree of the tree on which method `attachRight` is invoked. If the latter already has a right subtree, a tree structure violation is detected and an exception thrown. A null pointer check is made on `tree` before going ahead and setting up the parent to right child links.

The work of `attachRight` can be undone by its complementary method, `detach Right`.

The methods `attachLeft` and `detachLeft` are respectively symmetrical to the above pair.

Odds and ends.   Note that the method `isEmpty` returns `true` if `data` is null. Method `clear` sets all fields to null. This results in an empty tree, in a state identical to when a tree is constructed but the root has not yet been made.

Finally, the method `root` starts at the node on which it is invoked, and climbs the chain of parent pointers until a null pointer is encountered, which indicates that the root has been reached.

9.7   STACK-BASED TRAVERSALS

One way to speed up the traversals of a binary tree is to avoid using recursive calls. Every time a recursive call is made to the traversal method, the stacking of all local variables, parameters, and the return address, together with the transfer of control between different levels of recursion lead to high overheads in implementation.

We can reduce this overhead by implementing the recursion using a stack, as discussed in Section 8.5. In other words, we can convert a recursive method to a nonrecursive one, simply by doing all the stack-based work in the method itself, instead of leaving it to the compiler. While the stack still "memorizes" certain things for later recall, there is overhead of recursive method calls.

Let us learn how to write such a nonrecursive program for, say, inorder traversal.

9.7.1   Inorder Traversal of Binary Tree

Imagine again that the recursion unfolds as a series of "method boxes," as in the factorial computation shown in Section 8.2.1. There is one method box per node of the binary tree. A box is created when the node is first encountered—this is the *birth* of the node, the first milestone. The node is encountered again immediately after its left subtree is traversed—this is the *midlife* of the node, the second milestone, at which point the node is visited. Finally, the node is encountered for a third, and final, time immediately after its right subtree is traversed.

We need to translate the method boxes into things that will be stored on the stack as in the factorial stack illustration in Section 8.5. The lifetime of a method box would then be mirrored by the lifetime of its stack representative. Our strategy of operating a stack is the following:

- When a node is first encountered, stack it with a "birth certificate." This corresponds to the creation of a method box for that node.
- Change the state of a node *when it is retrieved from the stack.*

    - If it has a birth certificate, visit it and stack it back by replacing the birth certificate with a "midlife certificate." This corresponds to returning to the method box after traversing the left subtree.
    - If it has a midlife certificate, do not stack it back. This corresponds to leaving the method box for good (i.e., the end of the method box's life).

Starting by placing the root node on the stack with a birth certificate, our program will spin until the stack becomes empty (i.e., until every node has lived its life).

The approach outlined above is implemented in the following inorder traversal for a binary tree that stores Strings. This method uses an inner class called StackNode whose instances will be stored on the stack. It takes as parameter a Visitor object, whose role is explained after the code.

```
static void inOrder(BinaryTree<String> tree, Visitor<String> visitor) {

  class StackNode {
    BinaryTree<String> node;
    int milestone;
    StackNode(BinaryTree<String> node, int milestone) {
      this.node = node;
      this.milestone = milestone;
    }
  }

  if (tree == null || tree.isEmpty()) return;

  Stack<StackNode> S = new Stack<StackNode>();
  S.push(new StackNode(tree, 0));    // a box is born
  while (!S.isEmpty()) {
    StackNode snode = S.pop();
    switch(snode.milestone) {
      case 0: //birth
          snode.milestone = 1;
          S.push(snode);
          if (snode.node.left != null) {    //stack left child
              S.push(new StackNode(snode.node.left,0));
          }
          break;
      case 1: //midlife
          snode.milestone = 2;
          S.push(snode);
          visitor.visit(snode.node);
          if (snode.node.right != null) {    //stack right child
              S.push(new StackNode(snode.node.right,0));
          }
          break;
```

```
        case 2: //done
            break;
        default:
            break;
    }
  }
}
```

The final milestone (value 2) need not be recorded because there is nothing to be done on encountering it (i.e., there is no need to store the node on the stack). However, the code is written with this milestone duly recorded and stacked because it is then trivial to modify the code to conduct preorder and postorder traversals.

The inOrder method accepts a parameter visitor of type Visitor<String>. Recall our discussion about visiting a node in Section 9.2. The definition of visit is under the *control of the clients* of the binary tree—it is up to them to tailor the definition of visit to suit their needs. Thus, the parameter visitor is sent by the client, and the generic class Visitor is defined suitably by the client.

A simple default implementation of such a generic Visitor class follows.

9.7.2 A Visitor Class

Here is a visitor class defined in the structures.tree package:

Class File 9.4. *Visitor.java*

```
package structures.tree;

public class Visitor<T> {

  public void visit(BinaryTree<T> node) {
    System.out.println(node.getData());
  }
}
```

This Visitor class provides a default implementation of method visit that simply prints the data at the visited node. This method is invoked by the traversal process via the argument visitor object visitor:

```
visitor.visit(snode.node)
```

Later, we will see other instances where visitor classes are defined for traversals on other kinds of data structures.

9.8 GENERAL TREE

A complex system is often organized in the form of a hierarchy. Examples of such systems include the animal kingdom, business organizations, and academic institutions. In the computing world, operating systems such as UNIX and DOS organize files into hierarchies.

A general tree models a hierarchy. The root of the general tree is the top of the hierarchy, and each node may have any number of children. Several of the operations that may be performed on a general tree are typical of the kinds of questions we need to ask of the system being modeled or of the kinds of changes we may make to that system.

9.8.1   Example: Hierarchy in a University

Consider a university modeled by a general tree. At the root (level 0) is the president, under which are several nodes that stand for the colleges. Under each college, there are several divisions, each consisting of several departments, and so on. We may want to ask such questions as:

- *How many colleges are in the university?* Answer: Count the number of nodes at level 1.

- *What is the closest organizational connection between a pair of faculty members?* Answer: Find the nearest common ancestor of the nodes that represent this pair.

- *How many levels would a faculty member have to rise before he or she could become the president?* Answer: The depth, in the tree, of the node that represents that faculty member.

- *Are two specific faculty members in the same college?* Answer: Find whether the nodes that represent these faculty members are both in the subtree rooted at the node representing that college.

As described, the answers to these questions pertaining to the organizational hierarchy are determined by first transforming them to equivalent questions with respect to the general tree. These tree questions become the basis for the operations a general tree would need to support, since many systems would need to answer questions that can be transformed to this set of operations.

9.8.2   Example: UNIX Filesystem

The UNIX filesystem is an excellent example of a hierarchy put into practice with tremendous efficiency and flexibility of operations. It is well worth taking up a small example of a filesystem that is modeled as a general tree and seeing how some common file-manipulation operations can be transformed into general tree operations. Figure 9.5 is such an example.

For instance, the full pathname of `f1`, which is the path from the root to the node representing it, is:

```
/home/me/dir1/f1
```

Note that the same name (e.g., `bin`) can appear in different locations in the tree. However, no two instances of `bin` are the same, because each instance has a unique full path name. Obviously, whether a name in a general tree can be repeated or not depends on the system the general tree is meant to model.

Figure 9.6 illustrates a small set of core file operations in UNIX, and the corresponding access and/or modification actions that are to be performed on the general tree.

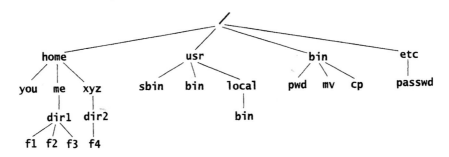

FIGURE 9.5: A UNIX filesystem Example. The root of the hierarchy is represented by '/', and each internal node is a directory. Each leaf node is either a directory or a nondirectory file. The full pathname of a file or directory is the path from the root to the node representing it, written with a '/' at the beginning and a '/' separating every two levels.

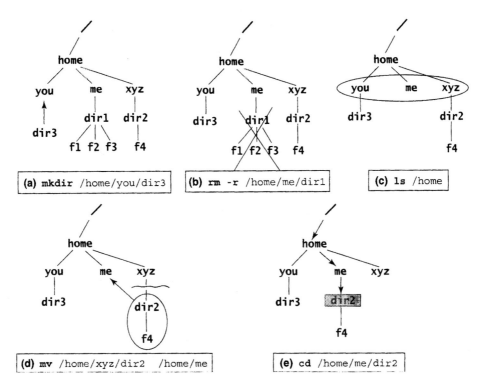

FIGURE 9.6: Examples of File Operations in UNIX. (a) Creating a file or directory. (b) Removing a directory and all the files under it. (c) Listing all the files and directories under a given directory. (d) Moving a directory into another. (e) Changing directories.

All these operations reflect a fundamental need: complete navigational freedom in the general tree. Therefore, the set of operations to be provided by a general tree implementation would be similar to the set of operations provided by the BinaryTree class. Which brings us to the question of *how* to implement a general tree.

9.8.3   Space Issues in Implementation

A node in a general tree has a variable number of children. Therefore, applying the idea of implementing a binary tree to a general tree (i.e., constructing a node with sufficient number of spaces for references to its children) is impractical.

Not knowing how many children a node might have, we would find it necessary to overestimate and allocate some *maximum* space per node. For example, we may assume that a node can never have more than 10 children, and allocate space for 10 references per node. This would, however, result in a severe wastage of space.

We can compute the exact wastage of space. If we assume that no node contains more than k children, and the tree contains n nodes in all, then the ratio, w, of space wasted to total space is:

$$w = \frac{nk - (n - 1)}{nk} \approx 1 - \frac{1}{k}$$

The total space allocated for links is nk. Every node except the root has one link to it, which means that $n - 1$ links are filled in. We arrive at the approximate figure by assuming n large enough that $(n - 1)/n$ is almost equal to 1.

An actual number or two might help at this point. If $k = 2$, we have a binary tree, and the ratio $w = 1 - 1/2 = 0.5$. In other words, 50% of the total space is wasted. Assuming $k = 5$ (a reasonably nontrivial hierarchy), we have $w = 1 - 1/5 = 0.8$, for a 80% wastage!

9.8.4   Correspondence with Binary Tree

There is a better alternative. Picture the implementation shown in the example of Figure 9.7. Implementation-wise, we now have a binary tree. A node has three links: one (*left*) to its first child if any, another (*right*) to its next sibling if any, and a third (*parent*) to either the previous sibling or the parent. All the children of a node (i.e., mutual siblings) are linked together.

Figure 9.8 gives another example of the correspondence between a general tree and its binary tree equivalent. The first child of a node in the general tree becomes the left child of the same node in the binary tree. The second child becomes the right child of the first, the third becomes the right child of the second, and so on.

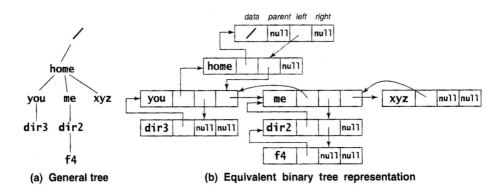

(a) General tree   (b) Equivalent binary tree representation

FIGURE 9.7: General tree implementation.

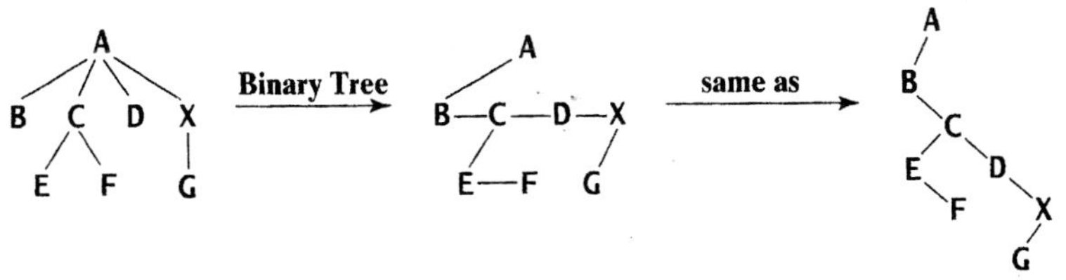

FIGURE 9.8: General tree to binary tree correspondence.

Most physical systems do not impose any order among entities under a common parent. For example, the files or directories under a directory in the UNIX filesystem are not ordered with respect to each other. However, for the convenience of implementation, the children of a general tree node are labeled in order as *first* child, *second* child, and so on.

CORRESPONDENCE BETWEEN GENERAL TREE AND BINARY TREE

A general tree may be represented by an equivalent binary tree as follows. For every node in the general tree: (a) the *first* child of the node becomes the *left* child of the same node in the binary tree, and (b) the *second* child of the node becomes the *right* child of the first, the *third* child of node becomes the *right* child of the second, and so on.

Two fundamental operations must be provided by the general tree: (a) finding the parent of a node, and (b) finding the *i*-th child of a node. They are worked out on the binary tree implementation shown in Figure 9.9. Finally, does a general tree possess a "signature" that can be stored in a file, and, if so, how can the equivalent binary tree be built from such a signature?

9.8.5 Signature of General Tree

Trying to relate the signature of a binary tree (pre + in or post + in traversals) to a general tree, our first thought would be to define equivalent traversals for a general tree. Here intuition works just fine.

The **preorder traversal** of a general tree is: visit the root, then recursively traverse the first subtree of the root, followed by the second, then the third, and so on.

The **postorder traversal** of a general tree: recursively traverse each subtree of the root in order of first, second, third, and so on, then finally visit the root.

Inorder traversal is not defined for the obvious reason: if a node has more than two children, should the root be visited between the first and second subtree traversals, or between the second and third subtree traversals, or ...? There is no definite answer.

Let us write down the traversals for the general tree of Figure 9.9:

General tree preorder: A B C E F D X G
General tree postorder: B E F C D G X A

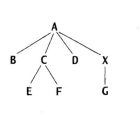

(a) General tree

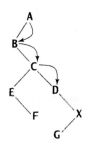

(b) Finding third child of A
in equivalent binary tree

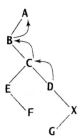

(c) Finding parent of D in
equivalent binary tree

FIGURE 9.9: **General Tree Parent and Child in Equivalent Binary Tree.** (a) General tree. (b) Find the i-th child of a general tree node by going to the left child of the corresponding node in the equivalent binary tree and following right links $i - 1$ times. (c) Find the parent of a general tree node by starting at the corresponding node in the equivalent binary tree and following the chain of parent links until a "right" turn is made.

and for its binary tree equivalent as well:

> Binary tree preorder: A B C E F D X G
> Binary tree postorder: F E G X D C B A
> Binary tree inorder: B E F C D G X A

Notice anything? **The preorder and postorder traversals of the general tree are the same as the preorder and inorder traversals of the equivalent binary tree.**

Thus the signature of a general tree is the pair of preorder and postorder traversals.

SIGNATURE OF A GENERAL TREE

The signature of a general tree is its pair of preorder and postorder traversals.

Building a general tree from its signature would then be translated into building its binary tree equivalent by treating the former's preorder traversal as the preorder of the latter, and the former's postorder as the inorder of the latter.

9.9   SUMMARY

- Binary trees model two-way decision-making systems.
- A binary tree consists of nodes and branches. There is a special node called the root.
- Every node in a binary tree has at most two children.
- Nodes that have no children are called leaf nodes, and the others are called internal nodes.
- There is a single path between any pair of nodes in a binary tree.
- A binary tree is defined by the relative positions of the data in its nodes, and the tree as a whole carries a meaning that would change if the relative positions of the data in the tree were to change.

- The depth of a node in a binary tree is the number of branches (distance) from the root to that node.
- Nodes at the same depth in a binary level are said to be at the same level.
- The height of a binary tree is the maximum level at which there is a node.
- A strictly binary tree is one in which every node has either no child or two children (i.e., no node can have only one child).
- In a complete binary tree, every level but the last must have the maximum number of nodes possible at that level. The last level may have fewer than the maximum possible, but they should be arranged from left to right without any empty spots.
- The maximum possible number of nodes at level i in a binary tree is 2^i.
- The maximum possible number of nodes in a binary tree of height h is $2^{h+1} - 1$.
- If N_{max} is the maximum number of nodes in a binary tree, its height is $\log(N_{max} + 1) - 1$.
- Recursive definition: a binary tree is either empty or consists of a special node called root that has a left subtree and a right subtree that are mutually disjoint binary trees.
- The number of nodes in an empty binary tree is zero. Otherwise, the number of nodes is one plus the number of nodes in the left and right subtrees of the root.
- The height of an empty binary tree is -1. Otherwise, the height is one plus the maximum of the heights of the left and right subtrees of the root.
- Recursive definition of inorder traversal of tree T: first recursively traverse the *L*eft subtree of T, then *V*isit the root of T, then recursively traverse the *R*ight subtree of T.
- Recursive definition of preorder traversal of tree T: first *V*isit the root of T, then recursively traverse the *L*eft subtree of T, then recursively traverse the *R*ight subtree of T.
- Recursive definition of postorder traversal of tree T: first recursively traverse the *L*eft subtree of T, then recursively traverse the *R*ight subtree of T, then *V*isit the root of T.
- The recursive traversals may be written in short form as follows: inorder is LVR, preorder is VLR, and postorder is LRV.
- Level-order traversal of tree T: Starting at the root level, go level by level in T, *v*isiting the nodes at any level in left-to-right order.
- The signature of a binary tree can be either of the following pairs of traversals: (a) preorder and inorder, or (b) postorder and inorder.
- Huffman coding is a statistical coding technique used for text compression.
- The Huffman coding technique assigns variable-length codes to text symbols such that the more frequently used symbols have relatively shorter codes.
- In the Huffman coding scheme for a given set of symbols, no code is the prefix of another.
- To enable clients to freely navigate through a binary tree, its Java class implementation makes its recursive structure publicly accessible.

- The overhead of recursive method calls in a tree traversal can be avoided by implementing an equivalent method that uses a stack to replace the recursive calls.
- A general tree models a hierarchy in which the root of the tree is the top of the hierarchy, and a node may have any number of children.
- A general tree may be represented by an equivalent binary tree as follows. For every node in the general tree: (a) the *first* child of the node becomes the *left* child of the same node in the binary tree, and (b) the *second* child of the node becomes the *right* child of the first, the *third* child of node becomes the *right* child of the second, and so on.
- The signature of a general tree is its pair of preorder and postorder traversals.

9.10 EXERCISES

E9.1. Give the preorder, inorder, and postorder traversals of the following binary tree:

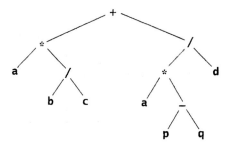

E9.2. You are given the following inorder and preorder traversals of an expression tree for a boolean expression:

Inorder traversal:

a || b > c && d < e || c != a == f && p < q

Preorder traversal:

|| && || a > b c < d e && == != c a f < p q

(a) Construct the expression tree from the traversals. Show your work (i.e., how you split the entries root, right subtree, and left subtree, as illustrated in Figure 9.4).
(b) Evaluate the tree for the following values of variables:

a = true, b = 15, c = 10, d = 10, e = 5, c = true, f = true,
p = 3, q = 4

E9.3. Radix Tree
The *radix tree* data structure shown below stores the bit strings 0, 1, 01, 011, 100, and 1011 in such a way that each left branch represents a 0 and each right branch represents a 1.

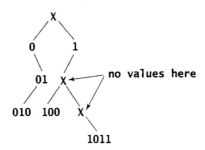

To find whether a bit string exists in this radix tree, start from the root and, scanning the bits of the string left to right, take a left turn if the bit is 00, and a right turn if the bit is 1. If a node can be reached using this sequence, and it does not contain an 'X', the bit string is found, else it is not found.

(a) Given the following strings:

    1011, 01, 0010, 1010, 011, 1000, 0101

Starting with an empty tree, build a radix tree to store these strings, showing the radix tree after *each* new string is inserted. (To insert a new string, you might have to insert more than one new node in the tree built thus far.)

(b) How much time did it take to build this tree? Treat scanning an existing edge and inserting a new edge as basic operations.

(c) How much time would it take to *lexicographically sort* these strings (print out the strings in the tree in order) once the tree is built, assuming the same basic operations as in the preceding question. The output of the sort in the above case should be:

    0010 01 0101 011 1000 1010 1011

(d) How much time would it take to insert one new binary string of k bits into a radix tree? An arbitrary number of binary strings but whose total length is n bits?

E9.4. (a) Build a Huffman tree for the following set of character-frequency pairs:

    (R,6), (C,6), (L,6), (B,10), (H,15), (A,20), (E,37)

(b) With the Huffman tree constructed above, encode the following text:

    CLEARHEARBARE

(c) If it takes 7 bits to represent a character without encoding, then for the above text, what is the ratio of the encoded length to that of the unencoded representation?

(d) Decode the following (the string has been broken up into 7-bit chunks for easy readability):

    1111011 1010111 1101110 0010011 111000

E9.5. With reference to the Huffman class of Section 9.5.4:

    (a) What is the worst-case running time (big O) to build a Huffman tree with n characters?

    (b) What is the worst-case running time (big O) to encode a text of length k if there are n distinct characters in the text?

    (c) What is the running time to decode a stream of length k?

    (d) Suggest how you might improve the efficiency of encoding by maintaining the array codes (and the arrays symbols and probs, which are parallel to codes) differently. What will be the running time of your more efficient scheme to encode a text of length k with n distinct characters? Would your answer to question (a) change for this new scheme?

E9.6. Answer the following questions for a binary tree of height h. Write all your answers in terms of h, with an explanation for each.

    (a) What is the minimum number of nodes this tree may contain? The maximum number of nodes?

    (b) What is the minimum number of nodes this tree must contain if it is a strictly binary tree? A complete tree? A strictly binary *and* complete tree?

    (c) Is the Huffman tree always a strictly binary tree? A complete tree? How about a radix tree—is it always strictly binary? Complete?

E9.7. A binary tree contains n nodes. Answer the following questions in terms of n, with an explanation for each.

    (a) What is the minimum possible height of this tree? The maximum possible height?

    (b) If this is a radix tree, what is maximum number of bit strings that can be accommodated in the tree?

    (c) If this is a Huffman tree, what is the maximum number of characters that can be encoded in it?

E9.8. Give the binary tree representations of the following general trees:

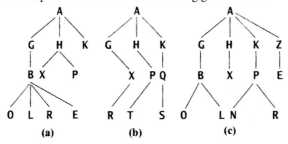

        (a)   **(b)**   **(c)**

E9.9. Give the general trees represented by the following binary trees:

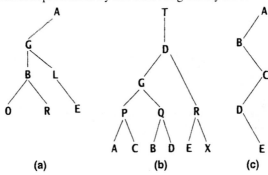

        (a)   **(b)**   **(c)**

E9.10. Give a recursive definition of a general tree.

E9.11. Give a recursive definition of the correspondence between a general tree and its equivalent binary tree representation.

E9.12. A general tree has a height h, and no node of the tree has more than k children. Answer the following in terms of h and k.

    (a) What is the minimum number of nodes the general tree can contain? The maximum?

    (b) What is the minimum possible height of the equivalent binary tree representation? The maximum height?

E9.13. Suppose a general tree represents the organizational hierarchy of a company. Every level represents a "rank" in the organization, with the root being the topmost rank. Give algorithms for the following, given the binary tree representation of this general tree. Also compute the worst-case running time (big O) of each operation, if the height of the general tree is h, and no node of the tree has more than k children.

    (a) Determine the total number of ranks in the organization.

    (b) Determine how many ranks have more than 50 employees.

    (c) Determine the rank (1 for the topmost rank) of a specific employee, given the employee's position in the binary tree representation.

9.11   PROGRAMMING PROBLEMS

P9.1. Two binary trees are *isomorphic* if they have the same shape.

    (a) Write a recursive definition of isomorphism for a pair of binary trees.

    (b) Write a *recursive* method:

```
public <T> boolean isomorphic(BinaryTree<T> tree1, BinaryTree<T>
tree2)
```

    that would determine whether two given binary trees, tree1 and tree2, are isomorphic. When you finish writing this method, go over it carefully to check whether it is the most efficient way of implementing a check for isomorphism.

P9.2. The mirror image of a binary tree swaps the left and subtrees of every node in the original tree:

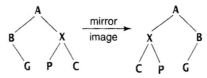

P9.3. The height of an empty binary tree is -1. The height of a single-node binary tree is 1. For a binary tree with two or more nodes, the height is the number of branches from the root to the farthest leaf.

    (a) Write a recursive definition of the height of a binary tree.

    (b) Write a *recursive* method:

```
public <T> int height(BinaryTree<T> tree)
```

    to return the height of a binary tree, tree.

P9.4. A binary tree is *height-balanced* if, for *every* node in the tree, the height of its left subtree differs from that of its right subtree by no more than one. In other words, either the left and right subtrees are of the same height, or the left is one higher than the right, or the right is one higher than the left.

(a) Write a recursive definition of a height-balanced binary tree.

(b) Write a *recursive* method:

```
public <T> boolean heightBalanced(BinaryTree<T> tree)
```

to tell whether a specified binary tree, tree, is height-balanced.

P9.5. Write a method:

```
public <T> void levelOrder(BinaryTree<T> tree)
```

that would perform a level-order traversal of the specified binary tree, tree, printing the entry at each node as it is visited. Use a queue initially containing the root of the tree. Iterate as long as the queue is not empty. Visit a dequeued node, and enqueue all its children.

P9.6. It would be useful to write methods in BinaryTree that give a client the ability to step through the nodes in inorder sequence. In order to do this, we could provide two methods, firstInorder and nextInorder. By invoking firstInorder, followed by successive invocations of nextInorder, the client can step through the entire tree. Add these methods to the BinaryTree class:

```
public BinaryTree<T> firstInorder()
```

which would return the node that would be visited first in an inorder traversal (null if the tree is empty), and

```
public BinaryTree<T> nextInorder()
```

which would return the node to be visited next in an inorder traversal (null if there are no more nodes to be visited).

P9.7. In Section 9.7 we wrote a method inOrder that uses a stack to explicitly implement the inorder traversal recursion. Now write methods preOrder and postOrder with a stack.

P9.8. In Section 8.2.1 we devised a recursive method to compute the factorial of a number. Write an equivalent nonrecursive method using a stack, along the lines of the inOrder method of Section 9.7. (Hint: Define an appropriate stackNode class to store the value of parameter *n* and determine how many milestones are required.)

P9.9. In Section 8.2.2 we devised a recursive method to compute the Fibonacci number for a given *n*. Write an equivalent nonrecursive method using a stack.

P9.10. In Section 8.4.2 we wrote a recursive method to solve the Towers of Hanoi problem. Write an equivalent nonrecursive method using a stack.

P9.11. In Problems P9.5 and P9.6 above, we have added traversal methods to the BinaryTree class. Another alternative is to not modify the BinaryTree class itself, but instead to create another class called TraversableBinaryTree (in the tree package) that would extend the BinaryTree class, inheriting all its fields and methods. Then, in TraversableBinaryTree, define the methods levelOrder, firstInorder, nextInorder, and the nonrecursive (explicit stack) versions of inOrder, preOrder, and postOrder. Implement the TraversableBinaryTree class.

P9.12. Implement an ExpressionTree class that can represent an arithmetic expression with binary operators and floating-point operands. Limit the operators to addition, subtraction, multiplication, and division. Operands can be either constants or variables. Your class should be able to build a tree from its signature, and evaluate it on a set of values for the variable operands.

P9.13. Implement a generic class GeneralTree<T> by using a component BinaryTree<T> to maintain the equivalent binary tree representation. With the BinaryTree<T> class as a guideline, implement a no-arg (default) constructor, and the following methods in GeneralTree<T>:

- Methods makeRoot, setData, getData, root, isEmpty, and clear, performing the same functions as their BinaryTree<T> counterparts.
- Access method:

  `public int numKids()`

  that would return the number of children of this general tree node.
- Access method:

  `public GeneralTree<T> getChild(int i)`

  that would return the node corresponding to the *i*-th child of this tree node. Children are numbered beginning with 1.
- Access method:

  `public GeneralTree<T> getParent()`

  that would return the parent of this tree node.
- Update method:

  `public void attachChild(GeneralTree<T> tree, int i)`

  that would attach the specified tree as the *i*-th child of this node.
- Update method:

  `public GeneralTree<T> detachChild(int i)`

  that would detach and return the tree rooted at the *i*-th child of this node.
- Tree building method:

  `public void buildTree(String[] pre, String[] post)`

  that would build this general tree from scratch, given its preorder and postorder traversals.

Have the methods throw appropriate exceptions where necessary.

P9.14. Having built a generic GeneralTree<T> class, we can build a class, FileTree extends GeneralTree<String>, for a UNIX filesystem. That is, FileTree is a class that extends a String instantiation of the generic GeneralTree<T> class.

FileTree will construct a hierarchy out a bunch of file and directory names, and provide a small set of operations that would implement those illustrated in Figure 9.6. Here is a specification of the specialization that the FileTree class provides, over and above the inherited methods of GeneralTree<String>:

- A no-arg (default) constructor that builds an empty filesystem.

- A constructor:

```
public FileTree(String[] pre, String[] post)
```

builds a filesystem, given its preorder and postorder traversals.
- A method that implements *mkdir:*

```
public void mkdir(String dir)
```

given the full pathname, dir, of the directory to be created.
- A method that implements recursive remove, *rm -r:*

```
public void rmR(String dir)
```

given the full pathname, dir, of the directory to be removed.
- A utility method:

```
static public String baseName(String file)
```

that would return the *base* name of the specified *file*. The base name of a file/directory is the last level of its full pathname.
- A method that implements *ls:*

```
public ArrayList ls(String dir)
```

given the full pathname, dir, of the directory to be listed. The returned array list consists of the base names of files and directories in the specified directory.
- A method that implements *mv:*

```
public void mv(String fromDir, String toDir)
```

given the full pathnames, fromDir and toDir, of the source and destination directories.
- A method that implements *cd:*

```
public void cd(String toDir)
```

given the full pathname, toDir, of the destination directories.

Have these methods throw appropriate exceptions wherever necessary.

C H A P T E R   10

Binary Search Tree and AVL Tree

A binary search tree is a binary tree that possesses an additional *ordering property* that maintains the data in its nodes in sorted order. This permits the clients of the binary search tree to perform a binary search on its entries. Since the search tree is a linked structure, entries may be inserted and deleted without having to move other entries over, unlike ordered lists in which insertions and deletions require data movement.

The AVL tree is a height-balanced binary search tree that delivers guaranteed worst-case search, insert, and delete times that are all $O(\log n)$.

Learning Objectives

- Explore the motivation for binary search trees by learning about the comparison tree for binary search.
- Use the comparison tree as an analytical tool to determine the running time of binary search.
- Describe the binary search tree structure and properties.
- Study the primary binary search tree operations of search, insert, and delete, and analyze their running times.
- Understand a binary search tree class interface and use it in application examples.
- Implement the binary search tree class with a binary tree class as the reused storage component.
- Study the AVL tree structure properties, the search, insert, and delete operations, and their running times.

10.1 COMPARISON TREE

We start by reexploring binary search on an ordered list implemented as an array. This provides the motivation and ideas for constructing a binary search tree.

COMPARISON TREE FOR BINARY SEARCH

A comparison tree for binary search on an array is a binary tree that depicts all possible search paths, i.e., it shows all the different sequences of comparisons undertaken by binary search when searching for keys that may or may not be present in the array.

Figure 10.1 shows the comparison tree for binary search on an array of 10 entries.

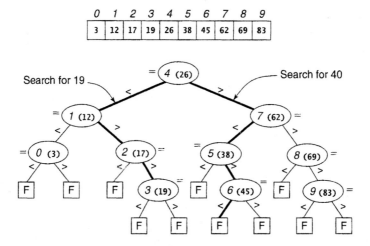

FIGURE 10.1: Binary Search Comparison Tree. Each internal node (oval) is an array position indicating a successful search. Each leaf node or external node (square) is a failure position (not in the array) indicating a failed search. A path from the root to an internal or external node at some position shows the number of comparisons made in searching for a key that ends up at that position.

In Figure 10.1, suppose we search for key 19 (*target*) located at index 3 of the array. The **binarySearch** algorithm of Section 5.2.2 would first compare 19 against the middle entry key (26, at index 4) for equality. This is indicated by the = symbol next to the root node.

Since the comparison fails, the search makes one more comparison to decide whether to go left or right. This additional comparison is indicated by the < symbol next to the left branch and the > symbol next to the right branch out of the root node. *This does not mean that two comparisons are made—the outcome of one comparison is sufficient to decide which way to go.*

Repeating this process, a path is traced down the comparison tree up to the node marked 3(19), which corresponds to the sequence 4 → 1 → 2 → 3 of array indices that are "hit."

The keys compared against the target, 19, in the above sequence of array positions are 26 → 12 → 17 → 19.

The equality comparison against 19 at position 3 results in success, and the search terminates at that point. The number of comparisons made for this search can be computed by counting the =, < and > symbols encountered along this path. In this case there were seven comparisons.

As an example of a failed search, consider searching for 40. The path followed by binary search is the sequence of indices 4 → 7 → 5 → 6, which corresponds to comparisons against the corresponding sequence of keys 26 → 62 → 38 → 45. After the final comparison for equality, an additional comparison leads to the failure node that is the left child of the internal node for index 6, discovered after making eight comparisons.

Failure nodes.   Observe that there are 11 failure nodes in this comparison tree. Each failure node represents one "failure position" in the array: there is one failure position sandwiched between every pair of indexes (accounting for nine such spots), plus one to the left of the first index and one to the right of the last index.

Each failure node acts like a trash bin, catching a range of search keys that fall between the entries in the array that sandwich this failure position. For instance, the failure node that we end up at in the search for 40 catches all keys between 38 (located at index 5) and 45 (located at index 6).

Another way to look at it is to focus on a failure node in the comparison tree and find its inorder predecessor and successor. For example, take the failure node that is the right child of the node marked 3(19). The parent of this failure node, 3(19), is its inorder predecessor, and the root node, 4(26), its inorder successor. Hence, this failure node will catch all keys that are strictly between 19 and 26, or between indices 3 and 4 of the array, respectively.

10.1.1 Search Time Using Comparison Tree

COMPARISON TREE AS A CONCEPTUAL TOOL

A comparison tree is simply a *conceptual* tool to analyze the time taken by binary search, and therefore is often referred to as an *implicit* search tree.

Let us see how the *worst-case* search time of binary search can be computed with the help of the comparison tree. Note in Figure 10.1 that we used the array locations to construct the tree, not the actual keys in these locations. In other words, the shape of the tree, and therefore the resultant sequences and numbers of comparisons, depends only on the size of the array. Changing the key values in the array will not change the shape of the comparison tree.

Worst-case search time.   The worst-case search time is divided into two cases: worst-case time for success and worst-case time for failure. The worst case for success would occur when searching for a value contained in an internal node that is *farthest* from

COMPARISON TREE INDEPENDENT OF DATA VALUES

The shape of the comparison tree, and thus the worst-case search time, depends only on the length of the array, and not on the key values.

the root. Similarly, the worst case for failure would occur when searching for a value that is caught by one of the failure-node trash bins that is farthest from the root.

The exact number of comparisons for each node in the tree of Figure 10.1 is shown in Figure 10.2.

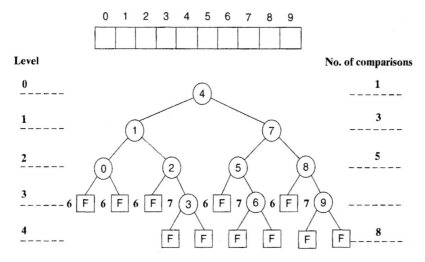

FIGURE 10.2: Time Analysis Using Comparison Tree. Levels 0, 1, 2 contain only internal nodes. The number of comparisons for success at each of these levels is shown at the far right. For instance, a successful search that ends up at any of the nodes of level 2 would consume five comparisons. All the nodes at level 4 are external nodes. Level 3 contains a mix of internal and external nodes, and the number of comparisons is individually listed beside each node.

The worst-case number of comparisons for successful search would result for the internal nodes at level 3, which are the nodes corresponding to array indices 3, 6, and 9. In other words, searching for a value that is at one of these three positions would use up more comparisons for successful search than any other.

The worst-case number of comparisons for a failed search would result for all the failure nodes at level 4. The rightmost failure node represents searches for values greater than the largest entry in the array—values that fall beyond position 9, which is the largest array index. The other five failure nodes, going from left to right, represent searching for values that are sandwiched between the following respective pairs of array positions: 2–3, 3–4, 5–6, 6–7, 8–9.

In general, if d is the depth (level) of a node V, then the number of comparisons to get to that node is $2d + 1$ if V is an internal (success) node, and $2d$ if V is an external (failure) node.

Let h be the height of the tree. Note that the deepest node in the tree is a failure node whose depth is equal to the height, h. The worst-case number of comparisons for an unsuccessful search is $2h$.

Observe, also, that the parent of such a deepest failure node is an internal node that must incur the maximum number of comparisons for a successful search. This parent's depth is $h - 1$, which means that the worst-case number of comparisons for a successful search is $2(h - 1) + 1 = 2h - 1$.

WORST-CASE COMPARISONS AS A FUNCTION OF TREE HEIGHT

If the height of a comparison tree is h, the worst-case number of comparisons is $2h - 1$ for successful search and is $2h$ for unsuccessful search.

The question is, what is h in terms of n, where n is the length of the array?

10.1.2   Height of Comparison Tree

Consider the pair of comparison trees shown in the following figure.

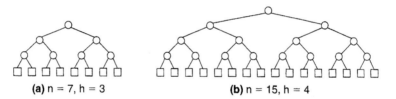

(a) n = 7, h = 3   **(b)** n = 15, h = 4

Tree (a) is the comparison tree for an array of length $n = 7$; for tree (b), $n = 15$. In either tree, all the failure nodes are at the last level, h, and $n = 2^h - 1$. This should be familiar from having seen something similar in Section 5.2. There we analyzed binary search by assuming that the number of entries, n, was a power of 2 minus 1 (i.e., n was of the form $2^k - 1$). Which implied that $k = \log_2(n + 1)$.

The analysis we are doing here is an alternative means of arriving at the results we obtained in that discussion. What was k there is h here, and we naturally come up with the same result for h:

$$h = \log(n + 1)$$

We will omit the explicit notation of base 2 for the logarithm, and simply assume that this is the case unless otherwise stated.

Now taking tree (a), increasing n from 7 to 8 would immediately place at least one internal node at level 3, and consequently increase its height by one, to $h = 4$. After this point, increasing n all the way up to 15 would keep the height steady at 4, while placing every additional internal node at level 3.

Thus, the height h for any general n (not necessarily a power of 2 minus one) is:

$$h = \lceil \log(n + 1) \rceil$$

where, as we know, $\lceil x \rceil$ is the smallest *integer* that is greater than or equal to x.

To summarize:

WORST-CASE COMPARISONS AS A FUNCTION OF INPUT SIZE

The worst-case number of comparisons made by binary search on an ordered array of n elements is $2\lceil\log(n + 1)\rceil - 1$ for successful search, and $2\lceil\log(n + 1)\rceil$ for unsuccessful search.

The *average number of comparisons* can also be computed using the comparison tree. The details are worked out in Section 10.8.

As we said earlier, the comparison tree is an *implicit* binary search tree, a conceptual tool that is not an actual binary tree with nodes and links. However, hidden in this conceptual tool is the glimmer of an idea: what if we make an *explicit* binary tree that mimics the comparison tree? We could call this a *binary search tree*.

10.2 BINARY SEARCH TREE PROPERTIES

We develop new tools and techniques when the old ones do not address all our concerns. For searching in an array, binary search is an excellent improvement over sequential search: the latter takes $O(n)$ time, while the former only takes $O(\log n)$ time. But there is no free lunch. Recall, from Section 5.4, the downside of maintaining an ordered list: inserting an entry takes up to $O(n)$ time, whereas inserting in an unordered list takes only $O(1)$ time.

In a nutshell, if we search an ordered list much more often than adding entries to or deleting entries from it, we are in excellent shape thanks to the superfast binary search. But if we ever need a much more *dynamic* data structure, one that constantly expands and shrinks due to frequent insertions and deletions, then we had better look for alternatives to the ordered list. This is where the binary search tree data structure comes in.

At the outset, let us state what we expect from a binary search tree:

WHAT WE EXPECT FROM A BINARY SEARCH TREE

Insertions and deletions should be faster than $O(n)$, and search time should not be slower than $O(\log n)$.

The binary search tree is a binary tree that mimics the comparison tree in the manner in which entries are ordered or positioned. Specifically, we allude to the following special *ordering* property, as defined below:

BINARY SEARCH TREE

A binary search tree is a binary tree whose entries can be arranged in order. For every node x in the tree, the value of the entry at x is greater than the values of all the entries in the left subtree of x, and smaller than the values of all the entries in the right subtree of x.

This ordering property has an important implication that we will remember and use frequently:

INORDER TRAVERSAL OF A BINARY SEARCH TREE

The inorder traversal of a binary search tree visits the nodes in ascending order of values.

For the most part, we will assume (as in the preceding definition) that there are no duplicate keys stored in the binary search tree. Here are some examples.

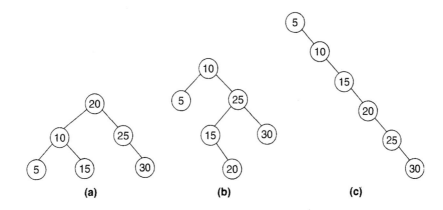

All three trees have the same set of keys. Their structures are different, depending on the sequence in which the keys were inserted and deleted. For all of these trees, verify that the ordering property is satisfied at *every node*. The definition makes it clear that the keys stored in a binary search tree must lend themselves to being arranged in order (i.e., they are *ordinal*). This means that we can use the equality, less than, and greater than comparators to order any pair of keys with respect to each other.

A major difference between a comparison tree and a binary search tree is the following:

COMPARISON TREES AND BINARY SEARCH TREES

For any given *number* of keys, n, there is only one binary search comparison tree. In contrast, there are as many binary search trees possible as there are different binary trees that can be constructed out of n nodes.

The binary search tree is a dynamic structure. Insertions and deletions are made at different points of time that are not known beforehand, and different structures arise out of different sequences of inserts and deletes. This will become clear immediately on seeing how to search, insert, and delete in binary search trees.

10.3   BINARY SEARCH TREE OPERATIONS

Binary search trees support three fundamental operations: *search, insert,* and *delete.*

10.3.1   Search

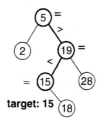

Searching in a binary search tree is identical to tracing binary search on a comparison tree, only this time the tree nodes are for real. As shown in the upper figure, the target key is first compared against the key at the root of the binary search tree. If these keys are equal, the search terminates successfully. If not, the search is recursively conducted on either the left subtree or right subtree of the root, depending on whether the target is respectively less than or greater than the key at the root.

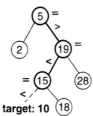

The search terminates with failure if the recursion hits an empty subtree. For instance, in searching for 10, as you can see in the lower figure, the last comparisons are against the key 15. First, the comparison $10 == 15$ is false. Then the comparison $10 < 15$ is true, and a left turn is made. However, since there is no left subtree at 15, the recursion terminates and the search ends in failure.

10.3.2   Insert

In order to insert a value, the search process is employed to *force a failure,* and the new value is inserted at the place where the search failed.

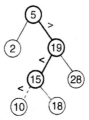

In the preceding example, the search for 10 failed at the left subtree of 15. If, instead, as illustrated in the next figure we needed to insert 10, we would make it the left child of node 15. Observe that a *newly inserted node always becomes a leaf node in the search tree.*

10.3.3   Delete

Deletion is somewhat more involved than insertion. The value to be deleted is first located in the binary search tree using the search process. Of course, if the value is not found, there is nothing to delete.

Let us assume that the value is found at node X. There are three possible cases, classified according to the level of difficulty of deletion.

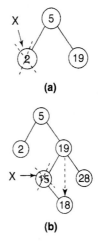

(a)

Case a: X is a leaf node. This is the simplest case. The action taken is to simply delete X (i.e., detach this node from its parent).

Case b: X has one child. This is a little more work. In the example, 18 is the child of 15 (X), the key to be deleted. First, make 18 the left child of 19 (parent of X)—shown by the dotted line. Then delete the node 15 by delinking it from its parent, 19.

(b)

Case c: X has two children. This is the most work. Unlike case (b) above, where the single subtree of X could be attached to X's parent, simply deleting X would leave *both* subtrees of X floating, with place only for one of them to get attached to X's parent. This will be the case, for instance, if 19 is deleted from the example of case (b).

An essential observation will help us solve this problem:

The inorder successor (predecessor) of a node in a binary tree does not have a left (right) subtree.

This observation helps us come up with a simple scheme to delete a node that has two children, illustrated with the following example of deleting 19.

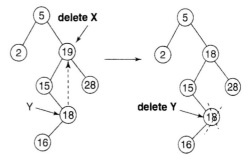

First find the inorder predecessor, Y, of X. Then copy the entry at Y into X, overwriting the previous entry at X. Finally, apply deletion on Y.

Applying deletion on Y will revert to either case (b) or case (a) because Y is guaranteed to not have a right subtree.

Verify that this deletion does not violate the ordering property. If Y is the inorder predecessor of X, T_l is the left subtree of X *except for* Y, and T_r is the right subtree of X, then *before* the delete, an inorder traversal would have visited the relevant nodes in the following order:

$$\ldots T_l\ Y\ X\ T_r \ldots$$

After copying the entry at Y into X, the old X effectively becomes the new Y, and the old Y is deleted. The new inorder traversal is now

$$\ldots T_l\ Y\ T_r \ldots$$

which is the previous traversal with X removed. Thus, the ordering property is maintained.

In the deletion scheme, we could alternatively find the inorder successor of X and proceed exactly as above.

Let us look at the running times of these fundamental binary search tree operations.

Running times. The worst-case running time is tied to the worst possible shape a binary search tree can attain.

For instance, starting with an empty binary search tree, if the keys 5, 10, 15, 20, 25, 30 were inserted in this order, we would get a completely lopsided, or *skewed,* binary search tree—a tree that is just a sequential chain of nodes.

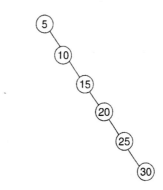

Consequently, searching in such a tree degenerates to plain old sequential search, with a worst-case time of $O(n)$. This is disastrous! An insertion in such a tree will also take $O(n)$ time in the worst case (go all the way down to the last node), and so will a deletion (delete the last node).

SKEWED TREE

The worst-possible binary tree structure is one that is completely *skewed* either to the left (no node has a right child) or to the right (no node has a left child). This happens when the values to be inserted arrive in descending or ascending order, respectively. Searching in such a tree degenerates to sequential search, with the attendant time of $O(n)$.

Let us take stock of the "progress" we have made so far by comparing the unordered list, ordered list, and binary search tree data structures on the basis of the time taken to search, insert, or delete a specified value. Table 10.1 summarizes our knowledge.

In the case of the ordered list (as also the binary search tree), both insert and delete consist of two parts: a search, followed by the actual insertion or deletion. Searching for the middle key in the ordered list gives the best time ($O(1)$), but deleting the middle key *does not*. In fact, deleting the middle key would consume $O(n)$ time, because $n/2$ keys would have to be moved over. The best time for delete occurs when the *last* key is deleted—the actual delete itself would take $O(1)$ time because nothing needs to be moved, but the search for this key would take $O(\log n)$ time. A similar argument may be made for insertion.

Now let us look at the best-case results for the binary search tree. The best-case search time is $O(1)$ in the case when the target is at the root. The best-case insertion

TABLE 10.1: Comparison of running times for search, insert, and delete in the unordered list, ordered list, and binary search tree.

Operation	Unordered List	Ordered List	Binary Search Tree	
Search	$O(1)$	$O(1)$	$O(1)$	Best
	$O(n)$	$O(\log n)$	$O(n)$	Worst
Insert	$O(1)$	$O(\log n)$	$O(\log n)$	Best
	$O(1)$	$O(n)$	$O(n)$	Worst
Delete	$O(1)$	$O(\log n)$	$O(\log n)$	Best
	$O(n)$	$O(n)$	$O(n)$	Worst

time is $O(\log n)$, which is obtained when the *tree is balanced* (i.e., its shape is similar to that of the binary search comparison tree). Recall from Section 10.1.2 that the height of a comparison tree with n nodes is $O(\log n)$. The height of a balanced binary search tree is therefore $O(\log n)$. Since an insertion is always done at the leaf level (bottom of the tree), the insertion process has to traverse an $O(\log n)$ "distance" before the actual insertion, for a time of $O(\log n)$. A similar argument can be made for the $O(\log n)$ best-case time for deletion.

Balancing. This best-case structure is our next goal. The objective is to keep the structure of the binary search tree *always balanced* in such a manner that the height never exceeds $O(\log n)$. After every insert or delete, we must somehow ensure that the tree does not get lopsided. If we could do this, the search, insert, and delete times would never exceed $O(\log n)$.

Remarkably, there *is* a way to keep the tree always balanced. In fact, there are at popular ways of constructing and maintaining balanced binary search trees. One of them is the **AVL** tree and the other is the **red-black** tree. The techniques used by these trees to maintain balance are fairly sophisticated. We will study one of them, the AVL tree, at the end of this chapter in Section 10.7.

Since the AVL tree is a binary search tree with "smarts," let us first study how to implement a simple binary search tree, which can then be used as a basis for building an AVL tree.

10.4 A BinarySearchTree CLASS

Figure 10.3 shows the public interface of a generic binary search tree class, BinarySearchTree<T extends Comparable<T>>.

The header of this class is similar to that of the OrderedList<T extends Comparable<T>> class described in Section 5.4, since both these classes store items in order of keys. Also, as in the OrderedList class, the BinarySearchTree class does not permit duplicate keys, and uses the structures.linear.Order

Class structures.tree.BinarySearchTree<T extends Comparable<T>>

Constructors

BinarySearchTree( )
Creates an empty binary search tree.

Methods

$O(n)$ **void insert(T item)**
Inserts the specified item into this binary search tree.
Throws **OrderViolationException** if this is a duplicate key insertion.

$O(n)$ **void delete(T key)**
Deletes the item from this tree with the given key, and returns the deleted item.
Throws **NoSuchElementException** if no item has given key.

$O(n)$ **T search(T key)**
Returns the item in this tree with the given key, null if no item has this key.

$O(1)$ **isEmpty( )**
Returns true if tree is empty. false otherwise.

$O(1)$ **int size( )**
Returns the number of items in this tree.

$O(n)$ **T minKey( )**
Returns the minimum-key item in this tree.
Throws **NoSuchElementException** if tree is empty.

$O(n)$ **T maxKey()**
Returns the maximum-key item in this tree.
Throws **NoSuchElementException** if tree is empty.

$O(n)$ **void preOrder(Visitor<T> visitor)**
Visits the tree in preorder.

$O(n)$ **void inOrder(Visitor<T> visitor)**
Visits the tree in inorder.

$O(n)$ **void postOrder(Visitor<T> visitor)**
Visits the tree in postorder.

FIGURE 10.3: A Generic Binary Search Tree Class. Only the public interface is shown. Duplicate keys are not permitted. Running times assume an implementation that keeps a running count of the number of items, n, in the tree.

ViolationException exception to detect attempted key duplication via the insert method.

Primary methods. The methods insert, delete, and search support the basic binary search tree operations.

One feature of this class is that the *structure* of the BinarySearchTree implementation is not visible to the client (i.e., there is no method that reveals the binary tree's structure). Therefore, the class has to provide methods (preOrder, inOrder, postOrder) that allow the usual tree traversals. Each of these traversal methods accepts as a parameter an instance of the generic Visitor<T> class, discussed and defined earlier in Section 9.7.2. This class is used by the traversal clients to determine exactly what action is to be performed at a tree node when it is visited. Each of the traversal methods invokes the method visit on the visitor instance parameter.

This class provides a pair of convenience methods, minKey and maxKey, that may be useful to clients.

The `search` method provides a way for the client to extract an item whose *key* part matches the specified key.

Recall our discussion in Section 4.4.5 about the key part of an item. That is, an item in general may consist of many components, of which a subset makes up the key. For instance, a binary search tree may store user accounts, and an account may have several components, such as user name, user email, and user address. Of these components, one or more may make up the key, such as the user email.

Say a client of this binary search tree wants to retrieve the entire account information for the user with email `user@somewhere.edu`. The client makes up a dummy account with only the email part filled in and all other fields set to null, and sends this dummy account as the search key parameter. The `search` method matches the given email with the email field of the accounts in the binary search tree, and returns the entire matching account.

The `delete` method is similarly designed to locate and delete the item in the tree whose key part matches the given key.

Running times of methods.   We have already seen that the worst-case running times of `search`, `insert`, and `delete` are $O(n)$. The running times of `size` and `isEmpty` are $O(1)$, given the assumption that the implementation keeps track of the number of entries in the tree at any time.

The traversals must visit every node in the tree, and the running times of $O(n)$ follow, assuming $O(1)$ time per visit.

The minimum (maximum) value is at the node that is visited first (last) in an inorder traversal. For `maxValue`, a worst-case tree would be one in which all the values are skewed to the right. Finding the maximum value would then involve scanning all n nodes in the path from the root to the leaf. The $O(n)$ time argument for `minValue` is symmetrical.

10.5   USING CLASS BinarySearchTree

The following examples illustrate how the `BinarySearchTree` class can be used in a couple of simple applications. They also illustrate the usage of the `Visitor` class, and its specialization, in extracting useful information from a binary search tree.

10.5.1   Example: Treesort

Recall from Section 10.2 that the inorder traversal of a binary search tree visits nodes in ascending order of the values they contain. Consider the following program segment:

```
BinarySearchTree<Integer> B = new BinarySearchTree<Integer>();
B.insert(15);
B.insert(8);
B.insert(10);
Visitor<Integer> visitor = new Visitor<Integer>();
B.inOrder(visitor);    // prints 8, 10, 15 in that order
```

The inOrder traversal method invokes visitor.visit() when a node is visited—recall the Visitor class introduced in Section 9.7.2.

What we have done here is interesting—we have sorted a set of entries using a binary search tree. The process we have implemented is called **treesort.**

TREESORT ALGORITHM

Insert the entries into a binary search tree, one by one, and when they have all been inserted, perform an inorder traversal on the tree to obtain the entries in sorted order.

What is the worst-case running time of treesort on a set of n entries? It is determined by the time taken to insert each of the n entries into the tree. In the worst case, the tree is completely skewed, which would happen if the entries were already sorted!

If we assume that duplicate keys are not allowed and then particularize the insertion code so that we avoid the equality comparison at every node, then inserting a key into an empty tree would be zero comparisons, into a tree with one node would be one comparison, into a *skewed* tree with two nodes would be two comparisons, and so on.

On the other hand, if we overlaid insertion on search, reusing the code for search with the additional equality comparison at every node, then inserting a key into an empty tree would be zero comparisons, into a tree with one node would be two comparisons, into a *skewed* tree with two nodes would be four comparisons, and so on. That is, we would need twice as many comparisons in this case, as compared to the previous "tuned" insertion implementation.

Since we are interested in the big O complexity, and the difference in the above implementations is a constant factor independent of the size of the structure, we can work with either. So, for instance, the latter scenario would result in the following sum to insert n entries, starting with an empty binary search tree, and building a *skewed* tree in the worst case:

$$2 + 4 + 6 + \cdots + 2(n - 2) + 2(n - 1)$$

which can be simplified to

$$2 * (1 + 2 + 3 + \cdots + (n - 2) + (n - 1))$$

Since the sum within parentheses is $n(n - 1)/2$, the total number of comparisons is $2n(n - 1)/2$, for a big O running time of $O(n^2)$.

10.5.2 Example: Counting Keys

Suppose we want to count the number of keys in a binary search tree that are less than a given key. A simple way to do this is to examine *all* the nodes of the tree and check whether the key at each node is less than the specified key.

To examine all the nodes, we can use any of the traversal methods. We need a specialized Visitor that, instead of printing data at a node in the visit method, would compare the key at a node against the given key and update the count if necessary. We can implement this specialization by defining a new class, CountVisitor, that extends Visitor and redefines the inherited visit method:

```
public class CountVisitor<T extends Comparable<T>> extends Visitor<T> {

  private int count;
  private T key;

  public CountVisitor(T key) {
    this.key = key;
    count = 0;
  }

  // overrides the superclass visit method
  public void visit(BinaryTree<T> node) {
    if (node.getData().compareTo(key) < 0) count++;
  }

  public int getCount() {
    return count;
  }
}
```

CountVisitor is only applicable to binary search trees, and its visit method must be able to compare keys for relative ordering (i.e., it can only work with objects that implement the compareTo method of the Comparable interface). This is why the header of CountVisitor is genericized not just with <T> but with the bounded <T that extends Comparable<T>>. Note that once the type *T* has been so bounded, the same *T* is also used to genericize the subclass Visitor. That is, we *do not* write:

```
CountVisitor <T extends Comparable<T>> extends
Visitor<T extends Comparable<T>>
```

and neither do we write:

```
CountVisitor <T> extends Visitor<T extends Comparable<T>>
```

   Following is a client program segment that builds a tree of integers and then counts the number of tree node values that are less than 50 using preorder traversal.

```
BinarySearchTree<Integer> B = new BinarySearchTree<Integer>();
// insert a bunch of integers into B
...
CountVisitor<Integer> cv = new CountVisitor<Integer>(50);
B.preOrder(cv);
System.out.println("count = " + cv.getCount());
```

There is one major assumption in the preceding example, namely, that the BinarySearchTree class is implemented using a BinaryTree class instance as component. This is clear in line 12 of the CountVisitor implementation, since the inherited (and overridden) visit method requires a BinaryTree instance as parameter.

10.6   BinarySearchTree CLASS IMPLEMENTATION

We use the BinaryTree class as a component in our BinarySearchTree class. This means that we will delegate much of the work to the methods of the BinaryTree class and reuse its code. Following is the BinarySearchTree class file.

Class File 10.1. *BinarySearchTree.java*

```
package structures.tree;

import structures.linear.OrderViolationException;
import java.util.NoSuchElementException;

public class BinarySearchTree<T extends Comparable<T>> {
  BinaryTree<T> tree;
  int size;

  public BinarySearchTree() { tree = new BinaryTree<T>(); size = 0; }
  public boolean isEmpty() { return tree.isEmpty(); }
  public int size() { return size; }
  BinaryTree<T> recursiveSearch(BinaryTree<T> root, T key) { ... }
  public T search(T key) { ... }
  public void insert(T item) { ... }
  void deleteHere(BinaryTree<T> deleteNode, BinaryTree<T> attach) { ... }
  BinaryTree<T> findPredecessor(BinaryTree<T> node) { ... }
  public T delete(T key) { ... }
  public T minKey() { ... }
  public T maxKey() { ... }
  void recursivePreOrder(BinaryTree<T> root, Visitor<T> visitor) { ... }
  public void preOrder(Visitor<T> visitor) { ... }
  void recursiveInOrder(BinaryTree<T> root, Visitor<T> visitor) { ... }
  public void inOrder(Visitor<T> visitor) { ... }
  void recursivePostOrder(BinaryTree<T> root, Visitor<T> visitor) { ... }
  public void postOrder(Visitor<T> visitor) { ldots }
}
```

Let us look at the fundamental operations, namely, search, insert, and delete, in that order.

10.6.1   Search Implementation

The public method `search` is supported by the nonpublic helper method `recursiveSearch` that performs a recursive search on the underlying binary tree.

Method `recursiveSearch` implements the process outlined in Section 10.3.1. The recursion terminates if the tree is empty or the target is found. Otherwise it recurses on the left or right subtree as appropriate. This recursive method has to be written separately instead of within `search` itself because it needs the additional `BinaryTree` root parameter to recurse on.

The public `search` method primes the recursion by sending in the root of the binary tree component. Alternatively, `search` could have been written as a single *nonrecursive* method using an iterative program structure to descend the tree.

```
public T search(T key) {
  if (tree.isEmpty()) {
    return null;
  }
  return
  recursiveSearch(
           tree, key).data;
}
BinaryTree<T> recursiveSearch(
  BinaryTree<T> root, T key) {
  if (root == null) {
    return null;
  }
  int c =
    key.compareTo(root.data);
  if (c == 0) { return root; }
  if (c < 0) {
    return
      recursiveSearch(
         root.left, key);
  } else {      // right subtree
    return
      recursiveSearch(
         root.right, key);
  }
}
```

10.6.2   Insert Implementation

The `insert` method, in contrast to `search`, is written in a nonrecursive manner. If the tree is empty, the root of the tree is set up with the data to be inserted, the size of the tree is incremented by one, and the method terminates. This early exit situation is implemented in the first `if` statement.

If the tree is not empty, an iteration is set up to descend the tree starting at the root. This is implemented by a `while` loop that follows the insert process of Section 10.3.2. The method must ensure that the item being inserted is not a duplicate; if so, it throws an `OrderViolationException`.

```
public void insert(T item) {
  if (tree.isEmpty()) {
    tree.makeRoot(data);
    size++;
    return;
  }
  // iterative descent
  BinaryTree<T> root = tree;
  boolean done=false;
  BinaryTree<T> newNode = null;
  while (!done) {
    int c = item.compareTo(
        root.data);
    if (c == 0) {   // duplicate
      throw new
      OrderViolationException();
    }
    . . .
```

The iteration stops (the done variable is set to true) when a null subtree is encountered in the direction in which the search is to be continued. At this point, a new node is set up and made a left child (if nested inside if) or a right child (if nested inside else) of the would-be-parent node, root.

The common code for both cases is written once, after the loop. This includes setting the fields of the new node, and incrementing the size of the tree by one.

Note that the left, right, and parent fields of the binary tree, tree, are directly accessed to carry out the actual insertion of the new node, instead of calling the attachLeft or attachRight methods. This approach is convenient, and, in fact, is expected for classes in the same package as structures.tree, while clients of BinaryTree that are not in its package are required to use the attachLeft or attachRight method.

10.6.3 Delete Implementation

As we have seen in Section 10.3.3, the delete operation is more complex than search or insert. We have two helper methods, findPredecessor and delete-Here, to assist delete in carrying out its task.

Case (c) of deletion, in which the node to be deleted has two children, requires that we find the inorder predecessor of this node. The method findPredecessor implements this requirement.

```
while (!done) {
  ...
  if (c < 0) {
    if (root.left == null) {
    // insert as left child
      newNode =
        new BinaryTree<T>();
      root.left = newNode;
      done=true;
    } else {    // go left
      root = root.left;
    }
  } else {
    if (root.right == null) {
    // insert as right child
      newNode =
        new BinaryTree<T>();
      root.right = newNode;
      done=true;
    } else {    // go right
      root = root.right;
    }
  }
}
// set fields of new node
newNode.data = item;
newNode.parent = root;
size++;
} // insert
```

```
BinaryTree<T> findPredecessor(
    BinaryTree<T> node) {
  if (node.left == null) {
    return null;
  }
  // turn left once
  BinaryTree<T> pred = node.left;
  while (pred.right != null) {
    // keep going right
    pred = pred.right;
  }
  return pred;
}
```

The method deleteHere is best explained by tracing it over an example. The following figure illustrates the deletion of a node (15) that has one subtree. The first two subfigures illustrate what happens in the delete method before deleteHere is called; the last two subfigures show what happens in deleteHere.

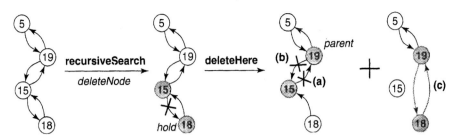

The first argument, deleteNode, to the deleteHere method is the node to be deleted. For the example in the preceding figure, this is node 15. The second argument to the deleteHere method, attach, is the subtree node (i.e., the root of the subtree) of deleteNode that is to be attached to the parent of deleteNode. In the example, this is node 18 (which is marked as hold by the delete method).

In deleteHere, the parent of deleteNode is first accessed, following which deleteNode is "cleared" (i.e., all its fields are set to null). Next, if deleteNode does not have a parent (i.e., it is the root of a binary tree that is itself not a subtree), nothing needs to be done, and the method returns.

Otherwise,
(i) The deleted node (15) is detached from its parent (19) by setting the deleted node's parent reference to null (mark (a) in the third sub-figure of the example), and setting the parent's child reference that refers to the deleted node to null (mark (b) in the third subfigure). This is coded in the second if statement. The symmetrical case, deleteNode, is its parent's right child and is coded in the second-to-last statement of the method.
(ii) The attach node which was sent in as argument to deleteHere (18 in the example) is attached to the deleted node's parent (19), as shown in (c) of the fourth subfigure in the example. In the method, these are the attachLeft and attachRight method calls, respectively.

```
void deleteHere(
    BinaryTree<T> deleteNode,
    BinaryTree<T> attach) {
  // deleteNode has only one
  // subtree, attach
  BinaryTree<T> parent =
      deleteNode.parent;
  deleteNode.clear();
  if (parent == null) {
    return;
  }
  if (deleteNode == parent.left) {
    // attach as left subtree
    parent.detachLeft();
    parent.attachLeft(attach);
    return;
  }
  // attach as right subtree
  parent.detachRight();
  parent.attachRight(attach);
}
```

Coming to the delete method proper, it first performs a search to find the node to be deleted by calling the recursiveSearch method.

After handling the erroneous condition of the node to be deleted being null, the method classifies the node to be deleted in one of the three categories we saw in Section 10.3.3: (a) leaf node, (b) node with exactly one subtree, or (c) node with two subtrees.

Case (c) is handled first, because it will be transformed into case (a) or (b), and in the code this is implemented as a graceful fall-through on control after case (c) is handled. Specifically, case (c) finds the predecessor of the node to be deleted with the call to findPredecessor, copies the data from this predecessor to the node to be deleted, and sets up the predecessor as the node to be deleted, deleteNode.

The leaf node situation (case (a)) is handled next. Whether the program control gets directly here or via case (c), delete Node is the node to be deleted. The method deleteHere is called with this leaf node that is to be deleted, and a second null argument, since there is no child to be attached to the leaf node's parent. The method terminates after this case is handled, returning the data in the node that was deleted.

Finally, case (b) is handled. The (one) subtree of deleteNode is identified as hold, and the deleteHere method is called, which will result in hold being attached to deleteNode's parent in place of delete Node, which is detached from its parent.

If the node that is deleted is itself the root of the binary search tree (represented by the tree class field), then the tree has to be reset to the subtree, which is done in the last if statement in the method.

```
public T delete(T key) {
    if (tree.isEmpty()) {
        throw new
        NoSuchElementException();
    }
    // find node containing key
    BinaryTree<T> deleteNode =
        recursiveSearch(tree, key);
    if (deleteNode == null) {
        throw new
        NoSuchElementException();
    }

    BinaryTree<T> hold;

    // case c
    if (deleteNode.right != null &&
        deleteNode.left != null) {
        hold =
        findPredecessor(deleteNode);
        deleteNode.data = hold.data;
        // fall through to case a or b
        deleteNode = hold;
    }

    // case a
    if (deleteNode.left == null &&
        deleteNode.right == null) {
        deleteHere(deleteNode, null);
        size--;
        return deleteNode.data;
    }

    // case b
    if (deleteNode.right != null) {
        hold = deleteNode.right;
        deleteNode.right = null;
    } else {
        hold = deleteNode.left;
        deleteNode.left = null;
    }

    deleteHere(deleteNode,hold);
    if (tree == deleteNode) {
        // root deleted
        tree = hold;
    }
    size--; return deleteNode.data;
}
```

10.6.4 Convenience Methods and Traversals

Of the remaining methods, minKey and maxKey are straightforward: essentially, minValue needs to find the "leftmost" node of the tree, and maxValue needs to find the "rightmost" one.

```
public T minKey() {                        public T maxKey() {
    if (tree.data == null) {                   if (tree.data() == null) {
        throw new                                  throw new
        NoSuchElementException();                  NoSuchElementException();
    }                                          }

    BinaryTree<T> root = tree;                 BinaryTree<T> root=tree;
    T min=root.data;                           T max=root.data
    root = root.left;                          root = root.right;
    while (root != null) {                     while (root != null) {
        min = root.data;                           max = root.data();
        root = root.left;                          root = root.right;
    }                                          }
    return min;                                return max;
}                                          }
```

Which leaves the traversals. Since the traversals are implemented as recursive processes, we need to break up the traversal implementation into two parts: a public method that is called by clients, and a nonpublic recursive helper method that is called by the public method. This is the same design technique we adopted for the search operation. So, for instance, the preorder traversal is broken up into the public preOrder method and the nonpublic recursive helper method, recursivePreOrder.

```
public void preOrder(                  void recursivePreOrder(
    Visitor<T> visitor) {                  BinaryTree<T> root,
    if (tree.isEmpty()) {                  Visitor<T> visitor) {
        return;                        if (root != null) {
    }                                      visitor.visit(root);
    recursivePreOrder(                     recursivePreOrder(root.left,
        tree, visitor);                        visitor);
}                                          recursivePreOrder(root.right,
                                               visitor);
                                       }
                                   }
```

We have already seen an application of the Visitor class in Section 10.5.2, where CountVisitor subclassed Visitor and defined a specialized visit method. The other traversal method pairs, inOrder/recursiveInOrder and preOrder/recursivePreOrder, are implemented in an analogous manner.

To summarize our discussion in this section, our implementation of the binary search tree hides the tree structure from its clients. All the client needs to see are the search, insert, and delete operations. By naming the traversal methods "preorder," "inorder," and "postorder," we allow the client a small window into the implementation structure, since these traversals are defined on binary trees.

However, we could very well have *replaced* these traversals with a single enumerator instead, that would implement inorder traversal, thereby enumerating the entries in ascending order of values. In particular, a first method could return the minimum-valued entry in the tree, and every subsequent call to a method next could return the preceding entry's inorder successor.

Having familiarized ourselves with an implementation of a simple binary search tree, we now turn to the AVL tree, a specialized binary search tree that guarantees $O(\log n)$ worst-case search, insert, and delete times.

10.7   AVL TREE

We return to the theme of binary search on an ordered list, and its representation as a comparison tree, which sowed the seeds for the growth of the binary search tree. On studying the binary search tree operations and their running times, we discovered, with dismay, that we were far from achieving our expectation of $O(\log n)$ time for search, insert, and delete.

We fell far short of our expectations because insertions and deletions into a binary search tree can play havoc with its shape. In the worst case, the tree could become completely lopsided, or skewed, on one side or the other, resulting in $O(n)$ time for search/insert/delete. To maintain the $O(\log n)$ time, the height of the tree would have to be maintained at $O(\log n)$—stated differently, it would have to be in a *balanced* condition. In order to achieve this balance, it was clear that the tree would have to be *rebalanced* after every insert or delete.

The **AVL** tree and the **red-black** tree are two kinds of balanced binary search trees that guarantee a worst-case search/insert/delete time of $O(\log n)$. The AVL tree was named after its inventors, the Russian mathematicians G. M. Adelson-Velskii and E. M. Landis, who described the tree and its balancing properties in 1962.

10.7.1   AVL Tree Structure

The AVL tree is a **height-balanced binary search tree.** What does it mean for the tree to be height-balanced? *Ideally,* it would mean that for every node, the heights of its left and right subtrees are equal. The AVL definition of height balance allows a small deviation from the ideal that works just as well.

AVL TREE
An AVL tree is a binary search tree in which the heights of the left and right subtrees of every node differ by at most 1.

Recall that the height of an empty tree is −1.

(a) and (b) are AVL trees. (c) and (d) are not AVL trees, and the node at which the AVL-ness is violated is shaded.

In (c), the node containing value 5 has a problem: its right subtree's height is 2, while its left subtree's height is 0, a difference of more than 1 between them.

Tree (d) is not an AVL tree—it does not violate the height-balance property, but it is not a binary search tree: the node containing the value 3 has a value (5) greater than 3 in its left subtree.

An AVL tree may also be defined recursively as follows:

RECURSIVE DEFINITION OF AVL TREE

An AVL tree is a binary search tree in which the left and right subtrees of the root are AVL trees whose heights differ by at most 1.

We will assume that all trees discussed here are binary search trees so that we can confine our attention to the height-balance property.

Balance factor. An AVL tree needs to keep track of the difference in the heights of the subtrees of every node. This is done by associating a *balance factor* with every node. There are three possible balance factors for a node:

- *Equal high,* '−': The left and right subtrees of the node are of equal height.
- *Right high,* '\': The height of the right subtree of the node is one more than that of its left subtree.

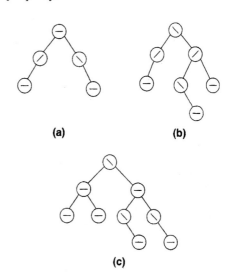

- *Left high, '/'*: The height of the left subtree of the node is one more than that of its right subtree.

The leaves of an AVL tree have an equal high balance factor because both the left and right subtrees of a leaf are empty.

Note again that an AVL *balance* is not necessarily a "perfect" balance in that its subtrees are not of equal height. Throughout this section, when we say that a node is "balanced," we mean that it is AVL-balanced.

10.7.2   Search, Insert, Delete Overview

Since the AVL tree is a binary search tree, searching proceeds as in any binary search tree.

Insertion also proceeds, in part, as in any binary search tree.

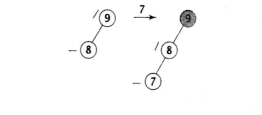

However, what if the sequence of insertions is a little different, say, 9, 8, 7, 5, 3? Then 9 and 8 would be inserted without any problem, but when 7 is inserted, it would lead to a height imbalance at node 9. The height of the left subtree of 9 is 1, while the height of its right subtree is −1 (empty), for a difference of 2 in subtree heights.

Or, if the sequence of insertions was 5, 3, 7, 8, 9, all except 9 would be inserted without any problem, but when 9 is inserted, it would lead to a height imbalance at nodes 7 and 5.

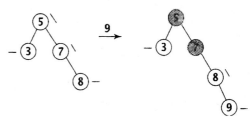

A node with a height imbalance like the ones in these examples is said to be *unbalanced,* or *out of balance.*

Height imbalances occur not only during insertions, but also during deletions. In these situations, at the time a node is detected to be out of balance, a rebalancing technique is applied at that node to restore the AVL height-balance property. This rebalancing technique is called **rotation**, and is a critical aspect of the AVL insertion and deletion processes.

10.7.3   Rotation

Rotation is a means of *locally* rearranging the structure of an AVL tree. It is performed on *on a tree link,* or branch. This link serves as a pivot about which the structure of the tree is locally rearranged.

A rotation is performed on link
S-V. T1, T2, and T3 are themselves
AVL trees, any of which could be
empty. The rotation breaks the links
$V \rightarrow S, P \rightarrow V$, and $S \rightarrow T2$, and makes
the links $S \rightarrow V, V \rightarrow T2$, and $P \rightarrow S$.

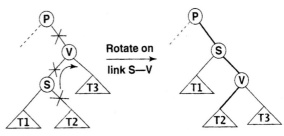

*It is important that the binary
search tree's ordering property be
preserved by the rotation.* That is why T2, the right subtree of S, is made the left subtree
of V after rotation.

Checking whether the ordering property is satisfied is easy. Since the inorder
traversal of a binary search tree visits the nodes in increasing order of values, simply
check whether the inorder traversal of the subtree at which the rotation is done is the
same before and after the rotation. In the rotation example, the inorder traversal of the
subtree at V before rotation is T1–S–T2–V–T3, which is the same as the inorder traversal
of the subtree at S after the rotation is done.

A rotation involves a certain *constant* number of steps, independent of the sizes of
the subtrees involved in the rotation. In other words, rotation takes $O(1)$ time.

In the example, the link on which the rotation is performed is a left branch. Rotation
on a right branch is symmetrical in nature. Next, we turn to a detailed examination of
insertion and deletion, where we will see more examples of rotation in action.

10.7.4   Insertion

Insertion in an AVL tree consists of the following sequence of steps:

- **Phase 1:** Insert the new value as in a regular BST by searching for its correct position
  and physically inserting a node containing the new value. The new node will always
  be a leaf node.
- **Phase 2:** Backtrack from the inserted (leaf) node up the chain of parents, correcting
  the balance factor of each node along the way. Stop at a node along the way if it is
  unbalanced, call this node X. Rebalance at node X.

Two observations about Phase 2:

- You may never have to stop and rebalance if no node along the backtracking path
  is unbalanced.
- Once you stop and rebalance a node, you do not have to continue backtracking.
  Insertion can terminate with the guarantee that the resultant tree is an AVL tree.

Rebalancing procedure in insertion.   Let us assume that an insertion is done in an
AVL tree, and in the backtracking phase a node (let us call it X) is found to be unbalanced.
Identify node R as the root of the taller subtree of X after insertion. There are two cases
for rebalancing at node X, depending on the balance factors of X and R.

**Case 1: The balance factor of X is the same as the balance factor of R. In other
words, the balance factors of X and R are both left high or right high. (The balance factors
of both being equally high will not be encountered.)**

Insert 9 as the right child of 8, following the regular BST insert procedure. Set the balance factor of 9 to '-'.

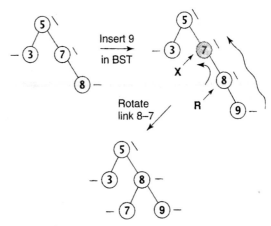

Then backtrack following the parent chain, first changing the balance factor of 8 to '\', and then stopping at 7 because it is unbalanced. This node has to be rebalanced.

Its child in the taller subtree is 8, whose balance factor is the same as that of 7. A rotation is applied on link 8-7 and the balance factors of 8 and 7 are updated. This completes the rebalancing process, and thus the insertion.

REBALANCING PROCEDURE, CASE 1:

1. Rotate about the link R-X.
2. Update the balance factors of R and X.

Insert 9 as the right child of 8, following the regular BST insert procedure. Set the balance factor of 9 to '-'.

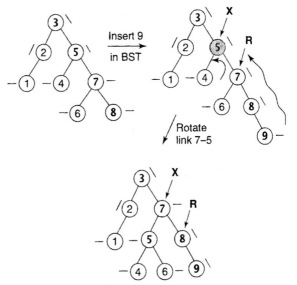

Then backtrack following the parent chain, first changing the balance factor of 8 to '\', then changing the balance factor of 7 to '\', and then stopping at 5 because it is unbalanced.

Apply rotation on link 7-5, and update the balance factors of 7 and 5. This completes the rebalancing process, and the insertion.

Note that the left child of 7, which is 6, is moved to the right child of 5 when the rotation is done. Since 6 is between 5 and 7 in value, it has to be either to the left of 7 or to the right of 5. But 5 is already to the left of 7 due to the rotation, so 6 becomes the new right child of 5.

Case 2: The balance factor of X is *opposite in orientation* to the balance factor of R. In other words, if X is right high, then R is left high, or vice versa.

Let Q be the root of the taller subtree of R.

Insert 6 as the left child of 7. Set the balance factor of 6 to '-'. Then backtrack following the parent chain, first changing the balance factor of 7, then changing the balance factor of 8, and then stopping at 5 because it is unbalanced. This node has to be rebalanced.

Its child in the taller subtree is 8, whose balance factor is opposite that of 5. Node 7 is the root of the taller subtree of 8. Rotate on link 7-8. Then rotate on link 7-5. Update the balance factors of 5, 7, and 8, and this completes the insertion.

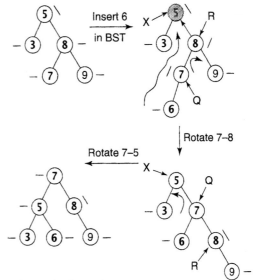

REBALANCING PROCEDURE, CASE 2:

1. Rotate link Q-R, which aligns nodes X, Q, and R in the same direction.

2. Rotate link Q-X.

3. Update the balance factors of X, Q, and R.

Insert 4 as the left child of 5, following the regular BST insert procedure. Set balance factor of 4 to '-'.

Then backtrack following the parent chain, first changing the balance factors of 5, 6, and 8, all to '\', and then stopping at 3 because it is unbalanced.

Apply rotation on link 6-8.

Apply rotation on link 6-3. Update the balance factors of 3, 6, and 8, and this completes the insertion.

Note that in the first rotation, the right child of 6, which is 7, is moved to the left child of 8. In the second rotation, the left *subtree* of 6, containing 5 and 4, is moved as a whole to the right subtree of 3.

10.7.5   Deletion

Deletion in an AVL tree consists of the following sequence of steps:

- **Phase 1:** Delete a value as in a regular binary search tree, with the three possible cases depending on whether the node to be deleted is a leaf, a node with a single subtree, or a node with two subtrees.
- **Phase 2:** Starting with the parent, P, of the deleted node, backtrack up the chain of parents, rebalancing every node along the way.

Observation about Phase 2: *Certain kinds of rebalancing cases will result in a legal AVL tree, in which case the backtracking can stop, and the deletion can terminate.*

    Notion of "shorter".   Consider Phase 1 of deletion. Let X be the node that is deleted in an AVL tree, and let P be the parent of the deleted node. The deletion is performed as in any regular BST, ultimately boiling down to either deleting a leaf node or deleting a node with one subtree. In either case, it is a fact that the subtree of P containing node X has become *shorter,* its size having been reduced by 1.

    The deleted node X is the right child of its parent P.

(a) X is a leaf node. After deletion, the right subtree of P reduces in height, to -1.

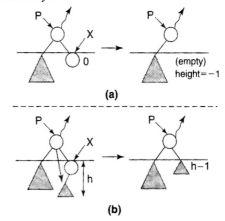

(a)

(b)

(b) X is a tree with one subtree. After deletion, the right subtree of P reduces in height, to h-1. In both cases, the right subtree of P is shorter by 1 after the deletion.

    Following is an algorithm for the deletion process.

algorithm delete_phase2

P : the parent of the deleted node X
shorter ← true

while (P is not null and *shorter* is true) do

  PP ← parent of P
  rebalance at P
    { rebalance may set *shorter* to false }
  $P ← PP$

endwhile

P starts out as the parent of the delete node. The variable *shorter* says whether the subtree of P in which the delete was made is shorter than before, and starts out by being true. However, when P is rebalanced, this variable may be reset to false. If this happens, the while loop terminates before the next iteration, which would go up a level higher in the tree. The loop would alternatively terminate if P cannot go any higher (i.e., it becomes null).

Rebalancing procedure in deletion. Assume that we rebalance at node P. There are three main cases of rebalancing depending on the balance factor of P and the relative heights of its subtrees.

REBALANCING PROCEDURE, CASE 1: THE BALANCE FACTOR OF P IS EQUAL HIGH.

Change balance factor of P to right high or left high according to whether the deletion has occurred in P's left subtree or right subtree, respectively.

When Case 1 is done, deletion can terminate right away without continuing to backtrack upward.

Delete 7 from BST, by copying the value of inorder predecessor, 5, and deleting node 5 instead. P, the node to be rebalanced, is the parent of the deleted node, in this case, 3. The balance factor of 3 is '-'.

Change the balance factor of 3 to '/'. The resulting tree is an AVL tree, and the backtracking process is terminated, which completes the deletion.

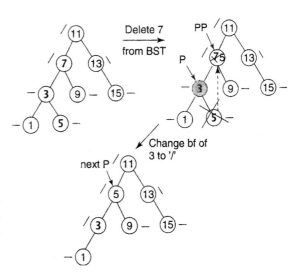

REBALANCING PROCEDURE, CASE 2: THE BALANCE FACTOR OF P IS NOT EQUAL HIGH, AND THE TALLER SUBTREE OF P IS SHORTENED BY THE DELETION.

Change balance factor of P to equal high.

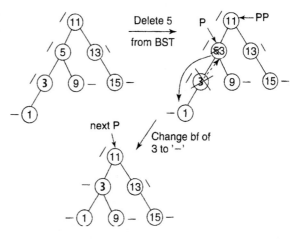

Delete 5 from BST, by copying the value of inorder predecessor, 3, and deleting node 3 instead. P, the node to be rebalanced, is the parent of the deleted node. In this case, it is the old 5, which is modified to 3, with 1 as the new child. The balance factor of P is '/'.

Change balance factor to '/'. The resulting tree is an AVL tree, but the balance factor of 11 is incorrect. It will be corrected when the backtracking process continues upward, with the next P set to node 11.

This case does not terminate the backtracking process. So after this case is applied, backtracking must proceed upward, and rebalancing must be applied to the parent of P.

Case 3: The balance factor of P is not equal high, and the shorter subtree of P is shortened by the deletion.

There are three subcases to be considered, depending on the balance factor of the root of the taller subtree of P. Let R be this root. In other words, R is the child of P on its taller subtree side.

REBALANCING PROCEDURE, CASE 3A: THE BALANCE FACTOR OF R IS EQUAL HIGH.

1. Rotate link R-P.
2. Set R's balance factor to left high or right high according to whether R is the right child or left child of P, respectively.

Delete 9 from BST. P, the node to be rebalanced, is the parent of the deleted node, which is 5 in this case. Its balance factor is '/'. R, its child in the taller subtree, is 3, whose balance factor is '-'.

Rotating 3-5 makes 4 move to the left of 5. Change the balance factor of 3 to '\'. The resulting tree is an AVL tree. Backtracking terminates, and along with it, so does the deletion process.

Applying this case terminates the backtracking process, and therefore the deletion.

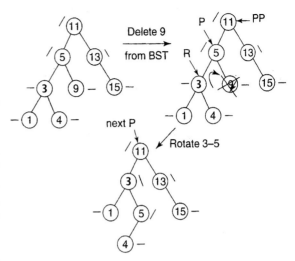

REBALANCING PROCEDURE, CASE 3B: THE BALANCE FACTOR OF R IS *NOT* EQUAL HIGH, AND IS ORIENTED IN THE SAME WAY AS P'S BALANCE FACTOR.

1. Rotate the link R-P.
2. Set the balance factors of both R and P to equal high.

Delete 9 from BST. P, the node to be rebalanced, is the parent of the deleted node, which is 5 in this case. Its balance factor is '/'. R, its child in the taller subtree, is 3, whose balance factor is also '/'.

Rotate 3-5, and change the balance factors of both 3 and 5 to '-'.

The resulting tree is an AVL tree, but the balance factor of 11 is incorrect.

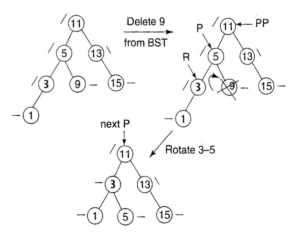

It will be corrected when the backtracking process continues upward, with the next P set to node 11.

REBALANCING PROCEDURE, CASE 3C: THE BALANCE FACTOR OF R IS *NOT* EQUAL HIGH, AND IS ORIENTED IN THE OPPOSITE DIRECTION TO P'S BALANCE FACTOR.

Let Q be the root of the taller subtree of R.

1. Rotate link Q-R, aligning P, Q, and R.
2. Rotate link Q-P.
3. Set the balance factor of Q to equal high.
4. Set the balance factors of R and P according to the heights of the subtrees of Q before deletion.

Delete 9 from BST. P, the node to be rebalanced, is the parent 5, of the deleted node. Its balance factor is '/'. Q, its child in the taller subtree, is 3, whose balance factor is '\'. R, the child of Q in the taller subtree, is 4.

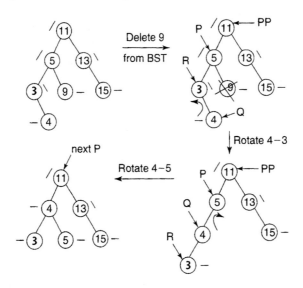

Rotate 4–3 counterclockwise to line up 5-4-3. Then rotate 4–5 clockwise.

The resulting tree is an AVL tree, but the balance factor of 11 is incorrect. It will be corrected when the backtracking process continues upward, with the next P set to node 11.

An AVL tree deletion exam-ple. We start with a tree in which node G is deleted. The initial parent is node F, whose balance factor is '/', while that of its child D on the taller side is '\' (i.e., opposite to F's). This sets up case 3c of rebalancing at F.

Two rotations are applied as prescribed by case 3c, first at link E-D, and then at link E-F. Subtrees that are not in the path of action have been replaced by triangles to lessen distraction. Since case 3c does not change *shorter,* the action moves up to C.

Node C is determined to fall into Case 2, since its balance factor is not '-', and its taller subtree has been shortened. This case simply resets the balance factor of C to '-'. Again, this case does not change *shorter,* so the action moves up to H.

The balance factor of H is '\' (not '-'), its shorter subtree has been shortened, and the balance factor of M, its child on the taller subtree, is the same, '\'. Thus, case 3b.

Actually, applying case 3b does not change shorter either, so the action must move up, but we have hit the root, so the deletion terminates. The height of the final tree is 4, one less than the height of the tree before deletion.

An AVL tree construction example. Let us build an AVL tree from scratch by inserting the values 9, 8, 3, 7, 5 in that order. Here is the first part of this construction, in which 9, 8, 3, and 7 are inserted.

Here is rest of the construction, in which 5 is inserted.

10.7.6   Running Times of AVL Tree Operations

Let n be the number of nodes in an AVL tree. Then its height is never more than approximately $1.44 \log n$. The analysis that leads to this is beyond the scope of our discussion. For the following discussion, we will take the height to be $O(\log n)$.

The search operation takes $O(\log n)$ time in the worst case, when it may have to go all the way down to a leaf node.

A rotation takes $O(1)$ time. An insertion would take $O(\log n)$ time for the search phase. For the second, rebalancing phase of insertion, the worst-case scenario is to back up all the way to the root, which would take $(\log n)$ time, and then rebalance at the root, which would take $O(1)$ time. This gives a total of $O(\log n)$ time for both phases of insertion combined.

Deletion is similarly analyzed. The first phase may involve a worst-case, $O(\log n)$ search, for deleting a leaf node. The second phase may involve a rotation or two ($O(1)$) at every node from the parent of the deleted node all the way to the root, for a time of $O(\log n)$. Again, the total time is $O(\log n)$ for both phases combined.

10.7.7   AVL Insert and Delete: Generalization

In our discussion of the insert and delete operations, we saw how each applicable scenario merits its own rules for rebalancing. We also saw that in the case of both insertion rebalancing scenarios, the insertion process stops after performing the required action, and does not have to go any further up the tree. How do we know this? Similarly, in two of the deletion rebalancing cases, the process stops after rebalancing, but in others, the process continues up the tree. Again, how are we assured that this holds for all possible AVL trees, and not just the instances we saw?

In this section, we will present a "defense" of these positions by means of a generalization of all the rebalancing cases of insertion and deletion.

Insertion rebalancing case 1.

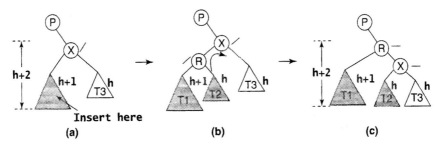

(a) AVL tree before insertion. (b) As a result of the insertion, the subtree with root R has increased in height by 1, thereby unbalancing R's parent, X. The balance factor of R is the same as that of X. A rotation is applied on R–X. (c) As a result of the rotation, T3 goes from being the right subtree of R to being the left subtree of X. The balance factors of R and X are both set to equal high. If P were the parent of X in (a), then as far as P is concerned, its subtree containing X has not changed in height. Thus the backtracking process can stop, and therefore the insertion can stop as well.

Insertion rebalancing case 2.

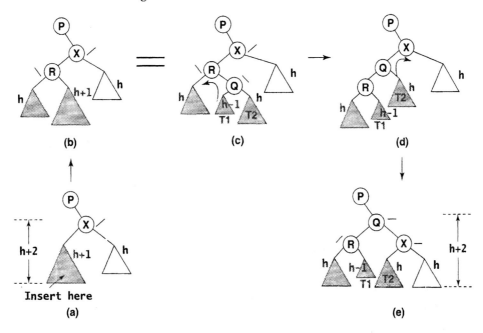

(a) AVL tree before insertion. (b) As a result of the insertion, the subtree with root R has increased in height by 1, thereby unbalancing R's parent, X. The balance factor of R is opposite that of X. (c) Q is the child of R in its taller subtree. A rotation is applied on Q–R. (d) X, Q, and R are aligned in the same direction, and T1 goes from being the left subtree of Q to being the right subtree of R. A second rotation, Q–X, is applied. (e) T2 goes from being the right subtree of Q to being the left subtree of X. The balance factors of X and Q are both set to equal high, and that of R is set at left high. If P were the parent of X in (a), then as far as P is concerned, its subtree containing X has not changed in height. Thus the backtracking process can stop, and therefore the insertion can stop as well.

Deletion rebalancing case 1.
(a) AVL tree before a deletion is made in the right subtree of P, whose balance factor is equal high. (b) As a result of the deletion, the subtree's height reduces by 1 (in this case). The balance factor of P is updated accordingly. If PP were the parent of P in (a), then as far as PP is concerned, its

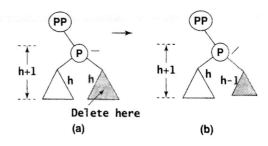

Delete here
(a)   (b)

subtree containing P has not changed in height (i.e., is not shorter). Thus the backtracking process can stop, and therefore the deletion can stop as well.

Deletion rebalancing case 2.
(a) AVL tree before a deletion is made in the right subtree of P, whose balance factor is right high. (b) As a result of the deletion, the subtree's height reduces by 1 (in this case). The balance factor of P is set to equal high. If PP were the parent of P in (a), then as far as PP is concerned, its

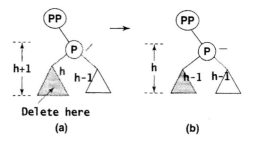

Delete here
(a)   (b)

subtree containing P has now reduced in height by 1, going from h + 1 before deletion to h after. Thus the backtracking process continues up to PP (which will become P for the next iteration), and the deletion process continues.

Deletion rebalancing case 3a.

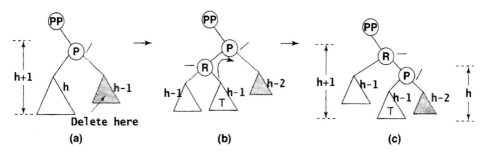

Delete here
(a)   (b)   (c)

(a) AVL tree before a deletion is made in the right subtree of P, whose balance factor is left high. (b) As a result of the deletion, the subtree's height reduces by 1 (in this case). Thus the shorter subtree of P is shortened. R is the root of the taller subtree of P, and its balance factor is equal high. A rotation is applied on R-P, which also results in T going from the right subtree of R to the left subtree of P. The balance factors of P and R are updated. If PP were the parent of P in (a), then as far as PP is concerned, its subtree containing P has retained its original height of h + 1. Thus, the backtracking process is terminated, and so is the deletion.

Deletion rebalancing case 3b.

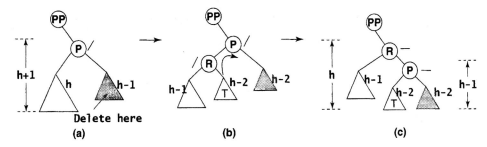

(a) AVL tree before a deletion is made in the right subtree of P, whose balance factor is left high. (b) As a result of the deletion, the subtree's height reduces by 1 (in this case). Thus, the shorter subtree of P is shortened. R is the root of the taller subtree of P, and its balance factor is left high, same as P's. (b) A rotation is applied on R-P, which also results in T going from the right subtree of R to the left subtree of P. The balance factors of P and R are updated, both set to equal high. If PP were the parent of P in (a), then as far as PP is concerned, its subtree containing P has now reduced in height by 1, going from h + 1 before deletion to h after. Thus the backtracking process continues up to PP (which will become P for the next iteration), and the deletion process continues.

Deletion rebalancing case 3c.

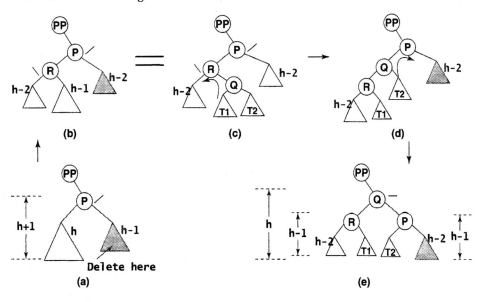

(a) AVL tree before a deletion is made in the right subtree of P. (b) As a result of the deletion, the subtree's height reduces by 1; the shorter subtree of P is shortened. R is the root of the taller subtree of P, and its balance factor is opposite P's. Q is the root of the taller subtree of R. (c) A rotation is applied on Q-R, which aligns P, Q, and R in the same direction. (d) A second rotation, Q-P, is applied. The balance factor of Q is set to equal high.

The balance factors of R and P will be updated as appropriate, *depending on the heights of* T1 *and* T2. What are the possibilities for the heights of T1 and T2?

Note that these are both subtrees of Q in (c). Also note that the height of the subtree for which Q is root is $h - 1$, because that subtree is the right subtree of R in (b). So here are the possibilities for their heights:

- T1 is $h - 2$ and T2 is $h - 2$, in which case the balance factor of Q would be equal high, in (c). Then, in (e), the balance factors of R and P would both be equal high.
- T1 is $h - 2$ and T2 is $h - 3$, in which case the balance factor of Q would be left high in (c). Then, in (e), the balance factor of R would be equal high, and that of P would be right high.
- T1 is $h - 3$ and T2 is $h - 2$, in which case the balance factor of Q would be right high in (c). Then, in (e), the balance factor of R would be left high, and that of P would both be equal high.

Finally, if PP were the parent of P in (a), then the subtree of PP containing P has reduced in height by 1, from h + 1 before deletion to h after. Thus, the backtracking process continues up to PP (which will become P for the next iteration).

10.8 BINARY SEARCH: AVERAGE NUMBER OF COMPARISONS

We are familiar with the general approach to determining the average search time, having applied it earlier to sequential search in Section 4.2.1. The average search *time* is equivalent to the average *number* of comparisons, since a comparison is the basic operation that contributes to the search time. In turn, the average number of comparisons, in general, is:

$$\frac{C_1 + C_2 + \cdots + C_n}{n}$$

where C_i comparisons are required to succeed (or fail) at the i-th element. Our task is to apply this general formula to binary search.

To start with an example, take the comparison tree of Figure 10.2. What is the average number of comparisons for failure in this tree? Assuming that the probability of failure at any *failure location* is the same as at any other, we have equal probabilities over five failure locations at level 3, and six at level 4, for a total of 11 failure locations. Noting that it takes six comparisons to fail at any failure node at level 3, and eight to fail at level 4, the total number of comparisons is $5 \times 6 + 6 \times 8 = 78$, for an average of $78/11 \approx 7$.

How about average comparisons for success? Again, assuming that every possibility of success is as likely as every other, we have equal probabilities over one, two, and four success locations at levels 0, 1, and 2, respectively, and three success locations at level 3, for a total of 10 success locations. It takes one comparison to succeed at level 0, three at level 1, five at level 2, and seven at level 3. Thus, the total number of comparisons is $1 \times 1 + 2 \times 3 + 4 \times 5 + 3 \times 7 = 48$, for an average of $48/10 = 4.8$.

Things get a little complicated when we want to extend this analysis to the general case: binary search on an array of n entries. (As you will recall, the average number of comparisons for sequential search on a list of length n was $(n + 1)/2$.) Let us start by working with the height of the comparison tree, h, and then later substitute a term in n for h.

Again, let us first analyze failures. To make it easier, we will assume that *all* failure nodes are at the last level. Since the height of the tree is h, this means that all failure nodes are at level h (i.e., there are 2^h failure nodes). To fail at any of these nodes would require $2h$ comparisons. The average number of comparisons is then

$$\frac{(2h \times 2^h)}{2^h} = 2h$$

This is easy to see to cross-check: every node requires the same number of comparisons, $2h$, so the average must be $2h$. Using $h \approx \log n$, we have:

> Average number of comparisons for failure $\approx 2 \log n$

Now let us look at successful search. The easy part is to count the number of internal nodes (i.e., all the places where one can end up successfully). For a tree of height h, we know that the number of internal nodes is $2^h - 1$. Let us now try to get a count of the number of comparisons at these nodes. If a node is at level i, the number of comparisons to succeed there is $2i + 1, 0 \le i \le (h - 1)$. Since there are 2^i nodes at level i, the average number of comparisons is:

$$\frac{\sum_{i=0}^{h-1} 2^i * (2i + 1)}{2^h - 1}$$

This can be evaluated as follows. Let S stand for the sum in the numerator. Thus, the above formula may be written as:

$$\frac{S}{2^h - 1}$$

Expanding the sum, we have:

$$S = 1 * 2^0 + 3 * 2^1 + 5 * 2^2 + \cdots + (2h - 1) * 2^{h-1}$$

What we will do next is to multiply this sum by 2 to obtain $2S$, and line up S and $2S$ as follows:

$$S = 1 * 2^0 + 3 * 2^1 + 5 * 2^2 + \cdots + (2h - 1) * 2^{h-1}$$

$$2S = \qquad 1 * 2^1 + 3 * 2^2 + \cdots + (2h - 3) * 2^{h-1} + (2h - 1) * 2^h$$

Now we subtract the second line from the first to obtain the following on the left- and right-hand sides of the equation:

$$-S = 1 * 2^0 + 2 * 2^1 + 2 * 2^2 + \cdots + 2 * 2^{h-1} - (2h - 1) * 2^h$$

Multiplying both sides by -1 and rewriting $1 * 2^0$ as $2 * 2^0 - 1$, we have:

$$S = (2h - 1) * 2^h - (2 * 2^0 - 1 + 2 * 2^1 + 2 * 2^2 + \cdots + 2 * 2^{h-1})$$

$$= (2h - 1) * 2^h - 2 * (\sum_{i=0}^{h-1} 2^i) + 1$$

We know that

$$\sum_{i=0}^{h-1} 2^i = 2^h - 1$$

so we have

$$
\begin{aligned}
S &= (2h - 1) * 2^h - 2 * (2^h - 1) + 1 \\
&= (2h - 3) * 2^h + 3
\end{aligned}
$$

Plugging this back into our formula for average number of comparisons, we get:

$$\frac{S}{2^h - 1} = \frac{(2h - 3) * 2^h + 3}{2^h - 1} \approx (2h - 3)$$

Finally, substituting $h \approx \log n$, we obtain:

$$\boxed{\text{Average number of comparisons for success} \approx 2 \log n - 3}$$

10.9 SUMMARY

- A comparison tree for binary search on an array is a binary tree that depicts all possible search paths. It shows all the different sequences of comparisons undertaken by binary search when searching for entries that may or may not be present in the array.

- A failure node in a comparison tree catches a range of values that lie between its inorder predecessor and its inorder successor in the tree.

- A comparison tree is simply a conceptual tool to analyze the time taken by binary search, and is therefore often referred to as an implicit search tree.

- The shape of the comparison tree, and thus the worst-case search time, is independent of the data entries in the array; it only depends on the length of the array.

- If the height of a comparison tree is h, the worst-case number of comparisons is $2h - 1$ for successful search, and $2h$ for unsuccessful search.

- The worst-case number of comparisons made by binary search on an ordered array of n elements is $2\lceil \log(n + 1) \rceil - 1$ for successful search, and $2\lceil \log(n + 1) \rceil$ for unsuccessful search.

- The values stored in a binary search tree must lend themselves to being arranged in order (i.e., they must be ordinal).

- A binary search tree is a binary tree whose entries can be arranged in order. For every node x in the tree, the value of the entry at x is greater than the values of all the entries in the left subtree of x, and smaller than the values of all the entries in the right subtree of x.

- An inorder traversal of a binary search tree will visit the nodes in ascending order of values.

- For any given number of values, n, there is only one binary search comparison tree. In contrast, there are as many possible binary search trees as there are different binary trees that can be constructed out of n nodes.

- The worst-possible binary tree structure is one that is completely skewed either to the left (no node has a right child) or to the right (no node has a left child). This happens when the values to be inserted arrive in descending or ascending order, respectively. Searching in such a tree degenerates to sequential search, with the attendant time of $O(n)$.
- The worst-case running times for search, insert, and delete in a binary search tree are all $O(\log n)$.
- Treesort is an algorithm to sort a set of values by inserting them one by one into a binary search tree, and then visiting them in inorder sequence. This algorithm has a worst-case running time of $O(n^2)$.
- The AVL tree and red-black tree are two types of balanced binary search trees that guarantee a worst-case search/insert/delete time of $O(\log n)$.
- An AVL tree is a binary search tree in which the heights of the left and right subtrees of every node differ by at most 1. It is referred to as a height-balanced binary search tree.
- Recursive definition: an AVL tree is a binary search tree in which the left and right subtrees of the root are AVL trees whose heights differ by at most 1.
- Rotation about a link in an AVL tree takes $O(1)$ time.
- Insertion in an AVL tree starts with a regular binary search tree insertion, followed by rebalancing.
- Deletion in an AVL tree starts with a regular binary search tree deletion, followed by rebalancing.

10.10 EXERCISES

E10.1. You are given a sorted array of length 11.
   (a) Draw a comparison tree for binary search on this array, along the lines of the one drawn in Figure 10.1
   (b) What is the worst-case number of comparisons for binary search on this array for a successful search? For a failed search?
   (c) What is the average number of comparisons for binary search on this array for a successful search? For a failed search? Assume that all possibilities of success are equally likely. Also, that all possibilities of failure are equally likely.

E10.2. Repeat each part of the preceding exercise for binary search using the *lazy binary search* algorithm of Exercise E5.4. (Hint: Failure and success occur only at leaf nodes. There are no comparison symbols next to any of the internal nodes.) Compare your answers to those obtained in the preceding exercise. Does this tree have more/fewer nodes?

E10.3. Repeat Exercise E10.1 for *sequential* search on a sorted array of size 11. Use the modified sequential search algorithm of Exercise E5.3.

E10.4. Binary search tree insertions/searches.
   (a) Construct a binary search tree by inserting the following in the given sequence:

   5, 10, 35, 15, 10, 70, 25, 30, 70

   Show the tree after every insertion.

(b) How many comparisons did it take overall to build the tree? Assume that the code to be inserted checks for duplicates and disallows them.

(c) What is the worst-case number of comparisons for a successful search in this tree?

(d) What is the worst-case number of comparisons for an unsuccessful search in this tree?

(e) What is the average number of comparisons for a successful search in this tree? Assume that all possibilities of success are equally likely.

(f) What is the average number of comparisons for a failed search in this tree? Assume the equal probability of hitting all possible failure *locations* in the tree.

(g) How would your answer to the previous part (average for failure) change if you assumed that searches are made on any integer between 1 and 100, and that all such searches are equally likely?

E10.5. From the binary tree constructed above, delete 35 by replacing it with its inorder predecessor and then deleting the predecessor. Show the resulting BST. How much work in all (location 35, then locating its inorder predecessor, etc.) did it take to complete the deletion? Assume two units of work to perform an item-to-item comparison, and one unit of work to write into a memory location.

E10.6. Repeat Exercise E10.5 to delete 35, but this time replace it with its inorder successor, and then delete this successor.

E10.7. Suppose a binary search tree stores integers in the range 1 to 1000. Which of the following search sequences are *not possible* when searching for the value 225 in this tree?

(a) 500, 355, 150, 320, 200, 225

(b) 500, 400, 200, 300, 200, 350, 225

(c) 50, 100, 600, 400, 40, 120

(d) 50, 500, 100, 400, 200, 300

E10.8. A binary search tree may be modified as follows: in every node, keep a count of the number of nodes in its right subtree. The following figure illustrates such a tree: the shaded part is the number of nodes in the right subtree; the unshaded part is the data. This modification is useful to answer the following question: what is the k-th largest element in the binary search tree? If $k = 1$, we are looking for the largest element: if $k = 2$, we are looking for the second-largest element, and so on.

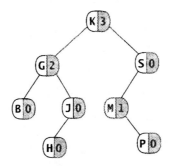

Write a *recursive* algorithm that would find the k-th largest element in this modified binary search tree. Assume that the tree contains n elements, and $k \leq n$. What is the worst-case running time (big O) of your algorithm?

E10.9. Suppose you are given two BSTs, the first with m entries and the second with n entries, with no duplicate keys in either. Describe an algorithm to merge the two trees into a new BST that contains all the entries of both the original BSTs. If the same key occurs in both trees, only one copy is retained in the merged BST. Your algorithm should be as fast as possible.

Analyze your algorithm for the worst-case big O running time.

E10.10. You are given the following AVL tree. Determine the height of the subtree rooted at each node in the tree, as well as the balance factor of each node.

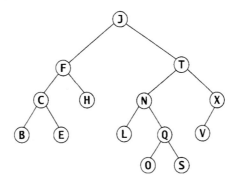

E10.11. In the AVL tree of Exercise E10.10, perform the following operations in the given sequence. Show the resulting AVL tree after every operation.
   (a) Insert Z
   (b) Insert P
   (c) Insert A
   (d) Delete T
   (e) Delete J

E10.12. Given the following AVL tree:

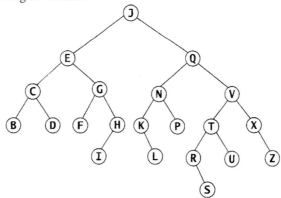

   (a) Delete J from the tree, using its inorder *predecessor* as replacement.
   (b) Delete J from the original tree, using its inorder *successor* as replacement.

E10.13. Build an AVL tree by inserting the following integers in the given sequence. Show the resulting AVL tree after every insertion:

96, 43, 72, 68, 63, 28

E10.14. Delete, one by one, all the entries from the AVL tree you built in Exercise 10.13. Show the resulting AVL tree after every deletion.

E10.15. In the AVL tree shown below, the triangles represent subtrees. Subtrees T1, T3, and T4 are of height $h - 1$, subtree T5 is of height $h + 1$, and all the other subtrees are of height h.

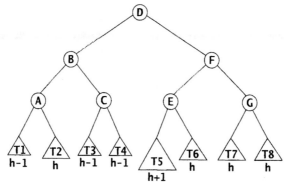

   (a) What is the height of the tree rooted at node D?
   (b) What is the balance factor of each node?
   (c) A deletion is made that decreases the height of subtree T2 to $h - 1$. Show the resultant AVL tree.

10.11 PROGRAMMING PROBLEMS

P10.1. Reimplement the method search in the BinarySearchTree class without using recursion.

P10.2. Reimplement the method insert in the BinarySearchTree class using recursion.

P10.3. Write a method for the BinarySearchTree<T extends Comparable<T>> class that would return a linked list of its entries in sorted order:

```
public LinkedList<T> sort()
```

(This method is a modification of the method inOrder.)

P10.4. The method inOrder of the BinarySearchTree class visits the entries in sorted order. Write another method for this class:

```
public void reverseOrder()
```

that would visit the entries in *reverse* sorted order.

P10.5. In Section 10.5.2 we presented a naive way of counting all the items in a binary search tree whose keys are less than a specified key. Naive because we visited *all the nodes* in the tree. Devise a more efficient means of computing this count, and write the following method in the BinarySearchTree class to implement your design:

```
public int countLess(T key)
```

What is the worst-case running time (big O) of your method?

P10.6. Add a method to the BinarySearchTree class:

```
public DLLNode<T> sort()
```

that would return a doubly linked list of all entries arranged in ascending order of keys. Use the DLLNode<T> class you devised in Problem P4.15, except that the type parameter T is now T extends Comparable<T>.

P10.7. Implement a class:

```
public class RichBST<T extends Comparable<T>> extends
BinarySearchTree<T>
```

by providing the following additional rich set of methods:

- A method to return, in an ArrayList, its items in sorted order:

  ```
  public ArrayList<T> sort()
  ```

- A method to return all items whose keys are greater than a specified key:

  ```
  public ArrayList<T> greaterThan(T key)
  ```

- A method to return all items whose keys are less than a specified key:

  ```
  public ArrayList<T> lessThan(T key)
  ```

- A method to return all items whose keys lie in a specified interval (including the ends) of keys:

  ```
  public ArrayList<T> inInterval(T key1, T key2)
  ```

  In other words, all items whose keys are greater than or equal to key1 *and* less than or equal to key2.

P10.8. In Exercise E10.8, we looked at a binary search tree in which every node maintained a count of the number of nodes in its right subtree. This helped us to determine the *k*-th largest entry efficiently. Can you modify the BinarySearchTree class to accomplish this? Explain clearly how, and if there are other related issues that need to be addressed, discuss them in detail.

P10.9. Reimplement the BinarySearchTree class *without* using the BinaryTree class as a component. Every node of the binary search tree must contain only two links, to its right and left children. It should *not* contain a parent link. Compare this implementation with the BinarySearchTree implementation of Section 10.6 with respect to both ease of implementation (simplicity of code) and space consumption. Does the efficiency of any of the operations in the new implementation differ from the old?

P10.10. Implement a *right* rotation on link q–x in a binary search tree, given a node x, with q as its left child. Use the following definition of a binary search tree node:

```
class BSTNode<T extends Comparable<T>> {
  T data; BSTNode<T> parent, left, right;
  BSTNode(T data, BSTNode<T> parent,
          BSTNode<T> left, BSTNode<T> right) {
    this.data = data;
    this.parent = parent; this.left = left; this.right = right;
  }
}
```

Complete this method:

```
<T extends Comparable<T>> void rightRotate(BSTNode<T> x)
```

P10.11. Implement your algorithm of Exercise E10.9. Use the BSTNode definition of Problem P10.10. Here is the header of the method you would need to implement:

```
<T extends Comparable<T>> BSTNode<T> merge(BSTNode<T> bst1,
                                           BSTNode<T> bst2)
```

P10.12. An inorder threaded BST is a BST in which every node has two additional pointers: a *previous* pointer that refers to its inorder predecessor, and a *next* pointer that refers to its inorder successor. The previous pointer of the minimum key node is null, and so is the next pointer of the maximum key node. The chain of next pointers, starting at the minimum key node, sets up an *inorder thread,* and the chain of previous pointers, starting at the maximum key node, sets up a reverse inorder thread.

Your task is to implement an inorder threaded BST. You will do this in two steps. First, create a class called ThreadedBinaryTree<T> that is a subclass of BinaryTree<T>. To the inherited fields, add the public fields previous and next for the thread. None of the inherited methods needs to be redefined, and no new methods need to be added.

Second, create a class called ThreadedBST<T extends Comparable<T>>, starting with the same interface as that of BinarySearchTree<T extends Comparable<T>> but replacing all instances of BinaryTree<T> by ThreadedBinaryTree<T>.

- The BinarySearchTree class uses a BinaryTree<T> class instance. Have the ThreadedBST class use a ThreadedBinaryTree<T> instance instead.
- Implement all the methods of the class, with special attention to insert and delete (and their helper) to maintain the thread pointers correctly.
- Implement the inorder method by using the inorder thread instead of traversing recursively.

CHAPTER 11

Heap

From a structural point of view, the heap is a special type of binary tree. From the functional point of view, it can be used either as a priority queue, which is a specialization of the regular FIFO queue we studied earlier, or as a tool for sorting. In this chapter, we will study in detail the role of the heap as a priority queue. Using the heap in sorting will be discussed at length in Chapter 13.

Learning Objectives

- Learn how the heap can play the role of a priority queue.
- Describe the structure and ordering properties of the heap.
- Study the characteristic heap operations, and analyze their running time.
- Understand the public interface of a heap class.
- Design a heap-based priority scheduler.
- Develop a priority scheduling package in Java that uses the heap class.
- Implement the heap class using an array list as the storage component for the heap entries.
- Appreciate the software engineering issues that inform the design of an updatable heap.

11.1   HEAP AS PRIORITY QUEUE

In the role of a *priority queue*, the heap acts as a data structure in which the entries have different priorities of removal: the entry with the highest priority is the one that will be removed next. This is a generalization of the regular FIFO queue. In other words, a FIFO queue may be considered a special case of a priority queue, in which the priority of an entry is the time of its arrival in the queue, and the earlier the arrival time, the higher the priority. Thus, the entry that arrived earliest is at the front of the queue.

The emergency room in a hospital is a quintessential priority queue. The patients who arrive at an ER require treatment with varying levels of urgency. The greater the urgency, the higher the priority with which a patient is treated.

Another use of a priority queue is in scheduling different processes in an operating system. Processes arrive at different points in time, and take different amounts of time to finish executing. The operating system needs to ensure that all processes get fair treatment in the amount of CPU time they are allocated. No single process should hog the CPU, nor should any process starve for CPU time.

There are various process-scheduling methods adopted by different operating systems. One method is to start off a newly arrived process at the highest priority, and to drop its priority by one level after every round of CPU time given to the process. A long-staying process will at some point plunge to the lowest priority possible, where it will stay for all future rounds until it completes execution. This particular method ensures that longer processes gradually receive less and less priority. A long process may still be in the process queue, waiting to finish, while a relatively short process that arrived later may finish execution and leave.

There is a crucial difference between the ER example and the CPU scheduling application that has a direct bearing on the implementation of the heap. Imagine a patient who arrives at the ER, and whose condition deteriorates while waiting for treatment. The priority of this patient must be increased according to the severity of his or her condition, and, in fact, may undergo several progressive increments.

Thus, an ER-like situation is best represented by a priority queue model in which the priority of an entry *may change while it is in the queue.* On the other hand, this is not a requirement in the scheduling application. The priority of a process may drop, but this happens *after* it has left the queue to be served by the CPU for some fixed time interval; if its current turn at the CPU is done, and it needs more time to finish, it *re-enters* the queue with a new, lower, priority.

In this chapter, we will mainly focus our attention on a heap that does not allow for the priority of an existing entry to be changed. In Section 11.8 we will see how to extend a heap to support efficient priority updates.

11.2   HEAP PROPERTIES

Following is the precise definition of a heap:

HEAP

A heap is a complete binary tree with the property that the key of the item at any node x is greater than or equal to the keys of the items at all the nodes in the subtree rooted at x.

Recall from Section 9.1.3 that a complete binary tree is one in which every level but the last must have the maximum number of nodes possible at that level. The last level may have fewer than the maximum possible nodes, but they should be arranged from left to right without any empty spots.

The property of being a complete binary tree is called the *heap structure property,* and the property of the relative ordering among the keys is called the *heap ordering property.* The heap ordering property guarantees that the key at the root of the tree (also called the *top of the heap*) is the maximum of all keys in the heap.

Structure (a) is a single-node heap. Structure (b) violates the heap structure property in that it is not a complete binary tree. Structure (c) is a heap. Structure (d) violates both the heap structure and the heap ordering properties.

Note that in a heap there is no specific relationship between keys in two disjoint subtrees. In (c), for example, keys 10 and 12 in the subtree rooted at 12 are both greater than key 8, which is at the level of their parent, but in a different subtree.

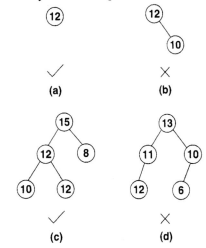

11.2.1   Max and Min Heaps

The heap definition given in the preceding section states that the key at a node is greater than or equal to the keys at the nodes in its subtrees. This makes for a **max heap,** to indicate the fact that the maximum key is at the top of the heap.

Alternatively, one could define a **min heap** which is the complement of the max heap:

MIN HEAP

A min heap is a complete binary tree with the property that the key of the item at any node x is less than or equal to the keys of the items at all the nodes in the subtree rooted at x.

This implies that the *minimum* key is at the top of the heap. In the rest of this chapter, we will be dealing with max heaps unless otherwise specified.

A priority queue can be implemented either as a max heap or a min heap, according to whether a greater key indicates greater priority (max heap) or smaller priority (min heap). For example, a min heap could simulate a FIFO queue by assigning priorities to entries based on time of arrival in the heap. The earlier the arrival time, the higher the priority, thus the entry with the minimum arrival time of all is at the top of the heap.

11.3   HEAP OPERATIONS

As a priority queue, a heap must provide the same fundamental operations as a FIFO queue. Specifically, it must provide an *insert* operation that inserts a new entry in the heap—this new entry must enter with a specified priority. Also, it must provide a *delete* operation that removes the entry at the front of the priority queue—this would be the entry that has the highest priority of all in the heap.

11.3.1   Insert

Inserting a new key in a heap must ensure that after insertion, both the heap structure and the heap ordering properties are satisfied.

First, insert the new key so that the heap structure property is satisfied, meaning that the new tree after insertion is also complete. In the example, 20 must be inserted as the left child of 8.

Second, make sure that the heap ordering property is satisfied by *sifting up* the newly inserted key, if need be. In the example, 20 is sifted up two levels.

Sifting up. Sifting up consists of comparing the new key with its parent, and exchanging them if the parent is less than the new key.

In the best case, no exchanges are done (a).

In the worst case, exchanges may have to be done repeatedly until the the new key reaches the root, as in example (b)–(c)–(d).

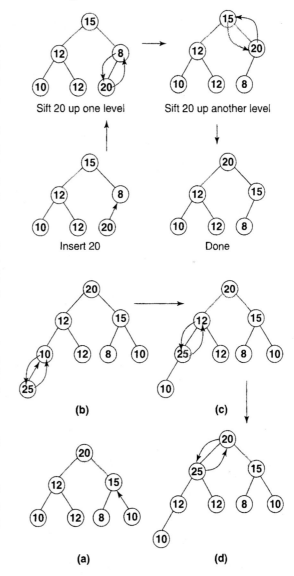

11.3.2 Delete

The entry at the top of the heap is the one with the maximum key. Deletion removes this entry from the heap. This leaves a vacant spot at the root, and the heap has to be *restored*.

Restoring the heap. (a) Delete 20. Remove the rightmost node in the last level, containing key 10, and write 10 into the root. This maintains the heap structure. Restore the heap order by *sifting down* 10.

(b) Compare 17 and 15, pick the larger, 17, and compare with 10. Since 17 is greater, exchange it with 10.

(c) Compare 12 and 12. Pick left 12, compare with 10. Exchange 12 with 10.

(d) Since 10 has reached a leaf, the heap restoration is done.

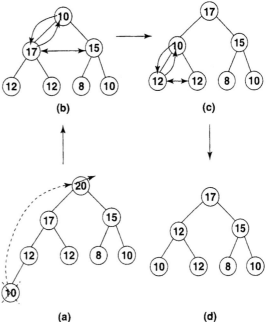

Sifting down. The key k that is extracted from the last node and written into the root is moved as far down as necessary to ensure that placing k in this spot will preserve the heap ordering property.

The children of k are first compared with each other to determine the larger key. This larger key is then compared with k. If k is smaller, it is exchanged with the larger key, which results in k sifting down one level. This process continues until either the larger of the keys of k's children is *less than or equal* to k, or k reaches a leaf node.

Deleting 17 results in the last node, containing 10, being removed from the heap, and 10 being written into the root. Then 10 is sifted down. 15, the larger of the keys of the children of 10, is exchanged with 10. The sift down stops after this exchange because 10 is greater than 8, its only child.

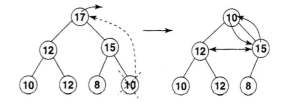

11.3.3 Running-time Analysis

The heap is a complete binary tree, so all levels but the last necessarily contain the full complement of nodes. Since we will be analyzing the worst case, we will assume that the last level also contains the full complement of nodes.

Let the height of the heap be h. In Section 9.1.3 we saw that the maximum number of nodes, N_{max}, in a binary tree of height h is $2^{h+1} - 1$. In a heap, if we assume that the last level is full as well, we have number of nodes $n = N_{max} = 2^{h+1} - 1$, which implies that $h = \log(n + 1) - 1$. (If we do not assume that the last level also has a full complement of nodes, we can restate this as $h = \lceil \log(n + 1) \rceil - 1$.)

Insert.   Sifting up during insertion takes one comparison per level between the new key and its parent. In the worst case, the new key may be sifted all the way up to the root, or h levels, for a total of h comparisons. In terms of n, therefore, insertion takes $\log(n + 1) - 1$ comparisons, for a big O running time of $O(\log n)$.

Delete.   Sifting down key k during deletion involves two comparisons per level, one between the children of k, and another between the larger child and k. In the worst case, k may be sifted all the way down to a leaf node, or h levels, for a total of $2h$ comparisons. In terms of n, this amounts to $2 * \log(n + 1) - 2$ comparisons, for a big O running time of $O(\log n)$.

11.4   A Heap CLASS

Figure 11.1 lists the public interface of a generic heap class.

The heap accepts items of any type, with the restriction that the type implements the compareTo method of the Comparable interface. This method will invoked on the items to compare priorities—in effect, the priority of an item is treated as its key.

Note that the enumeration methods first and next return the items of the heap in level-order. This means that first returns the top of the heap, and every subsequent call to next returns the item that would appear next in a level-order traversal going top to bottom, level by level, and left to right across each level.

Running times of methods.   The methods add and deleteMax correspond to the insert and delete operations, whose running times have already been analyzed in Section 11.3.3. Assuming that the heap keeps a running count of the number of items, the size and isEmpty methods each take $O(1)$ time.

Clearing the heap (i.e., emptying it out) can likewise be done in $O(1)$ time simply by setting the running count to zero. The enumeration methods first and next can be implemented in $O(1)$ time with a simple movement of a cursor that keeps track of the items in level order.

We can learn how clients can use this Heap class by studying a simulation of process scheduling.

11.5   PRIORITY SCHEDULING WITH HEAP

11.5.1   Overview

A process-scheduling system consists of a processor and a queue of schedulable processes that are waiting for their turn at the processor. The processes are given relative priorities of execution so that the process with the highest priority in the process queue is the first

Class structures.tree.Heap<T extends Comparable<T>>

Constructors

Heap(int cap)
Creates an empty heap with the specified initial capacity.
Heap( )
Creates an empty heap with a default initial capacity.

Methods

$O(\log n)$ **void add(T)**
Adds the specified item to this heap.
$O(\log n)$ **T deleteMax( )**
Deletes from this heap the item with maximum priority and returns it.
Throws **NoSuchElementException** if the heap is empty.
$O(1)$ **void clear( )**
Deletes all the items in this heap (i.e., empties it out).
$O(1)$ **int size( )**
Returns the number of items in this heap.
$O(1)$ **boolean isEmpty( )**
Returns true if this heap is empty, false otherwise.
$O(1)$ **T first( )**
Returns the top of the heap, null if the heap is empty.
$O(1)$ **T next( )**
Returns the next item in level-order from the heap, null if the end of the heap
is reached.

FIGURE 11.1: A Generic Heap Class. Only the public interface is shown. Multiple items may have the same priority (key), but will be relatively ordered in an arbitrary manner. Running times assume an implementation that keeps a direct reference to the top of the heap, a count of number of items, n, and a cursor that can enumerate items in level order.

one to be executed when the processor is free. This requirement is ideally met by the heap data structure used as a priority queue.

The scheduling simulation (using a heap) is controlled by several parameters, listed in Table 11.1.

TABLE 11.1: Scheduling simulation control parameters.

Parameter	Description
probOfArrival	Probability of a process arriving in the next interval
timeSlice	Time for which the processor executes a single process
maxExecTime	Maximum execution time of a process
maxPriority	Maximum priority of a process

The simulation proceeds in discrete time units. In each time unit, a new process may arrive in the system with a given probability that is determined by the parameter probOfArrival, an execution time, and a priority of execution. As soon as a process arrives, it is queued into the process priority queue/heap.

The process with the highest priority in the heap is sent to the CPU for execution at time *t*. In the example, the time-slice of the CPU is 2 units. The total time required by the process is 6 units. The process is executed for 2 time units by the CPU, and then sent back to the heap because it needs 4 more time units to finish.

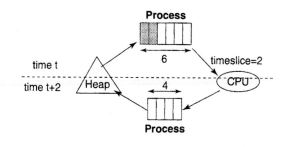

The following example traces a sample simulation session, with the control parameters probOfArrival = 0.3, timeSlice = 3, maxExecTime = 10, and maxPriority = 4. Say every simulation interval is one minute. In the table, a process is listed as a *(process id, execution time, priority)* triple.

Simulation

Time	CPU	Heap
2		(1,7,1)
2	(1,7,1)	
3	(1,7,1)	(2,4,1)
4	(1,7,1)	(2,4,1) (3,6,0)
5	(2,4,1)	(3,6,0) (1,4,0)
8	(3,6,0)	(1,4,0) (2,1,0)
11	(1,4,0)	(2,1,0) (3,3,0)
12	(1,4,0)	(2,1,0) (3,3,0) (4,7,3)

At the *end* of the second minute, two events take place: (a) a new process, (1,7,1), arrives at the scheduler and is placed in the heap, and (b) since the processor is free, this process is scheduled for execution. This is shown in the first two rows of the table.

While this process is executing, two more processes arrive, at the end of the third and fourth minutes, respectively. At the end of the fifth minute, two events occur. First, process id 1 finishes its turn (time slice is 3) at the processor. It is sent back to the heap as (1,4,0): the remaining execution time is 4 and the priority is decremented by one. Since the processor is now free, the second event takes place—process id 2 (higher priority than process id 3) is taken off the heap and scheduled for execution on the processor.

At the end of the eleventh minute, process id 3 is taken off the processor and sent back to the heap, but its priority is not decremented because it has already reached rock-bottom. Also, there are two contenders in the heap, 1 and 2 with the same priority, 0. Since 1 arrived earlier (end of fifth minute) than 2 (end of eighth minute), it is picked next. Thus, if all the processes in the heap are of the same priority, the heap behaves likes a simple FIFO queue.

In the following section we implement this scheduler using a Heap instance to maintain processes with priorities.

11.5.2   A Scheduling Package Using Heap

We will build a package called `apps.tree.scheduling` that consists of four classes: `Scheduler`, `ProcessSource`, `Proc`, and `Processor`.

Let us start with the `Process` class, which encapsulates processes in the scheduling system.

Process class.   The key implementation detail in the `Process` class is the priority comparison between `Process` instances. This is done in the usual manner, by having it implement interface `Comparable<Process>`, and thus the `compareTo` method.

Class File 11.1.   *Process.java*

```
package apps.tree.scheduling;

class Process implements Comparable<Process> {

    int pid; // process id
    int execTime; // execution time left
    int arrivalTime; // time of entry into heap
    int priority; // relative execution priority

    Process(int pid, int execTime, int priority) { ... }
    public String toString() { ... }
    public int compareTo(Process p) { ... }
}
```

All of the fields in this class, except `pid`, may change during the course of the simulation.

The constructor initializes the arrival time to zero for the start of the simulation.

```
Process(int pid, int execTime,
        int priority) {
    this.pid = pid;
    this.execTime = execTime;
    this.priority = priority;
    arrivalTime = 0;
}
```

Method `compareTo` is implemented in such a way that *if two processors have the same priority value, then the one with the earlier arrival time effectively gets higher priority.*

In other words, if all priorities are equal, then the priority queue degenerates into a simple FIFO queue.

```
public int compareTo(
            Process p) {
    int c = priority - p.priority;
    if (c != 0) {
        return c;
    }
    return p.arrivalTime -
            arrivalTime;
}
```

Method `toString` puts together all the attributes of a processor:

```java
public String toString() {
  return "(" + pid + "," + execTime + "," +
         priority + "," + arrivalTime + ")";
}
```

Processes are delivered to the scheduling system by the `ProcessSource` class.

ProcessSource class.

Class File 11.2. *ProcessSource.java*

```java
package apps.tree.scheduling;

import java.util.Random;

class ProcessSource {

  float probOfArrival; // probability of process arriving in next interval
  int maxExecTime; // maximum execution time of any process
  int maxPriority; // maximum priority of any process
  Random randomizer; // used with prob of arrival
  int pid; // unique processes id

  ProcessSource(float arrivalProbability, int maxExecTime,
                     int maxPriority) { ... }
  Process getProcess() { ... }
}
```

The constructor ensures that the arrival-probability parameter is in the legal range of 0...1 before proceeding.

```java
ProcessSource(float arrivalProbability, int maxExecTime,
                  int maxPriority) {
  if (arrivalProbability <= 0 || arrivalProbability > 1) {
    throw new IllegalArgumentException(arrivalProbability +
           " <= 0 or > 1");
  } else {
    probOfArrival = arrivalProbability;
  }
  this.maxExecTime = maxExecTime;
  this.maxPriority = maxPriority;
  randomizer = new Random();
  pid=0;
}
```

Method getProcess is called once in every simulation interval.

```
Process getProcess() {
  if (randomizer.nextFloat()
      > probOfArrival) {
    return null;
  }
  pid++;

  //scale random value to desired
  //execution time range
  int ptime = (int)
    (Math.random()*maxExecTime);
  if (ptime == 0) ptime++;

  //scale random value to desired
  // priority range
  int priority = (int)
    (Math.random()*maxPriority);

  return new Process(pid, ptime,
                     priority);
}
```

The first if condition checks whether a new process is deliverable in this call or not. The call randomizer.nextFloat() here returns a floating-point number between 0 and 1. Assuming that the randomizer distributes the numbers, it generates uniformly in the interval 0…1, comparing the number generated against probArrival results in processes being delivered at a rate that corresponds to the arrival probability.

Processes are assigned unique identification numbers in the sequence 1, 2, 3, …. The execution time, ptime, and the priority of a new process, priority, are randomly generated using the random method of the Math class.

The random method returns a random double value in the range 0.0 to 1.0, which is then appropriately scaled and converted to an int value. If ptime is computed to zero, it is incremented by one, to ensure that the execution time is strictly greater than zero.

Why do we use the java.util.Random class to determine whether a processor is deliverable, but use the Math.random method instead to randomize the execution time and priority of a process, even though both approaches give random numbers in the floating-point range 0 to 1? The reason is that the Random class delivers a *sequence* of numbers in which the next number in the sequence depends on the preceding numbers, and we need this sequence to be not disturbed by calls other than to check process deliverability.

Next, the Processor class, which represents the relevant aspects of a CPU for the scheduling system.

Processor class.

Class File 11.3. *Processor.java*

```
package apps.tree.scheduling;

class Processor {

  int timeSlice; // time slice given to a process
  int clock; // clock to track time slice
  boolean busy; // true if a process is currently executing
  Process currProc; // executing, or done but not removed from CPU
```

```
Processor(int timeSlice) { this.timeSlice = timeSlice; }
void startUp(Process currProc) { ... }
void stepTime() { ... }
boolean isIdle() { return !busy; }
Process getProcess() throws BusyInterruptionException { ... }
int getClockTime() { return clock; }
public String toString() {
    return currProc + "<" + clock + "," + timeSlice + ">";
}
}
```

When a process is to be executed on this processor, the method `startUp` is invoked with this process sent in as an argument.

```
void startUp(Process currProc) {
  // start cycle for new process
  this.currProc = currProc;
  clock = 0; busy = true;
}
```

Method `stepTime` is called at the end of every interval. It resets the clock if the current process has either exhausted the time slice limit or finished execution, whichever happens first. (It is possible for both these conditions to be simultaneously true.)

```
void stepTime() {
  if (!busy) { return ; }
  clock++;
  if (clock == timeSlice ||
      clock == currProc.execTime) {
    // process has finished its
    // allowed cycle
    clock = 0; busy = false;
  }
}
```

The `getProcess` method is needed in order to give back to the client the process that has finished executing, so that it can either be removed from the system or sent back to the process queue.

If this method is invoked while the processor is still busy executing, it throws a `BusyInterruptionException`. If the processor is not busy, it returns the stored process and sets the process reference field, `currProc`, to `null`.

```
Process getProcess()
throws BusyInterruptionException {
  if (busy) { // busy executing
    throw new
        BusyInterruptionException();
  }
  Process ret = currProc;
  currProc = null;
  return ret;
}
```

The setting to `null` indicates that apart from being idle, the processor has handed over the last executed processor to the client. This step is essential to ensure that the state changes are consistent. If `startUp` accepts a process from the client and starts executing it, then `getProcess` must complement it by delivering this process back to the client and "flushing" the processor.

The exception `BusyInterruptionException` is a checked exception, defined in the `apps.tree.scheduling` package as follows:

Class File 11.4. *BusyInterruptionException.java*

```
package apps.tree.scheduling;

public class BusyInterruptionException extends Exception {

  public BusyInterruptionException() {
    super();
  }

  public BusyInterruptionException(String s) {
    super(s);
  }
}
```

Following is the `Scheduler` class, which is the manager of the overall simulation.

Scheduler class. This class coordinates the scheduling activities, and thus interacts with all the other classes of the `apps.tree.scheduling` package. Since it is also the only class in the package that interacts directly with the `Heap` class, its methods are declared `public`. The other classes in the `apps.tree.scheduling` package do not interact with any class outside the package, and thus do not declare any `public` methods.

Here is the class outline, followed by a detailed explanation.

Class File 11.5. *Scheduler.java*

```
package apps.tree.scheduling;

import structures.tree.Heap;
import java.io.PrintWriter;

public class Scheduler {

    ProcessSource source; // where processes are created
    Processor cpu; // executing processor
    Heap<Process> procHeap; // priority queue of processes
    int thruPut, intervalThruPut; // process throughput numbers
    int numProcs, intervalNumProcs; // process arrival numbers
    int clock, intervalClock; // simulation and interval clocks

    public Scheduler() { procHeap = new Heap<Process>(); }
    public void init(float probOfArrival, int maxExecTime,
                     int maxPriority, int timeSlice) { ... }
    public void run(int howLong) throws BusyInterruptionException { ... }
    public void printStatus(PrintWriter pw) { ... }
    public void printHeap(PrintWriter pw) { ... }
}
```

Fields. The number of processes that have completed execution is called the *throughput*. This is measured on both a cumulative basis and a per-interval basis by the variables thruPut and intervalThruPut, respectively. Interval here refers to a certain number of time units for which the simulation runs and then pauses to observe the state. This is expanded on in the discussion of the run method that follows.

The fields numProcs and intervalNumProcs count the number of processes that arrive cumulatively and in the latest interval, respectively.

Initialization and status.   The init method sets up the environment of the simulation system by initializing the various components and control parameters. The code is self-explanatory.

```
public void init(float probOfArrival, int maxExecTime,
                    int maxPriority, int timeSlice) {
  // create system objects and initialize
  source = new ProcessSource(probOfArrival, maxExecTime,
                        maxPriority);
  cpu = new Processor(timeSlice);
  procHeap.clear();
  clock = 0; numProcs = 0; thruPut = 0;
}
```

The printStatus method prints various statistics that summarize the simulation process for the entire duration since the start of the simulation (cumulative), as well as the duration of the latest time period (interval) of interest.

```
public void printStatus(PrintWriter pw) {
  pw.println(" Interval Cumulative");
  pw.println("Processes Arrived " +
                intervalNumProcs + " " + numProcs);
  pw.println("Throughput " +
                intervalThruPut + " " + thruPut);
  pw.flush();
}
```

The printHeap method prints the contents of the process queue at the time it is called.

```
public void printHeap(PrintWriter pw) {
  pw.print("Heap: ");
  Process proc = procHeap.first();
  while (proc != null) {
      pw.print(proc + " ");
      proc = procHeap.next();
  }
  pw.println(); pw.flush();
}
```

Method run. The run method is the core simulation method, used to run the simulation for any desired number of time units, howLong. For instance, if you want to run a simulation for 50 time units, you may want to break it up into five periods of 10 time units each so that you can study the statistics at the end of each of these periods and look at the process queue. To do this, you would call run(10) five times, once for each period.

In each call to run, the simulation proceeds in steps of unit-time intervals. Each such unit interval is simulated by a while loop.

```
public void run(int howLong)
throws BusyInterruptionException {
   intervalClock = 0;
   intervalNumProcs = 0;
   intervalThruPut = 0;

   // run for given cycles
   while (intervalClock < howLong) {
      // PROCESS EVENT
      ...
      // step up the time
      clock++;
      intervalClock++;
      cpu.stepTime();
   }
}
```

In each time interval, one or more of the following events may occur. They are processed (PROCESS EVENT in the while loop above) in the given order.

1. A new process arrives.

Recall that the method getProcess of the class ProcessSource delivers a new process (with all but arrival-Time filled in) if one has arrived or returns null. On getting a new process, the run method fills in the arrival time and immediately adds this process to the heap.

The next two events occur if the processor is idle.

2. A process just finishes its turn at the processor.

If the processor is idle, it is checked (using the getProcess method) to see whether a process has just finished its turn. If so, this process may be completely done or may need to be rescheduled to finish up later.

If a process is to be rescheduled, its execution time is decremented by the processor time slice, its priority is decremented (but not below zero), and it is added back to the heap with a new arrival time.

```
// has a new process arrived?
Process process = source.getProcess();
if (process != null) {
   process.arrivalTime = clock;
   procHeap.add(process);
   intervalNumProcs++;
   numProcs++;
}


if (cpu.isIdle()) {
   // PROCESS CPU-IDLE EVENTS
   ...
}

process = cpu.getProcess();
if (process != null) {
   // remaining execution time
   process.execTime -= cpu.timeSlice;
   if (process.execTime > 0) {
      // decrease priority
      process.priority--;
      if (process.priority < 0) {
         process.priority = 0;
      }
      process.arrivalTime = clock;
      // reenter in heap with
      // decreased priority
      procHeap.add(process);
   } else {
      thruPut++;
      intervalThruPut++;
   }
}
```

The priority of a just-finished process is decremented before sending it back to the process queue so that newly arriving processes with the same priority as the original priority of the returning process get a shot at the CPU ahead of it. Otherwise, being of equal priorities, the FIFO rule would apply, and the returning process will have yet another shot at the CPU before the new process gets a chance.

3. A process is scheduled for execution on the processor.

Finally, if the processor is idle and the heap is not empty, the process with maximum priority is deleted from the heap (deleteMax) and is scheduled for execution on the processor.

```
if (!procHeap.isEmpty()) {
    // start executing
    // another process
    Process temp =
        procHeap.deleteMax();
    cpu.startUp(temp);
}
```

11.6   SORTING WITH THE Heap CLASS

At the beginning of this chapter we stated that the heap data structure can also play an important role in sorting. Here we explore one way a heap may be used to sort a set of items. In Chapter 13, we will explore another, more efficient sorting technique called *heapsort*.

Imagine that the priority queue operates in a more restricted manner, in two distinct phases. In the first phase, the "outlet" is shut off: entries are allowed to come in but not allowed to exit. In the second phase, the "inlet" is shut off: no entry is allowed in, and all the resident entries are let out one by one based on priority. *In effect, the entries have been sorted according to priority order.* The first phase may be referred to as the *build* phase, and the second, as the *sort* phase. This leads to a simple program to sort, say, a set of integers, using the Heap class.

11.6.1   Example: Sorting Integers

In the following code for the sorting program, an input file, "intfile", contains the integers to be sorted. It has $n + 1$ lines: the first line is the number of integers to be sorted, and the subsequent n lines are the integers themselves. We will print the sorted integers in *descending* order of values, which is easier to do since the Heap class implements a *max* heap.

```
class Sort {
  public static void main(String[] args) {
    Scanner sc = new Scanner(new File("intfile"));
    // first line in file gives number of integers to be read
    int n = sc.nextInt();
    Heap<Integer> sortHeap = new Heap<Integer>(n);

    // build phase
    for (int i=0; i < n; i++) {
        sortHeap.add(sc.nextInt());
    }
```

```
    // sort phase
    while (!sortHeap.isEmpty()) {
        System.out.println(sortHeap.deleteMax());
    }
  }
}
```

Running-time analysis.   Assume that we are sorting a set of n entries. The build phase is a sequence of n calls to the add method of the Heap class. Adding the i-th element takes up to $\log i$ time in the worst case. All n inserts would then add up to a worst-case time of

$$\log 1 + \log 2 + \log 3 + \cdots + \log(n-1) + \log n$$

which can be simplified to

$$\log(1 \times 2 \times \cdots (n-1) \times n) = \log n!$$

There is a mathematical result called **Stirling's formula** that proves the following approximation:

$$n! \approx (n/e)^n \sqrt{2\pi n}$$

Consequently, it can be shown that

$$\log n! = O(n \log n)$$

Thus, the build phase takes $O(n \log n)$ time.

The sort phase (which is, analytically, analogous to build) can also be shown to have a running time of $O(n \log n)$.

Thus this sorting program has a running time of $O(n \log n) + O(n \log n) = O(n \log n)$.

11.7 Heap CLASS IMPLEMENTATION

As far as the *conceptual* structure goes, the heap is a special type of binary tree, namely, a complete one. Therefore, one would expect that a heap could be implemented using a nonlinear linked binary tree structure, and perhaps that all the code of the BinaryTree class of Section 9.6 could be reused.

However, the fact that the heap is a complete binary tree has a very interesting consequence, and it is that *heap entries can be stored in a array*. This is quite a surprising twist, and we explore it in detail in the following section.

11.7.1 Array Storage

COMPLETE TREE STORED IN AN ARRAY

The entries of a complete binary tree can be stored in an array in such a way that stepping through the array from beginning to end is equivalent to the level-order traversal of the tree.

If we were to just look at the entries stored in the following array, how can we tell what the equivalent tree structure is?

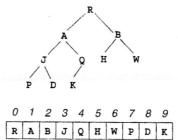

Determining the tree structure from the array. Determining the tree structure essentially boils down to determining the parent and the children of every node. The following properties of array storage tell us how this may be done in a very efficient manner.

- For a node of the binary tree at index k, its left and right children are at indices $2k + 1$ and $2k + 2$, respectively.
- The parent of a node at index k is at index $(k - 1)/2$ (integer division).

A couple of points can be deduced from the above:

- For a node at index k, if both $2k + 1$ and $2k + 2$ are beyond the upper limit of the array, the node is a leaf.
- If a node at index k has a child at $2k + 2$, then there *must* be a child at $2k + 1$ (otherwise the tree would not be complete).

When we say that we can find the children and parent of a node efficiently, we mean that we can do it with a *single* multiplication or division (and perhaps one addition), followed by a random access. That is to say, in $O(1)$ time.

It is possible to implement *any* binary tree as an array by storing the entries in level-order. The drawback is that we would have to skip cells of the array for which there are no corresponding nodes in the tree.

It is important to note that we have made a careful distinction here between the *conceptual* structure of the heap and its *physical layout*.

CONCEPTUAL STRUCTURE AND PHYSICAL LAYOUT

The physical layout of the heap is the array in which the heap entries are actually stored. This physical layout implements the conceptual structure of the heap, which is a complete binary tree on which the algorithms for the heap operations (and their running times) are based.

To consolidate our understanding, let us write an algorithm to sift down a key from the top of the heap. Assume that there are *n* entries in the heap.

The algorithm follows the procedure described in Section 11.3.2. In the main `while` loop of the algorithm, care is taken to ensure that there actually is a right child of *sift_key* before comparing it with *sift_key*'s left child.

algorithm sift_down(*H*, *n*)

H : the array storage of a heap
n : number of entries in *H*

> *sift_key* ← *H*[0], *key_index* ← 0
> *left_index* ← 1, *done* ← false
> while (*left_index* ≤ *n* and not *done*) do
> > *max_index* ← *left_index*
> > *right_index* ← *left_index* +1
> > if (*right_index* < *n*) then
> > > if (*H[left_index]* < *H[right_index]*)
> > > then
> > > > *max_index* ← *right_index*
> > > endif
> > endif
> > if (*H[max_index]* > *sift_key*) then
> > > *H[key_index]* ← *H[max_index]*
> > > *key_index* ← *max_index*
> > > *left_index* ← *key_index**2
> > else
> > > *done* ← true
> > endif
> endwhile
> *H[key_index]* ← *sift_key*

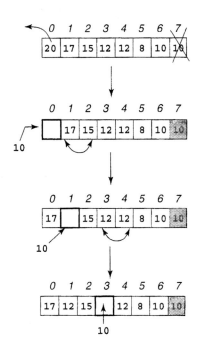

11.7.2   Implementation Using ArrayList

Class File 11.6. *Heap.java*

```
package structures.tree;

import java.util.ArrayList;
import java.util.NoSuchElementException;

public class Heap<T extends Comparable<T>> {

   ArrayList items;     // storage component
   int cursor;     // for enumeration

   public Heap(int cap) { items = new ArrayList<T>(cap); cursor = -1; }
   public Heap() { items = new ArrayList<T>(); cursor = -1; }
```

```
void siftUp(int index) { ... }
void siftDown(int index) { ... }
public void add(T item) { ... }
public T deleteMax() { ... }
public void clear() { items.clear(); }
public int size() { return items.size(); }
public boolean isEmpty() { return items.isEmpty(); }
public T first() { ... }
public T next() { ... }
}
```

Methods siftUp and siftDown.   The two methods discussed in this section implement the sift-up and sift-down processes we studied in Sections 11.3.1 and 11.3.2,
respectively. These are helper methods that support the public methods add and
deleteMax. They are visible only within the package structures.tree that contains
Heap, but not to clients outside this package.

The implementation of siftUp follows the
sift up process described in Section 11.3.1.

One useful extension here is that the
index of the item to be sifted up is sent as
a parameter to siftUp. If siftUp were to
be used only when inserting a new item
into the heap, then this parameter would
be redundant, since the index would always
be the last position, where the new item is
placed.

```
void siftUp(int index) {
  T me = items.get(index);
  while (index > 0) {
    int pindex = (index-1) / 2;
    T myparent = items.get(pindex);
    if (me.compareTo(myparent) > 0) {
      items.set(index, myparent);
      index = parent;
    }
    else break;
  }
  items.set(index, me);
}
```

However, siftUp can also be used in the situation where the priority of an existing
item in the heap is increased. In this case, the new priority of the item may no longer be
less than or equal to the priority of its parent (and potentially other ancestors in the path
from the item to the root), and this new item would then have to be sifted up, starting
from the current index of the item.

This is where the parameter to siftUp comes into play. A heap that allows updates
to the priorities of existing items is called an updatable heap, and is discussed in detail in
the following section.

The logic of the siftDown method is identical to that employed by the algorithm
in Section 11.7.1, with index playing the role of *key_index,* and me playing the role of
sift_key. Analogously to siftUp, siftDown allows the client to specify any position in the
heap (index in the array list) from which a sifting down may be done.

```
void siftDown(int index) {
  T me = items.get(index);
  int lindex = 2*index + 1;
  while (lindex < items.size()) {
```

```
        T maxChild = items.get(lindex);
        int maxIndex = lindex;

        int rindex = lindex + 1;
        if (rindex < items.size()) {
            T rightChild = items.get(rindex);
            if (rightChild.compareTo(maxChild) > 0) {
                maxChild = otherChild;
                maxIndex = rindex;
            }
        }

        if (maxChild.compareTo(me) > 0) {     // move down
            items.set(index, maxChild);
            index = maxIndex;
            lindex = 2*index + 1;
        }
        else break;
    }
    items.set(index, me);
}
```

Methods add and deleteMax. The add method is easy to implement because it relies almost completely on the siftUp method.

```
public void add(T item) {
    items.add(item);
    siftUp(items.size()-1);
}
```

Analogously, the deleteMax method relies on siftDown to do most of its work.

It throws an exception if the heap is empty. Otherwise, it gets a hold on the item to be returned from the top of the heap, and removes the last entry. If the heap had only one item before the delete, then it would now be empty. In this case, the last item would have been the same as the first (top) and is returned from the method.

Otherwise, the last item is moved to the top of the heap in preparation for siftDown, which is then called with the top index 0 as parameter. After the sift down is completed, the deleted item is returned.

```
public T deleteMax() {
    if (items.isEmpty()) {
        throw new
            NoSuchElementException();
    }
    T maxItem = items.get(0);
    T lastItem = items.remove(
                    items.size()-1);

    if (items.isEmpty()) {
        return lastItem;
    }

    items.set(0, lastItem);
    siftDown(0);
    return maxItem;
}
```

Enumeration. Here are the enumeration methods that complete the implementation.

```
public T first() {
  if (items.size() == 0) return null;
  cursor = 0;
  return items.get(cursor);
}

public T next() {
  if (cursor < 0 || cursor == (items.size()-1)) {
      return null;
  }
  cursor++;
  return items.get(cursor);
}
```

Running times. You may verify the running times of the methods listed in the Heap class interface in Figure 11.1 and discussed there.

There is only one issue: what happens when a new item is added, and the array list is full to capacity? In this case, as we know, the array list will be resized in order to accommodate the new item. If the heap had n items including the new item, then the resizing and internal copying would take $O(n)$ time, which would certainly violate the $O(\log n)$ expectation for insertion into a heap.

Since resizing happens very infrequently, especially if the initial capacity is assigned carefully, it causes little discernible change to the running times in general.

11.8   UPDATABLE HEAP

11.8.1   Designing an Updatable Heap

Toward the end of our introduction to heaps in Section 11.1, we described situations where it is required to update the priorities of items in the heap. In this section we will see how to design an efficient *updatable heap*.

In the example, when 7 is updated to 9, 9 is sifted up because it is greater than the key it replaced. On the other hand, if the new key is smaller than the old one, the new key would have to be sifted down the heap to its correct position.

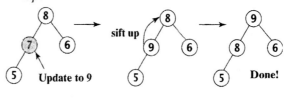

There is one crucial issue that affects the entire design. In order to update an entry, one would first have to locate it in the heap. If a heap had n entries, it would take upto $O(n)$ time to *find* that entry, since the heap is not tailored to perform fast searches. But this would prevent us from performing an update in $O(\log n)$ time.

11.8.2 Handles to Heap Entries

In order to achieve this $O(\log n)$ time, therefore, we need a *handle*—some kind of *direct* pointer to that entry so that we can avoid searching. Given a direct handle to any entry in the heap, one could access the item to be updated in $O(1)$ time, and then update that entry in $O(\log n)$ time, since a sift-up or sift-down can take at most $O(\log n)$ time on a heap of size n.

Every time an item is added, a handle to that item is returned, to be (possibly) used at a later time to update the item's priority. Exactly what should this handle be? Should we simply return the array list location (i.e., index) at which an item is stored in the heap?

In this next example, when 9 is added to the heap, a sift-up is performed, and the locations of 8 and 5 change, indicated by the shaded heap array list locations. If the location is used as a handle, the client is informed that the handle of the newly added item, 9, is 0. But how to inform the client that the handles of 8 and 5 have changed? Without this information, it would, for instance, use a "stale handle," 0, to update item 8, which is incorrect.

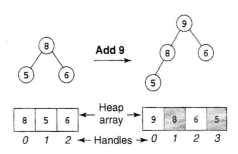

So simply equating the handle of an item to its location in the heap is not correct.

11.8.3 Shared Handle Array

The workaround to this issue is for the heap to maintain a separate handle array and share it with its clients. The handles of 8, 5, and 6 are at indexes 0, 1, and 2, respectively. A client can, for instance, update 8 by specifying index 0. This index is used to retrieve the handle to 8. When 9 is added, the client is informed that its index is 3. Meanwhile, the handles to 8 and 5 have changed, but the positions of these handles in the array

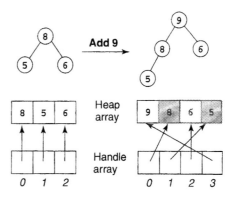

have not. Thus, the client can still update 8 using the handle at the same index as before, 0. Thus the client always has the correct handles.

The shared handle array scheme works. However, it sets up a closer-than-comfortable relationship between the heap and its clients. This inappropriate relationship and its antidote are both captured in the following design tip.

DESIGN TIP: AVOID SHARING SPACE BETWEEN OBJECT AND CLIENTS

Allowing a class to access its client's program space is a bad idea—both parties can make changes in the space with neither party taking complete responsibility. This is a potential security hole and may lead to sharing violations that are hard to detect and correct. The appropriate solution is to have one of the parties, either the client or the class, be solely responsible for handling the space, and provide controlled access via interfaces to the other party.

According to this design tip, a good solution to the stale-handle problem would be to encapsulate the handles within the heap itself.

11.8.4   Encapsulating Handles within a Heap

Encapsulating the handle array within the heap insulates the client program space from the heap and ensures that the handles are always fresh. When an item is added, the handle that is returned is an *index into the handle array* instead of a location in the heap array list. While the handle array entry at this index may change value, the index itself is always the same.

There is, however, one problem: wastage of space. Whenever an item is added to the heap, it is assigned a new handle by growing the handle array. In the example below, there are never more than four items in the heap, but the size of the handle array is 8 because eight adds were performed, and thus the first four spaces in the handle array are unused.

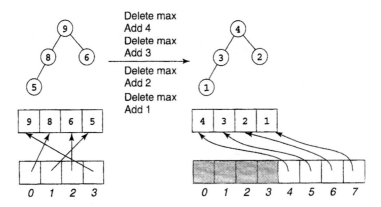

The size of the handle array is equal to the number of items *ever added* to the heap. This may be much more than the number of items *actually resident* in the heap at any given time. In general, if n items are added to the heap but there are never more than k items in the heap at any time, the original heap (of the Heap class) would have required exactly k units of space. Our updatable heap requires $n + k$ units of space. This can be quite bad, since n could be significantly greater than k.

11.8.5 Recycling Free Handle Space

The key here is to *carefully* recycle space in the handle array. When an item is deleted from the heap, it no longer needs space in the handle array, because the client will never access this item again. This space in the handle array can be marked *available* so that when a new item is added to the heap, the space can be reused as a handle to the new item.

Further, since we cannot afford to spend time searching in the handle array for such marked, recyclable space (remember our $O(\log n)$ requirement for insert/delete/update), we need to have a separate data structure that will keep track of all free spaces. A simple data structure that will achieve this is a list or a stack. Let us go with a stack.

Whenever an item is to be added to the heap, the free-space stack is first checked to see whether it is not empty, or put differently, whether there is some free space in the handle array. If so, the top entry of the stack is popped—this entry would contain the index of a free position in the handle array; the new item's handle would be in this position. If the free space stack is empty, the new item's handle would be added as a new handle entry at the end of the handle array. In any case, the new item itself is always added at the end of the heap array list. Finally, the client is passed back the index in the handle array where the new item's handle has been stored.

In summary, an updatable heap designed correctly, as described here, will support update of keys in $O(\log n)$ time, because every update results in either a sift up or a sift down. It would also ensure that the amount of space used is $O(m)$ where m is the maximum number of items ever in the heap.

11.9 SUMMARY

- A heap is a complete binary tree (heap structure property) with the (heap ordering) property that the value of the item at any node x is greater than or equal to the values of the items at all the nodes in the subtree rooted at x.

- The preceding statement defines a max heap. A min heap is defined symmetrically—the heap ordering property now requires that the value at a node be less than or equal to the values at the nodes in its subtree.

- A heap can be used as a priority queue. It can also be used to sort a set of values.

- One of the important uses of a priority queue is in scheduling a set of activities in the order of their priorities.

- The entries of a heap are stored in an array for maximum effectiveness in space usage.

- The (max) heap operations *delete_max* and *insert* both take $O(\log n)$ time.

- The heap data structure does not support a fast search operation, i.e., it is not a search structure.

- The updatable heap supports update of keys in $O(\log n)$ time, and uses $O(m)$ space, where m is the maximum number of items ever in the heap.

11.10 EXERCISES

E11.1. Given the following sequence of integers:

12, 19, 10, 4, 23, 7, 45, 8, 15

    (a) Build a max-heap by inserting the above set in the given sequence. Show the heap after every insertion. How many comparisons in all did it take to build the heap?

    (b) On the heap constructed above, perform successive *delete_max* operations. Show the heap after every *delete_max*. How many comparisons did it take in all to delete all the entries from the heap?

    (c) The above two steps essentially sort a set of entries, as described in Section 11.6. The total number of comparisons for both steps is the number of comparisons required to sort the set. Compare this with the *selection sort* algorithm of Section 3.5.1, which was discussed in the context of the quadratic running time order. How many comparisons does selection sort make on the above set?

E11.2. Repeat Exercise E11.1 above by building a *min heap* instead of a max heap. Assume that *delete_min* is the counterpart of *delete_max*.

E11.3. Rewrite the sift-down algorithm of Section 11.7.1 for a *min heap*.

E11.4. The notion of heap can be generalized to a *ternary* heap, in which each internal node has exactly three children except for the last internal node, which may have one, two, or three children. As usual, the key at an internal node is always greater than or equal to the keys of its children.

    (a) How would you store the ternary heap depicted below in a linear array?

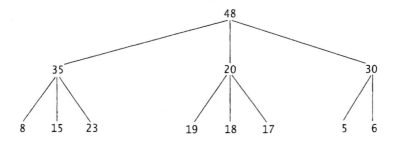

    (b) Draw the ternary heap resulting from deleting the largest value from the heap pictured above and then restoring the heap.

    (c) In an arbitrary ternary heap represented in an array H, what is the index of the parent of node H[k] for a general k?

    (d) For a ternary heap of depth d, what is the maximum number of comparisons required to restore the heap after a new value is placed at the root of the tree?

E11.5. It is often necessary to update (increase or decrease) the priorities of the entries in a heap. In order to do this, one has to first find the entry in the heap, and then update its priority. The only way a client of the (regular nonupdatable) heap can find a specific entry is to do successive *delete_max* operations until the entry is found, then update the priority entry and reinsert all the deleted entries, including the one with the updated priority. What would be the worst-case running time (big O) of a priority update, as described above, on a heap that contains n entries?

E11.6. Given a max heap that stores integers, and another integer k, we would like to print all the values in the heap that are *greater than k*. Give an efficient algorithm to do this by examining the least possible number of entries in the heap. Assume that the heap entries are stored in an array, as detailed in Section 11.7.1.(Hint: Use the heap ordering property to cut down on the number of entries to be examined. Try working with an example first.)

If the number of entries determined to be greater than k is m, how many comparisons does your algorithm make in the worst case?

E11.7. In Section 5.5 we saw how to merge two ordered lists. We can generalize this to merge k ordered lists. Assume that each list is stored in an array, and that there are N keys altogether in the k lists. Imagine auxiliary storage: an array of size N to receive the keys of the final merged list, and an array of k indices to tell you where to look in each list for the smallest unmerged key. We examine two ways of conducting the merge:

   (a) At every step of the merge, pick the smallest over all the lists using a simple sequential scan over the smallest remaining key in each list. What is the worst-case running time (big O) of this k-way merging algorithm? Explain.

   (b) Another approach is to first build a min-heap from the first key of each list. Then, in every step of the merge, extract the minimum key, say *min*, from the heap, transfer it to the output list, and insert the next element after *min* (in the input list where it came from) into the heap. (Assume that items installed in the heap carry information to identify the list from which they came.) What is the worst-case running time (big O) of this merging algorithm? Explain.

E11.8. A card game tournament is being played by a large number of players. Each game involves two players—the winner earns one point, the loser forfeits a point (deducted), and if the game is drawn, neither player's point score changes. Each player plays several games with other players. New players may join the tournament as they wish, and players may leave at any time. It is required to maintain a log of all players at any time, along with their current point tally in one or more data structures. A player's point tally may be updated (increased or decreased) at any time, players may be added or removed at any time, and the top four players need to be identified at any time.

What data structure(s) would you use to maintain the players' records? Describe how you would carry out the required operations, along with the running time (big O) of each.

11.11   PROGRAMMING PROBLEMS

P11.1. We said that the Heap class implements a max heap. If a min heap were required, you do not have to implement another class. Instead, you can appropriately implement the Comparable interface in such a way that the objects you store in the heap are compared in the *reverse* sense of the comparison required for the max heap.

Implement a client class that uses the generic Heap<T> class in the default max heap sense. Then *transform* this client class so that it can use the same Heap<T> class in the min heap sense. Show the transformed class code.

P11.2. Would it be possible to build a heap using the structures.linear.Queue<T> class (instead of the java.util.ArrayList class) to store the heap items? Why or why not?

P11.3. Modify the Sort class of Section 11.6.1 so that it prints the integer entries in *ascending* order instead, without changing the code for the loop that prints the entries. Use the ideas from your solution to Problem P11.1.

P11.4. Implement your algorithm of Exercise E11.6 as the following method:

```
T[] keysGreaterThan(T key)
```

in the Heap class. The method should return an array of all the items in the heap whose keys are greater than the given *key*.

P11.5. A priority queue may be implemented with an ordered list instead of a heap. Implement a class called PriorityQueue that provides the same interface as the Heap class, but uses an structurs.linear.OrderedList object as a component. Compare this implementation to the Heap class with respect to simplicity of coding and running times of the methods.

P11.6. We implemented the Heap class as a structure that contained Comparable items, where the Comparable interface actually prescribes methods to be implemented by a class whose objects are *ordinal* values (i.e., values that can be arranged in a sorted order).

It may be more appropriate to design a heap class to hold objects that have the priority part (*key*) separate from the actual data (*value*) stored. The key part can implement the Comparable interface. Reimplement the Heap class of Section 11.4 as a new class, KeyValueHeap, with the following header:

```
public class KeyValueHeap<T extends Comparable<T>, V>
```
That is, T is the type for the key, and V is the type for the value that goes with a key. Complete the implementation with the following methods:

- A method to add an entry to the heap:

```
public void add(T key, V value)
```

- A method to delete the maximum key item:

```
public V deleteMax()
```

where the deleted value is returned.

- A method to return the value associated with a given key:

```
public V getValue(T key)
```

You may add other methods as needed to make the class usable.

P11.7. Reimplement the Scheduling package using, instead of the Heap class, the KeyValueHeap class of Problem P11.6.

P11.8. Implement an UpdatableHeapclass according to the design of Section 11.8. Your implementation must maintain a handle array, as described in Section 11.8.3. It must also implement a stack to recycle free handle space, as described in Section 11.8.5.

It should have the same interface as the Heap class, except for the following changes:

(a) Change the add method interface to the following:

```
public int add(T item)
```

This method now returns an integer index into the handle array—recall the discussion in Section 11.8.3. This index will serve as a "coat check" that the client can use to update the item's priority at any time. You will need to reimplement this method to account for all the changes that have been made to the data storage scheme.

(b) Add a new method to update the priority of an existing item:

```
public void update(int index, T newItem)
```

The parameter newItem will replace the item whose handle array index is the first parameter, index.
You will need to reimplement siftUp, siftDown, and deleteMax as well, to account for the shared handle array and free handle array space.

CHAPTER 12

Hash Table

Until now, we have seen that the best worst-case time for searching in a set of n keys is $O(\log n)$, attributed to binary search of a sorted array and search in an AVL tree.

But why stop here? Wouldn't it be great if the search time could be even better than $O(\log n)$, say the ultimate best time possible of $O(1)$? It turns out that the **hash table** data structure comes close to offering such a guarantee: it delivers an $O(1)$ search time, but only on *average*. In the worst case, the search time could be as bad as $O(n)$.

Learning Objectives

- Develop the motivation for hashing.
- Study hash functions.
- Understand collision resolution, and compare and contrast various collision-resolution schemes.
- Summarize the average running times for hashing under various collision-resolution schemes.
- Explore the `java.util.HashMap` class.

12.1 MOTIVATION

One way of approaching the design of a data structure that would deliver an $O(1)$ search time is to trade space for time. We know that an array supports $O(1)$ time random access. But such a random access is based on the *position* of an entry in the array, and not on its *key*. Could we somehow use the *key* of an entry as a position index into an array? More generally, could we somehow design a data structure using an array for which the indices could be the keys of entries?

Let us think about this for a minute. Suppose we wanted to store the keys 1, 3, 5, 8, 10, with guaranteed one-step access to any of them. If we were to use these keys as indices into an array, we would need an array of size 10.

We would simply mark each cell of this array with *true* or *false,* depending on whether the index for the cell was one of the keys to be stored.

1	2	3	4	5	6	7	8	9	10
T	F	T	F	T	F	F	T	F	T

But there is a catch: the space consumption does not depend on the actual number of entries stored. Instead, it depends on the *range* of keys—the gap between the largest and smallest keys. For instance, if only two entries were stored, but they were 1 and 10,000, we would need 10,000 units of space.

Suppose we want to store 100 integers in such an array. Without any a priori estimate of the range, we have to be prepared to store pretty much any key that comes along, be it 1 or 1,000,000. Even if the range were estimated beforehand, there is no reason to expect it to be within a small multiple of 100 so that the space consumption is affordable.

What if we wanted to store strings? For each string, we would first have to compute a numeric key that is equivalent to it. How do we do this? Let us look at the approach adopted in Java, as implemented by the hashCode method in the java.lang.String class. This method computes the numeric equivalent (or hashcode) of a string by an arithmetic manipulation involving its individual characters. The resulting value is an integer. So, for instance, the hashcode for "cat" would be computed by an arithmetic manipulation involving the separate characters 'c', 'a', and 't'.

Say we want to store a set of five-character strings. The hashcodes of these strings may be in a very large range even though they are of the same length. Using the hashcode of a string as an index into its location in an array would therefore require a disproportionately large array for storage.

It appears that using numeric keys (i.e., hashcodes) *directly* as indices is out of the question for most applications. The next best thing is to select a certain array size, say N, based on space affordability, and use the key of an entry to *derive* an index within the array bounds.

HASHING AND HASH FUNCTION

A hash table is a storage array. Hashing is the process of storing an object in a hash table by deriving a numeric hashcode for it and mapping this hashcode to a location in the table.

Traditionally, the term *hash function* is used for the mapping of a number to a table location. However, we will use *hash function* to mean the combination of hashcode derivation and mapping.

Since the size of a hash table is finite, but the set of keys to be stored is drawn from an infinite *universe* of keys, it is quite probable, in general, that two keys can be hashed to the same location in the table, i.e., they *collide*. Then the hashing process must somehow figure out a scheme that will resolve collisions, so that a colliding entry is inserted at a distinct, empty location of the hash table.

COLLISION RESOLUTION

When a new entry hashes to a location in the hash table that is already occupied, it is said to collide with the occupying entry. Collision resolution is the process then used to determine an unoccupied location in the hash table where the new entry may be inserted.

We address both hash functions and collision-resolution schemes in the next two sections.

12.2 HASHING

Let us look at a simple hash function. Assume that the hash table size is 10, and that we are hashing the strings "cat", "dog", "mouse", and "ear". We will use the mapping function $h(k) = k \bmod 10$, where k is the hashcode.

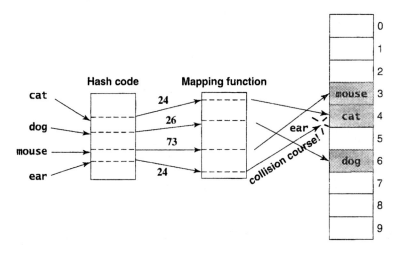

To convert a string to its numeric equivalent key (i.e., its hashcode k), we will add up the alphabetic positions of its constituent characters.

$$\text{cat} \equiv 3 + 1 + 20 = 24$$
$$\text{dog} \equiv 4 + 15 + 7 = 26$$
$$\text{mouse} \equiv 13 + 15 + 21 + 19 + 5 = 73$$
$$\text{ear} \equiv 5 + 1 + 18 = 24$$

The string ear collides with cat at position 4; however, there is empty space in the table, and it is up to the collision-resolution scheme to find an appropriate position for this string.

A different mapping function might try to reduce collisions by using more information to get a better distribution. For example, it might look at *all* the digits of the hashcode, k, and process them in some manner before taking the modulus. Say the hashcodes 14, 24, 34, and 44 are to be mapped into a table of size 10. The worst mapping function for these keys is the one given above: all the hashcodes would be mapped to the same location, 4. A different mapping function, say:

$$h(k) = (sum\ of\ digits\ of\ k)\ mod\ 10$$

would map these hashcodes to locations 5, 6, 7, and 8, respectively, which is a much better solution.

For any hash function you can devise, no matter how careful you are, there are always hashcodes that could force the mapping function to be ineffective by generating lots of collisions. In fact, it is more important to generate good hashcodes to begin with.

We are interested in hash functions that exhibit the following traits over a large number of inputs, although not necessarily *all* of them.

HASH FUNCTION REQUIREMENTS

- A good hash function must be *fast*—it must run in $O(1)$ time.
- A good hash function must distribute keys uniformly over the hash table. Ideally, every location in the hash table should have the same probability of being filled as any other location (i.e., the hash function should not favor one location over another).

A perfect hash function is one that would compute distinct indices into the hash table for all given inputs (no collisions at all), working within the limitation of the given array size, and performing the hashcode and index computation in constant ($O(1)$) time. In practice, there is no perfect hash function, only good-enough ones that have been determined (through a combination of mathematical analysis and experimentation) to work reasonably well on most input sets of keys. Therefore it is advisable to use an existing hash function that has proven to be good enough instead of trying to build one from scratch. No matter how good the hash function is, there must still be a way to handle collisions, which is our next topic of discussion.

12.3   COLLISION RESOLUTION

In this section, for the sake of simplicity and consistency with traditional language, we will use the term *key* to mean a numeric hashcode. Also, when we say that we are storing a key, we mean that we are storing the object whose hashcode is the specified key.

There are essentially two ways to resolve collisions. One is to find another location for the colliding key *within* the hash table. This is called **open addressing.** Another is to not store the keys in the table, but instead store all keys that hash to the same location in a data structure that "hangs off" that location. This is called **closed addressing.**

12.3.1 Linear Probing

The simplest form of open addressing is the following: when a collision occurs at index i of the table, *probe* (i.e., examine) the next location, the location after that, and so on, until either an open (unoccupied) location is found or you return to the starting location, i. Note that a sequence of such probes may involve wrapping around to the beginning of the table when its end is reached. This scheme is called **linear probing,** formally specified below.

LINEAR PROBING

Let the mapping function be h, the table size be N, and the key to be mapped be k. Then, if a collision occurs at the hashed location, $h(k)$, linear probing examines the sequence of locations $(h(k) + i) \bmod N, i = 1, 2, \dots$ until $(h(k) + i) \bmod N$ is an empty spot for some i, or $(h(k) + i) \bmod N = h(k)$.

The mod operator takes care of wrapping around to the beginning of the array. Linear probing is easy to implement. But there is a severe drawback to using linear probing, and it builds up in a most interesting manner: as more and more entries are hashed into the table, they tend to form *clusters* that get bigger and bigger. Consequently, the number of probes on collisions gradually increases, slowing down the hash time to a crawl.

Let us take an example to illustrate this clustering effect. We insert the words "cat", "ear", "sad", and "aid", in that sequence, into a hash table of size 10, using the sum of the positions of the letters in the alphabet as the hashcode for each: "cat" $\equiv$ 24, "ear" $\equiv$ 24, "sad" $\equiv$ 24, and "aid" $\equiv$ 14. We use a mapping function $h(k) = k \bmod 10$. The table is initially empty.

First "cat" hashes to location 4 in one step. Next, "ear" collides with "cat" at location 4, and linear probing takes a step forward to place it in location 5. Then "sad" collides with "cat", and linear probing finds an open spot at 6 after two probes. Finally, "aid" collides with "cat" and is placed in location 7 after three linear probes.

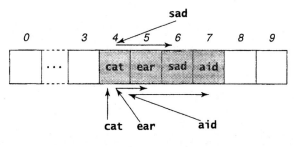

As we can see, every insertion adds another entry to the cluster. The crucial observation here is that clusters possess a self-aggrandizing quality, which only gets worse as they get bigger. We can show this mathematically, taking the preceding, table as an example.

Let us assume that our hash function is a good one in that it is capable of performing a uniform distribution of keys over the locations of the table. At the outset when the table is empty, each location has a 1/10 chance of being filled up. Now suppose `cat` is hashed and inserted in location 4. What are the new odds of the next key being inserted in some location of the table?

The hash function being the same, all locations *except* for location 5 can again expect a 1/10 chance of being filled. Location 5, however, can be filled because of two events: a key is hashed into location 5 (with a 1/10 chance), *or*, a key is hashed into location 4 (with a 1/10 chance), collides with `cat`, and is inserted in location 5 after linear probing. Summing up the probabilities of these two events, we have a 2/10 chance of the next key ending up in location 5.

After `cat` and `ear` have been inserted, all locations except 6 expect to be a filled with a 1/10 chance; location 6 has a 3/10 chance. It is almost as if the empty spot immediately following the cluster extracts a stronger magnetic pull on the next entry to be inserted, and this magnetic pull becomes stronger as the cluster becomes bigger, which in turn leads to the cluster's becoming even bigger. Witness the fact that after `sad` is inserted, location 7 exerts a 4/10 pull on the next entry to be inserted, four times as much pull as is exerted by any other location.

Running time.   We assume that the hashing process itself (hashcode and mapping) takes $O(1)$ time, independent of the size of the entry being hashed or the size of the hash table.

We start with the running time for insertion. The worst-case situation that ends in successful insertion occurs when all but one location is filled, and this empty location is farthest from the location to which the entry to be inserted is hashed. In other words, if the size of the table is N, then linear probing would take $N - 1$ steps to locate this empty spot. Obviously, then, the time spent is $O(N)$. A failed insertion would take the same number of steps in the worst case, with the difference that the last location is found to be occupied instead of empty.

Now let us consider searching for an entry in a hash table. This follows the same process as insertion—hash the target key, then search for it. The search process probes the locations of the table just as in insertion. If a match is found with the target, the search terminates with success. Otherwise, it either terminates with failure if it encounters an empty spot or it returns to the starting location. Since the worst-case running time for insertion is $O(N)$, the worst-case time for search is also $O(N)$ for both success and failure.

The worst-case times, bad as they are, are made worse by that fact that clustering accelerates the process toward the worst case. Clustering is the downfall of linear probing, so we need to look to another method of collision resolution that avoids clustering. Quadratic probing is one answer.

12.3.2   Quadratic Probing

Quadratic probing, another form of collision resolution by open addressing, aims to overcome the clustering problem that dogs linear probing. The idea of the quadratic probe is this: instead of probing in unit steps, as in linear probing, take steps of length equal to the *square* (hence quadratic) of the step number. This is expressed mathematically as follows:

It turns out that quadratic probing does avoid clustering. On the other hand, when the probing stops with failure to find an empty spot, as many as half the locations of the table *may still be unoccupied!* How does this happen?

QUADRATIC PROBING

Let the hash function be h, the table size be N, and the key to be hashed be k. Then, if a collision occurs at the hashed location, $h(k)$, quadratic probing examines the sequence of locations $(h(k) + i^2) \bmod N, i = 1, 2, \dots$ until $(h(k) + i^2) \bmod N$ is an empty spot for some i, or a location that has been already examined is examined again.

See the following example. The shaded locations in the array are filled. The hash location is 2.

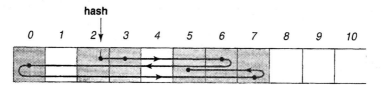

On collision, quadratic probing examines the shaded locations only, in the order 2, 3, 6, 0, 7, and 5. These locations are endlessly repeated, and an insertion is not done, even though half the table is empty.

You can verify that $(2 + i^2) \bmod 11$ gives the locations 3, 6, 0, 7 and 5, for $i = 1, 2, 3, 4, 5$, respectively. After this, for greater values of i, the locations are repeated in the reverse order (i.e., the values $i = 6, 7, 8, 9, 10$ probe the locations 5, 7, 0, 6, and 3, respectively).

In fact, it turns out that for any given **prime N,** once a location is examined twice, all locations that are examined thereafter are also ones that have already been examined. This means that only half the locations of a hash table of size N will be probed by quadratic probing, as will be proved in Section 12.5.

Running time.   As in the analysis of the running time for linear probing, we assume that the hashing process itself is $O(1)$ time.

Then, for insertion, if N is a prime, quadratic probing may end up looking at as many as half the entries of the table before succeeding or declaring failure. Thus, at most $N/2$ probes are made, with the resultant $O(N)$ time for both successful and failed insertion.

For searching, the analysis is similar to what we did for linear probing. The search process probes the locations of the table just as in insertion. If a match is found with the target, the search terminates successfully. Otherwise, it terminates with failure if it encounters an empty spot or it returns to a location that has already been probed (quadratic probing). Since the worst-case running time for insertion is $O(N)$, the worst-case time for search is also $O(N)$ for both success and failure.

12.3.3 Chaining

Unlike linear and quadratic probing, chaining is a closed addressing scheme to resolve collisions. If a collision occurs at location i of the hash table, it simply adds the colliding entry to a linked list that is built at that location.

All entries that hash to a specific location are stored in a linked list or chain hanging off that location. The entries cat, ear, sad, and jam all hash to location 4. Entries bed and pad hash to location 1. Each new entry is added to the beginning of its chain.

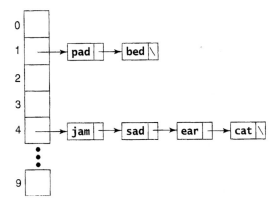

The term *bucket* is sometimes used to refer to the table locations—a number of entries may fall into the same bucket.

Running times. When a new entry is to be inserted, it is inserted at the front of the chain at the hashed location. (Alternatively, insertions may be made at the end of the chain if there is a direct reference to the last node in the linked list). This takes $O(1)$ time. Note that since a chain can (theoretically) grow indefinitely, there is no notion of failure in insertion.

The search process simply performs a sequential search of the linked list at the location to which the target is hashed, terminating with success or failure. Note that the number of entries, n, is not bounded by the capacity, N, of the hash table. The worst-case search time is $O(n)$ (not $O(N)$), and it happens when all n entries hash to the same location and are therefore in a single chain, with the entry searched for at the end of the chain.

12.3.4 Comparison of Running Times

We will now compare the running times for all the collision-resolution schemes. Except for the case of insertion with chaining, all other searches and insertions take $O(N)$ time in the worst case. So if we are only concerned about the worst-case performance, we may as well implement a simple linked list on which we can do insertions and searches in $O(N)$ time.

Where is the $O(1)$ time we are looking for? In order to get there, we need to consider a new quantity called the *load factor* of the hash table.

LOAD FACTOR

The load factor of a hash table, denoted by α, is the ratio of the number of entries in the table to its size. Let n be the number of entries in the hash table, and N be the size (or capacity) of the table; then $\alpha = n/N$.

Observe that $0 \le \alpha \le 1$ for open addressing because the number of entries n cannot exceed the capacity N. On the other hand, for chaining, $\alpha \ge 0$ because n is not constrained by N.

Donald Knuth, in *The Art of Computer Programming: Searching and Sorting* (Addison-Wesley, 1973), derives the *expected* or average search times for linear probing, quadratic probing, and chaining as a mathematical function of the load factor α.

Table 12.1 compares Knuth's analytical running times for successful search using linear probing, quadratic probing, or chaining by plugging in some specific values for the load factor α, $0 \le \alpha \le 1$.

TABLE 12.1: Comparison of the analytical search times for collision-resolution schemes in successful search.

α	Linear Probing	Quadratic Probing	Chaining
0.1	1.06	1.05	1.05
0.5	1.5	1.4	1.3
0.8	3.0	2.0	1.4
0.9	5.5	2.6	1.45
0.99	50.5	4.6	1.5

From Table 12.1, we can see that linear probing does not do badly at all until the load factor reaches 0.8, at which point it loses interest in the proceedings. Quadratic probing does much better, but chaining is the clear winner.

Thus chaining does deliver the promised $O(1)$ search time. The average search time for chaining is on the order of α, $\alpha \ge 1$. Assume that we want to store 10,000 entries, and are willing to allocate a table of size 1000, for a load factor of 10. Then the expected search time is about 10, or a *constant,* number of comparisons. The important thing to note here is that we can start with an a priori load factor we are willing to "tolerate" and size the table according to it. So, for instance, keeping the load factor at a maximum of 10, if we wanted to store 1,000,000 entries, we may allocate a table size of 100,000.

In order to clearly understand how all the concepts we have discussed can be integrated into a real hash table implementation, we will now examine the `java.util.HashMap` class. This class implements an interface, `java.util.Map`, which specifies the operations for an important abstract data type called *dictionary*.

12.4 THE `java.util.HashMap` CLASS

Consider a university-wide database that stores student records. Every student is assigned a unique *id (key)*. Associated with this are several pieces of information, such as name, address, credits, and gpa. Together, these pieces of information constitute the *value*. Students can be added, deleted, and searched for in this database. The association of every key with a corresponding value forms the basis of an abstract structure called a *dictionary*.

For the student database example cited above, one could imagine a *StudentInfo* dictionary that stores *(id, info)* pairs for all the students enrolled in the university.

The dictionary is abstract because it does not dictate *how* the key-value association is to be implemented. The `java.util.Map<K,V>` is an interface that defines the core

---

DICTIONARY

A dictionary is an abstract structure that stores a set of *(key,value)* pairs. Each entry in the set is identified by its *key,* with which a *value* is associated. There may be no duplicate keys in the set.

---

operations that would need to be supported by any concrete dictionary implementation, but does not itself implement all of them. The core operations and the corresponding methods in java.util.Map<K,V> are:

Operation	Map method
Adding a *(key,value)* pair	put(K key, V value)
Searching for the value associated with a given key	V get(Object key)
Deleting a *(key,value)* pair	V remove(Object key)

We have already encountered two implementations of the abstract dictionary structure in this book: lists (unordered and ordered) and binary search tree. Both structures support the defining dictionary operations of search, insert, and delete.

Apart from the core defining operations, the Map interface also provides operations to enumerate all the keys, enumerate all the values, get the size of the dictionary, check whether the dictionary is empty, and so on.

The java.util.HashMap class encapsulates a hash table and implements the dictionary abstraction as specified by the java.util.Map interface. It resolves collisions using chaining.

12.4.1 Table and Load Factor

Here is an example of creating a hash table with keys of type String and values of type String:

```
HashMap<String,String> phoneBook = new HashMap<String,String>();
```

When the no-arg HashMap constructor is used, a table of default initial capacity 16 is created, with a default load factor of 0.75. Note that what we referred to as table size in our earlier discussion is now the table capacity. The table size is defined as the actual number of key-value mappings in the hash table. The usage of capacity and size is thus analogous to the ArrayList.

In Section 12.3, we defined the load factor of a hash table as the ratio of the number of entries in the hash table to the table size. The load factor in HashMap, however, is used differently; it is a maximum limit, or *threshold,* placed on the actual load factor. In the rest of this discussion we will use n for the number of entries in the hash table, N for the hash table size (or capacity), α for the actual load factor, which is n/N, and t for the load factor threshold. The threshold can be any real number greater than zero.

We can choose an initial capacity that is different from the default by using the single-argument constructor:

```
HashMap<String,String> phoneBook = new HashMap<String,String>(101);
```

The HashMap class only uses capacities that are powers of 2. If we use 101 as the argument, the constructor will set the initial capacity internally to the smallest power of 2 that is greater than 101, which is 128. So we have set up a hash table with capacity 128 and default load factor threshold 0.75.

Suppose the load factor threshold in the hash table is set to $t = 0.75$ and the capacity of the hash table is set to $N = 128$, as above. Further, assume that the actual number of entries (size) $n = 64$. Then the load factor $\alpha = 64/128 = 0.5$. This load factor is less than the threshold $t = 0.75$.

Here is how we can set up a hash table with an initial capacity of 128 and a load factor threshold of 2.5:

```
HashMap<String,String>
phoneBook = new HashMap<String,String>(128,2.5);
```

The HashMap implementation guarantees that the actual load factor α will never exceed the threshold t. While the capacity of the table will grow as needed to accommodate entries, the load factor threshold cannot be changed after it is initially set.

12.4.2 Storage of Entries

Here is a set of relevant fields in the HashMap class. To retain the focus of the discussion, only the types and names of these fields (i.e., without modifiers) are shown.

```
Entry[] table;
int size;
int threshold;
float loadFactor;
```

The field called threshold is the *size threshold,* and is the product of the capacity and the threshold load factor: $N \times t$. This is the threshold for the number of entries—thus size can be at most equal to threshold.

Entry[] table sets up an array of chains. Each Entry object is therefore a node in the linked list that makes up a chain. Entry is for the use of the hash table only, and is not visible to the client:

```
class Entry<K,V> implements Map.Entry<K,V> {
  K key;
  V value;
  int hash;
  Entry<K,V> next;
  ...
}
```

The header shows that Entry<K,V> implements an interface called Entry<K,V> that is defined *inside* the java.util.Map<K,V> interface—thus the qualifier Map before the interface name.

The type parameter K is for the key, while V is for the associated value. The Entry implementation also stores the hash code for the key in field hash. The reason for this will become apparent in Section 12.4.4. The field next will hold a reference to the next Entry in its linked list.

12.4.3 Adding an Entry

The HashMap method put adds a *<key,value>* pair to the hash table. For example, here is how we can add a set of names and phone numbers to the phoneBook table we created earlier:

```
phoneBook.put("Nancy", "247-7257");
phoneBook.put("Bill", "647-9096");
...
phoneBook.put("Samir", "545-8192");
```

In each case, the name serves as the key, and the phone number is the associated value.

Another way to use the put method is to replace the value associated with an existing key. So, assume that after executing the above statements, we execute the following:

```
String oldValue = phoneBook.put("Samir", "545-0092");
```

Since the key "Samir" is already present in the table, the value currently associated with "Samir", "545-8192", is replaced with the new value "545-0092", and "545-8192" is returned as the old value. (If the key added is not in the table, the value returned is null.)

Following is the code for the put method as implemented in the Java SDK from Sun Microsystems:

```
public V put(K key, V value) {
  K k = maskNull(key);
  int hash = hash(k);
  int i = indexFor(hash, table.length);

  for (Entry<K,V> e = table[i]; e != null; e = e.next) {
      if ((e.hash == hash) && eq(k, e.key)) {
          V oldValue = e.value;
          e.value = value;
          e.recordAccess(this);
          return oldValue;
      }
  }

  modCount++;
  addEntry(hash, k, value, i);
  return null;
}
```

The very first statement is a call to the method `maskNull`, which is used to handle the case of the argument key being null. This is the code for `maskNull`:

```
static <T> maskNull(T key) {
  return key == null ? (T)NULL_KEY : key;
}
```

If the key argument is null, a special object, `NULL_KEY`, is returned, otherwise the argument key is returned as is. This `NULL_KEY` object is set elsewhere in the `HashMap` class to `Object()` (i.e., an instance of the `Object` class). This means that all null keys will be stored not as `null` references, but as references to one and the same `Object` instance.

The second statement in the `put` method is a call to the method `hash`, to compute a hash code for the key. For the sake of simplicity, we will not get into the details of the `hash` method, noting only that its implementation first invokes the `hashCode` method on the key, and then applies a "supplemental hash function" to defend against poor-quality hash coding.

After the hashcode is obtained, it is mapped to a table location with the call to method `indexFor`—the third statement in the `put` method. The `indexFor` method is defined as follows:

```
static int indexFor(int h, int length) {
  return h & (length-1);
}
```

Let us look at an example to see what this does. Say $h = 25$ and $length = 16$. Recall that the hash table capacity (which is the `length` parameter in this method) is always a power of 2. The & operator does a **bit-wise anding** of the operands.

The binary representations of h and $length - 1$ are respectively 11001 and 01111. A bit-wise **and** of these two operands basically keeps the last 4 bits of h as is, and sets all other higher-order bits to zero, since the corresponding bits in $length - 1$ are 0. So 25 & 16 = 11001 & 01111 =

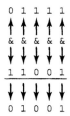

1001, which is the integer 9. This is the same as 25 mod 16, but doing a bit-wise and gets at the answer faster because no divisions are involved.

In general, since $length$ is a power of 2, say 2^k, the binary representation of $length$ will be $100\ldots0$, with k zeros. Then $length - 1$ is $011\ldots1$ with k 1's. Any h is expressible as a $2^c * k + r$, and the r part will be extracted as a result of the bit-wise and, since the $2^c * k$ part is a higher-order bit that will be zeroed out in the process. (Try this with $h = 41$ and $length = 16$, and verify that you get 9 as the answer after the bit-wise and.)

Another way to understand this is to draw an analogy with the decimal representation of numbers (i.e., numbers represented using base 10). For the analogy to be accurate, table sizes must be powers of 10. Then, if $h = 25$, and table size is 10, the result of 25 mod 10 is obtained by extracting the last digit (units place) of 25, which is 5. Or, if $h = 2556$ and the table size is 100, then the result of 2556 mod 100 is obtained by extracting the last two digits (units and tens places) from 2556, which is 56.

After the table index, i, is obtained as above, the for loop in method put searches the hash table to check whether the key that is sent as argument already exists. If it does, then the associated value is replaced with the new value sent in as argument, the old associated value is returned, and the method terminates. (Ignore the call e.recordAccess(this) in the loop because it is not relevant to our discussion.)

There is a call to method eq in the second part of the compound if condition. This method is defined as follows:

```
static boolean eq(Object x, Object y) {
  return x == y || x.equals(y);
}
```

The first part of the logical or in the return statement is needed in case y is null. Recall that null keys are stored as references to the special NULL_KEY object, so if x and y are null, the check x == y would return true. If they are not the same NULL_KEY object, the typical equals test is applied.

If the key does not exist, then the rest of the method (ignore the statement modCount++ because it is not relevant to our discussion) inserts the key and its value into the table at location i with a call to the addEntry method, and returns null.

Following is the code for the addEntry method:

We saw earlier that a table location is also called a bucket because it can hold many entries. The first statement gets a reference, e, to the first node in the bucket at index bucketIndex (i.e., the bucket into which a new entry is to be inserted). The second statement creates and adds a new entry to this bucket—the code must be familiar by now, an idiomatic one-liner that adds a node to the front of a linked list. Recall that an Entry (node) instance stores the hashcode of the key in addition to the *(key, value)* pair itself.

```
void addEntry(int hash, K key,
    V value, int bucketIndex) {

  Entry<K,V> e =
      table[bucketIndex];

  table[bucketIndex] =
      new Entry<K,V>(hash, key,
                     value, e);

  if (size++ >= threshold)
    resize(2 * table.length);
}
```

The if statement triggers a rehashing process if the size after adding this new entry is equal to or greater than the threshold number of entries permitted by the load factor threshold. Rehashing is performed by the resize method, which is sent as argument the new table capacity, twice as much as the old table capacity. This preserves the multiple-of-two constraint for table capacity.

12.4.4 Rehashing

The precondition to resizing is that the new capacity must be greater than the old. However, if there is no room for growth because the old capacity is already at the maximum possible value, then the method sets the threshold to the maximum possible integer value and returns.

Setting the threshold to the maximum integer value guarantees that no amount of adds to the hash table will result in a resize because the threshold will never be exceeded.

If all is well, and a resize is permitted, a new table is created with the given (new) capacity.

Method transfer is then called to rehash the contents of the old table to the new. Changing the size of the table results in a change in the result of the mapping function because the modulus (bit-wise and) is now taken with respect to a new number.

```
void resize(int newCapacity) {
    Entry[] oldTable = table;
    int oldCapacity =
            oldTable.length;
    if (oldCapacity ==
            MAXIMUM_CAPACITY) {
        threshold =
            Integer.MAX_VALUE;
        return;
    }

    Entry[] newTable =
        new Entry[newCapacity];
    transfer(newTable);
    table = newTable;
    threshold = (int)
        (newCapacity * loadFactor);
}
```

As an example, consider a key 25 that was mapped to location 9 when the table capacity was 16. If the table capacity is increased to 32, the bit-wise and of 25(11001) would now be applied with 31(011111). The result of this is 11001, which is 25 (as expected, since 25 mod 32 = 25). In other words, the key 25 that had earlier been mapped to location 9 must be rehashed (remapped) to location 25. Note that storing the hashcode of a key along with the *(key,value)* pair avoids a recomputation of the hashcode for rehashing—the hashcode is the same as before since the key has not changed.

Here is the code for the transfer method:

```
void transfer(Entry[] newTable) {
    Entry[] src = table;
    int newCapacity = newTable.length;
    for (int j = 0; j < src.length; j++) {
        Entry<K,V> e = src[j];
        if (e != null) {
            src[j] = null;
            do {
                Entry<K,V> next = e.next;
                int i = indexFor(e.hash, newCapacity);
                e.next = newTable[i];
                newTable[i] = e;
                e = next;
            } while (e != null);
        }
    }
}
```

The for loop goes through every chain in the original table, and remaps each entry in the chain to a new location. It first computes the new location index for the entry, with a call to the indexFor method, and the adds the entry to the chain at this location.

12.4.5 Searching

Searching is implemented by the get method:

```
public V get(Object key) {
  Object k = maskNull(key);
  int hash = hash(k);
  int i = indexFor(hash, table.length);
  Entry<K,V> e = table[i];
  while (true) {
    if (e == null)
      return null;
    if (e.hash == hash && eq(k, e.key))
      return e.value;
    e = e.next;
  }
}
```

It essentially follows the same process as the put method in obtaining the hash code for the key, then computing the hash location and searching for the key in the linked list at that location. If the key exists, the method returns the associated value; if not, it returns null.

Other methods. Method remove in the HashMap class removes a key and its associated value from the hash table:

```
public V remove(Object key)
```

Other convenience methods allow clients to enumerate all the keys, enumerate all values, clear the hash table, check whether it is empty, get the number of entries (size), and so on.

12.5 QUADRATIC PROBING: REPETITION OF PROBE LOCATIONS

In Section 12.3, we discussed quadratic probing as one of the possible open-addressing collision-resolution schemes. We discovered that if the size of the hash table is a prime number, N, then quadratic probing repeats already probed locations after probing only half the distinct number of locations in the table. In other words, it only examines $N/2$ locations of the table before starting to repeat locations. The following is a proof of why this is true.

Suppose a key is hashed to location h, where there is a collision. Then quadratic probing examines the following locations:

$$(h + 1) \bmod N, (h + 4) \bmod N, \ldots, (h + i^2) \bmod N, \ldots$$

Let us consider an instance where two different probes, i and j, end up at the same location:

$$(h + i^2) \bmod N = (h + j^2) \bmod N$$

which means

$$(h + i^2 - h - j^2) \bmod N = 0$$

which is the same as

$$(i + j)(i - j) \bmod N = 0$$

The key observation here is that *since N is a prime number, it must divide one of the factors $(i + j)$ or $(i - j)$.*

N divides $(i - j)$ only when at least N probes have already been made. On the other hand, N divides $(i + j)$ when $(i + j = N)$, at the very least. Which means $j = N - i$. This proves that the total number of distinct locations probed is only $N/2$.

12.6 SUMMARY

- A hash table implements the dictionary operations of insert, search, and delete on (*key, value*) pairs.
- Given a key, a hash function for a given hash table computes an index into the table as a function of the key by first obtaining a numeric hashcode, and then mapping this hashcode to a table location.
- When a new key hashes to a location in the hash table that is already occupied, it is said to collide with the occupying key.
- Collision resolution is the process used upon collision to determine an unoccupied location in the hash table where the colliding key may be inserted.
- In searching for a key, the same hash function and collision-resolution scheme must be used as for its insertion.
- A good hash function must be $O(1)$ time and must distribute entries uniformly over the hash table.
- Collision-resolution schemes fall into two broad categories: open addressing and closed addressing. Open addressing relocates a colliding entry in the hash table itself. Closed addressing stores all entries that hash to a location in a data structure that "hangs off" that location.

- Linear probing and quadratic probing are instances of open addressing, whereas chaining is an instance of closed addressing.
- Linear probing leads to clustering of entries, with the clusters becoming increasingly larger as more and more collisions occur. Clustering significantly degrades performance.
- Quadratic probing attempts to reduce clustering. On the other hand, quadratic probing may leave as much as half the hash table empty while reporting failure to insert a new entry.
- Chaining is the simplest way to resolve collisions and also results in better performance than linear probing or quadratic probing.
- The worst-case search time for linear probing, quadratic probing, and chaining is $O(n)$.
- The load factor, α, of a hash table is the ratio of the number of keys, n, to the capacity, N.
- The average performance of chaining depends on the load factor, α. For a perfect hash function that always distributes keys uniformly, the average search time for chaining is $O(1)$.

12.7   EXERCISES

E12.1. You are given the following keys to be hashed into a hash table of size 11.

96, 43, 72, 68, 63, 28

  (a) Assume that the hashcode for a key is the key itself. If in-table hashing is used, with the hash function being $H(key) = key$ **mod** 11, and collisions are resolved by linear probing, show the hash table after every key is hashed.
  (b) Repeat the above exercise, this time using quadratic probing to resolve collisions.
  (c) Repeat the above exercise, this time assuming that collisions are resolved by incrementing the table index by *key* **div** 11 as many times as required.
  (d) Assume that out-of-table chaining is used to resolve collisions. Using the same hash function as in the above exercises, show how the hash table changes after every key is hashed.

E12.2. Compute, for every table built in Exercise E12.1, the average number of comparisons required to successfully retrieve a key in the table.

E12.3. Using out-of-table chaining to resolve collisions, give the worst-case running time (big O) for inserting N keys into an initially empty hash table where the lists (chains) are:
  (a) Unordered
  (b) Ordered
  (c) AVL trees

E12.4. Suppose you have a list of 24 items and you want to have fast lookup times to access the items. You therefore decide to use a hash table to minimize the lookup time.

(a) The hash table uses open addressing combined with linear probing with an offset of 3; i.e., instead of examining entries $h, h + 1, h + 2, ...$, the entries $h, h + 3, h + 6, ...$ are examined. Which of the following is the best choice of hash table size? Why?

12, 13, 15

(b) The hash table uses closed addressing with chaining. Of the following, which is the best choice of hash table size? Why?

12, 13, 15

(c) You have a database of records where the keys are integers between 10 and 30 distributed uniformly. Of the following, which is the best hash function? Why? Assume that the hash table size, m, is much larger than the number of keys.

  i. Take the most significant (leftmost) digit of the key.
  ii. Take the least significant (rightmost) digit of the key.
  iii. Take the key modulo the table size.

E12.5. The figure below shows the current state of a 19-element hash table, with the occupied cells shown shaded. Assuming that collisions are handled using linear probing and that the hash function is perfectly uniform (i.e., it maps a key to any slot in the table with probability 1/19), calculate, for each of the remaining empty slots, the probability of that slot receiving the next item to be inserted into the hash table.

12.8   PROGRAMMING PROBLEMS

P12.1. Using the java.util.HashMap as a starting point, implement a Hashtable class that keeps the chains in ArrayList objects instead of linked lists. Make the following additional changes as compared to java.util.HashMap:
  (a) Add a constructor that accepts an initial capacity as well as an increment by which a table will grow every time a rehash is done. (That is, if the client uses this constructor, rehash does not automatically double the table size.)
  (b) Implement all other methods as appropriate to account for the ArrayList usage, as well as the new table size increment option.
  Analyze the worst-case and average big O running times of search, insert, and delete in your Hashtable class.

P12.2. Look at the source code for the java.lang.String class (it comes with the Java 5.0 installation from Sun) and see how the hashCode method is implemented. Describe how the hashcode is computed as clearly as you can—draw pictures if necessary.

P12.3. Your friend is starting up a new Web site which is going to have users register as members. He asks you to help implement an application that would validate a member's login. Your idea is to first create a class called Member that would hold a member's username (unique) and password. Then you want to store all Member objects in an instance of java.util.Hashmap so that when a user logs in, the username he/she types in can be checked against the members list, and then the associated password matches against the password that he/she enters.

Implement the Member class. Think of how a Member object's hashcode would be computed by the java.util.HashMap class, and how you can account for it in the Member class.

After implementing the Member class, write an application called Login, to perform login validation.

P12.4. Write an application, WordCount, to count the frequency of occurrence of each word in an input text file, using the java.util.HashMap class to store the words and their frequencies of occurrence. Compare this with a (hypothetical) implementation using the structures.tree.BinarySearchTree class. Which implementation would be better in the worst case? Which implementation would be better in *practice?*

CHAPTER 13

Sorting

In this chapter we are primarily interested in sorting algorithms that arrange a set of elements in order by repeatedly *comparing* pairs of keys. In this class of algorithms fall **insertion sort, quicksort, mergesort,** and **heapsort.** For contrast, we also present the **radix sort** algorithm, which does *not* compare keys—instead it sorts numbers according to their constituent digits.

For each of the above sorting algorithms, we perform a running-time analysis for the worst case. For insertion sort, mergesort, and radix sort, we also perform an analysis of the average-case running time.

Each of these sorting algorithms may be implemented by using the array, the array list, or the linked list data structure, as appropriate. We present an implementation of quicksort in Java that may serve as a useful guide for the implementation of any sorting algorithm.

Learning Objectives

- Study insertion sort, quicksort, mergesort, heapsort, and radix sort, and conduct a comparative analysis of their running times.
- Understand which sorting algorithm is most appropriate for a given situation.
- Learn how to implement sorting algorithms in Java.

13.1 INSERTION SORT

Insertion sort is an approach that we intuitively use to arrange things in order. Suppose you had a bunch of bills to sort in chronological order, and they were mostly in the right order except for a few that were out of place. You would go through this bunch, and when you encountered a bill that was out of place, you would *insert* it in its right place among those that were already in order.

When the algorithm starts, the first entry is treated as a sorted single-element array, shown shaded.

In the first step, the second element, 14, is inserted into this sorted array. This is done by comparing 14 against 5, and since 14 is greater, it is "inserted" in its own place. The sorted part is now the shaded two-element array.

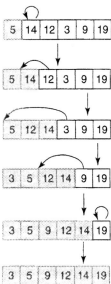

In the second step, the entry 12 is inserted into the two-element array. This is done by comparing 12 with 14 first. Since 12 is less, it has to go to the left of 14. Next, 12 is compared with 5, and since 12 is greater, it can be inserted at the second location of the array. This requires moving 14 over one step to the right to make room for 12.

The algorithm proceeds to insert 3, 9, and 19 successively into the growing sorted array to the left, making the required comparisons as in the earlier steps.

In every step of the insertion, the following process is applied:

1. Search in the partially sorted list $(0 \ldots i - 1)$ to find the correct position, p, for x.

2. Move all the entries between positions p and $i - 1$ (inclusive) over to the right by one place.

3. Write x into position p. The partially sorted list has now grown to occupy positions 0 through i.

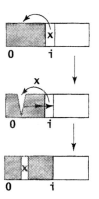

If n is the size of the list to be sorted, then the entire list is in sorted order after $n - 1$ steps.

We can gather all these ideas into an algorithm for insertion sort.

Algorithm insertionSort(A, n)

input: array A of length n
output: sorted A

for i from 1 to $n - 1$ do
    $x \leftarrow A[i]; p \leftarrow i - 1; done \leftarrow$ false
    while ($p \geq 0$ and not *done*) do
        if ($x \geq A[p]$) then *done* $\leftarrow$ true
        else $p \leftarrow p - 1$
        endif
    endwhile
    $p \leftarrow p + 1$
    for j from $i - 1$ downto p do
        $A[j + 1] \leftarrow A[j]$
    endfor
    $A[p] \leftarrow x$
endfor

The inner *while* loop first establishes the position, p, where the insertion will be made. Following this, the inner *for* loop moves entries over to accommodate the insertion.

Note the following in the algorithm if an entry to be inserted is already in its correct position:

(a) the inner *while* loop terminates after a single iteration where *done* is set to true;
(b) the inner for loop does not perform any iteration at all, since p is set to i, which is already greater than $i - 1$; and
(c) the new entry is simply written back over itself.

Analysis of running time.   There are two basic operations here that contribute to the running time: one, a comparison between a pair of entries in the list, and the other, a data move from one position of the array to another. (Equivalently, a data move can be counted as a write operation.) Each of these will contribute one time unit.

Let us start with the *best* case: what kind of input will lead to the fastest run of the algorithm? The answer is simple: an input that is already sorted. In this case, for every new entry to be inserted, one comparison is made with the entry just before it. Since the former is bound to be *not less* than the latter, it is left in place, which, following our algorithm, will result in the entry being written over itself. We can count this as one data move, or one write. For n entries, therefore, we have $n - 1$ comparisons and $n - 1$ data moves, for a grand total of $2n - 2$ units of time. Or, $O(n)$.

Now the *worst-case* scenario. For what kind of input will insertion sort be at its slowest, and exactly how slow is it? The intuitive answer is: an input sorted in *reverse order*. Then, every time an entry is to be inserted in the partially sorted list, it would have to go all the way to the front of the sorted list. If the partially sorted list is of length i, this would consume i comparisons followed by i data moves, for a total of $2i$ time units.

The total time would be the sum of the above for partially sorted lists of lengths 1, 2, and so on, all the way up to $n - 1$. In mathematical terms:

$$\sum_{i=1}^{n-1} 2i = 2 \sum_{i=1}^{n-1} i = 2 \times \frac{n(n - 1)}{2} = n(n - 1)$$

The worst case, therefore, consumes $O(n^2)$ time.

Somewhere between the best and worst cases is the average-case behavior. Unlike the best and worst cases, the average-case behavior is not restricted to a single characteristic "average-case input," On the contrary, what this means is that if we were to run insertion sort on a number of lists constructed "randomly," we would, over a large enough number of runs, average out the running time to some value. This value is the so-called average-case running time.

When we say a list is constructed randomly, we mean that there is no bias toward any one particular relative ordering among its entries. So a fully sorted list is as likely to be constructed as a list in which every entry is out of place, which is as likely to be constructed as any of the whole spectrum of in-between possibilities. Analyzing the average-case behavior is then a question of considering all possibilities with equal likelihood in every step of the execution of the algorithm.

Consider inserting an entry which is at position $i - 1$ into a partially sorted list of length $i - 1$ $(0 \ldots i - 2)$. There are i possible positions into which this entry can be inserted. On average, each of these positions is an equally likely candidate for the entry to be inserted in.

In this example, to place the entry in position $i - 1$ would take one comparison. This is the best case. The next position, $i - 2$, would take two comparisons. And so on. To place the entry in position 1 would take $i - 1$ comparisons. Position 0 would take $i - 1$ comparisons also, and *not* i. The reason for this is at the end of the $i - 1$-th comparison, 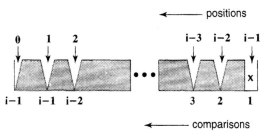 if the entry is found to be *not less* than the very first entry, it can be placed in position 1; if not, since there are no more entries to compare with, the entry is automatically placed in position 0.

There are i possible positions, each with a likelihood of $1/i$ of accepting the new entry. The average number of comparisons to insert this entry is therefore:

$$\frac{1}{i} + \frac{2}{i} + \cdots + \frac{i - 1}{i} + \frac{i - 1}{i}$$

The result of this sum is the following:

$$\frac{1}{i} \sum_{j=1}^{i-1} j + \frac{i - 1}{i} = \frac{1}{i} \times \frac{i(i - 1)}{2} + \frac{i - 1}{i}$$

which works out to:

$$\frac{i}{2} - \frac{1}{i} + \frac{1}{2}$$

This is the average number of comparisons required to insert the entry in position $i - 1$ of the list into the sorted sublist of length $i - 1$, to get a sorted list of length i.

To obtain the average number of comparisons for the entire algorithm, we need to sum up the above figure over i going from 2 to n:

$$\sum_{i=2}^{n} \left(\frac{i}{2} - \frac{1}{i} + \frac{1}{2} \right)$$

This may be broken up into three separate terms as follows:

$$\sum_{i=2}^{n} \frac{i}{2} - \sum_{i=2}^{n} \frac{1}{i} + \sum_{i=2}^{n} \frac{1}{2}$$

The first term is evaluated as:

$$\frac{1}{2} \sum_{i=2}^{n} i = \frac{1}{2} \times \left(\frac{n(n+1)}{2} - 1 \right) = \frac{n^2}{4} + \frac{n}{4} - \frac{1}{2}$$

What is important here is the leading term, $n^2/4$.

The second summation, $1/i$ summed from 2 to n, is not straightforward. It may be shown that this sum is *of the order* $\log n$. The third sum is clearly of the order n. Therefore, the average number of comparisons is $O(n^2)$, the same as the order of the worst-case number of comparisons. Since the number of data moves (or writes) is of the same order as the number of comparisons, the average running time of insertion sort is $O(n^2)$.

13.2   SORTING BY DIVIDE AND CONQUER

Divide and conquer is a powerful principle in computing. We have already seen an example of this principle in action, namely binary search of an array. Every comparison of the target item against the middle entry of the array resulted in dividing the array in half; half the array could be then discarded and the other half recursively searched using the same principle. We saw that this approach resulted in a tremendous saving in search time as compared to sequential search: $O(\log n)$ over (n).

It seems natural, then, to ask whether divide and conquer can be applied to sorting, with an analogous performance gain over, say, insertion sort, which takes $O(n^2)$ time in the worst case. The answer is yes, and there are two sorting algorithms that operate on this principle: **quicksort** and **mergesort.**

Divide and Conquer Algorithms

input: list L_in to be sorted
output: sorted list L_out

divide L_in into L_left, L_right
recursively sort L_left into L_left_sorted
recursively sort L_right into L_right_sorted
combine L_left_sorted, L_right_sorted into
         L_out)

The first step is to *divide* the input list, L_in, into two parts, L_left and L_right.

Each part is sorted recursively by applying the same divide-and-conquer strategy: the sorted parts are in L_left_sorted and L_right_sorted, respectively.

The last step is to combine these two sorted parts to produce the sorted list, L_out.

13.2.1   Quicksort

Quicksort is one of the most popular sorting algorithms in practice. This is strange, considering that its *worst-case* running time is $O(n^2)$, the same as insertion sort. However, it possesses a knock-out advantage: its *average* running time is $O(n \log n)$, a tremendous improvement over insertion sort.

The quicksort algorithm can be written using the general divide-and-conquer prescription.

Algorithm quicksort(A, left, right)

input: subarray $A[left \dots right]$
output: sorted subarray $A[left \dots right]$

$splitPoint \leftarrow$ **split**$(A, left, right)$
quicksort$(A, left, splitPoint - 1)$;
quicksort$(A, splitPoint + 1, right)$;

The *split* process selects a *pivot* entry, say x, in the given sublist and rearranges the entries of the sublist in such a way that all the entries less than x are to its left, and all other entries (greater than or equal to x) are to its right.

Split is explained in detail in the following discussion.

Pivot is chosen to be the first entry in the sublist, 9.

Index *left* starts at 1 and moves right as long as the entry it points to is *less than* the pivot, 9. It stops advancing at 14, which is not less than 9.

Index *right* then starts at the last position, and moves left as long as the entry it points to is *not less than* the pivot, 9. It stops advancing at 5, which is less than 9.

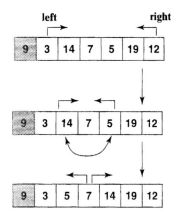

Entries 14 and 5 are exchanged, *left* is moved to the right by one, and *right* is moved to the left by one: both now point to 7.

Then *left* and *right* continue to advance toward each other. In the very next step, *left* moves to the right by one step, and crosses over *right: left* at 14 and *right* at 7. At this point, the pivot, 9, is exchanged with the entry at *right*, 7. Split terminates.

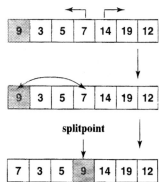

Note that the *left* and *right* indices stop moving once and for all when they eventually cross over. At this point, the *right* index points to the rightmost of the entries less than the pivot, and the *left* index points to the leftmost of the entries greater than or equal to the pivot. Finally, the pivot entry is placed at the split point by exchanging it with the *right* index entry. The *right* index then represents the split point.

Algorithm split(A, lo, hi)

input:
   subarray $A[lo..hi]$
output:
   sp that points to the pivot, and
   $A[lo \ldots sp - 1] < A[sp]$
   $A[sp + 1 \ldots hi] \geq A[sp]$

$pivot \leftarrow A[lo], left \leftarrow lo + 1, right \leftarrow hi$
while ($left \leq right$) do
    while ($left \leq right$ and
        $left \leq hi$ and $A[left] < pivot$) do
        $left \leftarrow left + 1$
    endwhile
    while ($left \leq right$ and
        $right > lo$ and $A[right] \geq pivot$) do
        $right \leftarrow right - 1$
    endwhile
    if ($left < right$) then
        swap $A[left]$ with $A[right]$
        $left \leftarrow left + 1$
        $right \leftarrow right - 1$
    endif
endwhile

swap $A[right]$ with $A[lo]$
$sp \leftarrow right$

The outer *while* loop spins until the indices cross over. The first inner *while* loop pushes the *left* index forward, while the second inner *while* loop pushes the *right* index forward.

In either of these inner *while* loops, the first condition is that *left* and *right* have not crossed over. The second condition for continuation is that the respective index does not cross the bounds of the subarray—*left* $\leq$ *hi* and *right* > *lo*. The *left* index would cross the array boundary if all entries are less than the pivot. Analogously, the *right* index would cross the array boundary if all entries are greater than or equal to the pivot. (The *right* index actually stops at *lo*, which is technically the array boundary because $A[lo]$ is the pivot, and does not participate in comparisons.)

If either index goes all the way across, as above, the condition *left* < *right* of the `if` statement is not true, and $A[left]$ is not swapped with $A[right]$. Instead, the outer *while* loop terminates, and $A[right]$ is swapped with $A[lo]$. You may want to trace the algorithm on a reverse sorted array and a sorted array to verify its correctness.

Analysis of running time.   All the running time is then essentially concentrated in the *split* process because the rest of the quicksort algorithm is simply the spinning off of recursive calls on the split-up subarrays. In the split process, as in insertion sort, comparisons and writes both contribute to the running time, and the number of writes is no more than the number of comparisons. Since we are interested in the big O order, we will only count comparisons.

The *quicksort tree* shows the entire recursive quicksort process. A recursion path terminates when the size of the subarray to be sorted is 1.

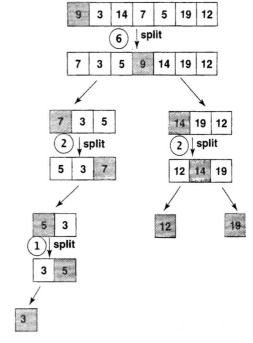

What is the number of comparisons in *split*? Every entry that either `left` or `right` points to is compared against the pivot element. So the number of comparisons is one less than the size of the subarray that is split, shown circled in the figure. The total number of comparisons over all splits for the example quicksort is $6 + 2 + 2 + 1 = 11$.

In general, for an array of size n, the number of comparisons made to split it is $n - 1$. This does not depend on how the array entries are ordered. In other words, the number of comparisons for a split does not break into different figures for the worst, best, and average cases. Then what, if anything, is the difference between the worst case and average case for quicksort overall?

At the beginning of our quicksort discussion, we said that the average running time of $O(n \log n)$ is a big improvement over the worst-case running time of $O(n^2)$. This distinction is in the only other possible place, which is the division of an array into subarrays. Thus the overall running time depends on the pattern of the relative sizes of the subarrays in the quicksort tree.

The quicksort tree we saw previously gets its shape because of the relative arrangement of entries in the input array. The same set of entries with a different relative arrangement will in general produce a different quicksort tree structure, and therefore a different number of comparisons overall.

The best- and worst-case possibilities are shown in the next figure. Instead of the entire subarray at every node in the quicksort tree, only the pivot element is shown.

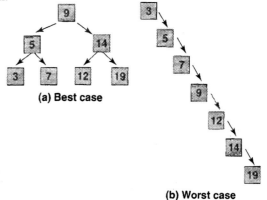

The worst case happens when the input array itself is sorted. Then the first entry, which is the pivot, is less than all the others, leading to a lopsided split. This lopsidedness happens at every split, resulting in a skewed quicksort tree. The total number of comparisons to quicksort the array in this worst-case example is $6 + 5 + 4 + 3 + 2 + 1 = 21$.

Can you construct an arrangement of entries in the input array that would lead to the example best-case tree?

There are a couple of useful observations we may make about this way of drawing a tree, with the nodes as the pivot elements:

- The tree obtained in this manner is a binary search tree: when a subarray is split, the values in the left subtrees are all less than the pivot, and the values in the right subtree are all greater than or equal to the pivot.

- The best case of quicksort is when the corresponding binary search tree is perfectly balanced, and the worst case is when it is completely skewed.

General worst case.   As we saw in the example, the worst case happens when the input is already *sorted*. Every time *split* is called, it ends up breaking up the array in the most lopsided way possible, because all the elements are greater than or equal to the first element, the pivot. Divide and conquer takes a bad beating.

In the general worst-case situation where the array is of size n, the first *split* would make $n - 1$ comparisons, the second, $n - 2$, and so on, all the way to one comparison on an array of size 1. This gives a total of

$$(n - 1) + (n - 2) + \cdots + 2 + 1 = \frac{n(n - 1)}{2}$$

comparisons. Or, $O(n^2)$.

General best case.   The best case, when the quicksort tree is perfectly balanced, occurs when every time *split* is called, it divides the array into two *equal* halves. We can derive an approximate figure for the number of comparisons in this case as follows.

At every level of the tree, there are at most n array elements. The root (level 0) represents the entire array (i.e., n elements). The level below the root, level 1, contains $n - 1$ elements, divided equally into the left and right children of the root, each of size $(n - 1)/2$. We can approximate this to $n/2$, for a total of n elements at this level.

Continuing in this fashion, at level 2, there are four nodes, each of size $n/4$, and so on. At the leaf level, there are n nodes, each of size 1. Since the tree is perfectly balanced, the number of levels is approximately $\log n$. Thus, there are $\log n$ levels, each containing at most n array elements.

Now consider the number of comparisons at each level. At the root, *split* makes $n - 1$ comparisons. At level 1, *split* is called on two subarrays of approximate length $n/2$ each, for $n/2 - 1$ comparisons in each case. That is, a total of at most $n - 2$ comparisons over both subarrays. At level 2, *split* is called on four subarrays, and on each one it makes approximately $n/4 - 1$ comparisons, for a total of $n - 4$ comparisons. This argument can be carried all the way to the last-but-one level. At the last level, there are only single-element subarrays, so *split* is not called.

We can ignore the subtracted constants (i.e., we can treat $n - c$ as n) because we are heading toward a big O summary, and the constants are a lower-order term than n.

Then, adding up the number of comparisons over all $\log n$ levels, we get $(n \log n)$. (The approximations we made along the way are conservative, in that the exact number of comparisons can only be less than this by a *constant factor*, never more.) In sum, the number of comparisons in the best case is $O(n \log n)$.

General average case.   Quicksort makes $O(n \log n)$ comparisons in the *average case*. As we remarked at the beginning, this is the primary reason for quicksort's great popularity. The analysis of the average running time that leads to this result is, however, beyond the scope of our current discussion.

Since quicksort is widely used in practice, several techniques have been applied to fine-tune its performance. Note that these techniques make quicksort more efficient, but only within the constraints of the big O running times that we have already seen. In other words, fine-tuning does not change the big O running times.

Choosing the pivot.   Let us start with the rule for picking the pivot element for *split*. In our discussions, we assumed that the pivot is always the first element, but this choice turned out to be the worst one could make for an input that is already in sorted order. There is no particular reason why the first element must be chosen as the pivot. A generally preferred alternative is the following:

Choose, as the pivot, the median of the first, middle, and last elements.

For example, if we are sorting integers, and the first, middle, and last elements of a certain subarray are 9, 12, and 10, respectively, then the median is 10.

For one thing, the median rule avoids the worst-case situation on a sorted input. In general, the idea is to use information about the input data (without spending more than constant time) to determine the pivot element in such a way that "pathological" cases are quickly rendered benign.

Another alternative is to choose the pivot randomly. Again, care must be taken to ensure that the random-number generation algorithm is fast. After the pivot element is chosen, it is exchanged with the first element in the subarray. The split process works just as before, using the first element as the pivot.

Edge effect.   The "leaf nodes" of the quicksort tree represent subarrays of size 1. A little higher up the tree we may have nodes with size 2, size 3, and so, to each of which we apply recursive quicksort until we get down to a subarray of size 1. For subarrays this small, the overhead of recursive calls far outweighs the benefit accrued from divide and conquer. In other words, for relatively small arrays, divide and conquer is more trouble than it is worth.

The solution that is commonly adopted is the following:

Use divide and conquer only if the subarray size is more than, say, 20. Otherwise, sort the subarray using insertion sort.

Note that the number 20 here is only an approximation. It can vary, depending on the speed of the machine on which the sorting is done.

Which subarray to sort first?   There are two recursive calls to quicksort after a subarray is split in two. Either of these could be done first without adversely affecting the correctness of the result. On the other hand, choosing which subarray to sort first could make for a significant difference in space consumption.

The space we refer to is the (*activation*) stack maintained by the compiler to keep track of recursive calls. Every time a recursive call is made, the current local state is stacked—let us assume that this consumes unit space.

The example here is a worst-case scenario: (a) the input array is already sorted, and (b) after every split, the algorithm chooses to first recurse on the *larger* subarray. Since the split is always going to be lop-sided, this leads to the local state of all $n - 1$ calls (before the last one, when the recursion stops) being stored in the stack—that is, at some point, the stack will consume $O(n)$ space.

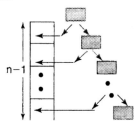

The remedy is:

Always sort the smaller subarray first.

Starting with an array of size n, the smaller subarrays are never larger than $n/2$, $n/4, \cdots, 2$. The longest activation "path," or "chain," in which the stack can keep growing is therefore never more than $\log n$. Thus, at no point during the execution of the algorithm is more than $\log n$ stack space required. This is a big win over the previous $O(n)$ worst case.

13.2.2 Mergesort

Mergesort provides an interesting contrast to quicksort. Both are divide-and-conquer algorithms, but mergesort insists that split be done across the dead center of the current sublist, so that two *equal* halves are produced, to then be recursively sorted. Then, after the two sublists have been sorted, they are *merged* to obtain a sorted version of the input sublist. Thus, most of the work is done in the merging step.

The mergesort algorithm can be written using the general divide-and-conquer prescription as follows.

Algorithm mergesort(A, left, right)

input: subarray $A[left \ldots right]$
output: sorted $A[left \ldots right]$

$splitPoint \leftarrow (left + right)/2$
mergesort$(A, left, splitPoint)$
mergesort$(A, splitPoint + 1, right)$
merge$(A, left, splitPoint,$
   $A, splitPoint + 1, right)$

The *split* part now is trivial: simply compute the midpoint of the subarray in question. (It is convenient to assume that the array to begin with is indexed from 0.) Then the divided subarrays are recursively sorted and merged together to obtain a sorted version of the input subarray.

All the comparisons in mergesort are done during the merge process. Merging two arrays requires additional array scratch space.

In the example below, the unshaded arrays with down arrows show the recursion going forward: at each step, the array is divided in two halves. The shaded arrays with up arrows show how the recursion backs out by merging sorted subarrays at each step. The number of comparisons for each merge is shown circled, for a total of 22 comparisons.

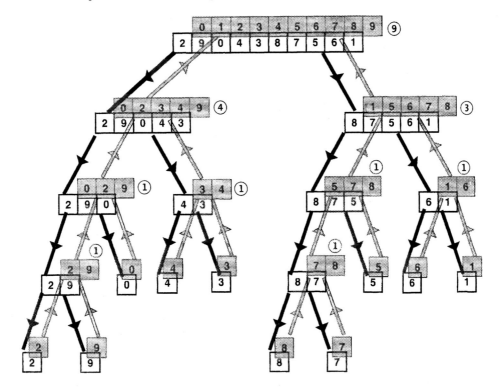

We are already familiar with the merging process, having covered it in great detail in Section 5.5. There, we noted that having maintained the lists in arrays of sizes m and n respectively, we needed additional array space of size $n + m$ to hold the merged output. In the **mergesort** algorithm above, we assume that once the merging is done in the scratch space, the merged list is copied back into the source subarrays, since the two source subarrays are simply adjacent halves of the "parent" array.

The mergesort tree in the previous example is almost perfectly balanced except for the last level. In the ideal situation, if the number of entries is of the form $n = 2^k$, a perfectly balanced tree of height $k = \log n$ is obtained. In general, the height of a mergesort tree for list of n entries (n is not necessarily a power of 2) is $\lceil \log n \rceil$. Thus, the height of the tree in the example is $\lceil \log n \rceil = \lceil \log 10 \rceil = 4$.

Linked lists.   Mergesort on an array needs additional space. If the array is large (as is typical in practical applications), this additional space may not be affordable. Mergesort works better with linked lists, and can be performed without any additional list space.

In the *forward* phase, dividing a linked list in half is not a single-step operation as in an array here. We need to traverse the list until we hit the middle node, incurring an additional penalty in running time.

In the *backing-out* phase, however, we have a clear winner. Merging two sorted linked lists is simply a matter of interleaving the nodes of the lists by readjusting the pointers, so that the resulting list contains all the nodes of the two previously disjoint linked lists in sorted order of values. No additional space is needed.

Analysis of running time.   Assume that we are sorting a list of n elements. We have already seen that the mergesort tree is always (nearly) perfectly balanced, so that the height of the mergesort tree is approximately $\log n$, with n elements at every level. Recall, from Section 5.5, that the worst-case number of comparisons to merge two sorted lists of length m and n, respectively, is $n + m - 1$.

Let us count the total number of comparisons first. Observe that the running-time analysis for the worst case can follow the same method as the best-case quicksort analysis. Instead of counting the number of comparisons for split going downward in the tree, as in quicksort, we count the number of comparisons for merge going upward, as illustrated in the earlier mergesort example. Moreover, if the quicksort split on a sublist of length k takes approximately k comparisons, so does merging two sorted sublists to obtain a consolidated list of size k. With this analogy, it is easy to see that mergesort takes approximately $n \log n$ comparisons in the worst case.

With linked lists instead of arrays, the split process also contributes to the running time. Every split of a linked list of size k takes $O(k)$ *pointer-pushing* operations, because the entire list has to be traversed in order to find the middle node. All the linked lists at any level of the mergesort tree add up to n nodes. Thus, at any level on the whole, splits over all the linked lists account for $O(n)$ pointer pushes. Over all $\log n$ levels, this adds up to $n \log n$, of the same order as the number of comparisons.

In sum, the worst-case running time is $O(n \log n)$, clearly beating the worst-case running time of quicksort, but on an equal footing with the latter's average-case running time.

What about the average case? To obtain the average case, let us first analyze the best case. In the best case, a list is still split in half, and the running time is the same as for the worst case: $O(1)$ for an array, and $O(n)$ for a linked list. Merging two sublists, each of length $n/2$, requires only $n/2$ comparisons in the best case, as compared to n for the worst case. However, as far as the big O complexity is concerned, it is the same, $O(n)$, as the worst case. Thus, the best-case time for mergesort is still $O(n \log n)$. Since the best case is the same as the worst case, the average case must also be $O(n \log n)$.

13.3 HEAPSORT

In Section 11.6, we saw an example of sorting using the Heap class, with the worst-case running time of $O(n \log n)$. This worst-case running time equals the best we have seen so far, which is heartening. However, the **build** phase of the sort, in which the entries are structured as a heap, can be done much more efficiently than in the method adopted in the program of Section 11.6.1. The running-time order of the new **build** followed by **sort** would still be $n \log n$. However, surprisingly enough, the new **build** method itself has a running time of only $O(n)$, down from $O(n \log n)$ for the old method.

In order to perform the new **build,** however, we have to go behind the Heap abstraction to get unrestricted access to the implementation. Henceforth, we will directly access the internal array, instead of going through the Heap interface methods.

13.3.1 Building a Heap in Linear Time

We start with the input array that contains the list of entries to be sorted. To keep the presentation simple, let us assume these entries are integers.

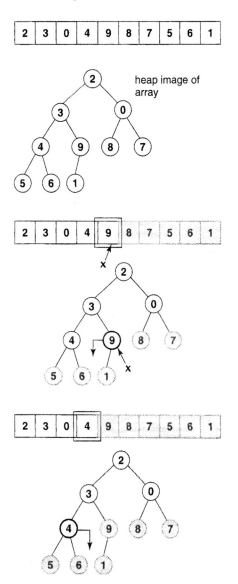

While the array has the heap structure (implicitly), it does not possess the heap order property. The work of **build** is to create precisely this by building a *max* heap out of the heap structure. To do so, it proceeds from the bottom to the top level in the heap structure, building bigger and bigger subheaps at higher levels out of the smaller subheaps already built at the lower ones.

To begin with, all the leaf nodes in the heap structure are trivially heap ordered, shown shaded. The first nontrivial heap structure that the **build** process works with is the "last" internal node (i.e., the bottommost and rightmost internal node). This is the node containing 9 in the example. The entry 9 is sifted down, but because it is greater than its only child, 1, it stays put.

Since the process goes bottom up, the subtrees of an internal node under consideration, say *x*, are guaranteed to be heaps by themselves. Thus, the only entry that could be out of order is the one at the root—namely, at node *x*. All the **build** process has to do is to sift down the entry at *x*. Let us refer to this incremental way of building a heap as *heapification;* thus, the subtree rooted at *x* has just been *heapified*.

After heapifying the subtree rooted at 9, the subtree rooted at 4 is heapified, which results in 4 sifting down. It is swapped with its larger child, 6, at which point 4 goes to a leaf node and the sift down stops. Following this, the action moves to the next level up, where the subtree rooted at 0 is heapified. This results in 0 sifting down. It is swapped with its larger child, 8, at which point it moves to a leaf node and the sift down stops.

Then the subtree rooted at 3 is heapified, which results in 3 sifting down. It is swapped with 9, but stays put after that because it is greater than 1. Finally, the root entry, 2, is sifted down. It goes all the way down to a leaf node, swapping successively with 9, 6, and 5.

Following is the *linear time* algorithm for the **build_heap** process.

Algorithm build_heap(A, n)

input: array $A[0 \ldots n - 1]$
output: max heap in $A[0 \ldots n - 1]$

$x \leftarrow n/2 - 1$
while $(x \geq 0)$ do
  $v \leftarrow$ value at x
  sift_down(v)
  $x \leftarrow x - 1$
endwhile

The *last* internal node is at index $n/2 - 1$. The succession of indexes from $n/2 - 1$ down to 0 corresponds to all the internal nodes of the heap image, going bottom to top among levels, and right to left in each level.

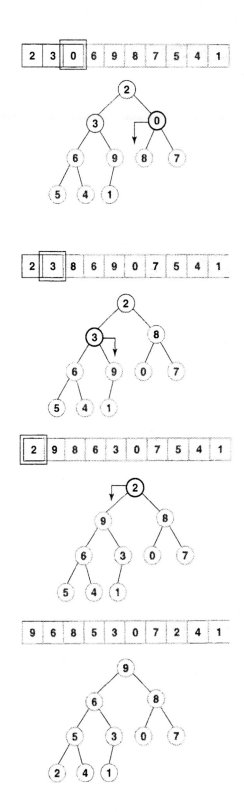

Intuitively, we would expect
the running time of *build_heap* to be $O(n \log n)$. Surprisingly, though, the running time is
better, it is $O(n)$. See Section 13.6 for a detailed analysis.

13.3.2 Sorting a Heap

Once the array entries are in a heap, sorting it is the next phase. This phase is fairly
straightforward, and consists of repeated sift downs.

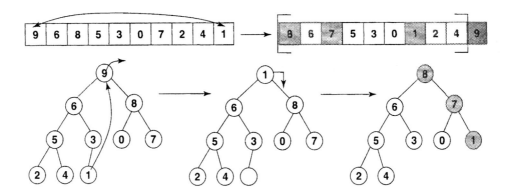

This is the first step of the sorting phase.
(a) Swap the top of the heap, 9, which is the first entry of the array, with the last, 1.
(b) Sift down 1 from the top, in a heap that effectively ignores the last entry.
Now the maximum entry is in the last (correct) position, and the rest of the array is
a heap in which this process can be repeated.

Algorithm and Running-Time Analysis.

Algorithm sort_heap(A, n)

input: max heap $A[0 \ldots n - 1]$
output: sorted $A[0 \ldots n - 1]$

$x \leftarrow n - 1$
while $(x > 0)$ do
    exchange $A[x]$ with $A[0]$
    $v \leftarrow A[0]$
    sift_down(v) in the heap $A[0 \ldots x - 1]$
    $x \leftarrow x - 1$
endwhile

The algorithm performs a sift-down
operation for heaps of sizes n, $n - 1$,
etc., all the way down to 2. From
Section 11.3 we know that sift down has
a worst-case running time of $O(\log k)$
on a heap of size k. Thus the worst-case
running time for the sorting phase is

$$\sum_{i=2}^{n} \log i$$

which is essentially the same as the
worst-case running time for the heapsort program described in Section 11.6.1,
namely, $O(n \log n)$.

13.4 RADIX SORT

Radix sort is a technique used to sort non-negative integers. Unlike the sorting algorithms covered so far, radix sort *does not* compare the values of the numbers to be sorted. Instead, it sorts by processing the numbers *digit by digit*.

Radix sort sorts a set of integers by making several passes over the set, one pass per digit. Each pass sorts the numbers according to a specific digit position, starting with the rightmost (least significant) digit in the first pass. As many passes are made as there are digits in the largest number. Numbers are implicitly left-padded with zeros as required.

In the first pass (*pass 0*), the numbers are sorted according to the last digit, in the second pass they are sorted according to the second-to-last digit, and so on.

Note that if there are several numbers with the same digit value for a certain pass, they will maintain the same relative ordering among themselves when that pass is done. For example, the numbers 862 and 222 have the same last digit, 2, for the first pass, and 862 comes before 222. Thus, 862 precedes 222 in the result of the first pass. Similarly, 222 and 225 have the same digit, 2, in the second pass, and 222 precedes 225. At the end of this pass, 222 still precedes 225.

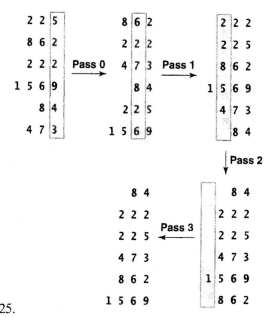

This property makes radix sort a *stable sort*.

The digit-by-digit sort restricts the kind of input to which radix sort can be applied. Specifically, radix sort may only be applied to non-negative integers in any *positional number system,* where the base of the number system is called the *radix,* thus the name. In the preceding example, we are sorting a set of decimal integers, so the radix is 10. Or, one may sort a set of binary integers (radix 2), or octal integers (radix 8), or hexadecimal integers (radix 16), and so on. The positional nature of the number system implies that digits increase in significance going right to left, which guarantees the correctness of the algorithm.

Scatter and gather. Each pass of the radix sort algorithm can be seen as a two-step process: *scattering* the integers into *buckets* based on the value of the digit in a given position, followed by *gathering* the entries in order of buckets.

Consider scatter and gather for *Pass 1* of the preceding example. One bucket is assigned for each possible digit value from 0 through 9.

In the gather process, the entries in a bucket must be gathered in the order in which they were scattered to maintain stable sort. For example, since 222 was scattered before 225 in bucket 2, it must be gathered before 225.

The radix sort algorithm follows.

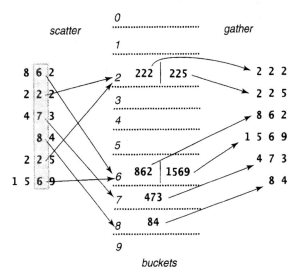

Algorithm radixSort(L, n, r)

input: List L, length n, radix r
output: sorted L

$d \leftarrow$ max # of digits in any number in L
$bucket[0 \dots r - 1]$

for p from 0 to $d - 1$ do

    clear all buckets
    for i from 0 to $n - 1$ do
        $next \leftarrow i$-th entry in L
        $v \leftarrow$ digit at position p of $next$
        append $next$ to $bucket[v]$
    endfor

    clear L
    for b from 0 to $r - 1$ do
        append all entries of $bucket[b]$ to L
    endfor

endfor

The first block of statements in the *for* loop scatters the entries of L into the appropriate buckets. The second block of statements re-creates L by gathering all the entries from the buckets.

There are three factors that determine the running time of this algorithm: the number of integers to be sorted, n, the maximum number of digits in any number, d, and the radix, r. So, for instance, if we were to sort 100 integers (represented in decimal notation), the largest of which is 8 digits long, then $n = 100$, $d = 8$, and $r = 10$.

We will assume that the entries in a bucket are stored in a circular linked list, and that the list L is also a circular linked list. This ensures that appending a single entry to the end of a linked list in the scatter phase can be accomplished in $O(1)$ time, and so can appending a linked list to another, which is done repeatedly in the gather phase.

Running-time analysis. *In each pass,* the scatter phase requires $O(n)$ time. Each number is added to the appropriate bucket in $O(1)$ time because it is a simple matter of indexing into the appropriate bucket of the bucket array in $O(1)$ time, followed by appending to that bucket, again in $O(1)$ time. Since there are n numbers, we obtain an $O(n)$ time for scatter. In the gather phase, a master list is progressively constructed by appending each bucket's linked list in turn, starting from bucket 0. Each append takes $O(1)$ time, and since there are r buckets, the total time is $O(r)$.

The sorting algorithm performs one pass per digit, so if there are d digits, d passes will be made. For all d passes, therefore, the running time is $O(d(n + r))$. The running time is not dependent on the actual distribution of values in the input. Thus, the worst, average, and best cases are all the same, $O(d(n + r))$.

But consider the fact that integers are represented in a fixed number of bits in a computer, say 32 (4 bytes). Then d above would be 32, a fixed constant. Also, $r = 2$ because the representation is in binary. Radix sort may be then applied to sort *n positive* integers, represented in binary form using just two buckets, in $O(n)$, or linear time!

13.5   IMPLEMENTATION: A `Quicksort` CLASS

In this section, we will go over a program that implements quicksort. Using this as a representational vehicle, we can then implement the other sorting algorithms.

Class File 13.1. *Quicksort.java*

```
package apps.sort;
import java.util.*;
public class Quicksort {
  private Quicksort() { }
  public static <T extends Comparable<T>>
        void sort(T[] list) { ... }
  static <T extends Comparable<T>>
        void quick(T[] list, int lo, int hi) { ... }
  static <T extends Comparable<T>>
        int split(T[] list, int lo, int hi) { ... }
  static <T extends Comparable<T>>
        int getMedian(T[] list, int lo, int hi) { ... }
  static <T extends Comparable<T>>
        void insertSort(T[] list) { ... }
}
```

The `Quicksort` class is a utility class that contains only static methods. Since the sort process simply takes an input and sorts it, there is no state that has to be maintained. The class cannot be instantiated—see the `private` constructor.

There is only one method that is callable by a client, and that is the `sort` method. The actual recursive quicksort is implemented by the helper method, `quick`, which in turn is helped by the other methods. The `sort` method accepts an array of entries of a generic type `T` as input, with the condition that `T` implement the `compareTo` method of the `Comparable` interface. The other supporting methods are all tied to this type `T`.

The sort method essentially takes the input from the client and passes it on to the recursive quick method, with the input array as the starting subarray.

```
public static <T extends Comparable<T>> void sort(T[] list) {
    quick(list, 0, list.length-1);
    insertSort(list);
}
```

The recursive quick method only works on subarrays of length greater than 10. So, after the return from the recursive quicksort call, there may be pockets of entries of length 10 or less in the original list that were not sorted. These are sorted by the call to insertion sort. This is one of the fine-tuning devices we saw, used to improve the real-time efficiency of quicksort.

Note that insertion sort is applied once to the entire list instead of once to each pocket. Doing the latter would incur the overhead of a method call (to insertSort) on every pocket; doing the former would incur the overhead of redundant comparisons that insertion sort would make even on the sorted parts of the list. A decision is made here that assumes that repeated calls to insertSort would add up to a larger overhead than redundant comparisons.

The quick method is more or less a verbatim rewrite of the **quicksort** algorithm we saw earlier, with one addition, which is to check that the length of the input subarray is greater than 10 before going ahead.

```
static <T extends Comparable<T>> void quick(T[] list, int lo, int hi) {
    if ((hi - lo) > 10) {
        int splitPoint = split(list, lo, hi);
        quick(list, lo, splitPoint-1);
        quick(list, splitPoint+1, hi);
    }
}
```

The workhorse of the implementation is the split method, which implements the **split** algorithm we discussed earlier.

```
static <T extends Comparable<T>> int split(T[] list, int lo, int hi) {

    int median = getMedian(list, lo, hi);
    T temp = list[lo];
    list[lo] = list[median];
    list[median] = temp;
    T pivot = list[lo];

    int left = lo+1;
    int right = hi;
    while (left <= right) {
        while (left <= hi && left <= right) {
            if (list[left].compareTo(pivot) >= 0) break;
            left++;
        }
```

```
    while (right > lo && left <= right) {
        if (list[right].compareTo(pivot) < 0) break;
        right--;
    }
    if (left < right) {
        temp = list[left];
        list[left] = list[right];
        list[right] = temp;
        left++;
        right--;
    }
}

temp = list[right];
list[right] = list[lo];
list[lo] = temp;

return right;
}
```

The first few statements implement one of the fine-tuning techniques we saw that protects against quicksort doing badly with sorted or nearly sorted arrays—using the median of the first, middle, and last entries as the pivot. Method getMedian is called in the first statement, which returns the index of the median value of the first, middle, and last entries in any given subarray. Once this index is obtained, the median (pivot) value is switched with the first, so that the pivot is always at the first position of the subarray before the actual split process is started up.

The heart of the split process that follows these fine-tuning statements is a faithful implementation of the **split** algorithm discussed earlier. Once the indices left and right have crossed over, and the while loop terminates, the pivot is swapped with the entry at right and the split point (right) is returned.

Following is the getMedian method:

```
static <T extends Comparable<T>> int getMedian(T[] list, int lo, int hi) {
    int mid = (lo+hi)/2;
    T low = list[lo];
    T high = list[hi];
    T middle = list[mid];
    if (low.compareTo(middle) < 0) {
        if (middle.compareTo(high) < 0) {
            return mid;
        } else if (low.compareTo(high) < 0) {
            return hi;
        } else {
            return lo;
        }
    } else {
        if (low.compareTo(high) < 0) {
            return lo;
```

```
        } else if (middle.compareTo(high) < 0) {
            return hi;
        } else {
            return mid;
        }
    }
}
```

There are six possible arrangements or permutations of three values, with the corresponding medians.

Last, the `insertSort` method is a concise implementation of the **insertionSort** algorithm seen earlier. Unlike the algorithm, the data movements here keep step with the comparisons, instead of leaving all data movements until after the insertion point is determined.

```
static <T extends Comparable<T>> void insertSort(T[]list) {
    for (int i=0; i < list.length; i++) {
        int j = i-1;
        T insertVal = list[i];
        while (j >= 0) {
            if (insertVal.compareTo(list[j]) >= 0) break;
            list[j+1] = list[j];
            j--;
        }
        list[j+1] = insertVal;
    }
}
```

13.6 HEAP BUILD: LINEAR RUNNING TIME

Consider the heap-building process described in Section 13.3.1, and, in particular, the **build_heap** algorithm. Let us analyze the running time of this algorithm—more specifically, the worst-case number of comparisons required to build the heap using this algorithm.

Assume a heap of height h. Recall that restoring the heap at a node involves sifting down the value at that node, which might percolate all the way down to the leaf level in the worst case. Sifting down between any pair of levels requires two comparisons. Thus, for any node at level i, $0 \le i < h$, it takes $2(h - i)$ comparisons, in the worst case, to restore the heap rooted at that node. There are 2^i nodes at level i, and each of these nodes contributes $2(h - i)$ comparisons to the heap-building process. Which gives us $2^i * 2(h - i)$ comparisons per level.

Adding this figure up over all levels except the last (the leaf nodes are trivial heaps), we get S, the total number of comparisons:

$$S = 2^0 * 2h + 2^1 * 2(h - 1) + 2^2 * 2(h - 2) + \cdots + 2^{h-2} * 2(2) + 2^{h-1} * 2(1)$$

by summing up over $i = 1, 2, \dots (h - 2), (h - 1)$.

Now we play the same game as in Section 10.8, multiplying S by 2, and lining up the product below S:

$$S \ = 2^0 * 2h + \ 2^1 * 2(h-1) + \ 2^2 * 2(h-2) \ + \cdots + \ 2^{h-1} * 2(1)$$

$$2S \ = \qquad\qquad 2^1 * 2h + \qquad\quad 2^2 * 2(h-1) \ + \cdots + \ 2^{h-1} * 2 + \ 2^h * 2$$

Subtracting the first line from the second, we obtain the following on the left- and right-hand sides of the equation:

$$S = -2^0 * 2h + 2 * 2^1 + 2 * 2^2 + \cdots + 2 * 2^{h-1} + 2^h * 2$$

The second through last terms form the sum:

$$\sum_{i=1}^{h} 2 * 2^i = \sum_{i=0}^{h} 2 * 2^i - 2 = 2 * (2^{h+1} - 1) - 2 = 2^{h+2} - 4$$

Plugging this back in S, and adding up the terms on the right-hand side, we obtain:

$$S = 2^{h+2} - 4 - 2h = 4 * 2^h - 2h - 4$$

Since $h \approx \log n$, we have $2^h \approx n$, so that $S \approx 4n - 2\log n - 4$.

Thus, the number of comparisons $= O(n)$, i.e. linear in the number of heap entries.

13.7 SUMMARY

- Following is a summary of the running times of the sorting algorithms, both worst-case and average:

	Insertion sort	**Quicksort**	**Mergesort**	**Heapsort**
Worst	$O(n^2)$	$O(n^2)$	$O(n \log n)$	$O(n \log n)$
Average	$O(n^2)$	$O(n \log n)$	$O(n \log n)$	$O(n \log n)$

This table has to be used with care because it only specifies the asymptotic *order* of running times. The figures can only be compared to each other fairly when n is "sufficiently" high.

- It turns out that insertion sort is not a bad algorithm at all, especially for n less than 20 or so, or when the array is mostly sorted to begin with. For such small n, the other algorithms incur a greater overhead than insertion sort. This is why the quicksort algorithm avoided using insertion sort when it encountered subarrays of size 20 or less, and instead "cleaned up" the mostly sorted array using insertion sort.
- If mergesort is implemented with linked lists, then all the sorting algorithms we have covered perform sorting *in place*. In other words, no additional space is used whose size depends on the number of elements to be sorted. Of course, this does not take into consideration space that the compiler can use to implement recursion. We have seen that this could be a problem with quicksort unless handled carefully.

- Compared to heapsort, a version of quicksort optimized with respect to the pivot choice as well as the clean-up phase has a much smaller overhead. This makes quicksort the sorting algorithm of choice in most situations in which fairly large arrays need to be sorted in place.
- Mergesort is mostly used for *external sorting* (i.e., sorting files stored on disk). The mergesort algorithm we discussed uses *two-way* merge in which two sorted lists are merged. An interesting related issue is that of $n - way$ merging, in which n sorted lists are merged into one consolidated sorted list.
- No sorting algorithm that sorts by comparing key values can *ever* run in time better than $n \log n$ in the worst or average case.
- Finally, radix sort is an alternative when the input consists of positive integers represented in some radix system, since it sorts digit-by-digit rather than comparing values as a whole. An efficient, linked-list-based implementation of radix sort for n numbers, none of which is more than d digits long, in radix r, takes time $O(n(d + r))$. If d and r are fixed a priori, radix sort is a linear time sorting algorithm.

13.8 EXERCISES

E13.1. Given an array containing the following integers:

```
3, 26, 67, 35, 9, -6, 43, 82, 10, 54
```

trace the **insertionSort** algorithm on this array. How many comparisons did it take to complete the sort?

E13.2. Repeat Exercise E13.1, using binary search instead of sequential search to find the position of an element to be inserted in the partially sorted subarray. How many comparisons did this modified insertion sort take? Does modifying insertion sort in this manner change the time-complexity order?

E13.3. What is the average number of comparisons (give an exact number, not big O) required to sort an array of 10 elements using insertion sort? Assume that every element to be inserted in a partially sorted subarray has an equal likelihood of ending up in any of the possible locations.

E13.4. The treesort algorithm to sort a set of values inserts these values one by one into a binary search tree, and then performs an inorder traversal of the binary search tree to obtain the result in sorted order. In some ways, the treesort algorithm is the dynamic-storage equivalent of insertion sort. How many comparisons would it take to build a binary search tree by inserting, one by one, the integers in Exercise E13.1?

E13.5. Repeat Exercise E13.4 using an AVL tree instead of a simple binary search tree. In general, what would be the worst-case running time (big O) of treesort on n entries, if one were to use an AVL tree? Is this a feasible alternative to the sorting algorithms presented in this chapter?

E13.6. On the input array of Exercise E13.1, trace the **quicksort** algorithm. Always choose the first element of a subarray as the pivot. Draw the quicksort tree. How many comparisons did it take to complete the sort?

E13.7. In Exercise E13.6, if the quicksort recursion had been stopped when the subarray size was 3 or less, and insertion sort had been applied at the end to sort the array, how many comparisons in all would it have taken to sort the array?

E13.8. Repeat Exercise E13.6, choosing as the pivot the median of the first, middle, and last elements of a subarray.

E13.9. Trace the **mergesort** algorithm on the input set of Exercise E13.1. However, instead of an array, a linked list is used to hold the input elements. Count the total number of comparisons required to sort the input.

E13.10. Sort the input array of Exercise E13.1 using heapsort. First, build a heap using the linear-time **build_heap** algorithm. Then sort the heap using the **sort_heap** algorithm. How many comparisons, in all, did it take to finish sorting the input?

E13.11. One could also sort a set of values using the Heap class of Section 11.4 as a min-heap. Starting with an empty heap, insert values one by one into the heap. When all the insertions are done, carry out successive *delete_min* operations—this gives the values in sorted order. How many comparisons in all would this sorting approach take?

E13.12. Given a *sorted* array of 10 elements, how many comparisons each would insertion sort, quicksort, mergesort, and heapsort make to "sort" this array?

E13.13. You are given the letters 'a', 'b', 'c', 'd', and 'e' to be sorted in alphabetical order. For each of the following algorithms, construct (a) a best-case input and (b) a worst-case input consisting of these letters.
(a) Insertion sort
(b) Mergesort
(c) The linear-time build-heap algorithm
What is the number of comparisons required for the best and worst case for each algorithm?

E13.14. Suppose we have two unordered lists of keys stored in arrays. The first list A contains *a* keys, the second list B contains *b* keys, and $a < b$. We would like to select only the keys that are common to both lists, and we propose four ways to do this:
(a) **Unordered:** For each key in A, scan B to see if that key is also in B.
(b) **Sortsmall:** Sort A, and for each key in B, see if that key is also in A.
(c) **Sortbig:** Sort B, and for each key in A, see if that key is also in B.
(d) **Merge:** Sort both lists, and use a merge-like scheme to find the common keys.
For each scheme above, give the order (big O) of the total worst-case cost in comparisons (in terms of a and b) to carry out the scheme, assuming that the various stages are implemented *as efficiently as possible*.

E13.15. Given a set of integers in the following sequence:

100, 23, 456, 9876, 259, 8654, 165, 81

Trace the **radixSort** algorithm on this array. How many time units did it take to complete the sort? Recall that each of the following operations takes one unit of time: (a) adding an integer to a bucket, (b) retrieving an integer from a bucket.

E13.16. An interesting sorting algorithm, **countsort,** that does not compare key values is described below on a list L[1..n] of integers.

- Find the values of the smallest and largest integers in the list, say *min* and *max*.
- Initialize a separate list C[*min..max*] to zero.
- Scan the list L for $1 \leq i \leq n$, and at each step, increment C at position L[i] by 1.
- Scan the list C from *min* to *max*. If C[*min*] = *m*, say, write *m* successive *min*'s into the first *m* locations of L. This continues from left to right: for every j such that $min \leq j \leq max$, write C[j] consecutive j's into L.

Answer the following questions about the countsort algorithm.

(a) Under what circumstances might countsort have a running time of $O(n)$?

(b) What are the memory (space) requirements for countsort?

(c) Will countsort always do the job in about n steps? Explain.

(d) Give a simple example for very small n where countsort requires a great deal of space and a great deal of time.

(e) Should we consider countsort as a competitor to, say, heapsort or quicksort? Explain.

(f) Can countsort be generalized to sort *any* set of values, not just integers? Explain.

E13.17. One way to sort an array of N elements is to divide it into k equal-sized blocks each of size N/k and do the following:

- Sort each block separately using quicksort.
- Use a k-way merge to merge the sorted blocks into a separate array.

Recall the k-way merge algorithms described in Exercise E11.7. We will refer to the first algorithm (using sequential scan) as the *linear* algorithm, and the second (using the min-heap) as the *heap* algorithm.

(a) What is the worst-case running time (big O) of the block-based sorting algorithm above if the *linear* k-way merge is used? Explain.

(b) Answer the same question, assuming that the *heap* k-way merge is used.

E13.18. In each of the following cases, explain what sorting algorithm you would use and why, assuming that the goal is to achieve the best possible worst-case running time for the type of input specified:

(a) A linked list of n records in random order where $n > 1000$.

(b) An array of n records in random order where $n > 1000$.

(c) An array of n records, none of which is more than two positions away from its correct position.

(d) A linked list of n last names, each at most 12 characters long.

(e) An array of n items, where $n < 10$.

13.9 PROGRAMMING PROBLEMS

P13.1. Implement a MergeSort class to sort an array of entries of type T, extends Comparable<T>. Copy the input array to a linked list, sort the linked list, and then recopy the sorted linked list back into the array.

P13.2. Implement a Heapsort class to sort an array of entries of type T, extends Comparable<T>, using the algorithms **build_heap** and **sort_heap.**

P13.3. Implement a Radixsort class to sort an array of integers. Internally, convert the input array into a linked list for all your work. Use linked lists for the buckets as well. When the sorting is complete, copy the resulting linked list into the original array.

P13.4. Integers are radix 10 numbers. But what if we have to sort hexadecimal numbers? Then the radix would be 16. Or binary numbers, for which the radix would be 2.

Modify your Radixsort class to handle any radix. Here are some helpful directions:

- Numbers will now be input as character strings because hexadecimal numbers would include the characters 'A' through 'F' in their representation.
- Pass an additional parameter, radix, to the sorting method.
- Digit extraction is more involved. In the scatter implementation, you may want to use the *static* method digit of class Character:

```
static int digit(char ch, int radix)
```

which, given a character and a radix, returns the equivalent integer value. So, for example, character '9' and radix 10 would give the integer 9; character 'E' and radix 16 would give the integer 14, because 'E' is the hexadecimal representation for the value 14.

P13.5. Implement a `Countsort` class to sort an array of integers using the countsort algorithm described in Exercise E13.16. Explain your choice of data structures to implement the class.

P13.6. In the quicksort algorithm, the partitioning part of the algorithm works by rearranging the keys in the array, so that all the keys to the left of the pivot element are less than the pivot, and all the keys to the right of the pivot are greater than or equal to the pivot.

Now consider the following partitioning problem: let L be an array of strings where each element in the array is either "red", "white", or "blue". Write a method:

```
public void rwbBand(String[] rwb)
```

to rearrange the strings so that all the "red"s are to the left of all the "white"s, which are to the left of all the "blue"s. Your method must make only a *single pass* through the array.

C H A P T E R   14

Graphs I: Algorithms

Graphs model the most general kinds of relationships between entities. A general tree is a specialized graph that only models hierarchical relationships; a binary tree is a specialized general tree that models hierarchies in which every entity may have at most two child entities.

In this chapter we will focus on the representational and algorithmic issues dealing with graphs. In the following companion chapter, we will delve into the implementation of graphs and graph algorithms in Java.

Learning Objectives

- Distinguish between trees and graphs, and between different types of graphs, including undirected, directed, and weighted graphs.
- Study two standard ways of representing graphs, namely adjacency matrix and adjacency linked lists, and understand the tradeoffs in using one representation over the other.
- Learn depth-first search and breadth-first search, two broadly different approaches to traversing graphs, and compare and contrast them with regard to usefulness and running times.
- Study three important graph algorithms, namely topological sorting, connected components, and shortest paths, and analyze their running times.

14.1 MODELING RELATIONSHIPS USING GRAPHS

Graphs model pair-wise relationships among a set of entities. Graphs may be categorized into two types, *undirected* and *directed*, based on whether they depict symmetric relationships or unsymmetric relationships. In either case, the graph may also be *weighted*. These different types of graphs, their properties, and their uses are described with examples in the following discussion.

14.1.1   Undirected Graphs

An undirected graph represents a symmetric relationship among entities.

The example graph models the symmetric relationship of "next to" among several rooms of a house. Each circled entry is called a *vertex,* and is labeled with the room it represents. The links between vertices, called *edges,* are used to represent the "next to" relationship between rooms. For example, the edge between *Den* and *Living* means that the den is next to the living room.

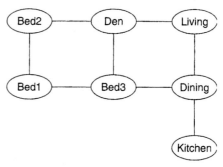

This example depicts a symmetric relationship. Saying that the living room is next to the den is the same as saying that the den is next to the living room.

The edge between *Den* and *Living* is denoted by $(Den, Living)$ or $(Living, Den)$—it does not matter which vertex is listed first. When two vertices are connected by an edge, each vertex is said to be a *neighbor* of (or *adjacent* to) the other. *Den* is a neighbor of (adjacent to) *Living,* and vice versa.

The *degree* of a vertex is the number of vertices that are adjacent to it (i.e., the number of its neighbors). The degree of *Dining* is 3, that of *Living* is 2, and that of *Kitchen* is 1.

A *path* is a sequence of edges, such as the one between *Bed*1 and *Kitchen* shown alongside. You can think of this path as a tour of rooms beginning at the first bedroom and ending at the kitchen, going through a sequence of rooms in which every next room is adjacent to the previous one. It may be represented by a *sequence* of vertices, *Bed*1, *Bed*2, *Den*, *Bed*3, *Dining*, *Kitchen*.

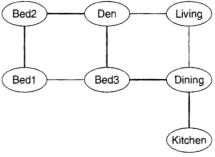

Alternatively, this path may be represented by a sequence of edges:

$$(Bed1, Bed2), (Bed2, Den), (Den, Bed3), (Bed3, Dining), (Dining, Kitchen)$$

A path does not have to go over all the vertices of a graph. In the tour above, we did not go through the living room.

In general, a path is a sequence of edges of the form $(v_1, v_2), (v_2, v_3), \ldots, (v_{k-1}, v_k)$, represented by the sequence $v_1, v_2, v_3, \ldots, v_{k-1}, v_k$. A path is *simple* if no edge and no vertex are repeated—the only exception is that the first vertex may be the same as the last. Henceforth, we will consider only simple paths.

The sequence of vertices *Bed1, Bed3, Living, Dining* is *not* a path, because a pair of consecutive vertices in the sequence, *Bed3* and *Living*, are not adjacent to each other. The sequence *Bed1, Bed3, Den, Bed3* is *not* a (simple) path, since it repeats the edge (*Bed3, Den*).

A *cycle* in a graph is a path that starts and ends at the same vertex. The path *Bed1, Bed2, Den, Bed3, Bed1* is a cycle. This graph has two other cycles: *Den, Living, Dining, Bed3* and *Bed1, Bed2, Den, Living, Dining, Bed3, Bed1*.

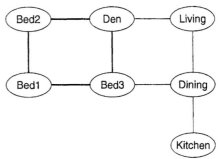

A graph that contains a cycle is called a *cyclic* graph. A graph that does not contain any cycles is called an *acyclic* graph.

A graph is said to be *connected* if there is a path between *every* pair of vertices; otherwise it is *unconnected.* The rooms-in-a-house graph is a connected graph. The following example shows an *unconnected* graph that represents "next to" relationships between some countries.

USA, Canada, and *Mexico* are in the same land mass, while *France* and *Spain* are together in a different land mass, and *Australia* is in a land mass by itself. For instance, there is no path from *USA* to *Australia.* In general, one cannot start from a country in a land mass and get to another country in a different land mass without "jumping" across

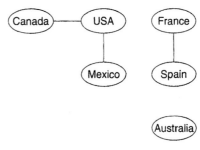

water. There is no overland path that can be taken from one land mass to another.

An unconnected graph is a collection of components. Each component is a subgraph that, by itself, is connected. These components are called *connected components.* Every vertex in the graph belongs to exactly one component. In the land masses graph, there are three connected components.

14.1.2 Directed Graphs

A *directed* graph represents an unsymmetric or asymmetric relationship among a set of entities.

This next example shows a directed graph representing the course prerequisite structure in a college. The vertices $C1$ through $C8$ represent courses, and the edges represent the prerequisite relationship between courses. The edges are all

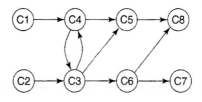

directed *from* a vertex *to* another vertex; a directed graph may not have any undirected edges.

The directed edge from $C3$ to $C5$ is denoted by the *ordered* pair $(C3, C5)$ and represents the fact that $C3$ is a prerequisite for $C5$. Note that $(C5, C3)$ is *not* an edge in the graph because there is no edge directed *from* $C5$ to $C3$.

Another example of a directed graph is the Web, where the vertices are the Web pages, and each edge represents a hyperlink link from one Web page to another. The graph shown alongside could be a model

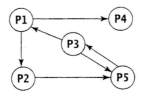

for a portion of a Web site, showing five Web pages, $P1$ through $P5$, and hyperlinks from each of these to other pages. So, for instance, page $P1$ has two links, one to $P2$ and the other to $P4$.

Yet another example of a directed graph is that of an electronic circuit in which the vertices represent various devices and the edges represent connections between devices. Each connection is directed from one device to another, representing the transmission of a signal *from* the output end of the first device *to* the input end of the second.

On occasion, one might need to represent a symmetric relationship in an otherwise unsymmetric relationship set. Take the example of two courses, $C3$ and $C4$, that are corequisites of each other (i.e., they have to be taken at the same time and may not be taken one before the other). The corequisite relationship is symmetric. How can this be represented in the prerequisite graph without using an undirected edge?

As shown below, a symmetric relationship between two entities may be represented in a directed graph by using a pair of edges between the corresponding vertices, in opposite directions.

We can restate the fact that $C3$ and $C4$ are corequisites of each other by saying that $C3$ is a prerequisite for $C4$, and $C4$ is a prerequisite for $C3$. This is then represented by drawing a pair of edges between $C3$ and $C4$, one directed from $C3$ to $C4$, and the other directed from $C4$ to $C3$.

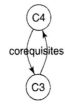

In the Web graph, there is an edge $(P3, P5)$ as well as an edge $(P5, P3)$, a pair of edges between the same vertices, in opposite directions. This is different from the course corequisites idea because there is no special meaning to this pair in the context of the Web except that there are a pair of Web pages that have links to each other.

All the graph terms that we defined earlier for undirected graphs are also defined for directed graphs, with some obvious and some not-so-obvious differences in interpretation. Vertex *w* is *adjacent* to (is a *neighbor* of) vertex *v* only if there is an edge from *v* to *w*.

In the course-prerequisite graph, *C6* is adjacent to *C3*, but *C3* is not adjacent to *C6*. Alternatively, *C6* is a neighbor of *C3*, but *C3* is not a neighbor of *C6*.

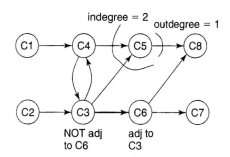

The *indegree* of a vertex is the number of vertices to which it is adjacent. In simpler terms, the indegree of a vertex is the number of edges directed into it. The indegree of *C5* is 2 because it is adjacent to two vertices, *C3* and *C4* (i.e., it has two incoming edges). The indegree of *C1* is 0.

The *outdegree* of a vertex is the number of vertices adjacent to it, or, the number of edges directed out of it. The outdegree of *C3* is 3, and the outdegree of *C7* is 0.

A path is a sequence of edges, *taken in the direction of the edges*, such as one from *C1* to *C6*: (*C1, C4*), (*C4, C3*), (*C3, C6*). This path may be alternatively represented by the vertex sequence *C1, C4, C3, C6*.

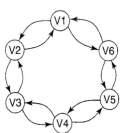

The sequence of edges (*C3, C5*), (*C5, C8*), (*C8, C6*) is *not* a path because (*C8, C6*) is not an edge in the graph.

A cycle is a path that starts and ends at the same vertex. There is one cycle, *C3, C4, C3*, in the course-prerequisite graph.

A graph that contains a cycle is called a cyclic graph. The course-prerequisite graph is, therefore, a cyclic graph. A graph that does not contain any cycles is called an acyclic graph. We can delete either the edge (*C3, C4*) or the edge (*C4, C3*) in the course-prerequisite graph to convert it to an acyclic graph.

The notion of connectedness in a directed graph is divided into two kinds: *strong* and *weak*.

A directed graph is *strongly connected* if there is a path *from* every vertex *to* every other vertex. This example shows a strongly connected graph: starting at any vertex, you can reach every other vertex. Note that there are two cycles that contain all the vertices of the graph and run in opposite directions, and six other cycles each of which contains two edges.

The course-prerequisite graph we saw earlier is *not* strongly connected, because, for instance, there is no path from C6 to C5.

A directed graph is *weakly connected* if, by ignoring the directions on the edges, the resultant undirected graph is connected. The course-prerequisite graph is weakly connected. Note that when the directions on the edges are ignored, there may be multiple undirected edges between some pairs of vertices. For the course-prerequisite graph, this happens between vertices C3 and C4. In this situation, multiple edges are treated as a single edge.

A strongly connected directed graph is also, by definition, weakly connected. The reverse is not necessarily true.

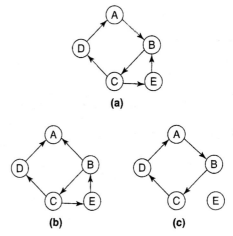

The directed graph of (a) is strongly connected because there is a path from every vertex to every other vertex. There are two cycles in this graph: A, B, C, D, A and B, C, E, B. Directed graph (b) is weakly connected, with one cycle: B, C, E, B. However, it is *not* strongly connected, because there is, for instance, no path from A to E. In fact, there is no path from A to *any* other vertex in the graph. Directed graph (c) is unconnected.

14.1.3 Weighted Graphs

A graph is *weighted* if each edge is labeled with a number, called the edge *weight,* indicative of the *cost* measure of the corresponding relationship. The meaning of the cost measure would depend on the physical system being modeled by the graph.

In an undirected graph, an edge weight could be a measure of the strength of the relationship between the vertices connected by that edge.

A molecule of some compound—like the ethane molecule shown alongside—can be represented by an undirected graph, with the vertices representing the different atoms of the compound, and the edges representing bonds between atoms. Every bond has a certain bond strength, which can be shown by placing a number equivalent to the bond strength on the edge representing that bond.

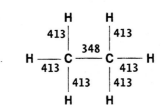

Directed graphs more commonly carry edge weights. A toll highway network is shown in this

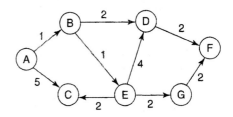

example. Each vertex represents a city, and each edge represents a road from one city to another. The numbers or weights on the edges represent the toll amounts in dollars.

14.2 GRAPH REPRESENTATION

To represent a graph, we have to choose one or more component data structures to store the vertices and edges. On what basis should we choose these data structures? It would help if we know the different ways in which graphs are used in applications.

Several important and fundamental graph algorithms need to scan all the neighbors of each vertex. A storage scheme in which all the neighbors of a vertex are stored along with the vertex would work best with these algorithms. Thus, for instance, every edge $x \rightarrow y$ of a directed graph would be interpreted as y being a neighbor of x and stored as such.

Once a storage scheme is chosen, it has to be implemented using an appropriate data structure. Again, there may be several alternatives to choose from, and our choice of structure would be based on the types of applications in which the graph is used. We discuss here two data structures that are most frequently used to implement the vertex-and-neighbors storage scheme: the *adjacency matrix* and *adjacency linked lists*.

Directed graph representation.   A graph which is stored using the vertex-neighbors scheme may be defined as a collection of sets.

Each vertex contributes one set of two members, of which the first is the vertex itself, and the second is the set of its neighbors:

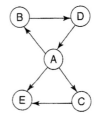

$\{A, \{B, C, E\}\}, \{B, \{D\}\}, \{C, \{E\}\},$
$\quad \{D, \{A\}\}, \{E, \{\}\}.$

The order in which the neighbors of a vertex is stored is irrelevant.

The user usually identifies vertices (and therefore edges) by means of name labels, like the alphabetic characters in the example. For the implementation, however, it is convenient to identify each vertex by an integer number, conventionally between 0 and $n - 1$, where n is the number of vertices. Let us number the vertices A, B, C, D, and E from 0 to 4 respectively.

Adjacency matrix.   A simple implementation of a graph with n vertices uses an array of arrays, or, in other words, a two-dimensional matrix of size $n \times n$. Each row of the matrix describes one vertex; the columns of the row list the neighbors of the vertex. The matrix is called an *adjacency matrix* or *adjacency table*.

Each entry of the matrix is a boolean value. Take the first row of the matrix, which lists the neighbors of vertex A. Columns 1, 2, and 4 contain a *true* value, *T,* indicating that the vertices numbered 1, 2, and 4 (B, C, and E, respectively) are neighbors of A. The other columns contain *false* values, *F.*

The vertex labels corresponding to the vertex numbers are shown both above the adjacency matrix and to its left. In the implementation, there will be an array that can translate between a vertex label and the number assigned to it.

		A	B	C	D	E
		0	1	2	3	4
A	0	F	T	T	F	T
B	1	F	F	F	T	F
C	2	F	F	F	F	T
D	3	T	F	F	F	F
E	4	F	F	F	F	F

To determine whether there is an edge from vertex 0 to vertex 3, one has to check whether the matrix entry $[0, 3]$ is T. Such a constant-time random access to any entry of the matrix is a major advantage of the adjacency matrix representation. On the other hand, the matrix representation is inefficient if one needs to scan all the neighbors of a vertex. To scan the neighbors of E, one has to go over *all* the columns of row 4, selecting only those that contain the value T. In the process, one is forced to examine columns that contain F, leading to wasted effort. This can considerably slow down applications that frequently need to scan all neighbors of vertices. Another related drawback is the excess space consumption. In the example, there are only six edges in the graph, while the matrix has 25 cells.

In sum, the adjacency matrix representation is most useful when the graph is sufficiently dense (i.e., there is a large number of edges). Or when the application needs to make a large number of random accesses to the structure to answer questions like: Is there an edge from x to y?

Adjacency linked lists. The disadvantages of the adjacency matrix can be eliminated if we choose an alternative representation in which the neighbors of a vertex are stored in a linked list.

Each vertex has an associated linked list of neighbors, called the adjacency linked list. A null list is associated with E because it has no neighbors.

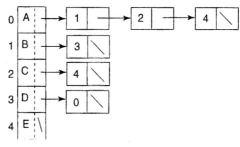

This representation is much more space-efficient, even though every neighbor that is represented carries with it a reference to the next node in its linked list.

Scanning all the neighbors of a vertex is a simple matter of going over all the entries of the adjacency linked list— there is no wastage of effort due to redundant checks.

However, we have lost the advantage of random access offered by the adjacency matrix. To determine whether there is an edge from vertex i to vertex j, one has to scan the adjacency list of vertex i looking for neighbor j. If vertex i has N_i neighbors, this scan could take N_i time in the worst case: j could be the last entry in the list.

14.3   GRAPH TRAVERSALS

Recall the graph that represented the "next to" relationship among the rooms of a house. How would you write a program to find a path from the kitchen to the den? You certainly would not have your program "walk" into the den directly from the kitchen, because these are not adjacent rooms. It would have to start at the kitchen and work its way to the den by following some sequence of edges and not going through any room more than once. In the worst case (for some "bad" graph), the program would have to go over the entire graph (i.e., all the vertices and all the edges) before it obtains a solution. Such a process is referred to as a *traversal* of the graph.

Conventionally, a traversal is said to *visit* the vertices of a graph. Every vertex is visited exactly once in a traversal. When a vertex is visited, some action is performed. This action could be as simple as printing the contents of the vertex, or it could be some complex action that updates the information stored at the vertex.

There are two standard graph traversals called Depth-First Search (DFS) and Breadth-First Search (BFS). The following subsections describe these traversals for undirected graphs, but they are applicable to directed graphs as well.

14.3.1   Depth-First Search for Undirected Graphs

Suppose the traversal starts at vertex *A*. It visits *A* and then has to choose a vertex to visit next. Vertex *A* has four neighbors: *B*, *D*, *E*, and *G*. Any one of these can be picked as the next vertex to visit without affecting the correctness of the traversal. In implementing the algorithm, which neighbor is picked next depends on the order in which the neighbors are stored.

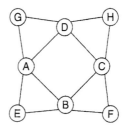

We will assume that the neighbors are stored and selected in alphabetical order. Thus, vertex *B* is picked. *Note that the other neighbors of A have not been examined yet by the traversal.* The traversal visits *B* next.

After visiting *B*, in order to decide which vertex to visit next, it first examines neighbor *A*. Since *A* has been visited, it is not considered further. The traversal keeps track of which vertices have been visited by appropriately "marking" a vertex when it is visited.

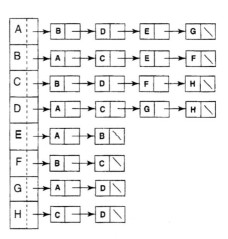

Continuing the forward motion in this manner, the traversal eventually reaches G, visiting intermediate vertices in the sequence A, B, C, D, G. What happens next? It examines the neighbors of G to select the next vertex to visit, but finds that both neighbors, A and D have already been visited. It is at a dead-end.

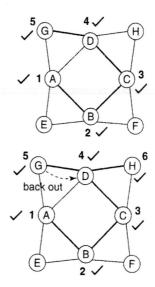

At G, the traversal starts *backing out* to try and visit unexamined neighbors of previously visited vertices. The traversal always backs out to the vertex from which it took a single step *in its forward motion* to visit the current vertex. From G, it thus backs up to D. Note that backing out does not follow an edge, it is simply a program-control jump.

At D, the traversal examines the first of the still unexamined neighbors, namely H. Since H has not been visited, the traversal moves forward and visits H.

After visiting H it examines the first neighbor of H, namely D, and finds that D has been visited. It examines the next (and last) neighbor, C, which has also been visited. The traversal is at a dead-end again, and it backs out to D only to come to a dead-end once more, since all the neighbors of D have been visited.

Backing up to C, it visits F, and then finds itself at a dead-end yet again. It backs up to C and then to B, from where it moves forward to visit E. It then backs up to B and then to A, upon which it terminates. The final sequence of visits is:
A, B, C, D, G, H, F, E.

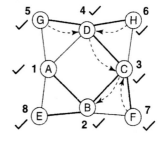

Starting at some vertex, depth-first search follows a path that goes as deep or far down the graph as possible, visiting each vertex along this path. This is the forward-motion phase. When the traversal cannot proceed any farther along the current direction, it backs out and tries to take another direction for traversal, again going forward as deep as possible before backing out. This depth-first forward motion gives the traversal its name.

Algorithm DFS(v)

visit v and mark v as visited
for each neighbor w of v do
    if (w is not visited) then
        DFS(w)
    endif
endfor

The DFS algorithm is easily expressible using recursion.

It is called with the start vertex, *v*, as argument. Every recursive call, *DFS(w)*, is a continuation of the forward motion. Every return from a recursive call indicates an implicit backing out, in which the traversal backs up from *w* to *v*.

14.3.2   Breadth-First Search for Undirected Graphs

The primary characteristic of breadth-first search, or BFS, is that it visits the vertices following a "wave-like" motion over the graph.

The traversal first visits *A*. Then it visits each neighbor of *A* in turn. These neighbors, *B*, *D*, *E*, and *G*, make up the first wave. To start the next wave, the traversal picks up *B*, the first vertex that was visited in the first wave. It examines all the neighbors of *B* and visits those neighbors that have not yet been visited. Of the neighbors *A*, *C*, *E*, and *F*, it visits *C* and *F* in that order. These vertices make up the second wave.

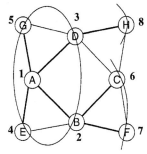

Continuing the process, the traversal picks the second vertex visited in the first wave, *D*, and examines its neighbors. Of these, only *H* has not been visited yet, so it visits *H* in the third wave. The traversal has visited vertices in the following sequence so far:

$$A, B, D, E, G, C, F, H$$

This sequence contains all the vertices of the graph. The traversal, however, continues looking for remaining unexamined vertices. It picks vertices *E* and *G* in that order from the first wave, examines their neighbors, and discovers that they have all been visited.

Next, it picks vertices from the second wave, *C* and *F* in that order, and examines all their neighbors. Again, since no unvisited neighbor is found, a new wave is not created. Finally, it picks vertex *H* from the third wave and examines its neighbors. No unvisited vertex is found, and the traversal terminates.

We saw that the DFS backing-out mechanism using recursion recalled vertices whose unexamined neighbors could provide new directions for forward motion. How does BFS recall vertices to continue where it left off? It does so by storing the waves in a queue.

Algorithm BFS(v)

visit v and mark v as visited
add v to the queue
while the queue is not empty do
       w ← vertex at the front of the queue
       delete w from the queue
       for each neighbor p of w do
           if (p is not visited) then
               visit p and mark p as visited
               add p to the queue
           endif
       endfor
endwhile

Visit A and place it in the queue

Remove A from the queue

Visit A's unvisited neighbors
B, D, E, G and add them to the queue

Remove B from the queue

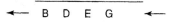

Visit B's unvisited neighbors
C, F and add them to the queue

Remove D from the queue

Visit D's unvisited neighbor
H and add it to the queue

Remove E, G, C, F, H from the queue

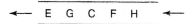

14.3.3   Traversal Driver

What would be the outcome of depth-first search on this unconnected graph, assuming that the neighbors of a vertex are stored in alphabetical order?

If *France* is picked as the start vertex, the traversal would visit *France* and *Spain* and terminate, because no other vertex can be reached from *France*. What about the other vertices? We can restart DFS from some unvisited vertex, as, for instance, *Australia*. Again the traversal would terminate immediately after visiting *Australia*. We can restart yet again from some unvisited vertex, say, *USA*. The traversal would now be able to visit all the remaining vertices, resulting in the following complete visit sequence: *France, Spain, Australia, USA, Canada, Mexico.*

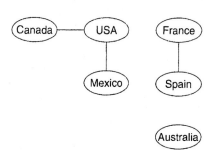

A similar restart mechanism is used for the BFS traversal of an unconnected graph.

In order to repeatedly restart the traversal process, we need a routine that would *drive* the DFS (or BFS) process and ensure that if it stalls, it is jump-started with a fresh, unvisited vertex. The following algorithm is generic for both DFS and BFS: replace 'X' with either.

Algorithm XFSdriver

for each vertex v in the graph do
  if (v is not visited) then
    XFS (v)
  endif
endfor

When the driver starts up, none of the vertices is visited. It picks the first vertex and calls the traversal algorithm with this as the start vertex. When the traversal returns, it has visited every vertex that is reachable from the start vertex. The driver, going over the remaining vertices in the for loop, skips over vertices that are now marked as visited. It picks the first unvisited vertex and uses it to restart the traversal.

For a general undirected graph, a traversal algorithm must always be accompanied by the corresponding driver, because it is not known beforehand whether the graph is connected or not. Even if the graph is connected, the driver does not introduce additionally significant running time, since the running time is principally determined by the traversal itself.

Running time.   Both depth-first search and breadth-first search scan all the vertices and edges of a graph, with the only difference being the order in which they are scanned. The adjacency linked list's representation is suitable because all the neighbors of a vertex are scanned.

The running time is computed by counting a unit of time for every vertex visit and a unit of time for every vertex inspection to see if it has been visited. We assume that the graph has n vertices and e edges.

First, each vertex is visited exactly once. The total time for the vertex visits is therefore n.

Next, how many times is a vertex inspected?

Consider vertex D in the graph shown alongside. During depth-first search, it is inspected once just before it is visited from C, and then three more times, once each when it is inspected from its other neighbors—G, H, and A—at different times during the traversal. Similarly, during the BFS traversal, it is 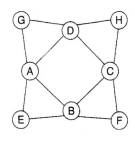 inspected once when it is visited from A, and then three more times, once each when it is inspected from C, G, and H.

In general, a vertex is inspected as many times as the degree (number of neighbors) of that vertex. The total number of vertex inspections is therefore the sum of the degrees of all the graph vertices. The sum of the vertex degrees is related to the number of edges, as follows.

In the graph above, the degree of A is 4 and that of B is also 4. The sum of the degrees of A and B is 8. However, this sum counts the shared edge (A, B) twice. Therefore, the sum of the degrees of *all* vertices counts every edge twice, giving an answer of $2 * e$.

The total time for traversal is therefore $n + 2 * e$ or $O(n + e)$. However, this running time holds only for graphs that are connected. We can extend this running time to general, unconnected graphs by applying it independently to each connected component.

If a component has p vertices and q edges, a breadth-first search or depth-first search of that component would take time $p + 2 * q$. Adding these times for all components gives the same result as before, $n + 2 * e$, for an unconnected graph with a total of n vertices and e edges.

In addition to the traversals, the driver takes up n units of time because it inspects every vertex to see if it has been visited. Thus the total running time for a traversal and its driver is $2 * n + 2 * e$, or $O(n + e)$.

14.3.4   Traversals for Directed Graphs

The depth-first and breadth-first search algorithms for directed graphs are identical to their respective undirected graph counterparts.

Assume the neighbors of a vertex are stored in alphabetical order. With $C1$ as the start vertex, depth-first search visits vertices in the following sequence:

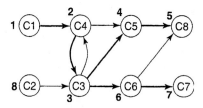

$$C1, C4, C3, C5, C8, C6, C7$$

What about vertex $C2$? It has not been visited because it is not reachable from $C1$. The traversal is thus restarted from $C2$. After visiting $C2$ it examines $C3$, and finding that $C3$ has been visited, it backs out to $C2$ and terminates.

The breadth-first search sequence on the same graph, starting with vertex $C1$, is $C1, C4, C3, C5, C6, C8, C7, C2$. Again, vertex $C2$ is visited by restarting the traversal from $C2$.

As with general undirected graphs, the traversal of a general directed graph requires a driver. Technically, a driver is not required if the graph is strongly connected. However, whether a general directed graph is strongly connected or not is not known beforehand and thus it is necessary to include the driver algorithm.

Running time.   The analysis of the running time follows the procedure used for undirected graph traversals with the driver. Let n be the number of vertices and e be number of edges in the graph.

The total time for traversal obtained in Section 14.3.3 was $2 * n + 2 * e$. The contribution of $2 * n$ due to vertex visits by the traversal and the inspection of vertices by the driver remains unchanged.

The contribution of $2 * e$ due to the inspection of vertices during the traversal was obtained by summing the degrees of all the vertices. For directed graphs, we add up only the *indegrees* of all vertices because a vertex x can be inspected from another vertex y only if there is an edge coming into x from y. Thus each edge is counted only once while adding the indegrees of all the vertices, thereby contributing a total of e to the time. Hence, the total running time for traversals is $2 * n + e$, or $O(n + e)$.

In the rest of this chapter, we will learn some "classic" graph applications. At the heart of a graph application is a model of the system under consideration using a (possibly weighted) undirected or directed graph. Once an appropriate model has been constructed, information may be extracted from it using one or more graph algorithms.

We present three graph algorithms that are used very often in practice: *topological sorting, connected components,* and *shortest paths.* The connected components and topological sorting algorithms are, in essence, extensions of the graph traversals presented earlier, while the shortest-paths algorithm introduces a new problem-solving technique called the *greedy* strategy.

14.4 TOPOLOGICAL SORT ON A DIRECTED GRAPH

Consider the course prerequisite graph again. If you need to take all those courses in order to graduate, you would have to schedule or arrange them in such a way that all the prerequisite constraints are satis-

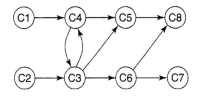

fied. For example, in your schedule, course $C1$ *must precede* course $C4$, and courses $C5$ and $C6$ must precede course $C8$.

Or consider a project that is divided into several activities, in which some activities can begin only when others on which they depend have been completed. For instance, if activity B depends on activity A, then B may be started only after A is completed. How can the activities be sequenced so that all the dependency constraints are satisfied?

Such systems of interdependent activities are modeled by directed graphs called *dependency* or *precedence* graphs. The course-prerequisite graph is a dependency graph.

14.4.1 Partial and Total Order

A dependency graph describes a *partial order* among a set of activities. In other words, not all activities are dependent on other activities.

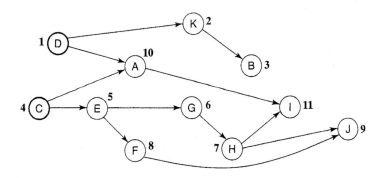

Activities C and D do not depend on each other. Neither do activities A and B. Such independent activities may be completed in any relative order.

In what order should one perform these activities? We need to arrange the activities in a sequence by assigning a sequence number to an activity that is greater than the sequence numbers of all the activities on which it depends. The numbers next to the vertices correspond to the following sequence that satisfies all dependency constraints:

$$D, K, B, C, E, G, H, F, J, A, I$$

Such a sequence is called a *total order.* Note that D precedes C in the total order (D has a lower sequence number) even though C does not depend on D. We can generate another equally valid total order in which C precedes D:

$$C, D, K, B, A, E, F, G, H, I, J.$$

14.4.2 Topological Numbering

As described above, a total order of the vertices of a dependency graph with n vertices may be constructed by assigning them integer numbers between 1 and n, referred to as *topological numbers.* The topological number (*topnum,* for short) of a vertex is its position in the total order, or *topological* order. The process of assigning topological numbers to the vertices of a dependency graph is called *topological sorting* because the topological numbers implicitly sort the vertices.

TOPOLOGICAL NUMBERS

Let *topnum(x)* be the topological number of vertex x. Then, if there is an edge from x to y in the dependency graph, *topnum(x)* < *topnum(y)* (i.e., x precedes y in the total order). The reverse is not necessarily true: *topnum(p)* < *topnum(q)* does not necessarily mean that there is an edge from p to q in the dependency graph.

In the precedence graph we just saw, there is an edge from E to F. Therefore, *topnum(E)* is 5 is less than *topnum(F)*, which is 8. On the other hand, *topnum(G)* is 6 is less than *topnum(F)*, which is 8, but there is no edge from G to F.

There is one potential problem in topological numbering: what if the dependency graph contains a cycle? In that case, there is no way to number the vertices in the cycle in order to obtain a valid total order.

To illustrate this, consider the acyclic graph of activities, and imagine that we introduce an edge from F to C to create the cycle $C \rightarrow E \rightarrow F \rightarrow C$. To number the vertices in this cycle, we start with any of the vertices C, E, or F and follow the sequence of edges, numbering vertices with increasing numbers.

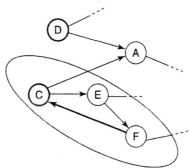

Suppose we start at *C* with the number 1. Then we can number *E* and *F* with numbers 2 and 3, respectively. However, on returning to vertex *C* to terminate the cycle, we face a dilemma. We have to assign number 4 to vertex *C* in order to satisfy the dependency $F \rightarrow C$. But this would violate the numbering rule for the edge $C \rightarrow E$, because *C* would get a number greater than *E*'s.

This dilemma *cannot* be resolved. Topological sorting is therefore restricted to directed acyclic graphs (DAGs).

Consider the task of scheduling the courses in the course graph so that all prerequisites are satisfied. Since vertices *C3* and *C4* form a cycle, we cannot use topological sorting to achieve our objective. (See the exercises for a way to overcome this problem.)

There are two variants of the topological sorting algorithm: one uses depth-first search, and the other uses breadth-first search. We will start with the more elegant alternative, the topological sorting algorithm that uses depth-first search.

14.4.3   Topological Sorting Using Depth-First Search

The intuition to the algorithm lies in the following observations. First, the algorithm needs to number vertices in such a manner that the topological number for vertex *v* is less than that of any vertex *reachable* from *v*. Second, depth-first search backs out from a vertex *v* *only when all vertices that are reachable from v have been visited*. In other words, all the vertices that are reachable from *v* are visited *before* the point when the traversal backs out of *v*. These two observations lead to the following rules of topological numbering.

TOPOLOGICAL NUMBERING RULES

- Number a vertex just before backing out from it.
- Assign topological numbers in descending order.

Numbering process.   Assume that the depth-first search begins at vertex *C* and that the neighbors of a vertex are stored in alphabetical order. In the first run starting at *C*, the traversal process goes all the way up to vertex I tracing the path $C \rightarrow A \rightarrow I$.

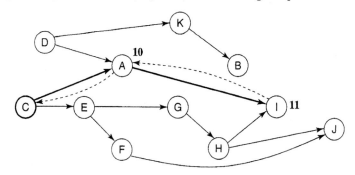

At this point, the traversal is about to back out of I. The vertex I is now numbered 11, and the next available topological number is immediately set to 10. The backing out carries the traversal to *A*, which is numbered 10, and back to *C*.

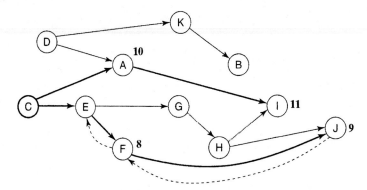

However, all the neighbors of *C* have not been examined yet, so the numbering of *C* must wait until they are. The next chain of vertices traversed is C → E → F → J. Vertices J and F are numbered when the traversal backs out of them. But vertex E cannot be numbered because not all of its neighbors have been examined yet.

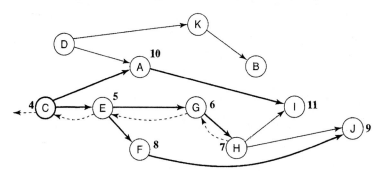

The next chain to be traversed is E → G → H. All these vertices are numbered, including E because the traversal finishes examining all the neighbors of E, and backs up to C. At this point, there are no more neighbors of C that are left to be examined, so C is numbered, and the traversal backs out of C.

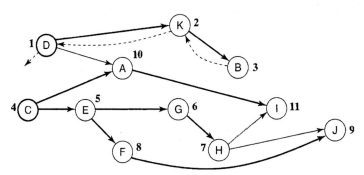

Since D, K, and B are not reachable from C, the traversal is restarted from D to complete the numbering.

Algorithm.   The topological sorting algorithm piggybacks on the depth-first search process, reaching out at the appropriate times to simply stick topological numbers on the vertices. The simple modifications made to the DFS algorithm are shown bold underlined in the driver as well as in the recursive traversal.

Algorithm DFStopsortdriver	**Algorithm DFStopsort(v, topnum)**

topnum ← n
for each vertex v in the graph do
    if (v is not visited) then
        DFStopsort(v, **topnum**)
    endif
endfor
	visit v and mark v as visited
	for each neighbor w of v do
	    if (w is not visited) then
	        DFStopsort(w, **topnum**)
	    endif
	endfor
	number v with topnum
	topnum ← topnum − 1

The first statement in **DFStopsortdriver** sets **topnum** to n, the number of vertices in the graph. The topological number is passed as a parameter to **DFStopsort**. The recursive **DFStopsort** algorithm backs out of a vertex v right at the end. This is the point where the numbering is done, and the topological number decremented.

14.4.4 Topological Sorting Using Breadth-First Search

Since BFS does not return to a vertex once it has seen it, a vertex may be numbered only after its *predecessors* have been numbered. If there is an edge $x \rightarrow y$, then x is a predecessor of y.

In the example graph we used to illustrate topological numbering, vertex A may be numbered only after its predecessors C and D have been numbered, and vertex I may be numbered only after its predecessors A and H have been numbered.

It is *safe* to number a vertex any time after *all* its predecessors have been numbered. By transitivity, this guarantees that a vertex will be numbered only after all the vertices from which it is reachable have been numbered. It is easy to see how this can be done manually, but how can an *algorithm* determine when it is "safe" to number a vertex? In other words, how can an algorithm keep track of whether all the predecessors of a vertex have been numbered? It does this by first counting the number of predecessors of each vertex, and decreasing this number every time the vertex is inspected from a predecessor.

Algorithm BFStopsort

for each vertex v in graph do
    compute pred(v),
        the predecessor count of v
endfor

for each vertex v in graph do
    if (pred(v) = 0) then
        add v to queue
    endif
endfor

topnum ← 1
while queue is not empty do
    w ← vertex at front of queue
    delete w from queue
    number w with topnum
    topnum ← topnum + 1

    for each neighbor p of w do
        pred(p) ← pred(p) – 1
        if (pred(p) = 0) then
            add p to queue
        endif
    endfor
endwhile

There is no separate driver for the BFS topsort process—the first two *for* loops may be treated as driver-like code.

The algorithm initially determines the indegree of each vertex and uses it as the *predecessor count* of that vertex. This is done in the first *for* loop.

The BFS process proper cannot be started at *any* vertex. In fact, every starting vertex must be guaranteed to not have any incoming edges. Thus, all vertices that have an indegree of zero are identified and enqueued in the second *for* loop.

In the main *while* loop, when a vertex *w* is dequeued, it is numbered. In the *for* loop inside this *while* loop, the predecessor count of each neighbor *p* of *w* is decremented by one. If the predecessor count of *p* goes to zero, this must mean that all its predecessors have been numbered and it is safe to number *p* any time between now and the termination of the algorithm. So *p* is enqueued.

For the graph we used to illustrate the DFS-based topsort, here is a possible topological sort of the vertices using the the BFStopsort algorithm:
C, D, E, A, K, F, G, B, H, I, J

14.5   CONNECTED COMPONENTS OF AN UNDIRECTED GRAPH

The application modeled by this graph may need to answer the following kinds of questions. In what land mass is *Mexico*? Are *USA* and *Canada* in the same land mass? How many different land masses are there? These kinds of questions are typical in applications modeled by unconnected graphs.

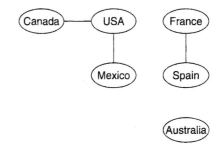

The last question, how many land masses are there, is the easiest to answer. Each land mass is a connected component in the graph. The number of land masses is therefore equal to the number of connected components. Actually, we have already seen how a traversal with its driver can be used to determine the number of connected components: simply count the number of times the driver needs to start the traversal.

To answer the other two questions, we need to mark every vertex with a component number. All vertices that belong to the same connected component are marked with the same number, and different connected components are marked with different numbers. Here is how the DFS driver and DFS traversal may be modified to carry out the marking. Modifications are shown in bold underline.

Algorithm DFSconndriver

compnum ← 0
for each vertex v in the graph do
   if (v is not visited) then
      compnum ← compnum +1
      DFSconn(v, **compnum**)
   endif
endfor

Algorithm DFSconn(v, compnum)

visit v and mark v as visited
mark v with compnum
for each neighbor w of v do
   if (w is not visited) then
      DFSconn(w, **compnum**)
   endif
endfor

Let us assume that the driver starts the traversal process first with *USA*, next with *France* and finally with *Australia*. Correspondingly, the traversal marks vertices *USA*, *Canada*, and *Mexico* with the number 1, vertices *France* and *Spain* with the number 2, and vertex *Australia* with the number 3. The BFS traversal may be similarly modified to identify the connected components of an unconnected graph. The details are left as an exercise.

14.6   SHORTEST PATHS IN A WEIGHTED DIRECTED GRAPH

A number of graph applications require the computation of the shortest path between a given pair of vertices in a directed graph with positive edge weights.

This is a weighted directed graph for a highway network. Vertices represent cities. Edges represent one-way roads. Weights on the edges are distances in miles. For the shortest route from city A to city F, you follow the route $A \rightarrow B \rightarrow E \rightarrow G \rightarrow F$ for a total distance of 12 miles. What about the shortest route from A to D? What is the distance covered along that route?

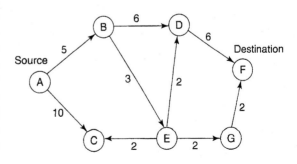

14.6.1   Dijkstra's Single-Source Algorithm

There is a well-known algorithm called *Dijkstra's shortest-paths algorithm* that computes the shortest route from the start vertex to the destination vertex. The algorithm begins at the start vertex and winds its way to the destination in a step-by-step manner, building a shortest path in increments as it progresses. Each vertex in the shortest path is treated as a "stop," and each edge is treated as a "step."

The start vertex is the first stop and the destination vertex is the last stop, with an alternating sequence of steps and stops in between. At each stop the algorithm "looks" ahead and examines the possible directions in which it could take the next step. It selects one direction to follow and takes a step in this direction to arrive at the next stop. The algorithm terminates when the destination stop is reached.

Greedy process. The interesting feature of the Dijkstra algorithm is that it somehow always manages to take the right steps. In other words, every step it takes becomes one more step in the shortest path, and it never has to retrace its steps. This property, known as the *greedy* property, is a distinctive feature of the algorithm.[1]

In order to ensure that it always takes the right steps, the algorithm does some work when it examines the possible directions for the next step. This work involves a mixture of estimation and correction guaranteed to keep the algorithm on the right track. For the highway network graph, the algorithm visits the start vertex *A* in the first step. It then 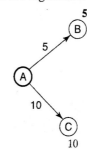 examines the neighbors of *A* (*B* and *C*) and labels them with their distance from *A*: label 5 for *B*, and label 10 for *C*.

The algorithm then uses these distance labels to pick the next vertex. *The vertex picked must bring it closer to the destination by traveling the smallest possible distance. B* is the vertex picked next, since its distance from *A* is less than that of *C*.

In the second step, the algorithm stops at vertex *B* and examines all its neighbors in order to determine new distances. The neighbors are *D* and *E*. The distance label of *D* is then set to 11, and that of *E* is set to 8. How does the algorithm arrive at these numbers?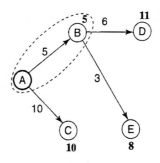

The algorithm labels a vertex with its distance from the start vertex, *A*. The distance of *D* is actually computed by summing the distance of *B* from *A*, which is already known, and the distance of *D* from *B*, which is simply the weight of the edge *B* → *D*. The same procedure is used to determine the distance of *E* from *A*. *The algorithm does not need to go all the way back to the start vertex in order to compute a new distance.*

---

1. There are other greedy algorithms in computing that function very effectively. However, there are many important problems where a greedy approach fails to work.

The circled vertices *A* and *B* are *done*. The distance labels of the done vertices are the final shortest distances from the start vertex and will not change during the rest of the algorithm. Dijkstra's algorithm terminates only when all vertices are added to the done set. As we shall see, any vertex that is not in the done set may undergo multiple corrections to its distance as the algorithm visits more vertices. The vertices *C*, *D*, and *E* are on the *fringe*. Each fringe vertex is connected to some vertex in the done set by a single edge.

To step forward once more, the algorithm picks one of the fringe vertices. Which vertex is picked next? The one with the minimum distance from *A*, namely, *E*. *E* is added to the done set; that is, the algorithm steps forward and stops at *E*. The neighbors of *E* are examined: *D*, *C*, and *G*.

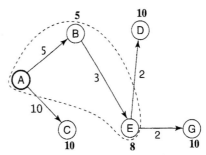

An interesting situation develops at *D*. The distance of the current shortest route from *A* to *D* ($A \rightarrow B \rightarrow D$) is 11 miles. But *E* offers a better deal: if the route were to go through E first ($A \rightarrow B \rightarrow E \rightarrow D$), the distance would be only 10 miles. In other words, the distance of the current shortest route from *A* to *D* is greater than the distance of the shortest route from *A* to *E* ($A \rightarrow B \rightarrow E$) plus the distance of the edge $E \rightarrow D$.

This situation clearly illustrates the greedy nature of the algorithm. The distance of a vertex is set to a certain value based on partial information gathered from the vertices visited thus far, which might seem greedy. However, when the algorithm has a chance to examine more vertices, it can correct a previous "mistake" by computing a new, shorter distance.

Continuing with the other neighbors of *E*, vertex *C* is examined and is seen to have a current distance of 10. An alternative route to C, via *E*, is: $A \rightarrow B \rightarrow E \rightarrow C$, whose total distance is also 10. This is a tie. Which route to pick? By convention, the old route is left intact. Last, the neighbor *G* is examined. A vertex such as *G* that is neither in the done set nor in the fringe is an *unseen* vertex. It is simply added to the fringe. Its distance is set to 10, obtained by adding the weight of the edge (E, G) to the distance from *A* to *E*.

There are two vertices in the fringe, *D* and *G*, both with the same distance. This is a tie, and may be broken by arbitrarily by picking either *D* or *G*. Independent of which vertex is chosen, the end result will still be a shortest path, but the actual path may be different. In this case, *D* is picked next. Picking *D* adds *F* to the fringe, with a distance of 16.

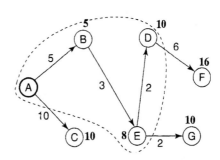

Now, of the two vertices in the fringe, F and G, G is picked because it has the shorter distance, 10. After G is picked, the distance of F is updated because going through G to F is better than getting to F via D. The new distance of F is 12.

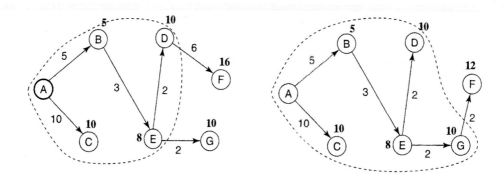

The final step picks the sole fringe vertex F. Since F has no neighbors, no new vertex is added to the fringe, and the algorithm terminates because the fringe is empty. There is only one way to reach from A to F, and that is the path $A \to B \to E \to D \to F$, of distance 12. This is guaranteed to be the shortest path from A to F.

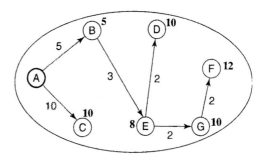

Shortest-path tree.   The final figure in the preceding section shows the *shortest-path tree* or *spanning tree* (SPT) that is *implicitly* described by the algorithm. The SPT is rooted at the start vertex, A, and contains every vertex of the graph.

The SPT provides a wealth of information. First of all, the SPT shows the shortest route from A to F, $A \to B \to E \to G \to F$, with a distance of 12 miles. Second, in the process of determining the shortest path from the start vertex (also called the *source* vertex) to the destination vertex, the algorithm ends up finding the shortest paths from the source vertex to all the other vertices in the graph. Observe that the SPT contains a unique, shortest path from the root, A, to every other vertex. Dijkstra's algorithm is therefore called the *single-source* shortest-paths algorithm.

Tabular trace of algorithm.

It is convenient to trace the sequence of steps in tabular form.

Step	Pick	D[B]	D[C]	D[D]	D[E]	D[F]	D[G]
1	A	5	10	∞	∞	∞	∞
2	B		10	11	8	∞	∞
3	E		10	10		∞	10
4	D		10			16	10
5	C					16	10
6	G					12	
7	F						

The second column lists vertices that are picked to be added to the *done* set. The other columns show the current shortest distances from start vertex A.

Vertices that are neither in the *fringe* nor in the *done* set have their distance set to infinity. The recording of distances in a vertex column stops when it is done.

Storage and retrieval of shortest paths.   What if the shortest route from *A* to *B* needs to be determined, instead of *A* to *F*? Can the algorithm be stopped after step 1? The answer is yes, it can. However, such a premature termination of the algorithm may be expensive in the long run. What if different users use the algorithm to determine the shortest route from *A* to different destination vertices, with several repeated requests? It is much more efficient to execute the algorithm once to compute all the shortest routes from *A* and store the output in a file. Then, whenever a new user needs to know the shortest path from A to any vertex, the answer can be retrieved from the stored output without recomputation.

Algorithm.   The graph algorithmic terms *vertex, edge, distance,* and *shortest path* carry different meanings depending on the physical system being modeled by the graph. Dijkstra's algorithm is used to find the *minimum cost* path, in general, where *cost* refers to the entity being minimized. In a highway or airline network, the cost could be the distance or the dollar amount. In a communication network, the cost could be the data transfer time.

Dijkstra's Shortest-Paths Algorithm

1. Place all the vertices in the **unseen** set by initializing the distance of each vertex to infinity.
2. Transfer the source vertex v_s from the **unseen** set to the **done** set and set its distance to zero.

3. For each neighbor w of v_s, transfer w from **unseen** set to the **fringe** by setting $d(w)$ = $wt(v_s, w)$.

4. While the **fringe** set is not empty do the following:

   (a) Select a minimum distance vertex, v_m, from the **fringe,** and transfer it to the **done** set.

   (b) For each neighbor w of v_m, do the following:

   - If w is in the **done** set, do nothing.
   - If w is **unseen,** then set $d(w) = d(v_m) + wt(v_m, w)$.
   - If w is in the **fringe,** then possibly update its distance by setting $d(w) = \min(d(w), d(v_m) + wt(v_m, w))$.

The input to Dijkstra's shortest-path algorithm is a directed or undirected graph with positive edge weights.

The *question* posed of the algorithm is: what is the shortest path from vertex v_s to vertex v_t? The start vertex v_s is referred to as the *source* vertex, and the end vertex v_t is referred to as the *target,* or *destination,* vertex.

The *answer* to this question has two components: (a) a path (sequence of edges) that needs to be taken from v_s to v_t in order to obtain the shortest distance, and (b) the distance along this path.

Each vertex v in the graph is labeled with a number, $d(v)$, which is the shortest distance from v_s to v. The algorithm starts by marking all the vertices with distance infinity, which implicitly places all the vertices in the unseen set. In the second step, it transfers the source vertex from the unseen set to the done set. The distance of the source vertex is set to 0. Subsequently, in the third step, the distance of each neighbor of the source vertex is set to the weight of the edge from the source to the neighbor. The weight of the edge $v \rightarrow w$ is denoted by $wt(v, w)$. Each neighbor is also transferred to the fringe.

The algorithm now steps into a loop, and in every iteration of the loop, a vertex v_m with minimum distance label is transferred from the fringe set to the done set. If there are several vertices with distance label equal to minimum distance, one vertex is picked arbitrarily.

Upon transferring vertex v_m, its neighbors are examined for distance computation. Each neighbor, w, could be in one of the three vertex groups. If it is already in the done set, it is left untouched. If it is in the unseen set, its distance, currently infinity, is replaced by the sum of the distance of v and the weight of the edge $v \rightarrow w$. If w is in the fringe set, it is possible that a new path to w via v has a shorter distance than the current distance of w. This is determined by comparing $d(w)$ against $d(v) + wt(v, w)$. If $d(w)$ is greater, it is set to $d(v) + wt(v, w)$. The algorithm terminates when there are no more vertices in the fringe set. The distance label of each vertex in the done set is its final shortest distance from the source vertex.

Running time. Let us assume that the graph consists of n vertices and e edges. Where does the algorithm do all its work? In steps 4a and 4b: every time it selects the vertex with minimum distance from the fringe, and every time it computes the distance for a vertex.

The distance computation is a single-step operation and may therefore be assigned unit cost. How many times is the distance computation performed? Every time a vertex is added to the done set, each of its neighbors is examined. If the neighbor is in the unseen set or in the fringe, a distance computation is performed. If the neighbor is already in the done set, a distance computation is not performed.

It is not possible to arrive at an exact figure for the number of neighbors that are not in the done set. However, note that if there is an edge $x \rightarrow y$, vertex y is examined for an update when x is added to the done set. After a possible update, this edge is never seen again because x will never be in the fringe. (The distance of y can be updated due to some other edge $z \rightarrow y$, but that is accounted for separately.) We can generalize this as follows: *every edge in the graph is used in at most one distance computation*. Therefore, the total number of distance computations is at most e.

The selection of the minimum-distance vertex from the fringe costs more than a unit. We know that the time taken to compute the minimum-valued item of a set of k items is k. In the algorithm, the items are the vertices in the fringe, and the minimum value is the minimum distance value among these vertices. The number of vertices in the fringe keeps changing during the course of the algorithm; it is not possible to arrive at an exact figure for the time required for selection. We can, however, make a conservative estimate by assuming that *all* vertices that are not in the done set are in the fringe. Certainly, the number of vertices in the fringe cannot exceed this.

Using this estimate, we can determine the total time for selection by finding how many times a selection is made. But that is easy. Every vertex added to the done set undergoes a selection, except for the source vertex. Thus selection is done $n - 1$ times. Starting with at most $n - 1$ vertices in the fringe, the number of vertices is reduced by one after every selection. Thus the total time for selection never exceeds:

$$(n - 1) + (n - 2) + \cdots + 2 + 1 = n(n - 1)/2$$

The total time for the algorithm is therefore $n(n - 1)/2 + e$, or $O(n^2 + e)$. Since the number of edges in a simple graph cannot exceed n^2 (can you see why?), the total time is $O(n^2)$.

Improvement by using updatable heap.   The running time can be reduced by maintaining the fringe vertices in a priority queue structure implemented using an updatable heap. In Section 11.8 we learned that an updatable heap allows the priority of an existing item in the heap to be updated in $O(\log n)$ time. We can store the fringe vertices in an updatable heap, using the current distance of the fringe as the priority. That is, the smaller the distance, the greater the priority, so that the fringe vertex with the smallest distance of all is at the top of the heap.

However, if the updatable heap is a *max* heap (the default situation), we need to somehow effectively switch the result of comparing distances. If the heap accepts priorities separately as integers with the items to be stored, then we can send in the *negative* of the distance as the priority. On the other hand, if the heap's client is responsible for comparing distances, we can simply switch the result of a distance comparison.

We now need to recompute the time it takes to do selections and distance computations. Let us do selections first. As before, we know that we need to make n selections. We will again use the same conservative estimate that *all* vertices not in the done set are in the fringe. Then we do $n - 1$ selections. Each selection is equivalent to a heap deletion, which we know takes $O(\log m)$ time in the worst case on a heap of size m. The first selection is on a heap of size $n - 2$, the second on a heap of size $n - 2$, and so on, until the last selection, which is on a heap of size 1. The total worst-case time for all selections then works out to:

$$\log(n - 1) + \log(n - 2) + \cdots + \log 1$$

(Each of these terms is really a big O order, but we have omitted the big O part for simplicity. We are working toward a big O result, and will bring the big O back at the end.)

This simplifies to $\log(n - 1)!$. From Section 11.6.1, we know that Stirling's formula makes $\log(n - 1)!$ equivalent to $O(n \log n)$. ($O((n - 1) \log(n - 1)!)$ is really $O(n \log n!)$.)

That is, the total worst-case time for all minimum-distance fringe vertex selections is $O(n \log n)$.

Let us now turn to distance computations. Again, we will start with the previous argument that every edge results in at most one distance computation. A distance "computation" can simply be a check of the old distance of a vertex against a new distance, and if the old distance is not less than the new one, then nothing further is done. If the old distance is greater than the new one, however, it is replaced by the new one. This will result in a priority-update operation being performed on the updatable heap for the updated distance.

For the worst-case time, we assume that every distance computation leads to a distance update. That is, there will be a total of e updates in all, which will result in e update operations on the heap. When we analyzed selections, we saw that the heaps are of sizes $n - 1, n - 2, ..., 1$. The e updates are distributed over these heaps, but we do not know how many exact updates are made in each of these heaps. Again, we will go for the most pessimistic estimate (for worst case) and assume that e updates are made on *every* one of these heaps. Clearly, this is an overcount, but we will use it with full knowledge.

Since the time to update priority in a heap of size m is $O(\log m)$, the total time for all e updates is (again dropping the big O temporarily):

$$e \log(n - 1) + e \log(n - 2) + \cdots + e \log 1$$

which results in $O(e \log n)$ after applying Stirling's formula.

Summing the times for selections and distance updates, we get a total worst-case time of $O(n \log n) + O(e \log n)$, or $O((n + e) \log n)$ for Dijkstra's algorithm. Note that this time is bounded by $O(n \log n)$ at one extreme for graphs that have 0 edges, and by $O(n^2 \log n)$ at the other extreme for graphs that have $O(n^2)$ edges. In actuality, most graphs have edges of the order of $O(n \log n)$, so the time then becomes $O(n \log^2 n)$, which is much better than the earlier time (fringe not stored in heap) of $O(n^2)$.

14.7 SUMMARY

- Directed and undirected graphs can be used to model pair-wise relationships among entities.
- Every undirected graph is a special kind of directed graph.
- The adjacency matrix representation of a graph is useful when the graph is dense or the application makes very frequent random queries on edges, such as "is edge (x, y) in the graph?"
- The adjacency linked-lists representation is useful when the graph is relatively sparse (fewer edges), and/or the application needs to access all or most neighbors of vertices.
- Both depth-first and breadth-first traversals are linear-time graph-traversal algorithms, with a running time of $O(n + e)$.
- Topological sorting is applicable only to directed acyclic graphs, or DAGs. It is a linear time $((O(n + e))$ algorithm that is typically used on precedence graphs.
- Dijkstra's shortest-paths algorithm is an instance of a greedy algorithm.
- The worst-case running time of Dijkstra's algorithm is $O(n^2)$ if the fringe is a simple unordered list. This time can be improved to $(O(n + e)\log n)$ if the fringe is implemented using a priority queue (updatable heap).

14.8 EXERCISES

E14.1. (a) List all the cycles in this graph. (b) List all the possible paths from *Bed*1 to *Kitchen*. How many of these paths go through *all* the vertices of the graph?

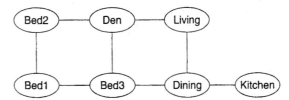

E14.2. Show the sequence in which the vertices of this graph are visited by the DFS algorithm, starting at D. Assume that the neighbors of the vertices are stored in *reverse* alphabetical order of their labels. Repeat for BFS.

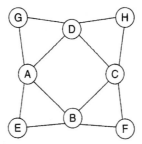

E14.3. Here is a precedence DAG.

Trace the breadth-first topological sorting algorithm, **BFStopsort** of Section 14.4.4, on this graph. Starting with the initial state of the queue, show how its contents change after every iteration of the `while` loop of the algorithm. Also indicate the vertex that is numbered in each iteration.

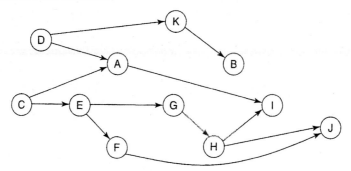

E14.4. This graph has $n + 2$ vertices and $2n$ edges. For every vertex labeled i, $1 \le i \le n$, there is an edge from S to i and an edge from i to T.

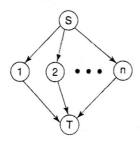

How many different depth-first search sequences are possible if the start vertex is S? How many different breadth-first search sequences are possible if the start vertex is S?

E14.5. The course-prerequisite graph we saw in Section 14.1.2 cannot be topologically sorted because of the presence of a cycle between vertices $C3$ and $C4$. We can overcome this problem by transforming the graph into a DAG by merging vertices $C3$ and $C4$ into a single vertex, $C34$.

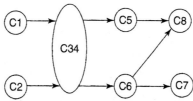

This graph can be topologically sorted. The position of $C34$ in the topological order indicates that courses $C3$ and $C4$ would have to be taken simultaneously at that time.

Trace the depth-first topological sorting algorithm of Section 14.4.3 on this graph.

E14.6. Algorithms **DFSconndriver** and **DFSconn** in Section 14.5 showed how the DFS driver and traversal could be modified to find the connected components of an undirected graph. How would you modify the BFS driver and traversal algorithms **XFSdriver** and **BFS** to do the same?

E14.7. In the shortest-paths example of Section 14.6, how would the shortest paths change if the tie in step 3 had been broken in favor of route $A \rightarrow B \rightarrow E \rightarrow C$? Also assume that the tie in step 4 is broken by picking vertex G over D. Draw the new shortest-path tree.

E14.8. In this weighted directed graph, each vertex represents a city, and each edge represents a toll road from one city to another.

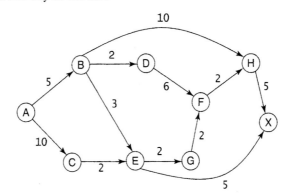

Use Dijkstra's shortest-paths algorithm to determine the minimum toll route from city A to city X. What is the total toll on this route? Show the shortest-path tree.

E14.9. In how many different ways can the vertices of the graph of Exercise 14.4 be topologically sorted?

E14.10. In an undirected *complete* graph, there is an edge between every pair of vertices. What is the running time of the depth-first search and breadth-first search algorithms for an undirected complete graph with n vertices? Your answer should only be in terms of n.

E14.11. Write an algorithm to determine whether there is a path from vertex v to vertex w in a directed graph. Your algorithm should print *yes* if there is a path, and *no* otherwise. What is the worst-case complexity of your algorithm for a graph with n vertices and e edges? Assume unit cost for every vertex inspection. (Hint: Use depth-first search and another vertex mark called "in-dfs". Set the "in-dfs" mark of a vertex to true when a depth-first search is initiated from that vertex, and set it to false as soon as the depth-first search backs out of that vertex. Use this mark to determine whether there is a path from v to w.)

E14.12. Topological sort works only on DAGs. What if we do not know whether a graph is a DAG, but use topological sort on it? The topological sorting algorithm must then terminate with an appropriate error message as soon as it detects a cycle in the graph. How would you enhance the depth-first-search topological sorting algorithm of Section 14.4.3 to detect cycles? Give the pseudocode code for your algorithm. (Hint: A small extension of the algorithm in Exercise 14.11.)

E14.13. Rewrite the DFS algorithm of Section 14.3.1 *without using recursion*. You will, instead, use a stack to simulate the recursion by pushing a vertex on the stack when it is visited and popping it off the stack when the algorithm backs out of that vertex.

E14.14. The adjacency matrix representation is handicapped by a slow all-neighbors scan process. What would be the time complexity of iterating over all the neighbors of a given vertex using an adjacency matrix?

E14.15. This exercise compares the space requirement of the adjacency matrix representation with the adjacency linked-lists representation.

Suppose a weighted undirected graph has n vertices and e edges. The weights are all integers. Assume that the space needed to store an integer is the same as the space required to store a reference, both equal to one unit. *What is the minimum value of e for which the adjacency matrix representation would require less space than the adjacency linked lists representation?* Ignore the space required to store vertex labels.

E14.16. For each of the following operations on an undirected graph, determine the running time, assuming that (a) it is represented as an adjacency matrix, and (b) it is represented as adjacency linked lists. Assume that there are n vertices (numbered 1 through n) and e edges in the graph.

(a) Determine whether the edge (i,j) exists in the graph.

(b) Add edge (i,j) to the graph. Assume that no duplicates exist.

(c) Add a vertex numbered $n + 1$ to the graph. Assume that no duplicates exist.

(d) Assuming that a vertex $n + 1$ has been added as above, add edge $(i, n + 1)$ for every vertex $i, 1 \leq i \leq n$.

(e) Delete edge (i,j) from the graph.

(f) Count the number of edges in the graph.

CHAPTER 15

Graphs II: Implementation

Designing and implementing a graph class and using such a class to implement various graph algorithms can be a fairly complex task. As always, the task becomes particularly challenging if the classes need to be designed in such a way that one can extend them to build other classes without much extra effort, reusing as much code as possible from existing classes.

Reuse of code is possible only when one can clearly understand the connection between what is being reused and what is being added on as an extension. Consequently, this chapter places considerable emphasis on understanding the connections between the various properties of a graph, as well between various graph algorithms, both at the design level and at the Java implementation level.

Learning Objectives

- Design the interfaces for the undirected and directed graph classes, keeping in mind that an undirected graph is a special kind of directed graph.
- Implement the depth-first algorithm, using the Visitor design pattern we encountered in traversing binary trees.
- Implement the topological sorting algorithm based on the depth-first search implementation.
- Implement the connected components algorithm using the depth-first search implementation.
- Implement Dijkstra's shortest-paths algorithm, carefully choosing the data structures, especially the fringe set of vertices, and paying special attention to code reuse.
- Implement undirected and directed graph classes, using a helper vertex class.

15.1   A DIRECTED GRAPH CLASS: DirGraph

All the graphs discussed in Chapter 14 (the unweighted and weighted variants of the undirected and directed graphs) arise from a common root: the directed graph. We will start by getting introduced to a directed graph class, DirGraph, followed by an undirected graph class, UndirGraph. These, along with other graph classes, are bundled in a package called structures.graph.

Figure 15.1 shows the public interface of a directed graph class named DirGraph.

Note that the vertex capacity is only an initial estimate that is used to allocate storage for the graph vertices. If more vertices are added than the estimated capacity,

Class structures.graph.DirGraph<T>

Constructors

> **DirGraph( )**
> Creates an empty directed graph with an initial default vertex capacity.
> **DirGraph(int vertexCap)**
> Creates an empty directed graph with the specified initial vertex capacity.

Methods

$O(1)$ **int numberOfVertices( )**
Returns the number of vertices in this graph.
$O(n)$ **int addVertex(T vertex)**
Adds the specified vertex to this graph only if the vertex does not already exist. Returns the number internally assigned to this vertex.
$O(n)$ **boolean containsVertex(T vertex)**
Returns true if this graph contains the specified vertex, false otherwise.
$O(n)$ **int vertexNumberOf(T vertex)**
Returns the number assigned to the specified vertex; -1 if vertex does not exist.
$O(1)$ **T vertexInfoOf(int vertexNumber)**
Returns the vertex whose number is specified.
$O(e)$ **boolean containsEdge(int vertexNumber, Neighbor nbr)**
Returns true if this graph contains an edge from the vertex with the specified number to the specified neighbor.
$O(e)$ **void addEdge(int vertexNumber, Neighbor nbr)**
Adds to this graph an edge from the vertex with the specified number to the specified neighbor only if the edge does not already exist.
$O(1)$ **Neighbor firstNeighbor(int vertexNumber)**
Returns the first neighbor of the specified vertex, null if there are no neighbors.
$O(1)$ **Neighbor nextNeighbor(int vertexNumber)**
Returns the next neighbor of the specified vertex, relative to a preceding call to **first** or **next;** null if there are no more neighbors.
$O(1)$ **void clear( )**
Empties out the graph (i.e., removes all vertices and edges).

FIGURE 15.1: A Generic Directed Graph Class. Only the public interface is shown. The type of vertex objects is parametrized with T. Duplicate vertices and edges are not permitted. Running times assume the adjacency linked-list representation for a graph with n vertices and e edges.

additional storage will be automatically allocated without the client having to take any special action.

15.1.1   Vertex Numbering

The client of the graph class can store any kind of application-specific information in a vertex—hence the generic definition with vertex type T as parameter.

For instance, take the example of a directed graph representing a Web site that we went over in Section 14.1.2. We can implement this graph, starting with adding all vertices, as shown alongside. Here the vertex objects are just strings that represent URLs.

```
DirGraph<String> webGraph =
        new DirGraph<String>();
webGraph.addVertex("P1");
webGraph.addVertex("P2");
webGraph.addVertex("P3");
webGraph.addVertex("P4");
webGraph.addVertex("P5");
```

In a variation of this application, it may be required to store the vertices as `java.net.URL` objects:

```
import java.net.URL;
...
DirGraph<URL> webGraph = new DirGraph<URL>();
webGraph.addVertex(new URL("http://www.dsoi.org/P1"));
...
```

Or, say a graph is used to model a network map of towns. Then the vertex object might encapsulate the name of the city, its population, its geographical coordinates, and the like.

No matter what the vertex object is, each vertex must be uniquely identifiable, since the `DirGraph` class does not permit duplicate vertices. It is up to the client to define an appropriate `equals` method in its vertex object class.

Internally, the graph class sets up a mapping from vertices to integer numbers. If there are n vertices in the graph, the vertices would be numbered from 0 to $n - 1$. The numbers are assigned arbitrarily (i.e., in no particular order). It is often easier for applications to deal with vertex numbers for the most part. The number of a vertex can be obtained through the `vertexNumberOf` method. Conversely, a vertex number may be used to retrieve the stored vertex information via the method `vertexInfoOf`.

In the Web site example above, say vertex numbers 0 to 4 have been assigned respectively to vertices $P1$ to $P5$.

```
System.out.println(webGraph.vertexNumberOf("P2"));
```

would print 1, and, conversely:

```
System.out.println(webGraph.vertexInfoOf(1));
```

would print "P2". If URL objects were used instead, we could write this:

```
...
URL p2url = new URL("http://www.dsoi.org/P2");
...
int p2num = webGraph.vertexNumberOf(p2url);
System.out.println(webGraph.vertexInfoOf(p2num));
```

The vertexInfoOf method would return a URL object in this case, and printing it out would invoke the getString method of the URL class.

15.1.2   Neighbor Class

The specification of method addEdge seems contrived. It would be more natural to specify a number for the second vertex, as, for instance:

```
void addEdge(int vertexNumber, int vertexNumber)
```

This would be quite alright, *except* if we want to store edge weights. In that case, we would have to specify yet another parameter, say:

```
void addEdge(int vertexNumber, int vertexNumber, int weight)
```

The graph class would thus have to provide both these methods, one with an edge weight parameter (for weighted graphs) and one without (for unweighted graphs). This is a bad idea, because by having these two methods coexist, the client may supply edge weights for some edges and not for others, thus violating the requirement that either all the edges must carry edge weights or none at all. These two methods are really *mutually exclusive,* but there is no clean way to enforce mutual exclusivity once both methods are provided.

As a workaround, we introduce a Neighbor class as part of the structures.graph package. It basically acts as a wrapper for a vertex number. However, its *real benefit is in enabling clients to extend it when weights on the edges are needed,* as we will see when we implement Dijkstra's shortest-paths algorithm on a weighted directed graph in Section 15.6.

Class File 15.1. *Neighbor.java*

```
package structures.graph;

public class Neighbor {

  public int vertexNumber;

  public Neighbor(int vertexNum) {
    vertexNumber = vertexNum;
  }
```

```
public boolean equals(Object other) {
    if ((other != null) && (other instance Neighbor)) {
        Neighbor another = (Neighbor)other;
        return vertexNumber == another.vertexNumber;
    }
    return false;
}
}
```

To complete the Web graph implementation, after having added vertices *P*1 through *P*5, we would add the edges as follows:

```
int p1num = webGraph.vertexNumberOf("P1");
... // numbers for other vertices
int p5num = webGraph.vertexNumberOf("P5");
webGraph.addEdge(p1num, new Neighbor(p2num));
webGraph.addEdge(p1num, new Neighbor(p4num));
... // add other edges
```

The addVertex method returns the number assigned to that vertex. We could have saved the vertex numbers when we added the graph, and used them when adding the edges. But this would be needlessly replicating storage in the client for information that is already stored in the graph. While the code given above looks tedious, it is typically more effective when actually reading a graph from file and implementing it, as you will see in the next section.

Running times of methods.   Both containsVertex and vertexNumberOf involve a sequential search on the vertices. The same goes for addVertex, because the method first checks whether the vertex to be added already exists. A sequential search on a list of *n* vertices takes $O(n)$ time.

Similarly, containsEdge and addEdge involve a sequential search of the neighbors of the specified first vertex. In the worst case, all the edges of the graph could be emanating from this vertex, leading to an $O(e)$ time measure. (For a simple graph, a vertex can have one edge to each of the other vertices, so the $O(e)$ is bounded by $O(n^2)$.)

15.1.3 Exercising the DirGraph Class

Reading a graph.   The following code will create a directed graph by reading from a file called "graphfile":

```
01 Scanner sc = new Scanner(new File("graphfile"));
02 int numVerts = sc.nextInt();
03 DirGraph<String> G =
04              new DirGraph<String>(numVerts);
05
06 int i;
07 String v1, v2;
08
09 for (i=0; i < numVerts; i++) {
10      v1 = sc.next();
11      G.addVertex(v1);
12 }
13
14 int numEdges = sc.nextInt());
15 for (i=0; i < numEdges; i++) {
16      v1 = sc.next();
17      v2 = sc.next();
18      Neighbor nbr =
19              new Neighbor(G.vertexNumberOf(v2));
20      G.addEdge(G.vertexNumberOf(v1), nbr);
21 }
```

```
6
A
B
C
D
E
F
6
A B
A E
B C
C E
C D
E F
```

Computing vertex indegree.   Recall that the indegree of a vertex in a directed graph is the number of edges coming into it. Directed graph applications often need to compute the indegree of each vertex. This is not hard to do. First, initialize all vertex indegrees to zero. Then, simply go over the neighbors of all the vertices, and if y is a neighbor of x, increment the indegree of y by 1. Following is the code for the graph G we created above:

```
int numVerts = G.numberOfVertices();
int[] indegree = new int[numVerts];
int i;

for (i=0; i < numVerts; i++) {
    indegree[i] = 0;
}

for (i=0; i < numVerts; i++) {
    Neighbor nbr = G.firstNeighbor(i);
    while (nbr != null) {
        indegree[nbr.vertexNumber]++;
        nbr = G.nextNeighbor(i);
    }
}
```

```
// print it all out
System.out.println("Vertex " + "Indegree");
for (i=0; i < numVerts; i++) {
    System.out.println(G.vertexInfoOf(i) + " " + indegree[i]);
}
```

The fact that vertices are assigned numbers enables us to use the vertex numbers as array indices to great advantage.

15.2   AN UNDIRECTED GRAPH CLASS: UndirGraph

The undirected graph class is derived from the directed graph class based on the observation that the undirected graph *is a special type* of directed graph.

A general directed graph models an asymmetric relationship. Now consider a special type of directed graph in which for every edge $x \rightarrow y$, there is a twin edge $y \rightarrow x$. The graph shown here (which we have already seen in another context) is an example of a special type of directed graph in which, for a given pair of vertices, either there is no edge between them, or there are two edges in opposite directions.

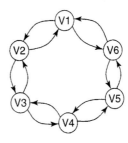

But this special type of directed graph models a symmetric relationship, *as would an equivalent undirected graph*. In an undirected graph, the edge (x, y) means that x is related to y, and y is related to x. We can think of the undirected edge (x, y) as equivalent to *a pair of directed edges: $x \rightarrow y$ and $y \rightarrow x$*. Just replace every pair of directed edges in the example with a single undirected edge, and you have an equivalent undirected graph!

While every undirected graph is a special type of directed graph, the converse is not true. Not every directed graph is a special type of undirected graph.

Our undirected graph class is called UndirGraph. In order to build UndirGraph by extending it from DirGraph, we must first very precisely state the way in which the undirected graph needs to specialize the directed graph. There is no specialization required for the vertices, because the vertices of an undirected graph behave just like the vertices of a directed graph. Specialization is required only for the edges. Table 15.1 gives us the equivalence between the edge-related functions of UndirGraph and DirGraph.

Figure 15.2 shows the public interface of our undirected graph class.

Imagine that the graph we used as an example in Section 15.1.3 was undirected instead of directed. Then, using the same input file, one could build an undirected graph by using the same code as presented there, save a single change at lines 03--04:

UndirGraph<String>   G = new   UndirGraph<String> (numVerts)

The interpretation of whether the graph is directed or undirected depends on only one thing: which addEdge method—the DirGraph one or the overriding UndirGraph

TABLE 15.1: Equivalence of UndirGraph and DirGraph edge functions. The set of methods of the UndirGraph class is identical to the DirGraph class set. addEdge is the only method that is specialized for the UndirGraph class, overriding its DirGraph counterpart.

UndirGraph	DirGraph
addEdge(x, y)	addEdge(x, y) + addEdge(y, x)
containsEdge(x, y)	containsEdge(x, y)
firstNeighbor(x)	firstNeighbor(x)
nextNeighbor(x)	nextNeighbor(x)

Class structures.graph.UndirGraph<T> extends structures.graph.DirGraph<T>

Constructors

UndirGraph( )
    Creates an empty undirected graph with an initial default vertex capacity.
UndirGraph(int vertexCap)
    Creates an empty directed graph with the specified initial vertex capacity.

Methods

$O(e)$ **void addEdge(int vertexNumber, Neighbor nbr)**
    Adds to this graph an undirected edge between the specified vertex and the specified neighbor, only if the edge does not already exist.

FIGURE 15.2: A Generic Undirected Graph Class. Only the public interface is shown. Nonoverridden inherited methods are not shown. The type of vertex objects is parametrized with T. Duplicate vertices and edges are not permitted. Running times assume the adjacency linked-list representation for a graph with n vertices and e edges.

one—is invoked when the graph is constructed. This, in turn, depends on whether the runtime type of the object is DirGraph or UndirGraph.

Here is a code segment that shows how to implement the rooms-of-a-house undirected graph shown in Section 14.1.1:

```
UndirGraph<String> roomsInHouse = new UndirGraph<String>();

// add rooms
roomsInHouse.addVertex("Living");
...

// add adjacency between rooms
roomsInHouse.addEdge(roomsInHouse.vertexNumberOf("Living"),
        new Neighbor(roomsInHouse.vertexNumberOf("Dining")));
roomsInHouse.addEdge(roomsInHouse.vertexNumberOf("Living"),
        new Neighbor(roomsInHouse.vertexNumberOf("Den")));
...
```

15.3 A DEPTH-FIRST SEARCH CLASS: DFS

At the heart of this class is an implementation of the **DFS** algorithm of Section 14.3.1. There are, however, several other considerations that will drive our DFS class design.

15.3.1 Design and Interface

- The class must do *only* what it is supposed to do, nothing more, nothing less. For instance, depth-first search *knows* about the graph, so it is solely responsible for traversing the vertices in depth-first order. However, it *does not know* about the application that will use it, so it cannot define what is to be done when a vertex is visited—this is left to the application.

- The class must be *flexible*—it must allow users as many "hooks" as possible where they can get control to carry out application-specific actions. As an example, we know that depth-first search marks a vertex as seen when encountered in the forward motion phase. But "seeing" a vertex can be decoupled from visiting it without affecting the correctness of depth-first search.

  Specifically, a vertex can be visited either when it is first seen (*preorder*) or when the search is just about to back out of it (*postorder*). This is entirely analogous to the preorder and postorder traversals of a tree. In sum, the DFS class will provide a preorder hook and a postorder hook where the application can hang its vertex visits.

- The class must be easily *extensible*. Consequently, it has to be designed as a careful collection of small interacting modules rather than a single monolithic method, so as to enable maximum reuse of code by other classes.

Class apps.graph.DFS<T>

Constructors

DFS( )
Creates a new DFS object.

Methods

$O(1)$ **init(DirGraph<T> G, Visitor<T> V)**
Initializes this DFS with the specified directed graph on which a depth-first search is to be conducted, and the specified visitor that is to be called whenever a vertex needs to be visited.

$O(n+e)$ **void preAction(int startVertex)**
Conducts a depth-first search starting at the specified vertex, visiting vertices in preorder. Only the vertices reachable from the specified vertex are visited.

$O(n+e)$ **void postAction(int startVertex)**
Conducts a depth-first search starting at the specified vertex, visiting vertices in postorder. Only the vertices reachable from the specified vertex are visited.

FIGURE 15.3: A Generic Depth-First Search Class. Only the public interface is shown. Visitor is a support class that is defined in the apps.graph package and may be extended by an application. The type of vertex objects is parametrized with T. Running times assume the adjacency linked-list representation for a graph with n vertices and e edges. It is also assumed that calls to the Visitor class methods take $O(1)$ time.

Our DFS class design will try to follow the above points as closely as possible. Figure 15.3 shows the public interface of this DFS class, implemented in the `apps.graph` package.

15.3.2 Visitor Class

An important element in the DFS class interface is the `Visitor` class. Recall from the preceding discussion of DFS class design that visiting a vertex is the responsibility of the application. On the other hand, it is the DFS class that is responsible for actually triggering a visit, since only the DFS class knows *when* it is at a certain vertex.

Therefore, the graph package defines a `Visitor` class with a prescribed set of methods, through which the DFS class can communicate with the application that uses it. Importantly, an application may extend `Visitor` to implement a specialized version of vertex visits.

The role played by `Visitor` here is analogous to that played by `structures.tree.Visitor` used in binary search tree traversals, discussed in Section 10.4.

Class File 15.2. *Visitor.java*

```
package apps.graph;

import structures.graph.DirGraph;

public class Visitor<T> {

  protected boolean[] visited;
  protected DirGraph<T> G;
  protected int numverts;
  protected int unvisitedIndex;

  public void init(DirGraph<T> G) {
    this.G = G;
    numverts = G.numberOfVertices();
    visited = new boolean[numverts];
    for (int i=0; i < numverts; i++) {
        visited[i] = false;
    }
    unvisitedIndex = 0;
  }
  public boolean isVisited(int vertex) { return visited[vertex]; }
  public boolean hasMoreToVisit() {
    for (; unvisitedIndex < numverts; unvisitedIndex++) {
        if (!visited[unvisitedIndex]) {
            break;
        }
    }
    return unvisitedIndex < numverts;
  }
  public int nextToBeVisited() {
    return hasMoreToVisit() ? unvisitedIndex : -1;
  }
```

```
public void visit(int vertex) { visited[vertex] = true; }
public void action(int vertex) {
  System.out.println(" " + G.vertexInfoOf(vertex));
}
}
```

You can see that the Visitor class takes over much of the bookkeeping that goes with the traversal process. The field visited keeps track of which vertices have been visited. Field G is the "target" graph on which the traversal is performed, set when its init method is called. The field numVerts is the number of vertices in the target graph G, and is separately stored to avoid the overhead of repeatedly calling the G.numberOfVertices method.

Note that the DFS class does not include a driver: the methods preAction and postAction only visit the vertices that are reachable from a specified vertex. The task of driving DFS is in fact delegated to the Visitor class, via the methods hasMoreToVisit and nextToBeVisited, and the field unvisitedIndex assists these methods by keeping track of the *lowest-numbered vertex* that has not yet been visited.

Here is an example of how the Visitor and DFS classes could be used together to implement *preorder* traversal of a graph such as the one used in the example of Section 15.1.3.

```
Visitor<String> visitor = new Visitor<String>();
visitor.init(G);
DFS<String> dfs = new DFS<String>(G, visitor);
while (visitor.hasMoreToVisit()) {
  dfs.preAction(visitor.nextToBeVisited());
}
```

The DFS traversal methods preAction and postAction call the Visitor class methods visit and action. Both traversal methods call visit as soon as the traversal is started at a vertex—note that the visit method simply marks the vertex as visited. However, action is called by the preAction method when the traversal is *started* on a vertex, while action is called by the postAction method when the traversal is *about to back out* of a vertex after looking at (and recursively traversing from) all its neighbors.

The following code ties all these pieces together.

15.3.3   DFS Implementation

Class File 15.3. *DFS.java*

```
package apps.graph;

import structures.graph.DirGraph;
import structures.graph.Neighbor;

public class DFS<T> {
  protected DirGraph<T> G;
  protected Visitor<T> V;
```

```
public void init(DirGraph<T> G, Visitor<T> V) {
   this.G = G;
   this.V = V;
}
public void preAction(int startVertex) {
   int numverts = G.numberOfVertices();
   // start up preorder recursive traversal process
   preTraverse(startVertex);
}
protected void preTraverse(int vertex) {
   V.visit(vertex);
   V.action(vertex);

   Neighbor nbr = G.firstNeighbor(vertex);
   while (nbr != null) {
       if (!V.isVisited(nbr.vertexNumber)) {
           preTraverse(nbr.vertexNumber);
       }
       nbr = G.nextNeighbor(vertex);
   }
}
public void postAction(int startVertex) {
   int numverts = G.numberOfVertices();
   // start up recursive postorder traversal process
   postTraverse(startVertex);
}
protected void postTraverse(int vertex) {
   V.visit(vertex);

   Neighbor nbr = G.firstNeighbor(vertex);
   while (nbr != null) {
       if (!V.isVisited(nbr.vertexNumber)) {
           postTraverse(nbr.vertexNumber);
       }
       nbr = G.nextNeighbor(vertex);
   }
   V.action(vertex);
}
}
```

Since we have not defined a constructor, the compiler supplies a no-arg constructor that does nothing. There are two fields: the graph on which the traversal is to be conducted, G, and the application-specific visitor, V. These components are passed in to this class via the init method; initialization involves setting the graph and visitor components to the supplied arguments.

Methods preAction and postAction complement each other: the former is invoked to conduct a "preorder" traversal, and the latter, to conduct a "postorder" traversal. These methods are organized in similar fashion.

Consider, for instance, method postAction. It calls on its helper, the nonpublic method postTraverse, which actually does all the work of traversal. This method, in turn, implements the old recursive DFS process that we are so very familiar with at this point. The most interesting aspect is, of course, the separation of *visit* from *action: visit* is always done in the forward motion, but *action*, in this case, is performed just before backing out.

Another look at our friendly Neighbor. Since we create edges by adding neighbors to a vertex, we can enumerate the neighbors as in the while loop of method postTraverse, and extract the vertex number component to make our recursive calls. The visitor V is totally responsible for making a meaningful connection between DFS and any client that uses DFS.

15.4 A TOPOLOGICAL SORT CLASS: DFSTopsort

We would like to design a class for topological sorting that essentially implements the algorithms **DFStopsortdriver** and **DFStopsort** of Section 14.4.3 by using the DFS class.

15.4.1 TopVisitor: Extending the Visitor Class

The topological sorting implementation can use the visitor pattern, with a modification. Since topological sorting needs to assign topsort numbers to vertices, it must define an action method that does exactly this instead of printing the vertex information. It does so by defining a TopVisitor class that extends Visitor.

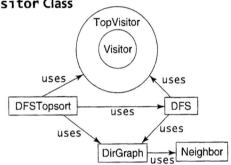

DFSTopsort defines, and uses, a TopVisitor instance. Its primary supporter, however, is the DFS class. DFS uses Visitor, but since TopVisitor extends Visitor, it actually uses TopVisitor when helping DFSTopsort. DFS, of course, uses DirGraph, and so does DFSTopsort. Finally, DirGraph uses Neighbor.

When all the vertices have been assigned topsort numbers, an array of these numbers must be returned for use in the application that calls for topological sorting. This array will be defined by the DFSTopsort class, and managed by the TopVisitor class. We look at the implementation, starting with the TopVisitor class.

Class File 15.4. *TopVisitor.java*

```
package apps.graph; import structures.graph.DirGraph;

public class TopVisitor<T> extends Visitor<T> {
  protected int[] topSequence; protected int topnum;

  public TopVisitor(int[] topSequence) {
    super(); this.topSequence = topSequence;
  }
  public void init(DirGraph<T> G) {
    super.init(G); topnum = numverts-1;
  }
  public void action(int vertex) {
    topSequence[topnum--] = vertex;
  }
}
```

The most notable feature of this class is its action method that overrides the Visitor class default implementation. It assigns a topological sequence number to the vertex on which the action is being performed. The action is performed when called by the DFS class.

The constructor and the init method will be used by the DFSTopsort class. The init method overrides the Visitor class's init. It performs the basic graph initialization by calling the superclass's (Visitor) init method, followed by setting the initial topological sequence number to $n - 1$, where n is the number of vertices in the graph; topological numbers will be assigned from $n - 1$ to 0.

Let us complete the picture by looking at the DFSTopsort class in its entirety.

15.4.2   DFSTopsort Implementation

Class File 15.5. *DSFTopsort.java*

```java
package apps.graph;

import structures.graph.DirGraph;

public class DFSTopsort<T> {

    protected DirGraph<T> G;
    protected int[] topSequence;
    protected TopVisitor<T> V;

    public void init(DirGraph<T> G) {
        this.G = G;
        topSequence = new int[G.numberOfVertices()];
        V = new TopVisitor(topSequence);
        V.init(G);
    }
    public int[] sort() {
        DFS<T> DFStraverse = new DFS<T>();
        DFStraverse.init(G, V);
        while (V.hasMoreToVisit()) {
            int vertex = V.nextToBeVisited();
            DFStraverse.postAction(vertex);
        }
        return topSequence;
    }
}
```

Initializing a DFSTopsort object involves creating an array for the topological sequence, as well creating a TopVisitor object and initializing it. The sort method creates and drives the postAction method of a DFS object. In these two methods, (init and sort), all the pieces of the topsort puzzle are fitted together to make a working whole.

15.5 A CONNECTED COMPONENTS CLASS: DFSConncomp

In a manner analogous to the design of the DFSTopsort class, we will build a class, DFSConncomp, that will use depth-first search (the DFS class) to find the connected components of an undirected graph. And, as in constructing the **DFSconndriver** and **DFSconn** algorithms of Section 14.5, our focus is primarily going to be on how we make those small modifications to the basic depth-first search process to achieve our goal.

Our task is made even easier at this point given that we have already built a topological sort class and can now use it as a reference model.

15.5.1 ConnVisitor: Extending the Visitor Class

Class File 15.6. *ConnVisitor.java*

```
package apps.graph; import structures.graph.UndirGraph;

public class ConnVisitor<T> extends Visitor<T> {
  protected int[] componentNumbers; protected int compNum;

  public ConnVisitor() { super(); }
  public void init(UndirGraph<T> G) { super.init(G); }
  public void initComp(int[] componentNumbers) {
    this.componentNumbers = componentNumbers;
    compNum = 0;
  }
  public void updateComp() { compNum++; }
  public void action(int vertex) {
    componentNumbers[vertex] = compNum;
  }
}
```

To make things somewhat more interesting (and to make a point), the creation of a ConnVisitor has been decoupled from the array in which it will store component numbers. The array is now supplied to the initComp method instead. This is a marginally better design than that of TopVisitor because it allows an application to create one component numbers array and reuse it for various connected components (on various graphs).

Second, an additional method called updateComp has been introduced. Since it is the driver that updates the component number every time it calls DFS to reenter the graph, updateComp is a hook for the driver to accomplish this update.

If you think ConnVisitor resembles TopVisitor, wait until you see DFSConncomp and its resemblance to DFSTopsort. In fact, to underscore this point, we will give a recipe to *syntactically* convert DFSTopsort to DFSConncomp.

15.5.2 DFSConncomp Implementation

Let's start cooking. Recipe for building this class from DFSTopsort:

1. Replace all occurrences of DFSTopsort with DFSConncomp, all occurrences of DirGraph with UndirGraph, all occurrences of topSequence with componentNumbers, and all occurrences of TopVisitor with ConnVisitor.
2. Remove the parameter from the call to the ConnVisitor constructor in init.
3. Add the line:

   ```
   V.initComp(componentNumbers);
   ```

   just before the end of init.
4. Write findComponents for sort.
5. Add the line:

   ```
   V.updateComp();
   ```

   at the end of findComponents.
   (There is no need to replace postAction with preAction.)

Class File 15.7. *DFSConncomp.java*

```
package apps.graph;
import structures.graph.UndirGraph;

public class DFSConncomp<T> {
  protected UndirGraph<T> G;
  protected int[] componentNumbers;
  protected ConnVisitor<T> V;

  public void init(UndirGraph<T> G) {
    this.G = G;
    componentNumbers =
      new int[G.numberOfVertices()];
    V = new ConnVisitor<T>();
    V.init(G);
    V.initComp(componentNumbers);
  }
  public int[] findComponents() {
    DFS<T> DFStraverse = new DFS<T>();
    DFStraverse.init(G, V);
    while (V.hasMoreToVisit()) {
      int vertex = V.nextToBeVisited();
      DFStraverse.postAction(vertex);
      V.updateComp();
    }
    return componentNumbers;
  }
}
```

15.6   A SHORTEST-PATHS CLASS: ShortestPaths

It would be useful to design a shortest-paths class that enabled clients to observe the gradual progress of the algorithm in order to get a better feel for how it works. For instance, an application could produce a sample run of the algorithm, as shown in Figure 15.4, on running shortest paths on the following sample graph that we saw in our discussion of Section 14.6.

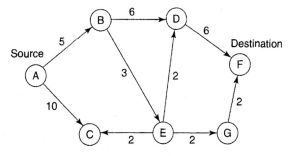

Once the run is completed, one can ask for the result for any destination vertex, because all shortest paths have been computed from the source vertex. The computation can be restarted on a different source vertex for the same graph, or on a different graph altogether.

```
Enter the graph file name ==> sptgr.dat
Enter the start vertex ==> A

DONE:(A,A,0)

FRINGE:(B,A,5) (C,A,10)

Choose one of the following actions:
      runall  runsome  result  restart  quit
           Enter action => runsome
           How many steps? => 3

DONE:(A,A,0) (B,A,5) (C,A,10) (E,B,8)

FRINGE:(D,E,10) (G,E,10)

Choose one of the following actions:
      runall  runsome  result  restart  quit
           Enter action => runall

Choose one of the following actions:
      runall  runsome  result  restart  quit
           Enter action => result
           Enter the destination vertex ==> D

Shortest path: A ---> B ---> E ---> D
Distance      : 10

Choose one of the following actions:
      runall  runsome  result  restart  quit
           Enter action => result
           Enter the destination vertex ==> F

Shortest path: A ---> B ---> E ---> G ---> F
Distance      : 12

Choose one of the following actions:
      runall  runsome  result  restart  quit
           Enter action => quit
```

FIGURE 15.4: Sample Run of Shortest Paths. The **done** and **fringe** vertices are printed as triples: (vertex, previous, distance). The status at the end of Step 1 is printed at the outset. After running three more steps, the status is printed again. This would correspond to the end of Step 4 of the algorithm sequence illustrated on this graph in Section 14.6, except that here the tie between C and D is broken in favor of C.

15.6.1 WeightedNeighbor: Extending the Neighbor Class

When we introduced the Neighbor class in Section 15.1.2, we said that one of the reasons for defining a class instead of simply using the vertex number was to enable applications to add weights to graph edges by appropriately extending this class. The time has come to put this into practice, since the shortest-paths algorithm works with weighted graphs. We extend `Neighbor` to a class called `WeightedNeighbor`, with the following definition that provides for integer weights to be assigned to the edges:

Class File 15.8. *WeightedNeighbor.java*

```
package apps.graph; import structures.graph.Neighbor;

public class WeightedNeighbor extends Neighbor {
  public int weight;
  public WeightedNeighbor(int vertexNum, int weight) {
    super(vertexNum); this.weight = weight;
  }
}
```

Two `WeightedNeighbor` objects are equal if their vertex number components are equal; hence the inherited `equals` method from the superclass `Neighbor` is reused as is.

15.6.2   ShortestPaths Implementation

Let us first figure out what data structures we need to implement the shortest-paths algorithm of Section 14.6.1 on any weighted directed graph.

Data structures.   We need to store the distance of each vertex and be able to update it when required. Since the update requires random access to the vertices, we will use an array for the distances. The unseen set is implicitly maintained: all the vertices that have a distance of infinity are in this set.

What about the fringe? We need to store the fringe vertices separately, because in every step we have to find the minimum distance vertex in the fringe. To keep things simple, we use an unordered list to maintain the fringe, with each entry in the list being a vertex number. However, an efficient implementation must use an updatable heap (Section 11.8), which supports updates in $(O \log n)$ time.

We need two more data structures to help us trace the shortest path from source to target. Recall that every vertex in the fringe is connected to some vertex in the shortest-path tree. When a vertex is finally moved out of the fringe to the done set, this connection becomes a link in the shortest-path tree. Thus every vertex has a *previous* vertex in the shortest-path tree; in fact, these *previous* vertices implicitly describe the shortest-path tree. We will use an array to keep track of the *previous* vertices.

Starting with the target vertex, we can follow the chain of previous vertices to trace the shortest path *backwards* from the target to the source—all the way up to the root of the shortest-path tree. In order to print the shortest path *from* the source vertex *to* the target vertex, we will use a stack to store the vertices during the backward trace, and then return them in the correct order.

ShortestPaths class.

Class File 15.9. *ShortestPaths.java*

```
package apps.graph;

import structures.graph.DirGraph;
import structures.linear.List;
import structures.linear.Stack;
import java.io.PrintWriter;

public class ShortestPaths<T> {
  DirGraph<T> G;
  int numverts;
  int sourceNum;
  int destNum;
  List<WeightedNeighbor> fringe;
  int Distance[]; int Previous[]; boolean Done[];

  public void init(DirGraph<T> G) { ... }
  public void from(T sourceVertex) { ... }
  public void runAll() { runSome(numverts-1); }
  public void runSome(int howManySteps) { ... }
  public int distTo(T destVertex) {
    destNum = G.vertexNumberOf(destVertex);
    if (destNum == -1) { return -1; }
    return Distance[destNum];
  }
  public Stack<T> pathTo(T destVertex) { ... }
  public void printStatus(PrintWriter pw) { ... }
  int fringeDeleteMin() { ... }
}
```

Let us do a quick check of all the fields: the graph, G, on which we need to run the shortest-paths algorithm; the data structures we discussed: `fringe`, `Distance`, `Previous`, and `Done`; the source and destination vertices `sourceNum` and `destNum`.

Methods. The method `init` sets G to the specified directed graph, and `numVerts` to the number of vertices in G. Apart from this, it creates `fringe` as well as the other arrays.

```
public void init(DirGraph<T> G) {
  this.G = G;
  numverts = G.numberOfVertices();

  // create all data structures
  fringe = new List<WeightedNeighbor>();
  Distance = new int[numverts];
  Previous = new int[numverts];
  Done = new boolean[numverts];
}
```

The method `from` is invoked by specifying the source vertex, and sets things into motion by executing Steps 1, 2, and 3 of the shortest-paths algorithm of Section 14.6.1.

```
public void from(T sourceVertex) {
  sourceNum = G.vertexNumberOf(sourceVertex);

  // initialize all data structures
  for (int i=0; i < numverts; i++) {
    Done[i] = false;
    Distance[i] = Integer.MAX_VALUE;
    Previous[i] = i;
  }
  fringe.clear();

  // do steps 1,2,3
  Done[sourceNum] = true;
  Distance[sourceNum] = 0;

  WeightedNeighbor nbr =
        (WeightedNeighbor)G.firstNeighbor(sourceNum);
  while (nbr != null) {
    int w = nbr.vertexNumber;
    Distance[w] = nbr.weight;
    Previous[w] = sourceNum;
    fringe.add(nbr);
    nbr = (WeightedNeighbor)G.nextNeighbor(sourceNum);
  }
}
```

The method `runSome` executes a specified number of steps of the algorithm. It stops either when these many steps have been executed or when the fringe is empty. In the latter case, the algorithm is done and all shortest paths have been computed—review step 4 of the shortest-paths algorithm.

```
public void runSome(int howManySteps) {
  int step=0;
  while (step < howManySteps) {
    if (fringe.isEmpty()) break;

    int minVertex = fringeDeleteMin();
    Done[minVertex] = true;
    WeightedNeighbor nbr =
          (WeightedNeighbor)G.firstNeighbor(minVertex);
    while (nbr != null) {
      int w = nbr.vertexNumber;
      if (Distance[w] == Integer.MAX_VALUE) {
          Distance[w] = Distance[minVertex] + nbr.weight;
          Previous[w] = minVertex;
          fringe.append(nbr);
      } else if (Distance[w] >
              (Distance[minVertex] + nbr.weight)) {
```

```
            Distance[w] = Distance[minVertex] + nbr.weight;
            Previous[w] = minVertex;
        }
        nbr = (WeightedNeighbor)G.nextNeighbor(minVertex);
      }
      step++;
    }
}
```

The nonpublic method `fringeDeleteMin` helps `runSome` by determining, and deleting, the minimum-distance vertex in the fringe.

```
int fringeDeleteMin() {
    int minWeight = Integer.MAX_VALUE;
    int minVertex = -1;
    WeightedNeighbor minnbr=null;

    WeightedNeighbor nbr = (WeightedNeighbor)fringe.first();
    while (nbr != null) {
        int w = nbr.vertexNumber;
        if (Distance[w] < minWeight) {
            minWeight = Distance[w]; minVertex = w; minnbr = nbr;
        }
        nbr = (WeightedNeighbor)fringe.next();
    }
    fringe.remove(minnbr);
    return minVertex;
}
```

Finally, the methods that give the result, `distTo` and `pathTo`, respectively return the shortest distance and shortest path to a specified vertex.

```
public int distTo(T destVertex) {
    destNum = G.vertexNumberOf(destVertex);
    if (destNum == -1) {
        return -1;
    }
    return Distance[destNum];
}
```

As described when we were selecting the data structures required, the method `pathTo` follows the chain of previous vertices starting from the specified destination. Every vertex encountered in this chain is stacked until the source vertex is reached. This stack is returned, with the source vertex at the top and the destination at the bottom.

```
public Stack<T> pathTo(T destVertex) {
  destNum = G.vertexNumberOf(destVertex);

  if (Distance[destNum] == Integer.MAX_VALUE) { return null; }

  Stack<T> pathStack = new Stack<T>();
  pathStack.push(destVertex);
  int prev = destNum;
  do {
      prev = Previous[prev];
      pathStack.push(G.vertexInfoOf(prev));
  } while (prev != sourceNum);
  return pathStack;
}
```

That about wraps it up for this class. The status of the done and fringe sets can be printed by invoking `printStatus`, as illustrated in the sample run of Figure 15.4.

```
public void printStatus(PrintWriter pw) {
  pw.println();
  pw.print("DONE:\t");
  for (int i=0; i < numverts; i++) {
      if (Done[i]) {
          pw.print("(" + G.vertexInfoOf(i) + "," +
                   G.vertexInfoOf(Previous[i]) + "," +
                   Distance[i] + ") ");
      }
  }

  pw.print("\n\nFRINGE:\t");
  for (int i=0; i < numverts; i++) {
      if (!Done[i] && (Distance[i] != Integer.MAX_VALUE)) {
          pw.print("(" + G.vertexInfoOf(i) + "," +
                   G.vertexInfoOf(Previous[i]) + "," +
                   Distance[i] + ") ");
      }
  }
  pw.println();
}
```

15.7 GRAPH IMPLEMENTATION

In this section, we will first implement the DirGraph class, and then we will use it to implement the UndirGraph class. Last, we make some observations regarding the implementation of weighted graphs.

15.7.1 DirGraph Implementation

A directed graph class may be implemented using either adjacency tables or adjacency linked-lists. We will discuss an adjacency linked-lists implementation.

The graph is an array list of adjacency lists, adjlists, which is declared protected so that it can be inherited by UndirGraph, which is subclassed from DirGraph. Each entry in this array list is a Vertex object constructed out of the vertex information supplied by the client.

Vertex class.   Let us first look at the Vertex class that is separately defined in the structures.graph package.

Class File 15.10. *Vertex.java*

```
package structures.graph;

import structures.linear.List;

public class Vertex<T> {

  protected T info;    // vertex object supplied by client
  protected List<Neighbor> neighbors;

  protected Vertex(T vertexInfo) {
    info = vertexInfo;
    neighbors = new List<Neighbor>();
  }
  public boolean equals(Object other) {
    if ((other != null) && (other instanceof Vertex)) {
        Vertex another = (Vertex)other;
        return (info.equals(another.info));
    }
    return false;
  }
}
```

There are two fields: an info part specified by the client when adding a vertex, and a neighbors part, which is a linked list of neighbors of that vertex. Observe that we have used the List class (Section 4.7), which provides a simple interface to the LinkedList class (Section 4.6), rather than using the LinkedList class itself. In addition to its simplicity, the List class provides the enumeration methods first and next, which are very useful in graph applications that need to iterate over the neighbors of a vertex.

The constructor creates an (initially empty) linked list to store the neighbors. The Vertex class simply wraps the information of a vertex along with its neighbors, and provides the nominal equals method: two Vertex objects are equal if their information components are equals.

The class itself is `public`, but all members (except `equals`) are `protected`, so clients cannot directly manipulate this class. The `DirGraph` class uses it internally.

Class File 15.11. *DirGraph.java*

```java
package structures.graph;

import java.util.ArrayList;

public class DirGraph<T> {

  protected ArrayList<Vertex<T>> adjlists;    // array of Vertex objects

  public DirGraph() { adjlists = new ArrayList<Vertex<T>>(); }

  public DirGraph(int vertexCap) {
    adjlists = new ArrayList<Vertex<T>>(vertexCap);
  }
  public int numberOfVertices() {
    return adjlists.size();
  }
  public int addVertex(T vertex) {
    if (!containsVertex(vertex)) { adjlists.add(new Vertex(vertex)); }
    return adjLists.size()-1;
  }
  public boolean containsVertex(T vertex) {
    return adjlists.indexOf(new Vertex(vertex)) != -1;
  }
  public int vertexNumberOf(T vertex) {
    return adjlists.indexOf(new Vertex(vertex));
  }
  public T vertexInfoOf(int vertexNumber) {
    Vertex<T> v = adjlists.get(vertexNumber); return v.info;
  }
  public boolean containsEdge(int vertexNumber, Neighbor nbr) {
    Vertex<T> v = adjlists.get(vertexNumber);
    return v.neighbors.contains(nbr);
  }
  public void addEdge(int vertexNumber, Neighbor nbr) {
    Vertex<T> fromVertex = adjlists.get(vertexNumber);
    if (!fromVertex.neighbors.contains(nbr)) {
        fromVertex.neighbors.add(nbr);
    }
  }
  public Neighbor firstNeighbor(int vertexNumber) {
    Vertex<T> v = adjlists.get(vertexNumber);
    return v.neighbors.first();
  }
  public Neighbor nextNeighbor(int vertexNumber) {
    Vertex<T> v = adjlists.get(vertexNumber);
    return v.neighbors.next();
  }
  public void clear() { adjlists.clear(); }
}
```

Vertex-Specific methods. The method `containsVertex` is used by `addVertex` because a vertex is added only if it does not already exist in the graph. Observe that addVertex implicitly assigns a number to a new vertex by adding it at the end of adjlists—the number of a vertex is its position in this array list.

The client adds a vertex to graph G by invoking addVertex and sending in the vertex information via an object that matches the template type T. The graph G takes this vertex object and calls on the Vertex constructor. A new Vertex object is constructed, with the info component set to this client vertex object, and the neighbors component set to a new empty linked list. This Vertex object is then added to the adjlists array list.

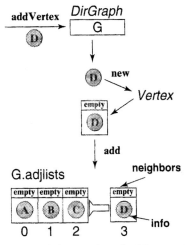

In this example, the information stored at a vertex is simply a string that uniquely identifies it, so the template type T is instantiated with type String.

The pair of complementary methods vertexNumberof and vertexInfoOf provide the necessarily translation between the client's means of identifying a vertex based on the information it stores, and the implementation's identification of a vertex by means of the number assigned to it.

Edge-specific methods.   The methods containsEdge and addEdge both conduct a sequential search of the neighbors list of a specified vertex. These methods require that both endpoints of the edge in question be already present in the graph.

The first argument of containsEdge, vertexNumber, is used as an index into the adjlists array list to access the corresponding Vertex element. This element's list of neighbors is then sequentially searched, by invoking the List method contains, to determine whether the second argument to containsEdge is in fact a neighbor of the first.

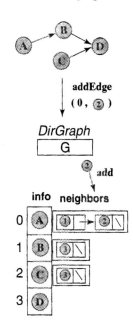

Not surprisingly, addEdge is almost identical to containsEdge. Again, the List method contains is invoked, this time to ensure that the second argument is not already a neighbor of the vertex specified in the first argument.

The client adds an edge to graph G by invoking addEdge and

sending in a vertex number (0), and a neighbor object (for vertex 2). G adds this neighbor object by invoking add on the `neighbors` component of `G.adjlists[0]`, which ends up adding the neighbor instance to the end of the neighbors linked list.

The methods `firstNeighbor` and `nextNeighbor` provide a means to enumerate all the neighbors of a specified vertex.

Running times.   Verify that the running times of the `DirGraph` methods presented here are as listed in the graph class interface of Figure 15.1.

There is room for improvement in how `adjlists` itself is implemented. With an array list implementation, the complexity of `vertexNumberOf` is $O(n)$. Since the vertices are not stored in any particular order, a sequential search is needed.

One possible improvement is to use binary search instead of sequential search, and this would, of course, require that we maintain the vertex labels in sorted order. This suggests that we use the `OrderedList` class instead of the `ArrayList` for `adjlists`. We will explore this option in one of the exercises, with particular emphasis on understanding the tradeoffs we would need to make if we choose this option.

15.7.2   `UndirGraph` Class Implementation

In Section 15.2 we observed that the undirected graph class is a special type of directed graph. Since every undirected edge is really two directed edges, we need to make sure, while adding an undirected edge (x, y) to the graph, that y is added as a neighbor of x, and x is added as a neighbor of y.

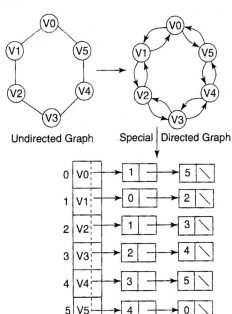

Each edge appears in two adjacency lists. For example, the edge between vertices $V1$ and $V2$ is represented once as the edge $1 \rightarrow 2$ and then again as the edge $2 \rightarrow 1$.

Recall, from Table 15.1, that `addEdge` is the only specialized method with respect to the `DirGraph` class. Thus, building the `UndirGraph` class as a subclass of `DirGraph` is simple, and leads to significant reuse of code.

Class File 15.12.   *UndirGraph.java*

```
package structures.graph;

public class UndirGraph<T> extends DirGraph<T> {
```

```
public UndirGraph() { super(); }
public UndirGraph(int vertexCap) { super(vertexCap); }
public void addEdge(int vertexNumber, Neighbor nbr) {
  super.addEdge(vertexNumber, nbr);
  super.addEdge(nbr.vertexNumber, new Neighbor(vertexNumber));
}
}
```

The field `adjlists` of `DirGraph` is inherited by `UndirGraph`. The constructors invoke their respective `DirGraph` counterparts.

Since all the methods of `DirGraph` are public, they are also inherited by `UndirGraph`. Of these, `addEdge` is overridden by the specialized `UndirGraph` version.

The running times of the `UndirGraph` methods are the same as those of their `DirGraph` counterparts.

15.7.3 Implementation of Weighted Graphs

The example graphs we have seen so far in this section did not carry weights on the edges. Each adjacency list entry contained a `Neighbor` object. The responsibility of adding a weight to every edge lies completely with the client of the graph class.

Each adjacency linked list entry consists of a `WeightedNeighbor` object and a reference to the next `WeightedNeighbor` in the list. `WeightedNeighbor` is a subclass of `Neighbor` obtained by adding on a weight to the core vertex number.

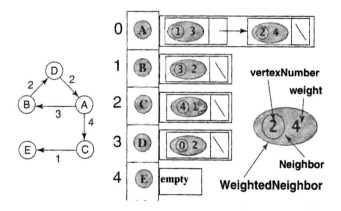

Since the edge functions accept a `Neighbor` argument, the only way for the application to introduce edge weights is to derive a subclass from `Neighbor` that incorporates edge weights. This gives the application complete freedom to define weights as it pleases without the graph implementation having to change at all.

The shortest-paths application, for instance, defined a subclass of `Neighbor` called `WeightedNeighbor` in which the weights were simply integers.

15.8   SUMMARY

- The class `DirGraph<T>` is a vertex-generic directed graph implementation, where the parameter type `T` is intended to be instantiated with the actual type of vertex objects.

- Since an undirected graph is a special kind of directed graph, the class `Undir-Graph<T>`, which implements a vertex-generic undirected graph, is a subclass of `DirGraph<T>`.

- Depth-first traversal is implemented as a generic class DFS<T>, with two targets: a directed graph `DirGraph<T>` (which by type extension includes undirected graphs), and a vertex-generic visitor class `Visitor<T>`.

- The class DFS<T> is designed in such a way as to be easily extensible to other DFS-based algorithms. Thus, it defines a general `preAction` method that sets up a framework to allow external action to be taken when a vertex is just visited, and a general `postAction` method that sets up a framework to allow external action to be taken when the DFS recursion is just about to back out of a vertex.

- The `Visitor<T>` class implements a client-specific version of vertex visits and does much of the work of keeping track of the progress of of depth-first traversal.

- The `DFSTopsort<T>` class is a vertex-generic class that implements DFS-based topological sort, and it also needs two targets: a directed graph, `DirGraph<T>`, and a visitor specialized for topological sort, `TopVisitor<T>`. It uses the DFS<T> class's `postAction` method framework.

- The class `TopVisitor<T>` is a subclass of `Visitor<T>`, specialized to take action at the point just before DFS recursion backs out of a vertex.

- The class `DFSConncomp<T>` finds the connected components of an undirected graph and needs two targets: an undirected graph, `UndirGraph<T>`, and a visitor specialized for connected components, `ConnVisitor<T>`. It uses the DFS<T> class's `postAction` method framework, but it could alternatively use the `preAction` framework without affecting the result.

- The class `ConnVisitor<T>` is a subclass of `Visitor<T>`, specialized to take action between traversals of connected graph components.

- The key decision in implementing Dijkstra's shortest-paths algorithm is what data structure to use to store the fringe vertices.

- The `Vertex` class encapsulates the actual vertex object sent in by the client (used to instantiate the type parameter of the generic `DirGraph<T>` and the generic `UndirGraph<T>`), and a list of `Neighbors` of this vertex.

- The `WeightedNeighbor` class is a subclass of `Neighbor` that stores integer weights on edges.

- The `ShortestPath` class uses a `DirGraph` with `WeightedNeighbor` instances to store the neighbors of each vertex.

- The `ShortestPaths` class may use the `Heap` class instead of the `List` to maintain the fringe vertices in a priority queue and thereby improve the efficiency of the shortest-path algorithm.

15.9 PROGRAMMING PROBLEMS

P15.1. Show how you would implement the ethane molecule graph of Section 14.1.3, using the UndirGraph<T> and WeightedNeighbor classes.

P15.2. Write a method, countEdges:

```
public <T> int countEdges(DirGraph<T> G)
```

that would return the number of edges in the specified directed graph.

P15.3. Write a method, countWeights

```
public <T> int countWeights(DirGraph<T> G)
```

that would return the sum of the weights of the edges of the specified weighted directed graph.

P15.4. Write a method, reverseEdges

```
public <T> void reverseEdges(DirGraph<T> G)
```

that would reverse the edges of the specified directed graph. Specifically, every directed edge (x, y) is replaced by the directed edge (y, x). What is the worst-case running time of your method on a graph with n vertices and e edges?

P15.5. Given two undirected graphs with the same vertex set, we would like to find the set of edges that are common to both graphs. Write a method:

```
public <T> ArrayList<String>
commonEdges(UndirGraph<T> G1, UndirGraph<T> G2)
```

that would return an array list containing edges that are in both G1 and G2. The result should code the edge (v1,v2) as a string "(v1,v2)", and must not contain any duplicate edges. What is the worst-case running time of your method on a graph with n vertices and e edges?

P15.6. Implement a class, BFS, that would perform a breadth-first traversal of a directed graph, following the algorithm **BFS** of Section 14.3.2. As in the DFS class of Section 15.3, your BFS class must provide a no-arg constructor and also a method init. Since there is no "backing out" in breadth-first search, there is no separation of preaction and postaction methods, as in class DFS. Instead, write a method called traverse that would perform the traversal. Use the same Visitor class as used in class DFS. Your BFS class would have to use the structure.linear.Queue class.

P15.7. Implement a class, BFSTopsort, that would perform a breadth-first topological sort of a directed graph, following the algorithm **BFSTopsort** of Section 14.4.4. You will have to do the following:
  (a) Define a class called BFSTopVisitor that is analogous to the TopVisitor class used by DFSTopsort. Use the init and action methods of TopVisitor as general guidelines; however, you will have to write methods init and action to reflect *increasing* numbers for vertices.
  (b) Provide a no-arg constructor in BFSTopsort, and methods init and sort.

P15.8. As outlined in Section 15.5, complete the implementation of class DFSConncomp.

P15.9. In Exercise E.14.6, you determined how breadth-first traversal could be modified to find the connected components of an undirected graph. Implement a class BFSConncomp that implements your algorithm from that exercise, and style it in the manner of the DFSConncomp class above. Can the class ConnVisitor be used here without any changes?

P15.10. In Exercise E.14.11, we explored how depth-first search can be used to determine whether there is a path from vertex *v* to vertex *w*. Implement your solution to that exercise by writing, in the DFS class of Section 15.3, a method called pathExists:

```
public boolean pathExists(int v, int w)
```

This method should accept two vertex numbers, *v* and *w*, and return true if there is a path from *v* to *w*, false otherwise. (Hint: write a supporting private recursive method along the lines of postRecurse that would carry out the business of marking a vertex as "in-dfs", etc. Note: your method(s) *must not* perform any "action" at the vertices, such as printing the vertex information.)

P15.11. Modify the ShortestPaths class of Section 14.6 by using an OrderedList for the fringe instead of List. Apart from storing the vertices in the fringe, along with each vertex you also need to store its current distances from the source vertex. In order to do this, define a class called FringeVertex that implements the interface Comparable. The OrderedList object used in ShortestPaths should store FringeVertex objects.

P15.12. At the end of Section 15.7.1, when we discussed the time complexities of the various DirGraph methods, we suggested that the running time of vertexNumberOf may be improved by using an OrderedList to maintain the adjacency lists, adjlists, instead of using a Vector.

    (a) Reimplement the DirGraph class using an OrderedList for adjlists. Which methods need to be reimplemented?

    (b) How does the change affect the vertex numbers?

    (c) Which methods have a better running time than before? Which methods have a worse running time than before?

    (d) Would you consider adding additional methods to the DirGraph class to offer the client better efficiency for certain operations? If so, what methods would you add?

    (e) Under what circumstances would it be preferable to use an ordered list instead of a linked list for the adjacency lists?

P15.13. Implement a DirGraph class using the adjacency table representation. Clients of this class must see the same interface as for the DirGraph class with the adjacency linked-lists representation. Specifically, any program that uses the DirGraph class must work with the new implementation *without any modifications*.

P15.14. Implement the UndirGraph class *without extending* it from DirGraph. Instead, use DirGraph as a component. In other words, the UndirGraph class may interact with the DirGraph class only through this component DirGraph object. Contrast your implementation with the one described in the text using inheritance.

Index